PAINE

Books by David Freeman Hawke

In the Midst of Revolution (1961)

American Colloquy (co-editor, with Leonard Lief, 1963)

A Transaction of Free Men (1964)

The Colonial Experience (1966)

U.S. Colonial History: Readings and Documents (editor, 1966)

Benjamin Rush: Revolutionary Gadfly (1971)

Paine (1974)

Those Tremendous Mountains:
The Story of the Lewis and Clark Expedition (1980)

COMMON SENSE:

ADDRESSED TO THE

INHABITANTS

OF

A M E R I C A.

On the following interesting

S U B J E C T S.

I. Of the Origin and Design of Government in general,
with concise Remarks on the English Constitution.

II. Of Monarchy and Hereditary Succession.

III. Thoughts on the present State of American Affairs.

IV. Of the present Ability of America, with some miscellaneous
Reflections.

Written by an ENGLISHMAN.

By Thomas Paine

Man knows no Master save creating HEAVEN,
Or those whom choice and common good ordain.
                                        THOMSON.

PHILADELPHIA, Printed
And Sold by R. BELL, in Third-Street, 1776.

Title page of the first edition of *Common Sense (Bettmann Archive)*

PAINE

by David Freeman Hawke

W. W. NORTON

New York • London

To
My colleagues on the Willy-Beekman committee
of Pace College

Benjamin T. Ford
Phyllis Mount
Thomas P. Robinson

First published as a Norton paperback 1992.

Designed by Sidney Feinberg

Library of Congress Cataloging in Publication Data

Hawke, David Freeman.
  Paine.

  Bibliography: p.
    1.   Paine, Thomas, 1737-1809.
JC178.V2H34   320.5'1'0924[B]   73–14264
ISBN 0-393-30919-3

W. W. Norton & Company, Inc.
500 Fifth Avenue, New York, N.Y. 10110
W. W. Norton & Company Ltd
10 Coptic Street, London WC1A 1PU

1 2 3 4 5 6 7 8 9 0

CONTENTS

IV. America: 1802–1809

ILLUSTRATIONS

PROLOGUE

"I HAVE RECEIVED your letter calling for information relative to the life of Thomas Paine," Joel Barlow wrote to a prospective biographer on 11 August 1809, only a few weeks after Paine had died. "It appears to me that this is not the moment to publish the life of that man in this country. His own writings are his best life, and these are not read at present."

Barlow, a native of Connecticut, had met Paine some twenty years earlier in London and had become his friend in Paris, where together they had lived through more than a decade of violent revolution. Then Paine's reputation had been great in Europe and America; now it had shriveled away and the world remembered only the worst of the man. "The greatest part of the readers in the United States will not be persuaded as long as their present feelings last, to consider him in any other light than as a drunkard and a deist. The writer of his life who should dwell on these topics, to the exclusion of the great and estimable traits of his real character, might, indeed, please the rabble of the age who do not know him. The book might sell; but it would only tend to render the truth more obscure for the future biographer than it was before."

In his writings Thomas Paine appeared to be a simple man. He was not, Barlow said, and to draw him "*complete* in all his character" challenged the talents of any author. "If this piece of biography should analyze his literary labors, and rank him as he ought to be ranked among the brightest and most undeviating luminaries of the age in which he has lived—yet with a mind assailable by flattery, and receiving through that weak side a tincture of vanity which he was too proud to conceal; with a mind, though strong enough to bear him up and to rise elastic under

I

the heaviest load of oppression, yet unable to endure the contempt of his former friends and fellow-laborers, the rulers of the country that had received his first and great services—a mind incapable of looking down with serene compassion, as it ought, on the rude scoffs of their imitators, a new generation that knows him not; a mind that shrinks from their society, and unhappily seeks refuge in low company, or looks for consolation in the sordid bottle, till it sinks at last so far below its native elevation as to lose all respect for itself, and to forfeit that of his best friends, disposing these friends almost to join with his enemies, and wish, though from different sources, that he would haste to hide himself in the grave —if you are disposed and prepared to write his life, *thus entire*, to fill up the picture to which these hasty strokes of outline give but a rude sketch with great vacuities, your book may be a useful one for another age, but it will not be relished, nor scarcely tolerated in this."

Barlow went on to speak of Paine's "mechanical genius" and of the iron bridge he had invented. He said that Paine "was not intoxicated" the night he was arrested during the Terror and began what turned out to be nearly a year in prison. "You ask what company he kept," Barlow continued, "—he always frequented the best, both in England and France, till he became the object of calumny in certain American papers (echoes of the English court papers), for his adherence to what he thought the cause of liberty in France, till he conceived himself neglected and despised by his former friends in the United States. From that moment he gave himself very much to drink, and, consequently, to companions less worthy of his better days."

Barlow rounded out the sketch of his friend with a few generous strokes he hoped would blot out the remarks about his drinking. "It is said he was always a peevish intimate—this is possible. So was Laurence Sterne, so was Torquato Tasso, so was J. J. Rousseau; but Thomas Paine, as a visiting acquaintance and as a literary friend, the only points of view in which I knew him, was one of the most instructive men I ever have known. He had a surprising memory and brilliant fancy; his mind was a storehouse of facts and useful observations; he was full of lively anecdote, and ingenious, original, pertinent remarks upon almost every subject.

"He was always charitable to the poor beyond his means, a sure protector and friend to all Americans in distress that he found in foreign countries. And he had frequent occasions to exert his influence in protecting them during the revolution in France. His writings will answer for his patriotism, and his entire devotion to what he conceived to be the best interest and happiness of mankind."

PART

I

England

1737–1774

CHAPTER

1

"WOUNDS OF DEADLY HATE"

JOHN ADAMS could never accommodate himself to man's perversity. He never, for instance, could calmly accept the fact that the age he had tried so hard to shape came to be called the Age of Reason, after the book by that "disastrous meteor" Thomas Paine.

> I am willing you should call this the Age of Frivolity as you do [he wrote at an unmellowed seventy-one to a friend], and would not object if you had named it the Age of Folly, Vice, Frenzy, Brutality, Daemons, Buonaparte, Tom Paine, or the Age of the Burning Brand from the Bottomless Pit, or anything but the Age of Reason. I know not whether any man in the world has had more influence on its inhabitants or affairs for the last thirty years than Tom Paine. There can be no severer satyr on the age. For such a mongrel between pig and puppy, begotten by a wild boar on a bitch wolf, never before in any age of the world was suffered by the poltroonery of mankind, to run through such a career of mischief. Call it then the Age of Paine.

Paine would have taken what Adams meant for insult as a compliment deserved. Why should the age not be named after him? Who had done more to shape it than Paine? "With all the inconveniences of early life against me," he once remarked, "I am proud to say that with a perseverance undismayed by difficulties, a disinterestedness that compelled respect, I have not only contributed to raise a new empire in the world, founded on a new system of government, but I have arrived at an eminence in political literature, the most difficult of all lines to succeed and excel in, which aristocracy, with all its aids, has not been able to reach or to rival."

Obviously, modesty never numbered among Thomas Paine's virtues.

The boast about "inconveniences" endured as a boy, which he surmounted by "perseverance," rings false. The evidence suggests he suffered a normally unhappy childhood and did his best to escape from rather than persevere against the troubles encountered. But the swipe at an aristocracy that had "not been able to reach or to rival" his achievements hints at the pool of bile stored up from a youth where he learned that the son of "a poor but honest man" rarely escaped the slot birth had assigned to him.

His father, Joseph Pain—thus the family name was spelled until the son came to America—was an impecunious resident of Thetford, a village located on the post road some seventy miles northeast of London. Of the two thousand or so inhabitants only thirty-one qualified to vote for the two men Thetford sent to Parliament. It perturbed few of Joseph Pain's contemporaries that over half of Parliament was elected by less than six thousand voters out of a population of some five million Englishmen, nor did stories they heard of the corruption that pervaded the government seed thoughts of revolt in their minds. "Almost without exception all classes of society were indifferent to the vast collection of abuses," a scholar of the age has remarked. "The first half of the eighteenth century showed a steady, if slow, increase in real comforts and in civilization for all classes in England. No one who benefited by this was inclined to oppose seriously the system which might be supposed to have produced this advance."

Joseph Pain worshiped with the nonconformist Society of Friends and earned his living as a staymaker. He fashioned for the ladies of the village, as Dr. Johnson's dictionary put it, "a kind of stiff waistcoat made of whalebone," or as a more imaginative definition had it, "an appliance for holding up or securing in position some part of a structure." At the age of twenty-six the meek and mild Pain took for a wife one Frances Cocke, a woman noted for her "sour temper and eccentric character," eleven years his senior, a member of the socially acceptable Church of England, and, as the daughter of an attorney, one of the village's elite. The marriage occurred in 1734. On 29 January 1737 the couple's only son, Thomas, was born.

The Pains were an anomalous couple. Differences that set the parents apart—class, age, religion, and temperament—might have been lost amid a cluster of children; but with only one child to focus upon—a daughter, born after Thomas, died in infancy—husband and wife smothered Paine with affection, each no doubt competing for what little love he was willing to spare them. According to the mother, "he never asked us anything but what was granted." He was reared as the mother wished, in the Church of England—"of which I profess myself a member," Paine said as late as 1776—but all his life he halfheartedly declared an affinity for his father's denomination, though he never joined it or practiced its precepts. He was forced so often to study the Bible that years after he had ceased to glance at it he could still quote long passages from memory. His father imposed upon him "an exceedingly good moral education" that cast Paine's conscience into a puritanical mold that remained intact to death. In old age, when he sought to pass along to the oncoming generation the standards handed down to him, he said of a godson in his care, "He shall not want for anything, if he be a good boy and learn no bad words."

Normally, a youngster of the lower class would at an early age have been put to helping his father in the shop, but the Pains "distressed themselves" in order to give their son an education. He attended the free school in the village—free because a local magnate had sufficiently endowed it to pay the teacher's salary—from the age of six to thirteen. He learned there to read and write, found that "the natural bent of my mind was to science," and also, so he thought, that he had a talent for poetry. He liked much about the school—the teacher's tales of a former life at sea; "a pleasing natural history of Virginia" found in the library, which aroused a desire "of seeing the western side of the Atlantic." But regularly during the seven years in school Paine botched his chief assignment, to learn Latin, a knowledge of which offered talented youngsters an escape hatch from the lower classes into a profession—medicine, law, or religion. Later he saw his failure in this department as a piece of good luck, for a child's genius, he said, "is killed by the barren study of a dead language, and the philosopher is lost in the linguist."

Paine's difficulty with Latin stemmed mainly from a lack of perseverance, not inaptitude. He was, it appears, a lazy student, however much his parents "distressed" themselves to educate him. "A sharp boy, of unsettled application," goes a contemporary estimate, a lad who "left no performances which denote a juvenile vigor of uncommon attainments."

It took seven years to convince the parents that their boy had lost the chance to rise to the role of gentleman in English society. At the age of thirteen his formal education ended. He was pulled from school and put to work as an apprentice in his father's shop. For a man whose words would one day shape history he had acquired "what was rare in Europe at the time, an education strictly confined to contemporaneous matters. No conservative, no evaluating discipline stood between his temperament and his times." His mind was empty of the cultural and political traditions that inhibited educated contemporaries against change. Ignorance, which carried lesser men into dark, narrow, and bigoted lives, freed Paine's lively intellect to look at the world in a fresh way.

Staymakers were skilled artisans, and the manual agility Paine displayed through life—it always surprised acquaintances to see the deft way he handled tools—must have owed much to the training he received in his father's shop. But staymaking ranked low on the social scale of crafts, and in later years detractors relished the chance to ridicule "Tom Paine the Staymaker." It demeaned a man to spend his days shaping and fitting rudimentary corsets to the women of a village. During the five years Paine worked with his father learning the trade, life, like the stays he made for Thetford's women, pressed in hard upon him. "The occupation of a hair-dresser, or of a working tallow-chandler, cannot be a matter of honor to any person—to say nothing of a number of other more servile employments," Edmund Burke would one day remark. Surely he would have added staymaking to the list had he known of Paine's past. "Such descriptions of men ought not to suffer oppression from the state; but the state suffers oppression, if such as they, either individually or collectively are permitted to rule." Paine seemed destined to live out his life as one of "the swinish multitude" that Burke deplored.

2

A single way to escape the predestined future lay open, and at the age of sixteen Paine ran away from home. "Raw and adventurous, and heated with the false heroism of a master who had served in a man-of-war," he recalled, "I began the carver of my own fortune, and entered on board the Terrible, privateer, Captain Death." Joseph Pain traced the runaway, and before the ship sailed his "affectionate and moral remonstrances" persuaded the boy to make another try at staymaking. Back home Paine kept track of the Terrible's career—she "stood the hottest engagement of any ship last war"—and its successes at sea, combined with the shrewish voice of his mother, served to undercut the power of his father's persuasion. Not long after he had been retrieved Paine absconded again, signing aboard another privateer, *King of Prussia,* and this time he "went in her to sea."

The sea failed to satisfy Paine. How long he remained afloat he never said nor did he ever reminisce about his days as a sailor, but the experiment served, so it seemed, to break his ties with home. In 1757 he turned up in London as a journeyman staymaker. A year later he deserted the city, surfacing next in Dover, a town from which thirty-five years later, after being harried from the land by the government for publishing *The Rights of Man,* he would depart England forever. Dover's location on the southeast coast had the virtue of being a long way from Thetford, but otherwise it failed to please Paine. After a year there as a journeyman staymaker, he pushed on to the village of Sandwich, a few miles up the coast. There he set up as a master staymaker and opened his own shop. A loan of ten pounds from his former master in Dover, which he never repaid, financed the venture. In September 1759, as his shop drifted toward bankruptcy, he married "a pretty girl of modest behavior" named Mary Lambert, a lady's maid and thus of his social class. A few months later, "embarrassed with debts, and goaded by duns, he was thus obliged to depart in the night" with his wife, his tools, and a few belongings. He moved to Margate, again only a short jaunt up the coast. There, less than a year later, Mary died, apparently during the premature birth of their child.

A haze shrouds the next four years, and only here and there does a fact emerge to mark Paine's movements. He abandoned staymaking in 1761, "disgusted with the toil and little gain" the craft offered; never in all his writings did he refer to his "late occupation." Doubly hit by the failure of his shop and the death of his wife, Paine, now twenty-four years old, buried his pride; he returned to Thetford and the home from which he had fled, ostensibly to prepare himself for a post in the excise service, "towards which, as his wife's father was of that calling, he had some time turned his thoughts." The excise was an internal customs duty imposed principally on alcoholic beverages but also on tobacco and a variety of other items carried by small shopkeepers. It was "a hateful tax," said Dr. Johnson, "adjuged not by the common judges of property, but wretches hired by those to whom excise is paid." The public hated the excise officers, and smugglers contributed risks that hardly made the low-paying jobs worthwhile, yet a line of applicants stood behind every opening. Paine hungered enough for the security the petty post offered to spend over a year studying for the qualifying examination. The examination tested an applicant's ability to write clear, readable English, for he would be required to turn in reports regularly to the London office. It also called for a sound knowledge of mathematics, and candidates, so one said later, spent weeks "cracking our brains over 'sets' of arithmetical questions of the most intricate and ingenious nature." The months Paine spent isolated in Thetford preparing for the exam may have been a turning point in his life, during which he laid the foundation for his skill as a literary craftsman and also as an amateur mechanical engineer well grounded in mathematics.

Paine passed the examination, but he did not receive a permanent appointment until 8 August 1764—to the town of Alford in Lincolnshire, some distance to the north of Thetford. His territory covered a wide stretch along the North Sea infested with smugglers from Holland bringing in contraband. Paine spent a year patrolling the Alford Out-Ride, as it was called, acquiring an intimate knowledge of the coastline. "The Dutch smugglers know every creek and corner of it," he said years later, when trying to convince Napoleon to invade England there. For more than two hundred miles the coast along the North Sea "is as level as a bowling-green, and approachable in every part," he went on. "The shore is a clear firm sand, where a flat-bottomed boat may row dry aground. The country people use it as a race-ground and for other sports when the tide is out."

Excisemen received fifty pounds a year, which worked out, after deducting the cost and feeding of the outrider's horse, to a shilling and ninepence a day, barely sufficient to keep a man alive, according to Paine. Bribery was common, and even an honest man, as Paine appears to have been, was pushed by the heavy workload into fraud; an indolent man, as Paine also was, found it impossible to avoid. To speed their inspections, excisemen often "stamped" a tradesman's accounts, that is, took his word for the amount of taxable goods he had in stock without checking his stores. In July 1765 Paine was accused of having *"stampt his whole ride."* He admitted the charge, and a month later, barely a year after receiving the appointment, he was removed from the service.

The dismissal forced Paine to fall back on staymaking. He worked for a time in the village of Diss, a few miles east of Thetford, moved back to the vicinity of Alford in Lincolnshire, then down to London. By now he was "reduced to extreme wretchedness," according to a contemporary who later dug into his past. "He was absolutely without food, without raiment, and without shelter." He somehow persuaded the headmaster of a private academy in London to take him on as an usher or teacher of English, at a salary of "twenty pounds a year, with five pounds for finding his own lodgings." He held this job until Christmas 1766, then for reasons unknown transferred to another school, where he taught for three months.

For a time he attempted preaching, but this venture fared no better than the others. Security continued to elude Paine, and on 3 July 1767 he petitioned his former superiors to be reinstated as an exciseman. Form required a humiliating penance to accompany the request. "I . . . humbly beg," he wrote, "I humbly hope . . . I humbly presume. . . ." He reminded the board that "no complaint of the least dishonesty or intemperance ever appeared against me." The only substantial charge was laziness, a charge others would level during a long life. If his "humble petition" succeeded, the suppliant concluded, "I will endeavor that my future conduct shall as much engage your honors' approbation as my former has merited your displeasure."

A decade later a critic of *Common Sense* remarked that the author "seems to be everywhere transported with rage—a rage that knows no limits, and hurries him along like an impetuous torrent. . . . Such fire and fury . . . indicate that some mortifying disappointment is rankling at heart, or that some tempting object of ambition is in view, or probably both." One source of that rage, the "mortifying disappointment," may have been Paine's experience with the excise board. His feelings about England from this point on could, perhaps, have been summed up in a quotation from Milton he used in *Common Sense:* "Never can true reconcilement grow where wounds of deadly hate have pierced so deep." ("It sometimes happens, as well in writing as in conversation, that a person lets slip an expression that serves to unravel what he intends to conceal," Paine said years later.)

Difficult as the letter was to write, it appears to have been a routine request for reinstatement. A year to the day after dismissal, he was promised a new post when a vacancy came up. Meanwhile, Paine kept alive by continuing to teach. He rejected the first opening offered by the excise board, praying "leave to wait another vacancy." On 29 February

1768 he accepted a post at Lewes, a town dead south of London a few miles in from the Channel.

3

Paine arrived in Lewes shortly after his thirty-first birthday. He slipped into the town's life easily and was soon friendly "with a very respectable, sensible, and convivial set of acquaintances, who were entertained with his witty sallies, and informed by his more serious conversations." He had a long face dominated by a large, drooping nose and blue eyes so lively and piercing that few failed to remark upon them after a first meeting. "His eye," said a friend, "of which the painter could not convey the exquisite meaning, was full, brilliant, and singularly piercing; it had in it the 'muse of fire.' " He preferred snuff to cigars or a pipe and used it to excess, he liked to drink with companions but not to a degree that raised comment, and he saw himself as something of a lady killer. "It is a whimsical weakness in Tom Paine, imagining that every woman who sees him, directly falls a victim to his charms," one of the non-charmed remarked.

Acquaintances found it easy to call him Tom. Later, it has been said, "good Englishmen expressed their disgust for the irreverent infidel by calling him Tom, and the name still warns all men that its proprietor does not deserve even posthumous civility," but contemporaries found that his amiability invited familiarity. People called him Tom, said a contemporary, "not out of disrespect, but because he was a jolly good fellow." Some may have thought him prudish, for he never swore or used "vulgar oaths," never told "indecent stories" or listened to them when told in his presence. He read few books but lived on an ample diet of newspapers. When an acquaintance came down the street, Paine never said, "How d'ye do?" but, instead, after a graceful bow of greeting, asked, "What news?" and if none came forth he gave what he had accumulated during the day.

Paine lived amid Lewes's five thousand inhabitants for six years, a long stretch for him in one spot. His work took him regularly to all parts of the town. He could be seen daily except Sunday moving about the streets, carrying in one hand a measuring rod, the tool of his trade, while a corked ink bottle bobbed from a string anchored in a buttonhole.

Paine admitted he probably made some enemies in Lewes, but he definitely made "many friends, rich and poor," several of whom stayed close to him throughout his life. He carried the nickname "Commodore" in honor of his "enterprise on the water and his intrepidity on the ice." He joined an informal club that met evenings at the White Hart Tavern, and there he became known for his skill with words. The "disputes often ran warm and high," according to one of the members, and Paine was usually the most obstinate of the debaters. The circulating title "General of the Headstrong War," given to the arguer of the evening who defended his view most vociferously, more often than not went to Paine. Occasionally he entertained the group with a poem of his making. The tenth anniversary in 1769 of General James Wolfe's death at Quebec (or possibly the unveiling in 1772 of Benjamin West's immensely popular painting of the event) evoked from him a string of stanzas which a few years later would lead to his first literary triumph in America. Another poem, longer and lighter in tone, emerged out of a news item about three justices of the peace who revenged themselves upon a local dignitary they disliked by hanging his dog for starting a hare from a barrow. The word got around of Paine's talent, and a candidate for Parliament paid him three guineas for a campaign song. Politics, however, then interested him little, presenting "to my mind," he said, "no other idea than as contained in the word 'jockeyship.' " Though no one in Lewes was "more firm and open in supporting the principles of liberty than myself," he later confessed that not until 1773 did he give any thought to matters of government. In that year, one day after a game of bowls, he heard a friend say that Frederick the Great of Prussia was *the right sort of man for a king for he has a deal of the devil in him*; this made Paine wonder "if a system of government could not exist that did not require the devil."

Paine lodged in Lewes with the family of Samuel Ollive, a Quaker who ran a tobacco shop. Ollive died in July 1769, leaving behind a widow, a daughter, two sons, and a declining business. Neither the widow nor her eldest child, Elizabeth, could cope with the business. After Ollive's death Paine, perhaps for propriety's sake, found rooms elsewhere, but in off-hours he helped run the shop, which meant he kept the accounts and also bought the tobacco in the leaf, then ground, shred, or cut it to suit the customers. He expanded Ollive's line into groceries, which in those days included "wet goods" or distilled spirits. Anyone but the impractical Paine and the innocent Ollive ladies should have known that disaster lay ahead. Both tobacco and spirits were on the excise list. In selling items as a private citizen that he must tax as a government official, he had involved himself in an enterprise contrary "to the maxims of the excise." Worse still, Paine was inept at business, though it would be many years before he could confess, in one of the few understatements of his life, that "trade I do not understand."

As the shop's income steadily deteriorated under his easygoing guidance, Paine compounded his original mistake by marrying Elizabeth Ollive on 26 March 1771. The marriage resembled that of his parents: At the age of thirty-four Paine, like his mother, acquired a spouse ten years his junior, and, like his father, one whom the townspeople had begun to regard as a spinster. The marriage differed from his parents' in that it was never consummated. Paine once admitted he "married for prudential reasons and abstained for prudential reason," and would say no more on the subject. It was clearly a union of convenience: The Ollives, mother and daughter, gained a man in the house and Paine, up to now destitute a good part of his adult life, acquired a roof over his head and the certainty of home-cooked meals. A few years after the wedding he revealed that though he "served in the humble station of an officer of excise," he was "somewhat differently circumstanced to what many of them are," implying that he had few if any financial worries.

Paine had not long been married when he became involved in a cause, the first of many. The impulse to act came, as it often would, from outside himself. "In 1772 the excise officers throughout the kingdom formed a design of applying to Parliament for some addition to their salaries," a friend reported. "Upon this occasion, Mr. Paine, who by this time, was distinguished among them as a man of talent, was fixed upon as a fit person, and solicited to draw up their case, and this he did in a very succinct and masterly manner." Paine corroborates this story: "I should not have undertaken it," he said of the cause and of his pamphlet *Case of the Officers of Excise*, "had I not been particularly applied to by some of my superiors in office."

George Lewis Scott numbered among the "superiors in office" who prodded Paine to lend his talents to the cause. Scott had been a commissioner of the excise board for fourteen years. Apparently a mutual interest in mathematics and science—Scott was once described as "perhaps the most accomplished of all amateur mathematicians who never gave their work to the world"—carried Paine into his orbit, and the two became friends. Paine judged him, as did most people, "one of the most amiable characters I know of." He abounded with "droll anecdotes and stories among the great and about the Court," where he had served as one of George III's tutors. From Scott, said Paine, "I obtained the true character of the present King from his childhood upwards." Scott was in his mid-sixties, and his circle of friends included Edward Gibbon, Samuel Johnson, Benjamin Franklin, and now the impecunious Thomas Paine.

The campaign to get excise officers' salaries raised began with a petition, probably written by Paine, which was circulated for signing by officers throughout the realm. A three-shilling assessment on every officer brought in five hundred pounds to cover expenses. Apparently not all the collected money went to the campaign, for later, upon separating from his wife, Paine was accused of "secreting upwards of £30 entrusted with him to manage the petition for advance of salary." Be that as it may, Paine's essay presenting the officers' case met with "much approbation while in manuscript," as well it might. It was a first-rate piece of work, restrained and respectful in tone, tightly and logically organized, and withal soundly reasoned. Even a churlish contemporary agreed that on the subject Paine said "all that the ablest writer could have said." No one within the government had reason to be offended by the essay, and the excise officers had every right to be delighted to see their case so well presented. Of the four thousand copies printed, three thousand went to colleagues in the service, and the remaining ones were distributed among government officials and members of Parliament. Paine, without obtaining official leave of absence, settled down in London to promote the officers' cause.

Though it must have soon been clear that nothing would come of the campaign—"A rebellion of excisemen, who seldom have the populace on their side, was not much to be feared," a contemporary remarked—Paine, perhaps enjoying the limelight on an expense account or pleased with an excuse to be out of his wife's hearing, refused to abandon it. December of 1772 found him still in London, and from the Excise Coffee House he dropped a few lines about his pamphlet to Oliver Goldsmith, remarking that the praise he had received was so great "that were I not rather singularly modest, I should insensibly become a little vain." Of course, neither then nor later did Paine let modesty flaw his character.

Paine continued through the winter to hustle about London selling his cause. Scott introduced him to his friend Benjamin Franklin, then serving as a colonial agent in England. Together Franklin and Scott sparked his interest in natural philosophy, as science was then called. Through them Paine became friendly with Dr. John Bevis, a distinguished astronomer in his seventies. He attended the lectures of James Ferguson and Benjamin Martin, two highly successful popularizers of Newton's principles. Martin, a mathematician and eminent instrument maker, had published a string of profitable books on science written for the layman. Ferguson, a good friend of Franklin, filled his lecture hall with intriguing machines he had constructed to illustrate his talks on astronomy. Ferguson was a placid man. Once during a lecture a woman stalked in and began demolishing his machines while he looked on quietly. "Ladies and gentlemen," he said after she had finished, "I have the misfortune to be married to this woman," then went on with the lecture.

Bevis, Martin, and Ferguson left an indelible impression on Paine. "After I had made myself master of the use of the globes, and of the orrery," he said later of his association with these gentlemen, "and conceived an idea of the infinity of space, and of the eternal divisibility of matter, and obtained, at least, a general knowledge of what was called natural philosophy, I began to compare, or . . . to confront, the internal evidence those things afford with the Christian system of faith." All three men gave short shrift to the Bible as the authoritative word of God. Instead, as Martin put it, all men "are without excuse who pretend to know God, and discuss of His attributes from any other principles than those of [natural] philosophy." Some twenty years later Paine would rephrase Martin's point in more incendiary language in *The Age of Reason.* However, for the time being Paine kept his deistical views to himself and publicly continued a respectable member of the Church of England.

The ferment stirred up in his mind by Bevis, Martin, and Ferguson helped to distract Paine from the failure of his mission in London. He learned during the winter of 1772–1773 that the treasury board had been "startled" by the excisemen's campaign, "as it might lead to similar expectations from the army and navy." But it was George III, Paine convinced himself, who ultimately brought about defeat, for "the King, or somebody for him, applied to Parliament to have his own salary raised a hundred thousand pounds a year, which being done, everything else was laid aside."

4

The vacation in London opened the door to a new load of troubles. The declining tobacco-grocery shop had drifted toward insolvency while Paine was away. Soon after returning to Lewes he learned that the home office wanted to inspect his books. There were only blank pages to offer for the months absent from duty. He asked a friendly superior officer to discover when the inspection would occur, "and if you can find out the examiner, desire you will drink a bottle or two of wine with him. I should like the character to go in as fair as it can." The bottle or two of wine, if consumed, did no good, and on 8 April 1774 Paine was again discharged from the excise service, "having quitted his business without obtaining the Board's leave for so doing, and having gone off on account of the debts which he hath constructed." Again, no hint of dishonesty appears in the rebuff. On the contrary, during this period of service he had, according to a friend, been several times praised by the London office for his "information and calculations forwarded to the office."

A discharge in the face of such praise, added to the tales heard about George III from Scott, and the suspicion that his campaign for the excise-men had lost out to George's need for a larger allowance, all intensified any bitterness Paine had accumulated toward the crown. A king who could dismiss a loyal and able servant must certainly be either stupid or wicked or both. "I rejected the hardened, sullen-tempered Pharaoh of England forever," he said less than two years later, "and disdain the wretch, that with pretended title of *Father of his People* can unfeelingly hear of their slaughter, and composedly sleep with their blood upon his soul."

With this second discharge Paine's life slid rapidly downhill. Soon afterward came a placard posted in Lewes announcing that "all the household furniture, stock in trade and other effects of Thomas Pain, grocer and tobacconist" were to be auctioned off. "Also a horse, a tobacco and snuff mill, with all the utensils for cutting tobacco and grinding off snuff; and two unopened crates of cream-colored stone ware." A month later, in June, "the said Thomas Pain and Elizabeth his wife . . . agreed to live separate," the legal notice read, "she engaging to pay her husband thirty-five pounds; and he promising to claim no part of whatever goods she might gain in the future."

Earlier, to scotch rumors about his virility, he had collected testimonials from two physicians who reported on his "apparent ability" and his lack of a "natural defect." He refused to tell friends why he would not sleep with his wife. "It is nobody's business but my own," he said. "I had cause for it, but I will name it to no one." Though his mother accused him of "vile treatment" toward his wife, there appears to have been little or no bitterness between Thomas and Elizabeth Paine. They were never divorced and neither ever remarried. She always spoke kindly of him and he "tenderly and respectfully of her." Years later when Paine heard she needed money, he "sent her several times pecuniary aid, without her knowing even whence it came."

At the age of thirty-seven Paine had lost two wives, a home, and every job he had held. Now, when his world looked darkest, he drifted toward Benjamin Franklin, to whom he confided a wish to embark for America. He wanted to start life afresh, to forget the miserable experience with the excise service, to wash away those years spent at a bench making ladies' stays. He dreamed of establishing "an academy on the plan they are conducted in and about London, which I was well acquainted with," but his school would differ in that it would be principally "for the instruction of young ladies," a curious goal for one who had recently escaped from an unconsummated marriage.

Shortly before Paine planned to sail he came around to collect letters of introduction from Franklin. On the last day of September 1774 Franklin wrote brief notes to his son-in-law Richard Bache, a Philadelphia merchant, and his son William, royal governor of New Jersey. As with everything he wrote, the letters were succinct, graceful, and informative:

> The bearer Mr. Thomas Pain is very well recommended to me as an ingenious worthy young man. He goes to Pennsylvania with a view of settling there. I request you to give him your best advice and countenance, as he is quite a stranger there. If you can put him in a way of obtaining employment as a clerk, or assistant tutor in a school, or assistant surveyor, of all of which I think him very capable, so that he may procure a subsistence at least, till he can make an acquaintance and obtain a knowledge of the country, you will do well, and much oblige your affectionate father.

Paine was anything but young—unless Franklin at sixty-eight thought a man of thirty-seven young—and nothing on the record hinted at his ingenuity or worthiness or that he was "very capable." Franklin was recommending to America, the land of the second chance, a born loser, yet he, like George Lewis Scott, must have spotted strengths in the man that life in England had repressed. What Paine later wrote of a wayward friend, Franklin may have perceived in 1774: "I thought I saw in you, young as you was, a bluntness of temper, a boldness of opinion, and an originality of thought, that portended some future good." Franklin's letter, in effect a protective passport that would incline the substantial people of Philadelphia to help the newcomer get settled, offered a last chance for another of England's castoffs to make something of what lay within him. The odds, however, were strong that Thomas Paine would vanish into the New World, as had thousands of other immigrants, never to be heard from again.

PART

II

The American Revolution

1774–1787

CHAPTER

2

A NEW BEGINNING

THE THIRTY-FIVE POUNDS wangled from his wife in the separation settle-ment permitted Paine to travel to America as a gentleman should—first class. He shopped around for a vessel that suited his taste, found one in late September 1774, rejected the choice a few days later and shifted to the *London Packet*, which, when it left in October, carried Paine aboard as one of five cabin passengers, along with 120 persons in steerage.

He quickly regretted the choice of ships. A "dismal and dangerous" putrid fever (presumably typhus) swept through the vessel, infecting nearly all on board. Paine "suffered dreadfully," so much that he all but gave up hope of living to see America. When the ship docked at Philadel-phia on November 30 he was still so weak that he could not turn over in bed without help. A physician from the city who checked over the passen-gers heard that Paine had come to America carrying letters of introduc-tion from Benjamin Franklin. He saw to it that the honored newcomer was carried ashore and given care and lodging.

Paine lay abed for six weeks, and not until mid-January of 1775 did he get around to visiting Franklin's son-in-law with the letter. (He missed Governor Franklin when he made a short visit to the city from New Jersey and never did meet him.) But the days in the sickbed were not wasted. While recuperating he wrote an essay—"Dialogue Between Gen-eral Wolfe and General Gage in a Wood near Boston"—which appeared in a local newspaper on January 4. No one would have guessed the author had arrived in America only a month earlier. The piece was almost *too* American, too much a slick piece of journalism that reflected fashionable opinions. It was as if Paine, in his eagerness to be welcomed in the new land, had dressed himself in the host's ideas, much as a man might don a new coat. He attacked the two recent royal governors of Massachusetts as men of "base and wicked qualities." He slashed out against the Quebec Act, by which Parliament had established the Catholic Church in Canada and accepted things French as appropriate for that colony. "But popery and French laws in Canada are but part of that system of despotism which has been prepared for the colonies," he said, adding, "The edicts of the British Parliament (for they want the sanction of British law) which relate to the province of Massachusetts Bay are big with destruction to the whole British Empire." Americans had been saying this since they first heard of the Quebec Act.

Perceptive readers saw that at one point the anonymous author did more than reflect American thinking: He carried the argument with England to new and dangerous ground. Twice he stated flatly that Massachusetts Bay had not only thrown off Parliament's jurisdiction but was "disaffected to the British crown." To break with the crown would in effect sever the colonies' last tie with England. A year and a half before America declared its independence and months before anyone even contemplated it Paine insinuated that the irrevocable decision had already been made.

2

Seeing his thoughts in print and perhaps hearing them discussed about town may have directed Paine's plans for earning a living into a new channel. He had not abandoned the scheme to set up a school; after he had spread word of his plan around the city, several gentlemen applied to him "to instruct their sons, on very advantageous terms to myself." But life as a schoolteacher held little attraction after Robert Aitken, a printer only a few years out of Scotland, invited him to join in the publication of a new venture, the *Pennsylvania Magazine: or, American Monthly Museum.*

Aitken was known for the quality of the work that came from his shop, and the first issue of the *Pennsylvania Magazine* helped to enhance his reputation. The device on the title page embraced a book, plow, lyre, anchor, and olive-twined shield, all tied together by the motto *Juvat in sylvis habitare* ("Happy it is to live in the woods"). Aitken was determined to produce an *American* magazine, one that depended only slightly on

England for material, but the then restless political climate presented difficulties. A year earlier England had attempted to force the colonists to drink the tea of the East India Company. The cities had reacted by prohibiting the tea ships from landing their cargoes. In Boston, however, the tea had been dumped overboard. Parliament had responded with a series of statutes aimed especially at breaking the recalcitrant spirit of the Bostonians. The city's port was closed to commerce until the tea had been paid for; troops were ordered in, to be housed and fed by the people; royal control over the Massachusetts government was tightened. The other colonies, sensing that these Intolerable Acts, as they were called, might be extended to their own bailiwicks, agreed that the situation called for joint consultation. The First Continental Congress, composed of delegates from the various colonies, met in Philadelphia in September 1774. The purpose of the meeting was to present a united front to the British government, and after weeks of debate the Congress sent across the ocean a string of "animated addresses" listing the rights that the colonists, as Englishmen overseas, considered were theirs—among them, the right to tax themselves, to choose their own political leaders, to be tried by their peers, to be free of standing armies. The Congress ended its eight-week session voting that, if the crown and Parliament refused to respect these rights, on 1 December 1774 the colonies would cease to import or consume goods coming from Great Britain, Ireland, or the British West Indies. The day after Paine arrived in Philadelphia the deadline came and went with no reply from across the sea. The new year began with all men uncertain of what lay ahead and sure of only one thing: "We are on the brink of a precipice."

Obviously, 1775 was not the happiest year to begin a literary journal, and Aitken knew it. Those who would normally write for the magazine "now turn their attention to the rude preparations for war," he said. "Every heart and hand seem to be engaged in the interesting struggle for *American liberty.*" Even so, he proposed to print mainly "original American productions" that would sidestep controversial issues. Comments on new British books would be printed "with remarks and extracts," but American publications would only be listed to "avoid the suspicion of party or prejudice." Disquisitions on religion, "particularly between the different denominations," would be excluded.

The lead essay in the first issue set forth Aitken's views perfectly. The pages of this magazine, the author said, would not retail the nonsense of its British counterparts or become "incentives to profligacy and dissipation." British wit, "one of the worst articles we can import," would be avoided. Indeed, all the vices of Great Britain should and would be shunned. "There is a happy something in the climate of America, which disarms them of all their power both of infection and attraction." The genteel style ("I consider a magazine a kind of bee-hive, which both allures the swarm, and provides room to store their sweets") hardly sounds like Paine, but Aitken years later attributed this opening piece to him. Paine also contributed a filler entitled "A Mathematical Question," signed "P." and a description of "A New Electrical Machine" that he had probably seen in James Ferguson's lecture hall.

Paine had taken rooms in a house next door to Aitken's bookshop. The shop offered a convenient browsing spot that led to an acquaintance with the bookseller-printer. Launching a new magazine gave Aitken more trouble than expected, and he soon saw he needed help. When the first issue came out—a month late—the publisher promised readers that others would follow on time, for, "having now procured additional assistance, he is better able to fulfill his engagements with greater punctuality." Paine, until then at loose ends, was the "additional assistance." The two men informally agreed on an arrangement in late January: Aitken would set policy for the magazine, deciding what should or should not run, while Paine handled the day-to-day details of the operation. Aitken left the question of salary unsettled; as a Scotsman he was not one to bring forth a subject Paine was too shy to mention. Eventually they agreed, after some hard words, on fifty pounds a year, exactly what Paine had earned in the excise service.

He took the job seriously and for a neophyte dealt out decisions with extraordinary confidence. A poem that held "some ingenious thoughts" was dismissed in the monthly column of "Notes *to our* Correspondents" as "a building of elegant materials unskillfully put together," and if the author "will please to call on us, we will point the defects out to him." Several of the rejections during the first month of editorship were scorching:

> ADONIS is too much *intoxicated* with love, to write a *reasonable* encomium on his mistress.

> The verses signed a SUBSCRIBER, are too imperfect for publication. We presume the author will think the same when his muse becomes a little calmer.

The piece signed *A high flyer* is lofty indeed! Our sober-paced muse is not capable of understanding it. If the writer will send us a key, and direct us how to use it, we will endeavor to make something of it.

Either pressure from Aitken or an injection of compassion led to less blunt remarks in later issues. Once Paine even made himself the butt of a tart remark. Of a poem he had written in England, which would soon appear in the magazine—"Farmer Short's Dog Porter: A Tale"—he said, "The verses on a *dead* dog, have no *life* in them; perhaps out of compliment to the animal they lament." The wit did not improve in succeeding issues. "We imagine some of our correspondents are tired of the hot weather," he commented after a torrid July, "as we have received three very *cool* pieces, beginning with Hail! Hail! Hail!" An essay on witchcraft satisfied as "a supplement to the life of Tom Thumb, or Mother Goose's tales, but cannot properly be admitted anywhere else." "Pro Bono's" piece on gunpowder, if printed, would "*blow up* his reputation, as he appears to know nothing of the matter."

In spite of the number of unsolicited pieces received, well over half the contents of every issue came from three men—Paine, who wrote under such pseudonyms as "Atlanticus," "Humanus," "Aesop," and "Vox Populi"; John Witherspoon, a clerical immigrant from Scotland and president of the College of New Jersey, who had encouraged his fellow countryman Aitken to undertake the magazine and used "Epaminonda" as his signature; and a witty lawyer named Francis Hopkinson, who signed his numerous contributions "A.B.," "C.A.B.," or "Philomenes." Paine produced something like a fifth of every issue from February through July. The essays varied from informative to uplifting, the poetry from lighthearted to lugubrious. The amount of his output convinced some, despite Paine's insistence that he had published nothing before coming to America, that in London he had been a Grub Street writer, which was then defined as a writer "of the lowest grade in the world of letters, a mere fabricator of false tales, wonderful narratives, the composer of common ballads, and of making the last dying words which never were spoken." Dr. Witherspoon seems to have originated the story and friends of his perpetuated it for years. A British spy passed it along to his superiors in 1777.

Shortly after Paine took over, circulation of the magazine jumped from around six hundred subscribers to over fifteen hundred, making it the most popular periodical thus far published in America. Dr. Benjamin

Rush, soon to be a friend, attributed the success principally to Paine's poem "On the Death of General Wolfe," written years earlier in Lewes. It appeared in the March issue of the magazine with accompanying music. The poem "gave a sudden currency which few works of that kind have since had in our country," according to Rush. Wolfe, hardly more than a youth when slain on the Plains of Abraham in 1759, had been mourned as no other man in the American past. Though a British general he became the first continental hero of the colonies, and Paine's poem came as only the latest of hundreds published in the succeeding sixteen years.

The elegy opens with Britannia wasting away "in a mouldering cave" festooned "with the feats of her favorite son." Jove takes pity and, as Mercury tells it, decrees "That Wolfe should be called to the armies above,/ And the charge was intrusted to me."

> To the plains of Quebec with the orders I flew,
>   He begg'd for a moment's delay;
> He cry'd "Oh! forbear, let me victory hear,
>   And then thy command I'll obey."
> With a darksome thick film I encompass'd his eyes,
>   And bore him away in an urn,
> Lest the fondness he bore to his own native shore,
>   Should induce him again to return.

The poem's success blotted out memory of all others that had honored Wolfe. It was universally praised. Even a scurrilous biographer confessed it was "a beautiful song." Later generations, for whom Wolfe had faded as a hero, supplanted by George Washington, thought otherwise. "If anything had been wanting to complete the climax of absurdity which marks this ballad, it is amply supplied in the four last lines," goes an 1815 judgment. "Where, we will not say in elegiac, but even in mock heroic poetry, can we find a more forced conceit, or a more ludicrous representation, than that of Mercury deliberately blindfolding the ghost of General Wolfe, cramming it into an urn, and, when thus disposed of, carrying it off under his arm, for the purpose of having it appointed generalissimo of the celestial armies." A still later critic dismissed the poem more harshly, ending his critique with the remark, "Dr. Rush must have been a better judge of pills than poetry, if he sincerely praised such stuff as this."

The bulk of Paine's contributions to the magazine are forgettably dull, as if writing on noncontroversial subjects bored him. His essays come alive only when he finds a chance to lash out at England. "When I reflect on the pompous titles bestowed on unworthy men, I feel an indignity that instructs me to despise the absurdity," he wrote in one piece. "The *Honorable* plunderer of his country, or the *Right Honorable* murderer of mankind, create such a contrast of ideas as exhibit a monster rather than a man." In another essay, which Rush coupled with the poem on Wolfe for giving the magazine "a sudden currency," Paine censures unmercifully as one of those monsters he has in mind Lord Clive, honored in England for fixing India firmly within the British Empire.

> Resolved on accumulating an unbounded fortune, he enters into all the schemes of war, treaty, and intrigue. The British sword is set up for sale; the heads of contending nabobs are offered at a price, and the bribe taken from both sides. Thousands of men or money are trifles in an India bargain. The field is an empire, and the treasure almost without end. The wretched inhabitants are glad to compound for offenses never committed, and to purchase at any rate the privilege to breathe; while he, the sole lord of their lives and fortunes, disposes of either as he pleases and prepares for Europe.

Ostensibly Paine was saying that Great Britain, through Lord Clive, had maltreated one of her richest colonies, India, but he had so designed the essay that alert readers could substitute the word "America" for "India" throughout, and the name "General Gage," who currently headed British troops in the colonies from his headquarters in Boston, for "Lord Clive." The popularity of the piece suggests his audience got the point.

In previous pieces Paine had wandered through "the groves of Arcadia," charmed by the "lovely appearance," the "air of pleasantness." There he had found girls "decorated with a profusion of flowers," living in "little cottages" adorned with "Jessamine and myrtle." Nothing coarse assailed the ears, only "a sweet confusion of voices mingled with instrument music." Paine wrote as expected when appealing to the genteel eighteenth-century audience that read periodicals. With the essay on Lord Clive, Paine, consciously or not, was beginning to pioneer "a style of thinking and expression different to what had been customary in England," as he later remarked. The writer, he said, must balance "warm passions with a cool temper," imagination with judgment, in order "to make a reader feel, fancy, and understand" exactly as the author wants him to. He experiments with these maxims for the first time on Lord Clive. The homely metaphors of his later work—"Let every tub stand upon its own bottom"; "Lay then the axe to the root"; "To use a sailor's phrase, he has *swabbed the deck*"—have yet to appear; but the lush, ornate prose affected in earlier pieces has been supplanted by lean, pungent sentences, each hammering out a new point as it unrolls across the page. Paine had, in short, begun to be himself, to direct his thoughts and shape his style to an audience he knew well—the plain people from whom he had sprung.

3

Those who missed the analogy between India and America in the piece on Clive surely caught it three weeks after the issue containing it appeared in the bookstalls. On 19 April 1775 Americans and British skirmished at Lexington and Concord. Up to this time Paine had made an effort to abide by Aitken's dictum of avoiding controversial political material. "As it is our design to keep a peaceable path, we cannot admit R.W. and M.N.'s political pieces," he announced in an early issue. (Apparently the essay on Lord Clive fell into the noncontroversial category.) If "R.W." refers to Reverend Witherspoon, the rejection did harm for later Paine was judged a belated supporter of the Revolution because "he struck out several passages in papers composed by Dr. Witherspoon as being too free." Also it was said "that no man was a warmer wisher for reconciliation . . . to monarchical government" than Paine, implying that the switch to independence had been sudden and more opportunistic than sincere. Paine admitted the charge was true, "but I reply that *war* ought to be no man's *wish*, neither ought any man to perplex a state, already formed, with his private opinions." Actually, political matters concerned him no more in 1775 than they had earlier in England; he preferred to explore other more intriguing aspects of American life. "I viewed the dispute as a kind of lawsuit, in which I supposed the parties would find a way either to decide or settle it," he said. "I had no thoughts of independence or of arms."

The fighting at Lexington and Concord ended fence-sitting for him. "Surely the ministry are all mad," he wrote back to George Lewis Scott in England; "they never will be able to conquer America." It also ended the ban on controversial material in the magazine. Paine included in the May issue an account of a dream that opened on "one of the most pleasing landscapes I have ever beheld," which suddenly turned into a virtual desert, then after a furious storm resumed its original shape. According to Paine's interpretation:

> The beautiful country which you saw is America. The sickly state you beheld her in has been coming on her for these ten years past. Her commerce has been drying up by repeated restrictions, till by one merciless edict the ruin of it is completed. The pestilential atmosphere represents that ministerial corruption which surrounds and exercises its dominion over her, and which nothing but a storm can purify. The tempest is the present contest, and the main event will be the same. She will rise with new glories from the conflict, and her fame be established in every corner of the globe.

The essay is a curious one from a newcomer to America. Paine's commitment to the Revolution was instantaneous and complete, undiluted with doubt or hesitation. Overnight he had become a superpatriot, and yet, as John Quincy Adams noted perceptively some twenty years later, Paine "has no country, no affections that constitute the pillars of patriotism." His rootless life gave him no platform on which to build a solid loyalty to America. "Loyalty to the nation must exist in the individual not as a unique or exclusive allegiance," it has been said, "but as an attachment concurrent with other forms of group loyalty—to family, to church, to school, and to the individual's native region." Lacking all these loyalties—and so aware of it that he would one day elevate his defect, if it could be called that, into a virtue by calling himself a "citizen of the world"—how could this stranger in the land easily give himself over to America's cause? Perhaps he was an opportunist who sensed that siding with the Americans would win him advancement and friends in the land. Perhaps a long-buried rage made it a pleasure to strike back at a homeland that had treated him ill for thirty-seven years. Perhaps gratitude for the way he had been accepted in Philadelphia made it imperative that he support America's cause as his own. It may even be that he saw a principle at stake—the rights of men—and that America's fight, if successful, might promote a similar uprising among the oppressed of England. Regardless of why he did so, Paine swung so swiftly to the colonial side of the dispute that within days after the news of the fighting outside Boston had reached Philadelphia he had become more American than most Americans.

In an essay entitled "Thoughts on Defensive War," published in the July issue of the magazine, he managed to be adequately belligerent without sounding radically dangerous. Readers must have noted that he called it a defensive war rather than a revolution. The king goes unmentioned; Parliament alone is blamed for sending troops to fight in America, "not for the defense of their natural rights, not to repel the invasion or the insult of enemies; but on the vilest pretense, gold." America must fight to defend her property, and for political liberty, which is important less for itself than for its influence on religion. "Political liberty is the visible pass which guards religions. It is the outwork by which the church militant is defended, and the attacks of the enemy are frequently made through this fortress." Paine's religious views, as he expressed them in public, satisfied the most devout. He revealed that until "the coming of Christ there was no such thing as political freedom in any known part of the earth," and elsewhere in the essay he predicted that "He who guides the natural tempest will regulate the political one, and bring good out of evil."

The July issue of the magazine also carried Paine's poem "Liberty Tree," which immediately became as popular and widely reprinted as the one on the death of General Wolfe. One quatrain contained a thought that would later become central to the argument in *Common Sense:*

> With timber and tar they Old England supplied,
>   And supported her power on the sea;
> Her battles they fought, without getting a groat,
>   For the honor of Liberty Tree.

The poem attacked those "tyrannical powers"—the king and Parliament —which in a version written after publication of *The Age of Reason* were broadened to include "Kingcraft and Priestcraft," who had joined "To cut down this guardian of ours."

"Liberty Tree" numbered among the last pieces Paine contributed to the *Pennsylvania Magazine,* though the periodical continued for a year longer. Editor and publisher, both prickly characters, got along badly. Success had swelled Paine's ego. "I was requested by several literary gentlemen in this city to undertake such a work on my own account," he said later, "and I could have rendered it very profitable." He complained repeatedly about his salary, and the publisher grumbled about the lateness of copy. Once, desperate for a particular essay that had been promised, he sat Paine at a table and produced a bottle of brandy, for, so he said years later when the word had got around that Paine was a drunkard, he "would never write without *that*," adding, "The first glass put him in a train of thinking," the second "illuminated his intellectual system," and the third produced a train of ideas that "appeared to flow faster than he could commit them to paper," all "perfectly fit for the press without any alteration or correction." John Adams repeated a version of this story that he had heard from John Witherspoon, who had said Paine was very intemperate and "could not write 'until he had quickened his thoughts with large draughts of rum and water.'"

The outbreak of war, coupled with the strain of working for Aitken, also hastened Paine's departure from the magazine. "When the country, into which I had just set my foot, was set on fire about my ears, it was time to stir," he said. "It was time for every man to stir. Those who had been long settled had something to defend; those who had just come had something to pursue; and the call and the concern was equal and universal. For in a country where all men were once adventurers, the difference of a few years in their arrival could make none in their right."

4

One way Paine stirred himself was to conduct with a friend, Captain Thomas Pryor, several experiments "for the purpose of fixing some easy, cheap, and expeditious method of making saltpeter [an indispensable ingredient in gunpowder] in private families." The experiments were published in the press under the by-lines of Captain Pryor and "Mr. Thomas Pain." Paine had proposed "a Salt-Peter Association, for voluntarily supplying the public magazine with gunpowder," and he banked on the findings of these experiments to promote his organization. Modern chemists do not dispute the success of Pryor's and Paine's investigations: They produced with a maximum of effort that extended over four days a modicum of the potassium nitrate crystals which, combined with charcoal and sulphur, would result in gunpowder. Even Benjamin Rush, trained as a chemist at the University of Edinburgh, offered few refinements on their process in his own set of experiments.

Experiments of all kinds—social and political as well as scientific—fascinated Paine. "We are a people upon experiments," he said; and in an early issue of the *Pennsylvania Magazine* he protested "against that unkind, ungrateful, and impolitic custom of ridiculing unsuccessful experiments," then added, "I am led to this reflection by the present domestic state of America, because it will unavoidably happen, that before we can arrive at that perfection of things which other nations have acquired, many hopes will fail, many whimsical attempts will become fortunate, and many reasonable ones end in air and expense."

A month after this prediction Paine made an experiment of his own in the social sphere, a "whimsical attempt" to right a wrong. Across from his lodgings stood a slave market. Aitken would let nothing so controversial as an attack on slavery appear in his magazine, but the *Pennsylvania Journal* on 8 March 1775 ran a piece written by Paine under the pseudonym "Humanus." He opened with a picture of the Negroes in Africa as "industrious farmers" who "lived quietly" before "Europeans debauched them with liquors." The observation that the English enslave "towards one hundred thousand yearly" makes it clear that blame for the evil rests on Great Britain rather than innocent America. The appeals to reason in the essay are few; those to "the sacred scriptures," the "gospel light," the "common Lord of all!" are numerous. Slavery, says Paine, is not "reconciliable with all those *divine precepts.*" But are Americans aware, he asks, that having "enslaved multitudes, and shed much innocent blood in doing it," God might seek retribution by allowing Britain to enslave them?

The question had been raised before—by Benjamin Rush three years earlier in his own tract against slavery and by virtually every American who had written against the institution since then. Nor were his ideas unique for dealing with the blacks once they had been freed. He suggested, as others had before him, that the old and infirm should be kept by their former masters, who would rent them land and employ them as free laborers. The view that some of the freed Negroes might "form useful barrier settlements on the frontiers" had a ruthless practicality that made it hard to think of Paine as a compassionate man. "Thus," he said, "they may become interested in the public welfare, and assist in promoting it; instead of being dangerous, as now they are, should any enemy promise them a better condition." The conclusion lacked bite: America would find itself on the road to happiness if it would Christianize the blacks, "taking some proper measures to instruct, not only the slaves here, but the Africans in their own countries."

Indeed, the essay rings false from start to finish. At one point Paine speaks of "a succession of eminent men"—among them Baxter, Durham, Locke, Carmichael, Hutcheson, Montesquieu, Blackstone, and Wallace—

who have proved slavery "contrary to the light of nature, to every principle of justice and humanity, and even to good policy." Since Paine later
confessed he had not read even the most accessible of this string of
scholars—John Locke—it is reasonable to assume he had read none. The
list, like parsley on a dinner plate, adds color but not content.

Though he knew little about slavery firsthand, Paine obviously detested it. "I despair of seeing an abolition of the infernal traffic in
Negroes," he later wrote Benjamin Rush from France. "We must push
that matter further on your side of the water." Later still he would be
hissed by Frenchmen for his praise of the free blacks of Santo Domingo.
Yet after the essay in 1775 he never again wrote an extended piece on
slavery. A friend once asked him why. "An unfitter person for such a
work could hardly be found," he said. "The cause would have suffered
in my hands. I could not have treated it with any chance of success; for
I could never think of their condition but with feelings of indignation."
The excuse from one known for his impassioned writing sounds flimsy,
but given his literary credo—warm passions must always be combined
with a cool temper—it may have been the truth.

5

On 5 May 1775 Benjamin Franklin returned from England, in time to
take the seat he had been elected to in the Second Continental Congress,
which would convene in a few days. On May 9 the New England delegates rode into town. Philadelphia greeted them solemnly to show its
sympathy for beleaguered Boston. Thousands of citizens watched silently from the curbs as several miles of carriages and horsemen and
soldiers with swords at salute position moved at a sedate pace through the
streets, accompanied by the tolling of muffled church bells. A few days
later George Washington arrived wearing the uniform of colonel of the
Virginia militia. Not long after Congress went into secret session behind
the closed doors of its chamber on the first floor of the State House it was
reported that the delegates had chosen "the modest and virtuous, the
amiable, generous, and brave George Washington, esquire, to be general
of the American army, and that he is to repair, as soon as possible to the
camp before Boston."

Congress could agree on Washington for commander-in-chief but on little else. John Adams believed America "ought immediately to dissolve all ministerial tyrannies, custom houses, set up governments of our own . . . confederate together like an indissoluble band, for mutual defense, and open our ports to all nations immediately." He found, however, that Congress was "not yet so much alarmed as it ought to be" and that a majority of the delegates still favored "negotiations for peace." Outside Congress hopes for reconciliation also remained high. The war mood had subsided in Philadelphia by late summer and the city had returned to its normal daily routine. Shiploads of immigrants from northern Ireland and Scotland continued to arrive at the wharves along Front Street. The shops were filled with goods that still flowed in from Great Britain. Prices remained steady.

Through these months Paine traveled about the city without leaving behind a trace of his movements. Then, in mid-October, again as "Humanus," he spoke up in the press. After ticking off charges against Great Britain's treatment of the Indians ("She has basely tampered with their passions, imposed on their ignorance, and made them tools of treachery and murder") and Negroes ("She has . . . ravaged the hapless shores of Africa"), he moved toward a conclusion that Benjamin Franklin, John Adams, and a few others had dared state in private but never in public. "When I reflect on the obloquies that Great Britain has heaped upon the colonies," he wrote, "I hesitate not for a moment to believe that the Almighty will finally separate America from Britain. Call it independence or what you will, if it is the cause of God and humanity it will go on."

CHAPTER

3

COMMON SENSE ON
INDEPENDENCE

JOHN ADAMS long after he had left the Continental Congress said with a sneer that Paine in 1775 "got into such company as would converse with him, and ran about picking up what information he could concerning our affairs." The company that would converse with Paine in those days was the same that talked with Adams—Philadelphians who were early and warm supporters of independence. The Independents, as they came to be called, had not by 1775 coalesced into a tight band. One wing worked away hardly aware of the other. A retired druggist named Christopher Marshall circulated about the city promoting independence along with James Cannon, an instructor at the College of Philadelphia; Dr. Thomas Young, a participant in the Boston Tea Party who had been hounded out of New England; and Timothy Matlack, a former brewer. These gentlemen rarely crossed the paths of David Rittenhouse, George Clymer, or Benjamin Rush, who agitated for independence among a more respectable circle of Philadelphians. Paine worked his way into the second group from the vantage point of his social center, Aitken's bookstore and printing shop. There he met Rush, who dropped in one day to browse and chat between calls on patients. An acquaintance ripened into friendship when Rush, who a few years earlier had written one of the first antislavery pamphlets published in Philadelphia, learned that Paine had authored the recent piece on the subject in the local press.

Friendship between Paine and Rush must have struck those who knew them as odd. Paine liked to drink, though at the time not excessively, otherwise the abstemious Rush, who had already declared himself in print on the evils of spiritous liquor, would have approached the friendship warily, or at least have commented on Paine's failing. Though both at the time were bachelors—Rush would marry the following year —they lived contrasting lives. Paine liked to sleep away the morning, talk through the day, end with a long evening in a tavern where more talk or perhaps a game of whist or checkers, mingled with liquid refreshment, occupied the hours. Rush, a young man on the make, rose with the sun, after no more than four or five hours' sleep, saw patients through the day, and passed the evenings quietly in his study writing articles to advance his professional reputation or the cause of America against England. Both men were considered above average height—somewhere around five feet eight or nine inches tall—but women found Rush handsome, a word never applied to Paine, whose large pendulous nose dominated a weathered face. Writing, generally a torture for Paine, came easily for Rush. A brief essay that might take Paine days, even weeks, built sentence by sentence, Rush could dash off in an evening, polishing it the next day between visits from patients. At the age of thirty Rush's published output tripled that of Paine's, a pace he would continue throughout his busy life.

Still, the two men had much in common. They were alike temperamentally, blunt and opinionated. Both had been befriended by Benjamin Franklin and revered him. Both felt spurned by the society they had been reared in. Rush, after studying medicine in Edinburgh and London, found in his first years of practice that not "one of my brethren ever sent a patient to me, and yet several of them had more applications daily than they were able to attend to." The antislavery pamphlet he published in 1772 received "the most virulent attack that ever was made upon me." He also believed that "by the persons who called themselves great in the city, I was at this time neglected or unknown."

These two much-put-upon gentlemen learned from their chats at Aitken's bookstore that they agreed, among many things, upon the necessity for independence. It distressed Rush to find "the public mind to be loaded with an immense mass of prejudice and error relative to it." He wrote an essay to put the people straight, then had second thoughts about publishing it, recollecting the setback handed to his medical practice by the antislavery pamphlet. "I shuddered at the prospect of the consequence of its not being well received." Why not let Paine, a stranger to Philadelphia, suffer the consequences? "I suggested to him," Rush later recalled without embarrassment, "that he had nothing to fear from the popular odium to which such a publication might expose him, for he could live anywhere, but that my profession and connections, which tied me to Philadelphia, where a great majority of the citizens and some of my friends were hostile to a separation of our country from Great Britain, forbade me to come forward as a pioneer in that important controversy."

Paine seized the suggestion "with avidity." He probably began to write soon after November 1, when word arrived in Philadelphia that the king had declared the American colonies in a state of rebellion. He blocked out a group of three essays which he originally planned "to have been printed in a series of letters in the newspapers, but was dissuaded therefrom on account of the impossibility of getting them generally inserted."

When the three were finished, Rush advised showing the work to Franklin, Rittenhouse, and Samuel Adams, as well as to James Wilson, the ablest of Pennsylvania's delegates in Congress and also a man who still hoped for reconciliation with Britain. Wilson was absent from home the day Paine stopped by, but the other gentlemen apparently saw his manuscript. (Rittenhouse definitely did, for Paine singled him out as "one of the very few to whom [I] showed some part thereof while in manuscript.") The changes made were few, the excision of one or two repetitions being the extent of the editing.

2

"The cause of America is in a great measure the cause of all mankind," Paine remarks in the introduction to *Common Sense*. Most Americans had assumed up to now that self-interest sufficed to justify their resistance to British encroachments or, at best, that they fought for the rights of Englishmen. Paine sought in a sentence to transmute a rebellion into a crusade. He gave warning at the start that he would argue not only for independence but for a revolution that would inspire mankind. He meant to invalidate the fundamental political assumptions every American had been reared to honor—the glory of monarchical government.

In the first essay Paine travels across dangerous ground as he moves in on the British lion, for a generation earlier Montesquieu had taught that England's government was the best yet created by man, a beautifully constructed Newtonian balance of diverse elements within society, a marvelously complex yet workable system of checks and balances. Paine finds the "boasted" constitution "imperfect, subject to convulsions, and incapable of producing what it seems to promise." Complex, yes, "so exceedingly complex, that the nation may suffer for years together without being able to discover in which part the fault lies." The supposed checks on the king are "farcical . . . a mere absurdity." A scathing assault on monarchical government—which Americans had been reared to honor—follows next. The king's power is absolute, his will "as much the law of the land in Britain as in France," says Paine. Worse still, this power too often falls into the hands of fools. "Nature disapproves" of hereditary monarchy, "otherwise she would not so frequently turn it into ridicule, by giving mankind an *ass for a lion.*" William the Conqueror is passed off as "a French bastard" who made "himself king of England against the consent of the natives." How does a monarch earn his keep? "In England a king hath little more to do than to make war and give away places, which in plain terms is to impoverish the nation and set it together by the ears," says Paine. Nothing justifies "the exalting one man so greatly above the rest." A short survey of the Old Testament leads to the proposition "that the Almighty hath here entered His protest against monarchical government is true, or the Scripture is false." Readers should now understand why in "popish countries" the Bible is withheld from the public, "for monarchy in every instance is the popery of government." By now it must be obvious that "the nearer any government approaches to a republic, the less business there is for a king."

Having rid Americans of reverence for the monarchical government and also the British constitution—according to one scholar, "Paine may well have been the first Englishman during the classical age of the constitution to ridicule its maxims publicly"—he shifts in the second essay to America, upon which he will "offer nothing more than simple facts, plain arguments, and common sense." One tight, direct sentence rolls out after another. "The sun never shone on a cause of greater worth. 'Tis not the affair of a city . . . 'Tis not the concern of a day . . . Now is the seed-time of continental union, faith and honor." One by one Paine cuts down every argument raised to promote reconciliation. "But she has protected us, say some." Alas, not so, says Paine, and facts follow. "But Britain is the parent country," say others. "Then the more shame upon her conduct. Even brutes do not devour their young." Those who talk of reconciliation are only "interested men, who are not to be trusted, weak men who *cannot* see, prejudiced men who will not see, and a certain set of moderate men who think better of the European world than it deserves." How can any American "hereafter love, honor, and faithfully serve the power that hath carried fire and sword into your land?" Paine asks. Anything short of independence offers "a mere patchwork" of compromise; "there is something absurd in supposing a continent to be perpetually governed by an island." There can be no reconcilement "where wounds of deadly hate have pierced so deep."

Tension builds as the argument moves from one nicely woven paragraph to the next. Paine slides to the edge of bathos—"The blood of the slain, the weeping voice of nature cries, 'TIS TIME TO PART"—but never slips over the side. He controls so effectively the material and in the process the reader that when he eventually remarks, "reconciliation and ruin are nearly related" the statement sounds sensible, and when a few pages later he calls George III "the royal brute of Great Britain," a treasonable phrase no American had dared put in print, the insult seems called for. Line by line the reader is swept along until Paine has prepared him for one of the most powerful battle cries ever uttered:

> O! ye that love mankind! Ye that dare oppose not only the tyranny but the tyrant, stand forth! Every spot of the old world is overrun with oppression. Freedom hath been hunted round the globe. Asia and Africa have long expelled her. Europe regards her like a stranger, and England hath given her warning to depart. O! receive the fugitive, and prepare in time an asylum for mankind.

Here Paine should have ended; unfortunately he still had much to say, and a variety of miscellaneous thoughts are tucked into a third essay. Artistically he erred; logically he had a point, for having made the case for independence he must tell America how to use its freedom. Earlier he had thrown out "hints" about the kind of governments to be erected —single-house legislatures unchecked by an upper chamber; representatives elected annually to prevent the corruption bred by long tenure in office ("When we are planning for posterity, we ought to remember that virtue is not hereditary"); governors with limited power to check the will of the people. The state legislatures should be subject to the Continental Congress, whose legislation would be the supreme law of the land. The new nation must have a constitution, for "our strength is continental, not provincial." The enlarged Congress—390 members seemed adequate— should be chosen by the broadest possible suffrage, for "a small number of electors, or a small number of representatives are equally dangerous."

Paine elaborates on these "hints" in the final essay. He reminds readers that without a strong central government "the vast variety of interests, occasioned by an increase of trade and population, would create confusion." He emphasizes the need for a powerful navy to protect America and its commerce. Fear of running the country into debt is dismissed with a line Alexander Hamilton would cherish: "A national debt is a national bond." After several such pages of disjointed comments, he glides to an end on a sensible rather than an emotional note: ". . . until an independence is declared, the continent will feel like a man who continues putting off some unpleasant business from day to day, yet knows it must be done, hates to set about it, wishes it over, and is continually haunted with the thoughts of its necessity."

3

Paine wanted to call the pamphlet *Plain Truth*. Rush preferred *Common Sense*, and this, as he remembered it, "was instantly adopted." Now only a printer was needed for the incendiary pamphlet. "There is Bell," Rush said. "He is a republican printer. Give it to him, and I will answer for his courage to print it." Rush disliked men of wit, deists, and those of loose morals. Robert Bell was known for his drollery, his religion "was at least doubtful," and by his mistress he had fathered an illegitimate daughter. But only he among Philadelphia's printers dared "to be as high-toned as Mr. Paine upon the subject of American independence." Paine ever after praised himself for daring to give the world *Common Sense* while it was still "unsafe for a man to have espoused independence in any public company," failing to note that his pamphlet came out under the by-line "written by an Englishman." Only Bell's name appeared on the title page; only he risked reputation and property for little in return. The obloquy meted out would come to him; the honor, if any, to the author.

Common Sense appeared in the bookstalls on 9 January 1776. "The book was turned upon the world like an orphan to shift for itself," Paine said. "No plan was formed to support it"—suggesting that none who had read the manuscript had been overwhelmingly impressed by it. If so, they all misjudged the public temper. With only word-of-mouth advertisement to promote it, the pamphlet burst from the press, said Rush, "with an effect which has rarely been produced by types and paper in any age or country," despite the relatively high price of two shillings Bell had placed on the work. Sales were helped by the timing of publication. This had been fixed to coincide with the arrival of the king's opening speech to Parliament, which, as expected, called for suppression of the American rebellion, "and so fortunate was I in this cast of policy," said Paine, "that both of them made their appearance in this city on the same day."

Within a week or so, author and printer had, by Paine's accounting, "upwards thirty pounds" in profits to divide between them. Paine refused to accept his half. Shortly after *Common Sense* had come out, news arrived in the city that American troops attempting to take Quebec had been repulsed. Paine stipulated that his share of the profits should go to two friends "for the purpose of purchasing mittens for the troops ordered on that cold campaign." He said, "I did this to do honor to the cause."

Bell determined to capitalize on his best seller by rushing out a second printing. This eagerness to cash in on his courage peeved Paine. He wanted to make revisions and additions to the original version, and when Bell refused to delay a new printing Paine, in the first of numerous quarrels with his publishers, broke with him. He got two other printers, eager for the job now that public response had made it clear no risks were involved, to produce three thousand copies each, all printed at Paine's expense. These were given to Thomas Bradford to sell at his London Coffee House at the cut-rate price of one shilling, even though the size had been increased by a third. Paine asked for no royalties, only enough return to pay the cost of paper and printing.

The new arrangement led to a lively if short-lived newspaper war between two "high-toned" gentlemen. Paine accused Bell of cheating on the share of profits he meant to devote to the purchase of mittens. Bell replied in kind, disparaging the pretensions of his "anonymous author," denouncing Paine as a "foster-father author" who falsely bragged in every alehouse that he had written every word of the pamphlet. Paine responded to "this noisy man" in injured tones. Despite the fuss, or perhaps partly because of it, *Common Sense* still sold so well that by the end of January both publishers could afford half-page advertisements in the *Evening Post*, along with smaller ads in the city's other newspapers. Since Paine later complained of his treatment from Bradford, the publisher of the third edition of the pamphlet—"He has a sufficiency in his hands to balance with and clear me, which is all I aimed at, but by his unaccountable dilatoriness and unwillingness to settle accounts I fear I shall be obliged to sustain a real loss exclusive of my trouble"—it would seem the dispute with Bell amounted to no more than the typical relationship of tender author with enterprising publisher.

Although the Bradford edition, published on February 14, offered a third more reading matter at half the price, none of the additions—a sprinkling of statistics, a new "appendix," a long "Epistle to Quakers"— strengthened the original version. However, close readers caught several significant changes. The original by-line, "written by an Englishman," had vanished and in its place came an admonition to cease worrying about the author's identity and attend to what he had to say. "He is unconnected with any party, and under no influence, public or private, but the influence of reason and principle." In the last line of the appendix every American was asked to become *"a virtuous supporter of the* RIGHTS OF MANKIND, *and of the* FREE AND INDEPENDENT STATES OF AMERICA," four and a half months before Congress made a similar request of the people. Scattered through the new pages were indications that in the six weeks since the first edition Paine had quietly stripped himself of English citizenship and now passed as an American. The revised preface told readers that "the author had studiously avoided everything which is personal among ourselves." And of the French and Indian War, fought while he served as an excise officer in England, he now said, "We had experience, but wanted numbers; and forty or fifty years hence, we shall have numbers, without experience."

Another change accompanied the quiet switch in allegiance. Two months before *Common Sense* he still spelled his name Pain. Now, without ceremony, as silently as it sounded, he tacked on an "e" to the end. The change was more than an affectation. The success of his pamphlet had, in a sense, made him a new man. "It appears to general observation, that revolutions create genius and talents; but those events do no more than bring them forward," he once observed. "There is existing in man, a mass of sense lying in a dormant state, and which, unless something excites it to action, will descend with him, in that condition, to the grave."

4

"The true prophet," it has been said, "is not he who peers into the future but he who reads and reveals the present." The true prophet had spoken in *Common Sense*. The pamphlet "struck a string which required but a touch to make it vibrate," a contemporary remarked. "The country was ripe for independence, and only needed somebody to tell the people so, with decision, boldness and plausibility." Aitken sensed his former employee's achievement and ordered two dozen copies the day after publication. Twelve days later he had purchased and presumably sold five dozen more. By the end of the year, said Paine, "I believe the number of copies printed and sold in America was not short of 150,000." This, he added, "is the greatest sale that any performance ever had since the use of letters"—a boast no one disputed.

The pamphlet spread through the continent with amazing rapidity. Ten days after Bell published it copies turned up in Alexandria, Virginia, and were already making "a great noise" there. Edmund Randolph of that colony later said that "the public sentiment which a few weeks before had shuddered at the tremendous obstacles, with which independence was environed, overleaped every barrier." But at the same time, he went on, *Common Sense* only "put the torch to combustibles which had been deposited by the different gusts of fury." Two of those "combustibles" were the recent firing upon Norfolk by British warships and the threat by royal officials to prod Virginia slaves to revolt from their masters. In New England a long train of abuses had been capped by the burning of Falmouth, an event that assured the pamphlet a popular reception. "A few more such flaming arguments, as were exhibited at Falmouth and Norfolk," said Washington from outside Boston, "added to the sound doctrine and unanswerable reasoning contained in the pamphlet *Common Sense*, will not leave numbers at a loss to decide upon the propriety of a separation." A citizen of Massachusetts wrote, "I believe no pages was ever more eagerly read, nor more generally approved. People speak of it in rapturous praise."

If books can convince, this one did. The war had yet to come to Pennsylvania, and sentiment for independence before Paine spoke forth lagged far behind that in Virginia and Massachusetts. "*Common Sense*, which I herewith send you," wrote a Philadelphian to a friend in London, "is read to all ranks; and as many as read, so many become converted; though perhaps the hour *before were most violent against the least idea of independence.*" A translation directed at the German-speaking part of the population, according to one man, "works on the minds of those people amazingly." Another gentleman reported that the pamphlet "seems to gain ground with the common people." In fact, he went on, "this idea of an independence, though sometime ago abhorred, may possibly by degrees become so familiar as to be cherished." When Samuel Adams sent a copy home, he remarked, "It has fretted some folks here more than a little."

The folks fretted may have been local citizens or possibly members of Congress. Whatever the delegates thought about the pamphlet, none except John Adams and John Hancock mentioned it in letters home until a month after it had been published. (Hancock spoke of it in a letter a week after publication and added what few others knew, that it had been written by "an English gentleman resident here by the name of Paine.") A member from North Carolina sent down a single copy as "a curiosity," adding in an accompanying note, "We have not put up any to go in the wagon, not knowing how you might relish independency." By the time Congressmen dared to speak out, printers in nearly all the colonies had set up their own editions for local distribution. Copies had been placed aboard vessels bound for Europe, and by midsummer a French translation, minus the section attacking hereditary monarchy, was having "a greater run, if possible, here than in America." (The expurgated version first appeared in *Affaires de l'Angleterre et de l'Amérique*, edited by Edmé Jacques Genêt, whose son would one day become a friend of Paine's. Genêt attributed the pamphlet to "le fameux Adams," that is, Samuel.)

With a single exception, those who had favored independence before *Common Sense* greeted Paine's work with unqualified praise. John Adams alone mingled reservations with admiration. Adams had come upon a copy in New York while riding back to Congress after a brief holiday at home. He reported to his wife that "the further encroachments of tyranny and depredications of oppressions" would soon make the doctrines put forth by Paine "the common faith." He found the pamphlet "a very meritorious production," envied the author's "elegant simplicity" and his "piercing pathos." The praise ended there. "The Old Testament reasoning against monarchy would have never come from me. The attempt to frame a continental constitution is feeble indeed; it is poor and despicable." No new arguments for independence were offered. "I believe every one that is in it has been hackneyed in every conversation, public and private, before that pamphlet was written." By mid-May he had no good at all to say for the work. "It is the fate of men and things which do great good that they always do great evil, too. 'Common Sense,' by his crude,

ignorant notion of a government by one assembly, will do more mischief,
in dividing the friends of liberty, than all the Tory writings together. He
is a keen writer but very ignorant of the science of government." Forty-
three years later he was still sputtering against the pamphlet. "What a
poor, ignorant, malicious, short-sighted, crapulous mass, is Tom Paine's
Common Sense," he wrote Thomas Jefferson, an observation Jefferson ignored in his return letter.

Soon after *Common Sense* had been published, friends at home guessed
it had been written by John Adams. "Poor harmless I!" he replied. " 'And
can I choose but smile / When every coxcomb knew me by my style.' "
Curiously, while Congress wondered for a month who the author was—
Samuel as well as John Adams, Benjamin Franklin, and Benjamin Rush
were all credited at one time or another with the work—native Philadelphians were circulating the word that "the pamphlet is said to be wrote
by one Mr. Paine." On February 6 Francis Hopkinson, who like John
Witherspoon apparently had accumulated grievances when Paine edited
the *Pennsylvania Magazine,* published a verse that revealed the author to
all who had a previous inkling:

> TOM mounted on his sordid load,
> And bawling d____n ye, clear the road;
> His shovel grasp'd firm in his hands,
> Which far and near the street commands,
> No hardy mortal dares approach,
> Whether on horseback, foot, or coach;
> None in his wits the risk would choose,
> Who either wears a coat or nose.
>   So _____ in pomp, on Billingsgate,
> His arms display'd in burlesque state;
> Scurrility and impudence,
> Bombast and Bedlam eloquence,
> Defiance bids _____ to COMMON SENSE.

5

Paine's sudden assumption of American citizenship obscured the ap-
propriateness of his original by-line, "written by an Englishman." Only
an Englishman could have written *Common Sense.* "It was in a great
measure owing to my bringing a knowledge of England with me to

America that I was enabled to enter deeper into politics, and with more success, than other people," he once told a friend. The "wounds of deadly hate" inflicted in England gave zest to the attack on monarchy no American from the distance of three thousand miles could emulate. Moreover, most enlightened Americans' affection for John Locke would have stunted the power of whatever they had to say about King George. Locke admired monarchical government so long as its power was checked. "I never read Locke, nor ever had the work in my hand," Paine said when accused of cribbing from *A Treatise on Government*, nor could he ever be induced to read it. "It is a speculative, not a practical work, and the style of it is heavy and tedious, as all Locke's writings are." No one in the eighteenth century could escape from Locke; his views on natural rights were part of the intellectual landscape. But lack of a firsthand acquaintance with his work gave Paine a freedom denied others. The revolution Locke had defended in 1688 encouraged reform, not overthrow, of the monarchy. It sought to conserve, not to root out, an institution England cherished.

If Paine owed nothing directly to Locke, indirect exposure came through the *Essay on the First Principles of Government* . . . by Joseph Priestley, a dissenting clergyman, England's greatest chemist, and a friend of Franklin. Paine, who read little except that pressed upon him, probably came across Priestley's work in a bundle of material to be used "towards completing a history of the present conflict" that Franklin had turned over to him in the fall of 1775. The early pages of *Common Sense* that explain the rise of representative government virtually paraphrase the *Essay*. In language more sedate than Paine's, Priestley questioned the validity of monarchical government, censured the corruption in British politics, deprecated England's complex arrangement of checks and balances, and favored a simpler form of government responsive to the will of the people. Style and tone rather than content set the two pamphlets apart.

Paine disguised his dependence on English thought and experience so effectively that few readers spotted it. John Adams believed his views on government came from and were included only to please "the democratic party in Philadelphia." This part of *Common Sense* particularly offended him. "His plan was so democratical, without any restraint or even an attempt at any equilibrium or counterpoise, that it must produce confusion and every evil work," he said. Some two months after Paine's pamphlet had come out, Adams wrote a letter to a friend giving his own conception of a sound government—a legislature of two houses that would check each other's excesses, a reasonably strong executive that worked with both houses but had veto power over their decisions, a strong judiciary appointed for good behavior, and the usual property qualifications for voters. The letter expounding this plan was published anonymously as *Thoughts on Government,* but informed men soon knew the author's identity. "Mr. Thomas Paine was so highly offended with it," Adams later said, "that he came to visit me at my chamber at Mrs. Yard's to remonstrate and even scold me for it, which he did in very ungenteel terms."

The meeting in Adams' room at Mrs. Yard's boardinghouse in Philadelphia ended with both men in good humor, for they could agree on the central issue—that a republican government, regardless of the form it took, suited America best. In conceding that, Adams also had to agree, grudgingly, that Paine had been the first to make a republic palatable to the people at a time when kings ruled everywhere and even enlightened men believed only a hereditary monarchy could give stability and continuity to a nation's government. But he refused, then or ever, to accept a greater achievement—that *Common Sense* had elevated a family quarrel, a "kind of lawsuit," into "the cause of all mankind."

CHAPTER

4

"A PASSION OF PATRIOTISM"

PAINE FINISHED REVISIONS of *Common Sense* on 14 February 1776. Five days later he set off for New York City carrying letters of introduction as "the celebrated author of *Common Sense*" from Rush, Franklin, and John Adams to Gen. Charles Lee, "a gentleman whose character he so highly regards." Paine and Lee, another transplanted Englishman, hit it off well when they soon after dined together. "He has genius in his eyes," Lee reported. "His conversation has much life." Paine praised Lee for his "sarcastic genius"—an apt phrase for the cantankerous general—and for his "great fund of military knowledge." But the acquaintance with Lee never amounted to more than that; both men may have sensed that two similar temperaments would soon rub against each other.

In March a series of letters appeared in the Philadelphia press signed "Cato," a pen name the informed in the city knew belonged to Dr. William Smith, provost of the College of Philadelphia. The letters advanced an able attack against Paine's arguments for independence. (A few weeks earlier a pamphlet entitled *Plain Truth* had appeared to rebut Paine, but even those for reconciliation judged it a shoddy work.)

A call from friends in Philadelphia went out to Paine in New York, urging him to speed back to the city to defend himself and the Independents against Cato's skillful attacks. About this time several gentlemen in Philadelphia, aware that Paine had no means of support and that he had relinquished all profits from *Common Sense* though still in debt for the six thousand copies printed at his own expense, sent him "by the hands of Mr. Christopher Marshall 108 dollars." The gift helped to pay his room and board; it also undercut his frequent assertion that he was only a disinterested observer of the Revolution.

2

Paine chose the pseudonym "The Forester" for his new series of essays. Here he both followed and broke with tradition; followed in that he varied his pen name from earlier productions in an effort to preserve anonymity, and broke with it in that he did not choose a classical name to mask his identity, almost as if he wished publicly to acknowledge his plebeian origins, his lack of classical learning. The earlier choices—"Atlanticus," "Humanus," and "Vox Populi"—though all appropriate for one who knew both sides of the Atlantic, considered himself humane, and immodestly posed as the voice of the people, would never again appear. "The Forester" must also have been selected to underscore the notion that wilderness-wise Paine would guide the innocent and ignorant through the wild thickets of politics to safe ground.

The new pen name did not shroud his identity. "The Forester writes with a spirit peculiar to himself and leads me to think that he has an intimate acquaintance with Common Sense," Abigail Adams told her husband. Her observation required slight perception. "I fear not the field of fair debate, but thou hast stepped aside and made it personal," Paine said at the end of the first letter. "Thou hast tauntingly called on me by name." Stung by Cato's continuing invective—which accused Paine of having neither "character nor connection"—Paine later took space in the press to say he had not come to America as a piece of flotsam washed up by the sea but as "a cabin passenger" recommended by Franklin *"as a worthy ingenious, etc."*

The first letter of reply to Cato begins and ends sententiously. "To be *nobly wrong* is more manly than to be *meanly right,"* goes the opening sentence; pomposity and arrogance characterize much that follows. "Thees," "thous," and "haths," rarely used by Paine, show he fumbled for his natural style. Cato had praised at length the glories of Pennsylvania's government, forcing Paine to write on a subject about which he knew little.

Weak arguments and affectations dulled but failed to smother the essay. Intermittently bright phrases kept it alive: Cato attempts to "catch lions in a mousetrap," he has "a curious way of lumping the matter," he hoodwinks the public "by the jingle of a phrase," his arguments "loiter in the suburbs of the dispute." Paine mints a new title for George III—

"sceptered savage"—so wickedly bitter it fails, for all its power, to outlive the hour. And twice he makes telling points. "It is now a mere bugbear to talk of *reconciliation* on *constitutional principles* unless the terms of the first be produced and the sense of the other be defined," he remarks at one spot of Cato's arguments. Elsewhere Paine reveals himself as perhaps the first colonist with a continental outlook; his English background kept him from local attachments and gave him a perspective most Americans lacked. He reprimands Cato for addressing his letters "To the People of Pennsylvania." This "hath mischief in its meaning," for "the great business of the day is continental." "And he who dares to endeavor to withdraw this province from the glorious union by which all are supported deserves the reprobation of all men. It is the true interest of the whole to go hand in hand; and dismal in every instance would be the fate of that colony that should retreat from the protection of the rest."

The Forester still gropes for a way to deal with Cato in the second letter, which rambles twice the distance of the first. He accuses Cato of "a cast of mind bordering upon impiety" and of "that Jesuitical cunning which always endeavors to disgrace what it cannot disprove," and he answers long quotations from Cato's own letters with a few spare, often ineffective lines. Even where he catches Smith in an "unnatural and distorted" simile that compares the dispute between Britain and America to a lovers' quarrel, the comment seems strained. "What comparison is there between the soft murmurs of an heart mourning in secret, and the loud horrors of war?" he asks, ending on an even falser note: " 'Get thee behind me,' Cato, for thou hast not the feelings of a man."

Paine admits in the third letter that Cato's attacks have made him "furious," but now his fury simmers rather than boils out of control. He handles with dispatch Cato's charge that to court foreign aid runs the risk of being overrun with European savages. "The assistance which we hope for from France is not armies (we want them not) but arms and ammunition," he writes. The dream that such assistance will lead to a political or military alliance is Cato's, "and is directly repugnant both to the letter and spirit" of common sense, which argues for isolation from "the political affairs of Europe." The jabs at Smith are surer now. "I have been the more particular in detecting Cato here," he says of the misrepresentations on foreign assistance, "because it is on this *bubble* that his air-built battery against independence is raised—a poor foundation indeed! which even the point of a pin, or a pen, if you please, can demolish with a touch, and bury the formidable Cato beneath the ruins of a vapor." Of Smith's habit of quoting from other authors, the unread Paine says, "I scarcely ever quote; the reason is, I always think."

He ends this letter with a brief essay directed "To the People," pointedly refusing to add "of Pennsylvania," though what follows is an election-eve sermon to that audience, for on May 1 Pennsylvania would vote for a new Assembly, enlarged to include deputies from the supposedly independent-minded backcountry colonies. *"It is not a time to trifle,"* goes the opening line. "Reconciliation will not now go down, even if it were offered." Only one question faces the people: What will best bring them happiness? America can be happy only under a government of her own: "As happy as she please; she hath a blank sheet to write upon. Put it not off too long."

The election came a week after Paine's third letter. In Philadelphia three of the four candidates who ran on the Independent ticket lost, and in the backcountry enough moderate deputies were elected to assure that control of the Assembly would remain in the hands of those who favored reconciliation with England. Paine took the results personally, for Pennsylvania had in effect repudiated the power of his pen. He had not voted in the election, probably because he could not meet the property qualification without lying—a voter had to own fifty pounds' worth of property to qualify—though he later said he stayed away from the polls to preserve his reputation for offering detached judgments. Nonetheless, in the fourth and final Forester letter he had plenty to say about why the Independents had failed to win; many good citizens were "now before the walls of Quebec"; Quakers and Catholics were leagued against them; Germans "zealous in the cause of freedom" were excluded from the polls; "the Tories by never stirring out remain at home to take advantage of elections." The Independents had failed to gain control of the Assembly. "We are got wrong . . . how shall we get right?" Paine asked. "Not by a house of Assembly," for that body will only perpetuate the evils of British rule as they currently exist. Without saying so specifically, he hints that a new government that draws its power from the people, not the crown, should be instituted, bypassing the Assembly and drawing up a constitution that owes nothing to Great Britain. Persuasion had failed; an overthrow of the government, violent if necessary, was the only recourse left.

3

Through May and June 1776 Paine's attention, like all Philadelphia's, swung between local and continental concerns. He roamed from one committee meeting to another and buttonholed congressmen at every chance, but he did little of importance, either through the press or in person, to shape events during these crucial months. On June 7 Richard Henry Lee, following instructions sent from Virginia, rose to request a declaration of independence from Congress, the creation of a continental constitution, and action on promoting commercial alliances with other nations. Congress voted to undertake items two and three at once, but on the first, independence, it procrastinated. Near the end of *Common Sense* Paine had suggested a "manifesto" be published that would set forth "the peaceful methods which we have ineffectually used for redress." This document should make clear "that not being able any longer to live happily or safely under the cruel disposition of the British court, we had been driven to the necessity of breaking off all connections with her." Congress now accepted the suggestion and appointed a committee of five headed by Thomas Jefferson to draw up the manifesto. Debate on independence was postponed until July 1.

Paine's only production during these weeks was a slim pamphlet that took the form of a dialogue between General Richard Montgomery, who had died before the walls of Quebec the previous year, and a delegate in Congress who balked at voting for independence. Paine said little new here. He wrote as if bored, and the essay drooped to a lackluster conclusion in which readers learned that heaven longed to see finished the ark where "all the liberty and true religion of the world are to be deposited."

During the three-week hiatus in the debate on independence ordered by Congress, the Independents in Pennsylvania managed first to hobble the Assembly, then to provoke from it a new set of instructions for the Pennsylvania delegation in Congress that would allow it to vote for independence—all this while plans went forward for a constitutional convention that would assure death for the nearly century-old legislature. Paine earlier had helped to clear the ground for the convention. If the people are "not so perfectly free as they ought to be," he had remarked in April, they have "both the *right* and the *power* to place even the whole authority of the Assembly in any body of men as they please; and whosoever is hardy enough to say to the contrary is an enemy to mankind." This has been called "one of his typically radical ultimatums that smashed the terms of a previous argument." The Independents Paine associated with saw the proposal instead as a plausible way to circumvent an Assembly dead set against independence. Benjamin Rush, for instance, rejoiced when the constitutional convention assembled; and when in an early session it chose him for the new delegation to represent Pennsylvania in Congress, he accepted the honor without compunction.

Paine was passed over as a delegate and "had no hand in forming any part" of the constitution the convention produced that summer, "nor knew anything of its contents till I saw it published." Later, when the constitution provoked criticism from such friends as Rush, he "kept clear of all argument" as long as he could, because "my personal attachments are equally balanced" between those for and those against it.

4

Congress declared the colonies free and independent states on July 2, and on July 4 it approved Jefferson's Declaration. A few days later Paine joined a body of Pennsylvania volunteers—or Associators, as they were called—that had been ordered to march to Perth Amboy, New Jersey, just off the southern tip of New York City, where the British were expected at any moment to launch an invasion. "The command was large, yet there was no allowance for a secretary," Paine said. He offered "my service voluntarily, only that my expenses should be paid," to Daniel Roberdeau, a well-to-do Philadelphia merchant who had recently been chosen to command the flying camp. (A flying camp comprised volunteers who enlisted for a brief time to cover or "fly" to a particular emergency, then disbanded when it or their term of duty ended.) Roberdeau accepted the offer. Paine spent the next three months at Amboy desultorily, watching British warships sail up New York Bay to unload troops on Staten Island. When the Associators began to desert in numbers, he moved among them passing out copies of *Common Sense* and repeating Roberdeau's plea to fight "for your honor's sake" against "an army of sixpenny soldiers." With the end of enlistments in September, the volunteers packed up and went home. Paine collected forty-eight dollars in expense money—he would take no more although Roberdeau "frequently pressed me to make free with his private assistance"—and from Amboy traveled up to Fort Lee, on the west side of the Hudson River just opposite the northern tip of Manhattan. There General Nathanael Greene took him on as his aide-de-camp. Greene, a large, heavy man with a stiff knee that forced him to walk with a limp, got along famously with Paine.

While at Fort Lee Paine served as field correspondent for the Philadelphia press, taking care in his dispatches to publicize the exploits of home-town boys. One Sunday in October Lord Percy sauntered up from lower Manhattan to engage a body of Pennsylvania troops on the plains of Harlem. Paine witnessed the skirmish from Fort Lee. Immediately after Lord Percy withdrew from the field, he had an account of the small victory under way. "The post being detained, by the desire of the General," he wrote, "gives me an opportunity (with a wooden pen on a drumhead) to acquaint you that the part of our army which was engaged today was . . ." and then followed the name of practically every Pennsylvanian involved in the fray. Long after the Revolution one of the participants remembered with pleasure the "handsome puff" Paine had given the men in the home-town press.

On November 16 the British captured Fort Washington, on the east bank of the Hudson. Washington ordered the evacuation of Fort Lee, but General Greene disobeyed, convinced he could withstand any assault. When on November 20 a British-Hessian army several times larger than the defending American force moved against the fort, no choice remained but to depart hastily. Paine's report of these events exonerated Washington and Greene, though both were culpable. Years later, in talking about the "black times of *Seventy-Six,*" he confessed to Samuel Adams that he had glossed over the military blunders of that campaign ("the country might have viewed them as proceeding from a natural inability to support its cause against the enemy, and have sunk under the despondency of that misconceived idea"). He made it appear that the evacuation went smoothly, when actually, as a British soldier reported, "the rebels fled like scared rabbits," leaving in their entrenchments not only several valuable heavy cannons but "some poor pork, a few greasy proclamations, and some of that scoundrel 'Common Sense' man's letters, which we can read at our leisure now that we have got one of the 'impregnable redoubts' of Mr. Washington's to quarter in."

The retreating army paused a day and a half at Hackensack, "when the inclemency of the weather, the want of quarters, and approach of the enemy, obliged them to proceed to Aquaconack, and from thence to Newark," and then on to Brunswick. Outside Brunswick the pursuing British advance guard began a "smart cannonade." Paine reacted calmly to the nerve-racking sounds: "I knew the time when I thought the whistling of a cannon ball would have frightened me almost to death, but I have since tried it, and find that I can stand it with as little discomposure" as any man. A colleague who accompanied him on the retreat remarked that "Paine may be a good philosopher, but he is not a soldier—he always kept out of danger."

December 1 marked the expiration of the enlistment term for volunteers from Maryland and New Jersey. Their departure and the failure of expected replacements to appear forced Washington to abandon all thought of making a stand. The retreat continued. The army pushed into Trenton on December 4 and rested there for three days. On "the approach of the enemy, it was thought proper to pass the Delaware."

Paine left the army at Trenton "on the advice of several principal officers, in order to get out some publications, as the printing presses were then at a stand and the country in a state of despair." He arrived in Philadelphia to find the public censuring the retreat "as pusillanimous and disgraceful." In a brief report for the press he passed over tactical errors that had given the British an upper hand and said that posterity would call the retreat "glorious"—and "the names of Washington and Fabius will run parallel to eternity."

Paine sensed the need for more than a straight factual account of the retreat to revive faith in the army. The enemy hovered on the east bank of the Delaware and might at any moment decide to attack Philadelphia. The people's spirit as well as the army's must be aroused. Once Philadelphia fell, Pennsylvania lay open to British ravaging, and with Pennsylvania, the keystone in the arch of states, occupied the Revolution might collapse. "The deplorable and melancholy condition the people were in, afraid to speak and almost to think, the public presses stopped, and nothing in circulation but fears and falsehoods" drove Paine to write ("in what I may call a passion of patriotism") an essay entitled "The Crisis." He wrote it to stir up the people of Pennsylvania, but clearly he spoke to all Americans. Nearly a century of repetition has reduced the opening sentences to a cliché, yet they still inspire men embarked upon desperate ventures. "These," said Paine, "are the times that try men's souls. The summer soldier and the sunshine patriot will, in this crisis, shrink from the service of their country; but he that stands it *now*, deserves the love and thanks of man and woman. Tyranny, like hell, is not easily conquered; yet we have this consolation with us, that the harder the conflict, the more glorious the triumph. What we obtain too cheap, we esteem to lightly; it is dearness only that gives every thing its value."

Paine wrote "in a rage," but a rage so controlled that it lent authority to all he said. Only when he spoke of Tories—all cowards motivated by "servile, slavish, self-interested fear"—and of the king—"a sottish, stupid, stubborn, worthless, brutish man"—did feelings get out of hand. Confidence in himself and in America (the careers of both were now joined) pervades every sentence. He confesses to "a secret opinion" that God had not given the world "up to the care of devils" and will not let perish a people "who have so earnestly and so repeatedly sought to avoid the calamities of war, by every decent method which wisdom could invent." Even if God remained neutral, the nation has Washington, whom "God hath blessed with . . . uninterrupted health and given him a mind that can even flourish upon care." Only the people of Pennsylvania give Paine doubt, and it is to them he directs his most inspiriting remarks. Have faith, he implores, and show that faith "*by your works,*" then goes on to admonish all laggards to the cause. "The heart that feels not now is dead; the blood of his children will curse his cowardice, who shrinks back at a time when a little light might have saved the whole, and made *them* happy. I love the man that can smile in trouble, that can gather strength from distress, and grow brave by reflection. 'Tis the business of little minds to shrink; but he whose heart is firm, and whose conscience approves his conduct, will pursue his principles unto death."

Given his purpose, Paine strikes no false notes. "As he passes on from paragraph to paragraph of this tremendous harangue," an admirer has written, "he touches with unfailing skill, with matchless power, the springs of anxiety, contempt, love of home, love of country, fortitude, cool deliberation, and passionate resolve." Paine closes "with such a battle-call as might almost have startled slain patriots from their new graves under the frozen clods." "This is our situation, and who will may know it. By perseverance and fortitude we have the prospect of a glorious issue; by cowardice and submission, the sad choice of a variety of evils —a ravaged country—a depopulated city—habitations without safety, and slavery without hope—our homes turned into barracks and bawdy-houses for Hessians, and a future race to provide for, whose fathers we shall doubt of. Look on this picture and weep over it! and if there yet remains one thoughtless wretch who believes it not, let him suffer it unlamented."

"The Crisis" appeared first as an essay in the *Pennsylvania Journal* on December 19, and four days later as a pamphlet, Paine having given it "to the printer gratis, and confined him to the price of two coppers, which was sufficient to defray his charge." Printers up and down the coast pirated the text as soon as it came to hand. The essay "rallied and reanimated" the people, according to a contemporary who had little good to say about anything touched by Paine. "Hope succeeded to despair, cheerfulness to gloom, and firmness to irresolution."

5

To avoid raising false hopes, Paine called his essay *American Crisis No. 1.* "The black times" had only begun; a string of unborn crises lay ahead, and he would have something to say about each of them as they took shape. He included the word "American" to distinguish his work from a similarly entitled series that had appeared in London in 1775 and been reprinted in the colonies the same year. The second *Crisis* came forth on 13 January 1777, this one an open letter to Richard Viscount Howe, whose fleet Paine had watched sail up New York Bay. Howe had arrived with peace offerings the previous July, just as his brother William, commander-in-chief of the British forces, prepared to open his summer campaign to take Long Island and New York City, a campaign that by autumn had sent Washington backtracking across New Jersey.

Although the new piece is more moderate in tone, Paine still gets off several good shots. "He that rebels against reason is a real rebel," goes one sentence, "but he that in defense of reason rebels against tyranny has a better title to *'Defender of the Faith'* than George the Third." Of Lord Howe's "drowsy proclamation" offering pardons to all rebels, he says, "Perhaps you thought America too was taking a nap, and therefore chose, like Satan to Eve, to whisper delusion softly, lest you should awaken her." He underscores the political theory Americans now practice by reminding his lordship that "we have learned to 'reverence ourselves' and scorn the insulting ruffian that employs you."

In the three weeks since the first *Crisis*, confidence of victory has replaced Paine's fear of defeat. Now he does not attempt to rally the people. America, he reminds Lord Howe, has a silent ally that assures her victory. "In all the wars which you have formerly been concerned in you had only armies to contend with; in this case you have both an army and a country to combat with. In former wars, the countries followed the fate of their capitals; Canada fell with Quebec, and Minorca with Port Mahon or St. Phillips; by subduing those, the conquerors opened a way into, and became masters of the country: here it is otherwise; if you get possession of a city here, you are obliged to shut yourselves up in it, and can make no other use of it, than to spend your country's money in it."

Paine here was not whistling in the dark to bolster American self-confidence. Nor did his perception that the land would swallow up the British originate with him. Two years earlier a youngster named Alexander Hamilton, then a student at King's College in New York, had made the same point. Washington was constructing his strategy around the insight by always drawing the British on, until their army became "like a stream of water running to nothing," as Paine put it. "By the time you extended from New York to Virginia, you would be reduced to a string of drops not capable of hanging together; while we, by retreating from state to state, like a river turning back upon itself, would acquire strength in the same proportion as you lost it, and in the end be capable of overwhelming you."

The two *Crisis* papers, bound together, went to Franklin, now in France negotiating a loan and a treaty, with Paine's suggestion they could be reprinted there, though possibly "some republican expressions should be omitted." An alert French censor would have been wise to have suppressed the entire second paper. "Universal empire is the prerogative of a writer," Paine said in the opening paragraph, announcing his plans for Europe. "His concerns are with all mankind, and though he cannot command their obedience, he can assign their duty." He gave fair warning early in the game who would be the first assigned to their duty: "I, who know England and the disposition of the people well, am confident, that it is easier for us to effect a revolution there, than you a conquest here." Once England had been set right, he implied, "the defense of reason" must be pursued throughout Europe.

6

Early in January of 1777 Congress learned that several tribes of Indians scattered along the west branch of the Susquehanna wanted to confer about their status with the new American government. A commission of six gentlemen—two from Congress and four from Pennsylvania—was appointed to treat with the Indians. A week after *Crisis No. 2* appeared, friends arranged for Paine, as usual short of cash, to fill the paid post of secretary to the commission. One of these friends may have been Lewis Morris of New York, a member of the permanent committee on Indian affairs. Morris was "a cheerful, amiable man," also tall, "singularly handsome," and rich. Paine considered him one of his closest friends.

The conference opened on January 27 at Easton, a village on the Delaware some fifty miles north of Philadelphia. "After shaking hands, *drinking rum*, while the organ played, we proceeded to business," the commissioners later told Congress in a report probably written by Paine, who may also have been responsible for underscoring the phrase "drinking rum." Over seventy braves with wives and children attended, together with at least six chiefs of various tribes. Paine circulated among them introducing himself as "Common Sense." After several days of palaver, a thousand dollars' worth of presents brought up from Philadelphia were distributed. "The Indians seem to be inclined to act the wise part with respect to the present dispute," the commissioners' report concluded. "If they are to be relied upon, they mean to be neuter. We have already learnt their good intentions." On January 30 the chiefs and the two congressmen signed a peace treaty—Congress later disavowed it, holding it had been made with Indians only "pretending to be a deputation from the Six Indian Nations"—and the delegation returned to Philadelphia.

Paine received, by his own accounting, $145 for the trip, paid months later in inflated currency. The venture, for all its brevity, made a lasting impression on him, perhaps because it served as his single extended contact with Indians. In 1786 he came upon a gathering of Seneca chiefs in Philadelphia. He made himself known "by past remembrance as Common Sense," shook hands all around, calling each one "brother," then treated the group to a two-shilling bowl of punch. Twenty-five years after the event he was still telling stories about the conference. During an evening in Washington when Jefferson was president he recalled one of the chiefs of the Six Nations reprimanding the Delawares, who were bridling under their subjugation to the Iroquois Confederacy. "You dogs," Paine remembered the chief saying, relishing the bluntness of his remarks, "if you do not be quiet, I will catch you by the hair of the head and throw you one by one over the Blue Mountains." Another he talked to, Chief Last Night, had been awed by the "great canoes" of the British on the rivers and lakes of Canada, but he doubted that their armies would subdue the Americans on land. "The king of England," he said, "is like a fish. When he is in the water he can wag his tail; when he comes on land he lays down on his side." That observation convinced Paine that "the English government had but half the sense this Indian had," and he never abandoned the judgment.

Nor did he ever comment on the Indians' duplicity. Less than two years after he had praised their "good intentions" the Iroquois Confederacy, led by American Tories, scalped hundreds of settlers along the west branch of the Susquehanna River. Paine's romantic view of the red man as a wise and noble savage allowed these actions to be washed from his mind.

7

Paine wrote little in the two months after returning from Easton. A brief piece of his in mid-March attacked a pseudonymous writer who, if he be "a man whom I have ever thought or called a friend, I spare him out of pity to myself." The essay is memorable only as a reminder that while opponents hid behind pen names, Paine regularly exposed himself in all he published. Pen names in a tightly knit society permitted a freedom of expression normally denied to the timid or cautious. Paine could have followed tradition here, as he did at first, but after *Common Sense* he dared—preferred, perhaps, for such was the size of his ego—to reveal his identity in all he wrote, regardless of how controversial its nature. He justified the innovation as expedient in time of war: "If men, under the hope of being concealed by a printer, are to publish what they dare not own, the public will forever be held in confusion." "British emissaries, British prisoners, and disaffected refugees will embarrass every measure, and endeavor to defame every character, however fair, that stands in their way, and for this reason, were it no other, I conceive that the name of no writer, in the present state of things, ought to be concealed when demanded."

Regardless of why he did it, Paine introduced into American journalism the personal report, whose authority stemmed as much from an awareness of who wrote it as from the strength of the thought and style. While leading a revolution on the political front, he had also initiated one in polemic literature.

On April 19, the second anniversary of the battle of Lexington, Paine produced *Crisis No. 3*, a discursive pamphlet of thirty-two pages designed to prod the Pennsylvania Assembly into passing, as it did two months later, a test law requiring an oath of loyalty to the new government. Tories, says Paine, are "a set of avaricious miscreants" motivated only by *"avarice, downright villainy,* and *lust of personal power."* Quakers who adhere to pacifism are "like antiquated virgins, they see not the havoc deformity has made upon them, but pleasantly mistaking wrinkles for dimples, conceive themselves yet lovely and wonder at the stupid world for not admiring them." Paine pauses once in the midst of this invective to lighten the piece with an unacknowledged borrowing from Chief Last Night, wherein the invading British are likened to "a wounded disabled whale" that "wants only time to die in; and though in agony of their exit, it may be unsafe to live within the flapping of their tail, yet every hour shortens their date, and lessens their power of mischief."

CHAPTER

5

AN UNSOLICITED HONOR

CONGRESS HAD RETREATED—some Philadelphians used a harsher word—to Baltimore before Washington, on Christmas day 1776, crossed the Delaware to raid the Hessians in Trenton. The delegates had lost faith in their general, and the capture of Philadelphia looked certain to them. Washington's foray into Trenton and a victory over the British at Princeton a few days later revived their spirits. That coupled with the discomforts of life in the village of Baltimore, where the boardinghouses were crowded and the streets clogged with mud, refreshed their memories of the amenities of city life. On 12 March 1777 Congress recovered its courage and reconvened in Philadelphia, somewhat abashed at its flight a few months earlier but glad to be back in the land of comfort.

Foreign affairs occupied its attention during the first month back in the city. The old Committee of Secret Correspondence, which had long served to handle these matters, now seemed inadequate to the task. A number of delegates believed that a larger committee with greater power to make decisions should be created, but a strong minority in Congress resisted the idea. Nonetheless, on April 17 Congress transformed the old group into the Committee for Foreign Affairs and also voted "that a secretary be appointed to the said committee, with a salary of seventy dollars a month." Soon afterward John Adams rose to nominate Paine, who knew nothing of his plan, as the paid secretary. Adams still doubted that *Common Sense* had been of "great importance in the Revolution," but he saw, so he later said, that Paine "had a capacity and a ready pen, and understanding he was poor and destitute, I thought we might put him

into some employment, where he might be useful and earn a living."
There was more to it than that. Paine was friendly with those in Congress
like Richard Henry Lee who opposed all attempts to strengthen the
continental government. The new committee had the marks of an embry-
onic executive department, a creation the Lee group wished to resist. By
placing Paine in a key role—he would be the only person permanently
attached to the committee—Adams, always the politician, may have
hoped to win votes to assure the new institution power and a long life.

The nomination provoked dissent only from the Reverend John
Witherspoon, who now sat in Congress as a delegate from New Jersey.
He objected "with an earnestness" most surprising, as John Adams
remembered it: "When [Paine] first came over, he was on the other side
and had written pieces against the American cause; that he had afterwards been employed by his friend Robert Aitken and finding the tide
of popularity run rapidly, he had turned about; that he was very intemperate and could not write until he had quickened his thoughts with
large drafts of rum and water; that he was, in short, a bad character and
not fit to be placed in such a situation." The accusations, when discussed outside Congress, must have planted in Paine his lifelong opinion that "parsons were always mischievous fellows when they turned
politicians."

Daniel Roberdeau, who had traded his command of the flying camp
for a seat in the Pennsylvania delegation, spoke in Paine's defense. Congress sided with him, and the nomination went through. Congress may
have wanted to express its gratitude for past services or it may only have
wanted to buy his pen for the nation. Whatever Congress' motives, Paine
was pleased. The post had been "unsolicited on my part," the first such
honor received during forty years of outrageous fortune. Congress had
handed him a responsible and sensitive post, requiring only that he swear
"to disclose no matter, the knowledge of which shall be acquired in
consequence of such his office, that he shall be directed to keep secret."
In addition to the honor and the money, Paine saw another virtue in the
job: it offered access to secret documents he could use in the history of
the Revolution he was planning to write. The clerkship had no more been
offered when Paine wrote Franklin in Paris, asking him to forward files
dating back to 1774 of several English reviews and of the relevant volumes
of Parliamentary debates for that period.

2

Paine assumed his new duties at a moment when domestic rather than foreign affairs occupied the attention of Congress. Late in the summer the British landed an army at the head of Delaware Bay and proceeded to march toward Philadelphia. On September 11 Washington met Howe's army southeast of the city at Brandywine Creek. Paine was sitting in his office preparing dispatches for Franklin in Paris "when the report of cannon at Brandywine interrupted my proceeding." That night he learned the Americans had lost the battle of Brandywine; the road to Philadelphia lay open to the British. By noon of the next day Paine had completed a new *Crisis* paper. He rushed the finished copy to a printer and "ordered 4,000 to be printed at my own charge and given away."

The British "band of ten or twelve thousand robbers," Paine proclaimed in the four-page paper, could never "conquer America, or subdue even a single state, unless we sit down and suffer them to do it." This time Paine's words reached a terrified populace who refused to be calmed or inspired. The band of robbers plodded on toward Philadelphia, and every mile they advanced spurred the departure of several hundred more citizens. Congress, recalling its demeaning flight the previous year, officially stayed in session, but by the evening of September 18, when Paine "was fully persuaded that unless something was done the city would be lost," most members had departed. He still believed salvation possible "if only an appearance of defense be made in the city by throwing up works at the heads of the streets."

The proposal failed to fit reality. The faithful had fled; those staying behind were pro-British or neutral, hardly a population to throw up barricades. Still, one or two city fathers saw enough sense in Paine's suggestions to encourage a visit to Gen. Thomas Mifflin, a renowned man of words whose passionate orations had attracted hundreds to the cause. Mifflin only days earlier had pleaded with Washington to defend Philadelphia. When the general refused to risk his army for a city, Mifflin declared himself "indisposed" and rode away to sulk in his town house, from where he "raised a prodigious clamor" against Washington. Now Paine came to the door, "acquainted him with our design," and asked "whether we might depend on him to command" the defense. Mifflin declined the offer, "not being then very well," though the next day he had recovered sufficiently to mount a horse and flee with the thousands of other citizens.

About one in the morning of September 19 an alarm sounded through the city signaling the enemy's approach. "A beautiful still moonlight morning and the streets as full of men, women and children as on a market day," said Paine. Full of despair, he sent off "my chest and everything belonging to the Foreign Committee to Trenton in a shallop." He lingered a day longer, retreated to the village of Bordentown, New Jersey, to the home of Col. Joseph Kirkbride, with whom he had struck up a friendship in Philadelphia. After a few days' rest, he set off in search of Washington's army. It took three days to find it, Paine "being unwilling to ask questions, not knowing what company I might be in." He arrived in time for the battle of Germantown.

The night the army moved out his solicitous friend General Greene ordered him to stay in camp until the following morning, when the front should be safe to visit. Paine set out at five A.M. Not far from Germantown he met wagons loaded with wounded, and further along "a promiscuous crowd of wounded"; both times he hesitated to ask who had won, fearing the answer. He learned of the defeat shortly when Colonel Biddle, an acquaintance from the retreat across Jersey, told him "that if I went further on that road I should be taken, for that the firing which I heard was the enemy's." (Spotting Paine far from the front may have prompted Biddle's recollection long after that "he always kept out of danger." Though he circulated only around the edges, the battle left a lasting impression on Paine. Seventeen years later, in Paris, he ended a letter to a friend with the remark that he planned to celebrate that night, for "today is the anniversary of the action of Germantown.")

The next day back in camp Paine breakfasted with General Washington, whom he found "at the same loss with every other to account for the accidents of the day." Washington had "supposed everything secure," when the retreat suddenly materialized. Still, he said, the troops had "gained what all young troops gain by being in actions," an observation Paine soon passed off as his own ("They seemed to feel themselves more important *after* it than *before*, as it was the first general attack they had ever made").

A few days later, after being shelled while crossing the Delaware in an open boat—he acted "*very* gallant," said a companion—Paine put the war behind him with another short visit to Colonel Kirkbride in Borden-town. There he received a letter from his friend Timothy Matlack, secretary of Pennsylvania's Executive Council. Matlack suggested that Paine attach himself to the army as a semiofficial observer to assure "more regular and constant intelligence of the proceeding of General Washington's army than has hitherto been had." The suggestion did not come from Matlack alone: "Everyone agrees that you are the proper person for this purpose." Paine returned to camp on October 22, a month after his departure from beleaguered Philadelphia, only to find the army pinned down by "the long and cold severity of the rains." Soon after he arrived word drifted in of Gen. John Burgoyne's surrender to Gen. Horatio Gates at Saratoga, the first major American victory of the war. The news received a mixed reception. Gates had not bothered officially to inform his superior, Washington, of the event, preferring to give word of it directly to Congress. The insult rankled, particularly as it came on the heels of two defeats for Washington and at a moment when, in the few weeks before winter hobbled the army, a deluge prevented further action.

An army trapped in a soggy encampment gave Paine little to report to the Executive Council. Early in November he retreated again to the comfort of Colonel Kirkbride's home, stayed "about a fortnight," then returned to camp as another packet of bad news reached headquarters— the fall of Forts Mifflin and Mercer to the British, which opened up the Delaware to the backed-up fleet of supply ships. Autumn blended into winter, and "the season passed barrenly away." Early in December Washington decided to wait out the winter at Valley Forge, close enough to keep an eye on the British in Philadelphia. "I was there when the army first began to build huts," said Paine. "They appeared to me like a family of beavers; everyone busy; some carrying logs, others mud, and the rest fastening them together. The whole was raised in a few days, and is a curious collection of buildings in the true rustic order."

A rustic life did not appeal to Paine, and he spent the rest of December and all of January 1778 at Colonel Kirkbride's. Shortly afterward he visited Valley Forge, then pushed on through the rolling snow-covered farm country of Pennsylvania to the village of York, where Congress was then sitting, to resume his duties as secretary to the Committee for Foreign Affairs.

3

Congress had dwindled to a rump body of some twenty members, barely enough for a quorum, with the retreat to York. With the army sealed up by winter in Valley Forge, the delegates had little to do in their isolation but talk about the past—Gates's victory at Saratoga, Washington's failure to save Philadelphia. The ice-blocked ports cut off news from the Committee for Foreign Affairs' agents in the West Indies and France, leaving Paine with nothing to do. Instead of taking rooms in York he settled at Lancaster, a larger town—the largest in inland America—and a center for refugees from Philadelphia.

"Just as I locked [the] front door to prepare for bed Thomas Paine came," Christopher Marshall wrote in his diary on 12 February 1778. "So there was supper to get for him; having been thus recruited, had his bed warmed, then to bed after he sat some time regaling himself." Marshall, along with David Rittenhouse and Timothy Matlack, were only three among several friends who had taken up residence in the town; their presence made the transition to the backcountry relatively pleasant for Paine, a city man at heart. The Pennsylvania Assembly as well as the Committee of Safety had set up operations there. Acquaintances from Congress and from Washington's staff passed through regularly on their way to and from York. By the time Paine arrived, Lancaster had come to resemble a diminutive Philadelphia.

Paine's companionable qualities made him a generally welcomed guest wherever he went; though he sometimes overstayed the welcome, he rarely wanted, in a long life of free-loading, for friends willing to put him up. This time it was William Henry, a gunsmith who had accumulated a small fortune from his armory in Lancaster, who invited him to join his household, which already harbored two other refugees—David Rittenhouse and Colonel Joseph Hart. Rittenhouse, at the moment treasurer for the state of Pennsylvania, was considered America's ablest mathematician and astronomer. Henry's hobby was chemistry; he had also experimented with steam engines for boats. All in all it was a congenial resting place for Paine.

The household found Paine a man of fixed habits. He slept late, had a leisurely breakfast, and then ordered his thoughts during a long walk.

Upon returning to his room, he would write down what he had composed during the stroll. After "an inordinate dinner," he would retire to his room, "wrap a blanket about him, and in a large armchair, take a nap, of two or three hours." Another walk followed in the afternoon, after which a few more sentences might be added to the essay in hand. After a light supper came a long evening of talk, suitably refreshed with drink but seldom enough to make him drunk. Those who knew him in Lancaster censured Paine for intolerable laziness. "His remissness, indolence or vacuity of thought, caused great heart-burning among many primary characters, in those days," said one.

Soon after moving in with the Henrys Paine began *Crisis No. 5.* The new essay deals with no specific or immediate crisis. Paine addresses it to Sir William Howe, who commanded the troops in occupied Philadelphia. He ridicules him as a man indolent, obstinate, and immoral, and as a general whose "military jig" with his army resembles "the labors of a puppy pursuing his tail." He censures him for encouraging "the forging and uttering of counterfeit continental bills," an act for which "the laws of any civilized country would condemn you to the gibbet without regard to your rank or titles." He tosses barbs in passing at the king and his ministry ("They have refined upon villainy till it wants a name") and at England ("Instead of civilizing others [she] has brutalized herself"). A postscript, in effect a second essay, addressed "To the Inhabitants of America," promises victory if "that virtuous ambition which first called America into the field" is revived. The piece ends urging the inauguration of a national draft in order that all citizens shall share equally the burdens of war, a suggestion Paine had made before and would make again, without success.

The rambling, disjointed essay is notable not for what it says but for what it ignores. In the months when the sentences were being forced out by a warm fire in Henry's house, Washington and his troops were enduring at Valley Forge "poor food—hard lodging—cold weather—fatigue—nasty clothes—nasty cookery." Nothing of their sufferings appears in the essay. Nor does Paine refer even obliquely to the talk against Washington he heard constantly in these months. Several of his friends—among them Benjamin Rush, Richard Henry Lee, and Thomas Mifflin—believed the victorious Gates should be brought in as commander-in-chief. At a time when he had a real crisis to write about Paine ignored it, preferring to let Washington stand alone against his enemies. He could have justified his silence as expedient, for to have brought the quarrel into the open could have harmed rather than helped the war effort. Instead, he later boasted he had written *Crisis No. 5* to bolster Washington's reputation, "to ward off that meditated blow" building up against him, although except for a passing reference to "the unabated fortitude of a Washington" the general goes unmentioned in the piece. He compounded the wrong by turning blame away from himself and toward John Adams, who he said *"did nothing"* to protect the general, forgetting that Adams at the time had been absent from Congress, preparing to depart for Europe.

4

Rumors were floating through Congress about the negotiations with France when the hard news arrived in April 1778 that a peace commission was on its way from England. The rusticated congressmen in York could do no more than wait to see what the two great nations had to offer the infant United States. One answer came on May 2 when a package of dispatches reached York that contained, among other items, two treaties with France—a commercial treaty and a treaty of alliance. With them also came the promise that words would soon be followed by deeds: France was sending an army and a navy to help speed America toward victory.

In the fall of 1776 the American commissioners had been instructed to seek only a commercial treaty with France; they were told to avoid a political alliance. The commissioners had ignored their instructions. The alliance they had negotiated required, among other things, that the United States must, if asked, help France defend her West Indian possessions if they were attacked. It was exactly the sort of entangling alliance against which Paine had preached in *Common Sense*, had dismissed as a fanciful "air-built battery against independence" when Cato had brought the matter up.

Paine conveniently forgot past remarks about foreign alliances and, along with everyone in Congress, rode high the wave of optimism, and during the ensuing weeks he launched a series of ludicrously wrong predictions. "I think the fighting is nearly over," he said, five years before it was. Early in June he told Washington the British would not evacuate Philadelphia because they wanted to hold on to all they had in America in order to bargain more effectively at the peace table. (The British left the city thirteen days later.) He predicted England would do everything possible to avoid a war with France. (True, but France declared war against England in July.) He was certain that the rumored arrival of the Carlisle peace commission, as it was called, would bring a recognition of American independence. (The commission offered full pardons to all rebels and little more.)

Congress was back in Philadelphia busying itself with other matters by the time it learned of the paltry concessions offered by the Carlisle commission. It had planned to assemble in its old home on July 2, but the State House proved uninhabitable. The British had used it during the occupation as "an hospital and left it in a condition disgraceful to the character of civility," Henry Laurens, Paine's friend and president of Congress, said. "Particularly they had opened a large square pit near the House, a receptacle for filth, into which they had also cast dead horses and the bodies of men." The first few days back in the city the delegates spent "shuffling from meeting house to college hall," holding little more than perfunctory sessions in these makeshift homes. In the midst of the shuffling to and fro word came from the mouth of Delaware Bay that the Count d'Estaing had arrived off the coast with a fleet of sixteen warships and carrying among its passengers Sieur Conrad Alexandre Gérard, the new minister plenipotentiary from France. The foreign minister, the Count de Vergennes, had honored America with one of his ablest diplomats. Gérard had been in the foreign service for thirty-one years, had negotiated the treaties with the United States, and had Vergennes' complete confidence. He was escorted into the city on July 12 with great ceremony. Formal presentation of his credentials was delayed until the innocent Americans, new at this business, figured out how a minister plenipotentiary should be received. On August 6, in a hastily scrubbed and fumigated State House, the ceremony was carried off with elegance. Gérard was accorded nothing but praise by the delegates. He was a wise, well-bred, modest man to all. No one sensed that behind his affable countenance hid a patronizing, almost arrogant attitude toward America and all its citizens whom he had met.

While Philadelphia adjusted to the presence of Gérard and the French fleet he had brought, the Carlisle commission from its base in New York worked to cut between the French and Americans with the pitiful proposals for reconciliation brought from England. When the commissioners found they could win no favor from Congress, even by attempted bribery, they appealed over the heads of the delegates directly to the people in a public proclamation that appeared early in October. Paine abandoned an open letter he had started to Lord North and addressed *Crisis No. 6* to the commissioners. He dismissed their "cargo of pardons" as unmarketable in America. "Remember," he admonished, "you do not, at this time, command a foot of land on the continent of America." A scattering of islands—Staten Island, Manhattan, small parts of Long Island and Rhode Island—"circumscribe your power." Like rats, the British have buried themselves "in corners of inaccessible security; and in order to conceal what everyone can perceive, you now endeavor to impose your weakness upon us for an act of mercy." The French are perhaps England's "natural enemy" but not America's. "There is a sociability in the manners of France, which is much better disposed to peace and negotiation than that of England." He ends on a patronizing note. Times have changed since England disdained even to listen to petitions from America; now she petitions us. Now she offers pardons, but we "offer her peace; and the time will come when she, perhaps in vain, will ask it from us." The essay ranked among Paine's best.

Crisis No. 7—the retitled letter to Lord North, now addressed "To the People of England"—followed three weeks later, on 12 November 1778, and it, too, was superb propaganda. It opens with a question—"Why is it that you have not conquered us?"—and answers it with a taunting revelation of America's weakness the previous year. "We had governments to form; measures to concert; an army to train. . . . Our nonimportation schemes had exhausted our stores, and your command by sea intercepted our supplies. We were a people unknown. . . . Could you possibly wish for a more favorable conjunction of circumstances? Yet all these have happened and passed away, and, as it were, left you with a laugh." America now hovered out of England's reach, "because the country is young and capable of infinite improvement, and has almost boundless tracts of new lands in store." Her people will no longer be dominated, for "domineering will not do over those, who, by a progress in life, have become equal in rank to their parents."

In this address to his former fellow citizens Paine felt the need to inject a rare personal note. "Perhaps it may be said that I live in America, and write this from interest," he said. "To this I reply, that my principle is universal. My attachment is to all the world, and not to any particular part, and if what I advance is right, no matter where or who it comes from."

5

"I am not much hurried in the secretary department, and have sufficient leisure for anything else," Paine had said early in July after returning to Philadelphia with Congress. He had not abandoned the idea of writing a history of the Revolution but continued to find new excuses why "I am unwilling to begin it too soon": The king's "*real motives* . . . in commencing the war" can be discovered from documents available only in England, and the plates and portraits needed to embellish the work "likewise cannot be perfected here." He lacked enough self-awareness to realize that as a man who lived in the present and with little respect for the past he was constitutionally incapable of writing history of any kind.

He did not dream away the time while searching for ways to delay beginning the history. On November 24, twelve days after publishing *Crisis No. 7*, he produced what has been called his best poem, "To the King of England," a scurrilous attack, so bitter that when later reprinted in England, the printer dropped the title to protect himself from being jailed for sedition. In it he compared George to Cain—"Alike in cruelty, alike in hate, / In guilt alike, and more alike in fate"—completing the quatrain with an ingenious allusion to the recent birth of the United States: "Both curs'd supremely (for the blood they drew) / Each from the rising world while each was new." The poem was widely reprinted in America and Europe, but only after Paine had pruned such awkward lines as "*Why lisps* the infant on its mother's lap, / And looking round the parlor—'*Where is pap?*' "

A week later Paine published the first of four essays on the merits of the Pennsylvania constitution. That document had created a one-house legislature, supreme in all legislation. It replaced the governor with an executive council of twelve members who had power to do little more than administer the assembly's acts. Both branches were elected by the people, as were all justices of the peace. The vote was extended to all men over twenty-one who had lived in the state one year and paid taxes of any kind. No special property qualifications hindered a man from holding public office. There were provisions for a system of free schools if the legislature provided the means to finance them (it never did), restrictions on bails and immoderate fines, abolition of imprisonment for debt. Since the constitution had been promulgated in September 1776 the once tightly unified band of Independents in Pennsylvania had split into two factions, one, the anti-Constitutionalists, holding that the democratic innovations broke with past political traditions and created a dictatorship of the people, the other, the Constitutionalists, that the innovations simply put into practice the principles that Americans were fighting for.

Paine stayed clear of the fight for over a half year, holding "no correspondence with either party, for or against, the present constitution." Finally, in March 1777, he tiptoed to the edge of the fray in a cautious public statement: "All that affects me on the matter, is, that a little squabbling spirit should at this ill-chosen time creep in and extinguish everything that is civil and generous among us. I cannot help conceiving it an excess of error and ill-judgment to be wrangling about constitution, till we know whether we shall have one of our own forming, or whether the enemy shall form one for us."

In May Benjamin Rush, as "Ludlow," came forth with the first of four articles that together presented the most thoughtful and convincing attack yet made on the constitution. He argued for a legislature of two houses that could check each other's excesses and for a strong executive with a limited veto and the power to appoint the judiciary and lesser officials. He held that the constitution as it stood violated the principles of the Revolution. The people were revolting against a king and Parliament whose unrestricted power had infringed on the rights of their subjects. An omnipotent assembly merely perpetuated the possibility of an old evil in a new disguise. Worse, safeguards against the rich capturing control of the all-powerful legislature and using it for their own ends existed nowhere in the constitution. The inequalities of property have "introduced natural distinctions in Europe," Rush said. "Where there is wealth, there will be power," and "the rich have always been an overmatch for the poor in all contests for power."

Rush's cogent arguments drew a philosophical rather than practical answer from Paine. Ludlow had confused natural and civil rights. "A *natural* right is an animal right; and the power to act it, is supposed either fully or in part, to be mechanically contained within ourselves as individuals. *Civil* rights are derived from the assistance or agency of other persons." The observation was acute—Paine would later elaborate for Jefferson in Paris and later still in *The Rights of Man*—but it did little to answer the point-by-point criticisms Rush had leveled at the constitution.

The assault by Ludlow—Paine never learned a friend lurked behind the name—helped to fuel the anti-Constitutionalists' fight, and in November 1778 they forced through the Assembly a resolution that called "for taking the sense of the state on the question *for* or *against* a convention" to create a new constitution. The Republicans appealed to Paine to lead the attack against the foe. "I did so, and the service was gratis."

The series opened with the usual disclaimer: that he wrote as a disinterested spectator, "perfectly cool and unfretted," determined to rest all arguments on "fair reasonings," never on "the arrogance of opinion, or the vanity of assertion." Critics of the constitution were, he hoped, disarmed with the reminder that "we are a people upon experiments."

Occasionally in the essays that follow, Paine gets down to specifics. He praises the much censured single-house legislature of Pennsylvania by arguing that it permitted speedy decisions, an asset in wartime when swift action is called for. A judiciary chosen by the people assures the state of judges who represent community rather than special interests. "If ever we cast our eyes towards England, it ought to be rather to take *warning*, than *example*," he says. There the justices of peace are appointed by the crown, with the result that "they are, in general, the bears of the country, and the spaniels of the government."

Despite these occasional nods toward concrete virtues in the constitution, Paine prefers to expound upon the political principles he cherished. He underscores his opinion, then not commonly held, that "*the sense of the majority is the governing sense.*" He finds it "disgraceful" that property qualifications should deprive half the state's adult white males of the vote. "Property alone cannot defend a country against invading enemies," and during a war to tell "men of their rights when we want their service, and of their poverty when the service is over, is a meanness which cannot be professed by a gentleman," he says in one passage, and in another, "Freedom and fortune have no natural relation," a thought that leads into this eloquent statement:

> I consider freedom as personal property. If dangerous in the hands of the poor from ignorance, it is at least equally dangerous in the hands of the rich from influence, and if taken from the former under the pretense of safety, it must be taken from the latter for the same reason, and vested only in those which

stand between the two; and the difficulty of doing this shows the dangerous injustice of meddling with it at all, and the necessity of leaving it at large. Wherever I use the words *freedom* or *rights*, I desire to be understood to mean a perfect equality of them. Let the rich man enjoy his riches, and the poor man comfort himself in his poverty. But the floor of freedom is as level as water. It *can* be no otherwise of itself and *will* be no otherwise till ruffled by a storm. It is a broad base, this universal foundation, that gives security to all and every part of society.

Though he had seldom said it better, there was nothing in these essays that Paine hadn't said before. From time to time he would be led by experience to change an opinion or two. But more striking than the adjustments made is the extraordinary consistency of his thought. All men, said Sir Isaiah Berlin, can be divided into two classes—hedgehogs and foxes. The foxes "pursue many ends . . . related by no moral or aesthetic principle." The hedgehogs "relate everything to a single central vision, one system less or more coherent or articulate, in terms of which they understand, think, and feel." Paine was a hedgehog. Wounds of deadly hate may have driven him to slash out at monarchy in *Common Sense.* "It is a decided point with me," he says now, though surely the wounds had healed, "that kings will go out of fashion in the same manner as conjurors did, and were governments to be now established in Europe, the form of them would not be monarchical." Why was he so certain? "The decline in superstition, the great increase and general diffusion of knowledge, and the frequent equalities of merit in individuals, would render it impossible to decorate any one man with the idolatrous honors which are expected to be paid to him under the name of a crowned head."

In the fourth and final essay praising Pennsylvania's constitution, published 12 December 1778, Paine promised to explore the virtues in later essays. But by the time the piece appeared he was brooding over what he regarded as a major political scandal, one that he, as America's self-appointed guardian of morality, must spread before the people. The crusade against evil he soon launched handed him the first setback since his arrival in America four years earlier.

CHAPTER

6

"A MOST EXCEEDING
ROUGH TIME"

IN LATER YEARS Paine always listed among his accomplishments on the title pages of his books "Secretary for Foreign Affairs to Congress in the American War." His pride seemed ludicrous. Congress assumed it had honored him for past service to the cause with a glorified clerkship that carried responsible duties but no substantive power, a sinecure that left him enough free time to continue turning out propaganda for the cause. Probably no more than two or three hours a day, if that, would be needed to take minutes of the committee's meetings, file papers, docket incoming dispatches, and prepare drafts of outgoing ones for approval.

Paine was made to see the assignment another way. Soon after assuming the post he received from Richard Henry Lee, then absent on a visit to Virginia, a letter that aired an irritation with "the procrastinating genius" of the committee. Lee thought it ought to be bolder in promoting an alliance with France and Spain. He held that Paine, as an "ex officio" member of the committee, could send to the American delegation in Paris all material that underscored British weaknesses and American strengths. The phrase "ex officio" bothered Lee; he crossed it out and urged that Paine on his own "officially transmit" the papers. If he acted promptly "France and Spain may come forward without much longer delay." Such advice from Lee, and no doubt other friends in and out of Congress, encouraged Paine to see his role as something larger than a mere clerk's, and his enemies had soon chalked it against him, as one sarcastically put it, for "styling himself *Secretary of Foreign Affairs.*"

Paine liked to boast that because he owned no property, called no place home, had never voted, he could "view the matter rather than the parties, and having no interests, connections with, or personal dislike to either, shall endeavor to serve all." He might have gotten away with his modest assumption of power on the Committee for Foreign Affairs— though the tight rein Congress held on the committee obviated any chance for him to exert real authority—if circumstances had not forced him to act as something less than the disinterested man he proclaimed to be. Congress had toward the end of 1778 divided into two semipermanent factions, a split the delegates themselves only dimly sensed until the Deane Affair rose to the surface.

2

Silas Deane came from Connecticut. He was forty-one years old and had married twice—once into wealth and then, as a widower, into society when he took for a wife the daughter of Connecticut's governor. He served as a delegate in Congress in 1776, when his home legislature rejected him. Deane had a reputation as a schemer. Originally John Adams found him "a very ingenious man and an able politician," but later, when he looked back, he appeared "a person of a plausible readiness and volubility with his tongue and his pen, much addicted to ostentation and expense in dress and living, but without any deliberate forecast or reflection or solidity of judgment or real information." Even a delegate from Deane's own state suspected his devotion to the American cause as "not genuine" and held that if sent overseas by Congress he would, once beyond the delegates' supervising eyes, place private interests above patriotism. Nonetheless, though he had never been abroad and spoke no French, he was sent to Paris early in 1776 as an agent to procure war material. For his service he would receive expenses and a commission of 5 percent on all supplies purchased for the nation. He was to pass as a merchant in the Indian trade, but at the first chance he was to inform the foreign minister that he was "in France upon business of the American Congress" and wished to purchase "clothing and arms for 25,000 men with a suitable supply of ammunition, and one hundred field pieces."

The foreign minister refused officially to receive Deane, but unofficially he directed him to Caron de Beaumarchais, a lively, litigious gentleman known to the court as a great wit and to the public as the author of *The Marriage of Figaro*. Beaumarchais knew nothing about business, but the government, displaying its own peculiar sense of humor, had placed him at the head of Hortalez and Company, a dummy organization through which war goods could be funneled to America without involving the crown. A subsidy of one million livres from France and another million from Spain financed the venture.

Ships loaded with guns and ammunition and other consignments from Hortalez and Company that would help win the Battle of Saratoga were sailing for America soon after Deane's arrival. All would have been well if Beaumarchais had not begun to use the company for his own ends. The courtly gentleman of "wit and genius," as Deane called him, sold gunpowder to Americans at a 500 percent markup and sent bills of lading with the shipments indicating these were not gifts. Muskets discarded by the French army and given to Beaumarchais for nothing were passed along to the United States at half their original cost. These shenanigans went unquestioned by Deane, possibly because his ignorance of the French language allowed Beaumarchais to hoodwink him. Possibly, too, Deane was using the company to feather his own nest, drawing on its capital to make private purchases for himself and friends in America like Robert Morris, who had told him before he left Philadelphia, "If we have but luck in getting the goods safe to America the profits will be sufficient to content us all."

The troubles brewing for Deane were further spiced by Arthur Lee, brother of that fiery presence in Congress, Richard Henry Lee. Lee, a haughty, suspicious Virginian, and Deane, a haughty, suspicious New Englander, took an instant and deep dislike to each other. Deane was a businessman, a calling Southerners as a rule held slight respect for, and he saw no conflict between serving the American cause and at the same time the interests of himself and his friends. Lee had studied medicine in Edinburgh and law in London and had been so long in Great Britain that Deane thought he "had a secret connection with the British." Lee, for his part, sent letters to his brother in Congress that made clear Deane was a man not to be trusted.

Late in 1777 an agent arrived in Philadelphia with vouchers and bills of lading from Hortalez and Company that totaled 4,500,000 livres, a debt, he said, that Congress owed Beaumarchais for goods purchased. The agent carried a letter from Deane saying that the debt was legitimate and should be paid. A puzzled Congress on December 8 ordered Deane to return home to "report on the state of affairs."

He lingered in Paris until the treaty negotiations with France had been completed. He collected testimonials of his services from Vergennes and Franklin and then accepted an invitation offered by the foreign minister, to set out as a passenger in the French fleet that was bringing the new ambassador, Conrad Alexandre Gérard, to America. He arrived in Philadelphia with Gérard late in the summer of 1778.

Silas Deane was a man "of strong self-esteem and unaccommodating manners," a scholar attempting a balanced assessment has said. "In several respects his conduct was lacking in judgment; nevertheless, for almost two years he [had] performed services of the utmost value to his country by getting into the United States large quantities of indispensable supplies." By his lights and those of his friends he had done well and expected a welcome equal to that of his traveling companion Gérard. Instead he ignited a political holocaust, the worst to strike Congress during the Revolution.

A number of forces contributed to the fury of what came to be called the Deane Affair. Congress had been shaken throughout 1778 by the revelation of several scandals. It had heard from one source that Dr. William Shippen, head of the medical department, had profited from the sale of hospital supplies; from another that Thomas Mifflin when quartermaster-general of the army had used government wagons to haul goods later sold on the open market; and from still another that Mifflin's replacement, Nathanael Greene, was "making a fortune too rapidly" by similar means.

By late 1778 the American Revolution for many had lost the quality of a crusade. Those who had prospered on wartime contracts now rolled about Philadelphia in gaudy coaches. While the ragged continental army survived on half rations, slim supplies, and often no pay, the city's rich, many of them friends of Deane, dressed their women in finery and loaded their tables with delicacies. "Speculation, peculation, and an insatiable thirst for riches seem to have got the better of every other consideration and almost of every order of men," Washington remarked while visiting the city to confer with Congress shortly after Deane's return.

War profiteering coupled with this display of conspicuous consumption convinced John Adams that unless something were quickly done to revive public morality "a civil war in America" was a distinct possibility. These forebodings were shared by Richard Henry Lee of Virginia and Henry Laurens of South Carolina. For these gentlemen Deane symbolized all the "avaricious and ambitious men" who, as one historian puts it, "sought to reverse the Revolution and to establish an aristocratic and mercantile society that would allow full play to private interests." The Deane Affair "went to the heart of the fundamental disagreement rapidly emerging among American leaders over the virtuous character of the American people and the nature of republican society being formed."

3

When Congress received Silas Deane in mid-August the delegates suddenly and somewhat to their own surprise crystallized into pro- and anti-Deane factions. Those hostile to him demanded to see his account books, only to learn that he had left them behind in France. Few of Deane's answers satisfied them, and they moved that he give Congress a written report of his activities during the past two years. Those favoring Deane blocked the motion and the interrogation ended with tempers high. "The storm increases," reported Gouverneur Morris, a pro-Deane man, "and I think some of the tall trees must be torn up by the roots."

Morris might have chosen an apter metaphor, for one of the "tall trees" was short, stocky Henry Laurens of South Carolina, who currently served as president of Congress. He was a tart, blunt man—delegates remembered the day he interrupted a speech of John Penn of North Carolina by singing from the chair, "Poor little Penny, poor little Penny; sing tan-tarra-ra-ra"—with none of the patience required to calm the mounting storm over Deane. His biographer has remarked that "Mr. Laurens, good man that he was, had quite a streak of self-righteousness and quite a stock of acid adjectives for those who differed with him." But there was this to be said: He cherished the Continental Congress as the embodiment of the new nation's interests and the mentor of its welfare. He had left the first session that quizzed Deane shocked that his "fellow-laborers had as absolutely taken sides as it can be supposed." In the days that followed he tried to shift discussion into other channels before news of the uproar tarnished Congress' reputation with the public. The public knew nothing about the furious debate behind closed doors until December 5 when the frustrated Deane, whose repeated requests to present his case before Congress had been ignored, published a long diatribe that accused the Lee brothers and a faction in Congress of favoring reconciliation with Britain and seeking to make a separate peace in violation of the treaty with France.

The letter convinced Richard Henry Lee that a conspiracy "plotted some months before" by merchants, war profiteers and evildoers in general was about to be consummated. He who had been among the first to encourage an alliance with France now saw the American delegation there (his brother excepted) as part of a "corrupt hotbed of vice" that "has produced a tall tree of evil, the branches of which spread over the great part of Europe and America, and unless it is speedily cut down and thrown away, I easily foresee extensive mischief to these states, and to the cause of human nature." Henry Laurens, on the other hand, reviled Deane's "highly derogatory" slurs against Congress and "the honor and interests of these United States." Congress, however, preferred to get on with the battle rather than worry about the insult to its dignity. On December 9 the disgusted Laurens resigned as president, ending his valedictory with a bitter denunciation of his colleagues. "I cannot," he said, "consistently with my own honor, nor with the utility to my country, considering the manner in which business is transacted here, remain any longer in this chair."

The pro-Deane faction assumed, correctly, that these remarks were directed at them. They reacted with two insults of their own—first by voting down a vote of thanks to the president for his service, hitherto a routine courtesy, then by electing John Jay of New York to replace Laurens in the chair, knowing that Jay looked kindly on Deane.

4

Thus far Paine had remained silent, preoccupied with his series on the Pennsylvania constitution then appearing in the press. But in an affair where one friend, Lee, saw at stake "the cause of human nature" and another, Laurens, "the honor and interests of the United States," silence could no longer be endured. Other factors helped speed his entrance into the battle. He had known for several weeks, thanks to the classified documents that had crossed his desk, "that the stores which Silas Deane and Beaumarchais pretended they had purchased were a present from the court of France, and came out of the king's arsenals." The appearance of copies of the missing dispatches had convinced him a conspiracy was afoot.

Paine fumed for several days after Deane's open letter appeared, then when no one rebutted the charges he cut short the series on the Pennsylvania constitution and on December 15 published his own reply. Of those to whom he had shown the manuscript "every man, almost without exception, thought me wrong in opposing" Deane. The essay, Paine's first attack against an American patriot and, for him, a restrained piece, accused Deane of little more than indiscrimination and poor taste. "You will please to observe," he told Laurens, "that I have been exceedingly careful to preserve the honor of Congress in the minds of the people who have been so exceedingly fretted by Mr. Deane's address, and this will appear the more necessary when I inform you that a proposal has been made for calling a town meeting to demand justice for Mr. Deane."

The judicious tone of the essay satisfied no one. Paine, to his astonishment, suddenly found himself the center of attack. "The poor fellow got a beating from an officer, it is said, for having wrote the piece," Richard Henry Lee reported. The beating occurred late one evening when a group of gentlemen were returning from a party given by James Mease, clothier-general of the army and rumored to rank high among the army's notorious speculators. "You may readily suppose," a contemporary said, "that the excellent wine of Mr. Mease exhilarated the company." While heading for their lodgings one of the men spotted Paine coming toward them down the street.

"There comes Common Sense," said one.

"Damn him," said another. "I shall common sense him."

As Paine came abreast, a foot went out and tripped him, and he fell "on his back into the gutter, which at that time was very offensive and filthy."

The attacks in the press were equally embarrassing. "Plain Truth" remarked on his "quaint conceit," his "solemn air of a person . . . deeply conversant in state secrets," and questioned his veracity. Paine answered pompously that as "I have been Secretary for Foreign Affairs almost two years, you will allow that I must be some judge of the matter," then tossed in the empty threat to prosecute "Plain Truth" for "publishing a false, malicious libel, tending to injure the reputation of the Secretary for Foreign Affairs."

Paine brooded until December 24, when he promised in a "card" to the public to "lay the facts fairly, with his usual candor, before the public." The first of a five-part philippic soon appeared. Even friends thought the essays bombastic and discursive. " 'Common Sense' has attacked Mr. Deane something in his own way," said one, "but I think has not made the best use of the materials." Part of the trouble was that he allowed himself to be deflected from the facts he had against Deane to innuendos against members of Congress with "mercantile connections," notably Robert Morris, who had until recently served as a delegate for Pennsylvania. There, as chairman of a committee that purchased military supplies, he had dispensed contracts to friends, among them Deane, as well as over a half million dollars' worth to his own firm of Willing and Morris. Paine thought his dealings should be investigated to determine whether there had been a conflict of public and private interests. Morris disagreed. Pennsylvania has no right "to inquire into what mercantile connections I have had or now have with Mr. Deane, or with any other person," he replied to Paine bluntly in an open letter. "If Mr. Deane had any commerce that was inconsistent with his public station he must answer for it; as I did not, by becoming a delegate for the state of Pennsylvania, relinquish my right of forming mercantile connections I was unquestionably at liberty to form such with Mr. Deane."

Friends congratulated Morris on his reply. "Paine, like the enthusiastic madmen of the East," said Thomas Mifflin, "was determined to run the *muck*—he sallied forth, stabbed three or four slightly, met with you, but missing his aim fell a victim to his own stroke; and by attempting too much will enjoy a most mortifying and general contempt." Morris refused to gloat. He respected Paine's marksmanship too much to enjoy serving as a target. Paine on the prowl could safely be confronted only when disarmed, and in the weeks that Paine shot at him Robert Morris gave a good deal of thought to doing just that.

Meanwhile, Paine continued to bore in on Deane. He promised to show any of Deane's friends who visited his office a report, "in handwriting which Mr. Deane is well acquainted with," that the supplies he said he had purchased "were promised and engaged, and that as a present, before he ever arrived in France." That seemingly innocent sentence undid Paine. In publishing it he had violated his oath "to disclose no matter" that as secretary "he shall be directed to keep secret."

Paine might have survived the indiscretion if it had not impugned the honor of France. A French citizen could legitimately sell goods to a citizen of the rebellious colonies; for the French government to sell or, worse, to hand over "as a present" such goods ranked as a dastardly act. Honor among nations had fled the world when one member of the European family, in time of peace, surreptitiously thrust a dagger into the back of another. Or so the stiff-necked, literal-minded Gérard thought. His contempt for American politicians convinced him the time had come to force them to play the game of diplomacy by the rule book. Moreover, America must be taught that in the partnership with France she played a subsidiary role in which the tunes would be called by France.

Later a British observer reported home that "Gérard has fairly bullied the Congress into the declaration of a falsehood under pretense of calling for an explanation of what 'Common Sense,' Mr. Paine, had wrote in his attack upon Deane." The bullying began immediately after Gérard had read Paine's essay, when he sent him a note calling for a retraction of the offensive revelation. Paine's reply showed he failed to understand what distressed the minister. "My design was and is to place the merit of these supplies where I think the merit is most due," he said, "that is, in the disposition of the French nation to help us." Gérard feared Paine served as the mouthpiece for the anti-French faction in Congress led by Richard Henry Lee and Samuel Adams. Let the minister relax; no faction had or ever would capture Paine's pen. "No member of Congress knows what I write till it appears in public," he said. Gérard should have suspected that he had not reached his man. Instead, he thanked Paine for the promise to be "more explicit" on the subject, which he interpreted to mean a retraction would be forthcoming in the next essay. The minister picked up his newspaper on January 5 to find Paine had retracted nothing. France had prefaced her alliance, one sentence went, "by an early and generous friendship." That did it. If Paine would not bend, he must be broken. Immediately after reading the latest effusion, Gérard officially protested to Congress against these "indiscreet assertions" and asked that "measures suitable to the circumstances" be taken.

5

Arrogance and self-righteousness had combined to put the normally accommodating Gérard—Europe regarded him as one of France's ablest diplomats—in an intransigent mood. Arrogance and self-righteousness blended with innocence had combined to blind Paine to what he had done. It took the curtness of Gérard's note to Congress to make clear he had somehow endangered relations between the United States and France. On January 6 he wrote Congress offering to resign as secretary. A gentleman could do no more. Moreover, as he had told Gérard, "I am under no obligation to Congress otherwise than the honor they did me in the appointment. It is in every other light a disadvantage to me. I serve from principle."

Congress did not answer his letter. Instead, President Jay ordered that "Thomas Paine do attend at the bar of this house immediately." When Paine stepped from his office into the chamber of Congress, Jay picked up a newspaper and said, "Here is Mr. Dunlap's paper of December 29. In it is a piece entitled 'Common Sense to the Public on Mr. Deane's Affairs'; I am directed by Congress to ask if you are the author."

"Yes, sir, I am the author of that piece," came the answer.

Jay put the same question about two other essays and received the same reply. He then said, "You may withdraw," allowing nothing more to be added to the exchange. After Paine left the room, John Penn of North Carolina moved that "Thomas Paine be discharged from the office of secretary of the Committee for Foreign Affairs." The motion lost when put to a vote, "the states being equally divided."

That night Paine drew up a memorial to Congress which he presented the next day, January 7. "I cannot in duty to my character as a freeman submit to be censured," he said. "I have evidence which I presume will justify me. And I entreat this house to consider how great their reproach will be should it be told that they passed a sentence upon me without hearing me, and that a copy of the charge against me was refused to me; and likewise how much that reproach will be aggravated should I afterwards prove the censure of this house to be a libel, grounded upon a mistake which they refused fully to inquire into." No hint of remorse, no sign of humbleness tinged the blunt sentences. Nor did it occur to Paine that without the change of a word his statement could have served Silas Deane three months earlier when he pleaded with Congress to let him present his case.

The memorial provoked Congress into a full day of debate on Paine's deportment. The issue involved more than an innocent indiscretion. The delegates faced a problem without precedent: Paine was the first public official the government had contemplated removing from office. Several members argued that Congress could not "punish a citizen unheard." But this is not a criminal case, answered Gouverneur Morris. The tenure of Paine's office is not "during good behavior; it is during pleasure," he went on. "And what are we? The sovereign power, who appointed, and who when he no longer pleases us, may remove him. Nothing more is desired. We do not wish to punish him." Paine is not an ordinary citizen, Morris said, but a public servant, and "the ideas annexed to such a character will serve to authenticate his assertions." The impression exists abroad that as Congress' servant he wrote with its consent, and therefore without "contradicting him, we shall not be believed." He pointed to "the threatening letter on your table" from Paine. "What! are we reduced to such a situation, that our servants shall abuse the confidence reposed in them, shall beard us with insolent menaces, and we shall fear to dismiss them without granting a trial forsooth?" Morris weakened his cogent argument for the right of Congress to dismiss one of its servants by sprinkling it with contemptuous references to that "mere adventurer *from England,* without fortune, without family or connections, ignorant even of grammar," that man full of "mad assertions" who has been "puffed as of great importance."

After the day-long discussion had ended, Paine's friends told him that evening that the decision would go against him the next day when the delegates voted. On the morning of January 8 Congress found on the table another letter of resignation from its obstreperous clerk. "I have betrayed no trust because I have constantly employed that trust to the public good," the still unrepentant Paine wrote. "I have revealed no secrets because I have told nothing that was, or I conceive ought to be, a secret. I have convicted Mr. Deane of error, and in so doing I hope I have done my duty." This second letter of resignation should have ended the matter, but the anti-Deane faction marshaled enough strength to mount a four-day debate on whether or not to accept it. Discussion opened with someone wondering how Paine had learned from the supposedly secret Journal of Congress that he had been denied a hearing. Charles Thomson, secretary of Congress, said he could not have seen the mentioned entry, for the Journal had never left Thomson's hands. It was moved that the delegates be "separately examined by the president on their honor" whether they had talked to Paine. A humiliated Henry Laurens stalled this procedure by confessing he had spoken to Paine. Embarrassment of all was buried by moving the debate to a new line of inquiry.

On January 12 it was unanimously resolved that John Jay assure the

French minister "that Congress do fully in the clearest and most explicit manner, disavow the publication referred to in his said memorials." The pro-Deane group demanded a fuller retraction—that Congress was "convinced by indispensable evidence that . . . the great and generous ally of these United States did not preface his alliance with any supplies whatever sent to America." In accepting the humiliating revision, Congress simultaneously repudiated Paine and its own reputation for integrity. Public disavowal of Paine's attempt to "injure the reputation" of France and America and "impair their mutual confidence" came a few days later when Jay's letter to Gérard was released to the newspapers.

Once Gérard had determined his course, Congress had no choice but to act as it did. Or so Gérard made it appear. It is doubtful that Vergennes would have forced the issue if Congress had refused to satisfy Gérard. But the delegates, innocent as Paine in international affairs, backed down. Many had been pleased to censure Paine for exceeding his authority as Secretary for Foreign Affairs. Others voted against him reluctantly and must have recalled as they cast their ballots the warning in *Common Sense* against entangling alliances.

On January 16 Congress again spent the day wrangling about Paine. It was agreed that all "public papers entrusted to him" as secretary be retrieved. The next question, whether to "discharge him from that office," was not so easily settled. Votes were cast by states, but John Penn demanded that on this issue he wanted the stand of individuals as well as states to be recorded, and it was so agreed. Every New Englander present and every man in the Pennsylvania delegation voted against the further humiliation of discharging Paine from office. Every delegate from New York and all the South except Richard Henry Lee—Laurens was absent—voted to discharge Paine. The states were evenly divided—New Jersey had no members present—and by the rules of Congress a tie vote defeated the motion. Paine's resignation was accepted. Two and a half months later when he received the final $250 due on his salary his official ties with Congress ended forever.

6

On January 8, during a private supper with an emissary from Gérard, Paine received "a very lucrative offer, to double the value of what I had resigned." The offer was repeated twice more, and finally, on January 14,

Paine accepted an invitation to visit Gérard himself. "I was sensible of a kind of shame at the Minister's door today," he said after the visit, "lest anyone should think I was going to solicit a pardon or a pension."

Paine and Gérard walked around the reason for theïr meeting through an afternoon of conversation. Only at the end did the minister come to the point. "Mr. Paine," he said, "I have always had a great respect for you, and should be glad of some opportunity of showing you more solid marks of my friendship." He went on to offer Paine one thousand dollars a year "to employ his pen chiefly with inspiring the people with sentiments favorable to France and the alliance, and in such a way as to foster hatred and distrust of the English." The offer was tempting, for it asked him to write only what he naturally was inclined to write. Also, he needed the money. Nonetheless, he refused it. "Any service I can render to either of the countries in alliance, or to both, I ever have done and shall do," he said, "and Mr. Gérard's *esteem* will be the only compensation I shall desire." Later, either to protect himself or to underscore his high-toned conduct, Paine told Congress of the proffered bribe, not implicating Gérard but saying only that it was "a private offer . . . amounting in money to £700 a year," adding that though the proposal was both polite and friendly "I thought it my duty to decline it; as it was accompanied with a condition which I conceived had a tendency to prevent the information I have since given [in regard to Deane], and shall yet give to the country on public affairs."

Gérard's graciousness mollified Paine sufficiently so that shortly after the conversation he began a new essay in which he said he "never *labored to prove* that the supplies *were* or *are* a present," but only that "there was a disposition in the gentlemen of France to have made America a very handsome present." Paine seemed to have accepted his new "task with pleasure," Gérard told Vergennes, his superior in Paris. "He has already entered on his duties," he reported, "by declaring that the matter of assistance did not concern the court, and was not a political affair." After writing this conciliatory statement, Paine came upon in the newspapers Gérard's thanks to Congress for "their frank, noble and categorical manner of destroying those false and dangerous insinuations which might mislead ignorant people." "I feel myself exceedingly hurt," he said after reading the lines. He determined to extract a retraction from Gérard. "I find myself obliged to tell him that I think it convenient to absent myself from the company even of my most intimate friends till he shall be pleased to explain that I am not personally alluded to in this paragraph."

Gérard refused to retract and Paine, as promised, absented himself from "even my most intimate friends." He shunned calling on Laurens because "I feel only an *unwillingness* to be seen, on your account." By the end of January he had not stirred from his rooms. "I have been out no where for near these two months," he told George Washington and Nathanael Greene in letters to them on January 31, by way of explaining why he had failed to call on them when they visited the city. "I have lately met with a turn, which, sooner or later, happens to all men in popular life," he wrote Franklin, "that is, I fell, all at once, from high credit to disgrace and the worst word was thought too good for me." At the end of the letter he added, "I have had a most exceeding rough time of it." (Franklin's daughter, Sarah Franklin Bache, had not helped ease Paine's rough time. Franklin liked Deane; in her eyes then Deane must be a good man. Upon meeting Paine one day in the street, she reprimanded him for his role in the affair, and since then Paine had "never even moved his hat to me," she told her father.)

Paine continued to write while he brooded, building his case in essay after essay. In the first three months after his resignation had been accepted he published eight long pieces. His excellent memory enabled him to quote from documents no longer in his possession which in his view showed how completely Deane had lied. As prosecutor out to convict he built a devastating if one-sided case that by mid-February had silenced Deane's allies. An unnerved Gérard was astonished at Paine's "inconsistency and obstinence" and wondered how the man could be muzzled. In March Paine turned to attack those in Congress who had maneuvered him out of office—Gouverneur Morris, John Penn, William Drayton—listing with acid comments virtually all who had voted to have him discharged. His nagging, "very impertinent" letters to Congress calling for facts to build his own defense—"it is necessary that my character stand fair as that of any member of this honorable House"—were "ordered to lay on the table." "Poor Paine, not the most prudent man in the world, is execrated by a number and much out of the books of Congress," a friend remarked. Congress bristled partly because Paine's campaign against members who had opposed him was succeeding. Maryland and Virginia passed laws prohibiting their delegates in Congress to profit from government contracts. Several delegates tainted by Paine's revelations were rejected by their legislatures for reelection to Congress. "The scale of affairs is now entirely turned as to the public sentiment," Paine said during a lull in the battle.

7

The Deane Affair did not fade from mind until two years later. In mid-1780 Deane had returned to Europe without receiving either censure or praise from Congress. He settled first in Paris, then moved on to Antwerp, from where in 1781 he sent a series of letters to American friends urging reunion with Great Britain. The British, who had encouraged the letters with a bribe, "intercepted" them and had them published in occupied New York's press. "Mr. Robert Morris assured me that he had been totally deceived in Deane; but that he now looked upon him to be a bad man, and his reputation totally ruined," Paine exulted after the letters had appeared. "Gouverneur Morris hopped round upon one leg" —he had recently lost a leg under a carriage wheel—"swore they had all been duped, himself among the rest, complimented me on my quick sight —and by God, says he, nothing carries a man through the world like honesty."

Over a century and a half passed before the full story of Deane's duplicity came out. Papers buried in the British archives eventually revealed that as early as 1777, before Congress recalled him, Deane had carried on traitorous negotiations with a British spy and that the letters of 1781 had been commissioned by the British government to promote disunion in the United States. Deane died in poverty in 1789 as he was about to set out for Canada, where he hoped to make a new start.

CHAPTER

7

"WE WANT ROUSING"

PAINE EMERGED FROM his lodgings early in April 1779 as he sensed public sentiment shifting from Deane's side to his. Owen Biddle, a merchant, offered him a clerkship in his office. Although an insignificant job, it allowed Paine to live without begging for room and board. Other friends in Philadelphia enticed him back into public life by voting him a seat on two committees created to investigate the affairs of Robert Morris. The committees met regularly through June and into July, but before their dossiers on Morris' dealings could be condensed into publishable reports, Paine had embroiled himself in another controversy, this one concerning the fisheries off Newfoundland.

The issue centered on whether Congress should make New England's traditional right to fish off and dry its catches on the coast of Newfoundland part of American demands when the time came to discuss peace terms with Great Britain. The debate opened within Congress in mid-February, rising to the surface off and on through the spring, until by the summer it occupied the delegates' full attention. It came alive outside Congress only in late June with a series of newspaper articles signed by "Americanus," who argued at length that to make the fisheries an ultimatum in the peace negotiations would prolong the war, exactly the point that Gérard had pressed upon delegates behind the scenes with a tactlessness that only inflamed the debate. Eagerness to strike back at Gérard, abetted by a suspicion that Gouverneur Morris lurked behind the pseudonym "Americanus," lured Paine into the battle. In the first of a three-part series he argued, without proving the point, that America had a natural right to the fisheries "so clear and evident that it does not admit of debate." What benefited New England benefited the nation, he went on, "for wealth like water soon spreads over the surface, let the place of entrance be ever so remote," but he failed to show how, at a time when interests were localized, that wealth would spread among the states. The second essay squandered space attempting to flush out the identity of "Americanus." Paine pinned the tag on Gouverneur Morris but later, when Morris shrugged it off, weakly insisted he had "replied to the piece rather than to the man." Only in the final essay did he produce substantial arguments—all of them lifted from debates in Congress. The fisheries provided a commerce "which interferes with none, and promotes others"; they composed a "fourth part of the staple commerce of the United States"; they enriched a part of the continent "inflicted [with] a degree of natural sterility"; they offered a nursery for seamen. As usual some of his best remarks came in asides. At one point he cleared away as rubbish the view that *the law of nations* was something "fixed and known like the law of the ten commandments," substituting a definition of international law difficult to improve upon: "It is a term without any regular defined meaning," he said, "in theory the law of treaties compounded with customary usage, and in practice just what they can get and keep till it be taken from them." Elsewhere in the essay he summed up his feeling for America in a sentence so apt that the new nation might well have taken it for its motto: "We covet not dominion, for we already possess a world."

2

The series on the fisheries revived smoldering animosities left over from the Deane Affair. On July 9 one who signed himself "Cato" unleashed a tirade surpassing anything that had gone before. Paine had "wormed into notice by a talent for abuse," then "had been raised to a confidential office by a faction who labored to undermine the great Fabius himself, the Saviour of his country." A string of questions to fertilize gossip—"Who was an Englishman? Tom P____. Who was a Tory? Tom P____."—ended with "Who maintains Tom P____? Nobody knows. Who is paid by the enemy? Nobody knows. Who best deserves it? Tom P____." Another assault followed a week later in the form of a poem that opened almost gently, considering what came later:

> Hail mighty Thomas! In whose works are seen,
> A mangled Morris and distorted Deane;
> Whose splendid periods flash for Lee's defense,
> Replete with everything but common sense.

The vicious cuts are saved for the end, where the anonymous author wonders about Paine's birth. He suggests "no mere mortal mother did thee bear." Instead,

> . . . as Minerva, queen of sense uncommon,
> Owed not her birth to goddess or to woman;
> But softly crept from out her father's soul,
> At a small crack in 't when the moon was full;
> So you, great Common Sense, did surely come
> From out the crack in grisly Pluto's bum.

"A Friend to Cato and to Truth" joined the battle, taunting Paine for having been discharged by Aitken for "your inveterate hatred to everything produced in favor of the liberty of these states" and comparing him to a drum—"the more you have been thumped and beaten, the greater noise you have made." In another piece, headed "The Galled Horse Winces," Cato sneered, "Thomas, you seem to be in a passion. Has Cato ruffled the smooth surface of your temper?" He had, as Cato knew. Two hours after the first piece had appeared Paine tried to extract Cato's identity from Benjamin Towne, whose newspaper had published the taunts. Towne said then "he had not liberty to give him up," and later that he had been tied down "to such strong obligations to conceal him, that nothing but a halter could extort it from him." Paine's friends on July 24 threatened Towne with the halter, and he quickly revealed the author as Whitehead Humphreys, a local merchant in iron and steel. That night a small mob with Captain Charles Willson Peale at their head gathered before Humphreys' house. Humphreys faced them down with pistols, and after some palaver all agreed to talk matters over the next morning at the London Coffee House. At the coffee house Humphreys was lectured on the phrase "liberty of the press," then, he said later, "I was delivered out of the hands of a lawless banditti (who repeatedly refused me the liberty of addressing my fellow citizens) and amidst the acclamation of a great majority of the most respectable citizens of Philadelphia." The show of force had its effect: Humphreys sputtered once more in print, then ceased the attacks on Paine.

Friends had silenced the opposition; now they set about to refurbish

Paine's reputation and shore up his ego. At nine o'clock in the morning, July 27, at a mass meeting in the State House yard, it was resolved, with "several thousand present," "that Mr. Thomas Paine is considered by this meeting as a friend to the American cause, and therefore . . . we will support and defend him, so long as his conduct shall continue to prove him to be a friend to this country."

These encomiums came as Paine's veracity was questioned again from another quarter. Cato's public flailing had provoked Charles Willson Peale to remark one day at the coffee house that Paine had refused a bribe from Deane's people for his literary services. Instantly, Deane demanded to know who had made the offer, and a short while later with John Nixon and James Wilson in tow he called at Peale's home to get the story firsthand. Paine came ambling down Market Street as they were leaving, "and as some of them saw me, they might have had the satisfaction from me, which they required, had they waited till I came up, which was within a few moments of their going away."

Instead, recriminations flashed again in the press. Paine, for his part, promised to tell all, then rambled on so vaguely that he later admitted his explanation offered "less . . . than was generally expected. . . . It is sufficient on my part that I declined the offer; and it is sufficient to Mr. Nixon and Mr. Wilson that they were not the persons who made it": a cheap exit from the squabble that left Deane guilty by implication. The rickety defense lent substance to the charge that Paine's "quibbling pen" seemed only "eager to traduce the worthiest men." Friends who had watched obloquy heaped upon Paine for over half a year spoke more charitably, and hoped he would soon again be himself.

3

Paine's troubles during June and July of 1779 absorbed only a portion of his time, the bulk of which went to resolving the ills besetting Philadelphia. He had never before been so directly involved in public affairs, caucusing almost daily with friends, serving on committees, writing reports—all while fending off attacks as best he could. Superficially his concerns seem multitudinous, varying from the price of salt to a rising sentiment against the French. Actually, everything that involved him focused on a single issue—the surging inflation currently sweeping the continent but bearing down especially hard on Philadelphians.

His slight salary as clerk in Owen Biddle's office made Paine sensitive to inflation. By the summer of 1779 the worth of a paper dollar had slumped to less than a copper penny, and the phrase "not worth a continental" had slipped into the language. As value fell, prices soared. Paine wanted the Pennsylvania Assembly to impose price controls, for Congress had refused to do so, insisting it lacked the power to demand them of the states. Paine argued that the unchecked prices acted as a tax on the plain people. The merchants answered that high prices did not cause, but resulted from, inflation, and that price controls could only bring ruin, forcing them to sell below cost. Also, enforcement of such controls in a loosely knit state with a weak government was impossible. No sane man would accept a fixed price and American paper money for the goods on his shelf when the French, with hard money in their pockets, were willing to pay what the market demanded to supply their sailors and soldiers.

French purchases entangled Paine in a direct confrontation with Robert Morris. Paine had a built-in antipathy toward men of wealth—"A rich man," he said, quoting James I, "makes a bonny traitor"—and Morris, as one of Pennsylvania's richest, offered a vulnerable target. Rumor had it that the French ship *Victorious*, which docked at Philadelphia in late April, carried a cargo owned by Morris that would be sold at inflated prices. Another rumor accused him of purchasing flour for the French navy at the going market price rather than the more modest one recommended by a citizens' committee.

At a public meeting on May 25 Paine was chosen to serve on one committee to investigate the consignment of the *Victorious'* cargo and on another to look into Morris' sale of flour to the French. Morris dealt cautiously with the committees—he met with them only when sympathetic witnesses were present and conducted nearly all his dealings in writing—but with sufficient courtesy and apparent sincerity to impress even Paine. The report on the *Victorious'* cargo, which cleared Morris of fraud, was probably written by Paine. But no businessman could completely satisfy Paine's high moral standards. "Though, as a merchant, he may be strictly within the rules," the report concluded, "yet when he considers the many public and honorary stations he has filled, and the times he lives in, he must feel himself somewhat out of character." The second committee, reporting on flour purchases for the French navy, also exonerated Morris.

The temperate judgments of these two reports, in which Paine must have had a large hand, are curious enough to deserve some speculation. It might be assumed that others on the committees had dictated the moderate conclusions, but all—among them David Rittenhouse, Timothy Matlack, and Daniel Roberdeau—were friends of Paine; his views and theirs seldom deviated. Perhaps Morris' affable, open, and frank disclosures to the committees convinced Paine that not all rich men were potential traitors, that they might even be as eager as the less endowed to promote the nation's interests. Perhaps, too, the persistent attacks against Paine, at their peak while the committee reports were being written, helped to undermine dogmatic assumptions he had made about the mercantile community. Paine never lacked the courage to speak out against any man he suspected of wrongdoing, but within the same skin lived a man eager to be liked by those he respected, and it soon became clear he respected Robert Morris. Regardless of the reasons, the committees' findings for Morris marked a turning point in Paine's attitude toward the established members of the community.

Publication of the committee reports coincided with an upturn in Paine's affairs. The assaults against him in the press ceased as abruptly as they began. On August 2 he was elected a member of an enlarged committee to control the price of flour and salt in Philadelphia and also to a committee created to find a way to raise taxes in Pennsylvania. For this second committee he produced a "Citizen's Plan," in which he proposed voluntary contributions in sound money to the government from citizens, the money received to be credited against their tax assessments. The state's Executive Council praised this laudable plan "to restore public credit," then rejected it as unworkable. Another plan he publicized to control prices proved equally unworkable. "The consequence was that no salt was brought to market," he said, and the price rose from one shilling and sixpence per bushel to thirty-six shillings per bushel; "and we regulated the price of flour (farina) till there was none in the market, and the people were glad to procure it at any price." From this he concluded that what had failed to work in Philadelphia would work nowhere else. Only later during the French Revolution was he to find, to his dismay, that an economic theory inapplicable in one society need not necessarily be inapplicable in another.

4

The extent of his public activities during the summer and fall of 1779 suggests that Owen Biddle demanded little of Paine's time and, to judge by his complaints of poverty, paid proportionally. "I think I have a right to ride a horse of my own," he said as autumn approached, "but I cannot now even afford to hire one, which is a situation I never was in before." Paine's pride did not help matters. When Timothy Matlack asked how he lived, he dodged an answer and became so fussed he failed to listen carefully as Matlack outlined a plan for Paine to "assist in arranging," for a fee, some of the busy Joseph Reed's papers for publication. In mid-August he came down with a fever that forced him to bed. Recovery in early September was followed by a relapse. "I know but one kind of life I am fit for," he wrote at the time, "and that is a thinking one, and, of course, a writing one—but I have confined myself so much of late, taken so little exercise, and lived so very sparingly, that unless I alter my way of life it will alter me."

Privately Paine talked in the fall of 1779 of abandoning the American Revolution. He wrote Franklin that he contemplated a visit to France and mentioned the plan again in a conciliatory note to Gérard. In another note he revealed a bitterness and slight attachment to the United States when he told Henry Laurens that "perhaps America would feel the less obligation to me did she know, that it was neither the place nor the people but the cause itself that irresistibly engaged me in its support; for I should have acted the same part in any other country could the same circumstances have arisen there which have happened here."

And yet as he talked of leaving he talked of staying. Perhaps Pennsylvania, whose government was in the hands of political friends, would help him. "I think I have done better by the state than the state has by me," he complained to Joseph Reed, president of the Executive Council. A few days later he asked the Council to subsidize publication of his collected works "with the loan of fifteen hundred pounds, for which I will give bond payable within a year." Nothing came of the request.

Meanwhile Reed, with a job in mind, had already written Gérard to check on the rumor that Paine was in the pay of the French. Gérard, in a carefully worded reply, said Paine had agreed to write for him and that he had a witness to the bargain in the person of Paul Fooks, official translator and interpreter for Congress. He did not say the agreement had been consummated, for it had not. Paine could be, and would be, bought. He had probably agreed back in January, after losing his job with Congress and with nothing to live on, to write for Gérard, then after Owen Biddle hired him as clerk had second thoughts. His series against the French position on the Newfoundland fisheries issue was convincing evidence that Gérard did not own him. But if Paine would not work for France, Gérard seems to have reasoned in his misleading reply to Reed, he should not work for any government.

Gérard's opinion soon became academic. In October, ill but joyful, he returned to France, having been replaced by a stocky, convivial diplomat named Anne-César, chevalier de la Luzerne. On November 2, a few days after Gérard's departure, the Pennsylvania Assembly chose Thomas Paine to serve as its clerk.

5

The clerkship gave Paine an adequate income and relieved him from the "idleness, uneasiness and hopeless thinking" which had "got so much the upper hand" since his illness in mid-August. It called for much shuffling of papers and little thought but offered "something like business," absorbing so much time that Paine wrote little while he held it. He gave "great satisfaction" to the Assembly, and from a friend who thought Paine might get a sinecure in the Land Office came the hint "that something further will be done for him at the close of the present sitting."

Two months after he assumed the post Washington revealed that the distress of the winter thus far exceeded even the dreary months at Valley Forge. Many of the men "have been four or five days without meat entirely and short of bread," he said, "and none but very scanty supplies." He went on to say, "Some for their preservation have been compelled to maraud and rob from inhabitants, and I have it not in my power to punish or to repress the practice. If our condition should not undergo a very speedy and considerable change for the better, it will be difficult to point out all the consequences that may ensue."

Crisis No. 8, completed on February 26, seemed frivolous against this backdrop. It was directed to the people of England, reminding them that John Paul Jones now roved off their coast. Paine made Jones's small force resemble a great invading fleet about to impose the miseries of war upon a hitherto spared and spoiled people. "To see women and children wandering in the severity of winter, with the broken remains of a well furnished house, and seeking shelter in every crib and hut, were matters that you had no conception of," he wrote. These ludicrous exaggerations were designed less to dishearten the safely ensconced English than to rouse the spirits of Americans during their current winter of discontent. But Paine sensed the inadequacy of his effort at a time when his friend Nathanael Greene was reporting of the troops in his command "more than half naked and two-thirds starved." He lopped off the second half of the essay and except for a single paragraph woven into a later piece never bothered to print it.

The army endured the winter, but Washington had little good news to announce with the arrival of spring. "Every idea you can form of our distresses will fall short of the reality," he wrote President Reed on May 28. "There is such a combination of circumstances to exhaust the patience of the soldiery that it begins at length to be worn out, and we see in every line of the army the most serious features of mutiny and sedition. . . . Indeed, I have almost ceased to hope." Reed passed the letter along to Paine, who as clerk read it aloud to the Assembly in a closed session. It is "vain to contend the matter any longer," Paine reported on one member's reaction. "We may as well give up at first as at last." Worse news came on the heels of Washington's gloomy report. The city of Charleston had fallen to the British on May 12 and word of the defeat filtered into Philadelphia early in June. The loss, said Paine, "is such a formidable blow that unless some very sudden and spirited exertions be made the distress that will follow will be long and heavy." The darkest hour of the war had come.

As Paine watched the line of bad news unreel during the spring of 1780, he again thought about leaving America, this time for England, where from within he imagined he might work more effectively as a propagandist and thereby hasten the war to an end. He confided the project to Nathanael Greene, who worried about the risk involved and urged Paine "to defer the matter" until he had weighed "it more seriously." Greene's advice came when it took little prescience to see that more than propaganda among the British was needed to defeat their armies in the field. Paine decided for the time being to stay put and do what he could to arouse a lethargic America.

His plan to win the war emerged in a long letter to Joseph Reed, written before the fall of Charleston had been confirmed. In it he revived his plea for a draft. Let all able bodied men be registered in groups of thirty within their towns or townships, he said; let each be assessed three dollars. When it comes time to offer up a soldier, let one of the thirty volunteer, with the collected money to be given him as a bounty. If none volunteers, let him be chosen by lot, still getting the bounty. That solved the manpower problem. The supply problem, equally crucial, received an even more imaginative solution. "Something must be done, and that something, to give it popularity must begin with men of property," he told Reed. Support from the wealthy could be won if they were shown that the army's reverses arose not from "defects in the departments of government as from a neglect in the country generally, in not contributing the necessary support in time," he went on. "If they have any spirit, any foresight of their own interest or danger, they will promote a subscription either of money or articles, and appoint a committee from among themselves to solicit the same in the several counties; and one state setting the example, the rest, I presume, will follow. Suppose it was likewise proposed to them to deposit their plate to be coined for the pay of the army, crediting the government for the value, by weight."

Paine spent two days drafting the letter. He ended with a plea for prompt, forceful action of some sort, regardless of how Reed felt about the suggestions he had made. "We must rise vigorously upon the evil, or it will rise upon us. A show of spirit will grow into real spirit, but the country must not be suffered to ponder over their loss for a day. The circumstance of the present hour will justify any means from which good may arise. We want rousing."

The proposal to lure cash from the well-to-do to back the war duplicated a plan offered by Henry Laurens two years earlier, which had died on the air. Now it might not. Wealthy men by mid-1780 controlled several state governments and were dominant in Congress; they felt confident they could control the course of the Revolution and held a less jaundiced view of schemes that called for their support. They wanted the Revolution to succeed now that it was in their hands. Paine told Blair M'Clenaghan, a wealthy Philadelphia merchant, that "as it is the rich that will suffer most by the ravages of an enemy it is not only duty but true policy to do something spirited," and the next day M'Clenaghan called a meeting to explain the scheme to the city's business leaders. Robert Morris initiated a second meeting a short while later. Out of these came pledges for some £300,000. Earlier Paine had withdrawn his accumulated pay from the state treasury—an inflated $1699—and five hundred of this he had given M'Clenaghan as his pledge to get the subscription going, promising five hundred more if called upon, "though the little gratitude I have received does not lay it upon me as a duty," he added gracelessly. Paine's name did not appear among the list of subscribers, probably because he was tactfully persuaded to withdraw his pledge and use it for his own needs.

A gratified Congress, unaware of Paine's role, praised the "patriotic scheme of the opulent merchants" of Philadelphia, and when the subscribers created the Bank of Pennsylvania, the first bank in America, to handle their contributions, Congress pledged the faith of the United States to protect them against loss. "By means of this bank," Paine later said with pride, "the army was supplied through the campaign and being at the same time recruited was enabled to maintain its ground."

The day after plans for the bank got under way Paine returned to the work he did best. *Crisis No. 9* was published on June 9. "Had America pursued her advantages with half the spirit that she resisted her misfortunes, she would, before now, have been a conquering and a peaceful people," went the opening lines; "but lulled in the lap of soft tranquillity, she rested on her hopes, and adversity only has convulsed her into action." The chastisement out of the way, the essay took a predictable course: the fall of Charleston "has at last called forth a spirit and kindled up a flame"; the British have won victories here and there, "but this piecemeal work is not conquering a continent"; "we are not now fighting our battles alone, as we were in 1776." And so on. It was an exemplary rather than brilliant piece that sought to do what no one in America could do better—rouse the people.

6

The summer of 1780 found Paine again with time on his hands. The Assembly had adjourned; no particular crisis called for the use of his talents. The University of Pennsylvania, recently created out of the old College of Philadelphia and controlled by the Constitutionalists, heightened the pleasure of celebrating the fourth of July by awarding him on that day an honorary master's degree. No other notable event marked the summer for Paine, and the arrival of autumn found him again restless.

Once more he revived the plan to return to England incognito. "Could a person possessed of a knowledge of America, and capable of fixing it in the minds of the people of England," he reasoned, "go suddenly from this country to that, and keeping himself concealed, he might, were he to manage his knowledge rightly, produce a more general disposition for peace than by any method I can suppose." He would slip in "under the cover of an Englishman who had made the tour of America incog." The scheme had the marks of an elaborate excuse dreamed up to give him an acceptable reason to leave America; he sounded at times when he tried to sell it as if he were homesick.

When President Reed heard of the idea he "scarcely knew what to say about it," except that he "thought it both difficult and dangerous." Paine saw no reason to temporize. He petitioned the Assembly for a year's leave of absence from the clerkship, concealing the nature of his plans by pretending he wanted to "collect and furnish myself with materials for a history of the Revolution." The house refused to grant the leave. Paine resigned. He had already booked passage when Nathanael Greene, hearing while passing through Philadelphia enroute to the South that Paine had revived the proposal, "expressed some apprehensions" and a few days later wrote a strong letter "dissuading me from it." The fate of Major André, who had recently been captured and hanged as a spy, convinced Paine he might become "an object of retaliation should I have been discovered in England when my first landing, and therefore gave the intention up."

La Luzerne, the new French minister, momentarily thought of subsidizing Paine's long-talked-of history of the Revolution, for if "composed under our eyes and according to our directions" it would help to preserve among Americans an affection for the French and distaste for the British, but nothing came of the idea. Once again, as Paine put it, he was "in the world without the least dependence on it," or as La Luzerne phrased it, he appeared "continually at loose ends."

CHAPTER

8

AN INTERLUDE IN FRANCE

THE PICTURE OF PAINE as a wild-eyed radical in the American Revolution dissolves under scrutiny. Instead, it could be said of him as has been said of the American he respected above all others, Benjamin Franklin, that he "was one of those men who achieve distinction by embodying completely the spirit of the society in which they live, rather than by deviating from it or going beyond it." Paine called for no fundamental changes in the forms of government once a republic had been established; he propagandized for no great social experiments. He rarely risked energy or reputation on lost causes. His writings, like a barometer, registered the current climate of opinion and also a hope of what it would be in the future.

Contemporaries occasionally accused him of being an opportunist. Some condemned him as impressionable, others as a huckster. Unquestionably he was flawed and often so were his writings. Unbridled invective diminished some of his essays. Others were filled with unfounded optimism. In still others passion often obscured the common sense of the matter. But when the time called for a dispassionate statement on an issue others dared not touch, Paine could rise to the occasion. He did so twice in the latter part of 1780—once in October with *The Crisis Extraordinary* and again with the pamphlet *Public Good*, published on the next to last day of the year.

Although *Public Good* came out at the end of the year, Paine had worked on it for some time. It resembled nothing he had previously published in America. It was carefully researched, tightly argued, controlled and reasonable in tone. The language as always is simple and direct. It reveals Paine at his best, cutting through a muddy complex of history and politics where he could as easily have used invective and innuendo to roil the stream. The result is one of his ablest pamphlets, though the ephemeral nature of the issue involved caused it to be quickly forgotten.

The title struck contemporaries as ironical, for it was assumed then, and has been since, that Paine wrote it more for private than public good, serving as a hireling for the Indiana Company, controlled by speculators anxious to turn a profit on their land holdings west of the Allegheny Mountains. Actually, the interests of the public were uppermost in Paine's mind, and the aid his essay might give friends in the Indiana Company was incidental to the main issue—that Virginia's refusal to abandon its claim to western lands harmed America. Paine had more to lose than gain by involving himself in this controversy. In attacking Virginia's claim he dared to anger such friends as Thomas Jefferson and young James Madison, a new delegate in Congress. He knew that what he wrote would set fire to the quick temper of his friend Richard Henry Lee, and it did. Lee never again spared praise for his companion of past battles.

Paine's interest in western lands dated from *Common Sense*, in which he had been one of the first to see them as an eventual source of income for Congress. Since then he had not expanded on the subject, even when urged to by friends in the Indiana Company. *"I never had nor ever would have anything to do in private affairs,"* he said emphatically. But Virginia's adamancy had by late 1780 changed his mind. As long as she refused to abandon her title to the West, tiny Maryland, fearful of being overwhelmed by her gigantic neighbor, would not ratify the Articles of Confederation, thus leaving the nation without a constitution. One day Colonel George Morgan, a friend, and several other stockholders in the Indiana Company brought Paine a batch of historical documents they thought undermined Virginia's western claims. Paine looked them over and saw that while incidentally they would promote the interests of the company they would also further what currently concerned him more— a stronger central government. He told Morgan he would use the material but "on *no account*" would he "mix the matter with anything relative to the private affairs of the company."

The bulk of *Public Good* offers a closely reasoned brief based on historical evidence against the Virginia claims. Paine argues that when the crown assumed Virginia as a royal colony the grant of land "from sea to sea" given in the royal charters lapsed, having been given only to the private company that founded the colony but eventually went bankrupt. Further, he says, the king's proclamation in 1763 fixed Virginia's western boundary to the eastern side of the Alleghenies. Having "proved" his case, Paine makes an emotional appeal. Virginia's claim, he says, "has a tendency to create disgust, and sour the minds of the rest of the states." More than any state, she has it in her power to promote a strong union. The lands she gives over to the nation Congress can sell, and those who settle on them will create "a frontier state for her defense against incursions of the Indians." Finally, he appeals to self-interest. Laying a new state on the back of the old one will double Virginia's trade; exports from the West will glide down the Mississippi River but imports must come in through Chesapeake Bay.

Paine ended the brief with two *obiter dicta*. In one he said that new states will eventually enter the union; this made him one of the first to go on record in favor of an expanding United States. A plan ought to be devised to bring these new states in gradually, "as new emigrants will have something to learn when they first come to America." The settlers might be allowed to send representatives to Congress, "there to sit, hear and debate on all questions and matters, but not to vote on any till after the expiration of seven years." Here in a rough way Paine anticipated ideas later embodied in the Northwest Ordinance of 1787, one of the most far-seeing enactments of the Confederation.

The second suggestion, bolder and even more irrelevant to the argument, called for a national convention to form a new constitution, the still unratified Articles in Paine's eyes being already outmoded. Time had shown that "the internal control and dictatorial powers of Congress are not sufficiently defined," he said. They "appeared to be too much in some cases and too little in others; and therefore, to have them marked out legally will give additional energy to the whole, and a new confidence to the several parts."

Everywhere except among Virginians *Public Good* received a respectful hearing, and a year and a half after publication it was still selling in Philadelphia for "a quarter of a dollar." James Madison's father thought "it unanswerable as to the main point," but Madison judged it a source "of calumny and influence" and determined "that an antidote should be applied." The antidote came in the form of a rumor that Paine had written the pamphlet as a paid lackey of the Indiana Company. After finishing the essay, he gave the documentary material used back to Morgan, and soon afterward the company gave him "a voter's share" in the company—twelve thousand acres of land. Paine waited nearly two years to apply for a deed, and when he did the gossip circulated about his paid pen. The gift, said Paine in defending himself, was unsolicited. "If there is any one circumstance in my character which distinguishes itself from the rest, it is *personal disinterestedness*, and an anxiety to serve a public cause in preference to myself," he said, adding, "I never took up a matter without fully believing it to be right, and never yet failed in proving it so." Still, though he had every reason to be proud of *Public Good*, Paine never again referred to it, as if the pamphlet reminded him of something best forgotten.

2

Except to enrage Virginians, *Public Good* had no discernible influence in the short run on either the public or Congress. The effect of *The Crisis Extraordinary* differed appreciably. The title came from a letter to Congress in May of 1780 in which George Washington reviewed again the sad state of the army's affairs. He particularly condemned the requisition system, whereby Congress assigned quotas to the states and left it up to each to fill the request in its own way; as a result virtually no state satisfied the demands placed on it. "The crisis, in every point of view, is extraordinary," Washington warned.

Paine had reacted to the admonition with the plan that led to the creation of the Bank of Pennsylvania. That project alleviated but did not end the crisis. The Assembly still refused to levy sufficient taxes to meet the quotas handed down from Congress, and in the fall of 1780 it went a step further in its insolence: It refused even to accept the quota assigned to it. John Muhlenberg, speaker of the house, asked Paine to write something that would persuade the Assembly to face up to its financial and continental responsibilities. Paine agreed. In *The Crisis Extraordinary* he attempted a miracle—to make taxation seem both palatable and painless. The annual cost of the war prorated among America's three million inhabitants, he said, came to thirteen shillings and four pence. The annual tax burden of Pennsylvania worked out to a trifling three shillings and five pence per person, slightly more than half the tax an Englishman paid for a gallon of rum. Paine tactfully avoided censuring the Assembly for not levying what was needed to perk up the "nerveless campaign" currently being waged by the army. Instead, he observed that "the people generally do not understand the insufficiency of the taxes to carry on the war"; his purpose was "to form the disposition of the people," who once enlightened would allow the Assembly to act.

"I knew I had the ear of the continent," Paine said later when explaining why he wrote the pamphlet and published it at his own expense, but except for an innocuous postscript dealing with Benedict Arnold's treason, which came to light while the essay was in the press, he spoke only obliquely to the continent. On one detour from the argument he applauded Congress "for taking up and funding the present currency at forty to one, and issuing new money in its stead," adding, "Everyone knows that I am not the flatterer of Congress, but in this instance *they are right.*" On another side trip he called for the imposition of import duties. Every state had contemplated such duties, for all fronted on the ocean, but Paine did not want the states to usurp this tax. At a time when Congress was judged weaker than water and when the Articles of Confederation still wandered about the land in search of states to ratify them, he dared to demand that the import duties "must be ascertained and regulated by Congress."

The Pennsylvania Assembly purchased ten dozen copies of the pamphlet from Paine—he turned the $360 received over to the printer in part payment of the debt he owed—to spread among its members. Paine had, as he put it, waded "through a tedious course of difficult business, and over an untrodden path," but once the legislators learned about the trail he had blazed they used it. A few evenings after *The Crisis Extraordinary* had been published John Muhlenberg told Paine "that all opposition had ceased and the house which before had been equally divided had that day been unanimous" in agreeing to impose new taxes and to accept the congressional requisition. The plea for a stronger central government received no encouragement from the Assembly.

It was one thing to legislate new taxes, another to collect them. Paine had skated lightly around this point in his tax lecture, knowing that "the scarcity of medium" in the country left the people with next to nothing for taxes. The nation needed a large and prompt infusion of hard cash into the economy. In Paine's view France alone could rescue the United

States, and to that end he "drew up a letter to Count de Vergennes, stating undisguisedly the true case; and concluding with the request, whether France could not either as a subsidy or a loan, supply the United States with a million sterling and continue that supply annually during the war." He showed the letter to a member of the French delegation, who doubted it would bring results. "A million sent out of the nation," the Frenchman said, echoing the standard mercantilist view of the day, "exhausted it more than ten millions spent in it." Paine carried his letter around to friends in Congress. The reasoning impressed, among others, Ralph Izard of South Carolina, who said, "We will endeavor to do something about it in Congress."

Congress had discussed calling on France for further "aids and supplies" for weeks after Washington had labeled the crisis extraordinary, but Paine's letter helped to focus the talk on a direct appeal for hard cash. On November 22 the delegates approved an address to the king requesting a loan of 25,000,000 livres, and two weeks later they voted to send a special envoy to Paris to plead the cause. The man appointed had to have a full knowledge of Washington's plans and military needs for the coming campaign, so on December 11, after rejecting Alexander Hamilton for the mission—he was "not sufficiently known to Congress to unite their suffrages in his favor"—the delegates chose another member of Washington's staff, John Laurens, the son of Paine's good friend Henry Laurens.

Laurens had been educated abroad—in Geneva, where he had studied law and learned to speak fluent French, and in London, where he completed his work in law at the Middle Temple. He joined Washington's staff early in the war and remained an aide until being detached to share in the defense of Charleston, where he became a British prisoner with its fall. He remained out of the war until exchanged a few months before Congress chose him for the trip to France. He had a bold, brilliant, and imaginative mind that charmed Washington and sometimes gave his father uneasy moments. Henry Laurens listened when his son had counseled support of Washington at the time others talked of supplanting him with Gates. He balked when the young man—then twenty-six—asked to have the slaves he would one day inherit trained as soldiers and assigned to the army. Those that survived the Revolution would be given their freedom. Henry Laurens said slavery had debased Negroes and blunted their ability to fight and nothing more was said on the matter.

Paine had met John Laurens early in 1778 when visiting Washington's headquarters. The two men seem to have liked and respected each other on sight. Now, two years later, Laurens told Paine he was "exceedingly averse" to accepting the congressional appointment. "He mentioned to me that though he was well acquainted with the military, he was not with the political line, and proposed my going with him as secretary." There may have been other reasons. A few days before Laurens had been appointed, Arthur Lee, back to report on European affairs to Congress, accused Franklin of being "neglectful of public business" and so "advanced in years" as to be incompetent. Paine could be counted on to help convince his old friend that Laurens' appointment was not intended as an affront. Laurens may also have wanted Paine along to help as a writer in the delicate negotiations with French officials he knew lay ahead. Possibly, too, Laurens did not make the offer to but received it from Paine, who had long been angling for a way to get to Europe. Regardless, it was made and Paine accepted with alacrity.

3

Shortly after the appointment by Congress John Laurens called on Paine, bringing along two Frenchmen eager to meet him—the Marquis de Lafayette and the Marquis de Chastellux. Chastellux had been in Philadelphia a month and a half and did not know "how it happened . . . I had not yet seen Mr. Paine, famed in America and throughout Europe," he confessed in his diary. "I discovered at his apartments, all the attributes of a man of letters; a room pretty much in disorder, dusty furniture, and a large table covered with books lying open and half-finished manuscripts." He found his "dress was in keeping with the room, nor did his physiognomy," said Chastellux, glancing at Paine's large red nose, "belie the spirit that reigns in his works." The Frenchman had heard that Paine at the moment was in "disgrace," owing "to his bad conduct" while serving Congress. The rumor led Chastellux to conclude that "the vivacity of his imagination and the independence of his character have rendered him better suited for reasoning on affairs, than for conducting them." The "animated" conversation ended when the visitors left to keep a dinner engagement with James Wilson, whom Chastellux characterized as "another literary man, more respected but less distinguished." Chastellux and Lafayette passed on their agreeable impression of Paine to La Luzerne, who two days later wrote Vergennes that he had decided, after keeping the writer at a distance, to use his talents to promote French interests.

Meanwhile, Congress was objecting to Paine's appointment as Laurens' secretary. Once more Witherspoon, who Paine believed would "never forgive me for publishing *Common Sense* and going a step beyond him in literary reputation," led the dissenters, rising to air again the old grievance—"that he doubted my principles," said Paine, *"for that I did not join in the cause till it was late."* Others advanced more convincing arguments. Paine's reputation for discretion still hung under a cloud. The noise raised over Deane's deportment and the attacks on Robert Morris continued to rankle many in Congress.

An incident that occurred on 19 January 1781 revealed something of the feeling against Paine. Dr. James Hutchinson, a Philadelphia friend who had sat on several city committees with Paine and shared his political views, on that day proposed him for membership in the American Philosophical Society. For most candidates election was virtually automatic. Among the seven accepted were Chastellux and Lafayette, eminent only as French noblemen. Among the blackballed was Paine. "There never was a man less beloved in a place than Paine is in this," Franklin's daughter Sarah remarked a few days before the society rejected him, "having at different times disputed with everybody. The most rational thing he could have done would have been to have died the instant he had finished his *Common Sense*, for he never again will have it in his power to leave the world with so much credit."

This rejection by the Philosophical Society increased Paine's eagerness to escape from Philadelphia. He told Laurens not to push for his appointment as secretary; he wished "to avoid contention" and to shun giving "umbrage to several who at that time, from mistake, were not my friends." Paine's name was withdrawn and twenty-three-year-old Captain William Jackson's submitted in its stead, a change Congress readily acceded to. Paine, however, would still accompany Laurens, only now as a friend and private citizen paying his own way. After collecting the salary the Assembly owed him, paying off all debts, and settling with his landlord, he had ninety dollars in bills of exchange, sufficient he thought to carry him through the stay in France. "I leave America with the perfect satisfaction of having been to her an honest, faithful and affectionate friend," he told Nathanael Greene when he still thought he would go as secretary to the mission, "and I go away with the hope of returning to spend better and more agreeable days with her than those which are past."

4

Paine, Laurens, and Jackson left Philadelphia in mid-January 1781. They spent three days conferring with Washington at his headquarters in New Jersey and assembling a list of supplies to ask the French for. "The impediment of floating ice" forced them to cross the Hudson River far above New York City. They reached Boston on January 25 only to find that the *Alliance*, which was to take them to France, lacked a crew. Local authorities promised to impress sailors for the ship, then did nothing. It took over two weeks of pleading by Laurens to get men enough for the *Alliance* to go to sea, and then it was "barely in condition." It left Boston February 11, under the command of Captain John Barry, who had been the first American naval officer to capture a British ship during the Revolution and who would later in the *Alliance* capture two more after bloody fights.

Paine, with one terrifying crossing behind him, embarked uneasy. His fears were justified the fifth night out when "a sudden tremulous motion" ran through the ship. He rushed topside to find "ourselves surrounded with large floating bodies of ice against which the ship was beating." As the captain sought to work free of the ice pack he had drifted into, the wind increased to gale force. "The sea, in whatever direction it could be seen, appeared a tumultuous assemblage of floating rocks, which we could not avoid and against which there was no defense." Paine and Laurens stayed on deck through the night. One thundering crash against the "icy rocks" ripped away part of the deck that Laurens only moments earlier had been standing on. It took nearly eight hours for the ship to ram its way through the field of ice—an adventure so impressive that for one of the few times in his life Paine recorded it in detail.

The trip continued eventful. A few days later they spotted two ships on the horizon. The *Alliance*, hoping for a British prize, gave chase, only to find that the hunted could outgun the hunter. Captain Barry stood off, "and they in their turn chased us." All passengers were equipped with guns and Laurens was placed in command over them. Tension ended when the enemy abandoned his quarry. The next day two more sails came into view. Once overtaken, one proved to be a British cutter, eight days out of Glasgow, which only two hours earlier had waylaid an unarmed Venetian-owned vessel bound for home with a cargo of pepper, indigo, glass bottles, and other noncontraband cargo. Barry ordered the captured crew of the Venetian unironed and after listening to the captain's story concluded "that the captivation by the cutter was contrary to the rights of neutral nations," words that Laurens had put in his mouth, for he had seen here "a happy opportunity for manifesting the determination of Congress to maintain the rights of neutral powers." Barry sent the Venetian on its way, "an act of humanity" that made Paine glow with pride, and took the privateer along as a prize of war.

Nothing further occurred to mark the voyage in Paine's memory. The *Alliance* docked at L'Orient, on the southern coast of Brittany, on March 9 after a swift crossing of twenty-three days. Paine found L'Orient "a clean, agreeable town." The joy of stepping once again on solid ground was heightened by finding fame had preceded him. "The commandant of L'Orient paid me very high compliments on what he called the great success and spirit of my publications." He found several Americans at the port and with one of them, Jonathan Williams, Franklin's grandnephew, he agreed to travel southward to Nantes while Laurens and Jackson set off straight for Paris. Paine suffered from a case of itch acquired aboard ship and his clothes after three weeks at sea were filthy, but the amiable Williams overlooked these shortcomings. "We agree exceedingly well together, and are growing intimate," he later told Franklin. "I confess I like him as a companion because he is pleasant as well as a sensible man, and I heartily wish that [the anti-Deane] party had not so good an assistant."

At Nantes the mayor, along with a covey of distinguished citizens, turned out to welcome Paine. His interpreter on this occasion was Elkanah Watson, another American who lived at the boardinghouse Paine had settled in. Watson, more fastidious than Williams, was "mortified" at Paine's seediness and, judging the book by the cover, later censured him for being "coarse and uncouth in his manners, loathsome in his appearance, and a disgusting egotist, rejoicing most in talking of himself and reading the effusions of his own mind." After the mayor and his companions had ended their welcome and departed, Watson, then twenty-three years old, took the forty-four-year-old Paine in hand. "I took the liberty, on his asking for the loan of a clean shirt, of speaking to him frankly of his dirty appearance and brimstone odor; and I prevailed upon him to stew, for an hour, in a hot bath. This, however, was not done without much entreaty; and I did not succeed, until, receiving a file of English newspapers, I promised, after he was in the bath he should have the reading of them, and not before. He at once consented, and accompanied me to the bath, where I instructed the keeper, in French (which Paine did not understand) gradually to increase the heat of the water, until 'le Monsieur serait bien bouilli.' He became so much absorbed in his reading, that he was nearly parboiled before leaving the bath, much to his improvement and my satisfaction."

5

To judge by later remarks made to Congress, Paine found nothing in the English papers Watson handed him in the bathtub to dispel the notion that the British people were "in a state of profound ignorance" about American affairs and supported the war "on the ground of delusion." It is hard to believe, however, that either then or later while in France he failed to hear about or to read a pamphlet by Thomas Pownall, former governor of Massachusetts and lieutenant governor of New Jersey and now a member of Parliament, that not only revealed understanding about the United States but promoted the cause of independence by drawing arguments from *Common Sense*. A half year earlier, as Paine knew, Pownall had introduced a bill in Parliament to enable the king to negotiate peace with America. The bill lost overwhelmingly. Pownall then took his case to the public in a pamphlet entitled *Memorial . . . to the Sovereigns of Europe*. John Adams, currently a member of the American commission to France, was so struck by it—*Common Sense*'s arguments in the hands of another somehow impressed him more deeply—that he immediately had it translated into French and also sent copies of it to friends at home.

The United States, Pownall insisted, had already "taken its equal station in the nations upon earth"; then in a remarkably prescient sentence he informed Europe that the United States was a "new primary planet" which inevitably would "have effect on the orbit of every other planet, and shift the common center of gravity of the whole system of the

European world." Much of the pamphlet from this point on is a gloss on the less emotional passages of *Common Sense*, but Pownall's use of them must at the time have made Paine wince. Pownall, for instance, praised America's detachment from Europe's "embroiled interests and wrangling politics," its happy freedom from "the entanglement of alliances." Since 1778 Paine had not only buried the arguments used earlier against entanglement with European affairs, but he was now in France doing what he could to tighten an alliance already made by enticing a great loan from France.

Pownall, like Paine, saw America's tie with Europe as commercial rather than political. She would, he believed, eventually become a free port for all Europe's products. In convoluted sentences that reflected Paine's thought if not his style, Pownall envisioned a magnificent future for the United States if such a policy was carried out. She will "become the arbitress of the commercial [world]," he predicted, "and perhaps the mediatrix of peace, and of the political business of the world."

Among the American commissioners in Paris, and later among politicians back in the United States, Pownall's *Memorial* became what has been described as "an official American propaganda piece." "There is something ironic in the fact," one scholar of American diplomacy has said, "that a treatise imbued with the spirit of the school of interests of the [European] states was the first programmatic exposition of American foreign policy with which the diplomats of the struggling young republic appealed to the Europeans of the *ancien régime*." From Paine's point of view it must have been even more ironic that his exposition on foreign affairs achieved dignity and influence—at least so far as John Adams was concerned—only when mouthed by a British aristocrat.

6

While Paine soaked in the bathtub at Nantes, John Laurens in Paris, guided by the knowledgeable Franklin, was traveling from one bureaucrat to another—from Necker to Vergennes, from the minister of marine to the director-general of finance—seeking a loan here, a gift there, and supplies from everyone. Although Vergennes dismissed him as a young man of "inexperience in affairs," and Franklin kept silent, Paine loyally said no man could have executed his assignment "with more address and alacrity." Actually, his success owed more to circumstances than to zeal. Upon arriving in Paris, he had handed Franklin a letter from Washington. It tactfully explained why Congress had chosen Laurens to report on "the present infinitely critical posture of our affairs." He was an informed eyewitness able "to give a military view of them and enter into military details and arrangements." In a second letter Washington wrote, "I beg leave to repeat to you, that, to me, nothing appears more evident than the period of our opposition will very shortly arrive if our allies can not afford us that effectual aid, particularly in money and naval superiority, which are now solicited." The French already had too much invested in the American cause to let all be lost for the lack of money and supplies. They were bound to react positively to Washington's assessment of the situation. Another circumstance that assured Laurens' success was the presence of Franklin. When the young emissary spoke brusquely to the dignified Vergennes, who had "exclaimed vehemently against the exorbitance of the demand" after their first meeting, the foreign minister warned Franklin to teach Laurens some manners, otherwise he would no longer be received by French officials. Franklin somehow satisfied Vergennes without ruffling Laurens. In spite of his gaucheries—once he cornered Louis XVI at a social function to press America's case, an act that left the court with its collective mouth hanging open—Laurens with Franklin's smooth cooperation "exacted" from the French, to use Vergennes' word, large amounts of arms, clothing, and ammunition together with loans and gifts totaling 25,000,000 livres.

It took two and a half months to conclude the negotiations. During this time Paine stuck closely to Passy, the suburb of Paris where Franklin lived and Jackson and Laurens had settled in. The direct and straightforward language of Laurens' reports back to Congress and to the French ministers he dealt with suggests that Paine had a large hand in them and that writing them kept him occupied. Later, when the small delegation moved into Paris to tie up loose ends of the mission, Paine stuck close to the hotel, hobbled by his ignorance of the French language. The language barrier, however, did not shake his determination to cut loose from America, though he seemed confused whether to make the separation brief or permanent. One moment he planned to remain in Europe "to write a pamphlet and send it over to Almon in London to be printed, and to return in the frigate which was to bring the second supply of money." But to Ralph Izard by letter and to John Laurens directly he resolved never to return, considering "the treatment I had received, and such hardships and difficulties I had experienced year after year." He wished the nation well and would continue to favor its cause—from a distance. The decision stunned Laurens. "His importunities for my returning with him were pressing and excessive," Paine said, "and he carried them to such a height, that I felt I should not be very easy to myself . . . and as he would have had nobody with him on the passage if any misfortune had befallen him, I gave in to his wishes and accompanied him back."

On June 1 Paine and Laurens embarked in the French frigate *Résolu* —Paine persisted in calling it the *Resolve*—convoying two transports loaded with military supplies and 2,500,000 livres. The voyage back took eighty-six days—"a passage in which we experienced every contrariety" —nearly four times as long as the trip over. The destination was Philadelphia, but midway across, "learning from a vessel which we pursued for the purpose of intelligence" that no French task force had arrived to clear the Delaware capes of British warships, Laurens "judged it most prudent to make a safe eastern port" and the three ships headed for Boston, arriving on August 25.

After rounding up wagons, sixteen teams of oxen, and an armed guard to transport to Philadelphia the cargo and cash they had brought, Paine and Laurens hired a sulky and started out ahead of the transports. They had learned upon landing that Washington was moving the army southward to Yorktown in the hope that, with cooperation from the French navy, he would be able to bottle Cornwallis up on the peninsula there. Laurens was eager to be in on the kill. Outside Providence the sulky broke down. Laurens borrowed horses from friends in Rhode Island and set out alone to catch up with Washington. "We parted the money he had with him," said Paine, "of which I had six guineas, and he not much more, with which I had to bear my own expenses and that of a servant he left with me and two horses, for three hundred miles, and I was obliged to borrow a dollar at Bordentown to pass the ferry with."

CHAPTER

9

SUBSIDIZED SERVANT

PAINE ARRIVED BACK in Philadelphia with empty pockets and nothing to do. In an attempt to edge back to the center of action, he again, this time humbly, offered his services to Congress, "if there is any occasion to send information to the army." No such occasion arose.

As the days passed he became preoccupied with poverty. A pair of boots Laurens had left to be repaired stayed at the shoemaker "as I must be obliged to borrow money to pay for them." The role of the literary man in a republic depressed him more than ever. If literature were to survive in America, he decided, it "must one day become the subject of legislative consideration." In Europe he had found the intellectual a cherished citizen. "It is well worth remarking, that Russia, who but a few years ago was scarcely known in Europe, owes a large share of her present greatness to the close attention she has paid, and the wise encouragement she has given, to every branch of science and learning; and we have almost the same instance in France, in the reign of Louis XVI."

Time hung heavy through the autumn of 1781, and as the empty days passed, self-pity set in, nourished by an awareness that as his fortunes dipped the nation's rose. News that Cornwallis and his army had been "nabbed nicely in the Chesapeake" filtered into Philadelphia in October. Soon after, Washington rode through the streets. The normally sedate city for the moment forgot itself and honored the event with a parade, a string of victory balls, a display of fireworks, illuminated windows, and gigantic bonfires.

Washington could look forward to a relatively carefree winter for the first time since taking command of the continental army. The tamed

British were for the most part penned up on Manhattan and nowhere presented a serious threat. No time would be better than now to bother the general with a man's personal problems, and on November 30, seven years to the day since he came ashore in Philadelphia, Paine composed a long letter full of sorrow for himself. He airs his feelings to Washington because as commander-in-chief his "situation detached him from all political parties and bound him alike to all and to the whole." He complains that he has "dealt generously and honorably by America," but she has not treated him similarly. This puzzles him, "for wherever I go I find respect." Friends censure the nation's neglect of him and yet do nothing to help, "so that their civility disarms me as much as their conduct distresses me." This situation cannot continue, and so he shall return to Europe, where "I have literary fame, and I am sure I cannot experience worse fortune."

Washington responded with an "affectionately interested" letter. He liked Paine and, equally pleasing, shared Paine's high opinion of Paine. No one appreciated more the effect his propaganda had had in marshaling support for the war. Once he had asked Congress for "a small traveling press to follow headquarters" and perhaps with Paine in mind "an ingenious man to accompany this press and be employed wholly in writing for it." Yorktown marked a great victory but not the end of the war, and until that came the nation could not, so Washington thought, afford to lose its most powerful spokesman. Immediately after receiving Paine's letter Washington, according to Paine, "concerted with a friend or two to make my continuance in America convenient to myself until a proper time might offer to do it more permanently."

One of those concerted with was La Luzerne; another was Robert Morris. Morris had recently been appointed superintendent of finance by Congress, and on September 18 he suggested Paine write an essay on taxation to rouse the people. No essay came forth—Paine had published nothing for nearly a year and perhaps found it hard to break his indolent ways—but off and on through the autumn the two saw each other socially. Publication early in November of Deane's "intercepted" letters calling for reconciliation brought them closer together when Morris assured Paine "he had been totally deceived in Deane." One evening in the course of "a long conversation" that strayed over a variety of subjects, Paine complained again of the neglect he endured. Morris said he wished "his pen to be wielded in aid of such measures . . . meant for the public good." Unfortunately, he went on, "I have nothing in my power at present to offer as compensation for your services," but whenever something turns up "I shall have you in my mind." In effect, said Morris, don't call us, we'll call you.

This conversation occurred on January 26. During the next two weeks the two men saw each other several times again. Both Morris and his assistant, Paine's old enemy Gouverneur Morris, who now "hopped round upon one leg," agreed that Paine's pen must be put at the service of the government. They told him he would be asked to support only "upright measures," then went on to list some of the things they had in mind. "We want the aid of an able pen to urge the legislatures of the several states to grant sufficient taxes" for the sole use by Congress; "to extend by a new confederation the powers of Congress"; "to prepare the minds of the people for such restraints and such taxes and imposts as are absolutely necessary for their own welfare"; and so forth. They were asking him to write only on issues he believed in. Paine said he was "well disposed to the undertaking."

Twice Washington had spoken to Robert Morris, urging "that some provision could be made" for Paine. Morris now visited the general and told him of the plan he had in mind. Washington approved. Morris then went to Robert R. Livingston, the newly appointed Secretary for Foreign Affairs, "and proposed that he should join me in this business, by furnishing from his department such intelligence as might be necessary from time to time to answer the useful purposes for which Mr. Paine is to write." Livingston agreed.

On 10 February 1782 Morris, Livingston, and Washington signed an agreement whereby Paine would receive eight hundred dollars a year to write for the government. He would be paid from a secret fund that the superintendent of finance could use without the need to give a public accounting. The agreement was to be kept absolutely secret since "a salary publicly and avowedly given for the above purpose would injure the effect of Mr. Paine's publication, and subject him to injurious personal reflections." However, someone talked. "Your old acquaintance Paine," Joseph Reed told Nathanael Greene, "is a hireling writer pensioned with £300 per annum, payable by General Washington out of the secret service money."

Perhaps Paine broke the secret, for he felt honored by the arrangement. He accepted it ten days after it was proposed, not in the spirit of a craven man about to become a party hack but as something long his due. His gratitude was muted, his arrogance intact. He knew the proposition had been made "not only out of friendship to me, but out of justice to me," he told Morris, "and without which I must be obliged to withdraw my mind from that line in which I can best serve the community and apply myself to the thought of getting a livelihood." He was, in short, doing America a favor in accepting the proposal. "I have the honest pride of thinking and ranking myself among the founders of a new independent world, and I should suffer exceeding to be put out of that track."

2

The agreement called for Paine to do what he had been doing—further the American cause by "informing the people and rousing them into action"—only now the rousing must promote a stronger union. He began to earn his keep immediately. The day the agreement was signed —February 20—he published in the press the first installment of an essay ridiculing King George's latest speech, which, though "hardly a line of it is true," is "as well managed as the embarrassed condition of their affairs would well admit of." It consists of a string of gibes at "one of the readiest believers in the world," a king who "sees not the plunge he is making, and precipitately drives across the flood that is closing over his head." Here and there in the second installment, which appeared a week later, Paine jabs at the "kind of trifling" in America that supposes "the danger past"—"this unsafe situation marks at this time the peculiar crisis of America"—but these touches seem added at the last moment to satisfy his employers and are irrelevant to the assault against George III.

Paine told Morris he would follow this essay "with another piece in next week's papers on the subject of revenue, of which I shall give notice," but before publishing it he promised to "take the liberty of consulting you and Mr. G. Morris." He finished the piece on March 5; later, tied with the attack on King George, it became the second half of *Crisis No. 10.* While, as promised, it dealt largely with the nation's need for taxes, Paine could not resist opening with a page on the Deane Affair. He reminded the public (and obliquely Messrs. R. and G. Morris) of his prediction, "*As he rose like a rocket, he would fall like a stick,*" and that during the time of troubles all Paine's friends except Henry Laurens "stood at a distance."

That off his mind, he swung with no effort at a smooth transition into the assigned topic. What followed revealed the peril, for Paine at least, of writing to satisfy someone other than himself. Until near the end of the essay he did little more than row through a sea of vacuous generalities. It took him ten pages to get to the point—that the states should levy one set of taxes for their own needs and another set to fulfill the quotas handed out by Congress. Too many states had reneged lately on their requisitions, using the excuse that the taxes they collected barely satisfied local needs. Separate tax budgets, said Paine, will let the people know what they are paying for, and they "will likewise know that those which are for the defense of the country will cease with the war, or soon after."

Paine sensed the inadequacy of this maiden effort for his employers. On April 3 readers of the *Pennsylvania Journal* got a revised version in which he spoke to the people of Pennsylvania, whose Assembly, prodded earlier by Paine, had levied new taxes to meet the quota of $1,120,000 placed on the state by Congress. The quota must be met. "Huzzas for liberty" no longer will do. Fine words won't "fill the soldier's belly, nor clothe his back; they will neither pay the public creditor, nor purchase our supplies." He who had said the least government is best now glows over the word "taxation." "We have given to a popular subject an unpopular name, and injured the service by a wrong assemblage of ideas." The man who signs a petition against higher taxes—and many such petitions were flowing into the Assembly—reveals a "meanness he would otherwise blush at." Taxes are needed "to protect the aged and the infant, and to give liberty a land to live in." Paine ended with an appeal to pride and common sense. "Let us be, in every respect, such a nation as we ought to be," he said. "The people of America are not a poor people, why should they appear so. We hurt our credit, our honor, our reputation in the world, by proclaiming ourselves what we are not."

Through the spring and summer of 1782 he checked everything he wrote with his employers. In mid-March he asked George Washington and Robert Morris "to spend part of an evening at my apartment and eat a few oysters or a crust of bread and cheese." He wanted to discuss business of an undisclosed "secret nature." An odor of sycophancy soon seeped into his relations with these gentlemen. Once, after several attempts to see Morris at his office, he dropped off the draft of an essay on commerce, with a brief letter attached: "I have closed it up without touching it over, but if you think it a convenient publication, being a better judge of the subject than myself, I will give it into Dunlap's paper on Tuesday morning. . . . Any time that will be convenient to you I will wait on you."

In June Paine published *A Supernumerary Crisis* at the urging of another of his employers, Robert R. Livingston. The tall, lean aristocrat from New York, already slightly deaf at thirty-five, got along well with Paine. Both shared an interest in practical science—Livingston would one day subsidize Robert Fulton's experiments with the steamboat—and, despite disparate backgrounds that gave them little else in common, regarded each other with mutual respect. As Secretary for Foreign Affairs, Livingston had become worried about the effect abroad of the so-called Asgill case. Captain Charles Asgill, the amiable nineteen-year-old son of a British nobleman, had, as a prisoner of war, been "doomed to death" by Washington in reprisal for a British atrocity. The death sentence still held when Washington learned that the captain's plight had stirred the French court, notably Louis XVI and his queen. Vergennes, in the name of Franco-American accord, requested clemency for the young man. At this point Livingston asked Paine to "state that unfortunate and distressing affair in its true light, so as to prevent mistakes taking place abroad or unjust reflection being cast on the temper of humanity of America." Paine's conception of the "true light" placed blame on the British, not where it belonged—on a dilatory Congress that had muffed a chance to reprieve Asgill. If you do not do something, he wrote in the open letter to the British commander, Sir Guy Carleton, Asgill "becomes the corpse of your will. . . . The evil *must* be put to an end; and the choice of persons rests with you." The essay convinced no one, and only months later when public sentiment on both sides of the Atlantic had mounted even higher did Congress finally lift the death sentence against Asgill.

3

In mid-July of 1782 Paine attended "a most splendid entertainment" given by La Luzerne to celebrate the birth of the dauphin of France. Over a thousand invitations had been sent out, and some ten thousand citizens gathered to watch the arrival at the minister's residence out near the State House of a mixed bag of guests—Whigs and ex-Tories, politicians and soldiers, the learned and those who knew not "whether Horace was a Roman or Scotchman." "The company was mixed, it is true, but the mixture formed the harmony of the evening," according to Benjamin Rush. Even Mifflin and Reed, though political enemies, "accosted each other with all the kindness of ancient friends." Paine alone among the multitude of guests elicited a snide comment from Rush, who had cooled somewhat toward Paine since the battle over the Pennsylvania constitution. "The celebrated author of *Common Sense,*" he said, "retired frequently from the company to analyze his thoughts and to enjoy the repast of his own original ideas."

Philadelphia never before had experienced such sumptuous entertainment, and perhaps it was this that made Paine ill at ease. A lavish display of fireworks interrupted the dancing, then the party resumed till midnight, when a supper prepared by thirty cooks borrowed from the French army was served. The awed crowd, reduced to near silence, "looked and behaved more as if they were *worshiping* than *eating,*" someone remarked.

The brilliant evening exemplified the change La Luzerne had worked in Franco-American relations, so cool when he had arrived that Paine had been embarrassed to be seen at the minister's door. In less than two years this fat, myopic gentleman had charmed the ladies of Philadelphia as "one of the most amiable, politest, easiest behaved men" they ever knew and won the confidence of the men "both as a private and a public man." He liked neither music nor dancing but agreeably spent most of his evenings surrounded by both, invariably returning late to the iron bed he slept in, "by way of security from the bugs." "Noble in his expenditures as befits the minister of a great monarchy, but as simple in his manners as a republican, he is equally well fitted to represent the king with Congress, or the Congress with the king." He was a shrewd, skillful diplomat, who succeeded where Gérard had failed largely because he liked Americans immensely and understood them better than any Frenchman of his day. He saw they had, as he put it, "an excessive attachment to liberty and an extreme suspicion of anyone who might endanger it," and guided by that insight he smothered the ill feeling Gérard had aroused. He accepted the United States as an equal partner in the alliance. On a sticky issue he won by tact what Gérard had tried to take by force. He stayed clear of domestic politics. By being "equally inaccessible to the spirit of party," Chastellux said, "it results, that he is anxiously courted by all parties, and that by espousing none, he moderates them all."

The decision to stay clear of all factions had led La Luzerne to keep

Paine at a distance until persuaded by Chastellux and Lafayette that he could be of use. "Few men," it has been said of La Luzerne, "were better versed in the arts of cajolery; few men could offer a bribe with such a delicate air of receiving a favor." Paine, susceptible to both, put up no resistance when approached, especially since La Luzerne asked him to write on an appealing subject—the "intercepted" letters of Deane then appearing in the New York press. Nothing came of this agreement, because Paine left almost immediately for France. After his return La Luzerne in December 1781 "engaged Paine to write a few articles on the advantages gained by the United States through the alliance." (Washington may have encouraged this arrangement, for it came soon after he had "concerted with" a friend or two in Paine's behalf.) Five months passed with nothing forthcoming, but La Luzerne was aware of "l'indolence naturelle de M. Paine" and waited patiently. Paine had rewarded him in May with *Crisis No. 11*, which was designed to silence talk that it would serve America's self-interest to make peace with Great Britain without consulting France. The thought that America might negotiate behind France's back proved "too bulky to be born alive," said Paine. France has treated us "nobly and generously," and we must return the favor. Do not forget that "the eye of the world is upon us to see how we act," he went on. "We have an enemy who is watching to destroy our reputation, and who will go any length to gain some evidence against us, that may serve to render our conduct suspected, and our character odious; because, could she accomplish this, wicked as it is, the world would withdraw from us, as from a people not to be trusted, and our task would then become difficult." Those words alone gave La Luzerne his money's worth.

La Luzerne paid 1530 livres or something like three hundred dollars for Paine's services in 1782, plus a bonus of fifty guineas when he read his *A Letter to Abbé Raynal.* The money helped to soften the needling remark in a British-controlled New York paper that "the *frenchified* politics of *Master Paine*, begin to peep through the threadbare disguise they have hitherto worn, under the name of *Common Sense.* "

4

Soon after the friendship with Morris blossomed in the fall of 1781, Paine borrowed from him a volume entitled *The Revolution in America* by the Abbé Guillaume Raynal, which had recently been translated from the French. He wanted it for background material for that history of the Revolution he perennially talked about when at loose ends. Raynal's book proved a pleasant find, for it deflected him again from a project he had no desire to carry out. "It is yet too soon to write the history of the Revolution," he said after reading it and noting the plethora of mistakes it contained, "and whoever attempts it precipitately, will unavoidably mistake characters and circumstances, and involve himself in error and difficulty." The volume in Paine's eyes had another virtue: "His mistakes afforded me, in part, the opportunity I had wished for, of throwing out a publication that should reach Europe, and by obtaining a general reading there, put the affairs of America and the revolution in the point of light in which they ought to be viewed."

Paine sent the volume back to Morris in November 1781 with the draft of a reply he had made to Raynal's inaccuracies and false interpretations. Eight months passed before he was sufficiently satisfied with his revisions to turn the manuscript over to a printer. It was in many ways a disappointing work, marred by stilted sentences, disconnected passages, and the usual digressions, but Paine liked it enough to sign his own name.

Paine had two points to make in the pamphlet. Raynal had argued that the American Revolution resembled all revolutions in history, differing only in that it was more senseless than most, arising out of a few insignificant taxes imposed on the colonies by Britain. "It is in vain to look for precedents among the revolutions of former ages, to find out, by comparison, the causes of this," Paine replied. The American Revolution differs from all others in history. "Here the value and quality of liberty, the nature of government, and the dignity of man, were known and understood, and the attachment of the Americans to these principles produced the Revolution, as a natural unavoidable consequence. They had no particular family to set up or pull down. Nothing of personality was incorporated with their cause. They started even-handed with each other, and went no faster into the several stages of it, than they were driven by the unrelenting and imperious conduct of Britain."

Paine then shows how the alliance with France has affected America. Raynal had judged it an unnatural union, arguing that close ties between a republic and a monarchy could only injure one or both nations. Paine thought otherwise, of course. "Perhaps no two events ever united so intimately and forcibly to combat and expel prejudice, as the Revolution in America and the alliance with France," he said. "Their effects are felt, and their influence already extends as well to the Old World as the New. Our style and manner of thinking have undergone a revolution more extraordinary than the political revolution." He never specifies how style and thought have altered. "We see with other eyes; we hear with other ears," is all he will say. He leaves unsaid an extension of that thought which must have been in his mind—France has changed us; surely we have worked changes upon France.

Paine had occasionally referred to himself as "a citizen of the world" without elaborating on the phrase. He does so now. "The true idea of a great nation," he says, "is that which extends and promotes the principles of universal society; whose mind rises above the atmosphere of local thoughts, and considers mankind, of whatever nation or profession they may be, the work of one Creator." Not only does nationalism indicate that "the progress of civilization has stopped," but it goes against the trends of the times. Science and commerce have made one world out of many. The unifying effect of commerce had been remarked by others but no one had attributed a similar influence to science. "Her influence on the mind, like the sun on the chilled earth, has long been preparing it for higher cultivation and further improvement," he writes. "The philosopher of one country sees not an enemy in the philosopher of another; he takes his seat in the temple of science, and asks not who sits beside him."

Science and commerce encourage one world of men. Why, then, does a world of war-making nations persist? Paine's answer is that prejudice blocks progress. The alliance between France and the United States begins to clear away this prejudice. As French ideas permeate America, a similar flow backwards across the Atlantic will eventually make the American Revolution "distinguished by opening a new system of extended civilization." Thus does America's cause become the cause of mankind.

Paine's *A Letter to Abbé Raynal* appeared in August, as usual published at his own expense. He gave fifty copies to Robert Morris "to send to any part of Europe or the West Indies," another fifty to Robert R. Livingston for the same purpose, and still another fifty to George Washington "for the use of the army, and to repeat to you my acknowledgment for your friendship." Thirteen dozen went to Charles Thomson, secretary of Congress, "to be sent as occasion might offer to the several governments, but from what reason I know not, they were not accepted." Altogether, by his own accounting, he gave away about five hundred copies, "for all I aimed at on this side the water was to reimburse myself the expenses of printing, which was about one hundred pounds" (he did not mention that over half of the cost was covered by the gift from La Luzerne). The minister remained openly warm but privately skeptical toward Paine— "He continues to gather material for the history of the Revolution," he reported to Vergennes, "but his natural indolence does not permit me to believe that he will ever reach the conclusion of his task, which is moreover beyond his talents"—but his pleasure with *A Letter to Abbé Raynal* prompted him to encourage the five French versions that appeared soon after copies arrived in Paris. French reviews were enthusiastic. "I have lately traveled much and find him everywhere," an American in France wrote of Paine's reputation there. "His *Letter to Abbé Raynal* has sealed his fame; and I am firmly persuaded that all the prolix writings of the present age, put together, will not contribute so effectually to eradicate ancient prejudices and expand a liberality of mind as his laconic epistle."

5

Paine marked the publication of his pamphlet by escaping from the heat of Philadelphia to Bordentown, where every year about this time he vacationed for two or three weeks with his friend Colonel Kirkbride. He was there in September when news arrived that the new Shelburne ministry, which had replaced the North regime that had carried Britain through seven years of war, appeared opposed to any peace overtures that involved recognizing American independence.

The news prompted him to revive in a letter to Robert Livingston the dream of another journey to France. "The scene of active politics is in my opinion, transferred from America to Europe," he wrote. It is there that American expectations "must be put into practice." Paine thought he might be able, from a base in France, to promote the idea of peace among Britons. Livingston and Robert Morris convinced him he could promote peace more effectively from his American base. By September only $125,000 of the $8,000,000 requisitioned from the states had been paid into the treasury, and Morris again wanted Paine to address the public "in terms to induce the payment of taxes, to establish better modes of taxation, etc." Paine preferred first to address Lord Shelburne, which he did in an open letter published at the end of October as *Crisis No. 12.* The essay repeated old arguments with a verve that made them seem new. Lord Shelburne had said England could still win the war. "Must England ever be the sport of hope, and the victim of delusion?" asked Paine. "Sometimes our currency was to fail; another time our army was to disband; then whole provinces were to revolt. . . . Sometimes this power, and sometimes that power, was to engage in the war, just as if the whole world was mad and foolish like Britain. And thus, from year to year, has every straw been catched at, and every will-with-a-wisp led them a new dance." Lord Shelburne had said an independent America would ruin England. "That a nation is to be ruined by peace and commerce, and fourteen or fifteen millions a-year less expenses than before, is a new doctrine in politics," said Paine.

Paine had enjoyed assembling these lighthearted taunts. He would have been crushed to learn that two old friends, Henry Laurens and Benjamin Franklin, at the moment negotiating terms for peace with England, were not pleased with the essay. Laurens said "it did not suit the present moment" and was "sorry for some things in it." Franklin had more to say: "I should think now that we are studying peace and conciliation that you had as good not send to England that printed paper addressed to Lord Shelburne," he told one of the English negotiators. "This rude way of writing in America will seem very strong on your side. Indeed it is true you have no idea in England of the animosity that has prevailed with us, owing to reiterated cruelties and ill treatment."

Morris wanted Paine to tackle the essay on taxes now that Lord Shelburne had been disposed of. Paine temporized. He was forty-five years old and uneasy, not knowing "where my home and dependence in the world is." He talked again of settling in France, that place "where I am not, and cannot pass unknown." "I see you are determined to follow your genius and not your fortune," Nathanael Greene wrote; then after a perceptive remark—"Your passion leads to fame, and not to wealth"— he ended by assuring his insecure friend, "Your fame for your writings will be immortal." By the time these flattering remarks arrived, Robert Morris, equally adept at reassuring Paine, had again deflected him from France.

6

In 1781 a Congress desperate for money had asked for power to levy a 5 percent duty on all imports, a request that required unanimous consent of the states. By the autumn of 1782 twelve states had, one by one, acceded to the resolution, largely under pressure from Robert Morris, who, in a barrage of letters to leaders around the country, suggested that anyone who opposed the impost "labors to continue the war, and, of consequence, to shed more blood, to produce more devastation, and to extend and prolong the miseries of mankind." In November the Rhode Island legislature flatly rejected approval; unless that body changed its mind the measure was dead.

On November 20 Paine sent Morris the first two of what would be a six-part series of essays directed to the people of Rhode Island. They began appearing in the Philadelphia press the next week, all unsigned, because, said Paine with unaccustomed modesty, "I do not wish to bring them into more notice than there is occasion for." Anonymity in this instance made common sense. Generally the essays dispense time-worn arguments, are discursive and listless, and come alive only when Paine forgets the virtues of the impost and wanders into a discussion of sovereignty and citizenship. In two striking passages Paine develops—invents might be an apter word—a concept later called dual sovereignty, after it was embodied in the federal Constitution of 1787. Hitherto men had conceived of sovereignty as indivisible. But the American situation is unique among nations, says Paine. "What would the sovereignty of any one individual state be, if left to itself, to contend with a foreign power?" he asks. "It is in our united sovereignty, that our greatness and safety, and the security of our foreign commerce, rest. This united sovereignty then must be something more than a name, and requires to be as completely organized for the line it is to act in as that of any individual state, and, if anything, more so, because more depends on it."

Paine saw more clearly than anyone at the time the uniqueness of an American's citizenship. "Every man in America stands in a two-fold order of citizen," he says. "He is a citizen of the state he lives in, and of the United States; and without justly and truly supporting his citizenship in the latter, he will inevitably sacrifice the former. By his rank in the one, he is made secure with his neighbors; by the other, with the world. The one protects his domestic safety and property from internal robbers and injustices; the other his foreign and remote property from piracy and invasion, and puts him on a rank with other nations. Certainly then the one, like the other, must not and cannot be trusted to pleasure and caprice, lest, in the display of local authority, we forget the great line that made us great, and must keep us so."

Paine sent his first three essays to the *Providence Gazette* for reprinting. When he learned that Congress, early in December, had appointed a delegation to visit Rhode Island in order to increase pressure on its leaders for an assent to the impost, Paine, too, decided he would be more effective at the scene. During a stopover in Providence with Laurens the previous year he had made several friendly acquaintances he thought would listen to reason. Also, he thought that the less Rhode Island's recalcitrance "was blazed about the world, the less would the reputation of America suffer." Whatever he had to say would be published only in Rhode Island newspapers without his usual pen name. Paine passed these "useful hints" along to Robert Morris on December 6 "and offered if needed to go thither." Three days later Morris "sent for Mr. Paine and encouraged him to go to Rhode Island respecting the impost." The next day they conferred again. Morris probably turned over some expense money, and Paine set out with his blessing. Clearly, Paine warped the truth when he said later that he set out for Rhode Island ahead of the congressional delegation "without the least intimation from any person whatever, and wholly and perfectly at my own expense."

His fourth essay on the impost appeared in the Providence press on January 11, and the fifth came a week later. The author was instantly identified, and with the disclosure that a visitor from outside the state was interfering in local affairs, shafts previously aimed at Congress shifted to Paine. Thereafter he lived out the stay in Providence in an isolation far from splendid. The congressional delegation never arrived, having learned enroute that Virginia had rescinded its approval of the impost, thus making the trip to Rhode Island meaningless. No encouraging word came from Robert Morris, despite four prodding letters from the lonely Paine. Local leaders set afoot a movement "to prevent the publication of any more of my pieces," spreading the story that Paine had been sent as a "mercenary writer" by well-heeled members of Congress to interfere in the affairs of a sovereign state. That barb hurt. No delegate in or out of Congress, said Paine in the sixth and final essay, choosing his words with care, "can say that the author of these letters ever sought from any man, or body of men, any place, office, recompense or reward, on any occasion for himself." He seeks only "the happiness of serving mankind, and the honor of doing it freely." (The identical words were used in defending himself against the accusation of serving as the Indiana Company's paid hireling.) These disingenuous lines appeared on February 1, and soon after he left Rhode Island.

7

Paine vanished for the rest of the winter, probably holing up with the Kirkbride family in Bordentown. He surfaced again on March 20 in Philadelphia when he stopped to pay his respects to Robert Morris. Three days later a ship dispatched from France by Lafayette brought news that the preliminary peace treaty had been signed. Paine began to work on *Crisis No. 13*, which was published on April 19, the eighth anniversary of the battles at Lexington and Concord.

Once again he rose to the occasion. " 'The times that tried men's souls' are over," he exulted in the opening lines "—and the greatest and completest revolution the world ever knew, gloriously and happily accomplished." He moves along into a stately elegy that blends joy with a somber awareness of America's responsibilities. "A new creation" has been entrusted to American hands. The people now have it in their power "to make a world happy—to teach mankind the art of being so—to exhibit, on the theater of the universe a character hitherto unknown." They have successfully concluded a revolution "which has contributed more to enlighten the world, and diffuse a spirit of freedom and liberality among mankind than any human event (if this may be called one) that ever preceded it." Nothing shall daunt the new nation. "She has it in her choice to do, and to live as happily as she pleases. The world is in her hands. She has no foreign power to monopolize her commerce, perplex her legislation, or control her prosperity." She must not rest on her laurels. "The remembrance of what is past, if it operates rightly, must inspire her with the most laudable of all ambition, that of adding to the fair fame she began with."

But dangers lie ahead. A long war "unhinges the mind from those nice

sensations which at other times appear so amiable." Constant exposure
to woe "blunts the finer feelings, and the necessity of bearing with the
sight, renders it familiar." War weakens the sense of moral obligations
within society, and these failings must be quickly repaired. But the fragile state of the union presents a more serious danger. We must strengthen
"that happy union which has been our salvation, and without which we
should have been a ruined people," Paine warns. "On this our great
national character depends. It is this which must give us importance
abroad and security at home," he goes on. "Our union, well and wisely
regulated and cemented, is the cheapest way of being great—the easiest
way of being powerful, and the happiest invention in government which
the circumstances of America can admit of. Because it collects from each
state, that which, by being inadequate, can be of use to it, and forms an
aggregate that serves for all." No one before had put the case for a strong
union better, and Paine had still more to say for it. "It is the most sacred
thing in the constitution of America, and that which every man should
be most proud and tender of. Our citizenship in the United States is our
national character. Our citizenship in any particular state is only our
local distinction. By the latter we are known at home, by the former to
the world. Our great title is AMERICANS—our inferior one varies with
the place."

CHAPTER

10

FROM RAGS TO RICHES

PAINE HAD COME ALIVE with the Revolution. For over seven years he had lived to rouse a nation. Now that nation wanted tranquillity, and peace cut him adrift to confront again the purposeless life he had hoped lay behind. Adjustment to life as it had been before the war came harder for Paine than for the man who had thrived on combat. The demobilized soldier at least had something to return to—a wife and family, a farm or shop. Paine had none of these. "Trade I do not understand," he said. "Land I have none, or what is equal to none. I have exiled myself from one country without making a home of another; and I cannot help sometimes asking myself, what am I better off than a refugee? and that of the most extraordinary kind, a refugee from the country I have obliged and served, to that which can owe me no good will." "Common Sense's" usefulness had ended. Both he and the people knew it, and for the next three years the signature virtually vanished from the newspapers.

Peace stripped Paine's life of purpose. It also left him consumed with worry about money. Morris had left the post of superintendent of finance, and with his departure had ended the flow of cash from the secret fund. Paine early in the summer of 1783 retreated from Philadelphia to Bordentown, possibly because it was cheaper to live with the Kirkbride family than pay room and board in the city. This time the country atmosphere failed to soothe. He brooded about the nation's failure suitably to honor him for services given to the cause. He knew that if he did not strike soon, before memory of his achievements waned, the nation would never reward him.

The trouble was he lived in a land that treated writers lightly. "Their works are read with more curiosity than confidence," Chastellux had remarked of America's attitude toward men like Paine, "their projects being regarded rather as an exercise of their imagination than as plans that are well grounded and authoritative enough ever to produce any real effect." England, too, seldom listened to its authors, but it at least saw that the good ones lived comfortably. No one considered it odd that Dr. Johnson existed on a gift from the crown or that Alexander Pope, a mere poet, had been offered by one of the king's ministers a pension of three hundred pounds with no strings attached. Paine yearned for a similar subsidy, but wangling one from a Congress that lacked a reliable income even for its own needs would not be easy.

A letter requesting advice went out to Robert Livingston, who conferred with Morris and other mutual friends. They concluded that Paine should apply directly to Congress for remuneration.

He took the advice. In a carefully worded letter he explained the uniqueness of his case deftly to a Congress reluctant to reward an individual while thousands of continental troops still went unpaid. "For besides the general principle of right, and their own privileges, they had estates and fortunes to defend, and by the event of the war they now have them to enjoy," he said. "They are at home in every sense of the word. But with me it is otherwise. I had no other inducement than principle, and have nothing else to enjoy." Paine may have miscalculated when he dropped the threat "that circumstances . . . may occasion my departure from America" and added the boast "I found her in adversity and I leave her in prosperity." Otherwise it was well done. It ended with a "humble request"—a phrase he had used sparingly since his days with the excise service—that Congress consider what he had freely rendered the nation and then judge a fitting reward for its "Humble Servant."

The letter was read aloud to the delegates. Without comment Congress created a committee of three to study his case and make recommendations. The timing of the appeal could not have been worse. In the summer of 1783 Congress' reputation had sunk low; states up and down the coast flouted its resolutions. Attendance was sporadic and the quality of the delegates second-rate. Then on June 21, two days before Paine was to confer with the congressional committee, a body of Pennsylvania troops surrounded the State House. The soldiers' wrath was not directed at Congress but at the state's Executive Council, also meeting in the building. From the Council they demanded an immediate settlement of their long overdue pay. The ultimatum was rejected. The abashed soldiers swallowed the threats they had made and allowed both the Council and Congress to walk away from the State House unharmed. Congress took the uprising as a personal insult and after reprimanding Pennsylvania for failing to protect its dignity decamped from the city, settling down in the country village of Princeton.

Philadelphia's attitude toward the mutiny divided along lines that had hardened years ago out of the debate over the state's constitution. But to lose Congress to a backwater village humiliated the city and diminished its prestige. The crisis called for a truce, and Paine, who had traveled both sides of the street in Pennsylvania politics, was asked—probably by Robert Morris—to draw up a conciliatory petition that would entice Congress back. He did, devising "a softening healing measure to all sides," or so he thought. Oliver Ellsworth in Congress found "nothing either in the matter, or composition to recommend it" and told Paine so. Joseph Reed thought it too conservative, rewrote parts of it, and dropped out a paragraph on the 5 percent impost that Paine had included to show that Philadelphia favored "doing justice to the foreign and domestic creditors of America." Reed was using the crisis to widen rather than compose differences. He "has catched at it as an opportunity of party," said Paine, sending his draft of the petition to Benjamin Rush to circulate about the city. He left it unsigned so that those who suspected anything by Paine might not be deterred from signing. The subterfuge worked in that all the principal men in the city, regardless of political leanings, added their names; it failed in that Congress ignored the plea from Philadelphia and continued to conduct its business, slight as it was, amid the flora and fauna of Princeton.

Meanwhile, the committee created to study Paine's request had suggested in its report that "a just and impartial account of our interest for public freedom and happiness should be handed down to posterity," an account best made by an official historian. The committee recommended him for the job, in his own words, as one "governed by the most disinterested principles of public good, totally uninfluenced by party of every kind," one who has never "sought, received, or stipulated for any honors, advantages or emoluments for himself." The recommendation grieved Paine. The committee had misunderstood his problem. He wanted some sort of immediate reward for past services, not a further assignment, especially one he knew, for all his talk, he had neither the interest nor talent to perform capably.

The time had come to confer again with Robert Morris. Morris advised Paine to compose a detailed account of his services to America. If Congress was disposed to honor him, it should know what he had done; if it was not so disposed, the narrative "will serve to exculpate me, in the opinion of future Congresses, from the implied demerit which the neglect of former ones serves to lay me under." Paine wrote the autobiography of his American career in September. Before giving it to the congressional committee he showed it to Washington, asking for his "confidential opinion whether I am acting in or out of character in what I have drawn up for that purpose." Washington's approval came by return mail, and the narrative was given to the committee in October.

It was a skillful plea. Paine reminded the committee that he had exposed Deane as a traitor, that his loyalty had been tested by "a very lucrative offer" from persons who tactfully went unnamed, because he preferred to hire himself out "at the usual wages of a common clerk to avoid running into debt." Boasting within bounds, he reviewed his publications, his part in establishing the Bank of Pennsylvania, his trip to France with Laurens. He mentioned in passing that Washington was "affectionately interested" in assuring his "continuance in America." He thanked the committee for recommending him for the post of official historian of the Revolution, but pointed out the yearly salary would not cover even the cost of collecting "materials and information from the different parts of America and abroad," let alone the cost of publication. Moreover, "For Congress to reserve to themselves the least appearance of influence over an historian, by annexing thereto a yearly salary subject to their own control, will endanger the reputation of both the historian and the history." He ended with a delicate hint that he wanted a pension. Out of "a disposition to serve others, I neglected myself for years together," he said. It is up to America "whether she will in return make my situation such, as I can with happiness to myself, and unconfined by dependence, remain in the rank of a citizen of America, or whether I must wish her well and say to her, Adieu."

"The constant coldness" Congress had shown him in the past did not lead Paine to expect much from his narrative, but the initial reaction looked good. The plan to appoint an official historian of the Revolution was abandoned, a new committee was created on October 31, and Paine's autobiography was turned over to it for study.

2

Washington had returned the autobiographical essay with an invitation to relax with a long visit to his current headquarters in a comfortable country mansion at Rocky Hill, not far from Princeton. "Your presence may remind Congress of your past services to this country," he added, signing the note, "by one who entertains a lively sense of the importance of your works." The visit was planned for October but had to be postponed. While in Philadelphia Paine was struck down with scarlet fever, or scarlet anginosa, as it was then called. The epidemic had appeared among the city's children in July and spread to the adult population in September. He was housebound for a month, though sufficiently recovered by mid-October to ask Robert Morris to send him a hundred dollars. Not until early November was he well enough to leave the city and venture on to Washington's headquarters.

Washington saw to it that he had a pleasant time. There was an easy, relaxed feeling between the two men, so much so that the general could even crack a joke over a minor misfortune. One Sunday when they were driving to church, Paine stopped off at a friend's place to leave his heavy overcoat with the servant. He then walked on to the meeting house and joined Washington there. On returning after the service to pick up the coat, Paine found that the servant had vanished with it and some of the master's silver plate. Ah, said Washington, with amusement, Mr. Paine ought to know "it was necessary to watch as well as pray." Later he gave one of his own coats to Paine, who wore it for several years before handing it over to a friend with the solemn pronouncement that the cloth about to warm him had once been owned by General Washington.

The highlight of the visit involved a scientific experiment instigated by Washington, whose curiosity and energy were boundless. "We had several times been told that the river or creek that runs near the bottom of Rocky Hill . . . might be set on fire," Paine later recalled, "for that was the term the country people used." Paine and Washington's aides argued one evening about the cause of the phenomenon. "Their opinion," said Paine, "was that, on disturbing the bottom of the river, some bituminous matter arose to the surface, which took fire when the light was put to it; I, on the contrary, supposed that a quantity of inflammable air was let

loose, which ascended through the water and took fire above the surface."
Washington suggested an experiment on the water should be conducted.

A scow was found and soldiers provided to propel it. "General Washington placed himself at one end of the scow and I at the other," Paine
remembered. "Each of us had a roll of cartridge paper, which we lighted
and held over the water about two or three inches from the surface when
the soldiers began disturbing the bottom of the river with the poles.
. . . When the mud at the bottom was disturbed by the poles, the air
bubbles rose fast, and I saw the fire take from General Washington's light
and descend from thence to the surface of the water, in a similar manner
as when a lighted candle is held so as to touch the smoke of a candle, just
blown out, the smoke will take fire and the fire will descend and light up
the candle. This was demonstrative evidence that what was called setting
the river on fire was setting on fire the inflammable air that arose out of
the mud."

3

Early in November news had reached Washington that the definitive
peace treaty had been signed and a few days later General Carleton
informed him that the British would evacuate New York City on November 25. Paine entered the city with the general or shortly afterward. On
December 4 he was established in a rooming house across from Fraunces
Tavern. The day before at the tavern Washington had bade farewell to
his officers, Gov. George Clinton, and other "citizens of the first distinction," and then walked between lines of his troops to a barge at the foot
of Broadway that carried him across the Hudson and on his way to
Mount Vernon.

No sentimental journey had brought Paine to New York. James
Duane, a squint-eyed gentleman from New York whom John Adams had
judged to be very shrewd, very sharp, had told Paine that the second
committee appointed to study his case planned to do nothing. His autobiographical narrative lay buried in its files. Duane outlined a new approach which he asked Paine to embody in a letter that could be used to
promote it in the New York legislature. Paine complied readily, sending
the letter from Mrs. Hamilton's rooming house the day after Washington
departed for home. "I candidly tell you," he wrote, as if Duane did not

know, "I am tired of having no home, especially in a country where, everybody will allow, I have deserved one. . . . I have but two resources left: the one is, to apply to the states individually; the other is, to go to Europe, for as matters are now circumstanced it is impossible I can continue here." If one state—meaning New York, of course—made "a beginning, it might have an effect on others." He had not "yet a fixed residence in any state. . . . I should prefer a residence in the state of New York to any other place, and as the state will have houses or situations to dispose of," he said, referring to the numerous Tory estates seques- tered by the government, "she will have an opportunity of remembering a friend who has not yet been to America the expense of a private sol- dier."

While Duane used the letter and the autobiographical narrative, which had been retrieved from the congressional committee's file, to build up sympathy among members of the legislature, Paine got his name before the public with *A Supernumerary Crisis*. It was written five days after the letter to Duane. The timing was opportunistic; the content was not. Two months earlier in letters to Washington and Morris, Paine had worried about rumors that Great Britain would refuse to make a com- mercial treaty with the United States. Early in December rumor became fact. Worse, it was learned Britain had also closed out the new nation from the West Indies, once one of the most lucrative ports of American commerce. The news presented America with its first postwar crisis, and Paine used it to pursue what had become a favorite hobbyhorse. Britain knew what she was doing, he said. She had in effect told the world that "it will be a long time before the American states can be brought to act as a nation, neither are they to be feared as such by us. . . . A certain state," meaning Rhode Island, had driven the truth home to the British. "The instance now before us is but a gentle beginning of what America must expect, unless she guards her union with nicer care and stricter honor," he said. "United, she is formidable . . . separated, she is a medley of individual nothings, subject to the sport of foreign nations." He gave the essay the authority of his wartime signature "Common Sense," which he would not use again for two years.

Paine spent the rest of December in New York. January saw him back in Philadelphia. The visit did not go well. He found that his alignment with those like Robert Morris who favored sound money, payment of war debts at face value, and a stronger central government had estranged him from his friends of '76, "the hot-headed Whigs," as he now called them. "It is the misfortune of some Whigs," he said, "to expect more than can or ought to be done and which if attempted will probably undo the government and place it in other hands." From February on he sat out the cold days of 1784's winter in Bordentown, where he owned property, agonizing through "a fit of gout," relieving his boredom and his spleen in letters to friends in New York. It is uncertain when he bought the small house and meadowland in the village, but he owned it by the end of 1783. Late in that year La Luzerne had given him 2400 livres as a gift for past services—Paine had written little during the year to justify a subsidy—and he may have used part of the money to make the purchase. Although neither house nor land was much in size, it was his first piece of real estate. If he bought it with the intention of settling permanently in Bordentown, the thought soon passed. He never became a legal resident there, never voted in the local elections. The house and grazing land were rented out, and the small income from them Paine probably turned over to Kirkbride, with whose family he continued to live.

Paine was incapable of living alone. He never learned to cook, knew nothing about keeping a house in repair, and grew despondent without company to amuse him. He ended his usual daily walk during the winter at Bordentown pushing through the snow for a few convivial hours at the local tavern run by Deborah Applegate. Otherwise he found little to amuse him. Books bored him; he never was and never would be much of a reader, except of newspapers. Country people with their talk about crops and the weather also bored him. "I am shut up here by the frost, and if my letter is tedious attribute it to my want of amusement," he told Lewis Morris.

Fortunately, before the snows had vanished from the ground friends in New York had relieved the tedium of his earthly purgatory with momentous news. In April Duane, with help from Morris, maneuvered through the New York Senate a bill that awarded Paine with a gift of land in the form of a sequestered farm. He was offered the choice of two sites, and on 16 June 1784 the New York legislature officially presented him with the one friends had advised him to select, the confiscated farm of a Tory in New Rochelle. Paine judged the gift "worth at least a thousand guineas."

4

Pleased but still not satisfied, Paine set out to use the New York gift as a precedent to persuade other states, one by one, to follow suit. This plan, rather than one that concentrated on Congress, had the additional merit, he told Washington, that "whatever I may then say on the necessity of strengthening the union and enlarging its powers, will come from me with much better grace than if Congress had made the acknowledgment themselves." James Madison approved this strategy when he heard of it, though for different reasons. A reward from Congress, he said, "might be construed into the wages of a mercenary writer," but those from the states "would look like the returns for voluntary services."

Jefferson opened the campaign in Paine's behalf, and Washington joined the enterprise in June, writing notes to James Madison, Patrick Henry, and Richard Henry Lee. "Can nothing be done in our Assembly for poor Paine?" he asked. "Must the merits of *Common Sense* continue to glide down the stream of time unrewarded by this country? His writings certainly have had a powerful effect upon the public mind. Ought they not, then, to meet an adequate return? He is poor! he is chagreened! and almost if not altogether in despair of relief." From a nation he had done so much for he asked little: "a decent independence is, I believe, all he aims at." For those who might judge Paine a radical, Washington took care to note that "his views are moderate."

On June 28 Madison introduced a bill in the legislature that would have offered Paine a piece of land with a market value of "about £4,000, or upwards," but the bill was defeated on the third reading by Arthur Lee. Lee argued that the man who had written *Public Good* deserved nothing from Virginia, and the desire for revenge that Lee "brewed up," as Madison told Jefferson, "put a negative on every form which could be given to the proposed remuneration."

Jefferson, who had been sent to Paris to replace Franklin as the American minister, could do little, but Washington continued his efforts on Paine's behalf. He spoke to John Dickinson, the current president of Pennsylvania's Executive Council. Dickinson sent a note to the Assembly informing it of Washington's interest and urging "that a suitable acknowledgment of [Paine's] eminent services and a proper provision towards a continuance of them in an independent manner, should be made on the part of this state." This was in December 1784. On 9 April 1785 the Pennsylvania Assembly awarded Paine five hundred pounds as a "temporary recompense." The legislature thought he deserved a larger stipend but before committing itself preferred to wait and see what Congress would do.

Congress, prodded by Washington, created a new committee to study his case, headed by a friend of Paine's, Elbridge Gerry. Since April 1784, when New York's gift came through, Paine had kept his pen in the inkwell and let others campaign for him in the state legislatures. The silence ended in 1785 with an ill-advised carping letter to Congress. He complained about how his salary as secretary had been "fretted down by the depreciation to less than a fifth of its nominal value." Gerry managed to silence him. On August 26 Congress resolved that "Mr. Paine is entitled to a liberal gratification from the United States." A month later, Paine, probably after being asked what he considered liberal, said he should be reimbursed for all his expenses since coming to America, which could "not possibly have been less than six thousand dollars." On September 28 Gerry moved on the floor of Congress that Paine be gratified with a gift of six thousand dollars. The resolution was defeated. Of the eleven states that voted, only Pennsylvania, Maryland, Virginia, and Georgia favored the motion. Congress, however, was determined to get Paine off its back. A new committee was appointed, and after listening to its recommendation Congress on October 3 voted to give Paine three thousand dollars.

After nearly two years of huffing and puffing, Paine's campaign for a pension had ended. Now that Congress had rewarded him, no state felt an obligation to add to the gifts he had already received. Paine had won less than he hoped for but more than he should have expected from a nation with heavy debts and thousands of grumbling soldiers still waiting to be paid for risking their lives. From a nation unaccustomed to honoring literary gentlemen with cash rewards Paine had received more than almost any writer would ever receive from a national or state government in American history. More astonishing still was the number of men who, in pleading his cause, had accepted as literally true the citation that accompanied New York's gift: "His literary works . . . inspired the citizens of this state with unanimity, confirmed their confidence in the rectitude of their cause, and have ultimately contributed to the freedom, sovereignty, and independence of the United States."

Paine accepted the gifts grudgingly, as something less than his due. "Men of letters suffer from conceit more than ordinary men," a man of letters once wrote. "They are an egotistic lot. Friendships between them are precarious. They are a little like bulls that way. The bull that was friendly and playful as a calf will gore the guts out of you at the drop of a hat when he's grown." A decade later George Washington would learn the aptness of that analogy.

5

Paine was never seriously in want the rest of his life, except for his last few months in prison during the Reign of Terror. Sometimes he would mismanage his affairs and find himself short of cash, but he would never again be down and out as in the past. He had no wife, no children to care for. Among his friends were always a number of substantial gentlemen who when pressed would usually lend him money. If he needed a place to stay, someone always came through with room and board.

In July 1786 Paine traveled to Morrisania, the country estate of Lewis Morris which lay a few miles north of Manhattan, and from there he traveled on his horse, Button, a gift from Morris, to New Rochelle to have a look at his land, then being farmed by a tenant who henceforth would pay his rent to the once impecunious Thomas Paine. With money in the bank—the Bank of North America, for which he would soon become a warm defender—he felt secure enough to indulge in some modest speculative ventures. In the fall of 1786 he learned about a tract of four hundred acres up for sale. A friend believed Paine "had no idea of purchasing" the tract when he first saw it, but before many hours had passed his name was signed to the deed. The cost in paper currency was £2,700, which worked out to something like $120 in specie, for this was the sum the friend a few days later brought to Paine from Philadelphia.

The song and dance Paine had handed friends in New York about his affection for that state became self-evident before the year 1786 had ended. He referred to New York as home and grumbled about the shabby treatment Pennsylvania had meted out, calling her gift of five hundred dollars a pittance to what he deserved. Yet Philadelphia, not New York, was the magnet that pulled him out of Bordentown and back into the field of politics. This time, as befitted one of the *nouveau riche*, he stepped out as spokesman for the Bank of North America.

CHAPTER

11

THE BANK WAR

THROUGHOUT THE REVOLUTION Paine wrote and talked eloquently but vaguely of the America he envisioned once victory had been achieved. Whatever corruptions had been imposed upon the land and the people by the war would be sloughed off, and a haven for mankind, swept clean of vice, would emerge. A number of contemporaries shared that vision. Some after the war sought to purify the language by forcing out English vulgarities and archaisms. Others worked to end slavery in this land of the free. Benjamin Rush initiated a temperance movement that called for moderation in rather than prohibition of the consumption of spiritous liquors. (Rush thought drinking more than a pint a day excessive, except in the case of fortified wine.) Those who believed that the nation's greatness would depend on an informed and enlightened public set about creating new colleges or worked to get state-financed public education. A few even dared to argue that the future depended on well-educated women.

Paine stood clear of this ferment of reform. The successful effort to revise Pennsylvania's penal code and to improve conditions in the prisons owed nothing to him. He who had once been a teacher wrote nothing to promote better schools. Those who worked through the legislature to bring about the end of slavery in Pennsylvania did so without his active support. He despaired "of seeing an abolition of the infernal traffic in Negroes" and his only suggestion to improve the black man's lot was to "wish that a few well instructed could be sent among their brethren in bondage; for until they are enabled to take their own part, nothing will be done."

These reforms had Paine's best wishes, but he would not write for them. When others cried out against the aristocratic tendency of the Society of Cincinnati, a fraternity of ex-officers that perpetuated itself through the members' eldest sons, he wondered "whether every part of the institution is perfectly consistent with a republic," but said nothing in print. Publicly he remained religiously orthodox, worrying about anything that might "extirpate religion and virtue from our country," but privately he now had "*common sense enough* to disbelieve most of the common systematic theories of divinity," a friend remarked, though he "does not seem to establish any for himself."

Those who knew him found it easy to explain why after the Revolution Paine retired to Bordentown "to the enjoyment of a quiet life" and kept his distance from the issues that stirred so many of his friends. He was preoccupied during the first two years of peace wangling rewards for himself from the states and the national government. He was not a joiner; rather, he was something of a prima donna, disinclined to share credit when honors were being handed out. No reform movement that required group action ever attracted his interest. He craved acceptance and knew that to denounce Christianity or the Society of Cincinnati would do little to win it for him. Paine wanted too much to be liked to rock the boat after independence, the port long aimed for, had been reached.

Those who thus explained Paine's postwar silence were startled when suddenly in the autumn of 1785 he emerged from Bordentown to joust publicly with friends he had worked with since the days of '76. Those friends, calling themselves Constitutionalists, had controlled Pennsylvania politics for nearly a decade, and Paine had been often their spokesman and always their ally through those years. He had not complained when they quashed the charter of the College of Philadelphia, then run by anti-Constitutionalists or Republicans, changed its name to the University of Pennsylvania, and issued a new charter that packed the state-appointed board of trustees with Constitutionalists. He had been delighted to accept an honorary master's degree from the politicized university. Disenchantment with "the hot-headed Whigs" began soon after the war but simmered out of sight until 1785 when they started talking about revoking the charter of the Bank of North America. That touched a nerve that propelled Paine out of retirement.

2

Robert Morris had proposed the Bank of North America when he served as superintendent of finances. Its purpose, he said, was to "facilitate the management of the finances of the United States," to "afford to the individuals of all the states a medium for their intercourse with each other," and "to increase both the internal and external commerce of North America." Congress issued a charter for the bank in 1781. Doubt that it had the power to do so led the directors in April 1782 to get a duplicate charter from Pennsylvania. The bank had opened its doors while Paine was in France, but only after he and Laurens had returned with the gold that provided the bulk of its capital did full operations get under way. If Morris could claim to be father of the bank, Paine was, in his own eyes, its stepfather.

The bank did much to stabilize currency and the nation's finances during the remainder of the war, and no one censured its work. When the war ended a recession set in. Land values slumped when the expected flood of immigrants failed to materialize, trade slowed, and prices, particularly on agricultural products, dropped nearly out of sight. The usual shortage of hard money became severe with the end of loans from France. In 1785 farmers in the backcountry of Pennsylvania, egged on by speculators who thrived on an inflated currency, pleaded with the Assembly to inject life into the economy with an emission of paper money. The bank feared it would be forced to redeem the currency in specie. By opposing the scheme it aroused the Constitutionalists, those "hot-headed Whigs" who controlled the Assembly and whose power centered in the backcountry. Petitions streamed into the Assembly denouncing the bank as a monopoly, dangerous to the state's and possibly the nation's welfare.

For those who knew him or had read his writings with care, Paine reacted predictably to the agitation. He detested paper money. As one who had been paid in nearly worthless continentals, he had in a sense been burned by it. He objected to it on ethical as well as practical grounds. Debased money evoked a passionate reaction from him. The man who passed counterfeit bills committed "a species of treason, the most prejudicial to us of any, or all the other kinds." The bank gave the people sound money, therefore it was morally defensible.

It had other virtues for Paine—it promoted commerce. "Our plan is commerce, and that, well attended to, will secure us the peace and friendship of all Europe," he had said in *Common Sense*, and the faith expressed then had strengthened in the years since. Also, the bank fit in nicely with his credo that the least government was the best; it was a private enterprise operated by private citizens for a profit, and though some complained that an annual dividend of 12 to 16 percent was excessive it did not perturb Paine. Finally, the fact that the bank transacted business in all the states and that its certificates were accepted as currency everywhere helped along another cause favored by Paine—a stronger union.

In April 1785 the antipathetic Assembly created a committee to inquire into the bank's affairs and consider the consequences if its charter was revoked. Paine for the time being hovered behind the battle lines. He had to tread cautiously, for the week the bank war flared up found the Assembly pondering a suitable gift for his services during the war. With a discretion incredible for him he watched silently while his welfare and the bank's future were pondered simultaneously.

The Assembly voted its gift of five hundred pounds to Paine on April 9. He felt free then to seek out two old friends who were leading the fight against the bank, John Smilie and Jonathan B. Smith. "I saw very clearly they were going to destroy themselves by a rash, sad, unjust, tyrannical proceeding, and that they might not, I endeavored in the most pressing and friendly manner to remonstrate with them, to point out the consequence, and caution them against it."

He told Smith and Smilie what would happen if they willfully drove through a repeal of the charter: "that in a government where nothing was certain the disposition to obedience would be so too—that acts, when so easily and frequently changed, lost the force and dignity of laws, and ceased to command respect—that their proceedings respecting the bank was a dangerous precedent—that it came under the description of *governing too much*—and that, however gratifying it might be to their prejudice, it would, in my opinion, be fatal to their power." They answered all this with "stress upon what they called the *dangerous influence of the bank*," and made it clear that Paine's remonstrance did not sit well with them.

Paine still said nothing in print. He wanted to revive his case with Congress for a pension; any outburst on the bank might damage his cause. Paine was about to set out for New York, where Congress was then sitting, when on April 19 he received a letter from Thomas Fitzsimmons, one of the original directors of the bank and a friend since 1776, asking his views on the battle over the charter. From Brunswick, where bad weather held up his stagecoach, Paine sent back his opinion on the bank war. It had placed him in a delicate predicament with old friends. "The house is composed of men, with whom I have lived with more intimacy than with the generality of the citizens of Pennsylvania, and who have shown more disposition to promote my interest than others have," he said. "But the house appears to me so exceedingly wrong in this business, both as to the matter and manner of it, that my private judgment on the case cannot go with them, and must go against them, disregarding consequences to myself."

On September 13 by a vote of fifty to twelve the Assembly rescinded the bank's charter. Paine still said nothing in public. Two weeks later Congress voted him the gift of three thousand dollars. Paine still kept silent, perhaps waiting to see if Congress had closed its file on him. It had. Finally, on December 21, he published the letter to Fitzsimmons in the Philadelphia press and at last took a public stand on the bank. The next day the Assembly recessed for six weeks. Paine used the holiday from politics to write a pamphlet of some fifty pages which he entitled *Dissertations on Government; the Affairs of the Bank; and Paper Money.* He finished it on 18 February 1786, and six days later the printer had bound copies to pass out to the returning members of the Assembly.

3

Of all those who wrote during Pennsylvania's bank war, "the most effective participant on either side was Thomas Paine," Bray Hammond, an authority on the subject, has said. Paine's arguments, as the heavy-handed title hinted, appealed to reason rather than emotion, to members of the Assembly rather than the general public. The opening pages focused on the different kinds of legislation the Assembly produced. First, there are bills which once enacted become laws. These "may be altered, amended, and repealed, or others substituted in their places, as experience shall direct, for the better effecting the purpose for which they were intended." Then there are bills which are in effect contractual agreements between the state and particular individuals. Charters fall into this category. "No law made afterwards can apply to the case, either directly, or by construction or implication: for such a law would be a retrospective law, or a law made after the fact." Thus, says Paine, without agreement from both parties to the contract a revocation of any charter can only be classed as unconstitutional. (Thirty-three years later Chief Justice John Marshall in the Dartmouth College case handed down a decision that elevated Paine's reasoning into constitutional law.)

It was not enough to tell the Assembly it had no legal power to revoke the bank's charter; it had done so, and the Pennsylvania constitution Paine had once praised was so constructed that there was no check on the Assembly's decisions. The deputies must be convinced of the Bank of North America's worth to the state and the nation. It was produced, he goes on, "by the distresses of the times and the enterprising spirit of patriotic individuals," a remark Bray Hammond finds especially congenial, for it "puts in a nutshell the circumstances in which American banking had its origins." Among the "patriotic individuals" Paine included himself, and not being one to indulge in false modesty he pauses to relate his role in founding the bank's progenitor, the Bank of Pennsylvania. He then moves on to show that the Bank of North America gives more than it receives. "The whole community derives benefit from the operation of the bank. It facilitates the commerce of the country. . . . The emolument, therefore, being to the community, it is the office and duty of government to give protection to the bank."

The Assembly talks of an emission of paper money, Paine continues, relishing what he is about to say. Paine often adjusted his opinions to time and place. Once, when addressing Frenchmen through the Abbé Raynal, he praised paper money as a way of financing the Revolution among a people who declined to tax themselves. "There may be cases in which paper money may be generally serviceable," he had told Fitzsimmons; "but it is an expedient, that should be used with the greatest caution, or we shall have all the evils of depreciation both of money and morals over again." In the *Dissertations* he spoke as he felt, allowing a moralistic fervor for the moment to supplant reason: "*Money is money, and paper is paper. All the invention of man cannot make them otherwise. The alchemist may cease his labors, and the hunter after the philosopher's stone go to rest, if paper can be metamorphosed into gold and silver, or made to answer the same purpose in all cases.*"

Here and elsewhere in the pamphlet Paine ground his ax too hard. The bank had been designed after the Bank of England, yet its powers exceeded those of the model. Pennsylvania lacked the right to supervise or inspect the operations of the most powerful institution within its borders. The cry of monopoly against it had validity, for as the government's banker its large capital placed it in a domineering position. The bank favored the farmer, said Paine, yet in fact it rarely granted commodity loans. One wild statement of his—"The republican form and principle leave no room for insurrection" in America—backfired within weeks after the pamphlet appeared, when Shays's Rebellion disrupted Massachusetts and terrified the elite of the nation into thinking that another revolution, this one internal, was about to commence.

The bank's opponents received only a single compliment from Paine, but that exception led to a remarkable aside. "The term 'forever' is an absurdity," he remarked in commenting upon the opposition's distaste for charters granted in perpetuity. "The next age will think for itself, by the same rule of right that we have done, and not admit any assumed authority of ours to encroach upon the system of their day. Our *forever* ends, where their *forever* begins." He had more to say on the point: "As we are not to live forever ourselves, and other generations are to follow us, we have neither the power nor the right to govern them, or to say how they shall govern themselves. It is the summit of human vanity, and shows a covetousness of power beyond the grave, to be dictating to the world to come." Paine estimated the average life of a generation to "be about thirty years." That being so, he suggested an amendment to Pennsylvania's constitution requiring "that all laws and acts should cease of themselves in thirty years, and have no legal force beyond that time."

"The question, whether one generation of men has a right to bind another, seems never to have been started either on this or our side of the water," Thomas Jefferson three years later remarked somewhat disingenuously, for he had read the *Dissertations* and more recently had talked with Paine on that question. Jefferson went on to say "that no society can make a perpetual constitution, or even a perpetual law. The earth belongs always to the living generation." Later, after Jefferson had sent these observations in a letter to James Madison, Paine developed his own earlier remarks in *The Rights of Man*. This has led at least one historian to conclude "that Paine saw a copy of Jefferson's letter to Madison," and that the borrowing of the phrase was "an altogether natural occurrence, an everyday borrowing from a cultural milieu to which Paine had contributed and in which he felt altogether at home."

4

Paine was in Philadelphia when the deputies assembled late in February, delighted with an excuse to escape the arctic gloom of Bordentown. He had a short piece directed at the backcountry members in the press on March 27, the day debate began on the resolution to restore the bank's charter. "Nothing is more certain than that if the bank was destroyed," he wrote, "the market for country produce would be monopolized by a few monied men, who could command the price as they pleased."

The debate lasted four days, and nothing "that has been agitated before the legislature of Pennsylvania ever drew together such crowded audiences." On the third day as discussion wound on into the evening Paine from the gallery heard John Smilie pause in a speech to call the writer of the *Dissertations* "an unprincipled author whose pen is let out for hire." The assault shook Paine. He had been pleased that not once in a war that divided friends of '76 had personal invective marred his campaign for the bank. Now Smilie, "sheltered under the sanctioned authority of a representative," had turned on him. The next morning during the Assembly's final session a motion to restore the bank's charter was defeated thirty-nine to thirty, a relatively slim margin compared to the overwhelming sentiment against the bank the previous year. Paine refused to exult, saying only "that the people are recovering from the delusion and bubble of the last year." He still smarted from Smilie's attack. On April 4, three days after the vote, he began a new series in the press, this time defending himself as he praised the bank. He admitted "that from the first establishment of the bank, to the present hour, I have been its friend and advocate; yet I have never made the least use of it, or received the least personal service or favor from it, by borrowing or discounting notes, or in any other shape or manner whatever of any person concerned with it directly or indirectly." Friends would have been happier if he had made a straight-out denial that he had received any money to write for the bank, but this he did not do. He sniped occasionally at Smilie, "who loves to talk about what he does not understand," but only in passing as he laid out before the public his dealings with the bank. "I have kept cash at the bank, and the bank is at this time in account to me between eight and nine hundred pounds, for money which I brought from New York, and deposited there ever since last September, and for which I do not receive a single farthing interest. This money the country has had the use of, and I think it safer under the care of the bank, until I have occasion to call for it, than in my own custody."

John Smilie, disguised as "Atticus," answered with a string of four open letters. The first ended excoriating Paine as one "who, having reaped a recompense more than adequate to his deserts, prostitutes his pen to the ruin of his country." The charge that his pen had been hired for the bank was dropped. The year before James Wilson had been paid four hundred dollars to write in favor of the bank. There is no reason to doubt that Paine would have accepted a similar offer if it had been made, but there is no evidence that such an offer was made.

5

Paine spent the summer in Bordentown. He dispatched an occasional missile to the press on the bank, but otherwise the days passed pleasantly in his workshop, where he was building a model for an iron bridge. The arrival of autumn found him refreshed and prepared again for battle. "I shall be backward and forward between here and Philadelphia pretty often until the elections are over," he told a friend in September.

The election that fall of 1786 would revolve around the inadequacies and virtues of the Pennsylvania constitution. In *Common Sense* Paine had said that a legislature composed of a single house and coupled to a weak executive offered the safest form of government. That same year Pennsylvania produced a constitution that followed his prescription. In 1778, when it looked as though the voters might throw out the document and call for a convention to construct a new one that created a two-house legislature and a strong executive, he had pleaded for the people to keep what they had. Now, eight years later, as he prepared to leave Bordentown for Philadelphia, Paine reversed field. He renounced his previous stand openly in an essay that appeared on September 20, fully aware of the opprobrium old friends would heap upon him. In 1778 he explained, "My aim was to quiet the dispute, and prevent it from entangling the country, at a time when the utmost harmony of its powers was necessary to its safety. The constitution was upon experiment, and the manner in which a single house would use an abundance of power would best determine whether it ought to be trusted with it." Then he had supposed that a single house would be responsive to the will of the people. Time and experience showed that a single legislature "is capable of being made a complete aristocracy," he now confessed. Then we believed that a strong executive "was the only dangerous part of a government, but we now see that quite as much mischief, if not more, may be done, and as much arbitrary conduct acted, by a legislature." A single house, annually reelected, subjects the state to "perpetual convulsions of imperfect measures and rash proceedings."

The Republicans won the election. They now had the power to revive the bank's charter and nearly enough to call for a new constitutional convention. Once the votes were counted Paine gave in, as always, to the desire to advise a friend in power. "Next to gaining a majority is to keep it," he told Thomas Fitzsimmons. "This, at least (in my opinion) will not be best accomplished by doing or attempting a great deal of business, but by doing no more than is absolutely necessary to be done, acting moderately and giving no offense." Neither Fitzsimmons nor his colleagues heeded this counsel. Once the Assembly convened, the dominant Republicans pushed at once for a convention to revise the constitution and also for a new charter for the bank. The Constitutionalists fought a bitter rear-guard action.

December found Paine again in Philadelphia. The question of the bank kept popping into conversations wherever he went, much as he tried to avoid the subject. One afternoon at a friend's house a dispute arose "between Mr. Paine and the Captain [Coltman] in which words were very high." Paine and Coltman had come to America on the same ship and they had remained friends ever since. Paine often stayed with Coltman's family when he visited Philadelphia. The captain suggested that Paine's articles on the bank had undermined the cause of liberty. Paine "swore by G—d, let who would, it was a lie," and with that they proceeded to quarrel "a considerable time." Finally, Paine departed, but the captain could not calm down. He continued to talk "about politics and the bank, and what he thought the misconduct of Mr. Paine in his being out and in with the several parties." A mutual friend who had arrived to share in the dinner then on the table, attempted to defend Paine, whereupon "the captain grew warm, and said he knew now he could not eat his dinner."

Anyone who went back to *Common Sense* or reread what Paine had written since could see that his defense of the bank dovetailed with his hopes for America. The bank was an engine, a machine that would make reality out of a dream. Under its aegis commerce would flourish and the union grow stronger. The change of mind about the constitution of 1776 was equally logical though harder to understand for those who knew his writings. It came suddenly when he saw that an all-powerful, unchecked legislature could be as tyrannical as an all-powerful, unchecked executive. When defending the constitution in 1778 he had asked only that the experiment be given a trial run. Eight years later he saw the experiment had failed and refinements and changes in the machinery were called for.

Friends of '76 found his new stance unforgivable. For some he had come to resemble two-faced Janus, and the analogy led to a scathing satire that circulated about Philadelphia years after Paine had departed for Europe:

> *Janus* is our own,
> Who props a bank, altho' he scorn'd a throne;
> And, should his heart with just resentments burn,
> Would scorn a bank and prop a throne in turn;
> But should both bank and throne reject the job,
> Would damn them both and idolize the mob;
> And if all three should scorn the honest fellow,
> For *Daniel Shays* and *Liberty* would bellow.

CHAPTER

12

EXPERIMENTS OF A
DIFFERENT KIND

PAINE HAD REMARKED during the Revolution that we are "a people upon experiments." Then the experiments had been political, and during the war they absorbed him. The day-to-day business of running a government bored him. Only when it seemed that republican principles were being traduced, as in the bank war, did he emerge from his workshop. Mr. Paine, a friend remarked, "seemed to delight in difficulties," but now "in mechanics particularly," not politics.

Visitors to his workshop found the political philosopher something other than expected. The routine of day-to-day living disconcerted Paine. He was indolent, sloppy, and absent-minded. He needed the care of a Mrs. Henry in Lancaster or a Mrs. Kirkbride in Bordentown to see that he ate regularly, that his clothes were laundered, that occasionally his room was cleaned and the bedsheets changed. Another man—deft, precise, and indefatigable—materialized in the workshop. His experiments were carried out with skill and imagination and reported with impeccable clarity. One day after the war, for instance, he and David Rittenhouse wanted to get some "noxious air" they had trapped in a bladder into a glass vial. "For this purpose," he explained to those who might wish to reproduce the experiment, "we took a vial of about three or four ounces, filled it with water, put a cork slightly into it, and introducing it into the neck of the bladder, worked the cork out, by getting hold of it through the bladder into which the water then emptied itself, and the air in the bladder ascended into the vial; we then put the cork into the vial, and took it from the bladder. It was now in a convenient condition for experiment." Paine and Rittenhouse went on to prove true what they already knew—"noxious air" burns, therefore it must be poisonous.

Natural philosophy had intrigued Paine from the time he had sat listening to Martin's and Ferguson's lectures in London. It had brought him into Franklin's circle, had strengthened friendships with Washington and Livingston and helped to build one with Thomas Jefferson, with whom by the end of the Revolution he was "on exceeding good terms." He continued to exchange ideas after the war with William Henry in Lancaster, continued to see David Rittenhouse and Benjamin Rush in Philadelphia. Occasionally these gentlemen devised gadgets, like Jefferson's pair of French doors that swung open together with a light touch to the handle of one. Occasionally they theorized about "noxious air," the cause of the common cold, or what happens when two pieces of iron are welded together. (Welding, said Paine, "appears to me no other than entangling the particles in much the same manner as turning a key within the wards of a lock, and if our eyes were good enough we should see how it was done.")

More often they joined to promote practical science. Whatever helped speed the settlement of the land—a better plow, a faster boat, a cheaper candle—won their approval. Science, as Paine put it, "lessened the catalogue of impossibilities." It allowed men to carry on the business of living more easily and efficiently. If the war "energized invention," peace did so even more, at least for Paine, who now had the time and money to devote to science. He assigned a lofty purpose to his new avocation—he would be as useful to America in the practical sphere as he had been in the political. Other less grand motives drove him into the workshop. A successful invention would reinforce his candidacy for immortality among men. Also it might bring to his door what had eluded him thus far—fortune. Money, however, meant less than the satisfaction Paine got from working with his hands. The long years as a staymaker had left him with an ability to use tools with a skill that still gave him great pleasure. Like his friend Benjamin Franklin, he continued in many ways to be what he had been—a craftsman at heart.

2

Franklin returned to Philadelphia in the fall of 1785 after nearly a decade in France. Paine had sought Franklin's approbation in all that he had done since coming to America, and he always got it. The relation between them was unique. Franklin called him his "adopted political son," and Paine in turn treated the old man like an adopted father. He even came in conversation to sound like Franklin, as when once he gave a friend a crafty piece of un-Paine-like advice. Never, he said, "give a deciding opinion between two persons you are in friendship with, lest you lose one by it; whilst doing that between two persons, your supposed enemies, may make one your friend."

Paine liked to drop in on Franklin after he had settled back in his house in Philadelphia. One day he found him rearranging his library, and the sage felt called upon to explain why. "Mr. Paine," he said, "you may be surprised at finding me thus busily occupied at my advanced state of life. Many might think me an old fool to be thus busied in the affairs of this life, while making such near approach, in the course of nature, to the grave. But it has always been my maxim to live on as if I was to live always." It may have occurred to Paine that a banquet he had recently attended honoring Franklin's eightieth birthday accounted for the reflective mood. "It is with such feeling only," he went on, "that we can be stimulated to the exertion necessary to effect any useful moral purpose. Death will one day lay hold of me, and put an end to all my labors; but, till then, it is my maxim to go on in the old way. I will not anticipate his coming." Paine relished the story and years later was still retelling it to friends in France who wanted to know what sort of man Benjamin Franklin had been.

In 1776 Paine had let Franklin edit *Common Sense* before sending it to the printer. A decade later he still came to him for advice, though he was now engaged in different kinds of experiments. In December 1785 he sent Franklin a packet of "smokeless candles." Each had a hole bored from end to end parallel to the wick. "In a little time after they are lighted," Paine explained, "the smoke and flame separate, the one issuing from one end of the candle, and the other from the other end." He wrote out some thoughts on the phenomenon: "Thoughts are a kind of mental smoke," he explained, "which require words to illuminate them." He wanted to hear what Franklin had to say about it. On New Year's Day 1786 Franklin had him to dinner. They talked away the afternoon, then after evening tea they experimented with the candles. They found that a gentle current of air "greatly improved the light." Franklin conjectured that the tin frame they were placed in "by internal reflections is heated and causes a constant current." Apparently it was agreed that the candles had no commercial value, for no more was heard of them.

3

Paine could take the snuffed-out smokeless candles calmly, for he had earlier involved Franklin in a grander project, one more suitable for men of vision—an iron bridge designed to span the rivers of an almost totally unbridged America. Paine said later that his conception had come to him one winter day while staring at an enormous ice jam in the Schuylkill River. The piers of any bridge across the river would have been crushed by the caked ice. Why not, he reasoned, produce a new kind of bridge— an American bridge suitable to the American environment. "The European method of bridge architecture, by piers and arches," he said, "is not adapted to the condition of many of the rivers in America on account of the ice in the winter." His bridge would "obviate that difficulty by leaving the whole passage of the river clear of the incumbrance of piers." It would be constructed of a single arch combining thirteen sections—"in commemoration of the thirteen United States," he noted, for this was to be a wholly American structure. Paine took the idea of his bridge "from a spider's web of which it resembled a section." He supposed that "when Nature enabled this insect to make a web, she taught it the best method of putting it together." He would call his bridge "a child of common sense."

Enemies later accused Paine of having stolen his idea from Abraham Swan's *Collection of Designs in Architecture*, published in 1757. This seems unlikely, for Swan's book contained plans only for stone and timber bridges. It is more likely that he borrowed from or was inspired by a French designer named Vincent de Montpetit, who in 1779 had constructed an iron model of a single-arch bridge. The model was on exhibition when Paine visited Paris in 1781. The bridge was designed like Paine's to be prefabricated at the iron foundry and then assembled on location. "The only novelty or discovery in Paine's bridge," Alfred O. Aldridge has pointed out, "was in the arrangement of the segments of the arch on the principle of a spider's web."

Paine never claimed he invented the iron bridge any more than he invented the arguments in *Common Sense*. In the pamphlet he reshaped what others had used before to transmute a lawsuit into a revolution. He spread before the people a vision of America's future greatness once free of Europe. Similarly, his vision of the iron bridge's role in the nation's future set him apart from others who may have conceived before him spanning rivers with girders of iron. Paine perceived long before most of his contemporaries that the world verged on a new age, one in which iron would replace stone and timber. As the American Revolution had for him heralded the death of a political age in which monarchs ruled men, so the industrial revolution signaled the birth of an epoch in which iron would dominate the material world. He had ushered in one revolution with a pamphlet; he would usher in another with a bridge.

Paine may have talked about his bridge to William Henry in Lancaster, whose experience as an armorer made him one of the most knowledgeable men in the land about the capacities of iron. He definitely talked to Lewis Morris on one of his visits to Morrisania. Morris encouraged Paine to go ahead. A bridge over the Harlem River would connect his estate with Manhattan. It was decided that Paine would return to Philadelphia and construct a wooden model to test out his ideas. In mid-November he rented a loft in Philadelphia and hired John Hall, a young mechanic who had recently emigrated from England, to assist him. By December nine of the thirteen sections had been pinned together in the, naturally, thirteen-foot model. As an employer he proved solicitous, bringing Hall wine and water, providing him with a foot stove, lending him stockings, giving him a coat. Visitors streamed through the shop keeping tabs on the experiment. Dr. Hutchinson stopped by, as did Franklin, Gouverneur Morris, Tench Francis, Robert Morris, David Rittenhouse, and Dr. John Redman. Paine welcomed them all as potential investors in or promoters of his scheme.

He had mixed feelings about the finished model. It held the weight of four men "without the least injury to it, or signs of any." As it was made of cherry, "not a very strong wood," Paine feared a heavier weight might ruin his and Hall's handiwork. He worried, too, that "the ends of the timber by continually pressing against each other will in time diminish something in their length either by splitting up or wearing away." After pondering all this, Paine decided to invest additional time and money in a second model, this one to be made of cast iron. Operations were moved to Kirkbride's house in Bordentown, where he and Hall could draw on a nearby furnace for their material.

4

In March 1786, before construction began, a tall, imposing man named John Fitch stopped by the shop in Bordentown for a visit. Fitch, too, was pioneering the new age. Within a few years he would put the first successful self-propelled steamboat on a trial run up and down the Delaware River, and it was about that still unfulfilled dream he had come to talk to Paine.

The two men hit it off well at once. Though reared an ocean apart, they shared much in common. Fitch years ago had walked away from a miserable marriage and had ever since professed "that the greatest torment that a man can have in this world is to be teased with women." He was a deist and when "middling glad in liquor," which was often, he tended to speak his "sentiments perhaps more freely than was prudent." He was determined to show the world that "little Johnny Fitch can do something of importance," but he was forty-three and success continued to elude him. His sense of superiority was, as a biographer puts it, "a rickety floor built over a deep well of uncertainty." After an expedition through the Northwest Territory, he had returned east in 1785 "to lay at the feet of Congress an attempt he has made to facilitate the internal navigation of the United States, adapted especially to the waters of the Mississippi." He described the steamboat to Franklin, who "spoke very flatteringly" of it to his face but behind his back said it would never work. As he canvassed the country in search of financial support, Fitch found, as Paine soon would, that everyone—Congress, state governments, and private individuals—was reluctant to put money in an untested pioneering venture.

After being dismissed by Congress, Fitch had visited William Henry in Lancaster. Henry said that ten years earlier he had thought of using a steam engine to push a boat along the water but except for inventing a "steam-wheel" had done nothing further with the idea. He also said that Thomas Paine had talked about designing a steamboat when he lived with the Henry family during the war. Now Fitch came to Paine with his model of a "machine to drive boats against stream," as Hall called it. He offered a partnership in return for financial backing. Paine said his own project absorbed the little cash he had to spare. Mr. Paine, said Hall, already "had enough hobbies of his own." But the two men talked; Paine suggested a way to simplify Fitch's complicated apparatus, and he paid five shillings for a map of the Northwest Territory that Fitch had drawn, etched, and printed himself. They parted friends, to meet a few years later in France, where each had gone in search of money to finance his dreams.

5

In May Paine and Hall began to work on an iron model of the bridge and by June had finished it. Both it and the wooden model were packed aboard a river boat and sent down to Philadelphia, where Franklin graciously allowed them to be displayed in his garden. His willingness to appear as Paine's patron meant much, for recently he had been elected to the highest office in the state, president of the Executive Council. (Paine was not the only one to use the old man. Though it was known that "the stone gave him uncommon pain," so excruciating that he could not stand being jolted over cobblestones in a carriage but had to be carried about the city in a sedan chair, the politicians forced him out of retirement with the hope that his presence at the head of the government would bolster its shaky reputation and pacify dissidents.)

If Pennsylvania subsidized construction of the iron bridge, "it would exceedingly benefit the city and county, and besides its usefulness would, I believe, be the most extensive arch in the world, and the longest bridge without piers," Paine told Franklin, adding an unctuous postscript: "I should therefore wish to see it undertaken and performed during your Presidency, as any share I might have therein would be greatly heightened by that circumstance." Paine, with Franklin's approval, invited the Executive Council to study the model. The Council encouraged Paine to hope the state might do something for him.

The project languished through the summer, and in the fall Paine was too busy getting Republicans elected to the Assembly to think about iron bridges. In November he learned that the Pennsylvania Agricultural Society had petitioned the Assembly for the exclusive right to build a bridge of three piers over the Schuylkill. This news drove him back to action, for the Schuylkill had supplanted the Harlem as the river he now wanted to arch with his bridge. Some of the visitors to Franklin's garden had told him that wrought rather than brittle cast iron was the material out of which his bridge should be constructed. Hall earlier in the fall had begun a model in the new material, working at a leisurely pace while Paine politicked for Republicans. Paine now stepped up the schedule, driven by the fear the Agricultural Society might frustrate his dream. "I am now flooring my model, which I hope to finish tomorrow," he wrote George Clymer, president of the Agricultural Society, on December 13. "I shall then have only the pallasadees [abutments] to put up, which I hope to get through in two or three days and shall bring it with me to Penn. You laugh perhaps at my pallasadees, but stay until you see them."

Paine's good humor vanished as the faster pace led to frayed tempers. "This day employed in raising and putting on the abutments again and fitting them," Hall wrote on December 14. "The smith made the nuts of screws to go easier. Then set the ribs at proper distance, and after dinner I and Jackaway [a helper] put on some temporary pieces on the frame of wood to hold it straight, and when Mr. Paine came they then tied it on its wooden frame with strong cords. I then saw that it had bulged full on one side and hollow on the other. I told him of it, and he said it was done by me—I denied that and words rose high. I at length swore by God that it was straight when I left it, and he replied as positively the contrary, and I think myself ill-used in this affair."

Tempers mended with a night's sleep, and within a few days the new model had been completed. It was loaded aboard a sled, hauled across the frozen Delaware River and down to Philadelphia. The day after Christmas Paine unveiled it in the presence of Franklin and Rittenhouse. After watching three men stand upon it, Rittenhouse said he thought it would be sturdy enough to carry traffic over the Schuylkill, but he feared that the cost of construction would be excessive. The plans, as drawn by Paine, called for 520 tons of wrought iron, and though Pennsylvania was the largest iron-producing region in the country, such an order would tax even its capacity. Nevertheless, Franklin and Rittenhouse encouraged him to solicit the Assembly for a subsidy.

On New Year's Day 1787 the wrought-iron model was exhibited in the State House yard. Members of an Assembly now controlled by Republicans Paine had helped elect, as well as the public, stopped by to look it over. Hall observed that "their sentiments and opinions of it were as different as their features. . . . The philosopher said it would add new light to the great utility. And the tailors (for it is an absolute truth) remarked it cut a pretty figure." A few days later the Assembly appointed a committee to inspect the model and test it. Paine estimated construction costs at $330,330. He was asking the state to spend a third of a million dollars, more than its current annual budget, to build an untested bridge at a time when the government was already burdened by a large debt.

The committee reported back within a week. It ostentatiously praised bridges generally but gave Paine's only a weak endorsement. Friends pushed through a resolution that created a second investigatory committee, but Paine expected little from it. There were too many ifs about the project. If the state had had more cash than debts, if private promoters had reacted with more interest and some cash of their own, if a smaller stream than the Schuylkill had been chosen to make the test, if the designer had been someone other than Thomas Paine . . . then possibly the first single-arched iron bridge in the world might have been built in Pennsylvania in 1787.

Franklin told Paine that if he could get approval from the Royal Society in London and the Royal Academy of Sciences in Paris it would improve his chance for a subsidy from the Assembly and might also encourage private investors to gamble on his bridge. By the middle of February, weeks before the second committee had brought in its report, Paine had completed plans to depart for France.

6

For over six years Paine had talked off and on of returning to Europe. He seemed puzzled himself by the strong pull the Old World exerted. He either could not or would not explain it. Possibly it could be said of Paine what was said of a later visitor, that he "was, in fact, not really interested in America at all" but only "in certain abstract propositions which America could prove."

On the previous trip to Europe he had planned an extended stay, but John Laurens had persuaded him to cut it short. This time, so he said, he would be gone only briefly. He was going only to visit his parents, "whom I am very anxious to see," and to get endorsements from European scientists for his bridge. He did not believe that the second committee assigned to study his bridge would have made any decision before "my return next winter." The convention that would meet in Philadelphia in May to amend the Articles of Confederation held no interest for him. The feeling around Philadelphia was that it would probably achieve nothing of lasting importance.

Paine dragged his feet leaving America, passing the days desultorily. He attended meetings of A Society for Political Enquiries that Franklin had organized and that met in his library. Among the members were Benjamin Rush, George Clymer, Gouverneur Morris, and James Wilson. The impetuous and garrulous Rush did most of the talking. Franklin said little and Paine "never opened his mouth," although he did furnish "one of the few essays which the members were expected to produce . . . a well written dissertation on the inexpediency of incorporating," the gist of which four years later turned up in *The Rights of Man.*

Paine planned to visit France first, then summer in England. He knew no one in France well except Jefferson and casually Lafayette and Chastellux. Franklin said that since he considered Paine "his adopted political son he would endeavor to write by him to his friends" there and a few days later sent along a packet of letters addressed to the Count d'Estaing, the Duke de La Rochefoucauld, Jean-Baptiste le Roy, and Le Veillard, all recommending Paine and his bridge warmly. "We want a bridge over our river the Schuylkill and have no artist here regularly bred to that kind of architecture," he explained to La Rochefoucauld, adding that he had intended to recommend Paine to Jean Perronet, the great French bridge builder, "but I hear he is no more." (Franklin had been misinformed; Perronet lived and was in the midst of building his greatest bridge.) Franklin wrote "more and longer letters," a biographer has observed, "than in any week since his return to America," partly to help Paine, partly to send a last word to friends he would never again see. To one he said reassuringly, "As I live temperately, drink no wine, and use daily the exercise of the dumb-bell, I flatter myself that the stone is kept from augmenting as much as it might otherwise do and that I may still continue to find it tolerable."

On April 19 Franklin added to the pile a letter addressed to Jefferson in which he urged him to introduce Paine "where it may be proper and of advantage to him." In passing, Franklin mentioned the latest political news. "Our federal constitution," he said, meaning the Articles of Confederation, "is generally thought defective, and a convention, first proposed by Virginia, and since recommended by Congress, is to assemble here next month to revise it and propose amendments. The delegates generally appointed as far as I have heard of them are men of character for prudence and ability, so that I hope good from their meeting. Indeed, if it does not do good it must do harm, as it will show that we have not wisdom enough among us to govern ourselves; and will strengthen the opinion of some political writers that popular governments cannot long support themselves."

Paine tucked this last letter in his valise and soon after left for New York, where he had learned a ship lay ready to sail for France. In New York friends in and out of Congress added more letters to the pile for Jefferson. James Madison gave a long one on politics, using a private code when he came to delicate matters. Another long letter from John Jay dealt with foreign affairs. The convention called to amend the Articles was on the minds of all. One gentleman wrote Jefferson that "not much" was expected of it. Another, who felt similarly, added, "I am rather a zealot in the measure, because it will operate, at least as an alarm, but whether it will be productive of any immediate effects I am doubtful." Paine seems to have shared the doubts. A month before he rode out of Philadelphia he had directed a final, furious letter at those "crazy brained politicians" in Pennsylvania with whom he had worked long enough to know "that a country under the management of their politics would be a perpetual scene of distraction and poverty." What help would an amended version of the Articles be in ejecting these misguided men from power?

On 26 April 1787 Paine sailed from New York. He had spent twelve and a half of the best years of his life in America. He had arrived poor. He left with over one thousand dollars in the newly created Bank of Philadelphia, £220 in cash held by friends in New York, a house in Bordentown, and a farm in New Rochelle, both of which brought in rent. He had arrived unknown. He left internationally famous. He was fifty years old and still a rootless and restless man who lived for the most part out of a suitcase. He owned a house he never lived in, a farm he seldom visited. He planned to be back before winter set in. He would be gone fifteen years.

PART

III

The French Revolution

1787–1802

CHAPTER

13

FRANCE TO ENGLAND
AND BACK AGAIN

PAINE EMBARKED with the usual trepidation. None of his three previous crossings had been pleasant. This one broke the pattern. He arrived at Havre-de-Grâce without incident on May 26, exactly a month after leaving New York. He spent four leisurely days sightseeing on the way to Paris. The countryside appeared "the richest I ever saw," the people "very stout," and "the horses of a vast size and very fat." He traveled light, for the superintendent at the customs house refused to release his bridge model until authorization had come down from above.

Paris produced a second disappointment: Jefferson was away touring southern France and northern Italy, scheduled to stop at a spa where he hoped the waters would speed the mending of a broken wrist. Paine found lodgings, then distributed the letters of introduction. "I have received visits and invitations from all who were in town," he wrote Franklin, adding that "your friends are very numerous and very affectionate." Jean-Baptiste le Roy, an eminent member of the Academy of Sciences and director of the king's laboratory at Passy, had been especially close to Franklin. "As he speaks English, there is scarcely a day passes without an interview," Paine said, hinting at the loneliness imposed on him by difficulties with the French tongue. Paine charmed le Roy—"The more I see of him, the more I must thank you," le Roy told Franklin—and he went out of the way to introduce him to important members of the Academy. One day they stopped at the home of the great naturalist Buffon, but the imperious old gentleman was too ill to receive them. Another time they chatted with Chrétien de Malesherbes. Six years later Paine would watch him defend Louis XVI in the trial before the National Convention. He would die in the Terror.

When Jefferson returned to the city early in June, Paine unloaded the letters and gifts from America. Although Paine claimed Jefferson as a close friend, they were only acquaintances. They had never corresponded and except for the American Revolution shared little in common. Paine was an indolent man who worked in spurts when he bothered to work at all, who knew nothing of classical literature, who drank too much, who lived contentedly in slovenly surroundings and kept irregular hours. Jefferson in contrast liked luxury, dressed fastidiously, drank moderately, and worked hard. "Determine never to be idle," he said. "No person will have occasion to complain of the want of time who never loses any. It is wonderful how much may be done if we are always doing."

Still, the two got along well. They were close enough in age—Jefferson had recently turned forty-four—to be contemporaries. Paine was an easygoing, comfortable companion. "His intelligence upholds its reputation perfectly," as le Roy put it, and among his worthy qualities was "the honest and profound spirit which he brings to bear upon every subject." Similar political views, a common interest in natural philosophy, delight in an evening of relaxed, open conversation created between them a relationship that was "cordial rather than intimate in nature." Jefferson gave Paine a gracious rather than a warm welcome. If he thought much of the iron bridge, he failed to say so. He introduced Paine around the city dutifully. To the Count de Moustier, who would soon leave for the United States as the minister replacing the Chevalier de La Luzerne, he dropped a short note saying only that Paine would like to meet him. "Je serai très flatté et très empressé de faire connaissance avec Mr. Paine" went the opening line of Moustier's immediate and gracious reply.

Over a month passed before the bridge model arrived in Paris and even then it had taken a stern note from the Abbé André Morellet, an old friend of Franklin's, to pry it loose from the customs house. "There is a great curiosity here to see it," Paine said before it arrived, "as bridges have lately been a capital subject." The city had recently commissioned a new bridge over the Seine, a river about the width of the Schuylkill; it would be built on piers and cost about five million livres. Paine knew his bridge could span the river more gracefully for less money. On July 21 he sent his model to the Academy of Sciences with a note that flattered the Academy's "skill in rendering judgments which enlighten the whole scientific world." The Academy in turn flattered Paine with the committee it selected to study his bridge. Le Roy was chairman and his colleagues were Jean Charles de Borda and Charles Bossut, both celebrated mathematicians. Le Roy assured Franklin that the committee would bring in a favorable report. "I should tell you further," he said, "that Mr. Paine's bridge has caused all the other iron bridges which were proposed before his to be brought out and examined, and it seems to me that people generally agree in considering his a simpler and more solid construction than any of those which I have just spoken of."

While waiting for the committee to render a report Paine had nothing to do but continue the round of visits among the enlightened people of Paris. Even now, after two months in the city, he seemed unaware that he had arrived in the midst of a revolution. The bridge had pushed politics from his mind. And he chafed to get out of Paris and over to London.

2

Paine spent the first thirty-seven years of his life pressed close to the bottom of Britain's lower class. In America, especially after publication of *Common Sense*, he circulated easily among all levels of society. France offered him an even headier experience, for here he cruised among an opulent elite comparable to nothing he had known before. Lafayette became his particular friend. Paine had known him in America as a tall young man on Washington's staff, "very elegant in his form," who talked in broken English. He appeared more impressive in his native habitat— a resplendent nobleman with an income of 140,000 livres a year. Then there were Chastellux and the Duke de la Rochefoucauld. The early judgments Paine formed of French society and politics came from gossip collected from the lofty circles these rich, successful gentlemen moved in. Of the Paris below this stratum, of the France that spread beyond the city's borders he knew nothing at all.

The opening scene of the French Revolution had ended on May 25, the day before Paine reached France, with the dissolution of the Assembly of Notables (or Not Ables, as some said). He had come to Paris an apolitical man, to promote a bridge, but everywhere he went people talked only of the government's financial predicament. Early in 1787 the minister of finance, Charles Alexandre de Calonne, had worked out the nation's first annual budget. The tally produced several surprises. Sumptuous Versailles, though a costly showpiece, took only 5 percent of the income, whereas the military required one quarter and, most surprising, the national debt over half of all money received. The debt stood at four billion livres, which, though a large sum, was less than half that of Great Britain and about equal to that of the Dutch Republic. But in those countries the budget was balanced by forcing the aristocracy to share in the cost of government; in France the aristocracy was virtually exempt from taxation.

The king had convened the Assembly of Notables on February 21— the first such gathering of noblemen and high churchmen in two and a half centuries—to present a tax reform program. Jefferson called the assembled aristocrats "the most able and independent characters in the kingdom." Calonne asked the Assembly to end all "abuses of privileges"; all three orders or "estates" were to share in the tax burden. Lafayette led the opposition to the reform program. He blamed the crisis on royal extravagance, and following his lead, the Assembly rejected Calonne's entire program. The king tried to break the impasse by dismissing Calonne and substituting in his place Loménie de Brienne, archbishop of Toulouse. The Notables now said they lacked authority to levy new taxes, and with that the king dissolved the gathering. Brienne now turned to the dozen or so parlements scattered throughout France. Unlike England's Parliament, these were essentially judicial rather than legislative bodies. They protected the "fundamental law" from incursions by the crown. The aristocracy dominated them, particularly the bellwether of the lot, the Parlement of Paris. That body, as expected, rejected the reform program peremptorily, saying that only the Estates-General, which had not met since 1614, could initiate new taxes.

The Assembly of Notables and the parlements fought to protect their privileged positions under an appealing banner—they were rebuffing the crown only to protect the rights of the people. They hoodwinked even the usually perceptive Jefferson. An American-bred distrust of a strong executive blinded him to the merits of the crown's reform program. He thought economies in the budget, coupled with a delegation of power to provincial assemblies, would solve all difficulties; and when the government inaugurated these reforms in the summer of 1787 he saw serenity around the corner. "I think that in the course of three months," he wrote in August, "the royal authority has lost, and the rights of the nation gained, as much ground by a revolution of public opinion only as England gained in all her civil wars under the Stuarts."

Paine echoed the opinion. "The people of France," he said, "are beginning to think for themselves." He, too, saw only clear skies ahead. "The appearance of disorder in France, is no more than one of the links in that great chain of circumstances by which nations acquire the summit of their greatness. The provincial assemblies begun in France, are as full, or rather a fuller representation of the people than the Parliaments of England are."

France had set her house at home in order, but abroad in the United Netherlands all was not well. There Paine unwittingly had helped stir things up. Some of his propaganda during the American Revolution had washed across the Atlantic and aroused the prosperous middle-class burghers to resist the autocratic rule of the Stadtholder, the Prince of Orange. By the summer of 1787 civil war had broken out. France supported the rebels, or Patriots, England the Stadtholder, a role William III had once held, and both secretly pumped large sums of money into the fight. The crisis ripened when the king of Prussia, whose sister had married the Prince of Orange, moved troops across the border. France had previously said she would counter a Prussian invasion with troops of her own; England promised that in that event she, too, would join the fray. The economy-minded Brienne saw to it that France reneged on its pledge to fight.

Jefferson reviled the decision with unaccustomed belligerence: "No nation makes war nowadays but by the aid of loans and it is possible that in a war for the liberties of Holland all the treasures of that country would have been at their service." In abandoning Holland, he continued with hardly the choicest of images, France had "lost the cow which furnishes the milk of war." Paine, on the other hand, applauded Brienne's move. He had "seen enough of war and the miseries it inflicts," he said. He found one day during a conversation with the Abbé Morellet that they "perfectly agreed with respect to the madness of war, and the wretched impolicy of two nations, like England and France, continually worrying each other, to no other end than that of a mutual increase of burden and taxes." (Paine must have hidden his contempt for monarchy from Morellet, who admired the British form of government and censured "superficial publicists" who spoke ill of it.) As he often did, Paine summarized the conversation on paper after returning to his lodgings, "that I might be assured I had not misunderstood him, nor he me." He sent the memorandum to the secretary with a promise that he would soon publish a pamphlet that might help alleviate tension between England and France. He knew that Morellet was a confidant of Brienne and he may have hoped, though there is no evidence to substantiate it, to revive a financial arrangement of the sort he once had with La Luzerne in America.

Paine began the pamphlet—he called it *Prospects on the Rubicon*—while waiting to hear the verdict on his bridge. " 'The Rubicon is passed,' was once given as a reason for prosecuting the most expensive war that England ever knew," went the opening sentence. "Sore with the event, and groaning beneath a galling yoke of taxes, she has again been led ministerially on to the shore of the same delusive and fatal river, without being permitted to know the object or the reason why." Holland, he says, is not worth a war, and to fight now when neither debt-ridden England nor France has recovered from past wars is senseless. They can float loans, Jefferson had said. Paine disparages the suggestion. "Credit is not money," he says. "It is the means of getting into debt, not the means of getting out." But a stronger argument than the money saved can be made for peace. "There is no real rivalship of interest" between England and France; "it is more the effect of temper, disposition, and the jealousy of confiding in each other, than any substantial cause that keeps up the animosity." There can be no war because it would be absurd.

If the minister of finance subsidized the pamphlet, he got little for his money. Paine appeals to the common Englishman—"I defend the cause of the poor . . . and of all those on whom the real burden of taxes falls" —but the plodding excursions into economics and foreign affairs blunted the chance for wide readership. He seeks the ear of the British government in one paragraph, then in the next assails "the pettish vanity of a young and inexperienced minister," William Pitt. Only when he speaks of events inside France does his enthusiasm bring the essay briefly alive. He grants that the ferment "may appear a kind of chaos" to Englishmen but begs them to remember that "the creation we enjoy arose out of chaos, and our greatest blessings appear to have a confused beginning." He ends with a rosy forecast. The people of France commence to think for themselves, and their affairs, "however confused they at present appear, are naturally approaching to a great and harmonious increase of its power."

3

Paine gave only half a mind to *Prospects on the Rubicon*. He worried through July about the reception of his bridge with the Academy of Sciences. Midway in August le Roy relieved his mind. Of all the models and plans for an iron bridge examined the committee agreed unanimously that Paine's was "the simplest, strongest, and lightest." What then was delaying their report? You must understand, said le Roy, that "an arch of four or five hundred feet is such an unprecedented thing and will so much attract notice in the northern part of Europe, that the Academy is cautious in what manner to express their final opinion." The truth was that le Roy's colleagues on the committee were tarrying. "I have pressed these two gentlemen to complete the report," he said out of Paine's hearing, "but since they did not finish, I took it upon myself last week."

Finally, on August 29, Paine was told officially that his bridge had received an unqualified endorsement from the Academy of Sciences. He packed his bags immediately for London, where he hoped to obtain similar approval from the Royal Society. Jefferson welcomed the chance of a "confidential conveyance" to London. He asked Paine to deliver a letter of political news to John Adams, the minister there; a bread-and-butter note to Abigail Adams; and a brief note to John Trumbull, the painter, with whom he had recently become friendly. He asked Trumbull please to commission Mather Brown, another artist, to do a portrait of Paine, "because Trumbull," Jefferson explained, "does not paint of the size of life and could not be asked to hazard himself on it." (Trumbull later did "hazard himself," rendering Paine as an almost handsome, well-dressed gentleman, the powdered shoulder-length hair neatly combed, the lips of his wide mouth pressed firmly together, the eyes radiating that piercing intensity that all who met Paine remarked on. Jefferson, upon receiving the portrait, called it "a perfect likeness.")

Paine also carried to London the memorandum he had written to Morellet, which had been returned to him with a note saying Brienne had read it, agreed with Paine's assessment of Anglo-French relations, and that it might be used in London to reassure any sympathetic British statesmen he met that there was "no disposition on the part of the French ministry to break terms with England, if England gives no cause of a rupture." The manuscript of *Prospects on the Rubicon,* which would be published in London, apparently had received Brienne's imprimatur. Along with all this came the albatross Paine had only begun to tote about the world—his bulky iron bridge model.

Paine left Paris on August 30, the day after he had been told of the Academy's approval of his bridge. Lafayette and Jefferson promised that while he was away they would encourage the French government to use his design for the bridge that was planned for the Seine.

4

Paine had stayed three months in France. His stay in England extended over a similar period—September, October, and November of 1787. Upon his arrival in London—last seen by him thirteen years earlier when he had left as an impecunious failure for America—he deposited the bridge model with the president of the Royal Society, Sir Joseph Banks, the famed botanist who had traveled to Tahiti with Cook in 1771. Then he delivered Jefferson's letters around the city and arranged for publication of *Prospects on the Rubicon.* Those errands completed, he called upon Edmund Burke, presenting a letter from Henry Laurens, whom Burke had befriended during the Revolution when Laurens had been imprisoned in the Tower of London after being captured while enroute to negotiate a treaty with Holland in 1780. Paine wanted to interest Burke in his bridge—Laurens' note introduced him as an ingenious inventor of mechanical contrivances—but they also talked politics. During the Revolution, Burke had been one of the few Englishmen Paine had referred to respectfully in his writings. He regarded him as a fair, generous, and open-minded gentleman, and for that reason trusted him before they had met. They got along well enough on this first meeting to plant the seed of what looked like a lasting friendship.

Early in his visit to England Paine traveled to his home village of Thetford. His father had died the previous year, but his mother, now ninety-one, still lived. The "good old woman" told her once "undutiful," now world-famous son that "she got an American newspaper during the Revolutionary war in which there was a proclamation of Congress for a Fast Day, and that she kept it very strictly." He settled on her a pension of nine shillings a week, an income then considered adequate for a comfortable retirement.

During the stay in Thetford Paine "seldom saw the *companions of his youth;* he went little out, being wholly occupied in reading and in writing." Among the letters he wrote was one to the marquis of Lansdowne, who fifteen years earlier during a five-day party at his estate had introduced Franklin and the Abbé Morellet to each other and since then had remained friendly with both men. Paine had once censured him in *Crisis No. 12* when the marquis had been the earl of Shelburne and prime minister. Lansdowne had ended the war with America and acceded to generous peace terms in the hope of keeping American friendship. George III hated him. Charles James Fox and Lord North had joined to oust him as prime minister in 1783, and he had been out of power since. He detested Pitt and his policies, and Paine expected him to be sympathetic to the views advanced in *Prospects on the Rubicon.* "With respect to France, I am certain the English entertain very wrong ideas," he wrote, reiterating that it was in "the true interest of the two countries to agree and trade, instead of fight with each other." He ended with an invitation: If Lansdowne came to London during the next few weeks, Paine would be pleased to meet him for a long talk on foreign affairs. No longer did the former staymaker want for confidence.

The weeks in London during the autumn of 1787 were drab compared to those in Paris but an elegant success compared to the years when he had last lived there. *Prospects on the Rubicon* stirred up some discussion when it came out—"He has scalded himself" with it, a mutual friend told Jefferson, adding, "John Bull is very wrath"—but sales lagged, the press virtually ignored it, and no one in government accepted Paine's implied offer to mediate between England and France. Paine reacted predictably to the reception. "The viciousness of that nation (Great Britain)—is inconceivable," he wrote back to America. Their "cowardly bravery" would vanish once the Quadruple Alliance, encompassing Russia, Austria, France, and Spain, materialized, for then "John Bull will be at last left in the lurch."

John Trumbull's home served as Paine's social center on this and later trips to London. Among the painters he met there was Benjamin West, who had grown up outside Philadelphia and shared many friends in common with Paine. Later he was introduced to Joel Barlow, a sometime poet and pamphleteer from Connecticut now in Europe peddling western lands for the Scioto Company. At Trumbull's he also met two other speculators, Daniel Parker and Peter Whiteside, who were involved in partnerships with Robert Morris. Neither was especially astute, and while Morris' affairs at home were sliding toward bankruptcy their shenanigans in London did little to help extricate him from the oncoming disaster. Paine asked Whiteside to handle the annuity he had settled on his mother.

Parker was present with Paine one evening when Trumbull told a story about John Adams. Shortly after a copy of the new federal Constitution had reached London he had heard Adams talk "of making the government hereditary and that as Mr. Washington had no children, it should be made hereditary in the family of Lund Washington." Paine believed the gossip and used it the rest of his life as a platform on which to build a monument of hate for Adams. Trumbull took it lightly. He regarded Adams with a respect mingled with amusement. One day when Adams was busy preparing to return home, he noticed that in the process of abandoning courtly life for the simplicities of America he had combed the powder from his hair. "Its color and natural curl were beautiful," the painter said, "and I took that opportunity to paint his portrait in the small Declaration of Independence."

Paine arrived at Trumbull's one evening wearing a snuff-colored coat, olive velvet vest, drab breeches, coarse hose, shoe buckles the size of a half dollar, and a bob-tailed wig more tattered than glorious. One guest, impressed to be sharing the room with him, spent the evening observing Paine. He found him a moody man who "often sat reserved in company; seldom mingled in common chit chat." Paine usually began an evening among strangers that way—sitting in silence. "Without wine or other liquor," according to one who admired him, "he was a but dull companion, but after a bottle, he would talk like an oracle, and surprise every company in which he sat." Soon the observing guest saw Paine blend into the party. "He delighted in advancing the most unaccountable, and often the most whimsical paradoxes, which he defended in his own plausible manner. If encouraged by success, or the applause of the company, his countenance was animated with an expression of feature, which, on ordinary occasions one would look for in vain in a man so much celebrated for acuteness of thought; but interrupted by extraneous observation, by the inattention of his auditory, or in an irritable moment, even by the accidental fall of the poker, he would retire into himself, and no

Nathanael Greene by Charles Willson Peale *(Independence National Historical Park Collection)*

Benjamin Rush by Charles Willson Peale *(The Henry Francis du Pont Winterthur Museum, gift of Mrs. T. Charlton Henry)*

Gouverneur Morris
(Bettmann Archive)

Robert R. Livingston
by Gilbert Stuart
*(New-York Historical Society,
New York City)*

Joel Barlow by Robert Fulton
*(New-York Historical Society,
New York City)*

Clio Rickman
(New York Public Library)

Richard Henry Lee
by Charles Willson Peale
*(Independence National Historical
Park Collection)*

Robert Morris
by Charles Willson Peale
(Bettmann Archive)

Second Street. Friday Evening —

Sir

Two letters of Mr S. Deane's having appeared in the N. y papers which are
variously commented upon, I should like
to converse a quarter of an hour with
you on that subject. — I hope this
Man's knack of creating confusion and
involving characters in suspicion is
at an end. — Whether the letters be
genuine or not I do not undertake to
give judgment upon, but his language
in France is equally as strange as any
thing contained in these publications.

I am Sir
your obdt Hble Servt
Thomas Paine

Hon. R. Morris Esquire

Thomas Paine to Robert Morris, November 2, 1781 (*Joseph Reed Papers, New-York Historical Society, New York City*)

Bust of Thomas Paine by John Wesley Jarvis (*New-York Historical Society, New York City*)

THE

AGE OF REASON:

BEING AN INVESTIGATION OF

TRUE AND FABULOUS

THEOLOGY.

BY

THOMAS PAINE,

SECRETARY FOR FOREIGN AFFAIRS TO CONGRESS

IN THE AMERICAN WAR;

AND AUTHOR OF THE WORKS ENTITLED

COMMON SENSE, AND RIGHTS OF MAN,
&c. &c.

PARIS: PRINTED BY BARROIS.
1794.

[SECOND YEAR OF THE FRENCH REPUBLIC.]

Title page of the first edition of *The Age of Reason (Richard Gimbel Collection of Thomas Paine, American Philosophical Library)*

John Adams by Charles Willson Peale
*(Independence National Historical
Park Collection)*

Thomas Jefferson
by Charles Willson Peale
*(Independence National Historical
Park Collection)*

Thomas Paine's cottage in New Rochelle (New-York Historical Society, New York City)

Robert Fulton by Benjamin West *(New-York Historical Society, New York City)*

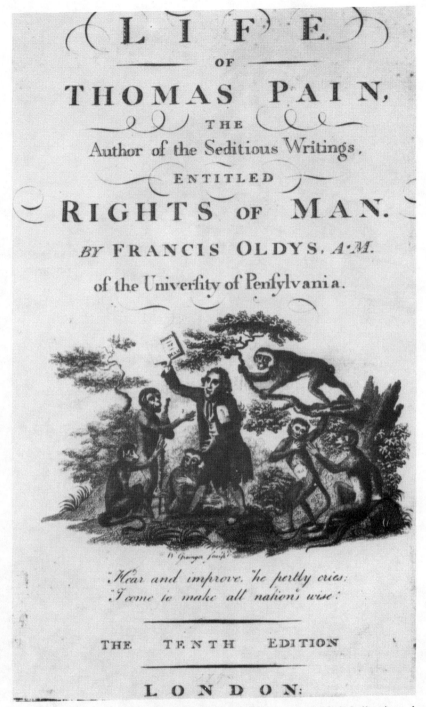

LIFE

OF

THOMAS PAIN,

THE

Author of the Seditious Writings,

ENTITLED

RIGHTS OF MAN.

BY FRANCIS OLDYS, A.M.

of the University of Pensylvania.

Hear and improve, he pertly cries:
I come to make all nations wise.

THE TENTH EDITION

LONDON:

Title page of Oldys' *Life of Thomas Paine (Richard Gimbel Collection of Thomas Paine, American Philosophical Library)*

Jean Paul Marat
(*Bettmann Archive*)

Georges Jacques Danton
(*Bettmann Archive*)

Maximilien Robespierre
(J. E. Bulloz)

Marquis de Lafayette
by Ary Scheffer
(Bettmann Archive)

Engraving of Thomas Paine by W. Sharp (*New-York Historical Society, New York City*)

James Monroe by Rembrandt Peale *(James Monroe Memorial Library)*

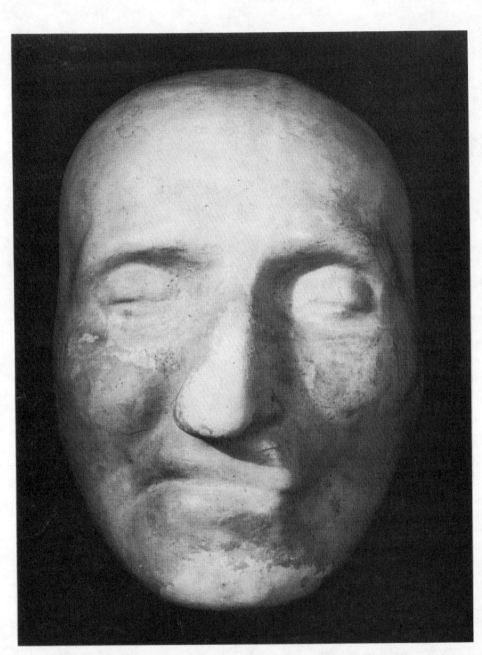

Thomas Paine's death mask by John Wesley Jarvis *(New-York Historical Society, New York City)*

persuasion could induce him to proceed upon the most favorite topic."

Another evening at Trumbull's brought Paine together with John Wolcot, a popular poet who wrote under the name of Peter Pindar. Paine that night, perversely and against all he had written, argued "that the minority, in all deliberative bodies, ought, in all cases, to govern the majority." Peter Pindar contributed nothing to the discussion. When all except he agreed with Paine, he said, "I am the wise minority who ought, in all cases, to govern your ignorant majority." His distaste for Paine, formed that night, lay buried until after *The Rights of Man* was published; then Peter Pindar let it out in a number of poems that treated Paine as a scourge, a "most delicious pest" determined "to set a realm on fire," a "son of sedition" who spoke only treason.

5

After three months in England Paine had failed to squeeze a decision on his bridge out of the Royal Society, and he had found no investors willing to risk their money on a full-scale version. For a time he hoped Robert Morris would back the project, "but his affairs appearing to be deranged lessens very considerably that dependence." Then over from Paris came worse news. Beaumarchais, who had worked with Silas Deane in the 1770s and still stood well with the king, had applied for the privilege of erecting an iron bridge over the Seine. Paine saw a double danger here: "It is very possible that after all the pains I have taken and the money I have expended, that some counterworking project will set itself up, and the hope of great gain, or great interest, will attempt schemes, that after some less pains will end in no bridge at all." Hoping to block Beaumarchais' project and find a way to substitute his own in its stead, he hurried back to Paris. He arrived in December and this time remained for half a year.

Paine returned frantic with worry. "If I can succeed only in one contract in Europe, it will very sufficiently answer my purpose," he said, "and I shall be able to build the Schuylkill bridge myself." In the haste to leave London he had forgotten to retrieve the model. He would send for it. No, he would go back himself to pick it up. He spread the story that he had returned to help Beaumarchais. After all, he decided, "my principal object is to get the bridge erected, because until then all conversation upon the subject amounts to but little." But he was not accustomed to sharing glory and soon dropped the idea of a partnership.

Lafayette advised "that it would be best to make some direct proposition to which either yes or no should be given." Paine talked to Éthis de Corny, who had been Lafayette's aide in America and now served as Avocat et Procureur du Roi. De Corny arranged an interview with the eminent engineer Jean Perronet, later known as the "father of modern bridge building." At the moment he was constructing what would be his most famous bridge, the Pont Sainte-Maxence in Paris. Paine told him that he proposed erecting an iron bridge over the spot Beaumarchais had chosen "for the same price as a wooden bridge." More than that, Paine promised to put it up "in three months time or less, as all the arches would be begun on at once, and the work would admit of as many hands being employed at the same time as you please." Could French foundries fabricate enough iron for the bridge? "The bridge is to be made in America," said Paine, "and sent to Paris ready to be put up."

Promises, promises. The French wanted to know what the bridge would cost, and on this point Paine hedged. Why worry about cost when "M. Le Coutenier, the banker, has proposed to furnish all the money?" Finally, Jefferson stepped in to give his older friend some fatherly advice: "You will not be able to get a step forward without an estimate." Then, gently, he tried to bring Paine back to earth: "A Frenchman never says No; and it is difficult for a stranger to know when he means it. Perhaps it is the longest to be learnt of all the particularities of the nation."

The bridge cemented Paine's friendship with Jefferson and Lafayette. Together they escorted him around to see high government officials, and afterward they would dine together. Often in the early months of 1788 their conversation turned to the virtues and defects of the new American Constitution. All three men admired it, with reservations. Paine thought "any kind of hooping of the barrel, however defectively executed, would be better than none," and he "could have voted for it myself, had I been in America." Like Jefferson he was sorry to see the principle of rotation of office abandoned. "The long duration of the Senate" especially bothered him. Unlike Jefferson, he thought the creation of a single executive the most serious flaw. "I have always been opposed to the mode of refining government up to an individual," he said. "Such a man will always be the chief of a party. A plurality is far better. It combines the mass of a nation together. And besides this, it is necessary to the manly mind of a republic that it loses the debasing idea of obeying an individual."

The arrival of transcripts of the debate over the Constitution in Pennsylvania's ratifying convention, which had met in November, stirred up further discussion around the dinner table. "Mr. Jefferson, Common Sense, and myself are debating in a convention of our own as earnestly as if we were to decide upon it," Lafayette wrote in February. James Wilson had led the fight for ratification in Pennsylvania, and in the state convention he had grown especially hot when the minority demanded that a bill of rights be added to the Constitution. In rejecting the demand, Wilson slipped in a few remarks about the natural rights of man. The right of an individual "to act as his pleasure or his interest may prevail" exists in a state of nature, he said, but it "is rendered insupportable, by the interfering claims and the consequent animosities of men, who are independent of every power and influence but their passions and their will."

These words vexed Paine. Wilson had got things all wrong. He talked gibberish about natural rights. These, he said to his friends across the table, are "the rights of thinking, speaking, forming and giving opinions, and perhaps all those which can be fully exercised by the individual without the aid of exterior assistance." When men banded together into a civil society it was not to impose restraints on these rights, but to protect them, "so that each individual should possess the strength of the whole number." The civil rights that emerge out of any social compact "are those of personal protection, of acquiring and possessing property." He had more to say:

> These I conceive to be civil rights or rights of compact, and are distinguishable from natural rights, because in the one we act wholly in our own person, in the other we agree not to do so, but act under the guarantee of society.
>
> It therefore follows that the more of those imperfect natural rights, or rights of imperfect power we give up and thus exchange the more security we possess, and as the word liberty is often mistakenly put for security Mr. Wilson has confused his argument by confounding the terms.

Paine knew that in the give and take among three brilliant talkers the subtle distinctions he had made might have been lost. That night after returning to his room, "being alone and wanting amusement I set down to myself (for there is such a thing) my ideas of natural and civil rights and the distinction between them." He sent the brief essay along to

Jefferson the next morning "to see how we agree." They agreed so fully that a century and a half later an eminent biographer who came across the essay in Jefferson's papers assumed, because it mirrored the Virginian's thoughts so completely, that Paine had copied down Jefferson's ideas after a night of talk. Actually, Paine had only amplified views that were first advanced in the debate in 1776 over the Pennsylvania constitution, but the restatement was so effective that it ever after became a fixed part of Jefferson's political philosophy.

This discussion of natural rights occurred against a dramatic backdrop. During those evenings of conversation at Jefferson's home France day by day edged closer to a real revolution. In January 1788 the Parlement of Paris, several of whose members had been exiled by the king, had censured the government for attempting to levy new taxes and, in passing, had talked eloquently about the natural rights of men. Neither Jefferson nor Paine nor even Lafayette perceived that the aristocratic Parlement had used an appealing abstraction to obstruct reform. Early in May the Parlement published a declaration listing what it considered to be the fundamental laws of the nation. Soon afterward the testy king issued a series of edicts that in effect hamstrung all the parlements by transforming them back to what they had originally been, mere judicial bodies. These May Edicts, as they were called, aroused the nation. Paine was on hand when the Count d'Artois, representing the king, brought the edicts to the Parlement in Paris.

> He came from Versailles to Paris, in a train of procession; and the Parliament was assembled to receive him.
>
> But show and parade had lost their influence in France; and whatever ideas of importance he might set off with, he had to return with those of mortification and disappointment. On alighting from his carriage to ascend the steps of the Parliament House, the crowd (which was numerously collected) threw out trite expressions, saying: "This is Monsieur d'Artois, who wants more of our money to spend."
>
> The marked disapprobation which he saw, impressed him with apprehension; and the word *Aux armes! (To arms!)* was given out by the officer of the guard who attended him. It was loudly vociferated, that it echoed through the avenues of the House and produced a temporary confusion: I was then standing in one of the apartments through which he had to pass, and could not avoid reflecting how wretched was the condition of a disappointed man.
>
> He endeavored to impress the Parliament by great words, and opened his authority by saying: "The King, our Lord and Master." The Parliament received him very coolly, and with their determination not to register the taxes; and in this manner the interview ended.

Nine-tenths of some five hundred pamphlets published during the next four months attacked the crown's policy. The parlements, long condemned for what they were, the strongholds of the aristocracy, suddenly became the bastions of liberty—to the people, to Lafayette, to Jefferson, to Paine.

Through all this, as Robert R. Palmer has said, "Jefferson's ideas continued to develop at deliberate speed, not an inch ahead of average opinion in France, and well behind a good deal of it." Presumably the same can be said for Paine. Few letters of his from this period survive, and those few give more space to his bridge than to French politics. He had arrived back from England determined, once plans for erecting the bridge were settled, to return to America in April or, at the latest, in May. May found him still in Paris; and though by the end of the month his bags were packed, the destination was England not America. From there he had heard that several well-heeled gentlemen liked the looks of his bridge and were considering investing in it. By mid-June he was back in London. "It is difficult to write about an affair while the event of it is depending because prudence restrains a man from giving an anticipated opinion," he wrote Jefferson, "but as matters at present appear the construction will take place here." He ended the note sending his regards to Lafayette. Of French politics he had nothing to say.

CHAPTER

14

"IN SOME INTIMACY
WITH MR. BURKE"

IN THE WINTER OF 1788 John Adams had departed for home, leaving America with no official representative in Great Britain. Paine filled the gap. When not huckstering his bridge, he circulated among the politicians, gleaning what he could about British affairs to pass along to Jefferson in Paris. Jefferson, for his part, dispatched full reports of political developments on the continent. Paine, in short, with Jefferson's connivance, now served unofficially as America's minister to Great Britain, a post he held for the nearly two years he remained there. The new assignment, if it could be called that, led to many visits with Edmund Burke, and those in turn allowed the acquaintance of the previous year to ripen into friendship.

Burke was fifty-nine years old when Paine came to know him, a somewhat seedy-looking gentleman in rumpled clothes. Of medium height, he wore spectacles that kept slipping down the bridge of his nose. He had come from Dublin as a young man to study law at the Middle Temple, eased early into politics, and by 1768 had, as a biographer put it, "blossomed, somewhat mysteriously, from a needy young Irishman into an English country gentleman" who owned an estate of six hundred acres that kept him perpetually in debt. He was an ambitious, serious, humorless man. ("I never heard him make a good joke in my life," Samuel Johnson, who admired Burke, said of him. "No, sir, he is not the hawk there. He is the beetle in the mire.") Paine had first heard of Burke in 1765 when he denounced the Stamp Act and befriended Americans—"this fierce people . . . sprung from a nation in whose being the blood of freedom circulates." Burke's opposition to the government's policy toward the colonies continued after the Stamp Act's repeal, culminating in his great orations *On American Taxation*, made the year Paine left England, and *On Conciliation with America* in 1775. He had been one of the few British politicians Paine referred to with respect during the American Revolution. Burke had opposed independence, but his affection for America survived the break and provided the foundation for a friendship with Paine.

Burke, like Paine, thought of himself principally as a writer, which he was. His speeches always read better than they sounded to English ears when he delivered them in a rapid harsh voice and Irish brogue. He matched Paine in courage, defending Catholics when others attacked them—though a Protestant himself he had married a Catholic—and assailing the government's barbarous treatment of homosexuals at a time when it was impolitic to do so. He, like Paine, favored free trade. Both men thrived on conversation, Burke being, according to a contemporary, "the best talker he had ever known." Always a preoccupied man, Burke lived on his great estate somewhat as Paine did in less magnificent surroundings—amid "dirt, cobwebs, pictures and statues," never noticing, as a sensitive visitor once did, that the Negro servant who brought tea had "wrapped a cut on his finger in a dirty rag."

In August 1788 Paine sent Burke a ten-page letter which, if it "happens to arrive in a leisure hour and find you unemployed under the shade of a tree, it may serve you to read in the room of a newspaper." Earlier he and Burke had met to talk about the iron bridge. Now he wished to speak of larger matters, notably of ways to bring England and France to a better understanding. "I had been educated, as all under English government are, to look on France as a wrangling, contentious nation striving at universal monarchy and oppression. But experience, reflection, and an intimacy with the political and personal character of that nation, removed those prejudices, and placed me in a situation to judge freely and impartially for myself." He enclosed a letter from the Abbé Morellet as proof of France's friendly attitude toward England. As he was rounding out his comments a long letter arrived from Jefferson. He extracted a paragraph of gossip Jefferson had picked up from the Russian minister in Paris that he thought might interest Burke.

Earlier Paine had planned to visit the Wilkinson ironworks about his bridge, but he had fallen ill in July and had to cancel the trip. Now he was better and ready to go, "but before I do this," he told Burke, "I promise myself the pleasure of enjoying a day or two at Beaconsfield," Burke's estate. Burke got the message and invited Paine—that "great American" he now called him—for a week's visit. During the visit the neighboring Duke of Portland, a very rich man and also titular head of the Whig party, invited both men to dinner. That evening Burke asked Paine how the American people felt toward George III. Paine thought it an indelicate question to ask the author of *Common Sense*, but he answered lightheartedly with an anecdote. "At a small town, in which was a tavern bearing the sign of the king's head," he said, "it was insisted on by the inhabitants that a memento so odious should not continue up; but there was no painter at hand, to change it into General Washington, or any other favorite, so the sign was suffered to remain, with this inscription under it—'This is the sign of the Loggerhead!' " The story apparently went down well; Paine was invited to stay a few days with the duke. He gathered enough news from socializing among the rich and powerful to fill a long letter to Jefferson. "Mr. B____ says" this. . . . "Sir George Staunton tells me that." . . . Such and such "gave Mr. Pitt cause and pretense for changing his ground."

As Paine used these gentlemen, they, too, used or hoped to use him. The Whigs were allied with the commercial interests of England, which were eager to heal the breach with America and revive the once profitable commerce with that country. Surely Paine, who had done so much to break the old ties, could, if persuaded, use his pen to renew them. In time they saw they had misjudged their man. "I believe I am not so much in the good graces of the Marquis of Lansdowne as I used to be," Paine told Jefferson in March 1789. "I do not answer his purpose. He was always talking of a sort of reconnection of England and America, and my coldness and reserve on this subject checked communication."

Paine on one side and Burke and his friends on the other talked at cross purposes. Also they talked over a wide gulf. The English politicians failed to see, or Paine hid from them and revealed only in letters to Jefferson, the distaste he still held for the government of his homeland. "I find the opposition as much warped in some respects as to continental politics as the ministry," he told Jefferson. The government indulges itself in a "triumph of presumption" toward France, and toward Russia the hatred "is as bitter as it ever was against America, and is carried to every pitch of abuse and vulgarity." The French Revolution had not yet developed to a point that revealed the distance between them. Meanwhile, they remained friendly, and Paine, with only half a mind on politics, fussed about his bridge. "He is not without some attention to politics," Burke remarked, "but he is much more deeply concerned about various mechanical projects."

2

Paine returned to England to find the bridge model had become "a favorite hobbyhorse with all who have seen it." Within a few days of his arrival he had even better news to report: "As matters at present appear the construction will take place here," he told Jefferson, adding, "I can raise any sum of money that I please, if a patent can be obtained for securing construction. A company has already offered themselves." The source for this optimism was Peter Whiteside, who offered Paine enough backing to start building an experimental arch. The knowledgeable Whiteside guided him to the proper government office to apply for a patent for his invention.

Paine's affidavit accompanying the request for a patent was impressive enough to serve as a prospectus. Would the iron arch rust? No, for "it is to be varnished over with a coat of melted glass." Would wooden pilings support the great weight? Yes, for they were to be encased in cement and then pinned together. The iron arch as Paine had conceived it offered countless virtues. It could be used in vaulted ceilings, thus allowing for large rooms unimpeded by supporting columns. It presented "a new and important manufacture to the iron works of the nation." Above all, it rendered "the construction of bridges into a portable manufacture, as the bars and parts of which it is composed need not be longer or larger than is convenient to be towed in a vessel, boat, or wagon, and that with as much compactness as iron or timber is transported to or from Great Britain; and a bridge of any extent upon this construction may be manufactured in Great Britain and sent to any part of the world to be erected."

Paine received his patent early in September, hardly a week after filing for it. A few days later the Walker ironworks in Yorkshire—"the most eminent in England in point of establishment and property," said Paine—agreed to construct the bridge, although the size of their foundry necessitated reducing the size of the bridge span from 250 feet to 90 feet.

Preparations for the great work absorbed the early part of November, but when actual construction began "we went on rapidly, and without any mistake, or anything to alter or amend." Burke visited the works, accompanied by Lord Fitzwilliams, whom Paine identified as "heir to the Marquis of Rockingham." After a tour, they tipped the workmen five guineas and carried Paine away for a few days of relaxation. The first half of the arch had been assembled by the end of the month. "In point of elegance and beauty it far exceeds expectations," a visitor remarked. Paine glowed, for he had striven to make his bridge a thing of beauty, once going so far as to rearrange a series of bolts in order that "the arch will appear handsomer."

He worked closely at the foundry with William Yates, the foreman, and had become "so confident of his judgment, that I can safely rely upon his going on as far as he pleased without me." Parliament would convene on December 4, and Paine, as America's unofficial minister in residence, had to be on hand to report pertinent news to Jefferson. Shortly after the first half of the arch had been assembled, he departed for London, leaving Billy Yates behind as "President of the Boards of Works."

3

During the recess of Parliament the king had gone mad. When members assembled in December many thought that his son should assume power. This put William Pitt in a delicate position. The Prince of Wales was known to be a good friend of Charles James Fox, who, along with Burke, headed the opposition. Once the prince became regent he would almost certainly supplant Pitt with Fox as prime minister. To block this maneuver, Pitt framed a regency bill that left George III on the throne and his son's powers as regent tightly limited. Burke said Pitt was "making a mockery of the king, putting a crown of thorns on his head, and a reed in his hand, and dressing him in the purple to cry 'Hail, King of the British.'" Fox argued that the king was legally dead and consequently the prince automatically acquired full sovereignty; all Parliament could do was fix the date for the formal transfer of power.

Paine had another suggestion. He urged Burke "to propose a national convention, to be fairly elected." This convention would discuss the constitutional questions involved and hand down a decision. Parliament, he said, had no right to make that decision, for if Parliament, as one part of the government, were "permitted to alter the other there is no fixed constitution in the country." Burke rejected the advice peremptorily. True, America had called a national convention when faced with a constitutional crisis, but what worked for a new country like America would not suit an old one like England. True, the Estates-General, a French version of a national convention, would soon convene to deal with a constitutional crisis, but Burke was not inclined to take England down any road traveled by France.

Paine predicted that out of the regency crisis "there will certainly be a change of the ministry." His forecast—as happened so often—was wrong. The adroit Pitt survived the onslaught. He stretched the debate through December and January. In February the king recovered his senses and began again to carry on business with his ministers. Talk about a regency ended. Curiously, at no time during the turbulent weeks had Paine mocked or reviled hereditary monarchy. Indeed, once in censuring the aristocracy, he remarked that "the monarchy is nearer related to the people than the peers are," a sentiment that John Adams had often expressed. He seemed to be saying the king served the nation's interests where members of Parliament worked only for their own. In his long war against monarchy it was a lapse he would not repeat.

During the regency bill debate Paine made another curious statement. He who had never in his writings expressed deep affection for America now suddenly bubbled with sentiment for the land he called home. "I had rather see my horse Button in his own stable or eating the grass of Bordentown or Morrisania, than see all the pomp and show of Europe," he wrote to a friend in New York. Again he quickly recovered himself. In the same letter he went on to say, "I am in as elegant style of acquaintance here as any American that ever came over." He boasted often in succeeding letters of the elegant circles he moved in. "I am in pretty close intimacy with the heads of the opposition," he said in one, and in another, "I am in some intimacy with Mr. Burke and after the new ministry are formed he has proposed to introduce me to them."

The winter of early 1789 saw Paine take his role as America's unofficial representative more seriously than ever. He urged Jefferson to discourage Congress from approving a successor to John Adams. "The greater distance Congress observes on this point the better," he said. "It will be all money thrown away to go to any expense about it—at least during the present reign," meaning under Pitt's leadership. In case Jefferson missed the point, he added, "I know the nation well, and the line of acquaintance I am in enables me to judge better than any other American can judge, especially at a distance."

Jefferson liked the suggestion enough to pass it along to Washington. Meanwhile, without waiting to hear from Washington, he continued to correspond with Paine as if he were the American minister in England, giving him full, uncensored accounts of the progress of affairs on the continent and especially inside France. Paine, for his part, continued through "the severest winter I ever knew in England" to work assiduously for American interests. "I have been to see the cotton mills, the potteries, the steel furnaces, tin plate manufacture, white lead manufacture," he told Jefferson. "All those things might be easily carried on in America." He talked with the American James Rumsey, another steamboat man, who had procured the model of a British mill in which the machinery "is worked originally from the steam."

Jefferson's letters from France were filled with news of larger moment. The Estates-General was about to convene for the first time in a century and a half, and the crown, to Jefferson's surprise, had said that the three estates, which traditionally met separately, should sit together and that half the seats should be allotted to the Third Estate, the bourgeoisie. The clergy of the First Estate and the nobles of the Second Estate "threaten scission," Jefferson reported. There "will be an awful crisis" if they refuse to back down. Paine "very much rejoiced" at the news. "The most effectual method to raise both the revenue and the rental of a country is to raise the condition of the people," he said, "or that order known in France by the Tiers Etat." He thought the people of France "are now got, or getting, into the right way, and the present reign will be more immortalized in France than any that ever preceded it."

Paine passed the gist of Jefferson's observations along to Burke, creating a curious situation. Both men were seeing the French Revolution through the eyes of Jefferson, who still believed that the liberal leaders of the French aristocracy were carrying their nation toward a constitutional monarchy, following a route marked out by the English in their Bloodless Revolution of 1688. When Paine in the spring of 1789 left for Rotherham to oversee the final assembly of his iron arch, he and Burke continued on the best of terms, neither man disturbed by forebodings about France.

4

As Paine looked back in old age he must have occasionally sensed that at several points his life lacked the artistic unity expected from the penman of revolutions. The summer of 1789, during which the French Revolution swept to a climax, found him shuttling between London and the ironworks at Rotherham, worrying about his bridge, not the rights of man. The final assembling of the experimental rib took place in late April. Six tons of pig iron were piled on the arch to test its sturdiness. The expansion rate of the plates under varying temperatures was checked to eliminate worry about buckling. Once satisfied, Paine shot off notes of the experiment's success to Sir Joseph Banks and Sir George Staunton, another influential member of the Royal Society.

Visions of glory and wealth danced before Paine's eyes. He saw an iron bridge based on his design arching over the Thames, and "if only a fifth of the persons, at a half penny each, pass over a new bridge as now pass over the old ones the tolls will pay 25 percent besides what will arise from carriage and horses." He caught the Walker brothers up in his dream. They saw their works becoming a center for the manufacture of prefabricated iron bridges around the world. Paine said that a complete bridge of five ribs and 210 feet long should now be attempted; they agreed immediately. The undertaking would be costly and something of a gamble. Let us spread the risk by taking "in one or two other ironworks with us," Paine said. The Walkers were insulted. "As our works are large," one said, "and capable of dispatching a considerable bridge in a short space of time we would not choose to be concerned with any other ironworks in this undertaking."

The agreement they arrived at called for the Walkers "to find all the materials, and fit and frame them ready for erecting, put them on board a vessel and send them to London," Paine explained to Jefferson. "I am to undertake all expense from that time and to complete the erecting. We intend first to exhibit it and afterwards put it up for sale, or dispose of it by private contract, and after paying the expenses of each party the remainder to be equally divided—one half theirs, the other mine."

Paine sent these lines to Jefferson on 13 July 1789. The next day the Bastille fell.

5

Throughout the spring of 1789 Jefferson continued in his letters to Paine to believe that the aristocracy would carry the revolution to a happy end. The duke of Orléans, one of the richest men in France, spoke thoughts, Jefferson said, "which would be deemed bold in England, and are reasonable beyond the reach of an Englishman, who slumbering under a kind of half reformation in politics and religion, is not excited by anything he sees or feels, to question the remains of prejudice." Only the clergy aroused his suspicion. He knew the nobility would work hand in glove with the Third Estate. When the Estates-General convened on May 6 he got the surprise of his life when a majority of the supposedly reactionary clergy voted to join with the Third Estate; the nobility refused to budge from its chamber.

Up to this point Jefferson had thought a few slight adjustments to France's political machinery by the liberal aristocracy would suffice to get it working smoothly again. He had accepted stratification as a fixed feature of French social and political life. He favored giving the French "as much liberty as they are capable of managing" but thought they could manage little. Now he quickly readjusted his ideas. By the end of May he had urged Lafayette to abandon his aristocratic colleagues and join with the Third Estate. He had once judged the leaders of the Third Estate too radical for his taste. Now he approved of all they did and said.

In July he sent Paine a résumé of the events of the past month, in order "that you may be able to separate the true from the false accounts you have heard." On June 17 the Third Estate had extended a final invitation to the remaining clergy and nobles to join with them and had been refused. "This done," wrote Jefferson, "they declared themselves the National Assembly, resolved that all the subsisting taxes were illegally imposed, but that they might continue to be paid to the end of their present session and no longer. A majority of the clergy determined to accept their invitation and came and joined them." They urged the nobles to follow suit, but "the aristocratical party made a furious effort, prevailed on the king to change the decision totally in favor of the other orders," whereupon the "common chamber," as Jefferson put it, gathered at a nearby tennis court and with the clergy "bound themselves together by a solemn oath never to separate till they had accomplished the work for which they had met." Fury against the nobility now boiled over into riots that swept through Versailles and Paris. The king sent a personal letter asking all three orders to gather in one chamber. This time the holdouts capitulated, and the Estates-General became the National Assembly, with power to create a constitution for France.

At this point in his résumé Jefferson dropped his dispassionate tone. The National Assembly, he said, sounding more like Paine than himself, "having shown through every stage of these transactions a coolness, wisdom, and resolution to set fire to the four corners of the kingdom and to perish with it themselves rather than to relinquish an iota from their plan of a total change of government, are now in complete and undisputed possession of the sovereignty. The executive and aristocracy are at their feet: the mass of the nation, the mass of the clergy, and the army are with them; they have prostrated the old government, and are now beginning to build one from the foundation."

The first article in the Assembly's creed, as Jefferson transcribed it, read, "Every government should have for its only end the preservation of the rights of man; whence it follows that to recall constantly the government to the end proposed, the constitution should begin by a declaration of the natural and imprescriptible rights of man." The list went on to declare that the monarchical form of government fit France well and the Assembly did not intend to abandon it; that the king's rights must be limited; that the citizens' rights must be explored and defined. "You see that these are the materials of a superb edifice," Jefferson concluded, "and the hands which have prepared them, are perfectly capable of putting them together, and filling up the work of which these are only the outlines." A pinch of doubt diluted the optimism. He still feared that an assembly of 1200 men "might lead to confusion," that the Assembly might refuse to accept the right of trial by jury, "and I consider that as the only anchor, ever yet imagined by man, by which a government can be held to the principles of its constitution." He said nothing about the mobs rising up everywhere around France, nor did he mention that on the day he wrote the king had dismissed his chief minister, Jacques Necker.

The Bastille fell on July 14, three days after Jefferson sent his long letter to Paine. Though a virtually empty prison, its squat dark bulk symbolized royal tyranny to the mob that stormed it. Paine accepted the event as a glorious act of defiance by an oppressed people. Burke said that if the assault had been "no more than a sudden explosion," it could be dismissed as trivial. "But if it should be *character* rather than accident, then that people are not fit for liberty and must have a strong hand, like that of their former masters, to coerce them."

Jefferson reacted like Paine to the storming of the Bastille and in succeeding letters applauded the course of the Revolution. After the fall of the Bastille the National Guard, a people's army, had been formed to keep order, and Lafayette was placed at its head. In Jefferson's eyes a constitutional monarchy had been virtually established by the end of July. The king had acknowledged his new role in an appearance before the Assembly. He had recalled Necker to appease the people. He had gone to Paris and accepted the cockade, symbol of the Revolution. In late August the Declaration of the Rights of Man and of Citizens came from the Assembly, and though it equivocated on religious freedom, emphasized the rights of property, and failed to provide for trial by juries, Jefferson regarded it as Frenchmen did—"the death certificate of the Old Regime." He viewed the riots proliferating around the nation as a passing phase. He played up the number of irreconcilables fleeing the country; their absence would make it easier to push through fundamental changes in the government. In his last letter to Paine from Paris—he would return to America at the end of September for what he thought was a brief vacation, unaware that George Washington had selected him to be secretary of state—he had only good news to report. Paine quoted his remarks to whoever would listen. "Mr. Jefferson concludes the letter," he wrote Thomas Walker, "by saying 'a tranquillity is well established in Paris and tolerable well throughout the kingdom, and I think there is now no possibility of anything hindering their final establishment of a good constitution which will in its principles and merits be about a middle term between that of England and America.' "

Paine's bridge, which he thought (wrongly, it turned out) would soon come down to London from the Yorkshire ironworks, kept him tied to England, out of the action in France. This bothered him little. He expected soon to be in the midst of another revolution closer to his heart. The one in France was having a yeasty effect on England. "There is yet in this country very considerable remains of the feudal system which people did not see before the Revolution in France placed it before their eyes," he told Jefferson. "While the multitude here could be terrified with the cry and apprehension of arbitrary power, wooden shoes, popery, and such like stuff, they thought themselves by comparison extraordinary free people. But the bugbear now loses its force, and they appear to me to be turning their eyes towards the aristocrats of their own nation. There is a new mode of conquering and I think it will have its effect."

6

Bread was the mainstay of a Frenchman's diet. He ate two or three pounds of it a day. By the autumn of 1789 the scarcity of flour made a loaf hard to come by, and when a housewife found one the price was, by her standards, astronomical. What had once cost half her husband's daily wages now cost 80 percent. Early in the morning of October 4 some six or seven thousand enraged women gathered in Paris to protest the situation, and after milling about in the rain for some time they decided, encouraged by, among others, a choleric little journalist named Jean Paul Marat, to march through twelve miles of mud to Versailles and protest to the National Assembly. A forehanded Lafayette with the National Guard ready to move at his command might have defused the mob; a dilatory Lafayette found himself several hours later trailing miles behind the women, more pushed by than leading some twenty thousand soldiers toward Versailles.

After the women reached Versailles and presented their grievances to the Assembly, they had nothing to do but stand in the rain waiting for a response. They became restless after one hour, and after two hours stormed the palace gates, streamed through the palace, and turned back only at the queen's doors. Herded into the courtyard, the women were momentarily mollified when Lafayette produced the royal family on a balcony to show that they had not fled. But the women wanted the king and his family and the National Assembly, too, where they could keep a close eye upon them. "To Paris!" the crowd roared. Lafayette advised the king to yield.

The exodus began the next day at one in the afternoon. Soldiers led the procession, one holding aloft a loaf of bread on his bayonet. Behind the troops came a string of wagons loaded with wheat and flour from the royal stores. Burly women, all in good humor now, waved ribbons and branches as they trudged alongside the wagons or rode atop their cargoes.

Another detachment of soldiers trailed the wagons, then came the royal carriage with Lafayette riding beside it as the guard of honor. At the rear came carriages bearing one hundred of the deputies to represent the Assembly. Rain fell steadily all the way into Paris. The October Days, as they came to be called, ended early in the evening of the fifth, when the royal family was safely installed in the old palace, the Tuileries.

In France, Burke said when he heard what had happened, "the elements which compose human society seem all to be dissolved, and a world of monsters is to be produced in the place of it." The news inspired Paine. He must leave at once for Paris. "A share in two revolutions," he said joyfully, "is living to some purpose."

7

A brief embarrassment delayed Paine's return to Paris. Early in October Peter Whiteside went bankrupt and was thrown into debtors' prison. When the creditors got hold of his books, they found he had charged the sum of £620 against Paine. The creditors asked satisfaction for the debt. Paine could not give it and was arrested on October 29. He was carried to a "commodious sponging house," a way station for debtors where they could negotiate with their creditors. Its name came from the excessive charges owners levied for food and lodging. "Here he lay for three weeks, in *durance vile*," a contemporary reported. "Those benevolent persons, Benjamin Vaughan, Mr. Hoare, the Quaker, and William Vaughan, all interested themselves in his fate. He now applied to Messrs. Clegget and Murdock, two American traders of great responsibility. They became his bail. And Paine, paying four [hundred] and sixty pounds, which he had at length received from America, and giving his own note for one hundred and sixty more, was set free in November 1789." He left at once for Paris.

8

He found that the Revolution had not put a dent in the full social life he had known on previous visits to Paris. Jefferson was gone, but his secretary, the affable William Short, just turned thirty, had stayed behind as the American chargé d'affaires. He continued to see the marquis de Chastellux, continued to be a confidant of Lafayette. He became friendly with Cornélie de Vasse, a Belgian baroness, who, though in her early fifties, apparently wanted to be more friendly than Paine wished. (She had written a book on *The Art of Reforming Men and making them Constant*, which may have put him off.) He regularly saw Gouverneur Morris, who had been in Paris for nearly a year on private business.

As in the past, Paine seemed drawn to Morris as a moth to a flame. He dropped by his place often to talk politics or, endlessly, about his bridge, never sensing Morris' cool feelings toward him. When Lafayette once asked for help on a constitutional problem, Morris warned him that Paine could "do him no good, for that although he has an excellent pen to write he has but an indifferent head to think." When Paine asked him to read an essay of his on the French central bank, Caisse d'Escompte, Morris, a knowledgeable man on financial affairs—indeed, he had written an authoritative essay on the subject—dismissed it as "an idle attempt, for in the first place the thing is at bottom false." He added, however, "His conceptions and expressions are splendid and novel but not always clear and just."

Trading London for Paris did not cause Paine to forget his friend Burke. In January 1790 he sent him a long letter on "how prosperously matters were going on" in France since the October Days. "If we distinguished the Revolution from the constitution," he said, "we may say that the first is complete, and the second is in a fair prospect of being so." He thought Burke should know that in France the word "aristocrat" had become synonymous with "Tory" in America—"an enemy to the Revolution." Schoolboys in France now paraded the streets carrying rifles and shouting, "The boys, like those in America, emulate men." Burke feared that the turbulence in France would contaminate England. Paine hoped it would. The French Revolution was certainly "a forerunner to other revolutions in Europe."

"Do you mean to propose," Burke replied, "that I, who have all my life fought for the constitution, should devote the wretched remains of my days to conspire its destruction? Do you not know that I have always opposed the things called reform; to be sure, because I did not think them reforms." With this he ended all correspondence with Paine. On February 9 he delivered in Parliament his first public blast against the Revolution. "The French have made their way through the destruction of their country, to a bad constitution, when they were absolutely in possession of a good one," he said. Melting down three orders into one "destroyed all the balances and counterpoises which serve to fix the state, and to give it a steady direction." He called the Declaration of Rights "a sort of *institute* and *digest* of anarchy. . . . By this mad declaration they subverted the state, and brought on such calamities as no country, without a long war, has ever been known to suffer, and which may in the end produce such a war, and perhaps many such." The speech was printed as a small pamphlet. A week later the public learned there was also "in the press and speedily will be published Reflections . . . concerning the Affairs of France. In a Letter from Mr. Edmund Burke to a Gentleman in Paris."

Paine, though not the "Gentleman in Paris," read Burke's "violent speech" there. A few days later he saw the advertisement for the second pamphlet, supposedly on the press. Paine decided immediately to leave for London to be on hand when the pamphlet came out, so he later said. For once his memory failed him. In March 1790 he told Benjamin Rush that he was going to London "expressly for the purpose of erecting an iron bridge." He would travel as an honored courier. "I take over with me to London the key of the Bastille which the Marquis entrusts to my care as his present to General Washington, and which I shall send by the first American vessel to New York." Another honor would soon be extended to him. When France completed its new constitution there would be a great parade, "and I am engaged to return to Paris to carry the American flag."

Paine had only good cheer to dispense as he prepared to leave for London. "I see very clearly," he told Rush, "that France through the influence of principles and the divine right of man to freedom will have a stronger part in England, than she ever had through the Jacobite bugbear of the divine right of kings in the Stuart line."

CHAPTER

15

BUSY WAITING

A "VERY PLEASANT" four-day trip carried Paine from Paris to London in the latter part of March 1790. He arrived with Burke very much on his mind. The morning after settling in he went around to the bookseller who usually published Burke's writings. "He informed me that Mr. Burke's pamphlet was in the press (he is not the publisher), that he believed Mr. Burke was much at a loss how to go on; that he had revised some of the sheets six, seven, and one nine times!"

From the bookseller's shop Paine set out on a round of visits. He called first upon Lord Charles Stanhope, an eminent eccentric of immense wealth. As an amateur inventor he had fathered stereotyping, built a variety of calculating machines, and designed a microscopic lens that had been named after him. In politics his fervent support of the French Revolution would one day make him a "minority of one" in Parliament and lead to the nickname "Citizen Stanhope." Despite the earl's warm welcome—"Have I the pleasure of shaking hands with the author of *Common Sense?*"—Paine came away from the meeting, after revealing his plan to answer Burke's pamphlet, with what for him was a curious judgment: Stanhope had "rather too much enthusiasm."

Next came a visit to Charles James Fox, one of the ablest, most cultivated, and most dissolute men in British politics. He was a heavy drinker, addicted to gambling, and a witty orator whose trenchant remarks in debate were often aimed at his perennial foe in the House, the younger Pitt. Paine had written a long letter to Fox from Paris in which he "laid down all the principal points . . . I intended for subjects for conversation when we met." The letter had never arrived, and so the conversation meandered over a wide field, as it could easily do when the fat and genial Fox found himself with someone he enjoyed talking to. The announcement that Paine planned to reply to anything Burke published on the French Revolution got slight reaction. If Stanhope had "too much enthusiasm," Fox "had little." From Fox he went to Sir George Staunton, an experienced diplomat, and repeated once more his decision to answer Burke in print.

During these visits Paine had grieved also about Burke's opposition to the Test Act, a statute that had been on the books since 1673. The Test Act forbade dissenters from the Church of England to hold any office in the government or in the army and navy, and, among other curious restrictions, it blocked them from taking a degree at Oxford or Cambridge and from serving in any responsible position in the Bank of England or the East India Company. The month Paine returned to England Fox was making the third attempt in as many years to get the act repealed. The previous year repeal had lost by only twenty votes. Since then the Bastille had fallen and the October Days had flashed by. Ten years ago, said Pitt, he would have favored repeal, but not now. Burke said that nothing in the Test Act infringed on religious freedom; all in England could worship as they pleased. The government had the right, especially in these parlous times, to keep from office any who might wish to overturn its institutions. Dissenters in England generally championed the French Revolution. They showed in their sermons and pamphlets that they had been "deeply infected by revolutionary impiety." They were, then, in a sense subversives whom the government should for its own health keep from public power. The bill for repeal lost by 188 votes.

"I am so out of humor with Mr. Burke with respect to the French Revolution and the Test Act that I have not called on him," Paine said in mid-April, soon after the repeal failed. "My idea of supporting liberty of conscience and the rights of citizens, is that of supporting those rights in *other people*, for if a man supports only his *own* rights for his *own sake*, he does no moral duty." Two days later he dined with Dr. Richard Price, a gentle, humane man but also a leading dissenter who the previous November had hailed the glories of the French Revolution in a speech that incensed Burke. Price remained as he had been since the fall of the Bastille, "all gay and happiness at the progress of freedom in France." He and Paine dined unaware that Burke had made the clergyman the "villain" in his essay on the French Revolution.

The promised but still unpublished pamphlet obsessed Paine. He queried everyone who might know something about it. One man told him Burke had stopped work on it. "I am now inclined to think that after all this vaporing of Mr. B. he will not publish his pamphlet." Paine refused to call upon Burke, but he could not resist talking about him. Coming upon "an intimate friend of Mr. Burke" in the street, he said, "I am exceedingly sorry to see a friend of ours so seemingly wrong."

"Time will show if he is."

"He is already wrong with respect to time past," said Paine, ending the exchange.

2

Paine had eight months to seethe before Burke published. During them he did little writing but much socializing, moving in and out of a number of circles. He continued to circulate in the American community. The renewal of an old tie with the Chevalier La Luzerne, who had been reassigned after America to the embassy in London, carried him into the French colony. He saw less and less of acquaintances met on the previous trip, the lords and earls and politicians Burke had introduced him to. Their interest in Paine had waned with their enthusiasm for the French Revolution. Joseph Johnson, a respected bookseller and publisher, filled the void by pulling him into his circle of friends. Johnson was known for his liberal politics, his "integrity and a virtuous disposition." He had published the works of the leading reformers and dissenting clergymen in London, and he wanted Paine as one of his authors. He extended an open invitation to the weekly dinners he gave for literary and political friends, and Paine accepted whenever he could.

At Johnson's he met William Godwin, the novelist, and Mary Wollstonecraft, the pamphleteer for the rights of women. Godwin had wangled an invitation just to meet Paine, but the formidable Mary Wollstonecraft dominated the evening. "Paine, in his general habits, is no great talker," Godwin recalled; "and though he threw in occasionally some shrewd and striking remarks, the conversation lay principally between me and Mary. I, of consequence, heard her, very frequently when I wished to hear Paine." Though he later married the lady, that evening "Mary and myself parted, mutually displeased with each other."

One of Johnson's authors, a young Scotsman named Thomas Christie, became a close friend. Christie earned his living as a banker but aspired to a literary career. He was at work on a volume of *Letters on the Revolution in France* when he met Paine. He intended "to have delineated at some length" on the origin and immediate causes of the Revolution, but when Paine said he intended to cover those points in his reply to Burke he graciously referred his readers to Paine's account, "which I am certain will be accurate and satisfactory."

The leading members of the Society for Constitutional Information —John Frost, Thomas Hollis, John Cartwright, Thomas Holcroft, John Horne Tooke—turned up one time or another at Johnson's dinners. Paine had been made an honorary member of the society in December 1787 before he knew much about it or its leaders. Gentlemen constituted it; they paid a hefty guinea a year to belong. They had banded together to promote reform, not revolution. They lobbied for "annual, equal, and universal representation of the Commons"; for public education; for the end of corruption in politics; for retrieving "the lost rights of the people." They revered the English constitution but only as it had existed in a pristine past when Anglo-Saxons roamed the land. Corruption had set in with the Norman invasion. The gentlemen of the Society for Constitutional Information wished to decontaminate it through their program of reform. They were in a sense latter-day Puritans, only they wanted to purify politics rather than religion.

John Horne Tooke exemplified these views and the later ambiguous relation between the society and Paine. In 1794, when on trial for sedition, he coined the image "fellow-traveler" to explain his and the society's attitude toward Paine. "Men may get into the same stage-coach with an intention of traveling to a certain distance; one man chooses to get out at one stage, another at another."

Tooke, like most members of the society, "was an old-fashioned British radical," it has been said, "who represented the solid tradesman's jealousy of the aristocratic patron rather than any democratic principle." The same could be said for Paine in 1790. No compassion for the peasant in France or the workingman in England had yet seeped into his writing. When he had told Jefferson that "the most effectual method to raise both the revenue and the rental of a country is to raise the condition of the people or that order known in France by the Tiers Etat," the people he referred to were shopkeepers and tradesmen. He worried at the time less about the rights of man than the rights of middle-class man. He and Tooke were "fellow-travelers."

And friends, too, so Paine thought. Tooke frequently invited him to his home at Wimbledon. Both liked to drink, and what was once said of Tooke—"His good humor and pleasantry increased with his cups"— could have been said of Paine. But behind his back Tooke ridiculed Paine. "He was accustomed to sneer both at his poetry and his prose." Once in company he repeated—"replete with the *bathos*"—a poem Paine had recited to him and "deemed . . . his masterpiece." He scoffed at his ignorance: "No man can reason but from what he knows," he said. "Paine knows but little, and is therefore to be trusted only within his own sphere of observation." Tooke courted Paine, as others had and others would, in order to use him; he would let him travel on alone after he had served his purpose.

3

Gouverneur Morris endured rather than courted Paine. He had come to England at the bidding of George Washington, to serve as America's unofficial representative. Washington wanted him to sound out the British government on a number of unsettled matters—their unwillingness to make a commercial treaty, their failure to send over a minister, their impressment of seamen, their retention of military posts on the northern frontier.

Paine submerged his disappointment when he learned Morris had received the assignment he had hoped for. Though he circulated easily among British politicians and knew more of them better, he never attempted to upstage Morris and always, on matters of import, deferred to him. Once when a British official wanted to confer with someone who could speak for the United States Paine said Gouverneur Morris was "the fittest person to step forward."

The entries in Morris' diary reveal Paine as a frequent but not always welcome visitor to Morris' lodgings: April 19 ("Paine comes in"), April 21 ("Paine comes and talks a long time about building bridges"), May 3 ("Paine comes in"), May 15 ("Paine calls upon me and talks a great deal upon subjects of little moment"), May 17 ("Mr. Paine called to tell me . . ."), May 21 ("Mr. Paine calls and breakfasts with me"), June 1 ("Paine visits me this morning but he has nothing to communicate worthy of notice"). The entries also reveal Paine as continually open, friendly, eager to pass along any news he had gathered on his rounds; Morris as cool, detached, and patient when he sensed Paine might be of some use to his mission. Morris rarely gave his visitor the benefit of the doubt. One day during the Nootka Sound incident Paine mentioned "that it appears from the king's speech that the British ministry have insisted upon satisfaction and restitution previous to discussion." Morris denied this, "ex absurditate," going on to say "that a remark upon it could not have escaped me." Later, on rereading the speech, he found Paine right, or "very nearly; the difference is that the claim is made for satisfaction and restitution previous to any *farther* discussion." Morris that day may have been a bit more testy than usual, for the Nootka Sound incident had been worrying both him and Paine throughout the summer of 1790.

4

On the morning of 3 May 1790, Paine found Gouverneur Morris in his study listening to John Paul Jones stammer out a string of woes. Jones had recently been dismissed from his post as an admiral in the Russian navy. Unemployment had left him with a small mountain of financial problems that he wanted Morris to reduce to manageable size. Paine broke in to announce that word had just arrived of a Spanish task force's attack upon a group of British ships at Nootka Sound, off Vancouver Island. Morris dismissed the news lightly, saying "I had learnt [it] long ago in Paris." If so, he had been obtuse to take it lightly. Paine, more astute, reasoned that Britain could use the incident to make serious trouble if she so chose. The next day the government justified his fear by announcing preparations for war. The confusion in France hobbled French movements abroad. If war came she would find it hard to give the traditional support to her ally Spain. Britain chose now to use the clash at Nootka Sound to challenge Spain's nearly four centuries' domination in the Pacific. France, hobbled by the Revolution, would be hard put to give help to her traditional ally. Without that help Spain might now be willing to relinquish her monopoly of the Pacific. Thus Paine read the situation—correctly, it turned out. He immediately dispatched the first of five letters to Lafayette explaining the British strategy. France, he said, must not knuckle under to the threat.

Lafayette had replied to none of the five letters by the first of June. Paine then applied to William Short, chargé d'affaires and thus the American spokesman in Paris until Washington appointed a new ambassador, hoping that through Short his message would reach French leaders. To force Britain to back down, "France has nothing to do but equip a navy," he wrote. Large navies, unlike standing armies, need not be feared. "They cannot be employed to the purpose of internal despotism. They can neither make nor overturn revolutions. They are fishes, and though a whale might swallow a Jonah at sea it could not hurt a pismire at land."

"The preparations for war here goes on," he said in the next letter, and "till France and Spain exert themselves fully England will ever be an insolent neighbor, bullying first one, and then the other." In a third letter he reverted to the venomous Paine of *Common Sense*. "I know the character of this country so well that nothing but carrying a high hand can manage them," he said. "Yet they are the greatest cowards on earth as all bullies are, if you impress them rightly. Unaccustomed to wars at home or on their own coast, they have no idea of a war but at a distance, and that they are only to read the accounts of it in the newspaper."

Between letters Paine worked on a pamphlet "recommending an attack in the Channel by the combined fleets" of France and Spain. He sent the manuscript to Short, told him to take it to Lafayette "and closet yourself for half an hour with him and read and talk over the contents, and do not forget to tell him at the same time that I have appointed you my Minister Plenipo to reproach him for his inattention to me for the letters I have written to him, which were merely for his service and not for my own." After the pamphlet was published he wanted the manuscript back. He would publish it in England as if it were a translation of the French version.

The letters to Short, sent in La Luzerne's diplomatic pouch, continued, all of them filled with forebodings: "The press gangs are at work again and the preparations for war are not slackened. . . . The English fleet, from every appearance, have received sailing orders, and it is expected it will sail this day." Between letters Paine continued to collect information, collaring friends in Parliament, visiting the French and Spanish embassies. In mid-July the king told Parliament, as Paine interpreted the speech, that "the British ministry have insisted upon satisfaction and restitution previous to discussion." Earlier Paine had resolved not to "call upon Mr. Burke . . . until his pamphlet comes out, or he gives it up." But the day after reading the king's bristling message he dropped a note to Burke saying "that upon the condition the French Revolution should not be a subject . . . I would call upon him the next day." He did. It was disgraceful, he told Burke, to " 'sleep obedience,' as Parliament was then doing, and run a nation into expense and perhaps a war, without so much as inquiring into the case, or the object, of both of which I had some knowledge." Burke, noncommittal, referred him to Charles Grey, a political ally and "the fittest member to bring such matters forward." Paine reported the conversation next day to Gouverneur Morris for what use it might be in guiding American conduct during the crisis.

Washington and Jefferson had watched from a distance with trepidation. Washington feared that if war occurred the British might march down from Canada through American territory to attack Spanish holdings in Louisiana and Florida. Worse, with "so formidable and enterprising a people as the British on both our flanks and rear, with their navy in front," America would be "surrounded" by her late enemy. In mid-August Jefferson instructed Morris to inform the British "we wish to be neutral, and we will be so"—then added an implicit threat—"*if they will execute the treaty fairly and attempt no conquests adjoining us.*" Morris conveyed the message in a way that satisfied Washington and Jefferson, though nothing came of the ploy to force a redress of American grievances.

Neither Washington nor Jefferson consulted Paine at any time. Perhaps they thought, as Morris did in London, that Paine's commitment to the French and his hatred of the British had warped his perception. By August Morris had ceased to confide in Paine—if ever he had confided to any extent. "I think I see this in its true light," Morris remarked after the two had discussed whether France would adhere to its alliance with Spain, "but do not mention to him my idea."

5

"I do not permit the *whole* of my mind, nor ever did, to be engaged or absorbed by one object only," Paine once said. He had a chance to test that precept during the Nootka Sound controversy, for the week it began, his long-awaited experimental iron arch reached London in the hold of a ship. "War, should it break out, will as in all new things, prevent its progress so far as regards profits," he said glumly as he watched the sections being unloaded onto a wharf along the Thames. Through June and July the portable ribs were trundled from dockside to a field just outside London in the village of Paddington, where the arch would be erected. He hired three carpenters, two laborers, and a foreman named Bull to direct the operation. Previously he had held "a slender opinion of myself for executive business," but the experience directing workmen at Rotherham convinced him "upon the whole that I have managed this matter tolerably well." He continued to manage well at Paddington.

Money, though, was a bit of a problem. Earlier he had asked Jefferson back in America to arrange for the transfer of two hundred pounds from his bank in Philadelphia to London, and now Gouverneur Morris, whether he liked it or not, served as his banker. Morris' diary captures the snug relationship: June 12 ("Paine calls upon me and asked the payment of money"), June 14 ("Paine calls on me and I give him an order for £22"), June 30 ("Paine calls to get money"), and so forth. The calls continued into July and August, but not always for money. August 1: "Paine comes again in the evening and sits till near eleven. His object is to get rid of himself." Morris endures these intrusions for two months before he loses his temper and tells Paine "he is a troublesome fellow." A few days later their relations are back to normal. "Paine calls on me to borrow money," goes the entry for August 14, "being as he says too much fatigued to go into the city. I lend him three guineas which I fancy will not be speedily repaid."

The abutments for the arch, the form or center on which the iron ribs would lay, and a fence around the site to keep the public out had all been completed by early August. The raising began on a rainy morning. Mr. Bull, the foreman, was moving along the scaffold when he slipped and fell, ripping his leg "up seven or eight inches like the flap of a saddle." With Bull out of commission, Paine was forced to be on the job from dawn to dark. "I come home sometimes pretty tired," he said, but pleased, he could have added. "Everything joints well and . . . what is somewhat extraordinary it has everybody's good word." One day some members of the Royal Society, headed by Sir Joseph Banks, came by to inspect the bridge. They appeared "as much pleased as if they had an interest in it."

Gouverneur Morris kept finding excuses to postpone a trip to the site. On September 11, when he had exhausted his store, he came out. He thought "Paine's bridge is not so handsome as he thinks it is." He also wondered "whether it be as strong," but added, "It has a very light appearance however."

Toward the end of September Paine added a flourish to his production. He put six carpenters to work—hang the expense!—flooring the arch so that visitors could walk across it. "I think the floor will be capital," he told the Walker brothers. "It is one of my lucky thoughts." As the work progressed he glowed with self-satisfaction. "I am always discovering some new faculty in myself either good or bad—and I find I can look after workmen much better than I thought I could."

In mid-October the bridge "was exhibited before a number of virtuosi, and gave infinite satisfaction," and thereafter the public was admitted—for a fee, of course. Country gentlemen with streams on their estates to span and delegations from towns fronting on rivers came to study it. The cost dissuaded all from ordering a duplicate from the Walker foundry. The bridge was displayed for a year, then, when no buyers appeared, dismantled and carted back to Rotherham. Paine had predicted his iron arch would "produce a pretty general revolution in bridge architecture." He turned out to be right. "Paine's bridge sired many others," an authority has said, "and the descent can be traced through the activities of William Yates, the foreman he had trained so well at Rotherham."

Yates's opportunity came through a man named Rowland Burdon, who in 1793 designed an iron bridge to span the River Wear at Sunderland in northern England. Burdon introduced "several new and original features" to Paine's basic design "for the purpose of resisting compression." The length of Burdon's arch was 236 feet, almost exactly the span Paine had contemplated for the Schuylkill. Burdon raised £22,000 to finance the project, and the Walker brothers won the contract to provide the iron ribs. Billy Yates and his son supervised the job at the foundry and on the site. All the ribs in Paine's experimental arch were incorporated in the Sunderland bridge. Work began in September 1793 and was completed three years later. The bridge instantly became famous, recognized then and ever since as "one of the most daring structures ever erected in [cast iron]." Robert Stephenson, the eminent British engineer, later called it "a structure which, as regards its proportions, and the small quantity of material employed in its construction, will probably remain unrivaled." Stephenson became curious to know who deserved credit for this remarkable bridge. To Burdon must be conceded his "careful elaboration and improvement" on Paine's design and his boldness in applying "this idea at once on so magnificent scale," reported the man assigned to come up with an answer. "But we must not deny to Paine the credit of conceiving the construction of iron bridges of far larger span than had been made before his time, or of the important examples both as models and large constructions which he caused to be made and publicly exhibited. In whatever shares the merit of this great work may be apportioned, it must be admitted to be one of the earliest and greatest triumphs of the art of bridge construction."

Paine heard about the Sunderland bridge in Paris, where as usual he was short of funds. A friend wrote one of the promoters of the bridge asking if they had "made free" with Paine's patent and whether Paine could expect a royalty for whatever of his had been used. Yes, came the answer, the bridge over the River Wear had been "suggested by Mr. Paine's" arch. No, there was slight chance of giving "any gratuity to Mr. Paine." And that was that.

6

Paine's "magnificent obsession," as it has been called, never completely obsessed him. While erecting the arch he worried steadily about events in France, about the Nootka Sound controversy, about Burke's still unpublished pamphlet. In September, while flooring the bridge walk, he used the spare hours to put the finishing touches on an essay entitled "Thoughts on the Establishment of a Mint in the United States." He sent it at the end of the month to Jefferson, who liked it well enough to have it published, and later told Paine that his "observations on the subject of a copper coinage have satisfied my mind on that subject, which I confess had wavered before between difficulties." Jefferson may have thought of urging Washington to appoint Paine director of the mint, then about to be established in Philadelphia and placed under the supervision of the secretary of state. The post would have been an ideal sinecure for Paine. It would have taken little of his time and left him free to write and experiment. If Jefferson suggested him for the post, he went unheeded. Washington never seriously considered him.

A year earlier, shortly before Jefferson had left for America, Paine had written, "I can scarcely forbear weeping at the thoughts of your going and my staying behind." Now he told Jefferson he intended "at all events to be in the United States in the Spring," before, he added optimistically, plans for the mint had advanced too far. The bridge was up. Burke apparently had abandoned publishing his views on the French Revolution. The war scare that had flared up over the affair at Nootka Sound had evaporated in October when Spain lost hope of aid from France and gave in to all British demands.

Paine was left with little to agitate his soul. In October, to take a vacation and possibly to promote the bridge, he traveled over to Paris. There he got long-awaited but unexpected news: On 1 November 1790 Edmund Burke would publish a book entitled *Reflections on the Revolution in France*. Paine hastened back to London to be on hand the day the book came out.

CHAPTER

16

REFLECTIONS ON RIGHTS
AND REVOLUTIONS

PAINE CALLED BURKE'S *Reflections on the Revolution in France* a "tribute of fear." Burke would have agreed, adding only that Paine had helped inspire that fear with his prediction that "the revolution in France is certainly a forerunner to other revolutions in Europe."

Through most of 1789 Englishmen gave desultory attention to the turmoil in France, a wait-and-see attitude prevailing. People thought the French government needed reforming. The French seemed to be going about it with a bit too much zeal for an Englishman's taste, but they were turning the country in the right direction—toward a constitutional monarchy. Burke glanced across the Channel when the Bastille fell, murmured that he hoped it was "an accident" and not indicative of "character," then said no more. A month later he still did not know whether "to blame or to applaud." He wished the National Assembly would shun theories about the rights of man and deal with "man in the concrete." He feared France must endure "more transmigrations" before order returned. Formation of the National Guard, an army independent of the crown's control, and creation of the self-governing Commune of Paris disturbed him. The "Great Fear" and the October Days horrified him. Yet at the end of October he still hedged, still refused to give "a positive opinion" about the Revolution.

Then on 2 November 1789 the Assembly confiscated lands of the church. Two days later Dr. Price hailed the Revolution as "the beginning of the reformation of the governments of Europe." "I looked on that sermon," Burke said, "as the public declaration of a man much connected with literary caballers and," he added, perhaps with Paine in mind, "intriguing philosophers, with political theologians and theological politicians both at home and abroad. I know they set him as a sort of oracle; because with the best intentions in the world, he naturally *philippizes*, and chants his prophetic song in exact unison with their designs."

Soon after Price spoke, Burke settled down to write the *Reflections*. If he still wavered about the Revolution, Paine washed doubts away with his prediction that it was the prelude of others, which he made to Burke in a letter sent 17 January 1790. "There is no foreign court, not even Prussia, that could now be fond of attacking France; they are afraid of their armies and their subjects catching the contagion. Here are reports of matters beginning to work in Bohemia, and in Rome. . . . Something is beginning in Poland, just enough to make the people begin to think." Now, if not before, Burke saw, as his biographer puts it, that "the Revolution was not a sequence of spontaneous happenings but a systematic plan to spread a false philosophy and to destroy the established European order."

On February 20 Burke promised that his book would be out "soon," but what had been set in type failed to satisfy him, no matter how much he revised the proofsheets. He wrote and rewrote through the spring and summer of 1790, while Paine worked on the bridge and fussed about Nootka Sound. He finished the book in September. After a month and a half of further revisions *Reflections on the Revolution in France* was published on November 1. It sold seven thousand copies the first week, twelve thousand before the month ended. The first printing in France of twenty-five hundred sold out in two days, and within three months sales there had reached sixteen thousand. German and Italian translations were out early in 1791, and reprints in Ireland and America followed later in the year.

Burke hoped he had written a manifesto for the Whig party. Instead, he found himself in the curious position of being praised by political enemies, condemned by friends. Fox considered the essay in "very bad taste." "Read it," said George III, who up to now had not been able to abide Burke. "It will do you good!—do you good! Every gentleman should read it." The king's endorsement helped boost sales; it did nothing to promote Burke's fortunes within the party. Whigs continued to defend or take a neutral stand on the French Revolution. Six months after publication Burke announced in Parliament that he could no longer stay allied with those who disagreed with him. *"There is no loss of friendship,"* Fox whispered from his seat. "I regret to say there is," Burke answered.

"I have done my duty though I have lost my friend. Our friendship is at an end."

Inside of two months Burke had provoked ten pamphlets in reply; over sixty more were to come before the battle of words ended in stunned silence with the Reign of Terror. Most of the authors were good Whigs who proclaimed their affection for English institutions and derided the absurd notion that they would soon be wiped away by revolution. They censured Burke as he had Price, as one who "naturally *philippizes*, and chants his prophetic song." Indeed, they found his assault on Price—"one of the best-hearted men that lives," Paine called him—particularly taste-less. Burke had reviled him as a "spiritual doctor of politics" who preached a "porridge of various political opinions and reflections . . . from the Pisgah of his pulpit." Price had to suffer partly because he served as a stalking horse for the real target—Paine, who had yet to expose his views in print. Occasionally though, Burke does fix his sights on Paine. The "literary men" promoting the revolution in France, he says at one point, "think that government may vary like modes of dress," a phrase sure to remind readers of the remark in *Common Sense* that "government, like dress, is the badge of lost innocence." He also probably had Paine, self-proclaimed citizen of the world, in mind when he added, "Their attachment to their country itself is only so far as it agrees with some of their fleeting projects."

All who answered Burke claimed they wished only to reform Parlia-ment. One of their planks called for manhood suffrage. No one, except Paine and Burke, saw the implications of the demand. To grant it would in effect bring the French Revolution to England. A society based on "orders," as England's was and France's had been, each with rights, privileges, and powers of its own, would be melted down into a single mass, politically equal. The framework of parliamentary government as it had developed out of the Middle Ages would buckle, and as it did, what began as a political reformation would end as a social revolution. Burke and Paine understood each other well. Both knew that reformation was a euphemism for revolution.

2

Burke tried in *Reflections* to build with words an impregnable defense of the status quo. "The total contempt which prevails with [the French], and may come to prevail with us, of all ancient institutions," he said in the opening pages, stating the theme early, "makes it not unadvisable, in my opinion, to call back our attention to the true principles of our own domestic laws." "To make a revolution is to subvert the ancient state of our country," he said elsewhere in the book; "and no common reasons are called for to justify so violent a proceeding." Although he admitted that "a state without the means of some change is without the means of its conservation," he came within a hair's breadth of arguing that what is, is right. He had little use for the common man, dismissing him as one of "the swinish multitude," and even less for abstract theories. "Power, not principles," as Paine put it, concerned Burke. He conceded few rights to men. "Whatever each man can separately do, without trespassing upon others, he has a right to do for himself; and he has a right to a fair portion of all which society, with all its combinations of skill and force, can do in his favor," but he does not have "a right to an equal dividend" of political power. He deprecated the efficacy of reason to order society. "We are afraid to put men to live and trade each on his own private stock of reason," he said, "because we suspect that this stock in each man is small, and that the individuals would do better to avail themselves of the general bank and capital of nations and of ages."

The strength of the *Reflections* owes little to Burke's brilliance as a political philosopher but much to his literary skill. "It is one thing to make an idea clear, and another to make it *affecting* to the imagination," he had said elsewhere. Englishmen *felt* his book because he had designed it to be felt—to affect their imaginations. He aimed at the heart more than the mind. Mention of Marie Antoinette carries him into a rhapsody calculated to make a stout-hearted Englishman weep: "I thought ten thousand swords must have leaped from their scabbards to avenge even a look that threatened her with insult. But the age of chivalry is gone. That of sophisters, economists, and calculators has succeeded; and the glory of Europe is extinguished forever."

The language rather than the logic carries his readers along. Every image, every metaphor is chosen with care. Revolution becomes a disease that prostrates a nation, the wise political leader a "physician of the state" who shows "uncommon powers." He links sympathy for the Revolution with drunkenness. It is hard "to secure any degree of sobriety in the propositions made by the leaders" of the National Assembly, whose members appear "intoxicated with their unprepared greatness." An address sent to the Assembly was "passed by those who came reeking from the effect" of Dr. Price's sermon, "the fumes" of which "were not entirely evaporated." Those who oppose Burke's views suffer from the "intoxication of their theories."

As a literary performance the *Reflections* was a stunning achievement. Early critiques chipped away at flaws in the book, but none came close to pulverizing it. An absurd defense of the rotten borough system as "perfectly adequate to all the purposes for which a representation of the people can be desired or devised," could be ridiculed. Outrageous praise for a parasitical French aristocracy that had slowly sucked the life out of a nation could be dismissed by Paine's devastating retort: "He pities the plumage but forgets the dying bird." But after hyperbole, misstatements of fact, and its sentimentality had been discounted, the book still stood like a boulder in the road that forces men to detour around it since they cannot demolish it. "The imperative tone, the cumulative effect of image and illustration, the apparently inexhaustible fertility of Burke's mind," Professor Boulton has remarked, "all combined to forbid effective reply except from the most incisive minds."

3

Paine had a good but not incisive mind, and in the early pages of *The Rights of Man* it looked as though he would follow the route others had taken—a point-by-point rebuttal of Burke's argument. He disputed Burke's view of a government's role in a nation's life:

BURKE: It is a partnership in all science; a partnership in all art; a partnership in every virtue, and in all perfection.
PAINE: Formal government makes but a small part of civilized life.

To Burke's central argument in the *Reflections*, "We wished . . . to derive all we possess as *an inheritance from our forefathers*," Paine retorted, "I am contending for the rights of the *living*. . . . Mr. Burke is contending for the authority of the dead over the rights and freedom of the living." An aristocracy, said Burke, "is a graceful ornament to the civil order." "Titles are but nicknames" suitable for children, Paine replied. "A certain writer, of some antiquity, says, 'When I was a child, I thought as a child; but when I became a man, I put away childish things.'"

But Paine abandoned the attempt to rebut Burke point by point before wasting much time on it. Instead, he produced a counter-manifesto. He would joust, but on his own terms. Burke spoke for government; he would speak for the governed. Burke spoke for the past; he would speak for the present.

Paine drew up new rules for the game, then invited in a new audience to watch. Burke had appealed to a sophisticated group of readers who could appreciate the subtleties of his argument and style; those who replied to him sought the same readers and, unable to match Burke's magnificent rhetoric, defeated themselves. Paine spoke to the governed in their own language. *Common Sense* had pioneered a new kind of political pamphleteering, one that presented a complex issue to a mass audience. No one had yet tried to reach "the swinish multitude" in England. Paine would conduct the experiment. "I wished to know the manner in which a work, written in a style of thinking and expression different to what had been customary in England, would be received," he said. Burke wrote for a ready-made audience; Paine created a new one.

4

Paine did not always deal fairly with Burke in *The Rights of Man*. Invariably he misquotes him, and at least once in a way that completely distorts his meaning. Occasionally he stoops to character assassination, as when he remarked that "Mr. Burke does not call himself a madman, whatever others may do." At another time, forgetting that he had once been "the pensioned pen" of Robert Morris, he accounts for the "strange doctrines" in *Reflections* by suggesting that Burke was on the crown's payroll as "a pensioner in a fictitious name," an allegation that proved true but hardly relevant to the issue. But all this was mild stuff to what Burke had handed Dr. Price. Given the generally high level of his attack, these barbs can charitably be dismissed as slips of the pen.

The praise showered upon Burke's work as a literary masterpiece has obscured the skill with which Paine replied. His boldest, most perceptive thrusts hit Burke where no one then, and few have since, dared to strike at him—as a literary craftsman. *Reflections*, says Paine, fails to distinguish between truth and fiction and thereby degenerates from history "into a composition of art." He makes of history a drama, "a theatrical representation, where facts are manufactured for the sake of show, and accommodated to produce, through the weakness of sympathy, a weeping effect." To carry off this "dramatic performance" he has taken to "omitting some facts, distorting others, and making the whole machinery bend to produce a stage effect." He produces "tragic paintings" rather than historical events. "It suits his purpose to exhibit consequences without their causes. It is one of the arts of the drama to do so."

Burke's style, too, is deftly punctured wherever it carries him into a ridiculous pose, as in his eulogy on the death of the age of chivalry:

> BURKE: Never, never more, shall we behold that generous loyalty to rank and sex, that proud submission, that dignified obedience, that subordination of the heart, which kept alive even in servitude itself the spirit of an exalted freedom.
>
> PAINE: In the rhapsody of his imagination, he has discovered a world of windmills and his sorrows are, that there are no Quixotes to attack them.

He chooses the passages for ridicule with care. At one point Burke makes a witty reference to Greek legend and quotes aptly from Virgil in alluding to the National Assembly's legislation regarding landed property: "They have reversed the Latonian kindness to the landed property of Delos," he writes. "They have sent theirs to be blown about, like the light fragments of a wreck, *oras et littora circum.*" Paine knew no Latin and little about ancient Greece. The passage must have been gibberish to him. He skips over it to light upon one written in seemingly comprehensible but convoluted English. "As the wondering audience, whom Mr. Burke supposes himself talking to, may not understand all this learned jargon," says Paine, "I will undertake to be its interpreter."

Burke draws from the classics to make a point, Paine from the language of the plain people. When something happens fast, it springs "up like a mushroom in a night." "To use a sailor's phrase," he says of Burke, "he has *swabbed the deck.*" "The duty of man is not a wilderness of turnpike gates, through which he is to pass by tickets from one to the other." The aristocracy becomes "a kind of fungus growing out of the corruption of society," a state church "a sort of mule-animal, capable only of destroying, and not of breeding up." The foreign phrases scattered by Burke go untranslated; to do so would insult his audience. When Paine uses "*Aux Armes!*" he has "*(To Arms!)*" trail it; after "*Le Roi à Paris,*" comes "The King to Paris." He relieves the "fatigue of argument" and enlivens dull passages with anecdotes. His historical account of the Revolution is deployed through the book rather than inserted as a single, possibly tedious, block. He lards the report with the I-was-there authority of a foreign correspondent—"I was there standing in one of the apartments through which [the king's emissary] had to pass"—whenever possible. Signposts are strewn along the way—"I will here cease the comparison . . . and conclude this part of the subject"; "it is time to proceed to a new subject" —to keep the reader oriented, and also to remind him he is not being hauled through Burke's "pathless wilderness." These guideposts ce- mented into the account give the appearance of organization to a book that is no better organized than Burke's. Paine here, as in *Common Sense,* tacks on to the end a fat "Miscellaneous Chapter" into which he stuffs all the facts and opinions he forgot to include in the text.

The Rights of Man amplified ideas expressed in *Common Sense,* but with less ferocity. "A French bastard landing with an armed banditti and establishing himself king of England, against the consent of the natives, is in plain terms, a very paltry, rascally original," he had written in 1776. "The plain truth is that the antiquity of English monarchy will not bear looking into." Now he writes more sedately, sensitive as always to the audience he addresses. He wants to win the English to his side, not antagonize them. His language is the vernacular, but he answers Burke's dignified indignation not with insolence or vituperation but with an equally dignified indignation toward those who cling to the past. Repre- sentative governments "are making their way in Europe," he says at the end; "it would be an act of wisdom to anticipate their approach, and produce revolutions by reason and accommodation, rather than commit them to the issue of convulsions. From what we now see, nothing of reform on the political world ought to be held improbable. It is an age of revolutions, in which everything may be looked for."

5

When Paine first read *Reflections* he said "he would answer it in *four days.*" He took nearly four months, though he had written something like a fourth of the book before Burke published. "Common Sense is writing for you," Lafayette told Washington in January 1790, "a brochure in which you will see a portion of my adventures. The result will be, I hope, happy for my country and for humanity." The brochure never appeared.

Instead, Paine incorporated Lafayette's adventures and his own account of the progress of the Revolution in *The Rights of Man.*

He had unexpected trouble getting the manuscript published. Joseph Johnson wanted it and accepted it. As the final sheets came from the printer, Paine saw that publication day could be tied to Washington's birthday, February 22. He hastily wrote out a dedicatory paragraph and the new page was tipped into the bound copies. Four hours after they were placed on sale Johnson recalled them, though over a hundred copies had already been sold. He had published earlier critiques of *Reflections*—those by Mary Wollstonecraft, Thomas Christie, and Capel Lofft—and assumed Paine's resembled them. Someone alerted him that it did not, that it contained some "obnoxious passages," and Johnson pulled the book from the market. J. S. Jordan agreed to take over the unbound sheets and to accept responsibility as publisher. Paine borrowed forty pounds from George Lewis Scott, his friend from days in the excise service, "to aid the publication of his pamphlet, suspended for want of money." Thereupon, for reasons unknown, he left London—possibly to raise more money, possibly to arrange for publication in France. Three friends —Thomas Brand Hollis, William Godwin, and Thomas Holcroft— agreed to see the book "fitted by them for the press."

Paine returned to London on March 7, handed Jordan a preface which he had set in type, and on March 16 *The Rights of Man* appeared in the bookstalls. The press reported that it had been "freed from some obnoxious passages." Actually, nothing had been changed. Jordan had only bound the new preface in with the sheets received from Johnson. "I have got it," Holcroft wrote to Godwin the day he picked up a copy. "Verbatim except the addition of a short preface, which as you have not seen, I send you my copy—Not a single castration (Laud be unto God and J. S. Jordan!) can I discover—Hey for the New Jerusalem! The millennium! And peace and eternal beatitude be unto the soul of Thomas Paine."

Shortly after the book came out there was "a consultation of the law officers to determine whether the author could be prosecuted," according to one newspaper. "The intention of doing so, whether in their power or not, has since been entirely dropped." The government had reasons for keeping its hands off the book. Paine had tempered argument and language so skillfully that it would be hard to make a charge of sedition stick in court. To prosecute would provide free advertising. Also it could lead to embarrassment; the book was dedicated to the president of the

United States, with whom the government now wanted to have good relations. Finally, there was the high price Jordan charged—three shillings. It was written in the plain people's language, but only the well-to-do could afford it. "Reprehensible as that book was (extremely so, in my opinion)," the attorney general said later, "yet it was ushered into the world under circumstances that led me to believe that it could be confined to the judicious reader."

An effort was made to restrict circulation. "I have got it," Holcroft reported. "But mum— We don't sell it— Oh, no— Ears and eggs." But curiosity and word-of-mouth advertising kept sales brisk. Jordan had set a new edition in type during Paine's absence from London and had it on the market three days after the first appeared. It sold out within a few hours. A third edition appeared on March 30, a fourth on April 14, a fifth on May 4, a sixth on May 28. All sold for three shillings.

The "judicious reader" reacted as expected. "It is written in his own wild but forcible style," said one; "inaccurate in point of grammar, flat where he attempts wit, and often ridiculous when he indulges himself in metaphors." The age "is too productive of aspiring, half-bred caitiffs, like him," said another. Still another deplored "the spirit of puritanic malignity" that seeps through the book, "and the language is the familiar, indecent slang of the conventicle." An uneasy feeling smoldered beneath this bluster. "What I own has a good deal surprised me," one man says. It is that the book "has made converts of many persons who were before enemies to the Revolution." More embarrassing, some of the *Reflections*' "warmest admirers at its first appearance begin to be ashamed of their admiration." One gentleman confessed that for all its roughness, the book was "full of spirit and energy, and likely to produce a great effect." Another feared that Paine's "coarse and rustic" language might "seduce his illiterate and unskillful" readers, who "may be easily duped to think seditiously, and of course to act rebelliously according to his wishes."

Paine set out early to satisfy the fears of his judicious readers. "Many applications were made to me from various parts of the country to print the work in a cheaper edition," he said, and as they arrived—from Sheffield, Chester, Leicester, Rotherham, from towns in Scotland—he granted them all, forgoing his royalty in every instance. One man asked "for leave to print ten thousand copies." As the requests mounted, "I concluded that the best method of complying therewith, would be to print a very numerous edition in London, under my own direction, by which means the work would be more perfect, and the price be reduced lower than it could be by *printing* small editions in the country, of only a few thousand each." The first cheap edition was run off early in April. From that day Paine expected the government to prosecute him. Instead, it chose to get at the book through the man. It hired a hack writer named Chalmers to rummage in Paine's past and print whatever dirt he could turn up.

Meanwhile, the respectable Society for Constitutional Information on March 23 had voted its thanks to Paine "for his most masterly book." Some members were uneasy about the endorsement. "There was certainly an apparent inconsistency in recommending a book which affirms we have no constitution, by a society instituted, as I conceive, for the preservation of one," a member remarked at the time, "but . . . previous to the publication, our society scarcely evidenced a particle of life." Horne Tooke admitted that certain parts of Paine's work were reprehensible, but then there were certain parts of the Bible "which a man would not choose to read before his wife and daughters." The society stayed friendly with Paine without embracing him. The two continued to travel in tandem down what one called the road to revolution, the other the road to reform.

CHAPTER

17

"BIG WITH A LITTER OF
REVOLUTIONS"

WHEN HE RETURNED TO PARIS, Paine moved into cheap lodgings with a friend named Hodges. A few days after the pair had settled in, Gouverneur Morris visited them, and he judged their apartment "wretched." Hodges spoke of Paine, then absent, "as being a little mad." Morris thought that was "not improbable."

Paine had been carried away by the success of *The Rights of Man*. "I could easily excuse, in an American, his prejudices against England," a French acquaintance wrote of him. "But his egregious conceit and presumptuous self-sufficiency quite disgusted me. He was drunk with vanity. If you believed him, it was he who had done everything in America. He was an absolute caricature of the vainest of Frenchmen. He fancied that his book upon the rights of man ought to be substituted for every other book in the world; and he told us roundly that, if it were in his power to annihilate every library in existence, he would do so without hesitation in order to eradicate the errors they contained, and commence with *The Rights of Man* a new era of ideas and principles. He knew all his own writings by heart, but he knew nothing else."

Through the spring Paine and Morris continued their uneasy friendship. Morris read *The Rights of Man* and found some "good things" in it but no more than he had found in Burke's book. Between almost daily visits to Morris and other Americans in Paris and to his numerous French friends, Paine used the pleasant spring days to work on a sequel to *The Rights of Man*, which he expected to complete by summer. The working title was *Kingship*. After finishing it he would drop the manuscript with a printer in London and then travel on to Ireland, where possibly he could stir that depressed country to throw off the British yoke. He had heard that twenty thousand copies of *The Rights of Man* had been sold in Dublin alone. The people should be ripe for revolt by summer.

Paine spent the month of May and the first half of June in Versailles working on his book. The peaceful routine ended early in the morning of June 21 when Lafayette rushed into his bedroom and shouted, "The birds are flown!" As commanding officer of the troops in Paris he had custody of the king and queen, who now lived adjacent to the Louvre in the palace of the Tuileries. The previous night the royal couple—the king disguised as a valet—had evaded the tight surveillance and were well on their way to the German border before their departure was noticed. " 'Tis well," Paine said. "I hope there will be no attempt to recall them." By fleeing, the king had destroyed what authority he could still command in the Assembly, had exposed his insincerity in pretending to support the Revolution, and had doomed the chance for a constitutional monarchy. Lafayette saw all this and something more. He would be held accountable if the escape succeeded. Rumors already abounded that his sympathy for the Revolution had diminished. The king's flight could be the lever to pry him from power into exile.

Later that morning Paine wandered about the city with Thomas Christie, whose work with his bank brought him to Paris. Agitated citizens filled the streets, all gossiping about the news. "You see the absurdity of monarchical governments," Paine said. "Here will be a whole nation disturbed by the folly of one man." With Christie and another friend he walked to the Tuileries, where they found an orderly crowd of curiosity seekers meandering through the royal apartments. In the afternoon they came upon a collection of citizens listening to a public reading of a proclamation from the Assembly, which promised that nothing that had occurred would interfere with the completion of a constitution for France. The crowd stood uncovered during the reading, their hats with the tricolor cockades pinned to them in their hands. The reading ended and, Christie reported, "in an instant all hats were on"—except Paine's, who had lost or forgotten his. *"Aristocrat! Aristocrat!"* someone shouted, and the crowd took up the chant. *"À la lanterne! À la lanterne!"* "Hang him to the lamppost! Hang him to the lamppost!" Christie explained Paine's situation to the crowd, and the trio of foreigners was allowed to go on their way unmolested.

The king and queen were retrieved and returned to Paris on June 25.

Lafayette hoped the flight had not wrecked plans for a constitutional monarchy. Paine hoped it had, and his pleasure at the thought marked a rift in three years of close friendship with Lafayette. "His flight is equivalent to abdication," said Paine; "for, in abandoning his throne, he has abandoned his office; the brevity of the period during which he was absent counts for nothing; in the present case it is the attempt to escape that counts for everything."

Several of Paine's friends agreed, among them Étienne Clavière, fifty-four years old and soon to become minister of finance; the Marquis de Condorcet, forty-eight, an aristocrat and a member of the Assembly; Jacques Pierre Brissot de Warville, thirty-seven, a journalist, and also a member of the Assembly; and Achille François du Chastelet, thirty-two, an impulsive, idealistic aristocrat. (Within two years all four would be dead, either by their own hand or the guillotine.) The five friends shared two things in common—all spoke English, a necessity if one were to work with and be a friend of Paine's; all were republicans. They joined in late June to form the Republican Club. "This society," Paine explained, "opposed the restoration of Louis, not so much on account of his personal offenses, as in order to overthrow the monarchy, and to erect on its ruins the republican system and an equal representation."

The club started a journal, *Le Républicain*, to spread their views. Condorcet edited it with Nicolas de Bonneville, a printer and journalist, and François Xavier Lanthenas, who would translate nearly all of Paine's works into French. *Le Républicain* lasted four issues, just long enough for Paine to contribute an essay.

In it he praises republican governments and then lets a cautionary note creep in: Frenchmen must not expect too much too soon. "During this early period of a revolution mistakes are likely enough to be committed," says Paine, "mistakes in principle or in practice; or perhaps, mistakes both in principle and practice." Men "in the early stages of freedom," he went on, thinking back upon the decade of political experiments in America, "are not all sufficiently instructed to be able to inform one another mutually of their several opinions, and so they become the victims of a sort of timidity that hinders them from reaching at a single bound that elevation which they have the *right* to attain. We have witnessed symptoms of this imperfection at the beginning of the present Revolution. Fortunately, they were manifested before the Constitution was fully established, so that whatever defects were apparent could be corrected."

Paine chose a sedate style in his appeal to the few intellectuals who read *Le Républicain*. In another essay written at the time, a manifesto directed at the people, he used a livelier approach to his subject. Here, in blunt words, without ceremony, he defrocks Louis XVI. For the first time the people of France heard their monarch called "simply Louis Capet," a man like all men. "The facts show that, if he is not a hypocrite or traitor, he must be a madman or an imbecile, and in any case, entirely unfitted to discharge the function confided to him by the people." But Louis Capet need not worry for his safety. France will not degrade her glorious cause, "will not step down from her lofty position in order to retaliate her wrongs on a miserable creature who is conscious of his own dishonor."

Du Chastelet translated the manifesto into French, signed it—the law required public pronouncements to carry the signature of a French citizen—then had it printed as a broadside to be plastered on the walls of Paris. In the early hours of July 1 he and Paine stretched their audacity to the limit by tacking one of the sheets to the doors of the hall where the National Assembly met. Thus, said a contemporary, an American and "a young thoughtless member of the French nobility, put themselves forward to change the whole system of government in France." *Common Sense* had been the first to challenge America to depose its king and create a republic. Paine's manifesto repeated the performance in France. But France, whose traditions and way of life had been entwined with the monarchy for centuries, was not America. It would take more than a handbill to persuade Frenchmen to abandon their king. A deputy ripped the manifesto from the Assembly door and denounced Du Chastelet for publishing seditious statements. The Assembly's wrath swung to Paine when he admitted being the author, but he was untouchable—an American who would soon leave for England. The uproar startled Brissot de Warville, and the strength of the king's support surprised him. He quickly moderated his talk about the glories of a republic.

Paine did not. Within a few days he was sounding off in the pages of the newspaper *Le Moniteur*, explaining why "against all the hell of monarchy . . . I have declared war." He lacked time to elaborate, for an earlier commitment "to spend a portion of this summer in England and Ireland" forced him soon to leave Paris. A few days before he departed William Short invited members of the American enclave to celebrate Independence Day at his house. Gouverneur Morris spotted Paine there, "inflated to the eyes and big with a litter of revolutions." He had put one behind him. He had currently circulated in the midst of a second and done much, he thought, to keep it rolling. Four days later he set off again for London, this time with the hope of inspiring a third revolution in England and, with luck, a fourth one in Ireland.

2

On his return to London Paine found the public still buying *The Rights of Man.* "The work has had a run beyond anything that has been published in this country on the subject of government, and the demand continues," he said. In Ireland it had gone through four editions, one of which numbered ten thousand copies. "The same fate follows me here as I *at first* experienced in America, strong friends and violent enemies, but as I have got the ear of the country, I shall go on, and at least show them, what is a novelty here, that there can be a person beyond the reach of corruption."

He returned a celebrity. Previously the public had heard about him as the author of *Common Sense;* now they had read him, and they wanted more. One printer brought out *Crisis No. 12,* the open letter to Lord Shelburne, as a pamphlet, including with it a portrait of Paine. Another reissued *Crisis No. 13* under the title *Thoughts on Peace.* Hardly a day passed in July without some item about him in the press. A sampling of the clippings revealed that neither friend nor foe took his presence lightly.

THE ORACLE   *July 8*
Paine is writing a new pamphlet to be entitled *Kingship* and its object is to demonstrate the inutility of kings.—It is to appear in November, in French, German, Spanish, Italian, and English at the same time, as persons are translating it into the four first languages as he advances in writing it. Such is the rage for disseminating democratic principles!

THE GAZETEER   *July 15*
Mr. Paine . . . arrived in town on Wednesday.

THE ORACLE   *July 16*
Paine was probably hindered from appearing at the Crown and Anchor, from apprehension that some aristocratic tipstaff should in person abridge the RIGHTS OF MAN!

LONDON CHRONICLE *July 19*
This day was published Oldys' Life of Paine.

THE TIMES *July 26*
The only property which Paine has left behind in this kingdom is an iron bridge, which the landlord, contrary to the Rights of Man on the levelling principle, holds in possession until the rent is paid at Lissing Green.

THE GAZETEER *July 28*
A highly finished portrait of Thomas Paine, Esq. copied from an original picture, in the possession of H. Laurens, Esq. painted by C. W. Peale, of Philadelphia, and engraved by Thomas Bassett.

THE ORACLE *July 30*
Paine, we are informed, speedily sets out on a journey through Ireland, where perhaps he expected to meet those congenial sentiments of sedition and turbulence which he has vainly sought in this kingdom.

He could shrug off the jibes about his bridge, his trip to Ireland, his absence from a banquet at the Crown and Anchor. The biography by "Francis Oldys" was harder to take for one as secretive of his personal life as Paine. "Oldys" was a pseudonym for George Chalmers, a Scots lawyer who had emigrated to Maryland, then on the eve of independence returned to England, a venomous foe of all politicians friendly toward the colonies. He attacked Burke first in a pamphlet in 1777 and five years later published another on *The Deformities of Fox and Burke*. He worked for the Board of Trade, and though Paine and his friends dismissed him as a mere clerk he was more than that. He had achieved a measure of fame with his *Estimate of the Comparative Strength of Great Britain*, a reliable compendium of facts about British trade that had gone through several printings since it had come out in 1782. He was also a cultivated man with a large and widely admired personal library. He had written a book on Shakespeare and a biography of Daniel Defoe and also edited Defoe's collected works. As a cultivated man he was infuriated by the way Paine handled the king's English. He gave over a large part—indeed, nearly half—of his biography to a line-by-line analysis of the grammatical and syntactical errors in *The Rights of Man*.

The government subsidized Chalmers to dig into Paine's past. He did the job so well that virtually everything known about the first thirty-seven years of Paine's life stems from his research. All the buried and hopefully forgotten failures—as a husband, staymaker, shopkeeper, excise officer, teacher—were dredged up. All the ill that had been said of him and little of the good were recorded. "This pamphlet is, in a high degree, uncandid and abusive," said a man who admired Paine. "However, the incidents which it contains seem to have been collected with care and assiduity, and to rest, as to their authenticity, on the evidence of dates and records. It should be remembered, likewise, that the particulars have not been contradicted, either by Mr. PAINE, or by any of his numerous admirers." The book sold well among those eager to learn the worst about its subject. Within a few months it had gone through five printings. Embarrassing facts such as the unconsummated marriage were now on public record, and none of Paine's enemies hesitated to throw them in his face the rest of his life.

Chalmers exposed all Paine's flaws in his book but one—his drinking. No hint appears in the first edition that he used alcohol to excess. Though he had always needed it to relax and though all his adult life he had relished the convivial atmosphere of taverns, apparently no one thought he drank too much, otherwise Chalmers would have lingered with pleasure over the fact. In the second edition of his book, published in 1793, he did, but all the anecdotes that tie Paine to the bottle take place after publication of the first edition. Paine's drinking appears to have slipped, or at least begun to slip, out of control with the public exposure of his past. He had run from it to America seventeen years ago. Fame had forced it upon him once again, only now he had to share it with the world.

3

The newspapers' curiosity about Paine diminished in August, and he spent the rest of the summer living quietly out of the public eye. He saw much of Clio Rickman, a friend from the days at Lewes, now a paunchy, middle-aged, moderately prosperous London bookseller. Paine's daily habits remained what they had been when he lived with the Henrys in Lancaster, the Kirkbrides in Bordentown. "At this time he read but little," said Rickman, "took his nap after dinner, and played with my family at some games in the evening, at chess, dominoes and drafts, but never at cards." (This disdain for cards was something new, for in days past he had enjoyed a game of whist with Hall when the two were building the early models of the iron bridge.) "Occasionally," Rickman continued, "we visited enlightened friends, indulged in domestic jaunts, and recreations from home, frequently lounging at the White Bear, Piccadilly, with his old friend the walking Stewart, and other travelers from France, and different parts of Europe and America. When by ourselves we sat very late, and often broke in on the morning hours, indulging the reciprocal interchange of affectionate and confidential intercourse."

He also saw a good deal of John Horne Tooke. Under the guise of friendship Tooke continued to hasten after Paine, hoping to discover how to control him. Tooke appeared for the moment to be having success. On August 4 one of the reform groups he was tied to—Friends of Universal Peace and Liberty—would meet at the Crown and Anchor to celebrate the French Revolution. Tooke was chairman and asked Paine to write his speech. Paine agreed and produced a most decorous statement for a man who had come to England "big with a litter of revolutions." It condemned "riots and tumults," for they only "seek to *stun* the sense of the nation, and to lose the great cause of public good in the outrages of a misinformed mob." It disparaged war and observed that Englishmen "are oppressed with a heavy national debt, a burden of taxes, and an expensive administration of government, beyond those of any people in the world." It censured the crown mildly for "extravagance, ambition and intrigue." It said nothing about deposing the king, nothing about the evils of hereditary monarchy. The pabulum ended with praise for the French Revolution—it offers England "an opportunity of reducing our enormous taxes."

The visits to Tooke's house at Wimbledon were a pleasant interlude in a bad stretch of weeks. The book on "kingship" went slowly, and the trip to Ireland had to be canceled. The iron bridge had not been the success expected. "Being on wood butments, they yielded and it is now taken down," he said. Burke replied to *The Rights of Man* patronizingly in August, giving it a dozen pages in his new book, *Appeal from the New to the Old Whigs*, without mentioning the author by name. After quoting liberally from some of Paine's more reckless paragraphs, he said daintily, "I will not attempt in the smallest degree to refute them. This will probably be done (if such writings shall be thought to deserve any other than the refutation of criminal justice) by others."

The times seemed on Burke's side. "I see the tide is yet the wrong way," Paine confessed in a weak moment, then quickly recovered with the inevitable "but there is a change of sentiment beginning." When depressed he boasted: "I have so far got the ear of John Bull that he will read what I write—which is more than ever was done before to the same extent." When disheartened he dreamed: "I intend, after the next work has had its run among those who will have handsome printed books and fine paper, to print an hundred thousand copies of each work and distribute them at sixpence apiece; but this I do not at present talk of, because it will alarm the wise mad folks at St. James."

The next work had advanced far enough along in November that Paine thought it would be in the bookstalls by Christmas or "soon after New Year's." It would not resemble his previous book. "I have but one way to be secure in my next work, which is, to go further than in my first," he said. "I see that *great rogues* escape by the excess of their crimes, and, perhaps, it may be the same in honest cases."

Paine now felt the English had singled him out for attack. "By what I can find," he said in November, "the government gentry begin to threaten. They have already tried all the underplots of abuse and scurrility without effect; and have managed those in general so badly as to make the work and the author more famous; several answers also have been written against it which did not excite reading enough to pay the expense of printing." Perhaps the "abuse and scurrility" of Oldys' government-financed book had got to him and reopened "the wounds of deadly hate."

4

Nine months after publication Paine learned of the reception of *The Rights of Man* in America. "I have received a letter from Mr. Jefferson who mentioned the great run it has had there," he told a friend in November. "It has been attacked by John Adams, who has brought an host about his ears from all parts of the continent. Mr. Jefferson has sent me twenty-five different answers to Adams who wrote under the signature of 'Publicola.' " In retailing rumor for fact Jefferson did great disservice to his friend John Adams. His gossip sealed Paine's hatred and Paine ever after pursued Adams with the ferocity he usually reserved for kings. John Quincy Adams was "Publicola," and he had begun his series against *The Rights of Man* before the father knew what his twenty-four-year-old son was up to.

A contemporary said that the French Revolution "drew a red-hot plowshare through the history of America as well as through that of France. It not merely divided parties, but molded them; gave them their demarcation, their watchwords and their bitterness." Eventually it did, but only after 1791. Until Paine's book appeared Americans paid little thought to the upheaval in France. A streak of reports filled the press after the Bastille fell, then the nation settled back to contemplate its own affairs. Early in 1790 John Adams published in the press a series of long, tedious essays, *Discourses on Davila*, attacking the Revolution. He ended them when "the rage and fury" they aroused "convinced me that to proceed would do more hurt than good." Perhaps so, but the rage, if expressed, came from a dedicated few; not the public at large, which remained uninterested until copies of Paine's book began drifting into the country.

A New York newspaper serialized *The Rights of Man* early in May, ending the last installment with an ode to Paine.

> Rous'd by the reason of his manly page,
>   Once more shall Paine a listening world engage;
> From reason's source a bold reform he brings,
>   By raising up mankind he pulls down kings.

While other newspapers reprinted parts or all of the book, Jefferson inadvertently helped to publicize the bound version. He had borrowed a copy from James Madison, who told him to send it along to the printer who was going to put out an American edition. Jefferson did so, attaching a brief note:

> I am extremely pleased to find it will be reprinted, and that something is at length to be publicly said against the political heresies which have sprung up among us.
> I have no doubt our citizens will rally a second time round the standard of Common Sense.

The printer published the note, along with an encomium on Jefferson's "republican firmness and democratic simplicity, which endear their possessor to every friend of the Rights of Man." Jefferson admitted privately he was thinking of *Discourses on Davila* when he wrote the note, but he had not expected or wanted the note to be published. It and the printer's praise were published around the land and helped to spur young Adams into answering Paine's book. The British, already affronted by the dedication to Washington, took the secretary of state's endorsement as an insult. Jefferson's friends were delighted until they heard he had apologized to Adams for the indiscretion. "He should have pointed out *The Rights of Man* as antidote" to Adams' arsenic. "There was no use in fighting eight years for liberty, if [liberty] must lick the spittle of the Vice President."

In the midst of this flurry of insults Jefferson did a curious thing. Samuel Osgood was resigning as postmaster general. The post office in those days was considered a profit-making enterprise, and its management came under the secretary of the treasury, Alexander Hamilton, whom Jefferson detested. Osgood's departure offered a chance to put a friend in the enemy's camp. "Mr. Jefferson and myself," Edmund Randolph, the attorney general, reported to Madison, "have attempted to bring Paine forward as successor to Osgood. It seemed to be a fair opportunity for a declaration of certain sentiments." The maneuver is curious in that it had no chance to succeed and exposed the lengths to which Jefferson was willing to go in order to undercut Hamilton. Washington already had trouble enough keeping peace within his official family without bringing in Paine. He handled the suggestion tactfully, saying, Randolph reported, "that it would be too pointed, to keep a vacancy unfilled, until his return from the other side of the water." The post went to Timothy Pickering, a devout Federalist and admirer of Hamilton.

Paine had sent Washington fifty copies of *The Rights of Man* in July 1791. On 6 May 1792 the president got around to thanking him. The letter sounds cautious and evasive, coming from one who nine years earlier had joyfully helped Paine set afire air stirred up from the bottom of a river.

> The duties of my office, which at all times, especially during the session of Congress, require an unremitting attention, naturally become more pressing toward the close of it; and as that body have resolved to rise tomorrow, and as I have determined, in case they should, to set out for Mount Vernon on the next day, you will readily conclude that the present is a busy moment with me; and to that I am persuaded your goodness will impute my not entering into the several points touched upon in your letter. Let it suffice, therefore, to say, that I rejoice in the information of your personal prosperity, and, as no one can feel a greater interest in the happiness of mankind than I do, that it is the first wish of my heart, that the enlightened policy of the present age may diffuse to all men those blessings, to which they are entitled, and lay the foundation of happiness for future generations.

Rarely has the recipient of a dedication responded so tardily or so circumspectly. Indeed, Washington failed even to thank Paine for the dedication. Possibly as a private individual he was pleased, but as president he was embarrassed, because at the time he was working to smooth relations with Great Britain in hope that she would negotiate a commercial treaty with the United States. He could not praise *The Rights of Man* in a letter he knew Paine would proudly show around London. He may have liked the book; he may have detested it. Paine would never know.

CHAPTER

18

HOUNDED BY THE GOVERNMENT

SOMEWHERE ALONG THE LINE Paine dropped the *Kingship* title. The new volume would come out as the second part of *The Rights of Man*. As with all his books, he had trouble getting it published. Booksellers, who then sometimes doubled as publishers, shied from having their names attached to it. J. S. Jordan and Joseph Johnson refused to allow theirs on the title page, though they agreed to the less risky venture of selling what was certain to be a profitable item through their bookshops. Johnson had been told by a friend who had read the unfinished manuscript that "if you wished to be hanged or inured in a prison all your life, publish this book." Finally difficulties ended, or so it seemed, when Thomas Christie turned up a venturesome printer—Thomas Chapman, an admirer of Paine's works who was delighted to bring out his new book.

Paine worked under a self-imposed deadline. He wanted the book out by Christmas of 1791, "when the town will begin to fill" with members of Parliament, whose new session opened the last day of the year. He hoped that the reform program he planned to present in the book would set the tone for the coming session.

Christmas came and went and the book still "loitered in the press," hardly more than half the pages set in type and some fifteen or so pages of manuscript yet to come in. Chapman seemed unperturbed by the delay. After reading only part of the manuscript, he had offered Paine a hundred guineas for the copyright. When Paine refused, he raised it to five hundred guineas. When Paine refused that, too, Chapman went to one thousand guineas, an extraordinary sum. Paine still balked. To sell away the copyright would give the printer, he said, power "to suppress or alter" passages in the work, the right to sell "it to any other person, or to treat as a mere matter of traffic, that which I intended should operate as a principle."

The finished book would extend to 174 pages. In mid-January 1792, proofsheets had been rolled on 112 pages, the compositors had set as far as page 146, and Paine had turned in enough additional manuscript to carry them to page 160. The afternoon Chapman read proof on pages 113 through 128, he suddenly sensed "a dangerous tendency" in the writing, which in "my weak judgment" made the work seditious. There appeared too "many observations in the [pages] directly personal against the king and government," he said. "I therefore immediately concluded in my mind not to proceed any farther in the work."

Thereupon, at two o'clock in the afternoon of January 16, Chapman wrote a note to Paine of his decision; then, without sending it, he brooded away the rest of the day, "fearful I should not have courage in the morning to deliver up the copy." He liked Paine and knew how eager he was to get his book before the public. Chapman unexpectedly found a way of ending the relationship "with satisfaction to myself." About six o'clock Paine showed up at the shop in a state that was "rather unusual, at least to my knowledge"—he was drunk.

"Being intoxicated, he introduced a subject we have unfortunately differed on several times; the subject of religion, a favorite subject with him when intoxicated," Chapman recalled. "The subject of debate ran very high; he opposed everything with great virulence, till at length he came to personal abuse, very much so, both to myself and Mrs. Chapman. An observation was made by Mrs. Chapman, late in the evening, I believe near ten o'clock, at which Mr. Paine was particularly offended; rising up in a great passion he said he had not been so personally affronted in the whole course of his life before." He was so offended that he wanted Chapman to proceed no "further in his work." The printer returned the manuscript the next morning. After receiving the bundle, the abashed Paine visited the shop, "and made many apologies for what he had said; he said that it was the effect of liquor, and hoped that I would pass it over, and proceed with the work; but being determined on the matter, I would not upon any account."

An argument fed by alcohol seemed to Paine a flimsy excuse for rejecting a book Chapman had offered a thousand guineas for. Certainly Chapman's sudden awareness when reading portions of the dangerous road Paine was carrying him down rings false. Any personal attacks "against king and government," any "dangerous tendency" in the work had been revealed much earlier in the manuscript, long before these few pages (a revision of the government's tax structure) which so angered and frightened Chapman. In this light, Paine's suspicion that the ministry had put pressure on Chapman to drop the book makes more sense.

Within a week Paine, or friends for him, had found another printer. The sheets already printed were carted to the new shop and the final pages of the manuscript were set in type as Paine delivered them. Johnson now agreed to help underwrite publication costs in return for the right to sell part of the first printing, and Jordan, reversing his earlier stand, allowed his name to appear on the title page as publisher for a similar right. To protect both men in case the government decided to prosecute the work as seditious, Paine signed a statement that he alone was both the "author and publisher of that work." With a curious pride, Paine identified himself on the title page as the erstwhile "Secretary for Foreign Affairs to Congress in the American War."

The second part of *The Rights of Man* was published on 16 February 1792, priced at three shillings, with a first printing of five thousand copies. Within two weeks the book had gone through four printings. The greatest best seller thus far in English history had been launched.

2

"It appears to general observation, that revolutions create genius and talents," Paine remarks midway through the second part, "but those events do no more than bring them forward." Twice before—in 1776 and 1791—revolutions had pushed Paine's genius to the surface. Now, early in 1792, the vision of a third revolution, this one sweeping the western world, produced the boldest, most indiscreet work he had yet written.

Indiscretion appeared on the opening page: Paine dedicated the book to Lafayette. He and Lafayette did not differ upon "the principles of government," but only upon the speed with which those principles should be implemented. "I am resolved to labor as fast as I can," Paine told his friend, "and as I am anxious for your aid and your company, I wish you to hasten your principles and overtake me." Changes Lafayette thought ought to take fifteen years to accomplish Paine wanted executed immediately, for "I think it equally injurious to good principles to permit them to linger, as to push them too fast." The dedication hastened Lafayette's fall from grace. By 1792 to call for a slowing of the Revolution had become as dangerous as to oppose it. When Paine's work was published in France later in the year, the translator ostentatiously omitted the dedication.

Throughout the new work Paine played with the word "revolution" as if he wished to sanitize it, sometimes equating it with mere change ("It is not worth making changes or revolutions, unless it be for some great national benefit"), sometimes with reform ("reforms, or revolutions, call them which you please"). The game could fool no one. Paine was issuing a manifesto that called for fundamental alterations "in the principles and practices of government." The English honored their Bill of Rights of 1688; that, he said, was only a political deal, "a bargain, which the parts of government made with each other to divide power, profits and privileges." In the context of his new book, revolution meant upheaval, however Paine sought to soften the word.

The early pages dispensed warmed-over Paine, old ideas in new words. Yet it is remarkable that Paine, who knew virtually all his own works by heart and could recite large chunks at the drop of a hint, rarely repeats himself. The old shibboleths, dusted off, emerge as if new. And all the old ones are here again. *Monarchy*—that "master fraud which shelters all others"; "political popery . . . a sepulcher of precedents." *The monarch*—"it requires some talents to be a common mechanic, but to be a king, requires only the animal figure of a man—a sort of breathing automaton." *Aristocracy*—"the drones of society"; "a seraglio of males, who neither collect the honey nor form the hive, but exist only for lazy enjoyment." *Constitutions*—"not the act of a government but of a people constituting a government; and government without a constitution, is power without a right." England's *Bill of Rights*—"a bill of wrongs and of insult." *Representative government*—produces wise laws "by collecting wisdom where it can be found." *Commerce*—"a pacific system operating to unite mankind by rendering nations, as well as individuals, useful to each other." The inevitable jabs at "Mr. Burke, who, I fear, is growing out of date like the man in armor," are here but now more deft. "The farce of monarchy and aristocracy, in all countries, is following that of chivalry, and Mr. Burke is dressing for the funeral."

The shibboleths are the same but the tone of the attack has changed.

The dignified indignation that marked the first part of *The Rights of Man* has been supplanted by an insolence, a contempt, a "jovial ferocity" toward sacred institutions. With this "terrific onslaught against the hereditary principle," Paine became "the first to dare to express himself with such irreverence," a historian has said. "Gentlemen," the attorney general remarked a year later to the jury at Paine's trial for seditious libel, "you will be pleased to take into consideration the phrase and the manner as well as the matter."

Equally unsettling in these early pages is the optimistic certainty that "monarchy and aristocracy will [not] continue seven years longer in any of the enlightened countries in Europe." Revolutions "may be considered as the *order of the day,*" says Paine. Freedom has "been hunted round the globe," but now "there is a morning of reason rising upon man." Later in the book he expands on this observation:

> To use a trite expression, the iron is becoming hot all over Europe. The insulted German and the enslaved Spaniard, the Russ and the Pole are beginning to think. The present age will hereafter merit to be called the Age of Reason, and the present generation will appear to the future as the Adam of a new world.

Hitherto Paine wrote mainly to promote a climate of opinion favorable to revolution. He offered reasons why men should revolt; he had little to say about what they should do once they had won their freedom. Now that revolution had become "the *order of the day,*" something more was called for. Paine had a plan, and at that point in the book—where the distressed Chapman had returned the manuscript—occurs a startling shift in the tone and content of the narrative that reveals a new Paine, a man with a social conscience. Earlier he had repeated his old belief that "formal government makes but a small part of civilized life." Now, like Condorcet and others he had come to know in France, he demands that government involve itself in the welfare of all its citizens.

Paine advances his plan in a string of extraordinary proposals that are essentially an Anglicized version of the program that the Revolution's leaders have in mind for France. The state should subsidize the poor in order that they might live in dignity and comfort. Children of the poor should be educated by the state, at the rate of "ten shillings a year for the expense of schooling, for six years each, which give them six months schooling each year, and a half a crown a year for paper and spelling books." Also for those in need twenty shillings ought "to be given to every woman immediately on the birth of a child." The government must care, too, for the aged. "It is painful," Paine said, "to see old age working itself to death, in what are called civilized countries, for its daily bread." He would have those over fifty receive six pounds a year from the state and those over sixty, an age when a man's "labor ought to be over," ten pounds annually until they died. This would not be regarded as charity, "but no more than the interest on the taxes he has paid from the day of his birth."

Further proposals follow. The excise officers' pay must be raised, a suggestion that led later in the year to the reprinting of the pamphlet he had written twenty years earlier. Workmen's wages, currently regulated by the government, ought to be allowed to seek their natural level. "Why not leave them as free to make their own bargains, as the lawmakers are to let their farms and houses?" he asks. "Personal labor is all the property they have. Why is that little, and the little freedom they enjoy, to be infringed?" Having suggested ways of raising the bottom of society, he calls next for the leveling of the top. The government should impose a progressive income tax on the rich and also inheritance taxes to break up their large estates.

Since implementation of these proposals is inevitable, "it would not only be wrong, but bad policy, to attempt by force what ought to be accomplished by reason," Paine says in a final effort to take the sting out of the word "revolution." He adds, "Rebellion consists in forcibly opposing the general will of a nation, whether by a party or by a government." That ingenious definition leads into a final, deceptively innocent proposal: Let conventions be held throughout the realm to discover "the state of public opinion with respect to government," and thus change, or reform, or revolution—call it what you will—can be brought about peaceably.

The rage of the early pages, directed against monarchs and aristocrats who impose their wills on the plain people, has diminished to a reasonable calm by the end of the book. Paine ends with an extended metaphor that encapsulates all that has gone before. The passage opens on a quiet, personal note that leads gently into one of the most graceful, powerful statements in all his writing:

> It is now toward the middle of February. Were I to take a turn into the country, the trees would present a leafless, wintry appearance. As people are apt to pluck twigs as they go along, I perhaps might do the same, and by chance might observe that a *single bud* on that twig has begun to swell. I should

reason very unnaturally, or rather not reason at all, to suppose *this* was the only bud in England which had this appearance.

Instead of deciding thus, I should instantly conclude that the same appearance was beginning, or about to begin, everywhere; and though the vegetable sleep will continue longer on some trees and plants than on others, and though some of them may not *blossom* for two or three years, all will be in leaf in the summer, except those which are *rotten*. What pace the political summer may keep with the natural, no human foresight can determine. It is, however, not difficult to perceive that the spring is begun.

3

The pleasures an author gets from bringing out a new book were this time diluted for Paine. A few days before publication he learned that Gouverneur Morris had been picked by Washington to serve as the American minister to France. On February 13 Paine sent a dozen copies of the second part of *The Rights of Man* to Washington and Jefferson. In a note to Jefferson he called the appointment of Morris *"a most unfortunate one."*

Paine promised, so he told Jefferson, to inform Morris exactly what he thought of his appointment "when I see him." Apparently he did nothing of the kind. Morris arrived in London the second week in February and Paine stopped by soon after he had settled in. Morris had already begun reading *The Rights of Man*, and the two talked about the book. He thought that this time Paine had gone too far and would be punished. Paine doubted it and said he would rely "on the force he has in the nation" to protect him. "He seems cocksure of bringing about a revolution in Great Britain," Morris wrote in his diary, "and I think it quite as likely that he will be promoted to the pillory."

Through the rest of February and until late March when Morris left to take up his assignment in France the two men carried on as before. Paine stopped by regularly to chat and Morris found it impossible to turn him away. They never wanted for things to talk or argue about. When Morris tried to enlighten Paine about the trend of events in France— order had vanished and violence had come in its place, he said—Paine responded lightly that "the riots and outrages in France are nothing at all." Morris replied that it was "not worthwhile to contest such declarations," adding good-humoredly that since he was sure Paine did "not believe what he says I shall not dispute it."

4

But Paine did believe what he said, and so did a good many others in England. Burke had predicted that "a revolution is the object which the reforming party really have in view." The second part of *The Rights of Man* seemed to confirm that view and discredit the movement to reform Parliament. If the "reform party" were to survive, it must make clear to the nation its distaste for Paine and his ideas.

In April a number of gentlemen who had joined the Society for Constitutional Information in order to promote a reformation of Parliament cut their ties and set up housekeeping under a new banner, Friends of the People, a title calculated to mislead. The members were friends of Parliament rather than the people. They proposed that the politicians clean their house before the people, aroused by Paine's book, did the job for them. Charles James Fox, once Paine's ally, looked favorably on their program. *The Rights of Man*, he said in the House of Commons, "was a performance totally different from all ideas of reform in our government."

Those who stayed behind in the Society for Constitutional Information believed that Parliament, incapable of reforming itself, would clean house only when forced to. Also, "they were critical of the kinds of men and institutions by which the monarchy was surrounded, they thought that church and state were controlled by aristocrats, and they regarded more equality as desirable." They had no intention of deposing the king, yet they continued to travel with Paine, uncomfortable companion that he was. The society had spent years propagating its program around the realm, all to little effect until Paine came along. To reject him now meant abdicating leadership of the national reform movement. And what if he lent his immense prestige to a truly revolutionary group? No, he must be kept within the fold.

The bottle Paine had uncorked appeared to have created a taste for politics among the plain people. In December "five or six mechanics . . . conversing about the enormous price of provisions," formed the Sheffield Constitutional Society, which three months later claimed two thousand members, all well organized and largely drawn from the working class. In January Thomas Hardy, a shoemaker who two months earlier had heard Paine call for "The Revolution of the World," formed in London an organization "for another class of people"—tradesmen, shopkeepers, and mechanics—too poor to pay the entrance fee other reform groups levied. Dues were a penny a year and it was agreed "the number of our members be unlimited." Hardy called it the Corresponding Society for the Unrepresented Part of the People of Britain, an awkward title soon shortened to the London Corresponding Society. The Society for Constitutional Information helped Hardy get his group under way. It established correspondence with the Sheffield society and with other reforming societies springing up around the country. These groups were self-sufficient and independent, but they looked to London for guidance. If London disowned Paine the reform movement would crumble.

Gentlemen everywhere thought they had reason to be uneasy as they watched the reform movement change as it expanded. Was the French Revolution about to be duplicated in England? "The endeavor to inflame the minds of the working class is one of the most malignant of Paine's daring attempts," wrote one man. Christopher Wyvill, who had earlier found much to admire in Paine's work now said, "If Mr. Paine should be able to rouse up the lower classes, their interference will probably be marked by wild work, and all we now possess, whether in private property or public liberty, will be at the mercy of a lawless and furious rabble."

The rabble bided its time. It refused to become furious or lawless and continued to shun the bait offered by Mr. Paine, partly because cheap editions of his work had yet to filter out, partly because the French Revolution still seemed irrelevant to their lives. What Paine and most of the reformers failed to consider was that Englishmen already had much of what Frenchmen were struggling for—religious toleration, freedom of speech, the right of assembly. "The countryside was ruled by the gentry, the towns by corrupt corporations, the nation by the corruptest corporation of all," Professor Thompson has remarked, "but the chapel, the tavern, and the home were their own." Until the government infringed on those " 'unsteepled' places of worship," the plain people would remain somnolent.

5

Here and there in the spring of 1792 signs cropped up that at least some of the natives were restless. Coal miners around Bristol threatened to strike; shoemakers at Liverpool pushed for higher wages; sailors in ports on the North Sea complained about working conditions. A jittery government misjudged these scattered grumblings; it smelled sedition on every breeze from the provinces. It reacted by using the press to stir up a storm against Paine, hoping that "the popular cry" would persuade him to decamp for France.

In April Paine's London friends decided he should take a vacation from the city until the storm passed. Joseph Johnson arranged for him to move in with a mutual friend, the engraver William Sharp, then living in Bromley, a village some ten miles southeast of London. Paine, who found it impossible to cope with "the common concerns of life," left all the arrangements to Johnson. "They went in a hackney coach, for such a vehicle could contain them, with all the movables which Paine possessed," an acquaintance recalled. "On their arrival at the new abode, Paine discovered that half a bottle of brandy was left behind; now brandy, being important to Paine, he urged Johnson to drive back to fetch it. 'No, Mr. Paine,' said he, 'it would not be right to spend eight shillings in coach-hire, to regain one shilling's-worth of brandy.' "

The villagers were not alerted that the famous Paine had settled among them. Sharp paid for his room and board, "for the purpose of concealing his character and name there," and Paine did nothing to attract attention to himself. "He went seldom into the town, but walked much into the fields, and often in the garden behind the house." The landlord reported later that he "behaved quietly, without complaining of his fare; drinking chiefly gin and water, of which he sometimes took copious drafts." Occasionally he slipped off to London, once to attend a meeting of the Society for Constitutional Information, only to be arrested at the door of the London Tavern for failing to make good on a debt of an additional two hundred pounds due Peter Whiteside's creditors. He was again carried to a sponging house, "wherein he was locked up, on account of his dishonesty, rather than his want," as an unfriendly biographer put it. This time Joseph Johnson and another bookseller bailed him out. Obviously the incident had been concocted as part of the government's campaign to harass Paine, and it surprised none of his friends that the story was leaked to the press. "Pretty gentlemen, indeed, to suffer their ADORED FRIEND to be bailed by two simple tradesmen, who sat at the lower end of the table, and who had got frisky from *bumbering*— to them poor souls—very un-constitutional toasts," ran one account. "It is very provoking—abominable and blasphemous towards the world's present divinity—that the bailiff's toast is—TOM PAINE'S Ça ira,—that is—'may nabbing go on!' "

In mid-May the government broadened its attack, this time indicting J. S. Jordan as the publisher of a seditious book. Again Paine came up to London, this time to persuade Jordan to fight the government's case. He promised to pay all legal expenses. Jordan would have none of this. It was simpler, he said, to plead guilty and pay a modest fine for having published the book. Fighting causes was not in his line.

On May 21, a week after Jordan received his summons, the government aimed two more shots at Paine—the first a summons calling him to be tried two and a half weeks hence for seditious libel, the second a royal proclamation that ordered all magistrates to search out the authors and printers of the "wicked and seditious writings" pervading the land and to send the facts they gathered to the king's ministers, "it being our determination . . . to carry the laws vigorously into execution against such offenders." Four days later, pressed by Fox, Pitt admitted that the proclamation had been directed at Paine. "Principles had been laid down by Mr. Paine," he said, "which struck at hereditary nobility, and which went to the destruction of monarchy and religion, and the total subversion of the established form of government." Why, someone asked, had the government waited so long to proceed against Paine? Henry Dundas, Pitt's friend and adviser and one of the ablest politicians in the land, rose to answer. The subversive passages were found only in the recently published second part of *The Rights of Man*, he said, speaking with a broad Scots accent. These passages were already being "sedulously inculcated throughout the kingdom," and the government would proceed against them in the courts. Dundas elaborated on a point made by Pitt—it was only when "societies were seen forming themselves upon those principles that alarm was excited, and preventative measures adopted." He waved before the House a petition circulated by the workingmen's group in Sheffield and said that the government had reason to be apprehensive "when great bodies of men in large manufacturing towns adopted and circulated doctrines so pernicious in their tendency, and so subversive of the constitution and government of the country."

Paine refused to be cowed. On May 27 an address he wrote was presented to the Jacobin Club in Paris. In it he boasted that there were societies "spread over all parts of Great Britain in almost unbelievable strength" dedicated to freedom, "peaceable principles," and the rights of man. On May 28 the press noted he had become one of the "frequent associates" of Talleyrand, whom the National Assembly had sent to London to promote better relations with England. On June 6 he sent a belligerent open letter to Dundas in which he welcomed the government's prosecution, ridiculed "hereditary nonsense," and compared England unfavorably with the United States, where "there is not that class of poor and wretched people that are so numerously dispersed all over England, who are to be told by a proclamation, that they are happy."

On June 8 the government announced that Paine's trial had been postponed until December. Perhaps it wanted time to prepare its case. It definitely hoped that as spies followed him wherever he moved about London he would crumple under the harassment and slip back to France. "It is earnestly recommended to Mad Tom that he should embark for France, and there be naturalized into the regular confusion of democracy," the government's mouthpiece, the *Times*, advised. Paine reacted by letting the press know on June 11 that he was "very quietly sitting to Mr. ROMNEY, the painter." Rickman had introduced him to Romney. "and it was by my earnest persuasion that he sat for him." The portrait that resulted, said Rickman, "is perhaps the greatest likeness ever taken by any painter." Sharp made an engraving of it that sold widely about England.

In the weeks that followed Paine made one concession to prudence. When the first six-pence edition appeared on August 3, the public found that those passages the government had labeled seditious had been omitted. In their stead Paine offered explanatory footnotes designed to send the curious reader to the original edition for enlightenment. The *Times* gloated that "the matter of charge against him is left out of the cheap edition," but Paine had compromised for a purpose. "As we have now got the stone to roll," he explained, "it must be kept going by cheap publications. This will embarrass the court gentry more than anything else, because it is ground they are not used to."

The royal proclamation against sedition signaled growing alarm, and from the month of May on the government bore down upon not just Paine but all political dissenters. Mobs were hired or inspired to attack the houses of such as Dr. Joseph Priestley, who had preached in favor of the French Revolution. Priestley soon emigrated to America, part of a small band of dissidents harried from the land. Hack writers were paid to write for the government in the people's language, as Paine had written. Tavern owners were pressured not to rent their rooms to the societies that had caused such "alarm and apprehension." The London Corresponding Society responded by setting afoot a subscription among the plain people to pay for Paine's legal defense. The Society for Constitutional Information denounced the proclamation and circulated six thousand copies of its reply to Pitt and Dundas. On July 4 Paine offered a thousand pounds of his profits from *The Rights of Man* to the society in support of its campaign against the government. The press reported the gift; it did not report that it was rejected. Paine was courteously told that he had never received adequate reward for his services to humanity and should therefore keep the money for his own use. He did, though curiously he ever after insisted the gift had been accepted.

6

During the spring of 1792 the French Revolution veered in a new direction. In April the Assembly, with only seven members dissenting, declared war against Bohemia, Hungary, and Prussia. Only a minority led by Robespierre opposed this policy. Brissot preached the gospel according to Paine—the Revolution must be extended to the people of all Europe. "No one loves armed missionaries," Robespierre answered. "To want to give liberty to others before conquering it ourselves is to assure our own enslavement and that of the whole world."

The sansculottes—those men whose long trousers identified them as shopkeepers, artisans, the "people of Paris without frosting"—grumbled as they saw the Revolution slide into a new channel before promised goals had been reached. On June 20 they aired their wrath with a march on the Assembly and then moved across the way to the Tuileries, where the king, wearing a red cap, drank a toast from a balcony to the people's health but refused with calm courage to renounce decisions he had made as a constitutional monarch. An offended Lafayette deserted his army, which had lain two months idle in the field, and rushed to Paris to denounce the mob's leaders. He who had once been the people's darling now became their villain.

On July 6 Prussian troops moved toward France. Five days later the Assembly proclaimed a state of emergency, this at a time when citizens were flooding into the capital from all parts of France to celebrate Bastille

Day. (A contingent that had trudged twenty-seven days from Marseilles arrived singing a new song—"Aux armes, citoyens. Formez vos bataillons!") Through the rest of the month the plain people of Paris seethed with a discontent that erupted on August 10, when the people's leaders moved into the Hôtel de Ville (city hall), put Mayor Pétion under house arrest, and substituted for the legal government of Paris the revolutionary Commune, representing the forty-eight sections or wards of the city. Simultaneously, a prefabricated mob marched on the Tuileries shouting, "Down with the fathead." The king and his family fled to the Assembly's hall for protection. At the palace the Swiss Guard fired into the mob; the mob fired back and when the smoke cleared some one thousand people lay dead. The guard retreated to the Assembly's hall and the people stormed through the empty palace.

A cowed Assembly now listened to the voice of Paris. It voted to suspend—the word "depose" was avoided—the king from office and to place him under guard. It decreed its own death by voting to call a National Convention to create a republican constitution for France. Lafayette reacted to all this by ordering his army to march with him to Paris. The troops refused. On August 19, as the Prussians prepared to move against Verdun, the last great fortress that blocked the road to Paris, Lafayette abandoned the Revolution he had helped to start. An attempt to escape through Belgium ended with his capture by the Austrians. Lafayette told them he should go free: "I am an American citizen, an American officer, no more in the French service." The Austrians did not buy the argument; Lafayette was imprisoned.

Back in Paris the Commune on August 22 demanded that henceforth the word "citoyen" be used in place of "monsieur." Four days later the Assembly announced that all priests who opposed the Revolution had two weeks to leave France. On the same day it voted honorary citizenship to seventeen foreigners "who, by their writings and by their courage, have served the cause of liberty and prepared the freedom of the people." Among the Americans honored were Thomas Paine, James Madison, Alexander Hamilton, and George Washington.

The efforts to placate the city came too late. On September 2 rumors circulated that Verdun had fallen. While the Assembly talked of fleeing a doomed city, the undaunted Commune proclaimed, "To arms, citizens! To arms!" Suddenly the people's fear and confusion exploded into violence. An orgy of slaughter ensued for three days.

Sunday, September 2: This afternoon [Gouverneur Morris wrote in his diary] they announce the murder of priests who had been shut up in the Carnes. They then go to the Abbaie and murder the prisoners there.

Monday, September 3: The murdering continues all day. I am told that there are about eight hundred concerned in it.

Tuesday, September 4: The murders continue. . . . The weather is grown very cool and this afternoon and evening it rains hard.

The rain helped to cool passions and awaken horror at what had been done. The September Massacres ended as abruptly as they began. Some 1300 prisoners had been murdered. The single woman among them, said Morris, had been "beheaded and emboweled, the head and entrails paraded on pikes through the street, and the body dragged after them."

During the bloody days in Paris electoral assemblies around the nation were meeting to choose deputies for the upcoming National Convention. Paine was selected by four departments—Aisne, Puy-de-Dôme, Oise, and Pas-de-Calais. Calais chose him as the last of five deputies— among the first had been a favorite son, Maximilien Robespierre, elected unanimously—and it took three ballots to put him across. In Oise he was the ninth of eleven elected and so little known to the assembly that the secretary spelled his name "Peenn" and identified him as "Anglo-Americain, naturalisé citoyen français." A Monsieur Salle offered to inform Paine of his election by Oise, but somewhere along the line it was decided Paine should represent Calais. Achille Audibert of that department left for London carrying a letter from the president of the Assembly urging Paine to accept his seat. Ahead lay "most interesting scenes for an observer and a philosopher." Another letter, from the electoral assembly of Calais, made the invitation irresistible: "Come, friend of the people, to swell the number of patriots in an assembly which will decide the destiny of a great people, perhaps of the human race. The happy period you have predicted for the nations has arrived. Come! do not deceive their hopes."

7

On September 6 Paine went to see his friend of bridge-building days, John Hall, currently on a visit to London. "Does not seem to talk much,"

Hall reported, "rather on a reserve, of the prospect of political affairs." Paine had applauded the August 10 uprising that overthrew the king, but the September Massacres had stunned him. "Scarcely had the fatal news of these massacres arrived [in England] when a general change in public opinion took place," he said later. "All the friends of France were in mourning; each feared to meet his friends. The enemies of the Revolution were triumphant; they hastened to reassert all the old anathemas and cries of horror against France, and these cries shattered every soul. In vain we claimed that the men who had perished were guilty; we repeatedly maintained that a prison was as sacred as an altar and that those who violated a prison were capable of betraying their country."

The arrival of Audibert helped to raise Paine's spirits. He accepted the invitation to represent Calais. He had heard that France "wished to gain all the assistance possible upon the subject of free constitutions," that it wanted in the Convention men skilled "in defending, explaining, and propagating the principles of liberty." Who better than he filled the bill? Besides, as he told Thomas Pinckney a few nights later, "it was to the interest of America that the system of European governments should be changed and placed on the same principle with her own." Pinckney "agreed fully in the same opinion." Pinckney had just arrived in London to take up his duties as the new American minister. He brought with him a letter to Paine from Jefferson ("Would you believe it possible that in this country there should be high and important characters who need your lessons in republicanism?") and Washington's cool thank-you note, both of which Paine packed in his luggage as he prepared to leave England.

Before departing he dropped off at the printers a last essay for the British people, entitled *Letter Addressed to the Addressers on the Late Proclamation*. Ostensibly it answered those who had addressed petitions to the government asserting their loyalty, but midway he swung into a plea for a national convention such as the one France had decreed. "By this, the will of the nation, whether to reform or not, or what the reform shall be, or how far it shall extend, will be known, and it cannot be known by any other means." In passing, Paine remarked on a new spirit abroad in England, which "moves along the country with the silence of thought." He wrote before learning about the September Massacres, but it was those massacres, at least one historian thinks, that pricked alive the spirit Paine prematurely sensed. "For all the echoes he sent reverberating around Britain, Paine was not enough," Professor Williams has said. The

London Corresponding Society, that "mother of all mischief," as Burke called it, had stagnated at around three hundred members. After the September Massacres it began to sign up something like three hundred new members a week. Similar societies of workingmen soon mushroomed through the provinces. Sales of *The Rights of Man* soared—helped along by the cheap editions and free publicity from the government—until by the end of the year they had reached over 200,000, this in a nation of less than ten million people, perhaps a third of them illiterate.

Paine left London on September 13—at night because he believed "it was necessary to take precautions for his personal safety"—accompanied by Achille Audibert and John Frost, a lawyer and friend who had been active in the Society for Constitutional Information. They detoured through Rochester, Sandwich, and Deal to shake off agents that might be trailing them. They planned to put up for the night at the York Hotel in Dover, surroundings considerably more plush than those Paine had known years ago when he had worked in the town as a staymaker, and catch the ferry for Calais the next day. Five minutes after they had settled in at the hotel a man who identified himself as the collector of the customs told them they were confined to their room until all personal effects had been examined, as he "had an information against us." Each of the three had to empty the contents of his pockets on a table, then the collector and his assistants opened their luggage and "took out every paper and letter, sealed or unsealed." When Frost demanded their authority to do all this, the collector answered "that the *Proclamation* gave him the authority." Paine observed "what passed and spoke but little"; Audibert stormed about the room and complained "violently of the ill treatment." Paine, when asked how much money he had on him, answered "about twenty-five guineas." The officer made him count it out. Obviously the collector acted under orders from some government official "then in the hotel," Paine noted, "but whom he did not choose we should see, or who did not choose to be seen by us; for the collector went several times out of the room for a few minutes, and was also called out several times." The ordeal ended an hour and five minutes after it began with some "trifling conversation, chiefly about the Proclamation." Except for the proofsheets of *Letter Addressed to the Addressers*, nothing of consequence was seized by the government. Once freed, the three men immediately boarded the waiting boat for Calais.

A crowd had assembled at the pier to stare as the infamous "Mad

Tom" Paine boarded the ferry. "He was hissed a great deal," an observer said, "and many ridiculous speeches made relative to his trade [as stay-maker]. The crowd increased very much; the wind being slack the packet was obliged to be towed out. I believe had we remained much longer they would have pelted him with stones from the beach."

Thus did Paine leave for the last time the land where he had been born.

CHAPTER
19

CITIZEN PAINE

PAINE, WITH HIS LARGE RED NOSE, his crimson cheeks, and his slouching walk, rarely made a good first impression. "He is the very picture of a journeyman tailor who has been drunk and playing at nine-pins for the first three days of the week, and is returning to his work on Thursday," said a gentleman who crossed with him to Calais. "We arrived at Calais," he added with a touch of disgust, "and as soon as he was known to be on the shore, the people flocked to see him, and it was talked of saluting him with the guards as he passed the Place d'Armes. It rained hard, and I left him."

The guards did salute Paine, despite the rain. Audibert was determined after the humiliating departure from England that France should welcome the man in style. Frost describes the scene: "All the soldiers on duty were drawn up; the officer of the guard embraced him on landing, and presented him with the national cockade, which a handsome young woman, who was standing by, begged the honor of fixing in his hat, and returned it to him, expressing a hope that he would continue his exertions in the behalf of Liberty, France, and the Rights of Man. A salute was then fired from the battery to announce to the people of Calais the arrival of their new representative." Citizens lined the streets shouting "Vive Thomas Paine!" as the procession moved toward the town hall, where the mayor embraced the hero "with the greatest affection" and welcomed him with a short speech that Audibert translated. Paine melodramatically laid his hand on his heart and replied "that his life should be devoted to their cause."

That night "a vast concourse of people" gathered in a meeting hall to cheer Paine again. He plowed with "the greatest difficulty" through the crowd toward the rostrum, where his chair had been placed beneath a bust of Mirabeau decorated with the flags of France, England, and the United States. Paine's election as deputy to the National Convention representing Calais was officially announced to the throng. "For some minutes after this ceremony, nothing was heard but 'Vive le Nation! Vive THOMAS PAINE!' "

Paine and Frost left for Paris on September 16. At each of the towns —Abbeville, Amiens, Clermont—they stopped at during the three-day trip the citizens overwhelmed Paine "with elaborate ceremonies." Frost looked on with good humor. The "flattering reception" had put Paine in high spirits, he said, though "I believe he is rather fatigued with the kissing." They reached Paris early in the evening of September 19. The September Massacres had ended only two weeks earlier, but they found Paris unexpectedly quiet, "though it was illuminated," said Frost, "and the guard under the arms from an apprehension of people visiting the Temple [the king's prison] to destroy Louis and his wife." After checking in at White's Hotel Philadelphia, they went to the Legislative Assembly, then winding up its affairs. Pierre Joseph Cambon, minister of finance, rushed forward to embrace Paine as he entered the great hall, and as he did the deputies and galleries exploded with cheers.

The next day Paine called on Gouverneur Morris and gave him letters brought from Thomas Pinckney. They talked about the course of the Revolution. Morris, with hardly disguised pleasure, said that "the Austrians and Prussians, who were then at Verdun, would be in Paris in a fortnight," adding, "I have no idea that seventy thousand disciplined troops can be stopped in their march by any power in France." As he made this glum prediction the Prussians, unknown to anyone in Paris, were engaged in an artillery battle against a French army under Gen. Charles François Dumouriez near the hamlet of Valmy, some hundred miles northeast of Paris. If Dumouriez' army were crushed, which Morris assumed it inevitably would be, the road to Paris lay open.

Paine at this point found himself confused. In Paris the Revolution appeared different than it had from London. In London Paine had applauded the August 10 uprising of the sansculottes, who, in a great gust of violence, had overthrown the king, forced a republic upon France, and brought about the calling of the National Convention. But the September Massacres had made the sansculottes despised as lawless rabble by his

French friends. Only a small minority, led by Paine's colleague from Calais, Robespierre, sanctioned their cause. Paine, the staymaker's son, was a sansculotte by background. But for seventeen years he had circulated among the gentlemanly class of three nations. Was he a sansculotte still or a bourgeois? Perhaps in the months ahead, as he applied his cherished principles to specific issues in the National Convention, he would discover who and what he was.

2

On September 21 Paine and 748 gentlemen from all parts of France walked through a blustery rain to the first session of the National Convention. Paine and Anacharsis Cloots were the only two foreigners in the procession. Cloots was a wealthy and ferocious Belgian nobleman, who early in the Revolution had dubbed himself "orator of the human race." After the September Massacres he became the self-appointed "orator of the sansculottes," though he continued to live in the baronial style to which he was accustomed. "He was also a preacher of blood," demanding that tyranny be snuffed out wherever it grew, "but cruelty being the order of the day," said a contemporary, "what most distinguished him from others was not the ferocity of his principles but the chimeras of his imagination." He despised Christianity and had published a book on the *Certainty of the Proofs of Mohammedanism*. Robespierre looked upon him as a madman.

The Convention supplanted the Legislative Assembly in the great hall, once the royal riding school, adjacent to the Tuileries, and after settling procedural matters and electing Pétion, the mayor of Paris, as their president, the session went smoothly. The Convention's first pronouncement seemed lifted from Paine's writings: "Kings are in the moral order what monsters are in the physical," it went in part. "Courts are workshops of crime, hotbeds of corruption, and the lairs of tyrants." After listening to these words, the deputies voted unanimously to abolish royalty in France. Paine, Gouverneur Morris took the trouble to note in his diary, was among those who "gave his voice" to the decision. What the king's fate will be "God only knows," Morris observed, "but history informs us that the passage of dethroned monarchs is short from the prison to the grave."

The day after this momentous decision the Convention heard good news. Word arrived from Valmy that after a tremendous artillery duel the French army of ragged sansculottes under Dumouriez had stood their ground and the Prussians had withdrawn from the field. For the moment Paris and the Revolution, too, had been saved. "From this place and this day dates a new era in the world's history," Goethe, it was said, remarked of the Prussian defeat at Valmy, and every deputy in the Convention was delighted to agree with him. With lighter hearts they declared on September 22 that all decrees passed henceforth should be headed "Year I of the Republic."

Thus far the Convention had proceeded harmoniously. George Jacques Danton broke the peace. "No man could make a greater show of zeal in the cause of liberty," Madame Roland once remarked of Danton, whom she did not like. His face, ravaged by smallpox, seemed "forbidding and atrocious" to her. "I could never associate anything good with such a countenance," she said. "Never did a face so strong express brutal passions, and the most astonishing audacity, half distinguished by a jovial air, and an affection of simplicity." Now, with that "astonishing audacity," Danton plunged the Convention into dissension. He proposed that judges throughout the land should be purged and that arbiters, plain men guided by common sense, be put in their places. "Let the people choose at its pleasure men of talent deserving of its confidence," he said. "Those who have made it their profession to act as judges of men are like priests; both of them have everlastingly deceived the people. Justice ought to be dispensed in accordance with the simple laws of reason." With bold jabs Danton swung against one of the last bulwarks of the old regime. The king had been toppled, but an entrenched judiciary still shored up and protected the aristocracy. Only by ousting the judges could the Revolution move forward.

Paine sat listening to the furious rebuttals, all in French, swirl around him. He sat next to Étienne Goupilleau, a deputy who spoke English and gave a running translation of the argument. Suddenly Paine asked for the floor, and with Goupilleau standing beside him to translate, he told the Convention that justice should be administered only by men who had a sound knowledge of the law. An Englishman in the galleries said the speech was "not fortunate." Paine erred in thinking that the French Revolution duplicated the one he had lived through in America, that his experience in one country with its own traditions could be transferred to another with a different history. His last battle in the United States —over the bank charter—had led him to distrust an unchecked legislature as completely as an unchecked monarch. Only a trained, disinterested judiciary could restrain both from trampling upon the rights of the people. It took a decade of experience in the American Revolution to acquire this wisdom, and he wanted to pass it along to the National Convention. Danton treated his remarks deferentially, but Paine returned to his seat knowing that somehow he had misjudged the situation. The proposal to overhaul the reactionary judiciary eventually passed.

Paine had meddled in something he knew nothing about and at the same time stepped into a dispute that had developed in his absence. After he had left for England the previous year, his friends Brissot, Pétion, Roland, and Lanthenas had associated with Robespierre, Marat, Danton, and others he did not know in an informal political society called the Jacobin Club. As the members rose to power in the Legislative Assembly, the club became a directing force in the Revolution. A rift developed when Brissot, against strong opposition from Robespierre and his followers, persuaded the club that the Revolution should be extended into foreign lands. It widened after the August 10 uprising of the sansculottes. Brissot's group favored holding the Revolution down to an orderly pace; Robespierre welcomed the people's demand that the pace quicken. The two factions strode into the National Convention's hall on opening day "at daggers' drawing," Gouverneur Morris observed, their dispute "very loud and open," and each claiming "the merits of having begotten the young republic upon the body of the Jacobin Club." Neither faction could count on a band of disciplined members who would react as one to a party whip. Robespierre's followers, no more than half a dozen when the Convention opened, took seats upon high benches to the left of the rostrum. Their lofty perches earned them the nickname Mountaineers. Eventually historians in search of a handy label called them the Jacobins. On the edge of the Jacobin orbit, sometimes within it, circled other splinter groups—the Enragés, the Hébertistes, the Dantonistes. The other notable faction, some fifteen or twenty in number, sat to the far right of the rostrum. Historians in time called them the Girondins, after the department Gironde from where their ablest orators came; contemporaries occasionally called them the Rolandists or more often the Brissotins, and even these labels meant little. The Brissotin party, Brissot used to say, "consists of three men—Pétion, Buzot, and myself." All that can reasonably be said about the two factions and their differences, according to one scholar, "is that the Girondins on the whole represented the 'men of '89,' who thought that the aims of the Revolution could be procured by good laws, an appeal to reason, and economic laissez-faire; whilst the Jacobins on the whole represented the more experienced and disillusioned view of 1791–1792, and believed in the need for a greater measure of central control."

The great majority of deputies sat between the extremes in a flat stretch of the hall that came to be called the Plain. The Mountaineers and Brissotins vied for their vote on every issue. As the Plain swung, so swung the course of the Revolution. When the Convention first met, the mass of uncommitted members, still haunted by the September Massacres, allowed the Brissotins to dominate the proceedings. Not always, however. Their vote carried Danton's proposal to clean up the polluted judiciary.

Danton, an amiable, mildly corrupt, exceedingly able man, leaned toward the Mountain but had not committed himself when the Convention convened. The Brissotins ignored a hint that he could be enticed into their camp. Instead, they demanded that the Convention investigate rumors that Danton had fattened his purse at public expense. On September 25, in a reckless attempt to demolish the Mountain, they accused Robespierre and Marat of aspiring to become dictators. The accusation landed on the Convention with the effect of a fire bomb. Paine had been burned once; this time he sat silent as some seven hundred Frenchmen raged around him, looking like "an owl in a room filled with monkeys and jackdaws."

On that day, September 25, his friend Nicolas de Bonneville had published Paine's latest essay, *Letter of Thomas Paine to the People of France*, a latter-day version of the "animated addresses" he had written during the American Revolution. He intended it as an innocuous plea for world revolution. "Liberty and equality are blessings too great to be the inheritance of France alone." Rejoice that foreign despots invade your land, "O! ye Austrians, ye Prussians! ye who now turn your bayonets against us, it is for you, it is for all Europe, it is for all mankind, and not for France alone, that she raises the standard of Liberty and Equality!" In view of the uproar in the Convention that day, the essay ended on a ludicrous note. "In entering on this great scene, greater than any nation has yet been called to act in, let us say to the agitated mind, be calm," he wrote, sounding like a benign parson speaking to his parishioners. "Let us punish by instruction, rather than by revenge. Let us begin the new era by a greatness of friendship, and hail the approach of union and success." Those who knew Paine wondered if election to the Convention had not carried him into water over his head.

3

On October 11 the Convention selected a committee of eight to draw up a constitution for the republic. The Brissotins placed their key men —Brissot, Pétion, Pierre Vergniaud, and Armand Gensonné—on the committee. The Convention's three philosophers—Condorcet, Paine, and Sieyès—were also included. ("I was elected the second person in number of votes, the Abbé Sieyès being the first," Paine reported.) To conciliate the opposition the last two seats were given to Bertrand Barère, who, though he sat in the Plain, leaned toward the Mountain, and to Danton, who, though he sat with the Mountain, still said he could deal with the Brissotins. Neither Robespierre nor any of his followers were chosen.

The Mountain never forgave the slight. The day after the selection a speaker at the Jacobin Club excoriated those "clever, subtle, scheming, and, above all, extremely ambitious men"—the Brissotins. "Look at the appointments," he said; "they are filled from among this faction. Look at the composition of the constitution committee; that is what did most to open my eyes. It is this faction, which wants liberty only for itself, that we must combat with all our might." Within a year and a half six of the nine members were dead—Brissot (guillotined), Pétion (suicide), Vergniaud (guillotined), Gensonné (guillotined), Condorcet (suicide), Danton (guillotined)—and a seventh, Paine, was in prison expecting death any day. Only Barère and Sieyès escaped.

Two men—Brissot and Danton—showed little interest in the assignment. Danton attended none of the committee's meetings and Brissot only a few. Brissot invited David Williams, an Englishman he greatly admired—Williams did not return the compliment, considering Brissot "an honest but weak man"—to advise him. Possibly Madame Roland's acerbic judgment of Paine influenced Brissot's curious decision. "I think him better fitted to sow the seeds of popular commotion, than to lay the foundations or prepare the form of government," she had said of Paine. "He throws light on a revolution, better than he concurs in the making of a constitution. He takes up and establishes those great principles, of which the exposition strikes every eye, gains the applause of a club, or excites the enthusiasm of a tavern, but for a cool discussion in a committee or the regular labors of a legislator, I conceive David Williams infinitely more proper than Paine."

Paine functioned badly in the committee meetings, as Madame Roland expected, but not because he failed at "cool discussion." "I always understand my own thoughts best when I see them in writing," he told Danton. Paine took his assignment seriously. He had, after all, come to France principally to give what he had learned about constitution making in America. He began by analyzing the defects in the constitution devised but never used by the Legislative Assembly. He distributed to the committee a French translation of his comments on the first forty-five pages of the discarded constitution and in English—the translator had not caught up with him—his views "Of the Distribution of Powers Delegated by the Nation."

Other members had specific assignments. Barère "was charged with the declaration of rights and the part concerning judicial power." Condorcet would edit and collate the members' work. Ten years earlier Condorcet's renown as a philosopher and mathematician had won him a seat in the prestigious French Academy. Until August 10 he regarded the Revolution "as a mathematical problem which could be solved by the formula of natural rights," but when "*le peuple* became a reality, instead of an abstraction, Condorcet experienced a sense of painful confusion." He boasted, like Paine, of being "a stranger to all parties, concerned with judging men and measures with my reason, not with my passions," a detachment that earned him contempt from Brissotins and Mountaineers alike. "One could describe Condorcet's intelligence in relation to his personality as that of a fine liqueur soaked in cotton," said Madame Roland. Robespierre dismissed him as "a great mathematician in the opinion of literary men, and a great literary man in the opinion of mathematicians."

Paine and Condorcet had been friends for nearly three years, sharing a fondness for mathematics and political abstractions. They agreed on the framework for the new constitution. Condorcet used the one Pennsylvania had produced in 1776 as a model. His version for France—and the final document seems to have been principally his—created a one-house popularly elected legislature and an executive council also chosen by the people. "The late constitution," Paine said, speaking of that by the National Assembly, "sacrificed too much to ceremony, and the impolitic apprehension of giving umbrage to foreign courts," and Condorcet had not repeated those mistakes. But he had fleshed out his skeleton with eighty-five pages of detailed directives. Paine had not counted on this sort of elaboration. "France is now in a situation to be the orator of Europe," he had told Danton. He had wanted a brief fundamental law which, with only a little tinkering here and there to adapt it to local circumstances, could serve other nations as a guiding light. France through this constitution "must speak for other nations who cannot yet speak for themselves. She must put thoughts into their minds, arguments into their mouths, by showing the reason that has induced her to abolish the old system of monarchical government, and to establish the representative." Condorcet had produced a document shaped to the needs of France instead of one of universal validity, useful for promoting world revolution.

4

While Condorcet struggled with the constitution, the Revolution inside and outside France rolled along nicely, so well that Paine enjoyed baiting Gouverneur Morris about its progress. "Paine offers a bet that the king of Prussia will soon be obliged to treat for the surrender of his army or leave to retire," Morris reported in October. A day later, hearing that the Prussians were retreating, he could only say, "This appears very extraordinary."

A month later Paine had further reason to twit Morris. On November 6 General Dumouriez' army of forty thousand ragged sansculottes won a great victory over the Austrians at Jemappes, near Mons in Belgium. The Austrian retreat left Belgium open to occupation by the French. Congratulations poured into the National Convention from English political societies. The jubilant Brissotins on November 19 decided the moment had come to internationalize the Revolution. "The National Convention declares in the name of the French nation," went the momentous decree, "that it will grant fraternity and assistance to all people desirous of recovering their liberty, and charges the executive power to give the generals the necessary orders to bear aid to these peoples and defend citizens who have been or may be molested in the cause of liberty."

Paine and his English-speaking friends celebrated the turn of events with a great banquet at White's Hotel. Two bands played and the company boomed out "Ça Ira" and the "Marseillaise" and other songs of the Revolution. Toasts were drunk to "The armies of France, and may the example of its citizen soldiers be followed by all enslaved countries, till tyrants and tyranny be extinct"; to "Thomas Paine, and the new mode of advertising good books by Proclamation and the Court of King's Bench"; to "The Republic of France, founded on the Rights of Man." Lord Edward Fitzgerald proposed one to "The speedy abolition of all hereditary titles and feudal distinctions." Fitzgerald, an Irishman, had served as a career officer in the British army. While on duty in America he had renounced his title. He would soon be cashiered from the army for his toast at the banquet.

Lord Fitzgerald had recently come to Paris specifically to ask Paine's advice on how to expand the Revolution into Ireland, where "the godlike author" was already something of a national hero. He had been elected an honorary member of the Society of United Irishmen of Dublin, and a number of ballads were spreading his fame among the plain people. In one the "brave Irish" were admonished:

> no longer inactive remain
> Attend to the dictates of Reason and Paine.

In another, a drinking song, the sentiment was less noble:

> The mighty Thomas Paine
>   Who Freedom did maintain,
> With energy of reason and sense,
>   Was stupid as an ass
> Till first he took a glass,
> Then truth sprung from his crusheen lan.

Upon first meeting him, Fitzgerald had been startled by Paine's fiery, weathered face. Soon he was saying that "the more I see of his interior, the more I like and respect him." The two men fell to eating all their meals together at White's. "I cannot express how kind he is to me," Fitzgerald reported; "there is a simplicity of manner, a goodness of heart, and a strength of mind in him that I never knew a man before to possess."

Paine drew up "a statement of the affairs of Ireland" based on the talks with Fitzgerald. In it he said there were several thousand volunteers at the ready in Ireland and that with a loan of 200,000 pounds sterling from France to buy arms and ammunition the uprising could get under way. He set up an appointment with Pierre Lebrun, minister of foreign affairs, to promote the project with the government. He told Lebrun he would bring along his friend Du Chastelet to act as interpreter, "as I do not speak French."

Language as much as ideology determined Paine's associations beyond the small group of British and American citizens who lived at White's Hotel. He circulated mainly among Frenchmen who spoke English and favored internationalizing the Revolution. (Marat and Danton spoke English, but Marat was a fanatical member of the Mountain and the practical Danton could not take Paine's philosophizing seriously.) Among the deputies he saw most were Condorcet, Brissot, Pétion, and Roland. Outside the Convention he saw Bonneville, who published all his writings, and Lanthenas, who translated them into French. Du Chastelet had calmed down since the day he and Paine had tacked the republican manifesto on the Assembly's door; he now served as a general in the army.

In October Edmond Genêt, an effusive gentleman of twenty-eight, joined Paine's group of French friends. Genêt had just returned from Russia, where he had been the French chargé d'affaires until Catherine asked him to leave. The Brissotins chose to push him for minister to the United States, and in late December he received the appointment. Among his duties there would be to further the Revolution in Spanish America. Once the groundwork had been laid, Francisco Miranda, who at the moment served as Dumouriez' second in command, would bring an army from Santo Domingo into the Mississippi Valley to detonate the uprising. Miranda was a wandering Venezuelan whom Paine had met in New York after the American Revolution, in which he had served with the French army. A desire to duplicate the success of the United States in Spanish America had driven him for a decade in search of money and men to realize his dream—first to England, now to France.

The victory at Jemappes secured the Brissotins' hold over the Convention. They claimed Dumouriez as one of themselves, and his success in the field had shown how easy it would be to carry the Revolution into other lands. On December 15 while the Mountain raged from on high, the

Convention adopted as its own an ideology Paine had been the first to articulate. "All who are privileged, who are tyrants, ought to be treated as an enemy in the countries we enter," went the new decree. The army wherever it marched must abolish all remnants of feudalism, destroy royalty, and establish popular governments. "When we enter a country," the Convention declared, "it is for us to sound the tocsin."

5

Three days after the December 15 decree Thomas Paine *in absentia* was put on trial in London. The government charged he was "a wicked, malicious, and ill-disposed person," and that he "seditiously and maliciously" had planned to "traduce and vilify" the government of England by writing and publishing a "seditious libel." Eight passages, some several paragraphs long, were cited in the indictment as seditious.

Paine's departure in September had led friends and foes to assume the crown would abandon its prosecution. With the viper gone from the garden surely the denizens would resume their slumbers. But they did not. They had been roused from their lethargy, and with the example of the sansculottes to inspire and Paine's book to instruct they began to speak up. Traditional deference toward their betters waned.

"Have you read this little work of Tom Paine's?" a spokesman for a grumbling crowd of working people asked a local magnate.

"No."

"Then read it—we like it much. You have a great estate . . . we shall soon divide it amongst us."

The government fought back with loyalty parades and petitions while the Society for Constitutional Information circulated through the autumn of 1792, so rumor had it, some 300,000 copies of *The Rights of Man* at three pence each and gave orders "to one printer alone to print one hundred thousand copies." In November the government decided that to contain the agitation it must proceed with the prosecution against Paine. A verdict of guilty would permit legal suppression of *The Rights of Man* and perhaps still the madding crowd. Paine caught the government's purpose at once. In an open letter to Sir Archibald Macdonald, the prosecutor, he remarked that since he could not be touched by a jury's decision, the object of the prosecution "can be no other than the people of England, for it is against *their rights*, and not against me, that a verdict or sentence can operate, if it can operate at all." Having exposed the government's intent, he went on to ruin his defense by admitting he looked forward to the overthrow of the English government—"the greatest perfection of fraud and corruption that ever took place since government began."

Paine here said only more bluntly than usual what he had said before, but the London Corresponding Society, thus far his staunch defender, thought he had gone too far. It issued its own public letter to the workingmen who predominated among its membership, stating that the society worked for reform, not revolution, that it continued to support the French Revolution but that Britain must not resort "to the same awful tribunal with our brethren on the continent." Thomas Hardy, who wrote the letter, saw as Paine did not that the English and French situations were not comparable. It had required violence in France to win freedoms that the English had accumulated gradually over a century. Change by peaceful means had been and would continue to be the English way. However, Hardy's eagerness to disassociate his society from Paine owed something, too, to the government's decision to clamp down on dissidents.

Paine's trial was held at the London Guildhall on December 18 before a blue ribbon jury notable for the lack of a workingman on its panel. "The court was crowded at a very early hour of the morning," the press reported, "and soon after nine o'clock the hall was filled even to the outside doors of the passage leading to it. We never saw so many people assembled on such an occasion." Sir Archibald was known for his blustery temper, his mediocrity as an attorney, and for a wife whose political influence had four years earlier won him the post of attorney general. Thomas Erskine, Paine's attorney, was England's most successful criminal lawyer, having the previous year made more money from his practice than any barrister in England's history. He was a friend of the Prince of Wales and also his attorney general. The prince said that he would dismiss Erskine from the post if he defended Paine. Shortly after the trial he did so.

The trial consisted of two lengthy speeches. Sir Archibald opened. He played to the fears of the propertied class, reading passages from Paine, then elaborating on the chaos that would ensue if such principles became practices. He talked of little children going to school with their sweetmeats wrapped in pages of *The Rights of Man*, lingering on the horrible effect such trash must have upon innocent minds. He read aloud Paine's brash letter to him, and at the point where Paine had dared him to say "whom it is you are prosecuting," Sir Archibald said, "Gentlemen, I certainly will comply with that request. I am prosecuting both him ar.d his work; and if I succeed in this prosecution, he shall never return to this country otherwise than *in vinculis* [in chains], for I will outlaw him."

When the attorney general began reading Paine's letter, Thomas Erskine had objected. Sir Archibald had not given him "the smallest notice of his intention to produce it," he said. "That letter contains the most atrocious calumny upon his Majesty and the princes. . . . If my client had been indicted for the letter you have read, I could not defend him. . . . I fear it is a foul forgery," he ended lamely. The judge allowed the letter as evidence because it "tends to prove that Mr. Paine is the author of the second part of *The Rights of Man.*"

Erskine, when his turn came, addressed the jury in a sharp, clear voice that betrayed no trace of his Scots background. He spoke for four hours. He knew the case was lost before he began, but he had worked more than a month on his speech and was determined "to astonish the world" with it. He went over the libelous passages one by one, asking the jurors to put them in context. He elaborated upon "the nature and extent of the liberty of the English press." Paine had written an abusive but not a libelous or seditious book; he had not sought to mislead but to enlighten. Where in the book, he asked, does Mr. Paine plead for the destruction of private property or sanction civil disobedience? Tampering with the freedom of the press is dangerous business; few men are wise enough to know where to stop. "Constraint is the natural parent of restraint," he said, "and a pregnant proof that reason is not on the side of those who use it."

When Erskine ended, Sir Archibald rose to reply. The foreman of the jury conferred with his colleagues in the box, then without waiting for Macdonald's rebuttal or the judge's summation, pronounced Thomas Paine guilty. Immediately after the verdict someone scattered a printed broadside among the people—"*The Confessions of Thomas Paine*, convicted of publishing a treasonable and seditious libel." A crowd outside the hall cheered Erskine when he appeared, took the horses from their traces and pulled his carriage by hand through the streets of London to his home. Erskine had achieved the personal triumph he sought, the government the power to suppress Paine's book. The day after the trial the *Times* reported that "Mr. Ridgeway, the bookseller, was sent to prison . . . for selling the second part of Paine's *Rights of Man.*"

Back in Paris Paine had absented himself from the city the day before the trial, being "unwell or pretending to be so," someone said. Two days later he was back in town attending a dinner Gouverneur Morris had arranged for several Americans. "Paine looks a little down at the news from England," Morris reported. "He has been burnt in effigy." Also, he had been exiled forever from England.

The government's victory opened a heresy hunt. Spies were assigned to the meetings of reform societies and told to report aberrant talk to their superiors. Booksellers who risked selling *The Rights of Man* under the counter faced jail sentences if caught. One man got four years for reprinting an innocuous address of the Society for Constitutional Information. The persecutions continued unabated through 1793 against *The Rights of Man*, and when in 1794 *The Age of Reason* was published the attack shifted to that pernicious volume.

6

Paine's trial in London coincided with Louis XVI's trial in Paris, although Louis' began a few days earlier—on December 11—and lasted much longer. The Mountain had pushed to bring the king to trial from the day the Convention convened. The Brissotins had fought an increasingly bitter delaying action. Some held with Paine that Louis was inconsequential. "It is the office of royalty rather than the holder of the office that is fatal in its consequence," he said, and the office had been liquidated. Others argued that the king's person was "inviolable"; still others that the legislature could not be accuser and judge at the same time. Also, a trial of the king would lead inexorably from a verdict of guilty ("If the king is not guilty," said Robespierre, "then those who have dethroned him are"), to a death sentence (the deputies could hardly treat considerately a man who would have guillotined them if he regained power and who had called upon foreign powers for help), and from there to a war with England (Pitt had promised that a precedent that threatened the heads of Europe would not go unpunished).

Brissot and his followers fought a delaying action through October and into November, but pressure from the Plain forced the issue into the open on November 13. The debate dragged on for a week. Paine remained silent throughout. On November 20 a secret wall safe discovered in the king's former apartment in the Tuileries revealed a cache of incriminatory letters showing that Louis had conspired with leaders inside and outside France to crush the Revolution while he served as constitutional monarch. The damning correspondence made the king's trial inevitable. Paine heard of the discovery before the Convention did, for immediately after the deputies were informed officially he gave an address "On the Propriety of Bringing Louis XVI to Trial." In it he handled a delicate issue with skill and perfect political pitch. Avoiding bluster and invective —the king was called Louis XVI, never Louis Capet—he worked to create a tolerant atmosphere in which the trial could take place. At the same time he gave the Brissotins a graceful way to retreat from their opposition to the trial.

He opened by retracting his previous stand. "I think it necessary that Louis XVI should be tried," he said, not out of "a spirit of vengeance, but because this measure appears to me just, lawful, and conformable to sound policy." The Convention must not "let slip so precious an opportunity," for "the trial of Louis XVI can serve to prove to the world the flagitiousness of governments in general, and the necessity of revolutions." The deputies know well Louis' guilt as a conspirator against the Revolution; a public trial will let the world know how despicable he has been as a monarch. But remember, Paine concluded, Louis XVI is "only a weak and narrow-minded man, badly reared," and the Convention must show "some compassion . . . when it decides his punishment."

The weather was foul on December 11 when the king came before the Convention. He was dressed in an olive-colored silk coat and looked pale from his months in prison. He stood quietly until Barère, who was presiding, had a chair brought for him. The galleries and the deputies' benches were packed, but Barère controlled the vast audience and the proceedings firmly. The relentless questioning lasted three hours. Louis stumbled over his answers. When it became apparent that the king had received no copy of the charges against him, the Convention voted to postpone the interrogation until he obtained counsel and had prepared his defense. Fifteen days later Chrétien Malesherbes—he had been one of the liberal lights of the old regime when Paine had met him six years before, had emigrated after the fall of the Bastille, and now had returned in case "the king might have need of him"—pleaded Louis' case before the Convention. He received a respectful but cool reception.

The Brissotins worked throughout December to delay a decision on Louis' guilt. They argued that the people in a national plebescite should determine his fate. During the weeks it would take to collect the people's opinion they would work up support for a plan to send the king and his family to America. Meanwhile, behind the scenes they tried to defuse the tense situation with the British government. Paine revealed to Gouverneur Morris that his friends among the French ministry were now willing "to make sacrifices for peace with England," namely, to give "Mr. Pitt the French West Indies to keep him quiet."

Paine these days had access to people that Morris, though he was the American minister, did not. It was through him that Morris met Edmond Genêt, the new ambassador to the United States, and thus was able to send on to Washington his perceptive judgment of the young man—"He has I think more of genius than ability and you will see in him at the first blush the manner and look of an upstart." Paine found it easier to see Lebrun, minister of foreign affairs, than Morris. He spent one evening at Lebrun's house listening to Brissot and others search for ways to stall a decision on Louis' fate. Since the guests spoke in French, Paine only listened, except at one point when young Genêt asked him what effect the execution of the king would have in the United States. "Bad, very bad," Paine answered.

The prestige of Paine in a land that esteemed writers led even the Mountain to treat him tenderly. On January 12 a Jacobin newspaper paid him an extraordinary compliment. "If we silence today the Vilettes and the Gauthiers [reactionary journalists]," the author wrote in an essay on freedom of speech, "tomorrow silence will be paid on the Thomas Paines, the J. J. Rousseaus; for a policy which begins by closing the mouths of servile and cowardly pamphleteers because they can do harm, will end by depriving of utterance the generous defenders of the rights of man, because they do not know how to flatter or to compromise with principles."

7

On January 15 Paine used his prestige in a final effort to save the king's life. His antennae were sensitive to a new mood in the great hall, and he adjusted his address to fit it. He called the king "Louis Capet" now; as a mere citizen his importance diminished and with it, he hoped, the need to vote his death. He appealed to the deputies' practical sense rather than their magnanimity; Louis' life should be spared because it is "the most politic measure that can be adopted." Every American, he went on, "feels the debt of gratitude which he owes to every Frenchman," and so "let these United States be the safeguard and asylum of Louis Capet." Trailing this plea for tolerance came a deft touch aimed at Robespierre, who had fought for the king's death since the Convention assembled. "It has already been proposed to abolish the punishment of death, and it is with infinite satisfaction that I recollect the humane and excellent oration pronounced by Robespierre on that subject in the National Assembly. This cause must find its advocates in every corner where enlightened politicians and lovers of humanity exist, and it ought above all to find them in this assembly."

Voting on Louis' fate began that evening. The deputies were given three questions to decide: Was the king guilty of conspiracy? Should the final decision of his guilt be left to the people? What should his punishment be? On the first question the 707 deputies present voted unanimously "yes." On the second, the vote was 424 to 287 not to refer the decision to the people. Paine here voted with the majority on an issue the Brissotins had fought for. The people had given the Convention power to declare "the *political* death of royalty," he said, and judging Louis guilty of conspiracy only completed the "execution of that decree."

The third, the crucial question—Should Louis be put to death, imprisoned, or banished?—was left to the next day, January 16. The deputies assembled that morning to find that the Brissotins had invented a new stalling tactic. Knowing the vote would be close, they now called for a two-thirds majority to impose any punishment. The debate meandered through the day, until at last Danton spoke. "What are you about?" he shouted at the deputies. "You have decided the fate of the nation by a simple majority. You required no more to declare the republic, or to declare war . . . and now you need a great majority to judge an individual." The Convention agreed a simple majority would be decisive.

The voting began in the evening, lasted all that night, all the next day, and into a second evening. Each of the 721 delegates present walked to the tribune to announce his decision, usually with a simple statement, sometimes with a long speech. The galleries were packed with Parisians who kept track of the count on scorecards, hissing or cheering as they heard each deputy speak. A lounge provided for deputies waiting their turn to mount the rostrum was furnished with soft sofas, food and drink, and attractive females. When the deputies' names were called they stepped to the center:

Abbé Sieyès: death. ("What were the tribute of my glass of wine in that torrent of brandy?")

Anacharsis Cloots: "Louis is guilty of lèse majesté. What punishment have his crimes merited? I answer, in the name of the human race, death."

Barère: "As a classical author said, the tree of liberty grows only when it is watered by the blood of all species of tyrants. The law says death, and I am only its voice."

Brissot de Warville: death. (Had the "honest but weak man" crumpled before the raucous galleries?)

Vergniaud: death. (He who had called it an insult to suggest a man might vote for the king's death.)

Condorcet: imprisonment.

Paine (speaking slowly in French): "I vote for imprisonment of Louis until the end of the war, and for his perpetual banishment after the war."

Others followed Paine's lead. "I rely on the opinion of Thomas Paine, and I vote like him for imprisonment," said one. "By the example of Thomas Paine, whose vote is not suspect," said another, "by the example of that illustrious stranger, friend of the people, enemy of kings and royalty, and zealous defender of republican liberty, I vote for imprisonment during the war, and banishment at the peace." The philosopher Bancal, Paine's friend, ended a brief speech calling for imprisonment with a prophetic statement: "I think that this judgment will be that not of kings, who prefer a dead king to a humbled king, but the judgment of the nations and of posterity, because it is that of Thomas Paine, the most deadly enemy of kings and royalty, whose vote is for me the anticipation of posterity."

The final vote was announced in the evening of January 17—334 for imprisonment or banishment; 26 for death with a plea for clemency; 361 for death. By a majority of one it was ordained that the king must die.

The next day the Brissotins called for a reprieve on the ground that Louis' death would lead to war with England. The Mountain insisted that humanity required that the king be put to death at once. "We must shorten his agony," one deputy said. "It is barbarous to leave him in doubt as to his fate." On January 19 another member warned against hasty judgment. "One of your members, Thomas Paine," he said, "has an important opinion to communicate to you. Perhaps it will not be useless to learn from him what in England—" Angry shouts cut him short. To hell with England. And: There has been too much delay already. Paine, however, ascended the tribune and stood there quietly as his friend Bancal, secretary of the Convention, began to read a translation of his speech. Though technically recognized on the motion for reprieve, Paine wanted a commutation of sentence and he spoke for the American people, not the English.

"The decision come to in Convention yesterday in favor of death has filled me with genuine sorrow," Bancal read from Paine's manuscript. Suddenly Marat shouted from the floor, "I deny the right of Thomas Paine to vote on such a subject; as he is a Quaker, of course his religious views run counter to the infliction of capital punishment." The Convention exploded in confusion—What was a Quaker? Has the Convention been harboring a subversive in its midst?—as Marat had calculated. "My reputation . . . rests upon the impetuous outbursts of my soul, upon my cries of rage, of despair, of fury," he had once told Robespierre. He had cried out at the first line of Paine's speech, knowing that given an attentive audience Paine's prestige and powerful rhetoric might sway the timid and humane to change their votes. The storm passed, but Marat had planted a suspicion about Paine that could not be erased as Bancal continued reading. When Paine told the deputies that the future would probably regard their vote of death for Louis as one "performed from a spirit of revenge rather than from a spirit of justice," angry murmurs ran through the hall. "My solicitude for the welfare of France has now been transformed into concern for her honor," he said. These were harsh words; they took courage to deliver. After telling the Convention the harm Louis' death would do to France's reputation in the United States, upon whom she depended heavily for naval stores, he said, "If I were able to speak in the French language, I would appear in person at your bar, and, in the name of the American people, ask that Louis be reprised." Now another Mountaineer, Jacques Thuriot, jumped up and shouted, "This is not the language of Thomas Paine." Marat, who made up in energy what he lacked in height—he was five feet tall—rushed up to the tribune and asked Paine several questions in English, then shouted out to the deputies, "I denounce the translator. Such opinions are not

Thomas Paine's. The translation is incorrect." Another deputy in effect called Marat a liar. "It is a correct translation of the original, which I have read," he shouted. Pandemonium broke loose again. Paine finally managed to tell the Convention that Bancal was reading a faithful translation of his views, and the reading continued—for a paragraph more, then Marat again rushed to the center of the great hall and screamed, "Paine voted against the punishment of death because he is a Quaker." Paine answered, "I have been influenced in my vote by public policy as well as by moral reasons." The reading continued, but it was obvious that on this day Thomas Paine's words would influence no one.

On January 20 the Convention voted 380 to 310 that Louis XVI should be put to death within twenty-four hours. He died the next morning under the guillotine. For the first time in the history of Europe "a king had been put to death like an ordinary man." The rest of Europe decreed a war of extermination against regicides.

CHAPTER

20

THE TERROR BEGINS

BEFORE HE LEFT LONDON Paine had said to a friend, "If the French kill their king, it will be a signal for my departure, for I will not abide among sanguinary men." The French had killed their king, but Paine remained in Paris. Where else could he go? He had been exiled from England. The constant postponement of his return to America showed he yearned little for that place. That left France. True, the king had died, but the Revolution inside and outside France had yet to be consummated. He never referred to the king's death in his correspondence, any more than he had ever mentioned other distasteful aspects of the Revolution, like the August 10 uprising or the September Massacres.

The Convention declared war against England and Holland on 1 February 1793. On the same day a committee of four—Condorcet, Paine, Barère, and Fabre—was chosen to write an address to the English people. (Fabre, a sometime poet who had added d'Églantine to his surname, was a friend of Danton and Robespierre, and his inclusion on the committee as a watchdog signaled the declining power of the Brissotins.) Condorcet wrote the address. "As to Thomas Paine," said Barère, "it was too hard for him to communicate his ideas, being unacquainted with our language." In the address Condorcet castigated the "execrable authors" of the September Massacres, which he blamed "on the hypocritical and atrocious enemies of our true principles and our liberty." Fabre refused to sign and the people of England never received their animating address. Barère later burned the only copy.

Paine allowed nothing—the death of the king, the war against England, the aborted address—to depress him. "The tyrants of the earth are leagued against France; but with little effect," he wrote. "Although single-handed and alone, she still stands unshaken, unsubdued, unsubduable, and undaunted: for our brave men fight not, as the troops of other nations, like slaves chained to the oar of compulsory power. They fight freely, and for conscience's sake. The nation will perish to a man or be free."

His hopes were high in February. In March the sky fell in. The call for a nationwide draft provoked a formidable uprising in the Vendée, a department that fronted on the Atlantic. General Dumouriez, desperate for a victory in Belgium, engaged the Austrians at Neerwinden, a village thirty miles southeast of Brussels. He lost. Soon after the defeat he saw the Jacobins gain strength in the Convention. He tried, like Lafayette earlier, to get the army to march on Paris. The troops refused to follow. Dumouriez deserted to the Austrians; and the Brissotins, who had allied their cause to his achievements on the battlefield, saw their hold on the Convention further weakened. Simultaneous with his defection England began to build up a coalition that would soon align all Europe's major and minor powers against France.

These disasters were accompanied by another on the economic front. By the end of March the assignat had plunged to a quarter of its value in gold. Prices soared and scarcities of necessities like bread became widespread. The Jacobins called for price controls; the Brissotins, who had always favored loosening the economic controls that had existed under the crown, resisted but offered no scheme to bring down prices or make more bread. The moderates in the Plain looked more and more toward the Jacobins for guidance.

In an effort to bring some order out of this chaos, the Convention on April 6, the day after Dumouriez' defection, created a Committee of Public Safety, which was designed to give firmer direction to the nation's affairs than had up to now been exerted by the executive. The nine members were empowered to supervise, expedite, direct, and even veto the administration's activities. None of the leading Brissotins won a scat on the committee. Barère did and so did Danton. Robespierre did not. But the swing of power had begun—away from the obstructionist leadership of the Brissotins up toward the Mountaineers on their high benches.

2

Paine contributed little to the Convention's decisions after the king's death. His French, still embarrassingly awkward after five years in the country, continued to hamper participation in debate. Joel Barlow, who had come to Paris a year after Paine knowing nothing of the language, could now speak it fluently, and sometimes Paine had to use him as a translator. The people he moved among remained those who spoke English—Audibert, Condorcet, Brissot, Bonneville, Bancal. His social life centered around the Anglo-American community at White's Hotel. John Frost had given up his rooms there and returned to London soon after the king had been guillotined. Clio Rickman and he exchanged places. Frost would soon be in jail, found guilty of sedition. Rickman had been indicted for selling Paine's works; he came to Paris to escape prison.

The prestige Paine's name carried in Paris impressed Rickman, who had known Paine when he had been down and out in Lewes and London. "He was so plagued and interrupted by numerous visitors, and sometimes by adventurers, that in order to have some time to himself he appropriated two mornings in a week for his levee days," Rickman reported. "To this he was extremely adverse, from the fuss and formality attending it, but he was nevertheless obliged to adopt it."

Partly to escape importuning visitors, in January 1793 Paine rented a small house at St. Denis, a remote, peaceful section of Paris. Rickman admitted later that Paine also moved "into the country for his health, which by this time indeed was much impaired by intense application to business." This may have been a euphemistic way of saying Paine needed a "rest cure" because his drinking had got out of hand. Certainly the routine he led in the country resembled nothing out of his past. All his life Paine had been a late riser. Now he got up "about seven," according to Rickman. "After breakfast he usually stayed for an hour or two in the garden," then through the rest of the morning "he would talk of his boyish days, play at chess, whist, piquet, or cribbage, and enliven the moments by many interesting anecdotes." Later he would retire to his study to write. "Here he remained till dinner time; and unless he visited Brissot's family, or some particular friend in the evening, which was his less frequent custom, he joined again the society of his favorites and fellow boarders, with whom his conversation was often witty and cheerful, always acute, and improving, but never frivolous."

The fellow boarders were two young Englishmen, William Johnson and William Choppin, whom Paine had met in London. Joel Barlow and his wife often visited the retreat, as did Brissot and Bancal. When Mary Wollstonecraft came over to Paris she occasionally spent an evening with Paine "in conversation and any amusement [that] might tend to dissipate those gloomy impressions" that the course of events produced among idealistic supporters of the Revolution in 1793.

Paine always remembered the place in St. Denis with affection. It was the only residence of many in a footloose life he ever bothered to describe. "The house, which was enclosed by a wall and gateway from the street, was a good deal like an old mansion farmhouse," he said, "and the courtyard was like a farmyard, stocked with fowls—ducks, turkeys, and geese; which for amusement, we used to feed out of the parlor window on the ground floor. There were some hutches for rabbits, and a sty with two pigs. Beyond was a garden of more than an acre of ground, well laid out, and stocked with excellent fruit trees. The orange, apricot, and greengage plums, were the best I have ever tasted."

Day by day during his stay in this tiny Eden Paine's hopes for the Revolution crumbled away, but the reality of events was not allowed to intrude in the description of his sanctuary. "My apartments consisted of three rooms; the first for wood, water, etc.; the next was the bedroom; and beyond it the sitting-room, which looked into the garden through a glass door; and on the outside there was a small landing place railed in, and a flight of narrow stairs almost hidden by the vines that grew over it, by which I could descend into the garden, without going down stairs through the house."

Paine excelled at self-deception, and nothing displays the flaw better than his recollections of the house at St. Denis. Here from April to the end of the year, he endured not the idyllic peace he recalled but one of the most depressing periods of his life, a period when fear for the Revolution's success became transmuted into fear for his own life.

3

On April 5, the day Dumouriez defected, Marat, as president of the Jacobin Club, sent a philippic to all departments. "Friends, we are be-

trayed," he said. "To arms! There is counter-revolution in the government and in the National Convention. There, in the citadel of our hopes,
our criminal representatives pull the strings of the plot they have con-
trived with a horde of despots coming to cut our throats!" He warned that
if the nest of traitors within the Convention was not soon exterminated
a dictatorship would have to be imposed to preserve the Revolution.

No one wondered who the traitors might be. Brissot and his colleagues determined to check Marat and at the same time use him for their
own ends. If they could silence the most incendiary of the Jacobins, they
could reassert their hold over the Convention. On April 12 they called for
Marat's impeachment; the next day a compliant Convention charged
Marat with inciting the nation to riot and anarchy. He would be the first
deputy brought before the Revolutionary Tribunal. A dangerous precedent had been initiated that the Jacobins leaped to use. On April 15 the
Convention received a petition from the sections of Paris. It demanded
the arrest of twenty-two deputies who were accused of presenting the
people of Paris to the world as "men of blood." Brissot, Condorcet, and
several other of Paine's friends were on the list. Paine was not. When "the
violence of party" first appeared in the Convention, Paine said later, "it
was impossible for me to see upon what principle they differed—unless
it was a contention for power. I acted however as I did in America, I
connected myself with no party, but considered myself altogether a National Man." Though most of his friends were Brissotins, the sansculottes took Paine for what he said he was—a man above party.

The Convention ignored the petition with its list of twenty-two
names. It lay on the table as an ominous warning of what would happen
if the Brissotins, or Girondins as members of the enlarged faction were
now more often called, lost their hold over the legislature. Meanwhile,
the city waited for Marat's trial. Paine, who had just escaped being
labeled one of the "men of blood," involved himself in it for personal
rather than party reasons. He did not like Marat. His affected apparel—
Marat stumped about Paris dressed as a sansculotte, his shirt open at the
neck, a folded cloth tied around his head, pistols in his belt—could be
tolerated, but those skillfully timed interruptions that had ruined Paine's
speech in the king's behalf could not. He had met the man privately only
once. "Is it really possible that you believe in republicanism?" asked
Marat, who then thought a constitutional monarchy would work best for
France. "You are too enlightened to be the dupe of such a fantastic
dream." In the house at St. Denis Marat's fiery letter to the departments

was interpreted by Paine and his friends, according to one visitor, as a call to massacre all foreigners in France, especially Englishmen. Paine's two fellow boarders—Johnson and Choppin—were English and also impressionable.

The day Marat was impeached Paine set out to get him. He wrote a letter to the Jacobin Club reporting Marat's treasonable comment on republicanism. He sent a copy of the letter to *Le Moniteur*, the city's leading newspaper. Nothing came of the charge. William Johnson offered Paine a second chance. Johnson, who thought Paine would be one of the first to die if the Jacobins came to power, decided to kill himself. Standing at the top of the stairs in the house at St. Denis, he stabbed himself twice, then, as he lay in his friend Choppin's arms, he gave Paine his watch and Choppin a farewell message to the world. Johnson lived, but the melodrama could not be played out until Paine had used it to cut down Marat. He gave the story to Brissot, who gave it to the editor of his newspaper, *Le Patriote*—"much to the displeasure of the supposed suicide, which by the bye is now alive and well," a friend remarked. The story sounded better with Johnson dead, so that is the way it ran. "Before dying, he wrote with his trembling hands these words which we have read on a paper now in the hands of an eminent foreigner: 'I came to France in order to enjoy Liberty, but it has been assassinated by Marat. Anarchy is even more cruel than despotism. I cannot endure the doleful spectacle of the triumph of imbecility and inhumanity over talent and virtue.'"

Both Brissot and Paine should have known better than to tangle with the adept Marat. The naïve ploy boomeranged to his advantage. Over two-thirds of the seven-hour trial centered on Johnson's attempted suicide. A friend of Paine, Sampson Perry, said on the stand that Johnson was unbalanced. When an attempt to bring Brissot from the Convention failed, the "eminent foreigner" Paine was called to the stand. Shown the note, he replied through an interpreter that he could not "conceive what it has to do with the accusation against Marat."

PRESIDENT OF THE COURT: Did you give a copy of this note to Brissot?
PAINE: I let him see the original.
PRESIDENT: You gave it to him exactly as it is printed?
PAINE: Brissot could only have written this note according to what I read to him and what I told him. I observe to the court that Johnson stabbed himself twice only after learning that Marat was going to denounce him.
MARAT *(interrupting):* The young man did not stab himself because I was going

to denounce him, but because I wanted to denounce Thomas Paine.

PAINE: For a long time Johnson had anxieties. As for Marat, I only spoke to him once, in the corridors of the Convention. He told me the English people were free and happy. I replied that they suffered under a double despotism.

Johnson admitted on the stand that he had been ill when he wrote the note. He had read in a newspaper that Marat had said that all those who had voted "for the appeal to the people would be massacred. The friendship I had for Thomas Paine led me to want to kill myself." (Johnson mistakenly assumed Paine had voted for a plebiscite after the king's trial.) After Johnson had testified, the trial finally moved on to the charges against Marat. Marat explained away each of the accusations, pausing twice to ask the spectators not to applaud while he addressed the court. The jury deliberated forty-five minutes. In announcing the acquittal, the chairman interrupted his praise for "the intrepid defender of the rights of the people" to remark, "It is difficult to contain one's just indignation when one sees one's country betrayed on all sides."

A raucous throng escorted Marat through the streets to the Convention's hall, where he spoke to the deputies with unaccustomed reasonableness as Brissot and his followers looked on. Meanwhile, Paine had gone to dinner at White's Hotel with Clio Rickman. At his table sat "a stout young man of about thirty" named Captain Grimstone, an English aristocrat who had fled to France to escape debtors' prison. After dinner, "when the glass had freely circulated," Grimstone "loudly and impertinently" denounced Paine's principles. Paine answered quietly. "The captain became more violent, and waxed so angry," said Rickman, "that at length rising from his chair he walked round the table to where Mr. Paine was sitting, and there began a volley of abuse, calling him incendiary, traitor to his country, and struck him a violent blow that nearly knocked him off his seat."

It was a capital offense to strike a member of the Convention, and Grimstone was immediately arrested. Paine went to Barère, who, as a member of the Committee of Public Safety, had the power to issue passports. According to Rickman, Barère was reluctant to help, but Paine "persevered and at length accomplished it, at the same time sending Grimstone money to defray his traveling expenses; for his passport was of so short a duration that he was obliged to go immediately to the *messagerie nationale* [stagecoach office]."

4

In May Paine came as a witness to another trial—that of Francisco de Miranda, who had been arrested in March after the disastrous defeat at Neerwinden. Dumouriez had blamed the defeat on Miranda's failure to rally his troops when they fled from the battlefield. In April an investigatory committee of the Convention cleared Miranda of all charges. Brissot made Miranda's cause the party's and lavished him with praise on the Convention floor. His remarks stirred the Jacobins, but not in a way Miranda could appreciate. Marat had been forced to stand trial; it was time for one of the Girondins' heroes to suffer. When the committee chairman attempted to read aloud the report that exonerated Miranda, the Mountain shouted him down. The Convention voted on April 20 that he must be tried. That same day he was removed from house arrest and put in prison.

The trial began on May 12 and lasted four days. Sansculottes composed the jury. Paine was one of a stream of friends who testified for the ebullient South American. He had known him for ten years, casually in New York and London, well in France, especially in the past year when the scheme to extend the Revolution into Spanish America began to take shape. Until his arrest the government had considered sending him at the head of an expedition into South America, while George Rogers Clark invaded Spanish holdings in North America. Clark's offer to head a French force was "actually under consideration," Paine reported in February, and would undoubtedly be accepted in the event of a war with Spain. Miranda's role depended on the outcome of his trial.

"It is impossible for one man to know another man's heart as he knows his own," Paine said from the witness stand; "but from all that I know of General Miranda I cannot believe that he wanted to betray the confidence which the republic has placed in him, especially because the destiny of the French Revolution was intimately linked with the favored object of his heart, the deliverance of Spanish America—an object for which he has been pursued and persecuted by the Spanish Court during the greatest part of his life." Thomas Christie testified "that Miranda did not come to France as a necessitous adventurer; but believed he came from public-spirited motives, and that he had a large sum of money in the hands of Turnbull and Forbes," the banking house Christie represented in Paris. The jury, after hearing an eloquent defense by the lawyer who would soon be defending Charlotte Corday and Brissot de Warville, voted unanimously to acquit Miranda.

Christie's testimony had surprised Paine. He did not know that Miranda was independently well off and wondered how he had accumulated his fortune. He found out during a visit with Miranda a few days after he had been released from prison. They were reminiscing about the Nootka Sound controversy, and in a file of letters Miranda had handed him Paine spotted one that revealed Miranda had been a well-paid employee of the Pitt ministry during the episode. "The dispute was then compromised; and Pitt compromised with Miranda for his services by giving him twelve hundred pounds sterling, for this was the contents of the letter."

Miranda remained free only two months. He returned to prison in July as an early victim of the Terror and stayed there until January 1795, when Paine helped effect his release.

5

The day the Convention voted to try Miranda Paine abandoned hope for the French Revolution. "Had this Revolution been conducted consistently with its principles, there was once a good prospect of extending liberty through the greatest part of Europe; but I now relinquish that hope," he wrote Thomas Jefferson on April 20. "As the prospect of freedom is now much shortened, I begin to contemplate returning home." Not seriously, though. He learned that day from Lewis Morris, who was keeping an eye on his farm at New Rochelle, that the house and barn had burned down, and Paine knew he did not have "money enough to build another."

The emerging ascendancy of the Jacobins filled him with despair. They are men, he said, "who act without either prudence or morality." The sansculottes' denunciation of the twenty-two leading Girondins disgusted him. "Most of the acquaintances that I have in the Convention are among those who are in that list, and I know there are not better men nor better patriots than what they are." He who had been born and reared in the working class now found that he loved man but not men.

The sansculottes—"the people of Paris," as he called them—were an abomination. Their "tumultuous misconduct" terrified him. The French Revolution resembled nothing out of his past. No mobs had assailed the Continental Congress. The fifty-five or so men who constituted it met behind closed doors, and although tempers often flared they worked reasonably well together. Here in Paris some seven hundred deputies debated under the surveillance of a hooting gallery. Men could not deliberate in such an environment. Only at "a distance from Paris," he decided, away from the raucous virulence of the sansculottes, could the deputies begin to deal sanely with matters of state.

Paine had been warned by a Jacobin journalist when he returned to join the Convention that this was a new kind of revolution—"a revolution of the poor." The poor, he now found, were not gentlemen. "If every individual is to indulge his private malignancy or his private ambition, to denounce at random and without any kind of proof, all confidence will be undermined and all authority be destroyed," he said in a letter to Danton. "Calumny is a species of treachery that ought to be punished as well as any other kind of treachery. It is a private vice productive of public evils." This must have sounded a bit prim to Danton, a tough politician accustomed to hard in-fighting. Burke would have smiled to hear Paine talk thus of his beloved sovereign people.

The letter could not have surprised Danton, who must have been one of the first to sense that Paine had stepped in over his head the day he joined the National Convention. He lacked the toughness, the talent, the experience to operate as a politician. He knew nothing about France; during some five years there he had rarely ventured beyond the borders of Paris. He continued to think the French Revolution was a reincarnation of the American Revolution. When the Jacobins tried to impose price controls to protect the people from profiteers, Paine objected, holding that such controls had not worked in America. He failed to see that France was not America, that it had a long tradition under a centralized government strong enough to enforce its decrees throughout the nation, that price controls had been tried here before and they had worked.

In the midst of the debate over the proposed constitution the people of Paris forced the deputies to ponder other matters. Throughout the month of May the sansculottes had repeatedly petitioned for the expulsion of the twenty-two Girondin leaders and also members of the Committee of Twelve, a recent Girondin creation designed to smother rebellion in Paris. The committee had interfered in the government of Paris by banning secret meetings and arresting several leaders of the sansculottes. At three o'clock on the morning of May 31 the sound of the tocsin turned Paris into an armed camp. The city gates were swung shut and the sansculottes seized key positions that made Paris theirs. Throughout the day delegation after delegation presented its demands. The Convention bowed to a few but ignored the crucial ones. June 1 passed quietly. The sansculottes' leaders kept tight control of their rebellion; no blood was shed, no property molested. On the night of June 1 François Hanriot, newly appointed commander of the National Guard, surrounded the Convention hall with four hundred soldiers who had orders to arrest specified Girondin leaders, "in case the Convention refused to accede to the request of the citizens of Paris."

On Sunday, June 2, the Convention again balked at the people's demands. A delegation of sansculottes left the hall shouting, "To arms!" and orders were passed to the soldiers to forbid any deputy to enter or leave the hall. Paine came upon the scene at this point. He showed his pass to Hanriot, who glanced at it and told him he could use it to make curling papers. Danton happened to be nearby at that moment and warned Paine in English not to think of going in. His presence might inspire someone to add his name to the list of distrusted Girondins. (Inside the hall his mild-mannered friend and translator Lanthenas had been saved at a humiliating cost. Marat got his name struck from the list by announcing that he was "too chicken-hearted to be worth worrying about.") Paine remarked to Danton that Vergniaud had been right when he said that the French Revolution was like Saturn, it devoured its own children. Danton said, "Revolutions cannot be made with rosewater."

Inside, the deputies voted to march as a body out past the guards and through the vast throng of some eighty thousand citizens dressed in their Sunday garb who had come to watch the show. The deputies got as far as the doorway. When they saw that Hanriot's soldiers would fire if they persisted, they returned to their seats and voted to accept all the people's demands. Twenty-nine members, all Girondins, were expelled. Seventy-five others departed in disgust from the Convention. The Girondins, largely through their own obtuseness and their own repressive measures, had fallen victims of what Robespierre called "a moral insurrection" of the people.

6

After being blocked from the Convention, Paine returned to the house at St. Denis and drank himself into a stupor. "At present," Gouverneur Morris reported nearly a month later, "I am told he is besotted from morning till night. He is so completely down, that he would be punished, if he were not despised." On June 6 and again on June 19 seventy-five deputies signed petitions condemning the invasion of the Convention as a violation of the rights of man and an insult to the majesty of the people. Paine's name appeared on neither petition. Instead he passed his days "in those childish amusements that serve to keep reflection from the mind, such as marbles, scotch-hops, battledores, etc., at which we were all pretty expert," he said. "In this retired manner we remained about six or seven weeks, and our landlord went every evening into the city to bring us the news of the day and the evening journal."

In the meantime the Jacobins produced a new constitution for France. Condorcet's handiwork was revised in eight days, submitted to the Convention on June 10, and accepted two weeks later. Condorcet's production was condensed rather than fundamentally altered, though there were some significant changes. In the old litany "Liberty, Equality, and Fraternity," Equality now received precedence. Whenever the government violated the people's rights, insurrection became "the most sacred . . . the most indispensable" of their duties. "Any individual who usurps the sovereignty of the people," went one ominous article, "shall be instantly put to death by free men."

On June 21 "two special deputies from the city of Arras are admitted to the bar," Le Moniteur reported. "They declare, in the name of the citizens of the Commune of that city, that Donoux, Personne, Maignan, Vailet, and Thomas Paine, deputies to the Convention from the Department of Pas-de-Calais, have lost their confidence." On July 9 Paine's name was linked to a conspiracy against the government, but the tie was so tenuous that even his accuser ended by rejecting it. "Respect a pillar of liberty from the other hemisphere," he told the Convention; "do not condemn him, for he has been deceived." Had a hint been dropped that the Jacobins would welcome Paine and his pen? Tentatively Paine began to venture into the city in August. He stayed clear of the Convention and did not advertise his presence, but one day he met Barère on the street. The Committee of Public Safety had recently been reorganized. Danton, too moderate for the Jacobins who now ran things, had been dropped and Robespierre elected in his place. The little bespectacled bachelor disliked Barère, considered him a weakling, but recognized his skill as an administrator and his brilliance as an orator. Barère the day Paine met him on the street was one of the most powerful men in France.

Paine's stumbling French made conversation difficult, and when it became evident that Barère had more in mind than polite chitchat they went to the foreign office to find an interpreter. Barère wanted Paine's opinion "upon sending commissioners to the United States of America," where Citizen Genêt's interference in that nation's affairs had stirred up a storm against France. Paine welcomed the query as a sign the Jacobins did not plan to proscribe him, and a few days later he sent Barère a twenty-page essay saying he thought "it would be proper to send commissioners," adding that "Congress had done the same thing during the American war." In a follow-up letter he promoted Jefferson as a friend of France and Gouverneur Morris as an enemy not to be trusted. Paine rejected the idea that he be included in the commission, but the foreign office thought that with his talent to awaken "the minds of men" he might be useful, though "not as a principal agent," according to a department memorandum. "To succeed with Americans, one must combine much dignity, a perfect self-possession," qualities it was thought Paine lacked.

Famine threatened France in the late summer of 1793, and Barère asked Paine "if fifty or an hundred shiploads of flour could be procured from America." Paine assured him they could. He "showed us the way to go to work, he aided in the correspondence and worked hard in the foreign office to bring about this extensive purchase of food," Barère said later.

Finally in the autumn of 1793 Paine made up his mind to leave France. He would "return to America in one of the vessels which will start from Bordeaux in the month of October," he told Barère on September 5. He chose an auspicious day to make the announcement. On September 5 the sansculottes again invaded the Convention, and while the deputies sat meekly a spokesman shouted that the time had come to impose "equality, by signal acts of justice, upon traitors and conspirators. Make terror the order of the day!"

7

From the autumn of 1793 to the fall of Robespierre a year later the Committee of Public Safety, using decrees passed by the Convention at its bidding, ran the nation from a small room in the Tuileries. It reorganized, the army, fixed prices and wages, instituted a planned economy. Terror, as a weapon to enforce its will on the nation, became official policy. "The National Convention was fighting hand to hand with all Europe," Barère said later, justifying the policy carried out by the Committee. "At all points it was fighting the bands of royalists, fomenting conspiracies at home and corruption abroad. Resistance produced excesses, while the plots to be baffled justified the measures employed by the Convention. For the nation it was a question of liberty and independence; for France it was a question of her existence and nationality. All means of general defense became legitimate and just."

On October 3 the Girondin leaders were officially accused as traitors to the Revolution on the floor of the Convention. Paine was included in the denunciation, which referred to him as an Englishman, an ominous label that leagued him with France's enemy. He had, it was said, "dishonored himself by supporting the opinion of Brissot, and by promising us in his fable the dissatisfaction of the United States of America, our natural allies, which he did not blush to depict for us as full of veneration and gratitude for the tyrant of France."

October was a bloody month. Marie Antoinette was guillotined on the 16th. At her trial Pierre Manuel was asked what had guided his decisions. "I trusted in the morality of Thomas Paine, master in republicanism," he said. "I desired like him to see the reign of liberty and equality established on fixed and durable bases; I may have varied in the means that I proposed, but my intentions were pure." Manuel shortly thereafter went to the guillotine. On October 31 Brissot, Vergniaud, Fauchet, Gensonné— all Paine's friends—were carted off to the guillotine, all singing the "Marseillaise" as the people of Paris taunted them from the sidewalks. Soon Condorcet, Buzot, Pétion, Guadet, Lebrun, Roland, and Madame Roland were dead, by their own hand or the guillotine.

Sometime during the month Robespierre, who suspected all foreigners, jotted down a reminder to himself: "Demand that Thomas Paine be decreed of accusation for the interests of America as much as of France."

CHAPTER

21

PRISON

DURING SEPTEMBER AND OCTOBER Paine sat out the Revolution in St. Denis while the Convention paused in a busy schedule to dechristianize France. It decreed on October 5 that hereafter time would be marked by a Revolutionary calendar that eliminated saints' days, fast days, and Sundays and substituted new names for the traditional months. Years were dated from the creation of the republic and began in September (Vendémiaire) and in blocks of thirty days moved through Brumaire, Frimaire, Nivôse, Pluviôse, Ventôse, Germinal, Floréal, Prairial, Messidor, Thermidor, ending at the peak of summer with Fructidor.

In November Notre Dame was transmuted into the Temple of Reason and a ludicrous pageant ensued, featuring an actress in the role of the Goddess of Reason and girls wearing tricolor sashes who posed as Liberty and the Torch of Truth. The dechristianization program had received wide backing in the Convention—Girondins as well as Mountaineers had favored it—but the Feast of Reason at Notre Dame embarrassed the deputies. Robespierre, who believed in a Supreme Being, an afterlife, and man's immortal soul, thought it smacked of atheism. The Feast of Reason made him see that dechristianization had gone too fast and that unless slowed down, the provinces, where a deep-rooted Catholicism prevailed, might reject the Revolution. Late in November he shifted the Convention's gaze from religion to a greater evil—foreign conspirators. "I demand that a purifying scrutiny be held at the tribune, to detect and drive out all the agents of foreign powers who under their auspices have introduced themselves into this society," he told the Jacobin Club. Robespierre detested Englishmen and suspected them especially of working to undermine the Revolution.

While Robespierre sent the Convention out on a witch hunt that would soon sweep Paine into prison—though an American citizen he spoke with an accent that caused casual acquaintances to think of him as English—Paine remained in the bucolic surroundings of St. Denis working on a book to further the dechristianization program, one that at the same time he hoped would appeal to Robespierre. The book had long been on his mind. In 1776 John Adams had scoffed at the arguments against monarchy in *Common Sense* drawn from the Old Testament. "Do you seriously believe, Paine," Adams had asked, "in that pious doctrine of yours?" "The Old Testament!" Paine replied, laughing. "I do not believe in the Old Testament. I have had thoughts of publishing my sentiments of it, but, upon deliberation, I have concluded to put that off till the latter part of my life."

Paine continued a good Christian in public, knowing that to air his thoughts would ruin his career. Privately—with Hall and Kirkbride, possibly with Franklin and Jefferson—he spoke as he believed, reverently of God, contemptuously of Christianity. But even among friends he was wary and talked about God only when drink had loosened his tongue. Then suddenly in the latter part of 1793, so he later said, he decided to put his thoughts on paper. Why? Now that he saw friends moving into prison or under the blade of the guillotine, "and I every day expected the same fate, I resolved to begin the work." While Brissot and Madame Roland in prison were writing their memoirs and Condorcet in hiding was composing his *Outline of the Progress of the Human Mind*, he, too, wanted to use what might well be his last days to empty his mind of what would have been impolitic to publish earlier in America or England. And so in the late autumn and early winter of 1793 Paine turned out *The Age of Reason, Being an Investigation of Truth and of Fabulous Theology*.

This tidy explanation has a flaw. Both Lanthenas and Paine later said he began the book *early* in 1793, months before the dechristianization program got underway, not long after the move to St. Denis following the king's death. Sometime before March he turned over the completed chapters to Lanthenas, who translated them and then passed them along to the printer. At some point Lanthenas showed a proof copy of the work to Georges Couthon, who with Robespierre served as the Committee of Public Safety's informal overseer of French religion. Couthon "seemed offended with me for having translated this," Lanthenas recalled. Yet, curiously, Paine's creed was Couthon's and Robespierre's. He believed in God and in life after death, as they did. He, like they, feared "the people of France were running headlong into atheism," and he wanted "to stop them in that career." He worried, as they did, "lest in the general wreck of superstition, of false systems of government and false theology, we lost sight of morality, of humanity, and of the theology that is true."

Lanthenas must have misread Couthon's reaction. Couthon did not try to block publication of the book when it came out a few months later. Nor did Lanthenas cease to translate the manuscript when pages began arriving again from St. Denis in the autumn. The course of events had stopped Paine's pen—as it had before with other books—for nearly a half year, this time sending him into a deep depression. In April he told Jefferson "I now relinquish . . . hope" for the French Revolution. He spent June and July in an alcoholic stupor. In August he edged tentatively back into the world and occupied himself with an assignment Barère had handed him. Sometime in September or possibly early in October, as the dechristianization program got under way, he resumed his work. The political climate, though still oppressive, now appeared salubrious for his sort of work on religion. England and America might regard his views on religion as radical; in France they seemed moderate, bound to offend few among the enlightened men who now ran the country.

2

It was a small book—no more than fifty-five pages in the original English edition—filled with a moral outrage directed mainly at the Old Testament. "Whenever we read the obscene stories, the voluptuous debaucheries, the cruel and torturous executions, the unrelenting vindictiveness, with which more than half the Bible is filled, it would be more consistent that we called it the word of a demon than the Word of God." Out of this "tail of the heathen mythology" sprang the Christian Church, which is no more than "a species of atheism—a sort of religious denial of God," said Paine. "It professes to believe in man rather than in God. It is a compound made up chiefly of Manism with but little Deism, and is as near to Atheism as twilight is to darkness." And what would he substitute for the Christian Church, the word of God as found in the Bible? He gives the answer in a vibrant, quietly eloquent passage that takes some of the sting from the blunt invective in earlier parts of the book:

It is only in the CREATION that all our ideas and conceptions of a *Word of God* can unite. The Creation speaks a universal language, independently of human speech or human language, multiplied and various as they be. It is an ever-existing original, which every man can read. It cannot be forged; it cannot be counterfeited; it cannot be lost; it cannot be altered; it cannot be suppressed. It does not depend upon the will of man whether it shall be published or not; it publishes itself from one end of the earth to the other. It preaches to all nations and to all worlds; and this *Word of God* reveals to man all that is necessary for man to know of God.

As usual, Paine said nothing in *The Age of Reason* that had not been said before. Deism traced back two centuries in Anglo-American thought, and even a devout John Adams dipping into deistical works as a youth became convinced the Bible was filled with "whole cartloads of trumpery." Paine's uniqueness, it has been suggested, "consists in the freshness with which he comes upon very old discoveries, and the vehemence with which he announces them." Or as the prosecutor at his trial had put it, it was not so much the matter as the manner that made readers sit up. There was more to it than that. Prior to Paine's writings deism had been a respectable creed, cherished quietly in private by sedate gentlemen like Thomas Jefferson and Benjamin Franklin. It was a gentleman's religion—until Paine gave it to the people. The elite, a historian remarks, "saw Paine's latest offense as surpassing all his previous outrages; he had taken the polite periods of the comfortable Unitarian ministers and the skepticism of Gibbon, translated them into literal-minded polemical English, and thrown them to the groundlings. He ridiculed the authority of the Bible with arguments which the collier or the country girl could understand." *The Rights of Man* had undermined traditional deference of the plain people in politics; *The Age of Reason* repeated the offense in religion.

Paine committed still a worse sin—he tossed out Christianity with the Bible. Anglo-American deism never publicly broke with Christianity, which the eighteenth century regarded as a form of social control over an unruly population. Churchgoing might not cleanse the soul, but it could inculcate manners and morals. Paine, drawing on a French version of deism established by Voltaire, dismissed this sophistry. But he was too much the earnest puritanical Englishman to treat Christianity in the jesting manner of Voltaire. To him it was wicked rather than ridiculous. Style sets *The Age of Reason* apart from other religious tracts, but the moral attack upon Christianity makes it peculiarly Paine's, a book in neither the

Anglo-American nor the French tradition of deism. His awful reverence for God unnerved those who took their religion lightly.

3

Robespierre's attack on foreigners made it clear that France was not the place for Englishmen. Paine used what influence he still had with the government to finagle passports for his friends Johnson and Choppin. The passports arrived late one evening, and by four the next morning the two had set out for Basel. Two days afterward Paine heard a rapping at the gate during the night. He got up and looked out the bedroom window. "I saw the landlord going with the candle to the gate, which he opened, and a guard with muskets and fixed bayonets entered. I went to bed again, and made up my mind for prison, for I was then the only lodger." But the guards had come for Johnson and Choppin. A month later the guards came again. This time they carried away the landlord.

Sensing that the end was near, Paine the next day wound up his argument in *The Age of Reason*. He had abandoned hope for a world revolution months ago, but perhaps what had proved impossible in politics might be achieved through religion. "It is certain that in one point all nations of the earth and all religions agree," he wrote.

> All believe in a God. The things in which they disagree are the redundancies annexed to that belief; and, therefore, if ever a universal religion should prevail, it will not be believing anything new, but in getting rid of redundancies and believing as man believed at first. Adam, if ever there was such a man, was created a Deist; but in the meantime let every man follow, as he has a right to do, the religion and the worship he prefers.

Paine ended his manuscript there and celebrated with an evening in town. He dined at White's Hotel with several fellow Americans and spent an agreeable evening in talk until midnight. He had drunk moderately, but the mile-and-a-half trip to the empty house at St. Denis seemed too much at that hour. He took a room for the night at the hotel and went directly to bed. About four o'clock in the morning there was a rap on the door. Paine opened it to confront the manager of the hotel, five policemen, and two agents of the Committee of General Security. The manager interpreted. The agents said the Committee had ordered Thomas Paine and Anacharsis Cloots to "be arrested and imprisoned, as a measure of general security; that an examination be made of their papers, and those found suspicious put under seal and brought to the Committee of General Security."

Paine invited the group into his room. He said politely he would dress and "go with them immediately," then played for time. Achille Audibert, who had brought him from London to Calais, was in the hotel and Paine asked to be taken to his room, ostensibly because he wanted a friend to interpret for him, possibly because he wanted Audibert to shoot out to St. Denis and remove incriminating material from his papers. Through Audibert he told the agents his papers were with Joel Barlow, who lived in the Great Britain Hotel. It was now nearly eight A.M. The agents, "worn out with fatigue" and hungry, did not reach Barlow's until eleven.

Barlow said he had none of Paine's papers except one proofsheet of *The Age of Reason* and the first thirty-one pages of the manuscript. Suspicious, the agents asked Barlow "to open for us all his cupboards; which he did, and after having visited them, we . . . recognized that there existed no papers belonging to him; we also perceived that it was a subterfuge on the part of Citizen Paine," who, it was obvious, wanted Barlow "to accompany him and be present at the examination of his papers." The agents granted the request, "as Citizen Barlow could be of help to us," and on the way to St. Denis they picked up their own interpreter at the office of the Committee of General Security.

In the house at St. Denis they "gathered in the sitting room all the papers found in the other rooms of the said apartment." Paine showed the interpreter the final forty-four pages of manuscript of *The Age of Reason*. "*It is an interesting work; it will do much good,*" Paine quoted the interpreter as saying. He also made sure the interpreter saw an essay written at the request of Barère, entitled "Observations on the Commerce between the United States of America and France." The agents gave the papers "the most scrupulous examination," and, having found nothing suspicious in them, agreed "that no seal should be placed" upon them. They then drew up a detailed account of the events that had taken place since they had knocked on Paine's hotel door twelve hours earlier. All present signed the document. Paine's name had been spelled throughout "thomas peine"; no one had the energy or concern to correct it. At four in the afternoon, 28 December 1793, Citizen Thomas Paine was "led to jail; to which he complied without any difficulty."

4

En route to prison Paine's guard stopped to pick up Anacharsis Cloots. The two foreigners were checked into the Luxembourg as the early winter darkness settled in. The Luxembourg, once a palace, had been renovated to accommodate up to a thousand prisoners. The jailer, a thoughtful old gentleman named Benoit, tried his best to give the place the relaxed routine of a communal boardinghouse. Too relaxed, some thought. When the authorities heard that the female prisoners' easygoing habits had given the prison a reputation as "the principal brothel of Paris," they clamped down to the extent of separating the sexes.

Paine was put in a damp room on the ground floor, "level with the earth in the garden and floored with brick." Mornings went to cleaning the cell, otherwise his routine had changed little from St. Denis. The afternoons were to spend as he wished—to write, to wander about the common room visiting with fellow prisoners, to take his daily walk in the courtyard. Prisoners paid for their own board, and Paine had brought enough money to eat well.

During the early weeks he assumed that his stay would be brief. Paine was the third American to be imprisoned by the Committee of General Security. Thomas Griffiths of Baltimore had spent nine weeks in jail and William Haskins of Boston five weeks. Gouverneur Morris, proceeding cautiously, had done nothing officially to effect their release, apparently holding with the view later expressed by President Washington: "If the citizens of the U[nited] States in foreign countries commit acts, which are repugnant to their laws or usages, they certainly expose themselves to punishment." The community of Americans in Paris had successfully petitioned the Convention for their release, and these people had told Paine soon after he had reached the Luxembourg and while he was still allowed visitors from the outside that they planned to use the same tactics to pry him from jail.

Sixteen Americans, including Haskins and Griffiths, marched as a body into the Convention on January 20 to plead for Paine's release. President Marc Vadier invited "us to the honors of the session, which meant seats within the bar," Griffiths said, but courtesy ended there. "Not a few members hissed during the reading of our memorial in which

Paine's attachment to republican principles was asserted." The petition claimed Paine as an American. It observed that he had been invited to France, and that the closest examination of his papers corroborated "the purity of his principles in politics and morals." It ended with the signers promising that with Paine's release "we shall make ourselves warrant and security for his conduct in France during the short stay he may make in this land."

The petition was answered a few days later by President Vadier, who doubled as head of the Committee of General Security and had signed the order for Paine's arrest. He phrased the reply with care. France now depended upon America for critical supplies. It could not afford to offend that nation by imprisoning one of her most eminent citizens without good cause. Vadier solved the dilemma by refusing to concede Paine was an American. True, he had "powerfully cooperated with the American Revolution," but in fact he "is a native of England," and this alone is damning "enough to apply to him the measures of security prescribed by the revolutionary laws." Besides, his principles were not pure; he has been deluded by "false friends." He has "nobly contributed to the liberties" of America, "but he has not so happily seized the genius of our Revolution." Sampson Perry, an English friend and admirer of "the talents, the splendid talents of Mr. Paine," thought Vadier's response "deserved respect." Also, said Perry, "whatever might be Paine's claim to the esteem and hospitality of the country in which he was a friendly, an invited sojourner, the *letter* of the decree against foreigners reached him, for he was *born in a country at war with France.*"

Gouverneur Morris alone offered hope. If officially he claimed Paine as an American and accompanied the claim with a reminder of France's need for American friendship, the government might back down. Paine and Morris were not, as Paine acknowledged, "on terms of the best harmony" at the moment. Morris had never liked him; he now looked upon him with contempt. "In the best of times," he said, "he had a larger share of every other sense than of common sense, and lately the intemperate use of ardent spirits has, I am told, considerably impaired the small stock, which he originally possessed." His personal judgment aside, Morris believed that Paine could not legally claim American citizenship after sitting in the Convention. He advised him that if he lay "quiet in prison" he might have "the good luck to be forgotten." Paine preferred to fight for release and "contrary to my judgment" Morris on 14 February 1794 wrote of the case to Chemin Deforgues:

Thomas Paine has just applied to me to claim him as a citizen of the United States. These (I believe) are the facts which relate to him. He was born in England. Becoming subsequently a citizen of the United States, he there acquired a great celebrity through his revolutionary writings. In consequence he was adopted as a French citizen, and then elected a member of the Convention. His conduct since that period is out of my jurisdiction. I am ignorant of the reason for his present detention in the Luxembourg prison, but I beg you, (if there are reasons unknown to me which prevent his liberation) please be so good as to inform me of them, so that I may communicate them to the government of the United States.

"The application, it must be confessed, was neither pressing in its terms, nor urgent in its arguments," an admirer of Morris has remarked. "It was little more than a statement of facts." The foreign minister replied that Paine had in effect renounced his American citizenship when he accepted a seat in the Convention. He promised to refer the case to the Committee of Public Safety. The cool answer indicated that the government did not plan to release Paine. It wanted him in jail and, regardless of how frail its case against him, in jail he would stay. But why, Paine kept wondering as the days in prison mounted into months, did the government want him behind walls? "They have nothing against me—except that they do not choose I should be in a state of freedom to write my mind freely upon things I have seen." That was it, of course. Obviously, they did not plan to guillotine him—though to Paine it was not obvious—or they would have brought him to trial. They wanted only to silence him. Set free, he would return to America and with that awesome talent of his to rouse the people he would speak "freely upon things I have seen" at a time when France, at war with the world, needed American friendship as desperately as America had once needed hers. In November, when many thought that war with the United States might come any day, the Convention at Robespierre's bidding reaffirmed French friendship with America and decreed that all treaties between the two nations were still in effect. Robespierre, Sampson Perry remarked, "has more than once been heard to say 'America has not clearly pronounced her opinion concerning the French Revolution.'" Paine must not be allowed to swing that opinion against France. That is what Robespierre meant in the memorandum to himself when he indicated that putting Paine in prison would be "for the interests of America as well as France."

In another memorandum, this one resembling a catechism, Robespierre asked himself what were the obstacles blocking the Revolution's success?

The paid journalists, who mislead [the people] every day by shameless impostures.

What conclusion follows?

That we ought to proscribe these writers as the most dangerous enemies of the country, and to circulate an abundance of good literature.

Robespierre counted Paine among the dangerous "paid journalists." Prison seemed the easiest, safest way to remove him from circulation, but he would probably have been willing to buy silence with the guillotine if Paine had continued to push his case from inside prison. Fortunately, silence was imposed another way. A few days after Morris had sent the foreign minister's reply to Paine, "all communication from persons imprisoned to any person without the prison was cut off by an order of the police," Paine reported. "I neither saw, nor heard from, anybody for six months."

5

"From about the middle of March 1794 to the fall of Robespierre July twenty-ninth (9th Thermidor), the state of things in the prisons was a continued scene of horror," Paine recalled later. "No man could count upon life for twenty-four hours. To such a pitch of rage and suspicion were Robespierre and his committee arrived, that it seemed as if they feared to leave a man living. Scarcely a night passed in which ten, twenty, thirty, forty, fifty or more were not taken out of the prison, carried before a pretended tribunal in the morning and guillotined before night."

The bloodbath began without warning. Through January and February the days passed uneventfully. Paine wrote a little, talked a great deal, and wandered about the courtyard for exercise. He and Anacharsis Cloots spent part of every day arguing about revolutions and religion. Cloots berated Paine "for his credulity in still indulging so many religious and political prejudices." The new policy closed off communication with the outside world in mid-March. Soon after, Cloots's old friend Jacques Hébert, hero of the sansculottes, arrived at the Luxembourg under arrest. Robespierre had determined to free the Convention from the people of Paris, and eliminating the Hébertistes, as they were called, was the swiftest route to that goal. The trial was short; on March 24 Hébert and several cartloads of his followers, Cloots among them, went to the guillotine.

Robespierre had now fixed his eye on the moderate wing of the Convention, and six days after Cloots departed Danton with a group of *his* colleagues entered the prison. Danton spotted Paine soon after iron doors clanged behind him. "That which you did for the happiness and liberty of your country, I tried in vain to do for mine," he said, taking Paine's hand in his. "I have been less fortunate, but not less innocent. They will send me to the scaffold; very well, my friends, I shall go gaily." He did. The trial lasted four days, and Danton fought hard every minute of it for his life. The Dantonists were found guilty on April 5, and at five o'clock in the afternoon of what had been a beautiful warm day that had brought the lilacs in early bloom they were sent to the guillotine, Danton ebullient to the instant the knife fell.

Paine lived through these days certain that every one would be his last, yet he lived each with a quiet courage that impressed the other inmates. "His cheerful philosophy under the certain expectation of death," said one of them later, "his sensibility of heart, his brilliant powers of conversation, and his sportive vein of wit, rendered him a very general favorite with his companions of misfortune, who found a refuge from evil in the charms of his society. He was the confidant of the unhappy, the counselor of the perplexed; and to his sympathizing friendship many a devoted victim in the hour of death confided the last cares of humanity, and the last wishes of tenderness."

Somehow he managed to keep writing. He revised *The Rights of Man* for "the use and benefit of all mankind," adding a new preface that was smuggled out of the prison. He wrote poetry and sentimental reminiscences, an "Essay on Aristocracy," and another "Essay on the Character of Robespierre." With Cloots gone he found a new companion in an English surgeon named Bond. They talked during the day in Paine's cell. Paine often read aloud from *The Age of Reason*, "and every night when Mr. Bond left him, to be separately locked up, and expecting not to see Paine alive in the morning, he always expressed his firm belief in the principles of that book, and begged Mr. Bond should tell the world such were his dying sentiments."

Robespierre had promised that with the purge of Danton and his followers the bloodletting would end, and for two months it did. Then on June 10 the Convention passed a law that deprived judicial protection —aid of counsel, the right to summon witnesses—to anyone accused of counterrevolution and allowed judges in their decisions the choice of only acquittal or death. The law gave birth to the Great Terror, which ended only when Robespierre fell from power on July 27. The Great Terror spanned forty-seven days. During it 1376 people of Paris were guillotined, over one hundred more than had been executed during the preceding sixteen months. From the Luxembourg alone on a single night in July 160 inmates went to the scaffold. "Many a man whom I have passed an hour with in conversation I have seen marching to this destruction the next hour, or heard of it the next morning," Paine recalled, "for what rendered the scene more horrible was that they were generally taken away at midnight, so that every man went to bed with the apprehension of never seeing his friends or the world again."

The first hint of the Great Terror came on June 19 when the genial jailer Benoit was replaced by a disciplinarian. The prison had become so packed with accused that the Committee of Public Safety feared a revolt under Benoit's lax rule. The new jailer imposed a tight surveillance. The courtyard was closed for strolling. Prisoners were forbidden to approach open windows on the upper floors, from which two inmates had already jumped to their deaths. In a surprise raid on all cells sharp instruments such as knives and forks were taken away and wooden ones given in their place. Paine had enough warning to hide his money behind the lock in the cell door.

Late in June Paine finally broke under the strain of six terrifying months in prison. He fell ill with a fever that "nearly terminated my existence." He was moved to a larger cell, where for five weeks he lay on a cot scarcely aware "of what was passing, or of what had passed." His cellmates, three Belgians, attended him around the clock; the prison doctor looked in only occasionally, for Paine was being well cared for by two fellow prisoners—Dr. Graham, an English physician, and Mr. Bond, the surgeon who had become his friend. The weeks left "a blank in my remembrance of life," Paine said. "My illness rendered me incapable of knowing anything that passed either in the prisons or elsewhere; and my comrades also made it a point all the time that my recovery continued doubtful not to inform me of anything that was passing. The first news they informed me of was the fall of Robespierre." Ironically, on the day Robespierre fell, July 27, he was brought to the Luxembourg. The jailer refused to receive him, nor would any jailer in Paris. He was executed the next day, and from that time on Paine's health began to mend.

6

Ten days after Robespierre's death Paine asked the government to free him. Still weak from his illness, he feared he "should not express myself with the energy I used formerly to do," and he did not. "That hypocrite" Robespierre was the strongest epithet he could call up. Though he wrote without self-pity, Paine made clear he had sacrificed "private tranquillity" during the past seven years "in the hope of seeing a Revolution happily established in France, that might serve as a model to the rest of Europe." He had "silently suffered" nearly eight months in prison and yet felt vindictive toward neither the government nor the people. "It is not the nation but a faction that has done me this injustice," he said. He emphasized his American citizenship, then ended "wishing fraternity and prosperity to France, and union and happiness to her representatives." For Paine it was a subdued, even tactful letter.

He sent it to the National Convention and a copy to the Committee of Public Safety. Neither responded. The day he wrote it, August 7, François Lanthenas used his recently published translation of *The Age of Reason* as an excuse to make an appeal for his friend. No response. A few days later Achille Audibert pled to Thuriot for Paine's release. Thuriot, who with Marat had interrupted Paine's plea for the king's life, now served on the still powerful Committee of Public Safety. "A friend of mankind is groaning in chains," Audibert told him, a friend who had been among the first who "dared to say that Robespierre was a monster to be erased from the list of men." No response. The enemies Paine had made still held power and, perhaps fearing his pen, preferred him in jail.

The government's pressing silence was relieved for Paine on August 17 when he spotted a garbled story in the newspapers. "As I believe none of the public papers have announced your name right, I am unable to address you by it," he wrote, "but a *new* minister from America is joy to me and will be so to every American in France." No matter who the replacement, he was bound to be an improvement over Gouverneur Morris, "*my inveterate enemy.*" The next day he learned the new minister's name—James Monroe. He spent the day jubilantly building his case for release in a long letter, rehearsing his career in France since election to the National Convention. He mentioned the Great Terror—that time when it seemed "to be a determination to destroy all the prisoners without regard to merit, character, or anything else"—but refused to linger over it. "Thank God times are at last changed," he said. With Monroe's "timely arrival" he could almost begin to taste his freedom.

A week passed. No response. Paine tried to seem insouciant in the next letter. "Having nothing to do but sit and think, I will write to pass away time, and to say that I am still here," went the opening sentence, but his anxiety burst out a few lines later. *"I shall be very glad to receive a line from yourself to inform me in what condition the matter stands,"* he wrote with emphasis. Monroe must do something "for me *now.*" Years among the French had made Paine suspicious of those mercurial people. "There is now a moment of calm," he said, but "the loss of a battle to the northward or other possible accident may happen to bring" about a new hurricane. "I am not out of danger till I am out of prison."

Paine heard nothing from Monroe all of September. Off and on, members of the Committee of General Security came to the Luxembourg to examine prisoners and clear those they thought safe for release. They ignored Paine on these visits, but on one trip they gave a clean bill of health to his Belgian cellmate Joseph Vanhuele. In desperation Paine wrote a brief note to the Committee: "Citizens Representatives: I offer myself for examination. Justice is due to every man. It is justice only that I ask. THOMAS PAINE." No response. He sent a second note, which the now free Vanhuele carried directly to the Committee, handing it over to Bourdon de l'Oise, the man whose denunciation on the Convention floor had sent Paine to prison. "Bourdon de l'Oise is the most inveterate enemy you can have," Vanhuele reported back. "The answer he gave me when I presented your letter put me in such a passion that I expected I should be sent back again to prison." (To strike a deputy was still a capital offense.)

By now Paine was "entirely without money" and had to borrow to buy food and firewood. From Peter Whiteside, friend from the bridge-building days in London, he heard that Monroe "has no orders respecting you" and that in America "you are not considered either by the government, or by the individuals, as an American citizen." Paine responded to this news with a forty-three-page essay regarding his citizenship. It was a lawyer's brief and a good one. He argued that the Constitution's article depriving a man of his citizenship if he accepts any title, place, or office from any foreign king, prince, or state does not apply to him. He accepted no honors but honorary citizenship from France, "took no oath of allegiance to France, or any other oath whatever," but only gave "his assistance in a convention chosen by the people, for the purpose of forming a government *de nouveau* founded on their authority." But all of this, Paine says around page forty, is beside the point, for "I speak as if the Federal government had made some declaration upon the subject of my citizenship," which it has not; "your saying that you have no order respecting me is a proof of it." Since Monroe had no instructions *not* to reclaim Paine, then he must have the discretionary power to reclaim him. Why, then, does he not use that power?

The confident tone was tinged with bluff. If Whiteside's information was correct, he confessed later, "my situation was without hope." He was now, in terms of both age and time served, nearly "the oldest inhabitant behind these walls." It looked as if he must live out his life in the Luxembourg. Monroe's silence and the other rebuffs sent Paine onto the sick list again. "The weather was becoming damp and cold, fuel was not to be had, and [an] abscess in my side (the consequence of these things and of the want of air and exercise) was beginning to form," he said. His larder was nearly empty. A lack of money reduced him to begging "for three or four candles, a little sugar of any kind, and some soap for shaving." Other prisoners had friends and families to supply them. "This is not the case with me," he said. "I have no person I can apply to but the American minister," and he refused to answer him.

Paine heard from Monroe on October 4. It had taken a month before his credentials were recognized by the French government and he could turn to Paine. He wrote to him in mid-September, but for some reason it took over two weeks for the letter to cross Paris and arrive in Paine's cell. It carried good news. Monroe said flatly he considered Paine an American citizen. "By being with us through the Revolution, you are of our country, as absolutely as if you had been born there; and you are no more of England, than every native of America is." Your letter, said Paine in reply, "has relieved my mind from a load of disquietude."

Another silence followed. The abscess in Paine's side continued to suppurate. When the sun went down he had to sit in the dark, for "I have not a candle to burn and cannot get one," he said. "Fuel can be procured only in small quantities and that with great difficulty and very dear." He was nearly fifty-eight years old. On October 13 he wrote Monroe a long, bitter letter, saying his patience was exhausted. For weeks friends kept saying "I shall be in liberty in two or three days," but the Luxembourg still claimed him. He had heard rumors "that I should have been in liberty long ago if the minister could have reclaimed me as an American citizen," the implication being that Monroe either could not or would not. "In short, sir, the case is now arrived to that crisis, that for the sake of your own reputation as a minister you ought to require a positive answer from the Committee." Monroe accepted the tongue lashing with understanding. Did Paine want him to take the case before the Committee of General Security regardless of the risk? Yes, replied Paine, "I cannot rest any longer in this state of miserable suspense, be the consequences what they may." As a precautionary measure, Paine suggested that Monroe "invite some of the Committee to your house" and air informally the arguments he planned to present formally. Monroe followed that advice and after the meeting had taken place passed word to Paine that it had gone well. Paine was elated and simultaneously cautious. "Matters and even promises that pass in conversation are not quite so strictly attended to here as in the country you come from," he said.

Monroe presented his petition for Paine's release to the Committee of General Security the day after his informal meeting. He was promised "an answer as soon as possible." That night the committee met with the Committee of Public Safety, and the next morning Monroe received an order for Paine's release. "I forwarded it immediately to Luxembourg, and had it carried into effect," he reported to the secretary of state back home, "and have the pleasure now to add that he is not only released to the enjoyment of liberty but is in good spirits."

Paine left the Luxembourg on November 4, ten months and nine days after his arrest.

CHAPTER

22

MR. MONROE'S DIFFICULT GUEST

MONROE REGARDED PAINE, who was more than twenty years his senior, as something of a national monument that deserved being preserved with affection. He invited him after the release from prison to stay as a guest in his house—he had taken over the one Gouverneur Morris had occupied—with him and his "young, beautiful, and affable" wife, unaware of Paine's talent for parlaying a casual invitation into a long stay. Over a year later Monroe wrote with resignation that it looked as though Paine would be his guest "till his death or departure for America, however remote either the one or the other event may be."

Paine's eagerness to see the city he had been denied for nearly a year made it impossible to keep him in bed, despite his feeble condition and the running abscess on his side. Two days after his release he was out and roaming the streets. As he tramped through the frozen slush—Paris was in the midst of one of the coldest winters of the century— he saw that the old elegance of the city had vanished. Trash littered the streets and empty shops everywhere caught his eye. Food and fuel were rationed and the allotments were meager. Monroe received for his staff of fourteen only two pounds of bread a day, less than a single Frenchman consumed in the old days. War and winter and the Terror had imposed misery upon all citizens of Paris, not just those inside the Luxembourg.

During one walk Paine met Hamilton Rowan, an Irishman of wit, charm and "commanding presence" with whom he had worked when there was hope France would subsidize a rebellion in Ireland. Rowan had mixed news about the progress of the revolution in Great Britain. People talked of calling a national convention of the sort Paine had proposed.

307

Sales of *The Rights of Man* continued high despite the ban, and *The Age of Reason*, in the face of even stronger efforts at suppression, was also selling briskly. Sunday schools, created to teach illiterate children to read the Bible, had, to the dismay of the devout, led the youngsters to sharpen their skills on Paine's works. The government tried to cope with the awakening masses by prosecuting their leaders. John Frost had been among the first after Paine to be tried. Erskine defended him, lost again, and Frost ended up serving an eighteen-month sentence that nearly killed him. Several victories against printers and booksellers followed; then in October 1794, as Paine negotiated for his freedom, the government put on trial Thomas Hardy, John Horne Tooke, Thomas Walker, and other leaders of the popular societies. Erskine defended them and this time won. All were acquitted. Paine had nothing to say about the contrast between the French republic's masquerade of judicial procedure during the Terror and monarchical England's state trials—all with juries, open to the public, and with defendants aided by competent counsel.

2

On December 8 the National Convention voted to recall seventy-three deputies who had been expelled during the Terror. Antoine Claire Thibaudeau, a moderate Jacobin still in his twenties, spoke for Paine, calling for repeal of the decree against foreigners that had led to his expulsion. The Americans in Paris, particularly Monroe, with whom he had become friendly, had asked Thibaudeau to testify for Paine. "I have never heard a single reproach uttered against Thomas Paine," he told the Convention, a rhetorical excess that the moment called for. "His expulsion from the Convention was merely the fruit of intrigue." The decree was repealed and Paine readmitted to the Convention, which continued to make amends for its past treatment of him. On 3 January 1795 it heard a plan to award pensions to citizens who had performed great literary service during the Revolution. Paine's name headed the list. Marie Joseph Chénier, whose more eminent brother had been guillotined on July 25, two days before Robespierre fell, presented the scheme, with the usual effusions. Thomas Paine, that "cherished colleague of all the friends of humanity," had used "the weapons of *common sense* against the sword of tyranny, the *sacredness of the rights of man* against the Machiavellism of

English policies." Among his "immortal works" *The Age of Reason* went unmentioned; the title might have caused laughter among deputies who had just lived through a year of terror.

Paine accepted these flourishes with perhaps bemused suspicion. He never received a sou from the proposed pension. He did not bother to attend the Convention during the first half of 1795. He did the little he could to promote the release from prison of Mme. Lafayette, who from her "abyss of misery" thanked him for taking a "great interest in my situation." He used his influence to help friends get passports from the foreign office. Otherwise he spent his time talking and writing and trying to decide whether to remain in France or return to America.

Early in January the Convention voted that an effort should be made to promote better political and commercial relations with the United States. This information "is of such great importance to my country," Monroe wrote to the Committee of Public Safety, "that I think it expedient to send it there officially, by some particularly confidential hand; and no one seems to be better fitted for this errand than Thomas Paine." The committee rejected flatly the suggestion, for Paine's post as deputy in the Convention would "not permit him to accept it." Monroe's proposal was inept, naïve, and even ridiculous. Paine's qualifications as an envoy for France had less now, after his ten months in prison, to recommend him than they had earlier when the foreign office had considered and rejected him as an agent to America. How could a man who had been brutally treated be trusted to represent France abroad? Moreover, Monroe should have known that Paine was no longer universally admired in America. His ties with the French Revolution made him odious to the Federalists; *The Age of Reason* made him detested by the devout.

Monroe had said that "if this affair can be arranged," Paine would "leave for America immediately *via* Bordeaux, on an American vessel, which will be prepared for him." Why, if Paine hungered for sight of the shores of America, did he linger in France? The trip was risky; Paine ranked high on Britain's list of wanted felons, and her navy would have been delighted to remove him from any ship that carried him. Then, too, Paine lived a comfortable life in Paris. The Convention owed him 1800 livres in back pay when he went to prison, and presumably he received it upon his release, and readmission to the Convention put him back on the payroll as deputy. Finally, the Convention was once again to decide on a constitution for the nation, and Paine, who believed that the lack of one had caused "the violences that have since desolated France and injured the character of the Revolution," wanted to have a hand in perfecting it.

These were his excuses for staying. The real reasons he kept to himself. If free to choose he would have settled down happily in London, but he had been exiled from England and the government showed no sign of lifting the ban. Paine talked of America as a refuge but rarely as the homeland he yearned to see again. The United States was a symbol for him rather than a place to live, a land where the principles he cherished were practiced but also a provincial land with more cows than people, a desolate spot for a man who seemed happiest amidst the turmoil of a London or a Paris. In a sense America was for him the Luxembourg enlarged. He would put off returning as long as he could find a plausible excuse to do so.

3

Paine came to France convinced it would take only a written constitution based on the rights of man to put the nation on the road to Eden. He still thought so eight years later. "Had a constitution been established," he said, "the nation would then have had a bond of union, and every individual would have known the line of conduct he was to follow. But, instead of this, a revolutionary government, a thing without either principle or authority, was substituted in its place; virtue and crime depended upon accident; and that which was patriotism one day became treason the next."

Now in the Year III (1795) of the republic a Convention cleansed of democratic Jacobins and idealistic Brissotins was about to give the nation a constitution that reflected the views of a new breed of leaders, men like Count François de Boissy d'Anglas, who had told the Convention, "We should be governed by the best. The best are those who are the most educated and the most interested in maintaining the laws. With few exceptions, you will find such men only among those who [own] property." In the new constitution citizenship was restricted to soldiers and those who paid direct taxes. Direct elections were eliminated; citizens voted for electors—some thirty thousand Frenchmen owned enough property to qualify as electors—who in turn chose a two-house legislature consisting of a Council of Five Hundred, all at least thirty years old, and a Council of Elders, consisting of 250 married or widowed gentlemen at least forty years of age. The Elders in their turn chose a Directory of five men, who also had to be over forty, a restriction that would have kept from power all but two of the twelve members who sat on the Committee of Public Safety in Robespierre's day. The Directory had the power to appoint ministers, issue decrees, run the war, diplomatic affairs, and the national police. It was the supreme authority in local administration.

The constitution had been created against a tumultuous backdrop. Between April 18 when a committee of eleven had been chosen to draw up the document and June 23 when it was presented to the Convention a well-organized mob had invaded the Convention's hall and terrorized the deputies for three days before the uprising was crushed and order restored. Paine had deplored an earlier invasion of the Convention by the sansculottes. Now, with his eye on a constitution "repugnant to reason and incompatible with the true principles of liberty," he ignores their rampages in his first publication since leaving prison, *Dissertation on the First Principles of Government.* Most of Paine's writings reflect events of the moment. This one does not. No hint of rioting sansculottes, no odor of the Terror penetrates here. Paine later explained why. He wrote the pamphlet soon after coming to France, in the first flush of revolution, and directed it "to the people of Holland, who . . . were determined to accomplish a revolution in their government." He resurrected it now as an apt sermon for deputies who had forgotten first principles. It excels as a gloss on the phrase "all men are created equal." Paine did not push his views to absurdity. "That property will ever be unequal is certain," he said. There are some men, he went on, surely speaking of himself, "who, though they do not despise wealth, will not stoop to the drudgery or the means of acquiring it, nor will be troubled with it beyond their wants or their independence." Others, who are not to be denigrated, make the seeking of property "the sole business of their lives, and they follow it as a religion." Paine complains only when property is "criminally employed [as] a criterion for exclusive rights." To make property the criterion of the right to vote "is dangerous and impolitic, sometimes ridiculous, and always unjust," he says; "it exhibits liberty in disgrace, by putting it in competition with accident and insignificance." This thought is followed with one of the apt and earthy metaphors that might have startled Paine's French audience: "When a broodmare shall fortunately produce a foal or a mule that, by being worth the sum in question, shall convey to its owner the right of voting, or by its death take it from him, in whom does the origin of such a right exist? Is it in the man, or in the mule? When we consider how many ways property may be acquired without merit, and lost without crime, we ought to spurn the idea of making it a criterion of rights."

On July 7 Paine appeared in the Convention hall for the first time since the fall of the Brissotins two years earlier; he had come to speak on the constitution. He stood silently on the tribune, as he had two and a half years earlier when pleading for the king's life, while a translation of his speech droned on to the audience. He urged the deputies in their reaction against the Terror and the insurrections of the sansculottes not to forget what the Revolution was all about. "In my opinion," he said, "if you subvert the basis of the Revolution, if you dispense with principles, and substitute expedients, you will extinguish that enthusiasm and energy which have hitherto been the life and soul of the Revolution; and you will substitute in its place nothing but a cold self-interest, which will again degenerate into intrigue, cunning and effeminacy." Muttering rippled through the hall during the reading of the speech. No one praised it and some objected strongly to the routine motion that it be printed.

Soon afterward the constitution of 1795 was sent to the people and ratified by them. In October elections were held for deputies to the Council of Five Hundred and the Council of Elders. Paine was chosen for neither body. His three years as a legislator had ended. The rights of man had gone out of fashion in France.

4

Paine emerged from prison to find that *The Age of Reason* had stirred ripples of anger in France and great waves in England and the United States. John Adams summarized one reaction: "The Christian religion is, above all the religions that ever prevailed or existed in ancient or modern times, the religion of wisdom, virtue, equity and humanity, let the blackguard Paine say what he will." Others, though they liked the book, found it unsuitable for plain people. "For the sake of public and private comfort and genial happiness," said one man, "it is better not to disturb the devout mind by fanciful and newfangled schemes of belief [which] should be open only to the eyes of the learned!" The public answers that had accumulated when Paine left prison were all by clergymen, pious gentlemen who "contend and wangle, and *understand* the Bible," said Paine; "each understands it differently; but each understands it best; and they have agreed in nothing but in telling their readers that Thomas Paine understands it not."

Paine understood the Bible as a fraud, and he had said so in *The Age of Reason*. But he had written that effusive essay under fearful circumstances and without a copy of the Bible handy. Living with the Monroes, he settled down with a copy in his lap to produce a fuller, more orderly indictment. The detailed analysis he now wrote became an elaborate footnote to previous remarks, and as footnotes tend to do, it stretched half again the length of the text. It was published in October as the second part of *The Age of Reason*.

This time he moved slowly from one Biblical book to the next, pointing to signposts along the way. "I proceed to examine the authenticity of the Bible, and I begin with what are called the five books of Moses. . . . Having thus far shown . . . that Moses was not the writer of these books . . . I proceed to the book of Joshua, and to show that Joshua is not the author of that book." In the solemn march he pauses occasionally, sometimes for a short sermon, sometimes to toss a taunt at clergymen ("Is it because ye are sunk in the cruelty of superstition, or feel no interest in the honor of your Creator, that ye listen to the horrid tales of the Bible, or hear them with callous indifference?"), then, with a "but to return to my subject," moves on. No wit or homely metaphors lighten this deadly serious attack, but the judgments are lively. The Book of Ruth gets short shrift: "an idle, bungling story, foolishly told, nobody knows by whom, about a strolling country girl, creeping slyly to bed with her cousin Boaz. Pretty stuff indeed, to be called the Word of God." Moses comes forth as one of the world's most "detestable villains," Solomon as a "witty, ostentatious, dissolute and at last melancholy" man who "lived fast and died, tired of the world, at the age of fifty-eight." The Book of Jeremiah is "a medley of unconnected anecdotes," and that of Isaiah "one of the most wild and disorderly compositions ever put together."

No hint of doubt tarnishes the pages. Paine insists he has "detected and proved" that none of the books were the Word of God, that none were written by their supposed authors, that all were riddled with contradictions and suspect even as history. Critics who assailed the first part of *The Age of Reason* "must return to their work, and spin their cobweb over again," he says when done. "I have now gone through the Bible, as a man would go through a wood with an axe on his shoulders and fell trees. Here they lie; and the priests, if they can, may replant them. They may, perhaps, stick them in the ground, but they will never make them grow."

Paine cuts deeper when he gets to the New Testament. "Were any girl that is now with child to say, and even to swear it, that she was gotten with child by a ghost, and that an angel told her so, would she be believed?" he asks contemptuously. "Certainly she would not." And what does such a fairy tale teach us?—"to believe that the Almighty committed debauchery with a woman engaged to be married, and the belief of this debauchery is called faith." He sneers even at the moral injunctions dispensed. "It is assassinating the dignity of forbearance, and sinking man into a spaniel" to ask him to turn the other cheek after being struck. "Morality is injured by prescribing to it duties that, in the first place, are impossible to be performed." Does Christianity offer the world nothing of value? Nothing, says Paine. "Of all the systems of religion that ever were invented, there is none more derogatory to the Almighty, more unedifying to man, more repugnant to reason, and more contradictory in itself, than this thing called Christianity," he concludes. "I here close the subject . . . certain, as I am, that when opinions are free, either in matters of government or religion, truth will finally and powerfully prevail."

5

Paine appears to have finished the second part of *The Age of Reason* early in August and then gone on a brief vacation while the manuscript was translated and set in type in English and French. He expected a large sale and ordered fifteen thousand copies for the American market alone. He underwrote the venture himself, probably in part with one of the loans Monroe "from time to time" made him. In August he "was out of cash and I know no method of supplying myself, but by having recourse to your friendship," he told Monroe. Eventually these loans totaled upward of 250 louis d'or, a debt that went unpaid until 1831, when Congress settled the account after Monroe had died in bankruptcy.

Paine's vacation began with a boat trip to Sèvres, and then on to Versailles, where he planned to remain for a while, but a week later he was back in Paris a very sick man. A drinking spree to celebrate completion of *The Age of Reason* may have helped to shatter his fragile health. Monroe was once praised by an acquaintance for "his conduct in preserving Tom Paine from the course of life he was too much attached to," an ambiguous remark that seems to refer to Paine's drinking. "At first he drank as he pleased, and therefore to excess," an unfriendly biographer remarked of Paine's stay with the Monroes. "But for his own good, as well as for the reputation of the mission, the minister found it necessary to stint him. Yet what he could not get in the house, he got out of it."

On the day that Paine, deathly pale, showed up on the doorstep the Monroes were in the midst of preparing for a long vacation. They planned to visit their young daughter who was in a boarding school at St. Germain. Paine's return caused them to cancel the trip. Mrs. Monroe found a nurse "who had for him all the anxiety and assiduity of a sister. She neglected nothing to afford his ease and comfort, when he was totally unable to help himself. He was in the state of a helpless child who has its face and hands washed by its mother." It seemed clear he was a dying man. In mid-September Monroe judged that "the prospect now is that he will not be able to hold out more than a month or two at the furthest."

Paine, too, thought he was about to die, and on September 24, hardly able to hold a pen in hand, he emptied his mind of accumulated bitterness in a long, acerbic letter to James Madison. "I owe this illness (from which I have not much prospect of recovering) partly to Robespierre and partly to Mr. Washington." Why, he asked, had the president done nothing to get him released from prison? "He ought to have said to somebody— inquire into the case of Mr. Paine and see if there is anything we can do for him." But he did nothing. "I ought not to have suspected Mr. Washington of treachery but he has acted towards me the part of a cold blooded traitor."

Paine had been storing up the vitriol in that last sentence for nearly a year, allowing it to emerge on paper only once before—in a quatrain composed soon after leaving prison:

> Take from the mine the hardest, roughest stone,
> It needs no fashion, it is WASHINGTON.
> But if you chisel, let your strokes be rude,
> And on his breast engrave *ingratitude.*

Later he wrote directly to Washington about his imprisonment, demanding an explanation for his "cool and callous" attitude. Monroe got wind of the letter and knowing it would compromise his position with the president told Paine he must not send it. Paine "did not entertain a favorable opinion" of this demand, as Monroe put it, but "he finally agreed" to withdraw the letter. Now that it appeared that he might die before speaking his mind, he reneged on the promise and surreptitiously sent the letter off, "for though my residence in Mr. Monroe's house makes a delicacy in the case I cannot abridge myself of my independence upon that account."

In November a visitor found Paine still suffering "incurably from the torture of an open wound in the side, which came," so the physicians told him, "from a decaying rib." Rumors by then had flown to England and America that Paine had died. At least twice earlier the world had been told of his death—his last words, according to one of the broadsides passed around England, were "I am a notorious liar"—but this time the story seemed true. James Madison assumed it was so as late as January 1796. However, by then Paine was on the mend and finding new ways to make life difficult for his host. This time he focused on the Jay Treaty.

Grievances had piled up to the point where the United States and Great Britain verged on war when John Jay arrived in London as Washington's emissary in the summer of 1794. He returned home at the end of the year, as Paine emerged from prison, with a treaty whose terms were still secret. Paine had disliked Jay since the abrupt, cool treatment he had received when Jay presided over Congress during the Deane Affair. Also, he deplored any accommodation with Britain. Regardless of the terms, he knew the treaty must be a bad one.

He did not know that the treaty would displease even Washington. The British promised to evacuate military posts on the American frontier and to open some ports in the Empire to American trade, a minor concession that let only small ships glide through the crack in the door but one never before granted to any country. But she refused to abandon the right to impress American sailors into the royal navy or to impound American ships trading with belligerents. She forced the United States to forsake the doctrine that free ships make free goods, but agreed to pay for all ships and cargoes impounded. America in return promised to prohibit French privateers from using her ports to reoutfit. Although the treaty contravened no treaty with France, it clearly contained much to displease the French.

When Washington eventually submitted the Jay Treaty to the Senate, a great political battle broke loose. By the time the Senate by a slim margin ratified the treaty the emotions engendered had spread through the nation and split the people into two camps. Paine in Paris railed against the treaty—it demeaned America, it insulted France, he said—but his heated reactions were no more extreme than those voiced by the opposition in America. Privately Monroe agreed with him but officially he could say nothing, and he told Paine to publish nothing on the treaty while living in the American minister's home. Paine promised not to. Then, in January Thomas Pinckney stopped in Paris on his way to England. Pinckney had just negotiated a treaty with Spain that opened the Mississippi to American shipping and preserved the principle that free ships make free goods. Paine asked him to carry a packet to his London publisher containing a diatribe against the Jay Treaty. Pinckney accepted it, then, after talking to Monroe, decided it was impolitic to serve as Paine's courier and returned it. Monroe again talked to Paine, "expressing my extreme concern that he pursued a conduct which, under existing circumstances gave me so much pain."

Paine's ingratitude for Monroe's hospitality soon took a more pernicious form. Early in 1796 he appears to have ingratiated himself with the new five-man Directory that now served as the government's executive. In The Hague John Quincy Adams heard a rumor that Paine had desisted from publicly attacking the Jay Treaty under pressure from members of the Directory who feared his invective might cause an irrevocable break with America. Monroe soon after began to suspect Paine of betraying private confidences to the Directory, particularly to Jean François Reubell, an "honest, obstinate and sour" man, a former Dantonist who had survived the Terror and now had a powerful voice in shaping French foreign policy. Monroe told a friend he thought Paine had "been the source of the information that had led the Directory to doubt his representations." He confronted the members with his suspicion and asked if "Paine had given them information contradictory to the representation" he had made. The directors evaded a direct answer.

A pamphlet Paine published in April, *The Decline and Fall of the English System of Finance*, has the mark of a work commissioned by the Directory. In it he handled an abstruse subject with his usual skill, but this time the deftness owed something to a silent collaborator—Sir Robert Smyth, an English banker whose sympathy for the French Revolution had several years ago brought friendship with Paine. In the essay Paine sought to convince the world "that the English system of finance 'is ON THE VERGE, NAY EVEN IN THE GULF OF BANKRUPTCY.' " He argued that England had a debt of nearly £400,000,000 in 1793, before it entered the new world war. The debt from this war would increase at a ratio of one and a half the cost of the previous war. ("I have not *made* the ratio any more than Newton made the ratio of gravitation," Paine said. "I have only discovered it, and explained the mode of applying it.") The Bank of England had no more than one million pounds in cash, "and on this slender twig, always liable to be broken, hangs the whole funding system of four hundred millions, besides many millions in bank notes." Increment to the debt from the latest war would push the financial system to the breaking point. Q.E.D.

Paine boasted that his pamphlet would be published "in all languages." Either he was prescient or privy to government plans. Lanthenas translated, changing the title to *Décadence et Chute de la Banque D'Angleterre*, and Bonneville printed it. The government ordered one thousand copies, calling it "the most combustible weapon which France could at this moment employ to overthrow and destroy the English government." Through the foreign office it sent a hundred copies to French agents scattered through Europe. A German translation subsidized by the Directory was aimed at bankers in Holland, Switzerland, and Germany who had large holdings of British bonds. An English edition, which may have been subsidized by the Directory, went through thirteen printings before the year was out. As if to vindicate the power of Paine's pen, the Bank of England suspended the convertibility of its bank notes into specie early in 1797. England and the Bank survived the crisis, but for the moment Paine appeared to the world as an acute economic prophet.

6

The side excursion into English finances only momentarily deflected Paine from a target that had come to obsess him—President Washington. "This subject warms him so much that he sometimes turns orator," an acquaintance of Paine reported to John Quincy Adams in The Hague, "and in a coffee house frequented by Americans, he has twice pronounced a string of the most virulent anathemas, concluding as proven that he was both a coward and a scoundrel." When Paine determined to transfer his barroom threats to paper Monroe called on Thomas Griffiths, one of the Americans who had signed the petition for Paine's release from prison, to intercede. "This I did, but all in vain," Griffiths reported. "He was, like many other geniuses advanced in life, both vain and obstinate to an extreme degree." At last, after tolerating his obstinate boarder for a year and a half, Monroe insisted that he find other quarters. Sometime in the spring of 1796 Paine took rooms in Suresnes, a suburb six miles from the center of Paris. There Monroe sent a mutual friend, Dr. Enoch Edwards, in a final effort to dissuade Paine from attacking Washington. Paine "most peremptorily refused."

The "Letter to George Washington," as Paine entitled it, was a ragbag into which he stuffed all the things Monroe had refused to let him publish while living in his house. Over half the seventy pages focused on the Jay Treaty, and given Paine's assumption—that the United States had erred in sacrificing French friendship in order to settle long-standing grievances with Great Britain—he presented a reasonable case against it. The remainder was a meandering, disjointed affair, shot through with venom and arrogant, self-righteous boasting. Monroe is treated generously, but there are sideswipes at old enemies like John Adams ("and John it is known was always a speller after places and offices, and never thought his little services were highly enough paid"), John Jay ("and this John was always the sycophant of everything in power, from Mr. Gérard in America, to Grenville in England"), and Gouverneur Morris (whose "prating, insignificant pomposity rendered him at once offensive, suspected and ridiculous"). Washington gets more space. He is painted in unrelieved black—a man who happily swallows "the grossest adulation," who is capable of "a cold deliberate crime of the heart," and so incapable of friendship that "he can serve or desert a man, or a cause, with constitutional indifference." As a general he has no "talent for inspiring ardor in the army" and between 1775 and 1780 contributed nothing commendable to the war effort. "You slept away your time in the field, till the finances of the country were completely exhausted, and you have but little share in the glory of the final event." Paine concluded the rambling remarks on Washington, who only a few years earlier he had praised as "a better man . . . and more of a gentleman, than any king I ever knew of," with a furious salvo: "And as to you, sir, treacherous in private friendship (for so you have been to me, and that in the day of danger) and a hypocrite in public life, the world will be puzzled to decide whether you are an apostate or an impostor; whether you have abandoned good principles or whether you ever had any."

There is a curious side to this assault. Throughout the essay enemies like Adams and Jay are referred to familiarly by their first names, but Washington is always addressed as "President," "General," "Sir," or simply as "Mr. Washington," never contemptuously or flippantly as "George." This formality may have been a literary device; to treat the man lightly would have diminished his importance. It may, too, have revealed a tacit emotional involvement with Washington. Paine never, at least on paper, addressed those he deeply admired by their first names— it was always "Mr. Franklin," for instance—and Washington up to now counted among the few he held in awe. Then came the time that tried Paine's soul—imprisonment. Washington responded with silence, Paine with unprecedented personal invective. Yet a lingering respect for the fallen idol inhibits his attack on "Mr. Washington." His remark that it was Washington's duty "to have made (at least) some inquiries about me" may be the plaintive cry of a man who had been spurned by a hero.

Strangely, there is no certainty that Washington ever knew Paine had been imprisoned. The event occurred three days before Thomas Jefferson retired as secretary of state, and Gouverneur Morris' letter reporting it landed on the desk of the new secretary, Edmund Randolph, who may have assumed the matter too trifling for the president's attention. But even if Washington had known, he would probably have done nothing personally to effect Paine's release. His circumspect handling of the imprisonment of Lafayette, who had asked for aid, showed him reluctant to use the presidency to help even a close friend. What he would not do for Lafayette he would hardly have done for Paine.

The open letter to Washington was finished 30 July 1796. A friend named Barnes carried it to London, where it would be easier to send to Benjamin Franklin Bache in Philadelphia, who would publish it. Before Barnes forwarded the essay a London publisher offered three hundred pounds for it. Paine refused the offer "because it was my intention it should not appear till it appeared in America, as that, and not England was the place for its operation." Bache released the letter in salvos—an excerpt in October, another in November just before election day, and the whole as a pamphlet in February 1797. The Jeffersonian Republicans treated it with embarrassed silence, the Federalists with disdain. "Tom, you are surely mad," one editor remarked. "Thou hast escaped the *guillotine*, but thy terrors have prepared thee for a *strait-jacket.*"

For several years America had thought little about Paine. His name seldom appeared in the press. The letter to Washington revived interest in him. Thomas Carey of Philadelphia, an admirer, published his complete works in two volumes in 1797. William Cobbett, an immigrant Englishman who wrote under the name of Peter Porcupine, reissued the "Francis Oldys" life of Paine "interspersed with remarks and reflections." Cobbett also responded to the letter with an essay that circulated widely. "How Tom gets a living, or what brothel he inhabits, I know not. Nor does it signify to anybody here or elsewhere. He has done all the mischief he can do in the world, and whether his carcase is at last to be suffered to rot in the earth, or to be dried in the air, is of little consequence. Wherever or whenever he breathes his last, he will neither excite sorrow nor compassion. No friendly hand will close his eyes, not a moan will be uttered, not a tear will be shed. Like Judas he will be remembered by posterity. Men will learn to express all that is base, malignant, treacherous, unnatural, and blasphemous, by one single monosyllable—Paine."

Washington read Paine's letter. He sent a copy to a friend, enclosing with it a copy of Cobbett's remarks. "Making allowance for the asperity of an Englishman," he said of Cobbett, "for some of his strong and coarse expression, and a want of official information of many facts, it is not a bad thing."

7

In November 1796 Monroe learned that he had been recalled. The news shook but did not surprise him. He had sensed for some time that Timothy Pickering, the current secretary of state, as well as President Washington were displeased with his diplomacy, as they had a right to be. In his efforts to retard a rupture, Monroe sometimes spoke indiscreetly, even disloyally, about the Washington administration, as when he suggested unofficially to the French foreign office that it might postpone action regarding relations with America until the November elections, when he hoped a pro-French administration headed by Thomas Jefferson might come into office.

In February the Directory told Monroe it considered the Franco-

American alliance as "ceasing to exist." In March it detailed its objections to the Jay Treaty, which Monroe answered in a lengthy statement that Pickering and Washington thought more conciliatory than forceful. In June the French learned that the House of Representatives had retracted its demand for a voice in ratification of the treaty, thus clearing the way for its implementation. In July, acting on a proposal put forth to the foreign office by a well-meaning busybody—Paine—the Directory decreed that henceforth France would treat neutral vessels "in the same manner as they suffer the English to treat them," meaning that all American shipping was liable to search and seizure by the French navy. Soon afterward Pierre Auguste Adet, French minister to America, was called home.

Charles Cotesworth Pinckney, Monroe's replacement, arrived in Paris on December 5. He had been preceded by a report from Adet, who dismissed him as a "deluded instrument" of Washington's administration. Monroe buried the bitterness over his recall and treated Pinckney courteously. Paine revealed less control over his feelings. A week after Pinckney's arrival he called, without warning, at the minister's apartment in the Hôtel des Tuileries. Mrs. Pinckney answered the door. Her husband was not at home, but Paine stayed to chat. Had Mrs. Pinckney heard that France had recalled her minister from America without sending a replacement? No, she said, though she had heard "some coolness" existed between the two countries. Coolness! said Paine. "No, it is indignation, and indignation well founded." Mrs. Pinckney suspected Paine had been drinking. She said nothing in reply to his outburst and he soon left to carry on his diplomacy elsewhere.

Paine probably had been drinking. He was distraught by the course of events. "The recall of Mr. Monroe cut everything asunder," he wrote Jefferson, "for though here they were enraged at the American government, they were not enraged with him. They had esteem for him, and a good opinion of him; they would listen to him, and he could soften them." Paine tried to persuade the Directory not to reject Pinckney out of hand. The results of the presidential election in America had not yet arrived in Europe. Moreover, Pinckney's appointment had not yet been confirmed by the Senate. Let France consider him in "suspension," he argued, or the office of the American minister as in "*vacance.*"

The government this time rejected Paine's advice. It refused to accept Pinckney's credentials. On the heels of this came news that John Adams had been elected president, by "the mercantile wiseacres," according to Paine. "I am mortified at the fall of the American character," he said in response to the news. "It was once respectable even to eminence; now it is despised; and did I not feel my own character as an individual, I should blush to call myself a citizen of America."

Ashamed as he was, Paine again talked of returning to America, and in March the Paris press reported he would soon depart. One of the papers, John Quincy Adams reported back to his father, "says that he is going with Mr. Monroe, *'to repair the mischief by the administration of Washington.'*" The report was correct. Monroe planned to leave from Bordeaux and Paine generously offered to go along to help defend his record in America. Monroe envisioned the public reaction when he stepped down the gangplank with the notorious "Mad Tom" at his side. He sent a mutual friend, Benjamin Vaughan, to dissuade without rankling Paine to postpone his return. Paine got the hint. He would still leave but separately and from Havre-de-Grâce. Necessity, not politics, convinced him he must not linger in France. He risked a new prison term if caught there when war broke out with the United States. Also, he needed money. "I have sustained so much loss, by disinterestedness and inattention to money matters," he said, "and by accidents, that I am obliged to look closer to my affairs than I have done."

A man who met Paine about the time he was packing his bags found him good company. "He is vain beyond all belief, but he has reason to be vain, and for my part, I forgive him," he said. "He converses extremely well; and I find him wittier in discourse than in his writings, where his humor is clumsy enough. . . . He drinks like a fish—a misfortune which I have known to befall other celebrated patriots. I am told that the true time to see him to advantage is about ten at night, with a bottle of brandy and water before him, which I can very well conceive."

Paine left Paris for Havre-de-Grâce in the third week of March 1797. He found that "ever since Mr. Jay's *treaty of surrender*" few American vessels came into the port. The *Dublin Packet* was leaving for New York early in April, "but I liked neither the captain nor the company," he said, "and besides this, the English cruisers are always at this port, and as I have lost all confidence in the American government, and had none in the captain, I did not choose to expose myself to the hazard of being taken out of the vessel." He hung around the city several weeks, undecided whether to leave or not. He later heard that Monroe's ship had been stopped on the high seas by a British warship "that searched every part of it, and down to the hold, for Thomas Paine."

Again Paine gave excuses rather than reasons for lingering in France. He wanted, as he admitted, to go to England, "and should a revolution begin in England," he said, while passing the days in Havre-de-Grâce, "I intend to be among them." That hope looked dimmer every day, and in the early summer of 1797 he again packed his bags and returned to Paris.

CHAPTER

23

GADFLY

ON 13 MAY 1797 the Directory paused in the midst of a new round of troubles to grant Thomas Paine permission to reside again in Paris. It had just crushed an insurrection led by François Noël Babeuf, and it could see looming ahead in the legislature another more serious threat to its authority. At the time Paine had been packing his bags for America in March, the first free elections under the republic were being held throughout France. The moment had seemed right to the Directory. The Austrians had recently been routed by Napoleon and the English were negotiating for peace with the French at Lille, a fortress city near the Belgian border. But the Directory miscalculated the people's affection for the republic. The new members elected to the Council of Five Hundred and the Council of Elders gave the antirepublicans in both bodies control, and they were determined to put France on the road to constitutional monarchy.

An early hint of their desire to resurrect the past came in June, less than a month after Paine's return to Paris, when Camille Jordan pleaded with the Council of Five Hundred to restore a number of privileges to the Catholic Church, among them the "innocent pleasure" of ringing church bells again. Paine replied to Jordan's proposal with a pedestrian essay in which he dismissed church bells as "a public nuisance." "It is a want of feeling to talk of priests and bells while so many infants are perishing in the hospitals, and aged and infirm poor in the streets, from the want of necessaries," he said.

Paine currently plumed himself "more on his theology than his politics," an acquaintance said, and in writing and conversation he had become a repetitive bore on the subject. He reprimanded in a tediously long letter his sometime friend Thomas Erskine, defender of *The Rights of Man* but lately prosecutor of a bookseller who had sold *The Age of Reason*. He talked incessantly of the reply he planned to the bishop of Llandaff's able attack on *The Age of Reason*.

Paine believed that a republic—at least in France—could not survive while the superstitions of Christianity prevailed, and the Directory shared his belief. In January he had joined the newly organized Society of Theophilanthropists, a name compounded "of three Greek words signifying God, Love, and Man," he explained. The sect promoted morality rather than religion. The congregation listened to didactic lectures, sang uplifting songs, and departed from the meetings certain they had helped strengthen the republic through their purified worship of God. Paine gave one of the edifying talks, a graceful essay that Joseph Johnson published under the sanitized title of *Atheism Refuted; in a Discourse to Prove the Existence of God*. Clio Rickman, now back in London, put out his own edition, calling it simply *A Discourse* and dedicating it "to the enemies of Thomas Paine. . . ." Government subsidies kept the sect alive, but it was apparent by the time the antirepublicans won control of the legislature that it would never threaten the power of the Catholic Church in France.

The antirepublicans failed to get the church bells ringing again, but they pushed through repeal of laws against refractory priests and those citizens who had emigrated from France. Late in the summer of 1797 the antirepublicans persuaded the legislature to vote for the disbandment of the Constitutional Club ("It is the only society of which I have been a member in France," Paine said, "and I went to this because it was become necessary that the friends of the republic should rally round the standard of the constitution"). It was outlawed so "that it might not give the example of exasperating matters already too much inflamed." The Directory moved twelve thousand troops to the outskirts of Paris. The legislature countered on September 3 by calling for the mobilization of the National Guard, but the next morning, September 4 (18 Fructidor), the deputies awoke to find that during the night the forehanded Directory had moved the army into the city. A few cannon were fired, and though no one died, the hamstrung legislature accepted defeat. The Directory purged the councils of two hundred antirepublican members; Barthélemy and Carnot were deported and their seats on the Directory handed to Philippe Antoine Merlin and Nicolas Louis François de Neufchâteau, both safe republicans.

Paine had aligned himself so completely with the republicans on the Directory that John Quincy Adams, observing events from The Hague, assumed he had been hired to write for them, "and in the style for which Madame Roland judged him peculiarly fitted, that is, to wind up the drunkenness of a club or a tavern into a frenzy." Paine supported the coup d'état and published a pamphlet defending it. "It was impossible to go on," he wrote. "Everything was at stake, and all national business at a stand. The case reduced itself to a simple alternative—shall the Republic be destroyed by the darksome maneuvers of a faction, or shall it be preserved by an exceptional act?" he asked. "If there are some men more disposed than others not to act severely, I have a right to place myself in that class; the whole of my political life invariably proves it; yet I cannot see, taking all the parts of the case together, what else, or what better, could have been done, than has been done. It was a great stroke, applied in a great crisis, that crushed in an instant and without the loss of life, all the hopes of the enemy, and restored tranquillity to the interior." He justified the coup by "the supreme law of absolute necessity." He acknowledged that the republic's first free elections had been violated and also its constitution, which he called the best that had "yet been devised by human wisdom." What he failed to see or admit was that the republic in order to save itself had become dependent upon the army. Perhaps the next time it was called in, the army would not return the government to the civilian leaders.

2

Paine had called the constitution of 1795 the best yet "devised by human wisdom." The remark needed amplifying—it hardly fit with an earlier judgment delivered to the National Convention—and he did so in a preface written after 18 Fructidor for a new edition of his pamphlet *Agrarian Justice*. Though the constitution had created "the *best organized system*" of government it was flawed, for "equality of the right of suffrage is not maintained." Babeuf wanted to correct this defect, but he erred by conspiring rather than "seeking remedy by legitimate and constitutional means." Babeuf also erred, in Paine's view, in thinking that communism would solve mankind's ills. But the two men shared a perception that came to them about the same time—political equality meant little as long as economic inequality prevailed in the world. This insight led Babeuf to rebellion and Paine to write *Agrarian Justice*.

He wrote the pamphlet in the winter of 1795-1796 as a reply to a sermon by the bishop of Llandaff on "the wisdom and goodness of God in having made both rich and poor." He did nothing with it until shortly before deciding to return to America; then, wishing to leave behind a last testament to the Revolution, he turned it over to a publisher. "Le départ precipité de Thomas Paine," the publisher explained, "ne lui a pas permis de faire traduire, sous ses yeux, cet ouvrage auquel il attachoit le plus grand prix." Upon returning to Paris in May he found that the pamphlet had done well enough to warrant a further printing, and this gave Paine the excuse to write a preface, which he inscribed to the legislature and the Directory.

Agrarian Justice ranks among Paine's greatest essays. He writes to the elite who run the world, not the plain people, and adjusts his style to please his audience and to coat the severest indictment he has yet directed against society. He begins with a simple premise: "The first principle of civilization ought to have been and ought still to be, that the condition of every person born into the world, after a state of civilization commences, ought not to be worse than if he had been born before that period." And yet look what we have—"spectacles of human misery which poverty and want present to our eyes in all the towns and streets of Europe." Among the paragraphs that follow come two, at once stately and severe, that say what no one had said before nor better since:

> The rugged face of society, checkered with the extremes of affluence and want, proves that some extraordinary violence has been committed upon it, and calls on justice for redress. The great mass of the poor in all countries are become an hereditary race, and it is next to impossible for them to get out of that state of themselves. It ought also to be observed that this mass increases in all countries that are called civilized. More persons fall annually into it than get out of it.

> It is not charity but a right, not bounty but justice, that I am pleading for. The present state of civilization is as odious as it is unjust. It is absolutely the opposite of what it should be, and it is necessary that a revolution should be made in it. The contrast of affluence and wretchedness continually meeting and offending the eye, is like dead and living bodies chained together.

Always before, weak-willed men unable to cope with life had been blamed for the poverty that engulfed them. Society had never been indicted. Having isolated the cause, Paine called for a heroic remedy. "It is only by organizing civilization upon such principles as to act like a system of pulleys, that the whole weight of misery can be removed." Did he plan to strip the rich? No. "Though I care as little about riches as any man, I am a friend to riches because they are capable of good," he said. "I care not how affluent some may be, provided that none be miserable in consequence of it." Did he favor some form of communism? No, he said. "It is necessary as well for the protection of property as for the sake of justice and humanity, to form a system that, while it preserves one part of society from wretchedness, shall secure the other from depredation." He thought that misery could be rubbed out by reforming the economic system, not demolishing it. He proposed the creation of a national fund to which all landowners contributed and out of which "shall be paid to every person, when arrived at the age of twenty-one years, the sum of fifteen pounds sterling, as a compensation in part, for the loss of his or her natural inheritance, by the introduction of the system of landed property." After the age of fifty everyone would receive ten pounds a year until death.

Paine had sketched the outlines of this program in *The Rights of Man*. Here he fleshed it out with a scheme for its execution. He wasted his energy. People bought the pamphlet, some were deeply influenced by it —William Blake in England classed Paine with Jesus as "a worker of miracles" after reading it—but the economic adjustments it called for, minor as they were, proved too much for those who ran the world in the eighteenth and nineteenth centuries. And few contemporaries saw what Paine, Babeuf, and a handful of others perceived: "A revolution in the state of civilization is the necessary companion of revolutions in the system of government." It had taken Paine ten years of living through the French Revolution to learn this, and now no one would listen. When society, he said to deaf ears, "shall be so organized that not a man or woman born in the Republic but shall inherit some means of beginning the world, and see before them the certainty of escaping the miseries that under other governments accompany old age, the Revolution of France will have an advocate and an ally in the heart of all nations."

3

With the ratification of the Jay Treaty, Paine's hatred for the Federalists, who had engineered the rapprochement with England, nearly consumed his common sense. In 1795 French cruisers had captured over three hundred American ships. The year 1796 had seen that pace continue. On 2 March 1797 the Directory annulled the doctrine that free ships make free goods—that is, neutral ships carrying no contraband of war are free to visit belligerents without fear of capture, a doctrine embodied in the commercial treaty with the United States in 1778—on the ground that since the Jay Treaty exempted Great Britain from the provision, France, to protect her own interests, must also reject it. The annulment set in operation a dragnet that scooped up hundreds of American vessels traveling to and from British ports. The Directory had in effect launched an undeclared maritime war with the United States. All this won Paine's full approval.

In 1797 his efforts to undercut American foreign policy edged perilously close to sedition for one who so loudly proclaimed his American citizenship. When John Adams announced the creation of a commission composed of Pinckney—who had settled down in The Hague—John Marshall, and Elbridge Gerry to resolve the differences between France and America, Paine derided the goodwill gesture. "It will be best," he advised Talleyrand shortly before the commissioners arrived in Paris, "to receive them with a *civil signification* of reproach." He added that in two or three days he would pass along to Talleyrand "some thoughts upon American affairs." Talleyrand had become foreign minister only three months earlier, shortly after returning from a two-year stay in the United States which had engendered in him no love for Americans.

In a follow-up letter to Talleyrand Paine put forth a plan—a Maritime Pact he called it—which he thought would promote international peace but which in the context of the moment could only be called anti-American; it advanced the interests of France rather than those of the United States. Differences between the nations could be settled by *"a non-importation convention,"* by which America *"agrees not to import from any nation in Europe who shall interrupt her commerce on the seas, any goods, wares, or merchandise whatever, and that all her ports shall be cut against the nation that gives offense."* Paine went on to say it would be better if this approach were incorporated in "a general convention of nations acting as a whole," but he did not insist upon it. Talleyrand thanked Paine for his thoughts and said they had been passed along to the Directory. Paine got the impression he was being listened to when in fact Talleyrand toyed with him, using him to promote French interests or at least dissension among the American commissioners.

The commissioners arrived in Paris early in October. They could not have chosen a worse time. In the month since 18 Fructidor the Directory had ejected dissidents from the government who earlier might have demanded a conciliatory policy toward the United States. On October 8 Talleyrand received them graciously but unofficially at his home. He told them in effect they must cool their heels until the Directory had reacted to a special report he was preparing for it on American relations. Paine, playing a self-assigned but indefinable role, seemed to think he should not call upon his fellow Americans. Instead, he sent John Marshall a packet containing his plan, supposedly before the Directory, and also page proofs of his pamphlet on the 18 Fructidor. Along with this background material came a letter. In it Paine condemned the Jay Treaty as a "sacrifice of neutral rights" which was "not consistent with the good of neutral nations considered collectively and as forming a common interest"; he warned that offering France the advantages England had gained under the treaty was not a bargaining point, for France already claimed them; he cautioned against demanding compensation for vessels and cargoes impounded by the French, for they were in no mood to pay. Paine ended by saying he thought the French wanted to heal the rift with the United States, but he saw no means by which this could be accomplished short of a general measure such as his proposal for organized neutrality.

Marshall forwarded Paine's letter to the secretary of state, "because from the continuance this man receives one has reason to suppose that it was not written without the knowledge and approbation of the [French] government." Privately he thought the letter "an insult which ought to be received with that coldness which would forbid the repetition of it."

Talleyrand had used Paine to make the point that France intended to push for a hard bargain with the United States. The next move was to send his own emissaries—later designated by John Adams as W, X, Y, and Z—to the commissioners. These emissaries said that before official negotiations could begin the commissioners must disavow President Adams' belligerent comments to Congress regarding France, promise a hefty loan, and also hand over a quarter of a million dollars "for the purpose of making the customary distribution in diplomatic affairs." "It is no, no, not a sixpence," said Pinckney when the demand for bribe money was made. Paine heard of the proposal only later. He condemned it, and said the identities of W, X, Y, and Z "ought to be known in order that suspicion may not fall on other persons," but he also wondered "whether it was prudent on the commissioners to hold conference with unauthorized persons."

The commissioners had no further contact with Paine after October nor, once he suspected that Talleyrand had used him, did Paine attempt to meddle with their negotiations. Not that there was much to meddle with; neither Talleyrand nor the Directory showed any interest in easing tensions with the United States. Napoleon's triumph over Austria, which culminated in a treaty at Campo Formio in mid-October, convinced the Directory it could deal with England without help from or fear of America. In November Napoleon was appointed commander-in-chief of the army of England. "England is now threatened with invasion," Marshall reported home. The Directory, he said, was so hostile to the United States that "the Atlantic only can save us." These developments delighted Paine. He shared the Directory's hostility toward the American government and he hoped soon to share in the invasion of England.

4

When Paine returned from Havre-de-Grâce his friend Nicolas de Bonneville offered to put him up for a week or two until he found a permanent place. Five years later Paine was still the Bonnevilles' guest. The ground floor of the house held Bonneville's print shop, where he did job work and published his newspaper, le Bien informé, to which Paine contributed most of his current writing. In the cramped quarters above, Paine had a bedroom and study. The Bonnevilles and their three young boys—there had been only one when Paine arrived—made shift as best they could.

Paine's daily routine remained what it had always been. "He rose late," Mme. Bonneville recalled. "He then used to read the newspapers, from which, though he understood little of the French language when spoken, he did not fail to collect all the material information relating to politics, in which subject he took most delight. When he had his morning's reading, he used to carry back the journals to Mr. Bonneville, and they had a chat upon the topics of the day." In the afternoon came the usual walk—"I do not believe he ever hired a coach to go out on pleasure during the whole of his stay in Paris," said Mme. Bonneville—and after dinner the long nap.

The day rarely passed without visitors. Joel Barlow, Robert Fulton, and Robert Smyth were the most frequent callers. General Bonaparte knocked on the door one day. Mme. Bonneville answered and found the general surrounded by a crowd from the neighborhood wondering what had brought him to this part of the city. He had come to see Thomas Paine. Bonneville came up from his shop and, sitting between Paine and Bonaparte, acted as interpreter. The general remarked that he had been greatly influenced by *The Rights of Man* and slept with it under his pillow every night. "A statue of gold should be erected to you in every city in the universe," he said. These effusions out of the way, he said he hoped Paine would visit him someday soon. He would like to talk over the scheme of using gunboats to invade England that Paine had devised.

In December 1797 Paine gave his ideas to the public in two articles for *le Bien informé*. The first one described the gunboats as he conceived them. They would have small sails, a bank of oars, and would draw at most four feet of water. A thousand such boats could put a respectable army ashore in England within twenty-four hours after they sailed from France. The second article offered a way to finance the building of the fleet. Voluntary contributions rather than new taxes would underwrite the cost. The trifling sum of twenty sous from only two and a half of the nation's twenty-five million citizens would produce enough to construct the fleet. To get the project moving Paine sent the Council of Five Hundred "a hundred livres, and with it all the wishes of my heart, for the success of the descent, and a voluntary offer of any service I can render to promote it." The "voluntary service" came in the form of a long memorandum to Bonaparte amplifying the plan in detail.

Some on the general staff favored an invasion by dirigible balloons, but the gunboat project impressed Bonaparte as more plausible. Paine claimed that some 250 boats had been built before "the expedition was abandoned for that of Egypt." Over fifty thousand troops were assembled near Brest for the invasion. Bonaparte, said Paine, promised "me at his own home I was to accompany him." But in late February, after an inspection tour of the army and the coastline, Bonaparte abandoned the project without telling Paine. In mid-March, while the general was working on plans for the invasion of Egypt, Paine was still rejoicing at the imminent "descent upon England."

5

New elections for the legislature were held in March. The previous year antirepublicans had given the Directory a hard time; in 1798 super-republicans, as they might be called, endangered the republic's fragile stability. These men wanted a new, more democratic constitution. The Directory saw that a fourth attempt in eight years to frame a constitution would throw France again into chaos. It fought these new antagonists on the left wherever they stood for office, but the superrepublicans triumphed in enough instances to gain control of both chambers of the legislature. This time the Directory responded with speed. In May it ejected 106 of the new members on the charge they planned to revive the Terror. Twice now the Directory had violated the constitution in order to protect it. Paine said nothing publicly on this second coup.

The Directory became sensitive to the slightest criticism. Bonneville published a lighthearted paragraph about Sieyès. The Directory found two of the sentences offending and ordered le Bien informé to suspend publication. "I am certain that Bonneville in inserting that paragraph meant only a witticism and not an injury; and never expected it would be taken seriously," Paine wrote the Directory. The suspension was lifted, but warning had been served that even old friends must tread warily.

Paine did not break with the government; the government broke with him. In August 1798 Dr. George Logan, a Philadelphia Quaker, came to Paris to see what he, as a private citizen, could do to end the brisk undeclared naval war France and America were fighting on the high seas. Paine, according to le Bien informé, introduced Logan to French officials and obtained for him a warm welcome. Talleyrand realized after Logan arrived that he had mishandled relations with Adams' three commissioners. Since the departure of two of them in March—Gerry had remained behind—the French fleet had been overwhelmed by Nelson in the Battle of the Nile, American harassment of French shipping had become a costly matter, and a growing Anglo-American accord held potential danger for all French holdings in the New World. Talleyrand was eager to settle differences with America before matters got out of hand. He knew that as the first step in a rapprochement he must disassociate the French government from Paine, whom the Adams administration detested. To that end Talleyrand denied Bonneville's item in *le Bien informé*. He said that Dr. Logan had met Paine only once and "found him so prejudiced against the United States, and so opinionative with respect to an influence he neither possesses among them nor us, that he abstained from conversing any more with him." The ploy worked to the extent that a few weeks later Logan left for home convinced that the French seriously desired peace with the United States.

Talleyrand chose wisely to break with Paine, whose anti-American feeling had become an unmanageable obsession. In September he published an essay in Bonneville's paper suggesting a practical way to conquer America. Don't attempt to invade the land, he advised; the British had tried that strategy and failed. Strike at the seaports, starting with Savannah in the south, moving along to Charleston, Georgetown, Wilmington, Norfolk, and on up the coast. A small fleet of gunboats could do the job adequately and inexpensively. "The master blow would be to finish at Halifax," he said, "then move down to New Orleans, take possession of the port of Natchez, call on the friends of liberty in the back parts of the United States, from Kentucky to the southern limits of English America." Nothing can excuse or explain away the essay. Hatred of the Federalists had propelled Paine into sedition.

6

Paine seldom "went into the society of French people," Mme. Bonneville reported, "except when, by seeing someone of office or power, he could obtain some favor for his countrymen who might be in need of his good offices. These he always performed with pleasure, and he never failed to adopt the most likely means to secure success." When Mary Wollstonecraft's brother was imprisoned Paine counseled patience. "Let them alone awhile, till their fury be somewhat dissipated in the violence of the proceedings," he said, and a short while later his boast "I shall not find any difficulty in obtaining his liberation" came true. When a stranger, Ebenezer May, wrote from Calais that he needed a passport for his wife, Paine spent a month cutting through red tape to expedite the request. Hearing that a friend had been forced to pay a bribe of 4600 livres in order to be cleared of a trumped-up charge, he sent off an indignant letter, for "the duty I owe to justice and to friendship makes it incumbent on me to state this case to the Directory." In a note to Sottin, the new minister of police, he said he would call the next day to introduce his friend Barlow, "who is just returned from Tunis, where he has been employed on a mission for the redemption of some American sailors. I want also to ask you if there are any new orders of the Directory respecting the Americans in Paris. They are in some difficulty about their [identity] cards."

Paine's name could still help friends in trouble, but otherwise he had no substantial influence. At the Irish Coffee House, where the author of *The Rights of Man* was universally admired, he compensated for the government's disdain. Dr. John Walker, an English Quaker who met him there, reflected the general judgment. For him Paine was "a man of gigantic political genius, that made, while other men took baby steps, the strides of a giant."

The coffee house served as a watering spot for English-speaking residents of Paris, particularly the small colony of Irish exiles who were waiting for France to sponsor a second descent—a previous one in 1796 had failed—upon Ireland. "They are," said a fellow Irishman, "sad, vulgar wretches." Paine's drinking with his Irish companions attracted attention in print for the first time. "Paine dines almost every day," an unfriendly English journal reported, "at Paris with MUIR, NAPPER TANDY, and some of other *persecuted patriots*, where he drinks brandy in such profusion, as to reduce him nearly to a state of insensibility." Paine, Tandy, and "the miserably mutilated" Thomas Muir formed a trio. Paine was especially fond of Napper Tandy, a wildly popular Irishman immortalized as the hero of "Wearing of the Green" and of whom it has been said, "He acquired celebrity without being able to account for it, and possessed an influence without rank or capacity." At a dinner Paine and Walker attended, Tandy toasted the French tricolor flag: Might it "float on the Tower of London, and on the Birmingham Tower of Dublin's Castle!" Paine joined in the toast; Walker, an abstainer, did not. "Walker is a Quaker with all its follies," said Paine, laughing. "I am a Quaker without them."

Paine served as the Irish revolutionaries' public relations man. In June he sent the Directory a memorial he had written for his friends asking for one thousand men and five thousand guns to promote an insurrection in Ireland. The Directory gave more than asked for. It sent an army to Ireland. Tandy had charge of a small force that landed at Donegal. The English repulsed the invasion and eventually Tandy, captured by subterfuge, landed in prison.

Paine's friends at the coffee house were probably the ones Joel Barlow referred to when commenting upon the low circles Paine moved in during his last years in Paris. When he dined with Barlow his companions were of a different order: eminent Frenchmen such as Volney and, after he returned to France in 1799, Lafayette, who had been freed from prison by Napoleon's victory over Austria in 1797; the Polish general Kosciusko; the American inventor Robert Fulton. Fulton had come to Paris in 1797 after a long visit in England. He settled in with the Barlows and would remain a permanent guest for seven years. He and Paine became especially friendly. The iron bridge brought them together. While in England, Fulton had published a book on canals in which he had remarked in passing on the English interest in iron bridges, apparently unaware that Paine had sparked that interest. These bridges, he said, "are progressively expanding as experience produces courage; nor should I be surprised, if genius in time gave the mechanic rainbow of one thousand feet to wide and rapid rivers." Now Fulton was working on a design for a submarine and trying to figure a way to propel it beneath the water. Paine suggested he find a large whale and hitch the underwater boat to it.

7

The year 1799 slipped along quietly for Paine. He still hoped "to return to America as soon as I can cross the sea in safety." That intention had to be postponed until peace with England came, and nothing in sight indicated that would soon occur.

In the autumn Paine went to Dieppe to visit Joseph Vanhuele, his former cellmate in the Luxembourg. When he left, French affairs were in a parlous state. The Directory, at odds with itself again, was failing to give decisive leadership. As antirepublicanism flourished both in the legislature and in the nation, restoration of the monarchy once again seemed inevitable. "I seek a sword," said Sieyès, now one of the directors. The sword arrived unexpectedly in Paris in mid-October in the form of Bonaparte, who had slipped away from his hamstrung army in Egypt. A coup d'état conceived and organized by Sieyès took place on November 9 (18 Brumaire). In the reorganization that followed five directors were replaced by three consuls, and a short while later when Sieyès, who thought he would control Bonaparte, was removed from power it was apparent that only one of the three—Napoleon Bonaparte—would rule. Paine said nothing in print about these developments. He did not bother even to return to Paris, remaining in Belgium through the winter of 1799–1800.

When he eventually did reappear at the Bonnevilles', he learned that on March 2 the Ellsworth commission had arrived from America. In an attempt to solve difficulties between France and America John Adams had persuaded Oliver Ellsworth, a Connecticut Federalist, to relinquish his post as chief justice of the Supreme Court and head a new commission to France. Bonaparte's coup d'état occurred while Ellsworth's party was at sea. They reached Paris as news arrived from America that Washington had died the previous December. Napoleon extended condolences for the French nation and in his message praised America as "the wisest and happiest nation on the face of the earth." Washington's "memory will forever be dear to the French people," he said in a decree to the army calling for ten days of mourning. The scene was set for settlement of the undeclared war.

A friendly welcome to a commission composed of three hidebound Federalists appalled Paine. He immediately paid a call on Ellsworth to offer his opinion on the matter. Ellsworth received him coolly. Apparently the French government got word of Paine's busybody activity, for in mid-April an order was passed down from the foreign office that he should be told "the police are informed that he is behaving irregularly and that at the first complaint against him he will be sent back to America, his country." The warning sufficed. During the remainder of the commissioners' nine-month stay in Paris, Paine had no further contact with them, nor did he write for publication anything on Franco-American relations.

After 18 Brumaire Paine's relations with Bonaparte were distant. At a public banquet the general noticed him and said to a companion loud enough for Paine to hear, "The English are all alike in every country— they are all rascals." Yet Bonaparte consulted him when he needed him. During the negotiations with Austria that resulted in the treaty of Lunéville he sent an emissary to ask Paine a question—"Whether in negotiating a treaty of peace with Austria it will be policy in France to enter into a treaty of peace with England?" Paine replied "no" in an essay he liked well enough to send to Jefferson.

In letters to America that were likely to be opened Paine spoke temperately of Bonaparte. Around a dinner table with friends he was of another mind. "Paine entertains the most despicable opinion of Bonaparte's conduct, military as well as civil," a visitor remarked, "and thinks him the completest charlatan ever existed." Barlow, too, shared this view and at a dinner where Paine was present he called Bonaparte "the greatest butcher of Liberty, the greatest monster that Nature ever *spewed!*," then extended his contempt to all France. "If it had not been for us they would literally have starved, and what return have we received for our kindness?" Paine, smiling, said, "It served the Americans right, they should have suffered the rascals to starve; slaves should not be fed by the hands of free men." The bitterness emerged at another dinner when Paine told his companion "to hold his tongue" over an outrageous statement another at the table had made, "as he might as well talk of honor to a gang of thieves as to contradict revolutionary Frenchmen in their notion of right and wrong."

Paine lived in comfortable boredom through the year 1800—silenced in France, exiled from England, isolated from America. The French cared nothing for what he had to say on political matters nor would they allow him to say it in print. The English continued to disappoint him by refusing to revolt. The Americans seemed content enough with John Adams to reelect him to a second term. Then in October Paine learned that Thomas Jefferson appeared certain to supplant Adams in the White House. He took heart. With a friend in power he could again be of use to America. The time had come to think of returning to the United States, regardless of the risks involved in venturing upon an ocean infested with British warships.

CHAPTER

24

MR. JEFFERSON SENDS A
PUBLIC VESSEL

PAINE ASSUMED JEFFERSON'S ELECTION to the presidency before it happened. On 1 October 1800, two weeks before the people cast ballots for presidential electors, he reopened communication after a long silence, laying the groundwork for future favors when Jefferson stepped into power. He spoke for friends: "If the chance of the day should place you in the Presidency," no better appointments could be made than Fulwar Skipwith as minister to France and Joel Barlow as minister to Holland. He spoke for himself: "If you should be in the chair, but not otherwise, I offer myself" for a sinecure he heard might open up for an American in Paris. "It will serve to defray my expenses until I can return, but I wish it to be with the condition of my returning. I am not tired of working for nothing, but I cannot afford it."

This passing reference to money cloaked the deplorable state of his finances. Paine had written three of the greatest best sellers of the eighteenth century—five, if the two parts of *The Rights of Man* and *The Age of Reason* are counted separately—and had nothing but debts to show for his success. He owed Monroe, Bonneville, Smyth, and God alone knew how many other friends, acquaintances, and strangers. The debt to a single casual friend—Capt. Nathan Haley, home port Stonington, Connecticut —alone should have staggered him. Haley paid Paine's board and lodging at Dieppe for forty-two days in 1799 (336 livres), for seventy-five days in 1801 (600 livres). The loans continued steadily over a stretch of three years, varying in amounts from 24 livres to 360 livres. In 1802 Paine's laundry woman had gone unpaid for three years; Haley settled the account (170 livres). He paid for the printing of *Pacte maritime* in 1800 (60 livres). The debt totaled 7177 livres when Paine left for America.

Understandably, Paine was eager to put France behind him, and he told Jefferson he would return to the United States "as soon as I can pass the seas in safety from the piratical John Bulls." But "if any American frigate should come to France," he added, "and the direction of it fall to you, I will be glad you would give me the opportunity of returning."

Paine sent Jefferson five letters in October alone—more than he had written to him in the previous five years. They were evasive on French domestic affairs but filled with perceptive comments about European events generally. Only when he touched on the Ellsworth commission did prejudice corrupt his reports. The commission on October 1, the day of Paine's first letter to Jefferson, concluded a convention that resolved French and American grievances. France in effect accepted the Jay Treaty and her loss as the most favored nation in American commerce. The treaty of alliance of 1778, the last America would make for over a century and a half, was abrogated. In return the United States agreed not to press for damages to ships and cargoes confiscated by France during the undeclared war. Paine had collected only vague gossip about these terms. Nonetheless, he suggested to Jefferson that in Europe's present unsettled state "it may be proper for America to consider whether it is worth her while to enter into any treaty at this moment"—Paine's discreet way of urging him to reject the treaty when he became president.

This snide comment on a triumph of diplomacy for which the Ellsworth commissioners deserved praise owes something to the "unfriendliness" they had shown Paine, something to his certainty that Federalists could do no good, and something to his international outlook. Paine was, as he had been saying for over twenty years, a citizen of the world, emotionally unattached to any nation. He saw all problems, particularly those related to commerce, from an international point of view. Also for over two decades he had argued that a free-flowing commerce promoted peace and inhibited war. The United States had entered world trade as a free nation with a unique doctrine for promoting it—free ships make free goods. She had retreated from that doctrine with the Jay Treaty; a similar agreement with France would kill it. American trade henceforth would become a pawn of European politics, and the United States would inevitably become involved in European wars. Rather than abandon the doctrine, he now wanted the United States to lead the way in creating "an association of nations for the protection of the rights of neutral commerce and the security of the liberty of the seas." Neutrals who joined the association would abandon a flabby compliance to belligerents who infringed on their rights to travel the seas freely. They would agree to "cease to import . . . any goods, wares, or merchandise, of whatever kind, forever from the nation so offending against the law of nations," said Paine. They would deny belligerents the right to visit and search their ships—"an insult," he called it—and monitor their own merchant fleets to assure those at war that they carried no contraband.

Out of these ideas Paine created a model maritime compact of ten articles published in French along with several other essays under the title *Pacte maritime* in the summer of 1800. In October, he sent Jefferson the English original along with two other fugitive pieces. The pamphlet, under the title *Compact Maritime*, was published in English soon after Jefferson received the essays.

After the initial flurry of five letters Paine sent no more for seven months, until at last in June he heard from Jefferson firsthand. However, in early February he learned from an American newspaper that what he had divined earlier was now fact—Thomas Jefferson had been elected the third president of the United States. Instantly he passed along the good news in a note to Fulwar Skipwith. With his usual thoughtfulness for the welfare of friends and his usual lack of common sense in practical matters, he went on to urge Skipwith to arrange to get his former cellmate Joseph Vanhuele, a Belgian, appointed American consul at Ostend.

2

On 18 March 1801, two weeks after his inauguration and only a few days after the Senate had ratified with slight modifications the convention worked out by the Ellsworth commission, Jefferson sent a brief but carefully composed reply to Paine's packet of October letters. He obviously spoke to the French government through Paine in the opening sentences, reaffirming as policy the sentiments of his inaugural address. We are determined not to waste "the energies of our people in war and destruction," and "we shall avoid implicating ourselves with the powers of Europe, even in support of principles which we mean to pursue," he wrote. The "frenzy" into which Americans "have been wrought, partly by ill conduct in France, partly by artifices practiced upon them, is almost extinct, and will, I believe, become quite so." The convention that settled Franco-American differences was being returned for the French to ratify by John Dawson, a member of Congress. Dawson would travel in the warship *Maryland*. "You expressed a wish to get a passage to this country in a public vessel," Jefferson said. "Mr. Dawson is charged with orders to the captain of the *Maryland* to receive and accommodate you back if you can be ready to depart at such a short warning." After mentioning that an old friend, Robert R. Livingston, would be the next minister to France, he ended on a flattering note: "That you may long live to continue your useful labors and to reap the reward in the thankfulness of nations is my sincere prayer."

Upon arriving in Paris, Dawson gathered up General Kosciusko and the two went around to the Bonneville house to deliver Jefferson's letter. Paine received them in his workshop-study-parlor, a slovenly room filled with his modest accumulation of possessions. Along one wall stretched three shelves of cardboard boxes, each of them labeled, as one visitor remarked, "after the manner of a minister of foreign affairs, *correspondance Americaine, Britannique, Française; Notices Politiques; Le citoyen Français*, etc." In one corner stood several large, curiously shaped iron bars; in another were the omnipresent models of the iron bridge. Opposite a fireplace heaped with ashes lay a board on sawhorses "covered with pamphlets and journals, having more the appearance of a dresser in a scullery than a sideboard." During his fourteen years in France "time seemed to have made dreadful ravages over his whole frame, and a settled melancholy was visible on his countenance."

Paine's melancholy vanished, for a time at least, when he read the letter Dawson handed him. It "gave me the real sensation of happy satisfaction," he wrote back to Jefferson, "and what served to increase it was that he brought it to me himself before I knew of his arrival." Paine turned down the offer of the *Maryland*, giving no reason except to say he preferred to "wait the return of the vessel that brings Mr. Livingston." Perhaps he hoped that by lingering in France he would give Jefferson time to find a sinecure that would let him stay in Europe long enough to pay off his debts. "It would be a curious circumstance, if I should hereafter be sent as secretary of legation to the English court, which outlawed me," he told a later visitor, laughing as he spoke. "What a hubbub it would create at the King's levee, to see Tom Paine presented by the American ambassador! All the bishops and women would faint away; the women would suppose I came to ravish them, and the bishops, to ravish their tithes. I think it would be a good joke."

Dawson and Kosciusko were hardly out the door before Paine had a copy of Jefferson's letter translated and ready for the press. A France that no longer revered him must hear what the president of the United States thought of him. Paine wanted attention, and he got it. France was puzzled by the respect and affection extended to this American gadfly. England, as the newspapers there interpreted the letter, was surprised that a warship would be sent expressly to take Paine home. That the president would write "a *very affectionate letter* to that living opprobrium of humanity, TOM PAINE, the infamous scavenger of all the filth which could be raked from the dirty paths which have been hitherto trodden by all the revilers of Christianity" boggled the imagination of the *Gazette of the United States*, bellwether of the Federalist press. "What! Invite to the United States that lying, drunken, brutal infidel?" asked one editor, that "scavenger of faction," a drunken atheist loathsome to all Americans, remarked another. Curiously, none attacked him for sharing in the French Revolution. His crimes were writing *The Age of Reason* and the letter to George Washington.

The Republican press reacted limply, as if embarrassed to be saddled with Paine. The president's offer of a free trip in a public vessel implied "no more than that Thomas Paine had an equal claim to it with any OTHER AMERICAN CITIZEN." The *National Intelligencer*, party organ for the Republicans, asked Americans "to feel charity for the misfortune of a fellow mortal," and suggested that the "country might feel grateful for the distinguished services of a man, rendered in a period of difficulty and danger, though such a man might afterwards avow opinions which some might think good, others might think bad." A friend embarrassed by this timid defense from the party's leading paper told Paine it "appeared like a half denial of the letter or as if there was something in it not proper to be owned, or that needed an apology."

3

Back in Paris Paine awaited the ship that would bring Livingston to France and carry him home to America. He no longer wrote on politics, even in letters, though among friends he aired his disillusionment freely.

"I give up all hope that any good will be done by France," he told Skipwith. "That honor is reserved for America." His opinion of Napoleon—"There is not on record one who has committed so many faults and crimes with so little temptation to commit them"—had not mellowed, nor his opinion of Frenchmen. "Why, they are worse off than the slaves at Constantinople," he told a visitor; "for there, they expect to be bashaws in heaven, by submitting to be slaves below, but here, they believe neither in heaven nor hell, and yet are slaves by choice." His indifference about English affairs startled those who had known him over the years. "Indeed, he seemed to dislike the mention of the subject," said one. He would not be provoked to discussion even when a friend said he had altered his opinion on the applicability of Paine's principles to English society. "You certainly have the right to do so; but you cannot alter the nature of things," Paine answered mildly. "The French have alarmed all honest men; but still truth is truth. Though you may not think that my principles are practicable in England, without bringing on a great deal of misery and confusion, you are, I am sure, convinced of their justice."

He could, though, be provoked when talk turned to religion. "*The Age of Reason* has lost you the good opinion of numbers of your English advocates," he was told one day. "In a tone of singular energy" and with uncommon warmth he said he had written the book to "inspire mankind with a more exalted idea of the Supreme Architect of the universe, and to put an end to villainous imposture." He vowed he was willing to lay down his life for his creed and "the Bishop of Llandaff may roast me in Smithfield, if he likes, but human torture cannot shake my conviction." The gentle bishop, a humane and tolerant man, had published a reply to *The Age of Reason* that angered Paine as none other had. He had interleaved his copy of the bishop's work with remarks on almost every page and he delighted in reading aloud his comments to any visitor who would listen. He planned to publish his comments as the third part of *The Age of Reason*, "which, if I mistake not, will make a stronger impression than anything I have yet published on the subject."

Alcohol only increased his ardor on the subject. One evening at a dinner party where he had promised "*to be discreet*" because one of the ladies present was a devout Catholic, "he kept everyone in astonishment and admiration of his memory, his keen observation of men and manners, his numberless anecdotes," the host recalled. "Thus far everything went on as I could wish; the sparkling champagne gave a zest to his conversation, and we were all delighted. But alas! alas! an expression relating to his *Age of Reason* having been mentioned by one of the company, he broke out immediately. He began with astronomy. Addressing himself to Mrs. Y., he declared that the least inspection of the motion of the stars, was a convincing proof, that Moses was a liar. Nothing could stop him. In vain I attempted to change the subject, by employing every artifice in my power, and even by attacking with vehemence his political principles. He returned to the charge with unabated ardor. I called upon him for a song, though I never heard him sing in my life. He struck up instantly one of his own composition; but the instant he had finished it, he resumed his favorite topic. Every time he took breath, he gained fresh strength, and on he went, with inconceivable rapidity, until the ladies gradually stole unobserved from the room, and left another gentleman and myself to contest, or rather to leave him master of the field of battle."

Though ignored by the politicians of France, Paine did not want for flattery these days. "Many travelers called upon him," Mme. Bonneville reported, "and, often having no other affair, talked to him only of his great reputation and their admiration of his works. He treated such visitors with civility, but with little ceremony, and when their conversation was mere chit-chat, and he found they had nothing particular to say to him, he used to retire to his own pursuits, leaving them to entertain themselves with their own ideas." He sparkled when ladies called. "He received us with the greatest good humor, and instantly set about exhibiting his playthings," the bridge models, said one who paid a visit with Edward P. Livingston, the son-in-law of the new minister. The Bonneville boys, then four and five years old, were on hand when they arrived. "During the entire morning that we spent with him, they were playing about the room, over-turning all his machinery and putting everybody out of patience except himself, who exhibited the most incorrigible good temper."

Like everyone else, the lady could not help remarking on Paine's appearance. "Drinking spirits has made his entire face as red as fire and his habits of life have rendered him so neglectful in his person that he is generally the most abominably dirty being upon the face of the earth. He complimented us with a clean shirt, and with having his face washed, which Mr. Livingston said was one of the greatest efforts he ever was known to make." As the visit progressed, she soon found herself under Paine's spell. "In spite of his surprising ugliness, the expression of his countenance is luminous, his manners easy and benevolent, and his conversation remarkably entertaining," she admitted somewhat to her consternation. "Altogether his style of manner is guileless and good-natured, and I was agreeably disappointed in him, considering the odiously disagreeable things I was led to expect."

4

Completion of the iron bridge over the River Wear that incorporated his experimental arch helped to reawaken Paine's interest in the project that had brought him to Europe. England had excelled where he led the way. Surely now that the worth of his design had been proved, America would rush to execute it. He told visitors that when he returned to the United States he would supervise the erection of an iron span over the broad Delaware and the narrower Schuylkill.

Before returning he would have to improve his design. He made a new model in pasteboard, five feet long, five inches high from the cords. After bringing it "to high perfection," he reproduced it in metal. "This was the most pleasant amusement for him," said Mme. Bonneville. "Though he fully relied on the strength of his new bridge, and would produce arguments enough in proof of its infallible strength, he often demonstrated the proof by blows of the sledgehammer, not leaving anyone in doubt on the subject." Late one night after the Bonnevilles had gone to bed they heard him pounding away on the bridge with his hammer. Suddenly the noise stopped and Paine appeared at the bedroom door. "Come and look," he said, "it bears all my blows and stands like a rock." The Bonnevilles rose and dutifully followed their guest to his room. "Nothing in the world is so fine as my bridge," he said, then glancing at the silent Mme. Bonneville, added, *"except a woman!,"* a compliment "he seemed to think," said Mme. Bonneville, "a full compensation for the trouble caused by this nocturnal visit to the bridge."

The frequent visits of Robert Fulton kept Paine from focusing solely on his bridge. Fulton thought a steam engine turning paddle wheels would one day propel a boat over water. Paine doubted it, "because, I suppose, that the weight of the apparatus necessary to produce steam is greater than the power of the steam to remove that weight, and consequently that the steam engine cannot move itself." But what about gunpowder? "If the power which an ounce of gunpowder contains could be detailed out as steam or water can be [somewhat as gasoline is exploded in an internal-combustion engine, he would have added from the vantage point of a later century], it would be the most commodious natural power because of its small weight and little bulk."

Paine's mind teemed with projects, much as it had after the American Revolution when there was nothing on the political scene to stir his mind. He turned out a long essay—inspired perhaps by Fulton's book or by conversations with him—on the need for a system of canals and iron bridges to unify France and promote her industries. He constructed a crane to lift materials more efficiently than could those then in use. He wrote an essay on "a method of building houses without permitting damp to penetrate"—by covering the outside walls with plaster of paris rather than the limestone mortar used in America. He invented a machine for shaping boards into wheels. Because he thought this creation might make his fortune, he guarded its secret by having the machine "executed partly by one blacksmith and partly by another." Fulton drew blueprints that could be used for a patent application. (The specifications, along with Fulton's drawing, were submitted at Washington two years after Paine's death; nothing further came of the invention.)

5

Robert R. Livingston arrived in Paris early in December 1801. Paine called on him and his family soon after they had settled in. There was an easy, relaxed relationship between them, friendly rather than intimate but close enough that they could joke on matters they took seriously. When Paine was laid up for a week with a sore throat, Livingston stopped by with a "collection of discourses preached by Elihu Palmer," a former clergymen who, as Paine put it, "is now one of my converts and has opened a meeting house at New York, to expose the lies of the Bible and to show it is a forgery." Another time Livingston came for breakfast when Charles François Dupuis, author of *Origin of Worship (Origine de tous les cultes)*, was also a guest. Naturally, the talk centered on religion, but Paine also showed off his bridge models, his crane, and his planing machine. When Livingston got up to go, he turned to Paine and said with a smile, "Make your will; leave the mechanics, the iron bridge, the wheels, and so forth, to America, and your religion to France."

When Livingston some time later set out to see England, Paine urged him to visit "the numerous and respectable list of friends" he had there, among them his bookseller Johnson ("an honest worthy man") and Rickman ("a good fellow"). He gave him a letter of introduction to two others, Colonel William Bosville and Sir Francis Burdett, but feared he would miss them, for they were on their way to Paris. Sir Francis was a friend of Thomas Hardy—he later settled a pension upon him—but his claim to fame was that his beautiful mistress, Lady Oxford, later became the mistress of Lord Byron. Colonel Bosville—though never more than a lieutenant in the Coldstream Guard he was always known as colonel—was immensely rich and known for his generosity to unpopular causes. He admired Paine but disparaged his tendency to drink too much.

The colonel's and Sir Francis' visit to Paris proved fortunate for Paine. Before they departed for home the two showed their appreciation for the author of *The Rights of Man* by presenting him with five hundred louis d'or, a gift that would let him return to America in style once peace allowed him to set out, for now he would have to pay his way. The frigate that had brought Livingston to France had been diverted to the Mediterranean as part of a task force created to subdue the Barbary pirates that had been harassing American shipping.

Peace came in March 1802 when the French and English signed a truce at Amiens. "As it is now peace, though the definitive treaty is not yet signed," Paine wrote at once to Jefferson, "I shall set off by the first opportunity from Havre or Dieppe after the equinoxial gales are over." The "first opportunity" came six months later. During these months Paine tied up the loose ends of fifteen years in France. It was agreed that Mme. Bonneville and the three boys would follow Paine to America at the first chance and Bonneville would come when the government gave him permission to emigrate. Earlier Bonneville had been imprisoned for calling Napoleon a "Cromwell" in *le Bien informé*. Since then he had been under surveillance, and his paper had been suppressed. He earned his living by working here and there in printing offices, by writing articles, and translating books from German and English into French.

Sometime in August 1802 Clio Rickman came over from London to bid Paine farewell. After a few days in Paris together the two friends set off for Havre-de-Grâce, with Paine's few personal belongings, the bridge models, the planing machine, and his cartons of personal papers loaded into a carriage. Aware that he had been drinking too much, Paine planned to use the ocean trip as a health cure. He had, said Rickman, "objected to any spirits being laid in as a part of his sea stock" and packed only wine for the long trip.

PART
IV

America

1802–1809

CHAPTER

25

THE "LOATHSOME REPTILE" RETURNS

THE DAY PAINE'S SHIP docked at Baltimore, 30 October 1802, he found a storm brewing. Rumors had continued to float about that "our pious President thought it expedient to dispatch a frigate for the accommodation of this loathsome reptile." One wit wondered how Paine would get his baggage ashore, for "we know it is requisite to make oath at the custom-house, upon *the Holy Evangelists,* that the trunks contain no articles for sale."

The reception at dockside belied what lay ahead. A small crowd of the curious, among them even a few Federalists with "smiling friendly expressions," turned out to watch the old man, now sixty-five but still slender, step ashore. No one joked about his bulbous nose or his scarlet face. The welcoming party accompanied Paine to a convenient tavern, and there, "after sipping well of brandy, he became somewhat fluent in conversation, and readily declared that Mr. Jefferson's invitations were the cause of his returning to this country." He showed off the bridge models, said he was sending them along to Washington, and that he would soon follow to visit the president.

According to one reporter, "The writings of Mr. *Paine* on religious subjects were not even mentioned, and the right of private opinion was neither assailed, nor brought into question." The lapse was momentary, as Paine learned before the week was out. Friendly papers praised him as a man "whose writings *vindicated America* and the *Rights of Mankind,*" but the Federalist press would not let the public forget that the author of *The Age of Reason* was Christianity's "most rancorous, though by no means its most *decent, refined, or elegant foe.*"

353

Paine at first seemed pleased with "the agitation my arrival has occasioned," telling a friend that every newspaper from New Hampshire to Georgia "was filled with applause or abuse." The abuse persisted. One editor called him an "obscene old sinner," another an "infamous scavenger," and still another suggested Jefferson might use him for manure. How did "*so notorious a drunkard,* and *so impious a buffoon*" gain such ascendancy over people's minds, asked one writer? A line from a satirical poem informed those who had not seen him that "His nose is a blazing star!" His presence had struck the Federalists "as with an hydrophobia," Paine said shortly after leaving Baltimore for Washington; "it is like the sight of water to canine madness." But the barbs cut deep and soon drew blood. These Federalists, he cried out at last, sounding like a wounded animal, "these Terrorists of the New World, who were waiting in the devotion of their hearts for the joyful news of my destruction, are the same banditti who are now bellowing in all the hackneyed language of the hackneyed infidelity, and they finish with the chorus of *Crucify him, crucify him.* I am become so famous among them, they cannot eat or drink without me. I serve them as a standing dish, and they cannot make up a bill of fare if I am not in it."

2

Not all the press was bad. "Years have made more impression on his body than his mind," the Philadelphia *Aurora,* a Republican paper, reported. "He bends a little forward, carries one hand in the other when he walks. He dresses plain like a farmer, and appears cleanly and comfortable in his person, unless in the article of snuff which he uses in profusion. His address is unaffected and unceremonious. He neither shuns nor courts observation. At table he enjoys what is good with appetite of temperance and vigor, and puts to shame his calumniators by the moderation with which he partakes of the common beverage of the boarders. His conversation is uncommonly interesting, he is gay, humorous, and full of anecdote—his memory preserves its full capacity, and his mind is irresistible and I may say its obstinate determination to pursue whatever object it embraces."

The transition from Paris to bucolic Washington staggered even Paine's ability to be gay and humorous. The official community numbered 291 persons. Of these, 152 were congressmen, all of whom were absent when Paine arrived. Congress normally convened sometime after the harvest season and sat until it was time for spring planting. The president and his cabinet, except for the hard-working secretary of the treasury, Albert Gallatin, vanished during the humid summer months, leaving the government to be run by clerks. No one had anything good to say for the town. "It may be compared to a country seat where state sportsmen may run horses and fight cocks," a contemptuous Philadelphian said. In the midst of a desolate landscape the president, he added, sits "like a pelican in the wilderness, or a sparrow upon the housetop." As if to emphasize the separation of powers, congressmen lived in boardinghouses scattered around the unfinished capitol, while across a mile-wide malarial swamp another community orbited around the executive mansion. Both were self-contained hamlets with their own markets, craftsmen, and servants, and both were uninviting. "Where monuments had been planned brush piles moldered and rubbish heaps accumulated," a historian of the town has remarked. "Where majestic avenues were to sweep, swaths of tree stumps stood, rough quarried stone marking the intersections. Cows grazed on future plazas and bullfrogs chorused on the mall. Wildlife overran the premises."

In such a place gossip was a mainstay of life and Paine's arrival added considerably to the town's store of it. Rumors floated about that the residents of two taverns had "refused to remain in the house if Tom were admitted to the public table." He finally found quarters at Lovell's Hotel —a boardinghouse, traveling under an assumed name—but even there he was harassed. "The members who are there are not willing to acknowledge they have any society with him," a prejudiced Federalist reported. "He dines at the public table, and, as a show, is as profitable to Lovell as an *Ourang Outang*, for many strangers who come to the city feel a curiosity to see the creature. They go to Lovell's and call for the show."

Paine had arrived in Washington expecting to stay at a boardinghouse. Even in Paris he had only visited, never lived in, Jefferson's home. But if the president's conscience had, by chance, made him think it necessary to put up the much-abused Paine at the executive mansion, he had a good reason not to extend an invitation: Jefferson's two daughters, together with his grandchildren, had chosen this time, when Congress was out of session and executive business at an ebb, to visit him. The daughters would have preferred not to have had Paine pay even a social call. One of them told her father as much. "Mr. Paine is not, I believe, a favorite among the ladies," he replied to her, "but he is too well entitled to the hospitality of every American not to cheerfully receive mine." Paine came, and while the Federalists grumbled that the president "admits him freely and frequently to his house and his table" the ladies "found his manners sober and inoffensive; and he left Mr. Jefferson's mansion the subject of lighter prejudices than he entered it."

Paine was "civilly received by the President whom I suspect he will much embarrass," a Federalist reported. He "is not despised, neither is he the bosom friend of Mr. Jefferson," a mutual friend remarked. Paine continued to be the man he had always been, an easygoing companion who liked to pass an evening in good talk laced with brandy. (He appeared to have his drinking under control. "Mr. Paine is not now, whatever he might have been," a friendly paper reported, "inclined to inebriety, but is as abstemious as the *tories* would wish him otherwise.") Jefferson the private citizen could still enjoy his company; Jefferson the president had to be circumspect with a man whom the bulk of America regarded as an "outrageous blasphemer." Considering the vituperation then being heaped upon Paine, Jefferson showed courage as well as courtesy by inviting him to visit. The invitation, said one writer, only proved that the president, like Paine, believed "that *the story of the birth of Jesus Christ is an* OBSCENE, BLASPHEMOUS FABLE . . . that the Virgin Mary was a woman of bad fame, and that her husband was cornuted." A less violent reaction to Paine's presence came from another Federalist who had been taken to the executive mansion to be introduced to the president. "In a few moments after our arrival, a tall high-boned man came into the room," he related. "He was dressed, or rather undressed, in an old brown coat, red waistcoat, old corduroy, small clothes much soiled, woolen hose, and slippers without heels." The supposed servant turned out to be Jefferson. Within a few minutes his charm had all but disarmed the suspicious Federalist, who later confessed Jefferson had been "easy of access, and conversed with ease and freedom." Then in came Paine, seated "himself by the side of the President, and conversed and behaved towards him with the familiarity of an intimate and an equal!" The sight caused the Federalist later to wonder: "Can virtue receive sufficient protection from an administration which admits such men as Paine to terms of intimacy with its chief?"

3

The Age of Reason gave Federalists excuse enough to abuse Paine. A few days after he had brushed the dust of Baltimore from his feet and settled in at Lovell's Hotel he handed them another, this time in an open letter, the first of a series addressed "To the Citizens of the United States." The letters proved, in case anyone had forgotten, that the old man had not mellowed with age and that his style had lost none of its force.

The opening sentence of the first letter set the tone for all that followed: "After an absence of almost fifteen years, I am again returned to the country in whose dangers I bore my share, and to whose greatness I contributed my part." The Federalists ranted about his religion or lack of it. Let them know that he owed his survival "through a thousand dangers" endured in the French Revolution "not to the prayers of priests, not to the piety of hypocrites, but to the continued protection of Providence." And who were these Federalists? No more than "little barkings of scribblings and witless curs who pass for nothing," a faction who contemplated "government as a profitable monopoly, and the people as a hereditary property." What about the Federalist newspapers, those loud mouthers of "noisy nothingness"? "It is on themselves the disgrace recoils," said Paine, "for the reflection easily presents itself to every thinking mind, that *those who abuse liberty when they possess it would abuse power could they obtain it.*" Rumors had circulated that Paine would accept a sinecure in the government. Not so. "I have some manuscript works to publish, of which I shall give proper notice, and some mechanical affairs to bring forward, that will empty all my leisure time."

Republicans chuckled to see "with what dignity" Paine had walked "over the federal curs of America" in this opening barrage, "scarce deigning to glance at this puny and bastard breed, which is only calculated to make a *noise* and wear *collars,* the badges of their slavery and *dependence.*" The Federalists dismissed the *"chosen vessel* of our beloved President!" as a hack limited to calling his adversaries *"mad dogs!"*

In the second letter a week later he violated a rule of his—to "be always master of one's temper in writing." At the outset it appeared his purpose was to flay Federalism again, but he had not got far into the discussion before he descended to castigating poor John Adams—a man "of a bewildered mind," "of paradoxical heresies," a man "not born for immortality." The diatribe ended on an even crueler note: "Some people talk of impeaching John Adams; but I am for softer measures. I would keep him to make fun of." Adams, who must have wondered what prompted the assault, could never erase it from his mind, partly because "I never had one friend in the world to contradict the lying rascal, though hundreds were able to do it of their own knowledge."

Paine's rage slips out of control again in the third letter, as he moves in on George Washington. He makes a witless comparison of the Reign of Terror in France, where thousands lost their lives, to "the Reign of Terror that raged in America during the latter end of the Washington administration, and the whole of that of Adams," then remarks that the leaders in both countries were "in character the same sort of men." He judges Washington "of such an icy and death-like constitution that he neither loved his friends nor hated his enemies." And what has the great Washington done to merit idolatry? "That gentleman did not perform his part in the Revolution better, nor with more honor, than I did mine, and the one part was as necessary as the other." Paine ends in a fury so great that he refuses to give the dateline "City of Washington," as in the previous letters, but now signs it from "Federal City." (Ironically, in calling it Federal City Paine had chosen the name Washington wished it to be called.)

Paine's rage had now spent itself. The fourth letter, published from "Federal City" on December 6, two days after Congress reconvened, offers little more than a potpourri of remnant thoughts. He gloats in his role of being "a living contradiction of the mortified Federalists." Look at my surpassing good fortune, he says. "I am now in my circumstances independent; and my economy makes me rich. As to my health, it is perfectly good, and I leave the world to judge of the stature of my mind."

The Federalists did just that. The diatribes embarrassed Republicans, who urged the president to muzzle Paine. The president listened, then let William Duane, editor of *Aurora*, speak for him. Mr. Jefferson "has seen him devoting his time, health, and talents to promote freedom," Duane wrote shortly after the fourth letter appeared, "he has seen Mr. Paine's return to this country with pleasure, and will not by a line of conduct recommended, and which could only be pursued by *tories*, send him in his old age with sorrow to his grave; but by showing a respect, merited from Americans, will evince the goodness of his own heart, and fulfill the wishes of his constituents."

4

After Congress assembled early in December, Jefferson treated Paine more circumspectly. Paine's visits to the executive mansion continued so quietly, if at all, that one Federalist remarked, "I have not heard of his being at the President's since the commence of the session, and it is believed that Mr. Jefferson sensibly feels the severe, though just remarks which have been made on his inviting him to this country."

The president's discretion did not mean Paine lived cut off from society. Stephen R. Bradley, president pro tem of the Senate, "in imitation of the President, admits that miscreant Paine to his table," a disgruntled congressman reported. But Bradley, as had Jefferson, invited only Republicans when Paine came to dinner, "and in this they show their prudence." The Whigs of '76 and the Republicans of 1800 gave him "a cordial reception"; they marred the occasion slightly by their self-conscious boast of "independence to feel and avow a sentiment of gratitude for his eminent revolutionary services." Henry Dearborn, secretary of war, had him to dinner and so, too, did Albert Gallatin, who had married Hannah Nicholson, whom Paine had known when she was a youngster growing up in New York City.

"This extraordinary man contributed exceedingly to entertain the company," one of the guests at Gallatin's party said. "We had some conversation before dinner, and we sat side by side at the table. He has a red and rugged face, which looks as if it had been much hackneyed in the service of the world. His eyes are black and lively, his nose somewhat aquiline and pointing downward. It corresponds in color with the fiery appearance of his cheeks." Paine's conversation ran the spectrum of his life. He told anecdotes about Indians he had met at Easton in 1777, recited a poem attacking Gouverneur Morris—"You would have been pleased to hear this old schoolboy speak his piece"—and rambled on about "things not in print concerning the American Revolution."

The party at the Dearborns' had gone equally well—so much so that after dinner when it came time for the ladies to retire Mrs. Dearborn "intimated that the conversation would be acceptable in the drawing room." The Federalists twisted the pleasant occasion into an attack on Paine, using a letter supposedly by Dr. Manasseh Cutler of Massachusetts. "After dinner, Paine began to ridicule *religion*, and blaspheme the

Nazarene in the most *shocking* manner. Mrs. D——n, with an air of dignified authority, arose, opened the door, and *bid him Begone!* Paine and his
friends feared and looked thunderstruck!" Mrs. Dearborn said she could
endure no more, "then pointing to the door commanded him to *begone that
moment!* He then left the room, while the company sat in amazement!"
Cutler later solemnly declared "that he never wrote or insinuated anything which could countenance such a falsehood," but the harm had been
done. The forgery traveled from newspaper to newspaper through the
continent. Paine saw now that unless the attacks against his religious
views were contained he would become a liability to Jefferson's party and
of no use as a propagandist. He and Duane agreed that "all this *war-hoop*
from the pulpit" served as a stalking-horse behind which the Federalists
concealed their true purpose—"to prejudice the president in the eyes of
his constituents." Paine saw a deeper conspiracy—"to overthrow the
Federal Constitution established on the representative system, and place
government in the New World on the corrupt system of the Old."

Regardless of why the Federalists kept firing away, clearly their guns
must be spiked before the Republicans could use Paine. The chance to
do so came in December when he received a letter from his old friend
Samuel Adams, now eighty and retired from public life. It had grieved
Adams, it had astonished him, to learn that Paine had turned his "mind
to a defense of infidelity." "Do you think," he asked, "that your pen or
the pen of any other man can unchristianize the mass of our citizens, or
have you hopes of converting a few of them to assist you in so bad a
cause?"

Paine pondered his reply for a month. He showed friends a draft to
make sure he had hit the right tone, then before mailing the final version
he turned a copy over to the press. He had aimed this artful, dignified
statement of his religious views at the public rather than Adams. The
theme developed out of a remark by Samuel Adams—the duty of public
men in America was "to *renovate the age* by inculcating in the minds of
youth *the fear and love of the Deity and universal philanthropy.*" "Why, my
dear friend," said Paine, "this is exactly *my* religion, and is the whole
of it. . . . *I believe in God!* . . . do you call believing in God infidelity?" And
how does one serve God? Exactly as Adams had urged, through universal
philanthropy, or as Paine preferred to put it: "not by praying, but by
endeavoring to make his creatures happy." So far so good. Adams had
worried that *The Age of Reason* might "unchristianize" Americans. Paine
tiptoed around this point. "The case, my friend," he said, "is that the

world has been overrun with fable and creeds of human invention, with sectaries of whole nations against all other nations, and sectaries of those sectaries in each of them against each other."

The letter ended with one of the finest sentences Paine ever wrote. "Our relations to each other in this world," he told Adams, "is as men and the man who is a friend to man and to his rights, let his religious opinions be what they may, is a good citizen to whom I can give, as I ought to do, and as every other ought, the right hand of fellowship, and to none with more hearty good will, my dear friend, than to you."

The care poured into the letter went for nothing, so far as Paine could tell from the public's reaction. Adams, who died a few months later, never replied.

5

An incident that occurred during the Christmas season revealed the distance between Paine and Jefferson and how much their relationship had changed since the days of London and Paris when neither man held back political secrets. The revelation came about by accident, the result of a conversation in Lovell's Hotel between Paine and a congressman from Pennsylvania, Dr. Michael Leib. Word had crossed the ocean that Spain had ceded the Louisiana Territory to France. Simultaneously, the Mississippi had been closed to American traffic, provoking a stream of protests into Washington from settlers in the regions affected. Federalists in Congress, hoping to embarrass the peace-minded Jefferson, called for a declaration of war. Paine thought the difficulty could be solved another way.

The United States, he said, might begin by sending to France and Spain a "remonstrance against an infraction of a right," but he doubted this would achieve much. The other course "is by accommodation—still keeping the right in view, but not making it a groundwork." Paine's approach to the problem impressed Leib. "By beginning on this ground anything can be said without the appearance of a threat," he went on. "The growing power of the Western Territory can be stated as a matter of information, and also the impossibility of restraining them [the United States] from seizing upon New Orleans, and the equal impossibility of France to prevent it."

Having laid this groundwork, Paine continued, the United States should then offer to buy the entire territory from France. The purchase price could "be estimated between the value of the commerce and the quantity of revenue that Louisiana will produce." Leib asked why France would be receptive to this "monied proposal." "The French treasury," replied Paine, "is not only empty, but the government has consumed by anticipation a great part of the next year's revenue. A monied proposal will, I believe, be attended to; if it should, the claims upon France can be stipulated as part of the payment, and that sum can be paid here to the claimants."

The conversation ended with Dr. Leib suggesting that Paine pass his thoughts on Louisiana along to the president. On December 25 he did so, sending his essay to Jefferson as a Christmas present "on *The Birthday of the New Sun.*" The next morning he visited the executive mansion to find out how his essay had been received. Jefferson said "that measures were already taken in that business," a vague remark that glossed over the more limited plans he had in mind for Louisiana. Robert R. Livingston had been instructed to buy if he could only the island on which New Orleans lay, not the Louisiana Territory. Paine's bolder proposal would be the one eventually adopted, not because Jefferson pushed for it, but because, as Paine had said, the French treasury was empty and Napoleon needed cash to pursue his war against England.

After the chat with Jefferson, Paine returned to Lovell's. He searched out Leib and told him of the conversation with the president. Leib nodded and said he had known all about the negotiations for New Orleans.

"Why, then," said Paine, "did you not tell me so, because in that case I would not have sent the note."

"That is the reason I would not tell you," Leib replied, "because two opinions concurring on a case strengthen it."

The incident left Paine with a sour taste. Now, if not before, he realized how far removed he was from the confidence he once enjoyed with Jefferson. He brooded for three weeks, then, on 12 January 1803, sent a brief note to the president. "I will be obliged to you to send back the models, as I am packing up to set off to Philadelphia and New York," he said, referring to his bridge models. "My intentions in bringing them here in preference to sending them from Baltimore to Philadelphia, was, to have some conversation with you on those matters and others I have not informed you of. But you have not only shown no disposition to-wards it, but have, in some measure, by a sort of shyness, as if you stood in fear of federal observation, precluded it. I am not the only one, who makes observations of this kind.''

Jefferson replied the following day: "You have certainly misconceived what you deem shyness. Of that I have not had a thought towards you, but on the contrary have openly maintained in conversation the duty of showing our respect to you and of defying federal calumny in this as in other cases, by doing what is right. As to fearing it, if I ever could have been weak enough for that, they have taken care to cure me of it thoroughly." He reminded Paine of the pressure of public business, which had been unrelenting since the return of Congress; he said he had been obliged to forgo mechanical and mathematical matters since he had become president. However, he thought well of the models, especially the one for planing wheels. He would like a couple of them if ever they should be made and sold. Jefferson may, as a biographer has said, have "been merely going through the motions with Paine, impelled by a sense of duty, but he appears to have done as much as could have been expected of a busy chief magistrate. It appears, also, that neither at this time nor thereafter did he utter a word of complaint against one who was doing him far more political harm than good."

The note mollified Paine. He stayed in "Federal City" nearly a month more and wrote an essay on iron bridges he hoped would convince Congress to appropriate money for an experimental span of four hundred feet. Should it do so, "I will furnish the proportions for the several parts of the work and give my attendance to superintend the erection of it." He was advised—by whom he did not say—not to submit the proposal now because the current "session would necessarily be short, and as several of its members would be replaced by new elections at the ensuing session."

This was balderdash. There were those among the Republicans, notably in the northern states, who favored federal aid for internal improvements, but so long as Jefferson remained president no Congress under his thumb would sanction such a program. Paine seems not yet to have caught on—perhaps he never did—that Jefferson and his followers still held to a doctrine he had discarded years ago—"the least government the best." They wanted a central government weaker than water. If canals were to be dug, if roads were to be cut through the forests, if iron bridges were to span the rivers—the states must foot the bills. Jefferson was engaged in dismantling as much as he could of the foundation built by the Federalists during twelve years in power. He and Paine agreed on the conduct of foreign affairs—be lenient toward France, hard on England —and that assured Paine's loyalty to the party. The obloquy showered upon him by the Federalist press and hatred for Washington and Adams also helped to keep him within the fold. But if he had ever inquired deeply into Jefferson's views on the role of the central government in the life of the nation Paine would have had at least a few misgivings about the banner he traveled under. He was a Republican as much by default as by conviction.

CHAPTER

26

AN "OBSCENE OLD SINNER" SETTLES IN

PAINE LEFT WASHINGTON in mid-February 1803, paused in Baltimore, and then moved on to Philadelphia, where he expected to renew friendships made a quarter of a century earlier during the days that tried men's souls. Some old friends, like Benjamin Rush, revolted by the blasphemous *Age of Reason*, refused to speak to him; others, like Charles Willson Peale, welcomed him back warmly. Peale gave him a tour of his museum—a conglomeration of dinosaur bones and other artifacts, mechanical models, and a multitude of Peale's paintings, all nicely housed in the American Philosophical Society's hall. Peale promised to add Paine's bridge models to the collection when they arrived from Washington.

The tour of the museum exposed Paine to an insult of the sort "good" people would hand out to him the rest of his life. While watching a young lady having her profile made by a machine called a "phisognotrace," he said by way of being friendly, "They take off *heads here*, with great expedition, Miss." "Not quite so fast, sir, as they once did in France," the girl answered, a reply that, according to an observer of the exchange, "so discomfited Paine, that he turned on his heel, and walked to another part of the room." An old man standing nearby whispered to the girl, "Excellent! Excellent! young woman! The Lord is merciful, or the earth would open and swallow up that wretch."

Paine spent three days in Philadelphia before crossing the Delaware to Bordentown, where he arrived on February 24. Colonel Kirkbride as usual put him up. There also to meet him were Mme. Bonneville and her three boys—Benjamin, Thomas, and the infant Louis—who had landed in America early in November at Norfolk, Virginia. Paine had not encouraged her to stop off at Washington. Though Mme. Bonneville had landed in a strange world where she barely understood the language, he told her to borrow money from a friend of his in Norfolk and find her way to the home of Colonel Kirkbride, "from whom you will receive every friendship." Somehow she had managed.

A few days after reaching Bordentown Paine got another example of the reception he could expect from strangers. He and Kirkbride had gone to Trenton, where Paine planned to catch a stagecoach to New York. "I'll be damned if he shall go in my stage," one man said when Kirkbride tried to book a seat. "My stage and horses were once struck by lightning, and I don't want them to suffer again," said another. By the time Kirkbride had hired a chaise word had spread through town of Paine's presence. A mob led by a drummer beating out the "rogue's march" surrounded the carriage. Paine scanned the jeering crowd without "the least emotion of fear or anger, but calmly observed that such conduct had no tendency to hurt his feelings or injure his fame."

He arrived in New York on March 2 and immediately went round to see James Monroe, who expected to sail for France the next day. Jefferson had recently appointed him minister extraordinary to France, where, working with Livingston, he would help negotiate the Louisiana Purchase. Paine handed over a packet of letters for Monroe to deliver to friends in France. One of these was to Nicholas Madgett, an Irishman who worked for the minister of marine and with whom Paine was "on very friendly terms." Madgett had been assigned by his minister, when Paine still lived in Paris, to collect all the information he could on Louisiana, and at one point in his research he had asked Paine to draw up a constitution for Louisiana, a request refused on the ground "that it was impossible to draw up a constitution for a people and a country that one knew nothing of," a remark he would not have made ten years earlier. Paine now urged Monroe to call on Madgett. He would not have to pump him for facts; "only give him the opportunity of telling, and he will make a merit of it, and the more so, if he joins to it the idea that you come on the good mischief of preventing mischief."

All this Paine put in a long memorandum to Monroe that he could read at leisure on the crossing. At the end he suggested that it would "be a measure of precaution to get Spain to sign or attest the cession," for if the monarchy were ever restored in France it might assume that nothing done since Louis XVI's overthrow was binding on the nation. The advice was sound and pointed up the contrast between Paine's public and private character. Publicly he saw all issues, all men, in black and white: Federalists evil, Republicans good; England wrong, France right; Jefferson a saint, Adams a devil. Privately, when emotions were not involved, he invariably showed a sound understanding of the complexities of the problem at hand, when accommodations should be made, where a gamble should be taken. In Paris Monroe pressed for Spain's approval of the sale of the Louisiana Territory but pressure from Napoleon for an instant decision made it impossible.

2

The trip to New York was the best thing that had happened to Paine since his return to America. The city was filled with immigrants from the British Isles, and it seemed all of them had read *The Rights of Man* and all were eager to stand the author to a drink. "One day laborer would say, drink with me Mr. Paine; another, drink with me," an unfriendly biographer reported, "and he very condescendingly gratified them all." On March 18 Paine was honored with a banquet. "A numerous company of republicans" gathered at the City Hotel at four o'clock and six hours later, after many, many toasts, all "accompanied with appropriate songs and music"—among the songs was "The Fourth of July" (tune: "Rule Britannia") by Thomas Paine—the company retired, so the news account said, "in perfect harmony and order." A few days later Paine returned to Bordentown bubbling with good spirits. "He was well and appeared jollier than I had ever known him," said his old friend John Hall, who visited him there. "He is full of whims and schemes and mechanical inventions, and is to build a place or shop to carry them into execution, and wants my help."

Apparently the citizens of Bordentown had come to accept the infidel in their midst as something less than the sinner advertised. Tradition holds that he continued to be "by the mass of the people held in odium," but it also holds that he had a large number of friends with whom he met regularly at the Washington House, where "his drink was invariably brandy" and he talked freely "with any proper person who approached him." He visited the tavern daily, at the end of his afternoon walk. Residents of Bordentown, as had those of Philadelphia, Lancaster, London, and Paris, remarked that "in walking he was generally absorbed in deep thought, seldom noticed anyone as he passed, unless spoken to, and in going from his home to the tavern was frequently observed to cross the street several times."

Soon after returning to the village Paine involved himself in an election campaign by writing two essays. The first, his best piece since returning to America, was written in March at Bordentown and published as the sixth letter to the citizens of the United States. In it he defended Jefferson's first two years as president. To him "the United States owe, as far as human means are concerned, the preservation of peace, and of national honor." Under Adams' administration, by contrast, America had been "kept in continual agitation and alarm; and, that no investigation might be made into its conduct, it entrenched itself within a magic circle of terror, and called it a SEDITION LAW." He ended calling again for an investigation of Adams, "not to punish, but to satisfy; and to show, by example, to future administrations, that an abuse of power and trust, however disguised by appearances, or rendered plausible by pretense, is one time or another to be accounted for."

Federalists everywhere, but particularly in New Jersey, were using his association with Jefferson as a weapon to win seats in Congress. In his second campaign piece on April 21 Paine sought to still the attacks by publishing the letter Jefferson had sent to him in France offering homebound passage on an American warship. The essay was long, temperate, and dull, full of lengthy excerpts from the *Compact Maritime*. The point of the piece was to push into the shadows Jefferson's invitation of a free trip home and emphasize the "peaceable principles" contained in the president's letter. The essay contributed little to the Republican victory that spring in New Jersey.

A lazy summer followed. In June Congress disbanded, having of course done nothing about his request for a subsidy to build an iron bridge. Paine at last abandoned hope for his dream. He sent the memoir on iron bridges he had planned to present to Congress to the press, hoping, he said, it would help guide those who someday would span the rivers of America with iron bridges. A month later the two bridge models he had shown Jefferson arrived in Philadelphia. Along with the invoice that would allow Peale to pick them up at the freight office he sent a note warning that "the models to be viewed in a proper position should be placed as high as the eye." He ended on a wistful note: "With respect to the Schuylkill Bridge, it would have been constructed in a single arch. It would then have been an honor to the state."

On his first Independence Day in America since 1787 Paine was invited as one of the guests of honor to a banquet in New York. His contribution to the affair was an "extempore" poem. Paine loved to recite his poetry to an audience and pulled out all the stops when performing. The poem he gave this day allowed ample room to display his talents. A typical stanza ran:

> Palled with streams of reeking gore
> That stain the proud imperial day,
> He turns to view the western shore,
> Where freedom holds her boundless sway.

Paine's most substantial work that summer came in three long letters on Louisiana. The first, a public letter, appeared in May. In it he attacked the Federalists as warmongers for encouraging Western farmers to seize New Orleans.

By August the purchase of Louisiana Territory had become known but not yet approved by Congress. Paine worried that the Federalists might be able to defeat the accession treaty in the Senate. "I love the restriction" the Constitution has imposed on the president's treaty-making power "because we cannot be too cautious involving and entangling ourselves with foreign powers," he told Henry Brackenridge in the second long letter, but the agreement to purchase Louisiana is not a treaty and thus does not require approval of two-thirds of the Senate. "We are the sole power concerned after the cession is accepted and the money paid, and therefore the cession is not a treaty in the constitutional meaning of the word, subject to be reviewed by a minority of the Senate," the minority, of course, being Federalists. "The object here is an increase of territory for a valuable consideration. It is altogether a home concern— a matter of domestic policy."

He made the same point in his third letter, to Jefferson, then offered the president advice on how to incorporate within the Union a body of foreigners who not only were unacquainted with American traditions but were also Catholics. He worried how to "hold the priests in a style of good behavior." Let the people be initiated into American practices by giving them "the right of electing their church ministers, otherwise their ministers will hold by authority from the Pope," he suggested. "I do not make it a compulsive article, but to put it in their power to use it when they please," if only to give them "an idea of elective rights."

3

Late in August Paine set out for Stonington, Connecticut, to visit his friend Captain Nathan Haley. Though it was a backwater fishing village, Captain Haley called it home port for his small ship *Brutus*. Paine's presence created a stir there; the curious from surrounding villages as far away as New London came to see and listen. Originally he had planned to stay three weeks; he lingered on well into autumn relishing the attention he received.

Jefferson unwittingly contributed to his celebrity. Shortly after Paine turned up in Stonington, two letters arrived addressed to Mr. Thomas Paine from the president of the United States. In them Jefferson discussed the problems involved in annexing Louisiana. Paine read the letters aloud whenever he had an audience, always interjecting his views on the questions raised by the president. Jefferson had worried about the constitutionality of annexation. A procedure "with which the Constitution has nothing to do, and which can be judged only by the circumstances of the times when such a case shall occur," said Paine. "The cession makes no alteration in the Constitution; it only extends the principles of it over a larger territory, and this certainly is within the morality of the Constitution, and not contrary to, nor beyond, the expression of intention of any of its articles." (These "sensible comments" came from "one of the few correspondents of Jefferson to tackle the constitutional question," according to the president's biographer.)

Paine carried the farmers and fishermen who came to listen out of their narrow lives and into the world of international affairs. He painted England's government as "tottering" and predicted that a touch from Napoleon would topple it. "In that case it is not improbable we may obtain Canada," he said. He thought that Bermuda, "a nest for piratical privateers," also ought to be added to the American empire. He predicted Napoleon would attempt the invasion in November, landing somewhere along the more than two hundred miles of flat sandy beaches that lined the English coast on the North Sea which he had come to know well as an excise officer who had to patrol them.

Paine's conversation with his Stonington visitors sometimes moved into the delicate area of religion. One day a group of Baptists, "among whom were three ministers," showed up. Talk turned to the upcoming presidential election.

"They cry out against Mr. Jefferson because, they say, he is a deist," one of the Baptists said. "Well, a deist may be a good man, and if he think it right, it is right to him. For my own part, I had rather vote for a deist than for a blue-skin Presbyterian."

"You judge right," said Paine, "for a man that is not of any of the sectaries will hold the balance even between all; but give power to a bigot of any sectary and he will use it to the oppression of the rest, as the blue-skins do in connection."

As the autumn wore on, Paine realized he must soon leave Stonington. That meant he must also begin to foot his own bills, and to that end he conceived a get-rich-quick scheme that seemed foolproof. "I shall be employed in the ensuing winter in cutting two or three thousand cords of wood on my farm at New Rochelle for the New York market, distant twenty miles by water," he explained to a friend. "The wood is worth 3½ dollars per load as it stands. This will furnish me with ready money, and I shall then be ready for whatever may present itself of most importance next spring." The plan called for him to stay in Stonington until "the wood cutting time comes on," then he would "engage some cutters here and then return to New Rochelle."

4

Nothing came of the wood-cutting scheme. Paine had no more arrived at his farm in New Rochelle than he came down with what he called a severe "fit of gout," but what another described as "a sort of paralytic affection, which took away the use of his hands." Obviously, he could not live alone on his farm. He stayed for several weeks in the house of Capt. Daniel Pelton, who kept a store in the village, and later for two months with one of Pelton's clerks, Mr. Staple. When weather permitted he lounged away the day in front of the store trading memories with other old-timers, joshing the children, whose mothers had talked of Paine in a way that made them think *Tom* Paine must be a very bad and brutal man." Every afternoon Staple piled him into a gig for a ride through the countryside. Staple found him "the reverse of morose, and though careless in his dress and prodigal of his snuff, he was always clean and well-clothed." He drank so little at the time that Staple considered him "as really abstemious, and when pressed to drink by those on whom he called during his ride, he usually refused with great firmness but politely."

By January Paine had had enough of a country winter and moved down to New York. He put up for a while at the City Hotel. The proprietor, who had heard of Paine's capacity for alcohol, reported that his renowned guest drank less than any of the other boarders. At this time he was welcomed in the city's best homes. Dr. Nicholas Romaine, one of the leading physicians, often had him to dinner. Dr. Romaine was learned and bulky, weighed over three hundred pounds and loved to eat. John Pintard, one of the "enlightened citizens" who sometimes shared Paine's afternoon walk about the city, joined them once at the table. He had known Paine since the American Revolution, and they bantered good-humoredly together.

"I have read and re-read your *Age of Reason,*" Pintard said, "and any doubts which I before entertained of the truth of revelation, have been removed by your logic. Yes, sir, your very arguments against Christianity have convinced me of its truth."

"Well, then," said Paine, "I may return to my couch tonight with the consolation that I have made at least *one* Christian."

Soon after Paine moved into the City Hotel Mme. Bonneville, distraught with loneliness in Bordentown, came to New York with the three boys. Paine, though displeased, took rooms for himself and her family at James Wilburn's boardinghouse. Now the problem of money became pressing—and irritating, for Mme. Bonneville's "notions of economy" did not square with Paine's. When Wilburn presented a bill for thirty-five dollars' worth of extra charges she had incurred, he refused to pay. Wilburn sued. The court found for Paine, but no sooner had the verdict been delivered than Paine paid the bill, hoping the public humiliation had persuaded Mme. Bonneville to adopt thriftier habits.

The deaths of old friends, silence from others, contributed to Paine's discontent that winter. Samuel Adams had died the previous October, Colonel Kirkbride a few weeks later. The ice-blocked harbor closed off contact with Europe for over three months. "What is Barlow about?" he wondered in a letter to a friend in Paris. "I have not heard anything from him except that he is *always* coming. What is Bonneville about? Not a line has been received from him." Paine filled the gap with a new set of friends—John Fellows, a veteran of the Battle of Bunker Hill, who had published the first American edition of *The Age of Reason* but now ran the city's waterworks; William Carver, a blacksmith and veterinarian, who as a boy in Lewes had held Paine's horse when he served in the excise service; Elihu Palmer, a blind ex-Presbyterian minister, who now headed the Deistical Society of New York and published a journal called *The Prospect, or View of the Moral World.*

Paine sent several pieces to *The Prospect*, most of them culled from the manuscript of the third part of *The Age of Reason.* He signed the first one with his full name and the second "T.P." Thereafter, heeding an admonition handed to him in Stonington that his deistical works would harm the Republicans at a time when Jefferson was up for reelection, he resorted to a variety of pseudonyms—"A Friend to the Indians," "An Enemy to Cant and Imposition," "A True Deist," "A Member of the Deistical Church," "A Member of the Deistical Congregation." These brief essays only repeated or elaborated less trenchantly what Paine had said before.

In March Paine dictated—a fall on the ice had again incapacitated him —an open letter "To the People of England on the Invasion of England," a discursive, uninspired piece notable only for its praise of Napoleon. ("France has now for its chief the most enterprising and fortunate man, either for deep project or daring execution, the world has known for many ages.") In this essay, as in the ones for *The Prospect*, Paine appeared to be unloading a few items from his accumulated literary luggage, as if he were eager to keep his name before a public who had not heard from him for some time. At best they were finger-exercises from an old master.

5

In the spring of 1804, once again at his farm in New Rochelle in a small cottage that had escaped the fire, Paine found the farm more a burden than a boon. His tenant for the past eighteen years had given notice he planned to leave, and "instead of paying his rent, brought Mr. Paine a bill for fencing which made Paine his debtor." Paine had never been able to cope with the minor harassments of life. Wherever he had wandered someone—Colonel Kirkbride, Joseph Johnson, Nicolas Bonneville—had cared for and protected him. Now it was John Fellows' turn. Paine asked Fellows to come out from the city and "help me settle my accounts with the man who lives on the place," confessing that "you will be able to do this better than I shall." He wanted to be free to write—to get "on with my literary works, without having my mind taken off by affairs of a different kind."

He wrote steadily that summer. At least six essays, the authorship of all disguised, turned up in *The Prospect*. Early in August he sent a piece to a friendly editor in Connecticut in which he told the people there how they should go about forming a constitution for their state. The task was less awesome than they might think. "There has been so much experience on the principles and manner of forming constitutions since the Revolution began that no material error can now take place"—especially if they heeded his advice.

On July 12 Alexander Hamilton died from the wound received in his duel with Aaron Burr. The stream of eulogies in the Federalist press failed to provoke Paine until he came upon Gouverneur Morris' funeral oration. Morris' praise was fulsome; Paine's rebuttal was tasteless. Morris made Hamilton the hero at Yorktown; Paine held that the gold he and Laurens had brought from France had "enabled Congress to go on, and the army to proceed to Yorktown." From the battlefield, Paine continues, "our orator conducts Hamilton to the convention which met in Philadelphia in 1787, to form the federal constitution. *'Here,'* says he, *'I saw him labor indefatigably'*—for what?—*'for his country's good,'* continues the orator. No, sir. He labored to establish a constitution that would have deprived the citizens of every description of the right of election, and have put *himself,* and you too, Mr. *Prate-a-pace,* in possession of part of the government for life." From this point the essay deteriorates into slander against Morris, a man of "*conceits* instead of *principles,* and *vanity* instead of *wisdom.*" He had decamped from France with "wagon loads of fine French furniture, for Gouverneur Morris knew how to feather his nest. In business he is a babe, and in politics a visionary; and the older he grows the more foolish he becomes."

September found Paine attacking missionaries who used the Bible to proselytize among Indians ("Will the prisoners they take in war be treated the better by their knowing the horrid story of Samuel's brewing Agog in pieces like a block of wood, or David's putting them under the harrows of iron?"), the books of the New Testament ("They come to us on no other authority than the Church of Rome, which the Protestant priests, especially those of New England, called the *Whore of Babylon*"), and Sundays in Connecticut. "The word Sabbath, means REST," he said in this last piece; "that is, cessation from labor, but the stupid Blue Laws of Connecticut make a labor of rest, for they oblige a person to sit still from sunrise to sunset on a Sabbath-day, which is hard work."

At the end of the month he responded to a memorial that had been sent to Congress by the French inhabitants of Louisiana in which they called for protection "of our rights" and indulgence of their slave trade. Earlier Paine had worried about incorporating foreigners within the United States without their consent. Now he took a patronizing attitude toward their uneasiness. "You are arriving at freedom by the easiest means that any people ever enjoyed it," he said; "without contest, without expense, and even without any contrivance of your own. And you already so far mistake principles, that under the name of *rights* you ask for *powers; power* to *import and enslave Africans;* and *to govern* a territory *we* have *purchased.*"

At last Paine had written something to please all Americans. John Randolph of Roanoke, otherwise no admirer of his, urged on Albert Gallatin "the printing of . . . thousands of copies of Tom Paine's answer to their remonstrance, and transmitting them by as many thousand troops, who can speak a language perfectly intelligible to the people of Louisiana, whatever that of their governor may be."

6

Jefferson was reelected with ease. With the Federalists in disarray, Paine had nothing left to write about. Now that everything is "on a good ground," he said, "I shall do as I did after the war, remain a quiet spectator and attend now to my own affairs."

He had become resigned to the farm as a permanent home. His possessions were few enough to embarrass the poorest farmer in the neighborhood, but for one who had lived his life out of a trunk they seemed abundant. "I have six chairs and a table, a straw bed, a feather bed, and a bag of straw . . . a tea kettle, an iron pot, an iron baking pan, a frying pan, a gridiron, cups, saucers, plates and dishes, knives and forks, two candlesticks and a pair of snuffers." He owned three hundred acres, "about one hundred of which is a meadow land." And there was more. "I have a pair of fine oxen and an ox-cart, a good horse, a chair, and a one-horse cart, a cow, and a sow and nine pigs."

Through the eyes of others Paine's place seemed something less than the Garden of Eden. "At our arrival," said a friend, who called at the cottage with a companion one morning around breakfast time, "we found the old gentleman living in a small room like a hermit, and I believe the whole of the furniture in the room, including a cot-bed, was not worth five dollars." Paine politely invited the visitors to breakfast. The table-cloth was "composed of old newspapers," and after a Negro woman who cooked Paine's meals had set two extra places she asked if she should boil fresh tea. "The reason why the servant made this inquiry was, that Paine's general method was to re-dry the tea leaves before the fire, and have them put in the tea pot again the next time he drank tea," the visitors learned later. "Our tea at that time was common bohea, and coarse brown sugar, and a part of a rye loaf of bread, and about a quarter of a pound of butter. The black woman brought in a plate of buckwheat cakes, which Mr. Paine undertook to butter; he kept turning them over and over with his snuffy fingers, so that it astonished my companion and prevented him from partaking of them."

The farm, like the buckwheat cakes, was more than Paine could cope with. He had trouble finding a suitable tenant. Christopher Derrick, who replaced the previous one, proved contentious and incompetent and he was dismissed. With no tenant the farm produced no income, and in the summer of 1804 Paine sold off some sixty acres to make ends meet. He got $4020 for the land and with the cash in hand he began to dream again—this time of building an annex to the cottage. "The additional part will be one room high from the ground (about eleven or twelve feet) divided into apartments with a workshop for mechanical operations," he told Jefferson. "The upper part of this will be flat as the deck of a ship is, with a little slope to carry off the rain. It will be enclosed with a palisade all round and down to within about seven feet of the deck or floor. This part will then serve for an observatory and to live on in summer weather, and with screens, or light shrubs in light cases on casters to move easily I can set off what rooms I like in any part, alter them and choose, and be as retired in the open air as I please." Jefferson did not think much of the plan. "I much doubt whether the open room on your second story will answer your expectations," he wrote. "There will be a few days in the year in which it will be delightful, but not many. Nothing but trees, or Venetian blinds, can protect you from the sun." Jefferson need not have cautioned Paine; the addition was a dream that never materialized and the money from the land sale went to pay debts.

The autumn passed desultorily, except for a brief trip to New York in November to answer in court for his nonpayment of Wilburn's bill on Mme. Bonneville's extra charges. The stagecoach picked him up in front of the post office in New Rochelle. "Tom Paine, as I am a sinner," the driver whispered to those in the coach. Paine, looking somewhat seedy, climbed up on the front seat with the driver. When the coach stopped for breakfast he talked about the American Revolution and the ineptness of Washington's leadership. Later, back on the road, someone in the coach talked loudly of Alexander Hamilton's virtues. "Rank nonsense," Paine shouted back from his perch. A young man in the coach, beside himself with fury, said no one could harm Hamilton's reputation any more than Thomas Paine could undermine Washington's.

"Let me tell you I am that Thomas Paine," Paine answered, unaware he had been recognized.

"Well, sir," said the young man, "if the garment fits you, you are welcome to wear it." Others in the coach joined in harassing the old man up front, and so it went all the way into New York. Paine won his suit against Wilburn and returned to the quiet of his farm.

The days passed uneventfully until December 24. Two friends who were staying with him had "gone out to keep Christmas Eve," leaving behind a neighbor's boy to keep him company. Around six o'clock the dismissed tenant, Christopher Derrick, carrying a musket and half drunk with rum, approached the cottage, saw Paine sitting near the window, and fired at him. The buckshot lodged in the windowsill and wall, missing Paine. "I ran immediately out," Paine said, "and one of Mr. Dean's boys with me, but the person that had done it was gone. I directly suspected who it was, and I hallowed to him by name, that he *was discovered.*" A warrant was issued for his arrest, but Paine refused to press charges and Derrick went free.

Paine did nothing to dramatize his narrow escape. "I am exceedingly well in health," he told friends who asked after him. The shooting went unmentioned a week later in a long letter to Jefferson on Santo Domingo; The only personal aside was to say that he wrote during a snowfall, "and if it continues I intend to set off for Philadelphia in about eight days, and from thence to Washington." Paine wanted to talk the president into having the United States serve as a mediator between France and the black revolutionists on Santo Domingo who had proclaimed the Republic of Haiti. He visualized America's role in the New World as it would be presented eighteen years later in the Monroe Doctrine. "She is now the parent of the western world," he told Jefferson, "and her knowledge of the local circumstances of it gives her an advantage in a matter of this kind superior to any European nation. She is enabled by situation and growing importance to become a guarantee, and to see, as far as her advice and influence can operate, that the conditions on the part of Domingo be fulfilled. It is also a measure that accords with the humanity of her principles, with her policy, and her commercial interest."

Paine also hoped to talk over his plan with the French minister, Louis André Pichon, a friend from Paris days, but he never got to Washington. "I have given up the intention," he wrote Jefferson, because the "state of the weather renders the passage of the rivers dangerous and traveling precarious." In the latter part of January he accepted an invitation to live with William Carver and moved back to New York. Carver idolized the old man. "Have you forgotten my care of you during the winter you stayed with me?" he asked later when all was not well between them. "How I put you in bed every night, with a warm brick to your feet, and treated you like an infant one month old?" Once, for his afternoon nap, Paine heated the brick himself, only he overheated it, and the brick, wrapped in cloth, "communicated fire to the bed," and "the smell of fire led Mr. Carver to his room, the door of which he broke down, and dragged Paine out of it."

From Carver's house Paine continued to pass along his thoughts to the president. From a sea captain he heard that slave traders from Liverpool were doing a lively business with New Orleans. He worried that slavery would be impossible to eradicate in the territory if the trade continued much longer. Why not settle the land with free Negroes? he wondered. "The best way that occurs to me is for Congress to give them their passage to New Orleans, then for them to hire themselves out to the planters for one or two years; they would by this means learn plantation business, after which to place them on a tract of land." Better yet, why not populate the land with refugees from Europe? "Were I twenty years younger," said Paine as he approached his sixty-eighth birthday, "and my name and reputation as well known in European countries as it is now,

I would contract for a quantity of land in Louisiana and go to Europe and bring over settlers."

But he was not twenty years younger. Instead, he had to content himself with an old dream—"a collection of all the pieces I have published." The edition now would come to five volumes of four hundred pages each and would sell for two dollars a volume. The first three would contain political pieces and the last two "will be theological and those who do not choose to take them may let them alone." After further thought he decided to add a sixth volume of miscellaneous pieces—"correspondence, essays, and some pieces of poetry, which I believe will have some claim to originality." Thus did Paine while away the winter of 1804–1805.

7

April found him back on the farm. He fussed as he settled in about a favorite penknife left behind at Carver's—"a small French penknife that slides into the handle"—about some lost papers he thought might have slipped behind the chest in his bedroom there, about the Bonneville boys' summer visit to New Rochelle. "The boys will bring up with them one pair of the blankets Mrs. Bonneville took down and also my best blanket which is at Carver's," he wrote to John Fellows. "I wish you to give the boys some good advice when you go with them [to put them on the boat to New Rochelle], and tell them that the better they behave the better it will be for them. I am now their only dependence, and they ought to know it."

The visit did not work out well. Mme. Bonneville accompanied the boys, and Paine found her "an encumbrance upon me all the while she was here, for she would not do anything, not even make an apple-dumpling for her own children. It is certainly best that Mrs. Bonneville go into some family, as a teacher, for she has not the least talent of managing affairs for herself. She may send Bebee [Benjamin] up to me. I will take care of him for his own and his father's sake, but this is all I have to say." In another letter in which he enclosed fifty dollars to pay the rent on Mme. Bonneville's house, he snapped at Fellows, whom he had asked to perform some errands in the city. "I supposed, as you have a good deal of leisure, that the little commissions I asked you to do and which were not disagreeable, especially to a man in your line, would not have been troublesome to you."

The querulousness spilled over into his writing that summer. In June he wrote another letter "To the Citizens of the United States," the eighth in the series and in his mind "the most important of any I have published." It was a limp piece that rehashed old grievances against the Federalists and John Adams. As in earlier letters, he argued again that there was "no ground for suspicion" that France intended to launch an invasion during its undeclared war with America. Federalists used the specter to justify a large standing army which would be turned against dissident Americans, not an invading enemy. The argument had merit; it also sounded hollow coming from one who had published an essay in Paris telling the government how few troops and ships would be needed to invade the United States successfully.

In June he published a brief pamphlet on *Constitutions, Governments, and Charters.* A New York bank had recently bribed several members of the legislature in order to get a lucrative charter. The offending lawmakers had been defeated at the next election. "Of what use is it to dismiss legislators for having done wrong," Paine asked, "if the wrong is to continue on the authority of those who did it? The solution was to have one legislature propose special acts such as incorporation of companies and the next one enact it into law. If the proposal was bad, "the election then ensuing would, by discarding the proposers, have negatived the proposal without any further trouble."

In July hatred of England led to comment on the "madness in her councils (besides the royal madness) that has no foresight, and cannot calculate events," and those remarks led to others that Clio Rickman, who had heard Paine sound off at length on Napoleon, refused to believe his friend wrote. "France, at this time, has for its chief the most enterprising man in Europe, and the greatest general in the world," Paine now said; "and besides these virtues or vices (call them what you please, for they may be either), he is a deep and consummate politician in everything which relates to the success of his measures. He knows how to plan and how to execute. This is a talent that Pitt is defective in, for all his measures fail in execution."

Also in July he attacked a pair of blackguards, *"two skunks who stink in concert,"* who had sprayed "promiscuous abuse" upon Thomas Jefferson. He wrote under the pseudonym "A Spark from the Altar of '76," because "I found myself obliged, in order to make such scoundrels feel a little smart, to go somewhat out of my usual manner of writing." Another spark from the altar of '76 came in August in the form of a long essay on Pennsylvania politics. Two months earlier he had tried to explain to a new generation what the American Revolution had been all about:

> The independence of America would have added but little to her own happiness, and been of no benefit to the world, if her government had been formed on the *corrupt models of the old world.* It was the opportunity of *beginning the world anew,* as it were; and of bringing forward a *new system* of government in which the rights of *all* men should be preserved that gave *value* to independence. . . . *Mere* independence might at some future time, have been effected and established by arms, *without principle,* but a *just* system of government could not. In short, it was the *principle* at *that* time, that produced the independence; for until the principle spread itself abroad among the people, independence was not thought of, and America was fighting without an object.

The unprincipled Federalists, who aped British customs, beliefs, and traditions, had traduced that heritage, and now, quietly, his rage reined in, Paine proceeded to show the people of Pennsylvania where they had been led astray. They had replaced their constitution of 1776, whose "groundwork . . . was good," with one in 1790 that created an unjust, un-American government. It gave the governor a veto power "copied from England," and this negativing power in the hands of an individual "ought to be constitutionally abolished." It also handed him "a great quantity of patronage," and this, too, was "copied from the corrupt system of England." The Senate, whose members served for four long years, "is an imitation of what is called the House of Lords in England." Worst of all, the new constitution "makes artificial distinctions among men in the right of suffrage. . . . We have but one ORDER in America," said Paine. "Why then have we descended to the base imitation of inferior things? By the event of the Revolution we were put in a condition of thinking originally. The history of past ages shows scarcely anything to us but instances of tyranny and antiquated absurdities. We have copied some of them and experienced the folly of them."

Several times in the essay Paine paused to praise "the greatest and most useful man America has yet produced"—Benjamin Franklin. "Everything that Franklin was concerned in producing merits attention." Surely voters would see the piddling shadow cast by Gov. Thomas

McKean, up for reelection, alongside this giant. They did not. McKean two months later was reelected, and talk of calling a convention to revise the constitution died away. The times, Paine could see, were not made for him. The spirit of '76 was dead.

The revelation contributed to his peevish mood that autumn, which also owed something to his health—"his health is, I think, declining," said Elihu Palmer, who saw him in September and was certain that this "firm cog in the wheel of human life" would soon die, unaware that his own death lay only months away—and something to the need for money. In the autumn of 1805 he asked Jefferson to put pressure on Congress to "grant me a tract of land that I can make something of." After hearing nothing for six weeks he sent a curt follow-up note. Jefferson replied immediately, saying he had delayed comment until Congress met and he could sound out the members. He gave Paine little hope of success. A few months later Paine tested out another proposal on Jefferson. "I think you will find it proper, perhaps necessary, to send a person to France in the event either of a treaty of peace or of a descent [upon England], and I make you an offer of my services on that occasion to join Mr. Monroe. I do this because I do not think there is a person in the United States that can render so much service on the business that will come on as myself." Jefferson treated the old gentleman's offer respectfully, telling him gently that discussions were needed only with Spain and England, and that qualified American plenipotentiaries were already on the scene.

Times had changed. No one seemed interested in listening to Thomas Paine. A lonely, private misery set in. He became apathetic and ceased to write. Robert R. Livingston had returned to New York in the summer of 1805 and Fulton the following winter; neither man took the trouble to look Paine up. He began again to drink heavily. In the spring of 1806 William Carver drove out from the city and found Paine disheveled and drunk at a tavern in New Rochelle. He had not shaved for a fortnight. His shirt was in tatters, "nearly the color of tanned leather, and you had the most disagreeable smell possible, just like that of our poor beggars in England," Carver said later. "Do you recollect the pains I took to clean you? That I got a tub of warm water and soap, and washed you from head to foot, and this I had to do three times, before I could get you clean. I likewise shaved you and cut your nails, that were like birds' claws. I remember a remark that I made to you at that time, which was, that you put me in mind of Nebuchadnezzar, who is said to be in this situation.

Many of your toenails exceeded half an inch in length, and others had grown round your toes, and nearly as far under they extended on top."

Once he had Paine clean and sober, Carver invited him to come again and live with his family. Paine accepted the offer and let Carver bundle him into a carriage and carry him back to the city.

CHAPTER

27

POWDERED WITH SNUFF,
STUPEFIED WITH BRANDY

PAINE LIVED WITH the Carver family on this visit some five months. The house was at once the best and worst place for him. Best in that Carver and his friends among the workingmen of the city gave the adulation an old man needed and listened to his talk with respect; he was always "Mr. Paine" to them. Worst in that they indulged his drinking. Most of his visitors were from "among the lower orders, and most of them drunkards like himself," a staid young man named Grant Thorburn reported. Most of the refined citizens who in other years had invited Paine to dinner now snubbed him. "The only persons wearing superfine coats I ever saw in his company," said Thorburn, were John Fellows, Walter Morton, a former official in the customs house who now ran the Phoenix Insurance Company, and Thomas Addis Emmet, a distinguished Irish lawyer who had recently emigrated to New York after being imprisoned for revolutionary activities. This trio of protectors, who would stay loyal to the end, seemed resigned to letting Paine drink himself to death. Fellows supplied his liquor, which averaged something like a quart of brandy a day.

Thorburn found Paine physically repulsive—"his countenance was bloated beyond description; he looked as if God had stamped his face with the mark of Cain"—but could not resist visiting him at the Carver house, drawn by his wit, his humor, his "clear, strong head." It was impossible to dislike the man. They argued religion steadily, but "always in a friendly way," Thorburn, a devout Presbyterian, trying to trip the master with the Bible he regularly brought to their discussions. He still believed—"a young *enthusiast*" Paine called him with a smile—the old man could be saved. "Mr. Paine," he said with exasperation one day, "here you sit, in an obscure, uncomfortable dwelling, powdered with snuff and stupefied with brandy; you, who were once the companion of Washington, Jay, and Hamilton, are now deserted by every good man; and even respectable deists cross the streets to avoid you."

Paine listened to the reprimand, then looked at Thorburn across a wide gulf and said, "I care not a straw for the opinions of the world."

Paine did most of his drinking at night. During the day he still wrote and in the latter part of June 1806, soon after returning to Carver's house, he sent an essay to James Cheetham, whose newspaper *The American Citizen* published most of his work now. The essay carried him into a decade-old controversy—the cause of yellow fever. Physicians agreed the disease was not communicable and that it originated from "putrid air" injected into the atmosphere. They divided over the source of the "infected air." One group held it came from swamps and marshlands bordering the coastal cities. Chauvinists were certain nothing so evil could originate in America, and Paine, siding with this faction in 1803, argued it came "barrelled up" in the cargo ships from the West Indies. (He was close to the mark; infected mosquitoes brought the disease from the Caribbean to the United States.) Now, in 1806, he had changed his mind. He recalled the experiment made with Washington twenty-three years earlier when with long poles they had stirred up a muddy pond bottom and as air bubbled to the surface it had burst into flame when touched by a torch. Here was the putrid air that produced yellow fever. The disease's recent appearance in America meant that "some new circumstance not common to the country in its natural state" had produced it. And the "new circumstance"?—the numerous wharves built in New York and Philadelphia, where yellow fever centered, to accommodate "the vast increase of commerce" since the Revolution. These wharves, solid embankments that extended into the rivers, disturbed the flow of the water over the mud bottoms. Build them instead in the form of stone arches, he advised, "and the tide will then flow in under the arch, by which means the shore, and the muddy bottom, will be washed and kept clean, as if they were in their natural state, without wharves."

2

The essay on yellow fever was widely reprinted. Jefferson called it "one of the most sensible performances on that disease that had come under his observation." A visiting Scotsman told Paine the piece had "attracted considerable attention in the southern states," and that even his "most strenuous political opponents" found the argument "ingenious." The news pleased Paine, "and in the course of conversation on the subject [he] discovered a good deal of that literary vanity of which he has been accused."

Other visitors that summer reported his ego intact and his health tolerably good, though he "begins to feel the effects of age." He was still slender, still had "an uncommonly penetrating eye," and once he started talking one forgot the flaming "scorbutic eruption" of his face. He celebrated July 4 with a stroll "in the midst of the hustle" down Broadway with two Englishmen who were surprised to find Paine lived "quite retired, and but little known or noticed."

Occasionally he kept to Carver's house because of "his health," but whenever up to it, even on hot, humid days, he took the usual afternoon walk about town. On Sunday, July 25, he "felt exceedingly well." After a light supper of bread and butter, he was climbing the stairs to bed when "I was struck with a fit of an apoplexy that deprived me of all sense and motion." He fell "headlong over the banisters as suddenly as I had been shot through the head" and lay sprawled on the floor with "neither pulse nor breathing, and the people about me supposed me dead." Three weeks later he reported he had "not been able to get in and out of bed since that, otherwise than being lifted out in a blanket by two persons."

The old man was too proud to be depressed. He had endured "an experiment on dying, and I find that death has no terrors for me," he boasted, and "my mental faculties have remained as perfect as I ever enjoyed them." He passed off the illness as "a hurt in his leg" to a visitor who found him in bed surrounded by newspapers, eager to talk, and as opinionated as ever. After pointing to an outrageous item in one of the papers, he "declared decidedly" that the rumors of peace between England and France were baseless. "The war must inevitably go on till the government of England falls," he said; "for it was radically and systematically wrong, and altogether incompatible with the present state of society." The visitor thought the new Whig government would repair past mischiefs. Paine shook his head. *He* knew the British government well, knew "that no man, or set of men, would ever be able to reform it; the system was wrong, and it never would be set right without a revolution, which was as certain as fate, and at no great distance in time." The peppery opinions continued until the visitor shifted the conversation into another channel.

Mrs. Carver had a family to care for and little time to spare for the invalid. Mrs. Elihu Palmer, widow of the friend who had edited *The Prospect*, came in as a part-time nurse. She made the bed, swept the room, and served his meals, but when absent, "which often happened," Paine complained, "I had a great deal of trouble" getting those things done. "Sometimes the room became so dirty that people that came to see me took notice of it and wondered I stayed in such a place." He was still bedridden in mid-September but well enough to vent his grievances in a series of essays on a newcomer to the city named Samuel Carpenter, whose "flowery embellished language" offended Paine's literary sensibilities. The vendetta against Carpenter—it eventually drove him from New York—was senseless, but it served as a tonic for Paine. In October he left his bed. He stuck close to Carver's house but felt well enough to publish "A Challenge to the Federalists to Declare Their Principles" and a brief piece on the liberty of the press. A friend passing by came upon him nosing about Carver's blacksmith shop. Another friend, who was returning to Europe that month, came around to exchange snuff boxes with him. He found "the old philosopher in bed at four o'clock in the afternoon" but "talkative and well."

Paine had a setback—psychological rather than physiological—in November. He had felt well enough early in the month to travel up to New Rochelle to vote for members of Congress and the state assembly. The supervisor of the inspectors was a man named Elisha Ward, whose father and brothers, according to Paine, had served with the British during the Revolution, "but this one being the youngest and not at that time old enough to carry a musket remained at home with his mother."

After Paine had filled in his ballots, he "tendered [them] separately, distinguishing which was which, as is the custom." Ward refused to accept them. "You are not an American," he said. A lie, said Paine, and promised that if Ward persisted in this "injustice I would prosecute him." Ward rose, called for a constable, announced, "I will commit you to prison," then had second thoughts, for he soon afterward chose "to sit down and go no farther with it." But the disputed ballots were not counted. Paine "commenced a prosecution" against Ward, and when the case was placed on the docket for 20 May 1807 he began rounding up affidavits from those who could testify to his citizenship—Vice President George Clinton; James Madison, who as secretary of state had in his office Monroe's report claiming him as a citizen; Joel Barlow, still in Paris. "As it is a new generation that has risen up since the Declaration of Independence, they know nothing of what the political state of the country was at the time the pamphlet *Common Sense* appeared," he wrote forlornly to Clinton; "and besides this there are but few of the old standers left, and none that I know in this city."

3

By this time Paine had determined to leave Carver's house. He resented the way he had been treated. "In no case was it friendly, and in many cases not civil," he said. His grievances were many. Mrs. Carver did not give him his "tea or coffee till everybody else was served, and many times it was not fit to drink." He had been obliged to furnish his own bedding, his room was nothing but a closet to the front room. Carver had left him alone on the night he was stricken with apoplexy. When Mrs. Palmer came to care for him, she was given neither a room of her own nor access to a fire when the weather grew cold. "As to myself, I suffered a great deal from the cold. There ought to have been a fire in the parlor."

When Carver presented a bill of $150 for Paine's room and board for twenty-two weeks and Mrs. Palmer's for twelve, Paine refused to pay, itemizing his complaints in a long, plaintive letter. ("Mr. Paine's extreme parsimony," a warm friend said, "which disposes him to live on his friends while he has plenty of his own, together with his intemperance has alienated a great many of his friends who were firmly attached to him for the good he had done for mankind.") Carver in his answer reminded Paine, with justification, of all he had done for him, then, without justification, intimated "some criminal connection" between Mme. Bonneville and Paine, adding, "whether the boys are yours, I leave you to judge."

Carver aired what must have been common gossip about Paine and Mme. Bonneville. After three years of hearing that any day now her loving husband in Paris would join the family, citizens began to doubt the story, and, understandably, replace it with one of their own. While Paine tried to hold her at arm's length, his affection for the boys, especially his namesake Thomas, must have caused talk. "I am glad to hear that Thomas is a good boy," the childless Paine wrote Andrew Dean in New Rochelle while still bedridden. Dean, who had a farm adjacent to Paine's and had been keeping Thomas at his place, had written that the boy needed a new outfit—a pair of trousers, shirts, and a hat. "You can take the horse and chair and take Thomas with you and go to the store and get him some strong stuff for a pair of trousers, hempen linen for two shirts, and a hat," Paine said. "He shall not want for anything if he be a good boy and learn no bad words." When Dean spoke of paying a visit to the city, Paine urged him to do so, and "when you come take Thomas with you."

None of the Bonnevilles moved in with Paine, however, when he left the Carvers'. John Fellows worked out an adjustment of the bill with Carver, and found rooms for Paine and Mrs. Palmer at a rooming house in Corelear's Hook, across the East River in Brooklyn. Before the two settled in there, more convenient lodgings turned up in Manhattan, where John Wesley Jarvis agreed to share his bachelor quarters with Paine. Jarvis was twenty-five years old and a competent, well-regarded portrait painter. He worked "hard and faithfully," a friend said, "but would not have it known," for he cherished his reputation as an easygoing man about town. He liked to drink and later his career was "broken by dissipation." He enjoyed women and his penchant for "mysterious marriages," some said, made it difficult for him to establish "respectable communion with ladies." Friends considered him "the best story-teller that ever lived" and "one of the greatest humorists of the age"; the residue of wit that survives fails to justify his reputation. When people talked about great men, he always pointed to a nutmeg grater on the mantelpiece and said, *"There's a greater."*

Though divided in age by a half century, the two men hit it off at once. Jarvis found Paine "one of the most pleasant companions I have met with for an old man," and the five months they shared the apartment counted among the happiest of Paine's last years. During the stay Jarvis flattered Paine with a portrait that softened his flaming face into a healthy glow and caught the keen eyes of a man who seemed much younger than his sixty-nine years. A single flaw marred the relationship: Paine got lonely at night while Jarvis was out on the town. One night Jarvis returned around four and found Paine on the floor.

"I have the vertigo, the vertigo," said Paine.

"Yes," said Jarvis, eying the bottle on the table, "you have it deep—deep." In telling the story, Jarvis insisted Paine was not a drunkard: "He did not, and could not, drink much." Loneliness drove him to the bottle, but in company he almost always kept within his capacity.

Paine's homes varied but not his habits. The long nap after dinner remained fixed in the daily routine. One afternoon an old lady came to see him. Told he was asleep, she said, "I am sorry for that, for I want to see him very particularly." Struck by her urgency, Jarvis broke a house rule and took her into the bedroom.

Paine rose on one elbow and "with an expression of eye that staggered the old woman back a step or two," asked, "What do you want?"

"Is your name Paine?"

"Yes."

"Well, then, I come from Almighty God, to tell you that if you do not repent of your sins and believe in our blessed Saviour Jesus Christ, you will be damned and. . . ."

"Pooh, pooh, it is not true. You were not sent with any such impertinent message. Jarvis, make her go away. Pshaw, He would not send such a foolish ugly old woman as you about with His message. Go away. Go back. Shut the door." The old lady, stunned into silence, raised her hands high in dismay and left.

Toward the end of the stay with Jarvis, Paine published an "Essay on Dreams," in which he analyzed the dreams used in the Bible to reveal Christian doctrine. The essay met a silent reception in the press. His enemies grew cunning, Paine said. "They know that if they abuse it, everybody will obtain it." If you want to be read, Jarvis said, write a book entitled "Paine's Recantation." "You know the time must soon come, when like Voltaire and others," he went on, "you will recant all you have said on the subject of religion."

"I do not know what I may do when infested by disease and pain," Paine said; "I may become a second child; and designing people may entrap me into saying anything; or they may put into my mouth, what I never said. . . . I don't believe what the priests reported of Voltaire's confession on his deathbed." Paine went on to declare himself in perfect health and soundness of mind and solemnly repeated to Jarvis "his belief in his already written opinions."

4

In April 1807 Jarvis moved to new quarters. Paine found—more likely someone found for him—rooms with Zakarias Hitt, a baker who lived on

Broome Street, then near the outskirts of the city. Hitt was a disciple of Paine's and protective of the old gentleman's reputation. To those who asked about his drinking habits he would say only that "he did not drink more than three quarts of rum a week."

Paine ate with the Hitt family. He had a tiny bedroom and a small parlor adjoining it where he could write. Few people bothered to visit him, perhaps no more than four or five during the ten months he lived with the Hitts. His letters reflected the loneliness. "My dear Bonneville, why don't you come to America?" went an opening line in one of several he sent his old friend in Paris. "You sometimes hear of me but I never hear of you," he wrote Barlow. "What is Fulton about? Is he taming a whale to draw his submarine boat?" He asked Barlow to have the *National Intelligencer* sent to him, for "I am somewhat at a loss of want of authentic intelligence." From Thomas Hardy in England he heard "that your labor is not altogether lost in this country for all the gloom that overshadows us. There are many who are silently reading and meditating on what you have written and lamenting that those pure principles are not put in practice." But these contacts with old friends were few. No one told him that Robert Fulton had returned to New York in the winter of 1806, interested now in steamboats, not submarines. *The Clermont*, as it was later called, built by Fulton, financed by Robert R. Livingston, successfully traveled up the Hudson River in August 1807.

Forced in upon himself, Paine pumped out essays as never before— more in the last three years of his life than in any comparable period. Little of the work was distinguished. Most of it dealt with one or another of the petty feuds he pursued intently. In April he ridiculed the Federalist governor of New York, Morgan Lewis, then suing for $100,000 the chairman of a political meeting that had censured him. Lewis, a mediocre politician, would be hard put to prove he had suffered that much injury, said Paine. In May he directed blunt shafts at "shanny-brained Rufus" King and at the Federalists, whom he reviled as "British agents, or old tories employed as such, to make confusion in the country by any means." In June James Cheetham was his target. That feud had begun over a half year earlier when Cheetham tampered with the master's prose; it rapidly descended to name-calling, with Paine labeling Cheetham a disgrace to the Republicans, and Cheetham accusing the old man of drunkenness.

"I, sir," Paine said, "never permit anyone to alter anything that I write; you have spoiled the whole sense that it was meant to convey on the subject."

"It was too harsh to appear in print," Cheetham said.

"That was not your business to determine," Paine said, and with that remark transferred his allegiance to Jacob Frank's *Public Advertiser*.

In July two Englishmen visited Paine in the rooms on Broome Street. "He looks better than last year," they decided. "He read us an essay on national defense, comparing the different expenses and powers of gunboats and ships of war and batteries in protecting a seacoast." Gunboats had been Paine's minor obsession for over a decade. In the past he had viewed them as an offensive weapon, perfect for invading England. Now he saw them as a defensive weapon to protect the American coast. Gunboats were maneuverable, drew little water, required few repairs, and above all they were inexpensive. A fleet of seventy-four would cost only $296,000, compared to the $500,000 required to build a single ship of the line carrying seventy-four guns. Moreover, "gunboats, being moved by oars, cannot be deprived of motion by calms, for the calmer the weather the better for the boat," said Paine. "But a hostile ship becalmed in any of our waters, can be taken by gunboats moved by oars. . . . And besides this, *gunboats in calms are the sovereign ships.*" These lines inspired a lighthearted retort from a New England Federalist.

> TOM PAINE has exploded the old-fashioned notion,
> That ships of the line are the lords of the ocean;
> And shows how a gunboat with only one gun,
> *In a calm* can occasion a *first-rate to run;*
> Nay more, he had prov'd (to cut the thing shorter)
> The gunboat can blow the first-rate out of water;
> Then let nations be told, who *great navies* have arm'd,
> The Sovereign of Ships, is a—*gunboat becalmed!*

The gunboat campaign gave new purpose to Paine's life. Through the summer and into the autumn of 1807 he polished and elaborated his ideas. He devised a scheme to finance the boats. Originally they were to carry a single gun "fixed in a frame that slides in a groove." Now he constructed a model for a gunboat with twin mounts and sent it along to Jefferson for his appraisal. The model "has all the ingenuity and simplicity which generally mark your inventions," Jefferson replied. "Believing myself that gunboats are the only *water* defense which can be useful to us, and protect us from the ruinous folly of a navy, I am pleased with everything which promises to improve them." The president added that he had sent the model to the Navy Department for the judgment of experts there. A month later he forwarded their report to Paine without comment: It recommended against approval of his design.

5

In January Hitt said he must raise the weekly charge for room and board from five to seven dollars. Paine said he could not afford it, although he had in assets a house and lot in Bordentown and his farm in New Rochelle. He did not want to sell them now, for "he expected to live to a very great age, as his ancestors had before him," Mme. Bonneville explained, and "he saw his means daily diminish, while he feared a total palsy." It terrified him to think he would have no money to pay for constant care when the affliction came. Someone managed to calm his worries about the future and Paine accepted an offer of ten thousand dollars for his farm. At the same time he wrote to Congress asking to be reimbursed for the trip he had made with Laurens to France in 1781, though he had gone as a private citizen. Not a line of humility seeped into the petition. "All the civilized world knows," he said near the end, "I have been of great service to the United States, and have generously given away talent that would have made me a fortune." Before he heard from Congress, the prospective buyer of the farm died, the widow asked to be relieved of the contract, and Paine complied.

Totally at loose ends, he moved in February to a cheap tavern on Partition (Fulton) Street, a small place "where a sixpenny show was daily exhibited," a contemporary remarked. "Here he had no care taken of him; he was left entirely to himself." During the next six months he pressed his claim with Congress, writing to the speaker of the house, the vice president, and, finally, President Jefferson. Only after a kind but firm letter from Jefferson telling him he stood no chance of being rewarded did he finally accept defeat. "He was deeply grieved at this refusal," Mme. Bonneville said.

In July "one or two of his disciples" stepped in and took Paine away from the tavern, "as it were by force." First they persuaded him to sell the house and seven acres of meadowland in Bordentown; he got eight hundred dollars for them, and confirmed the sale with a bold, firm signature. Next, they got a man named Ryder who lived in Greenwich, a village a mile and a half north of the city, to agree to board him for ten dollars a week. He stayed at Ryder's ten months. Within a few weeks of his arrival he seemed something like his old self and sent off to the press one more blast at that "ignorant, conceited, headstrong Englishman" James Cheetham, who at last "has run his length, and is now posted in every meeting in the city, as a professed British hireling would be." It was the last piece Paine ever published.

He lived an isolated existence at Ryder's. He had to shave himself, for no barber would make the trip from the city. He had lost the use of his legs and had to spend the days in a chair with a table before him to hold the book or newspaper he was reading. In pleasant weather table and chair were placed before an open window of his first-floor room. Almost no one from the city called on him. Ryder often came upon him in tears, but except to complain about the inability to walk, Paine kept his self-pity to himself. The few visitors he had still found him a witty, cheerful companion. "His conversation was calm and gentleman-like, except when religion or party politics were mentioned," one remarked. "In this case he became irascible, and the deformity of his face, rendered so by intemperance, was then disgusting." The visitors were still struck by his keen blue eyes. They "were full, lucid, and indicated his true character," said one man. "The penetration and intelligence of his eye bespeak the man of genius and of the world," said another, who arrived at Ryder's to find Paine "sitting wrapped in a nightgown, the table before him covered with newspapers—with pen and ink beside them."

He weakened steadily through the autumn. By January 1809 he required constant attention. Walter Morton arranged for Ryder to get twenty dollars a week to care for him. On January 18, sensing the end was near, Paine wrote out his last will. Twice before he had made out a will, each time "saying he had believed such and such one to be his friend, and that now having altered his belief in them, he had also altered his will." He prefaced the final one with a summary of his literary achievements, beginning with *Common Sense*, "which awaked America to a declaration of independence." Except for bequests to his executors, Walter Morton and Thomas Addis Emmet—he no longer regarded John Fellows as a friend—and to Mrs. Elihu Palmer and Clio Rickman, all of which bequests were to come from the sale of half his farm, everything went to Mme. Bonneville in trust for the education of the boys. He wanted his body to lie in the Quaker cemetery, but if this were not possible then he desired to be buried on his farm, the grave "to be a square of twelve feet, to be enclosed with rows of trees, and a stone or post and rail fence, with a headstone with my name and age engraved upon it, author of *Common Sense.*" The will ended with Paine's credo: "I have lived an honest and useful life; my time has been spent in doing good, and I die in perfect composure and resignation to the will of my Creator."

6

No one thought Paine would live out the month of February. He continued, though extremely weak, not only to live but to amaze visitors. "When he could no longer quit his bed he made someone read the newspapers to him," said Mme. Bonneville, who came out at least twice a week from the city to see him. "His mind was always active. He wrote nothing for the press after writing his last will, but he would converse, and took great interest in politics." On February 25 Dr. James R. Manly found Paine "indisposed with fever and very apprehensive of an attack of apoplexy," so much so that for a few days he had dispensed "with his usual quantity of accustomed stimulus," only to resume it when he felt no better. Later Manly spoke to Paine's friends in the city—probably Morton and Emmet—and at their urging agreed to take him on as a patient.

In March ulcerous sores appeared on Paine's feet. His abdomen began to swell, which "indicated dropsy, and that of the worst description," said Manly. Bed sores, exacerbated by the water he passed in bed, added to his "infinite pain." Yet never, according to Mme. Bonneville, did Paine complain of "his bodily sufferings, though they became excessive."

On March 19 Willet Hicks, a neighbor and a member of the Society of Friends, called at Paine's request. "I am now in my seventy-third year, and do not expect to live long," the old man told him. "I wish to be buried in your burying ground. I could be buried in the Episcopal church, but they are so arrogant; or in the Presbyterian, but they are so hypocritical." The Quaker congregation denied the request, giving as its reason that Paine's "friends might wish to raise a monument to his memory, which being contrary to their rules, would render it inconvenient to them." Mme. Bonneville saw that the news distressed Paine. She promised to see him safely buried on his farm. "I have no objection to that," said Paine, "but the farm will be sold, and they will dig my bones up before they be half rotten." One night soon after he had been turned down by the Quakers he said to Dr. Manly, who was sitting with him, "I think I can say what *they* make Jesus Christ to say—My God, my God, why hast thou forsaken me?"

Loneliness overwhelmed him. "I am here alone, for all these people are nothing to me," he said to Mme. Bonneville. He pleaded with her to take a house in Greenwich so that she could be with him constantly, and "I, at last, consented," she said. On May 4 he was loaded into an armchair and carried to the house she had rented at 59 Grove Street, "after which he seemed calm and satisfied, and gave himself no trouble about anything." A Mrs. Hedden was hired as nurse. She read the Bible to him by the hour, while he said nothing. "He was very feeble," she remarked later; "quite to all appearance, exhausted. Poor man, how I felt for him! How I wished he was a Christian! He would be a day without speaking a word, except asking—'is nobody in the room—who's there?'" Earlier he had not minded being alone during the day; now he wanted someone always near. Also, "he must see that he or she was there, and would not allow his curtain to be closed at any time," Dr. Manly said, "and if, as it would sometimes unavoidably happen, he was left alone, he would scream and holler, until some person came to him."

Now he did not want for visitors. The collector of customs for New York City came one day saying he had received a letter from Monroe asking Paine only "to acknowledge his debt so that [Monroe's] children could get the money." Carver and he were reconciled. Kitty Nicholson Few, whom he had known since her childhood, called. "You have neglected me," Paine said to her, "and I beg you will leave the room." She left weeping. Her sister, Hannah Nicholson Gallatin, called with her husband Albert. "*I am very sorry that I ever returned to this country,*" Paine said to Gallatin. Dr. Nicholas Romaine, a friend from better days, stopped by twice a week. Willet Hicks visited him daily and was there when two clergymen pushed their way past Mrs. Hedden. "You have now a full view of death, you cannot live long, and whosoever does not believe in Jesus Christ will assuredly be damned." Weak as he was, Paine raised up on an elbow. "Let me have none of your popish stuff," he said. "Get away with you. Good morning, good morning." Then, to Mrs. Hedden: "Don't let 'em come here again, they trouble me."

On May 12 Jacob Frank, the single journalist in America who felt the need to honor Paine as the end approached, reprinted *Crisis No. 13* in the *Public Advertiser* in order to show "that Mr. Paine had entertained a proper idea of the interests and destinies of the whole United States, while many of us were in the day of early infancy, in *other countries,* or rocked in our cradles during the period that 'tried men's souls.' "

From May 15 on Dr. Manly expected Paine to die at any moment. The ulcers on his body had "assumed a gangrenous appearance" and became "excessively fetid and discolored." But the tough constitution inherited from his parents forced him to endure three weeks more of agony. The pain often made him involuntarily cry out, "Oh, Lord help me!" He drowsed most of the time, but when he woke his voice was strong and his mind clear. Even his sense of humor remained alive, as Dr. Romaine observed. Not long before the end came the bulky Dr. Romaine on one of his regular visits said to Mme. Bonneville, "I don't think he can live till night." Paine, hearing voices, opened his eyes.

" 'Tis you, doctor; what news?" he said, uttering the question he had always asked when coming upon a friend.

"Mr. such and one is gone to France on such business."

"He will do nothing there," said Paine.

"Your belly diminishes," said the doctor, glancing at Paine's distended abdomen.

"And yours augments," said Paine.

Old friends called shortly before he died. Captain Daniel Pelton came from New Rochelle. Jarvis visited and came away saying Paine "expressed a continued belief in his written opinions" on Jesus Christ. Dr. Manly made a last effort to have him recant. "Do you believe? or let me qualify the question—do you wish to believe that Jesus Christ is the son of God?" Several minutes of silence passed, then "with much *emphasis*" Paine said, "I have no wish to believe on that subject."

On his last night Mme. Bonneville asked Paine if he was satisfied with the treatment he had received. "*Oh! yes!*" he said, then mumbled a few incoherent words. He spent the rest of the night tranquilly and died at eight o'clock in the morning 8 June 1809.

EPILOGUE

THE DAY PAINE DIED Jarvis came out to the house in Greenwich to make a death mask. "I shall secure him to a nicety," he said with a weak try at humor, "if I can get plaster enough for his carbuncled nose." Those who had known Paine said the completed mask was "remarkable for its fidelity to the original." "Death had not disfigured him," said Mme. Bonneville. "Though very thin, his bones were not protuberant. He was not wrinkled and had lost very little hair."

Mme. Bonneville purchased a mahogany coffin for Paine; she had been told this was the American custom. She dressed him in a muslin gown with black ribbons at the neck and wrist and put a cap under his head as a pillow, for "he never slept in a night cap." The day of the funeral, June 9, Jacob Frank published a brief but affectionate tribute. "This distinguished philanthropist" devoted his life "to the cause of humanity," he said, and "if ever a man's memory deserved a place in the breast of a freeman, it is that of the deceased, for

> Take 'em all in all
> We ne'er shall look upon his like again!

Frank invited the city to turn out for the funeral. Few made the effort. Before the coffin was placed on the wagon that would carry it to New Rochelle, Mme. Bonneville went into the parlor to take a last look at Paine, "and having a rose in my bosom, I took it out, and placed it on his breast." She, her sons, two Negroes, Willet Hicks, a carriage loaded with six Irishmen, and a chaise with Emmet and Morton made up the cortege to New Rochelle. Along the way someone remarked to Hicks "that if

399

there was any purgatory [Paine] certainly would have a good share in it before the devil would let him go."

"I would sooner take my chance with Paine than any man in New York on that score," Hicks said.

At the farm a few local friends joined the small group from Greenwich. After the coffin had been lowered into the earth, Mme. Bonneville stood at one end of the grave and told her son Benjamin, "Stand you there, at the other end, as a witness for grateful America." She looked around at the small collection of mourners, and as the gravediggers shoveled in the dirt she said, "Oh! Mr. Paine! My son stands here as testimony of the gratitude of America, and I, for France!"

The next day James Cheetham published a short account of Paine's burial. "I am unacquainted with his age," he wrote, "but he had lived long, done some good, and much harm." The nation's press ignored Frank's farewell tribute; Cheetham's was reprinted throughout the land. Cheetham began at once to collect material for a biography of Paine. Joel Barlow was among the first to answer his queries. Two and a half months later someone else asked Barlow why Paine, alone among the heroes of the American Revolution, had gone unmentioned in his poem "The Columbiad." "I knew him well," Barlow said in a brief but pointed reply that reaffirmed what he had written Cheetham, "and no man has a higher opinion of the merit of his labors in the cause of liberty, in this country and throughout the world—But he was unjust to himself. His private life disgraced his public character. Certain immoralities, and low and vulgar habits, which are apt to follow in the train of almost habitual drunkenness, rendered him a disgusting object for many of the latter years of his life, though his mental faculties retained much of their former luster."

Cheetham's biography came out before the year ended and with it he got the revenge he had been unable to achieve when Paine had been alive and able to defend himself. He pictured Paine as America wanted to remember him—as a drunkard and an atheist. The nation, it turned out later, could tolerate a drunkard as a hero but not an atheist. "Didst thee never hear him call on Christ?" people would pleadingly ask Willet Hicks. Hicks was told that Dr. Manly was willing to say that Paine had recanted before he died "if I would engage to be silent only." Hicks refused to be silent, and so, too, did Dr. Manly. He swore under oath that Thomas Paine had at no time said that he believed Jesus Christ to be the Son of God.

As the years passed, people became uneasy when reminded they had been friendly with Paine. In 1813 Mme. Bonneville asked Jefferson for permission to publish his letters to Paine. "While he lived," Jefferson answered, "I thought it a duty, as well as a test of my own political principles to support him against the persecutions of an unprincipled faction." But now that he has "retired from the world, and, anxious for tranquillity, it is my wish that they should not be published during my life, as they might draw on me renewed molestations from the irreconcilable enemies of republican government."

Paine had known virtually every important political figure in England, France, and the United States during his lifetime. Not one of them publicly praised him after his death.

Worse lay ahead. The humiliation he dreaded most came to pass as he had feared. In 1819 William Cobbett, who as Peter Porcupine had assailed Paine when he lived, became a disciple. One night he traveled out to the plot at New Rochelle and dug up Paine's bones, carried them to England and lost them.

William Carver fell apart sometime after Paine died and lived out his life as a street beggar and a drunkard. His home was a hovel for which the Tom Paine Society of Free Thinkers paid the rent. He lived until 1840, bragging to the end that "old Billy Carver was the friend of Tom Paine" and that was "glory enough for any man."

ACKNOWLEDGMENTS

LET ME BEGIN with two tales about the manuscripts, letters, and whatever else Paine valued enough to haul about the world. When he died all belongings were entrusted to Mme. Bonneville. She in turn passed the collection on to her son Benjamin, the same Captain Bonneville whose adventures Washington Irving would one day memorialize. While on his explorations through the Rocky Mountains and the Far West, Captain Bonneville stored the material in a barn in St. Louis. The barn burned down, and everything that Paine had saved vanished in smoke.

The second story is only slightly less sad. A few years ago workmen were clearing out a shed in York, Pennsylvania, when they came upon a stack of books and a bundle of "many letters" addressed to Thomas Paine, all, according to report, "in the same handwriting and written by a woman in London." The workmen had never heard of Paine and only dimly of the American Revolution. The letters were moldy, damp, and hardly readable. They spread them in the sun, and once all were nicely dried they burned them.

Between these two burnings several gentlemen have made extensive efforts to overcome the obstacles that time, accidents, and Paine, an exceedingly private man, have erected against the biographer. Moncure Conway gave a good part of his own life to researching the two-volume study he published in 1892. Next came Frank Smith in 1938 with a relatively brief but very readable work for which he has never received the credit deserved. Smith added no annotation or even a bibliography to his book, and only those with an intimate knowledge of Paine's life were aware of the considerable amount of new material he had unearthed. A doctoral dissertation in 1951 by Arnold Kinsey King covered Paine's years in America during the Revolution more fully than will perhaps ever be done again. In 1959 Alfred Owen Aldridge capped a string of scholarly articles with his own biography of Paine. The bibliography revealed that he had traveled far beyond Smith and Conway and along the way had uncovered a large amount of new information, much of it fugitive writings by Paine unknown to all editors of his works.

Even today no full, let alone adequate, collection of Paine's public and private writings exists. The latest and best is that of Philip S. Foner, published in 1945. Foner did a competent job, considering that he worked alone and without financial assistance. But his edition is seriously flawed. Sometimes letters are misdated; occasionally they are given in an abbreviated form, with no warning to the reader, or split apart and presented as separate letters in different parts of the work. The topical organization hampers the scholar who wants to study the material in chronological order. The index is inadequate, to put it courteously. No serious effort has been made to ferret out hitherto uncollected material.

Obviously a new edition of Paine's writings is in order. Whoever attempts the task will find it has been immeasurably eased by one more of Paine's scholarly friends—Colonel Richard Gimbel. During his lifetime Colonel Gimbel collected every available scrap of published and unpublished material by and about Paine he could lay hands upon. His vast collection, formerly at Yale University, is now at the American Philosophical Society in Philadelphia. A catalog is in preparation. After it is completed scholars will find that they will have easily accessible under one roof a staggering amount of material that once upon a time they would have had to travel thousands of miles to study. Here are only a few of the nuggets the collection contains—complete files of *le Bien informé* and the *Moniteur* for the years Paine was in Paris; citations of virtually every reference to Paine in London newspapers during the 1790s; photostats, microfilms, or Xerox copies of relevant material from British and French archives. Every biography of Paine and every edition of his works is also there, together with hundreds of volumes dealing with events and men with which Paine to the slightest degree was involved.

Now to more specific debts. My principal thanks go again to the New York Public Library, where, in the Allen Room, the bulk of this book was researched and written. The library's gracious help extended to a letter of introduction that opened doors in Europe, notably those of the British Museum in London and the Archives Nationales in Paris.

I am also grateful, as in the past, to the New-York Historical Society, the American Philosophical Society, and Pace College. Finally, my thanks to the two readers—Ruth Ann Lief and Alfred Young—who did much to improve the manuscript.

NOTES

The spelling in all quotations has been standardized according to modern American usage, but in no instance has Paine's language been modernized.

Full citations for all material quoted from or referred to will be found in the Basic List of Books and Articles.

All material from Paine's collected works has been taken from the two-volume Foner edition. The citations are unusually full for a reason. Those who wish to trace a particular quotation but do not have the Foner edition available can, knowing the document and date, still do so in other editions. Moreover, if the Foner edition is superseded by a fuller collection of Paine's writings, the detailed references will still let the reader track down the sources.

Page

PROLOGUE

1 Joel Barlow to James Cheetham, 11 August 1809, Vale, *TP*, pp. 135–137.

I. "WOUNDS OF DEADLY HATE"

7 "disastrous meteor": Butterfield, *Adams Diary and Auto.*, vol. 3, p. 330.
Adams on Age of Paine: to Benjamin Waterhouse, 29 October 1805, Worthington Chauncey Ford, ed., *Statesman and Friend* (1927), p. 31.
"With all the inconveniences": *Rights of Man*, vol. 1, pp. 405–406.

8 On spelling of Paine's name see Aldridge, *TP*, p. 19. It was still Pain in the *Pennsylvania Journal*, 22 November 1775.
On number of Thetford voters see Palmer, "*TP*," p. 165.
"Almost without exception": Cole-Postgate, *British Common People*, pp. 91, 96.
The definitions of stays come from Samuel Johnson's dictionary and from the *Oxford English Dictionary*.
"sour temper": Chalmers, *TP* (1791 ed.), p. 3.

9 "he never asked": Frances Pain to daughter-in-law, 27 July 1774, Chalmers, *TP*, p. 38n.

9   "I profess myself": Forester letters, vol. 2, p. 84.

"an exceedingly good moral education": *Age of Reason*, vol. 1, p. 496.

"He shall not want": Paine to Andrew Dean, 15 August 1806, vol. 2, p. 1485.

"distressed themselves": quoted in Conway, *TP*, vol. 1, p. 11.

"natural bent of my mind": *Age of Reason*, vol. 1, p. 496.

"a pleasing natural history": *Crisis No. 3*, vol. 1, p. 88n.

genius "is killed": *Age of Reason*, vol. 1, p. 492.

"A sharp boy": Chalmers, *TP*, p. 5.

10   "what was rare in Europe": Brinton, *Dict. Am. Biog.*

"The occupation of a hair-dresser": Burke, *Reflections*, p. 49.

"Raw and adventurous": *Rights of Man*, vol. 1, p. 405.

"she stood the hottest engagement": *Common Sense*, vol. 1, p. 33.

11   "went in her to sea": *Rights of Man*, vol. 1, p. 405.

"a pretty girl": Chalmers, *TP*, p. 8.

"embarrassed with debts": *ibid.*, p. 11.

"disgusted with the toil": Rickman, *TP*, p. 36.

excise service, "towards which": *ibid.*, p. 36.

"a hateful tax": Johnson quoted in *Oxford English Dictionary*, under "Excise."

12   "cracking our brains": "The Exciseman," *Excise Life As It Is* (1878), p. 2.

"The Dutch smugglers know": "To the People of England on the Invasion of England," 6 March 1804, vol. 2, pp. 679–680.

"stampt his whole ride": minute of the excise board, quoted in Aldridge, *TP*, p. 17.

13   "reduced to wretchedness": Chalmers, *TP*, p. 20. TP as preacher, *ibid.*, pp. 21–22.

"humble petition" in Aldridge, *TP*, pp. 17–18.

"transported with rage": Charles Inglis, *The True Interest of America . . .* (1776), quoted in Bernard Bailyn, *The Ideological Origins of the American Revolution* (1967), p. 18n.

"It sometimes happens": *Origin of Freemasonry*, vol. 2, pp. 833–834.

14   "with a very respectable": Rickman, *TP*, p. 38.

"His eye": *ibid.*, p. xv.

"It is a whimsical weakness": Wilmot, *An Irish Peer*, p. 57.

"good Englishmen expressed": Stephen, *English Thought*, vol. 1, p. 387.

"not out of disrespect": Walter Savage Landor, "Imaginary Conversations," quoted in Conway, *TP*, vol. 2, p. 294.

"What news?": Cobbett-Bonneville manuscripts, Conway, *TP*, vol. 2, p. 457.

15   Nickname "Commodore": Chalmers, *TP*, p. 22.

"disputes ran high": Rickman, *TP*, pp. 38–39.

"jockeyship": *Age of Reason*, vol. 1, p. 496.

On TP and politics at this time, Henry Collins in his introduction to a paperback edition (1969) of *Rights of Man* on page 19: "It was almost certainly Ollive who aroused Paine's interest in local government, as a result of which he was elected to the Lewes Town Council, then known as the Council of Twelve." Collins adds that "the discovery that Paine served on the Lewes Town Council was made as recently as 1965 by Leslie Davey of Lewes, a member of the Thomas Paine Society. See Bulletin of the T.P.S., vol. 1, no. 2, 1965." Neither Chalmers, who dug deeply into Paine's years at

Lewes, nor Rickman, who was eager to publicize the best of Paine's past, nor Paine himself, who never shied of bragging on his accomplishments, mention this honor. Indeed, in *Rights of Man*, vol. 1, p. 406n., he says he did not enter "public life" until 1775.

16 "trade I do not understand": TP to a committee of Congress (October 1783), vol. 2, p. 1228.

"married for prudential reasons": Chalmers, *TP*, p. 34.

"somewhat differently circumstanced": TP to Goldsmith, 21 December 1772, vol. 2, p. 1129.

"In 1772 the excise officers": Rickman, *TP*, pp. 40–41.

"I should not have undertaken it": TP to Goldsmith, 21 December 1772, vol. 2, p. 1130.

On Scott see *Dict. of Nat. Biography.*

17 "one of the most amiable characters": TP to Henry Laurens, 14 January 1779, vol. 2, p. 1162.

case of the officers of excise, vol. 2, pp. 3–15.

"secreting upwards of £30": Mrs. Pain to daughter-in-law, 27 July 1774, Chalmers, *TP*, p. 38n.

"all that the ablest writer" and "A rebellion of excisemen": Chalmers, *TP*, p. 28.

Chalmers, *TP*, pp. 36–37, says Scott introduced TP to Franklin.

18 For sketches of Bevis, Ferguson, and Martin see *Dict. of Nat. Biog.* and also Clark, "An Historical Interpretation of Paine's Religion," from p. 67 of which comes the quotation of Martin.

"After I made myself master": *Age of Reason*, vol. 1, p. 498

On treasury board and George III: *Rights of Man*, vol. 1, pp. 441–442.

19 "if you can find out the examiner": Chalmers, *TP*, p. 32n.

"having quitted his business": quoted from the board's records, Aldridge, *TP*, p. 23.

TP praised for "information": Rickman, *TP*, p. 45.

"I rejected the hardened Pharaoh": *Common Sense*, vol. 1, p. 25.

"all the household furniture": Chalmers, *TP*, p. 31n.

20 Chalmers' comments on TP's virility and separation, p. 34, are substantiated by Rickman, *TP*, p. 46. See also Cheetham, *TP*, pp. 30n.–31n.

"an academy on the plan": TP to Laurens, 14 January 1779, vol. 2, p. 1161. The remark that it would include "young ladies" comes from Corner, *Auto. of Rush*, p. 113. See also Rush to Cheetham, 17 July 1809, in Butterfield, *Rush Letters*, vol. 2, p. 1007.

The original letters of introduction are lost. One is printed in Sparks, *Franklin Works*, vol. 8, pp. 137–138. For evidence there were more see TP in *Pennsylvania Evening Post*, 30 April 1776.

21 "I thought I saw in you": TP to John King, 3 January 1793, vol. 2, p. 1327.

2. A NEW BEGINNING

25 TP on voyage and arrival in Philadelphia to Franklin, 4 March 1775, vol. 2, pp. 1130–1133. Number of German and English servants given in Christopher Marshall diary, 30 November 1774, Historical Society of Pennsylvania,

quoted in Smith, "TP's First Year in America," p. 318. TP gives date of
arrival to Washington, 30 November 1781, vol. 2, p. 1203.

25   "Dialogue Between Wolfe and Gage" in vol. 2, pp. 47–49.

26   "to instruct their sons": TP to Franklin, 4 March 1775, vol. 2, p. 1131.
      On Aitken see Thomas, *History of Printing*, vol. 2, p. 152.

27   "Every heart and hand": Publisher's Preface, *Pennsylvania Magazine*, vol. 1,
      January 1775. All references hereafter are to vol. 1.
      To "avoid suspicion": "Proposals," *Pennsylvania Packet*, 21 November 1774.
      The lead essay: "The Magazine in America," vol. 2, pp. 1109–1113; quotations
      from pp. 1110, 1113.

28   "having now procured": Aitken's advertisement in January issue. Rush says
      Aitken "applied to" TP, Corner, *Auto. of Rush*, p. 113. King, "TP in Amer-
      ica," correctly observes that TP was not the editor of the magazine. He
      regards him as an editorial assistant. Executive editor might be an apter
      title. On the question of salary see TP to Laurens, 14 January 1779, vol. 2,
      p. 1161. In letter to Franklin 4 March 1775, he says regarding salary, "I have
      not yet entered into terms with him," vol. 2, p. 1131. Scharf and Westcott,
      History of Philadelphia, vol. 1, p. 309, say that Paine became editor "at a salary
      of 25 pounds a year." They give no source.
      "Notes *to our* Correspondents," "a building," March, p. 144.
      "ADONIS," "The verses," February, p. 98.

29   "The piece," "The verses on a *dead* dog," *ibid.*
      "Hail! Hail! Hail!," July, p. 338.
      "Life of Tom Thumb," "Pro Bono's," June, p. 290.
      TP's pseudonyms are discussed in Richardson, *History of Early American
      Magazines*, pp. 180–181, 181n.–182n. TP's pen names were first identified by
      Aitken in 1797 when James Carey of Philadelphia published a two-volume
      edition of his writings. See Smith, "Light on TP's First Year in America,"
      p. 352. For Hopkinson see *ibid*, pp. 186n.–187n., and for Witherspoon see *ibid*,
      pp. 183n.–184n. Definition of a Grub Street writer from William West, *Fifty
      Years' Recollections of an Old Bookseller* (1837), p. 68. The British spy's comment
      is in B. F. Stevens, *Facsimiles of Manuscripts in European Archives Relating to
      America 1773–1783* (1895), item #2062, Ambrose Serle to the Earl of Dart-
      mouth, 11 June 1777. John Jay refers to TP as one "who had been a hackney
      writer in London," Jay, *Life of John Jay*, vol. 1, p. 97.
      On circulation of magazine see TP to Franklin, 4 March 1775, vol. 2, p. 1131.

30   "gave a sudden currency": Rush to Cheetham, 17 July 1809, Butterfield, *Rush
      Letters*, vol. 2, p. 1008.
      "On the Death of General Wolfe": vol. 2, pp. 1083–1084. Aldridge, "Poetry
      of TP," pp. 82–83, offers a modern commentary on the poem. Deprecatory
      judgments are from the *Port Folio* in 1815 and the *North American Review* for
      1843, both quoted in Aldridge, *ibid.*, pp. 83–84.

31   "When I reflect": from "Reflections on Titles," vol. 2, p. 33.
      "Resolved on accumulating": "Reflections on the Life and Death of Lord
      Clive," vol. 2, p. 24.
      Clark culled the lush examples of TP's prose in "TP's Theories of Rheto-
      ric," pp. 322–323.

Page

31 "a style of thinking": *Rights of Man*, vol. 1, p. 348.
"warm passions with a cool temper": *Letter to Abbé Raynal*, vol. 2, p. 214.

32 "As it is our design": February, p. 98.
"he struck out several passages": Jay, *Life of John Jay*, vol. 1, p. 97.
"I reply that *war*": Forester letters, 24 April 1776, vol. 2, p. 80.
"I viewed the dispute": *Crisis No. 7*, vol. 1, p. 143.
"Surely the ministry are all mad": TP to Laurens, 14 January 1779, quoting from his letter to Scott, May 1775, vol. 2, p. 1162.

33 "The beautiful country": from "The Dream Interpreted," vol. 2, pp. 51–52.
Paine "has no country": John Quincy Adams to John Adams, 3 April 1797, Ford, ed., *Writings*, vol. 2, p. 157.
"Loyalty to the nation": "The Historian's Use of Nationalism and Vice Versa," in David Potter, *The South and the Sectional Conflict* (1968), pp. 37–38.
"Thoughts on Defensive War": vol. 2, pp. 52–55.

34 "Liberty Tree": vol. 2, pp. 1091–1092. Commentary on the poem with later revised versions of it in Aldridge, "Poetry of TP," pp. 84–86.
"I was requested": TP to Laurens, 14 January 1779, vol. 2, p. 1161.
Aitken on TP's writing habits: Thomas, *History of Printing*, vol. 2, p. 152.

35 "could not write": Butterfield, *Adams Diary and Auto.*, vol. 3, p. 334.
"When the country": *Crisis No. 7*, vol. 1, pp. 143–144.
Essay on saltpeter in *Pennsylvania Journal*, 22 November 1775. On gunpowder production see Orlando W. Stephenson, "The Supply of Gunpowder in 1776," *American Historical Review*, vol. 30 (1924–1925), p. 227.
"We are a people upon experiments": "A Serious Address to the People of Pennsylvania," vol. 2, p. 281.

36 "I am led to this reflection": "Useful and Entertaining Hints," February 1775, vol. 2, p. 1022.
TP on slavery: vol. 2, pp. 16–19.

37 "I despair": TP to Anonymous (i.e., Rush), 16 March 1789 (1790), vol. 2, p. 1286. The full letter with recipient identified and dated correctly has been reprinted by Butterfield, *Library of Congress Journal of Acquisitions*, vol. 1 (1943–1944), pp. 17–22.
TP hissed by Frenchmen: Yorke, *Letters from France*, vol. 2, pp. 337–338.
"An unfitter person": quoted in Epps, *Life of Thomas Walker*, pp. 140–141.
"the modest and virtuous Washington": John Adams to Abigail Adams, 17 June 1775, Butterfield, *Adams Correspondence*, vol. 1, p. 215.

38 America "ought immediately": John Adams to James Warren, 6 July 1775, Ford, *Warren-Adams Letters*, vol. 1, p. 75.
"Humanus" published: "A Serious Thought" 18 October 1775; it appears in vol. 2, pp. 19–20.

3. COMMON SENSE ON INDEPENDENCE

39 "got into such company": Butterfield, *Adams Diary and Auto.*, vol. 3, p. 330.
On Marshall, Matlack, and Cannon see Hawke, *In the Midst of a Revolution*, pp. 102–105.

40 "one of my brethren": Corner, *Rush Auto.*, pp. 81–82.

Page

40   "the most virulent attack": Rush to Noah Webster, 29 December 1789, Butterfield, *Rush Letters*, vol. 2, p. 528.
"by the persons": Corner, *Rush Auto.*, p. 85.
"the public mind": Rush to Cheetham, 17 July 1809, Butterfield, *Rush Letters*,
vol. 2, p. 1008.
"I shuddered": Corner, *Rush Auto.*, p. 114.
"I suggested": *ibid.*, p. 114.

41   "to have been printed": TP in *Pennsylvania Evening Post*, 30 January 1776,
quoted by Aldridge, "Some Writings of TP," p. 837.
"one of the very few": Forester letters, *Pennsylvania Journal*, 10 April 1776,
vol. 2, p. 67.
Common Sense appears in vol. 1, pp. 3–39.

42   "Paine may well have been": Corinne C. Weston, *English Constitutional
History*, p. 192, as quoted in Wood, *Creation of the American Republic*, p. 224n.

44   "There is Bell": Conway, *TP*, vol. 1, p. 66, quoting from a contemporary
pamphlet. On Bell see "McCulloch's Additions," pp. 97, 176, 232.
"to be as high-toned": Rush to Cheetham, 17 July 1809, Butterfield, *Rush
Letters*, vol. 2, p. 1008.
"The book was turned upon the world": Forester letters, vol. 2, p. 67.
"with an effect rarely produced": Rush to Cheetham, 17 July 1809, Butterfield, *Rush Letters*, vol. 2, p. 1008.

45   "and so fortunate was I": TP to Laurens, 14 January 1779, vol. 2, p. 1162.
"upwards thirty pounds" and "for the purpose of purchasing mittens": TP
in *Pennsylvania Evening Post*, 30 January 1776, as quoted in Aldridge, "Some
Writings of TP," p. 837. See also TP to Laurens, 14 January 1779, vol. 2, pp.
1162–1163.
On the newspaper war see Hawke, *In the Midst of a Revolution*, pp. 90–91. See
also Gimbel, *Bibliographical Check List of Common Sense*, pp. 22–49.
"He has a sufficiency in his hands": TP to Laurens, 14 January 1779, vol. 2,
p. 1163.

46   "He is unconnected with any party": *Common Sense*, vol. 1, p. 4. Other
quotations are on pp. 46 and 42.
"It appears to general observation": *Rights of Man*, vol. 1, p. 368.
"The true prophet": Eric Hoffer, *The Passionate State of Mind* (1955), p. 133.

47   "struck a string": *The Life of Ashbel Green . . . Written by Himself* (1849), p. 46.
Aitken's orders: Gimbel, *Bibliographical Check List*, p. 20.
"I believe the number of copies": TP to Laurens, 14 January 1779, vol. 2, p.
1163.
"a great noise": *The Journal of Nicholas Cresswell* (1925), p. 136. An extensive
account of the reception of *Common Sense* can be found in King, *TP*, pp.
72–83.
"the public sentiment": Edmund Randolph, "Essay on the Revolutionary
History of Virginia, 1774–1782," in *Virginia Magazine of History and Biography*,
vol. 43 (1935), pp. 306–307.
"A few more such flaming arguments": Washington to Joseph Reed, 31
January 1776, Fitzpatrick, *Washington Writings*, vol. 4, p. 297.
"I believe no pages": Deacon Palmer, 19 February 1776, quoted in Smith,
John Adams, vol. 1, p. 239.

47 "*Common Sense*, which I herewith send you": letter dated 16 May 1776, quoted in Margaret Wheeler Willard, ed., *Letters on the American Revolution* (1925), pp. 274–275.

"works on the minds": Edward Burd to James Burd, 15 March 1776, quoted in Hawke, *In the Midst of a Revolution*, pp. 91–92.

"seems to gain ground": Edward Shippen, Jr., to Jasper Yeates, 19 January 1776, quoted in *ibid.*, p. 92.

"It has fretted": Samuel Adams to James Warren, 10 January 1776, Ford, *Warren-Adams Letters*, vol. 1, p. 204.

"by an English gentleman": John Hancock to Thomas Cushing, 17 January 1776, Massachusetts Historical Society *Proceedings*, vol. 60 (1925–1927), p. 100.

"We have not put up": Joseph Hewes to Samuel Johnson, 13 February 1776, quoted in Burnett, *Continental Congress*, p. 131.

"a greater run": Silas Deane to Secret Committee of Correspondence, 18 August 1776, Wharton, *Revolutionary Diplomatic Correspondence*, vol. 2, p. 124. Information on publication of the pamphlet in France found in Butterfield, *Adams Diary and Auto.*, vol. 2, pp. 351, 352.

"the further encroachments of tyranny": John Adams to Abigail Adams, 18 February 1776, Butterfield, *Adams Correspondence*, vol. 1, p. 348.

"The Old Testament reasoning": John Adams to William Tudor, 12 April 1776, quoted in Smith, *John Adams*, vol. 1, p. 240.

"It is the fate of men and things": John Adams to James Warren, 12 May 1776, Ford, *Warren-Adams Letters*, vol. 1, pp. 242–243.

"What a poor, ignorant": John Adams to Thomas Jefferson, 22 June 1819, Cappon, *Adams-Jefferson Letters*, vol. 2, p. 542.

"Poor harmless I": John Adams to William Tudor, 12 April 1776, quoted in Smith, *John Adams*, I, p. 240.

Hopkinson's poem: 6 February 1776, *Pennsylvania Evening Post*.

"It was in great measure": TP to Nathanael Greene, 9 September 1780, vol. 1, p. 1189.

"I never read Locke": New York, *Public Advertiser*, 22 August 1807, reprinted by Aldridge, "TP and the N.Y. *Public Advertiser*," p. 377.

50 On Priestley's *Essay* see Gilbert, *Beginnings of American Foreign Policy*, pp. 41–42.

"His plan was so democratical": Butterfield, *Adams Diary and Auto.*, vol. 3, p. 333.

51 "Mr. Thomas Paine was so highly offended": John Adams to Rush, 12 April 1809, Schutz and Adair, *Spur of Fame*, p. 144.

4. "A PASSION OF PATRIOTISM"

52 Letters of introduction: Adams to Lee, 19 February 1776, *Lee Papers*, vol. 1, p. 312; Franklin to Lee, 19 February 1776, *ibid.*; Rush to Lee, 19 February 1776, Butterfield, *Rush Letters*, vol. 1, p. 95; Franklin to Lee, 19 February 1776, John Bigelow, *Works of Benjamin Franklin* (12 vols, 1904), vol. 7, p. 113.

"He has genius in his eyes": Lee to Rush, 25 February 1776, *Lee Papers*, vol. 1, p. 325–326.

"by the hands of Marshall": TP to Laurens, 14 January 1779, vol. 2, p. 1165.

Page

53 "The Forester writes": Abigail Adams to John Adams, 21 April 1776, Butterfield, *Adams Correspondence*, vol. 1, p. 390.

The Forester letters are found in vol. 2, pp. 61–87. They originally appeared in the *Pennsylvania Journal* on 3, 10, 24 April and 8 May 1776. Cato's letters appeared in the *Pennsylvania Packet* 11, 18, 25 March and 1, 8, 15, 29 April 1776. "To be *nobly wrong*": vol. 2, p. 61.

54 "It is now a mere bugbear": vol. 2, p. 62.

"And he who dares": *ibid.*

"that Jesuitical cunning": vol. 2, p. 73.

"What comparison is there": vol. 2, p. 74.

"The assistance which we hope": vol. 2, p. 77.

"I have been the more particular": vol. 2, p. 78.

55 "I scarcely ever quote": *ibid.*

"*It is not a time*": vol. 2, pp. 81, 82.

TP admitted he did not vote in "A Serious Letter," 7 April 1786, vol. 2, p. 280.

Reasons why Independents lost: vol. 2, p. 86. "We are got wrong": *ibid.*, p. 85.

56 a dialogue: vol. 2, pp. 88–93.

"not so perfectly free as they ought to be": Forester letters, 3 April 1776, vol. 2, pp. 62–63.

57 "one of his typically radical ultimatums": Wood, *Creation of the Republic*, p. 335.

"had no hand in forming": "To the People," 18 March 1777, vol. 2, p. 270.

"kept clear of all argument": *ibid.*, p. 272.

"The command was large": TP to Laurens, 14 January 1779, vol. 2, p. 1163.

TP passes out copies: Smith, *TP*, p. 36.

58 "frequently pressed": TP to Laurens, 14 January 1779, vol. 2, p. 1163.

"The post being detained": *Pennsylvania Journal*, 6 November 1776, under dateline October 28.

"handsome puff": Alexander Graydon, *Memoirs of His Own Time, with Reminiscences of the Men and Events of the Revolution* (1846 ed.), p. 188.

"black times": TP to Samuel Adams, 1 January 1802, vol. 2, p. 1434.

"the rebels fled": Moore, *Diary of the American Revolution*, vol. 1, p. 350, quoted in Tyler, *Literary History of the American Revolution*, vol. 2, p. 37.

Retreat across New Jersey reprinted in Almon, *The Remembrancer or Impartial Repository of Public Events for the year 1777* (1778), pp. 28–29. Paine said later that "I began the first number of the Crisis . . . at Newark, upon the retreat from Fort Lee, and continued writing it at every place we stopped at and had it printed at Philadelphia the 19th of December." (*Public Advertiser*, 22 August 1807, quoted in Aldridge, "TP and the N.Y. *Public Advertiser*," p. 378.) My own guess is that he began the journal of the retreat, later published in the *Pennsylvania Journal* and Almon's *Remembrancer*, at Newark and that *Crisis No. 1* was dashed off in a single burst of passion.

59 "when the inclemency of the weather": *Pennsylvania Journal*, 29 January 1777, reprinted vol. 2, pp. 93–95.

"I knew the time": *Crisis No. 2*, vol. 1, p. 63.

Page

59 "Paine may be a good philosopher": Biddle, *Autobiography*, p. 87.
"on the advice of": undated fragment of letter to John Bayard, Gimbel collection, American Philosophical Society.
"The deplorable and melancholy condition": TP to Laurens, 14 January 1779, vol. 2, p. 1164. *Crisis No. 1* appears in vol. 1, pp. 50–57.

60 "in a rage": TP to Franklin, 20 June 1777, vol. 2, p. 1133.
"As he passes": Tyler, *Literary History of the American Revolution*, vol. 2, pp. 38–39.

61 "to the printer gratis": TP to Laurens, 14 January 1779, vol. 2, p. 1164.
"Hope succeeded to despair": Cheetham, *TP*, p. 56.
Crisis No. 2: vol. 1, pp. 58–72.
"He that rebels against reason": p. 58.
"Perhaps you thought": p. 59.
"In all the wars": pp. 67–68.
"like a stream of water": p. 68.
"some republican expressions": TP to Franklin, 20 June 1777, vol. 2, p. 1133.
"Universal empire": *Crisis No. 2*, vol. 1, p. 58.
"I who know England": *ibid.*, p. 71.

63 Lewis Morris: Corner, *Rush Auto.*, p. 146; John Sanderson, *Biography of the Signers of the Declaration of Independence* (9 vols., 1820–1827), vol. 9, p. 122.
The account of the Indian conference at Easton is taken from Godcharles, *Daily Stories of Pennsylvania*, pp. 70–71, and Condit, *History of Easton*, pp. 60, 117–180. TP's appointment to the committee as secretary in *Pennsylvania Colonial Records*, vol. 11, p. 98. For rejection of treaty see Ford, *Journals of Congress*, vol. 7, p. 166, under date 27 February 1777.
"by past remembrance": Hall manuscripts, Conway, *TP*, vol. 2, p. 462, under date 15 April 1786.

64 During an evening in Washington: "Dr. Mitchill's Letters from Washington, 1801–1813," p. 746.
On Chief Last Night: "On the Question, Will There Be War?" 15 August 1807, vol. 2, p. 1013.
"a man whom I have ever thought": "To the People," 18 March 1777, vol. 2, p. 270.
"If men": to Whitehead Humphries, 16 July 1779, vol. 2, p. 171.

65 *Crisis No. 3* is in vol. 2, pp. 73–101.
On Tories: p. 90.
"a wounded whale": p. 75.

5. AN UNSOLICITED HONOR

66 Creation of Committee for Foreign Affairs: Ford, *Journals of Congress*, 17 April 1777, vol. 7, p. 274.
Adams still doubted: Butterfield, *Adams Diary and Auto.*, vol. 3, p. 334.

67 Witherspoon objected: *ibid.*
"parsons were always": Yorke quoting TP in *Letters from France*, vol. 2, p. 360.
"unsolicited on my part": TP to Franklin, 20 June 1777, vol. 2, p. 1132.

Page

67 TP's oath: Ford, *Journals of Congress*, vol. 7, p. 274.

TP on plans for history: to Franklin, 20 June 1777, vol. 2, p. 1133.

68 "when the report of cannon": TP to Franklin, 16 May 1778, vol. 2, p. 1146.

"ordered 4,000": TP to Laurens, 14 January 1779, vol. 2, p. 1164.

Crisis No. 4 appears in vol. 1, pp. 102–105.

"if only an appearance": TP to Franklin, 16 May 1778, vol. 2, p. 1146.

On Mifflin: see Flexner, *Washington and the Revolution*, pp. 20, 253, 255, 256.

69 TP reports on his movements after fall of Philadelphia in letter to Franklin, 16 May 1778, vol. 2, pp. 1144–1151.

"he always kept out of danger": Biddle, *Autobiography*, p. 87.

The troops had "gained": Flexner, *Washington and the Revolution*, p. 257.

"They seemed to feel": TP to Franklin, 14 May 1778, vol. 2, p. 1147.

acted *"very* gallant": Conway, *TP*, vol. 1, p. 99.

70 Letter from Matlack: Conway, *TP*, vol. 1, p. 94.

Valley Forge: TP to Franklin, 16 May 1778, vol. 2, p. 1150.

"So there was supper": Marshall diary, 12 February 1778, Historical Society of Pennsylvania.

72 "his remissness": Henry, *Campaign Against Quebec*, p. 149n. Henry recounts TP's way of life as he saw it in Lancaster.

Crisis No. 5 appears in vol. 1, pp. 106–129.

"military jig": p. 115.

"counterfeit bills": p. 108.

"They have refined": p. 118.

"Instead of civilizing others": *ibid.*

"that virtuous ambition": pp. 127–128.

"to ward off that meditated blow": Letter III, "To the Citizens of the United States," 29 November 1802, vol. 2, p. 922.

Adams *"did nothing":* *ibid.*, p. 922. For Adams' reaction to the insinuation see Butterfield, *Adams Diary and Auto.*, vol. 4, pp. 5–6.

73 Dispatches reach York: Burnett, *Continental Congress*, pp. 231–232.

74 TP's predictions in letter to Washington, 5 June 1778, vol. 2, pp. 1152–1153.

State House as "an hospital": Henry Laurens to Rawlins Lowndes, 15 July 1778, Burnett, *Letters of Congress*, vol. 3, p. 333.

"shuffling from meeting house": *ibid.*

75 *Crisis No. 6* appears in vol. 1, pp. 130–139.

"Remember, you do not": p. 132.

"There is a sociability": p. 137.

"offer her peace": p. 138.

Crisis No. 7 appears in vol. 1, pp. 140–157.

"Why is it": p. 141.

"We had governments": *ibid.*

"because the country is young": p. 149.

"Perhaps it may be said": p. 146.

76 "I am not much hurried": TP to Franklin, 24 October 1778, vol. 2, pp. 1153–1154.

"To the King of England": reprinted in Aldridge, "The Poetry of TP," pp. 90–92.

77 "no correspondence with either party": "To the People," 18 March 1777, vol. 2, p. 270.

"All that affects me on the matter": *ibid.*

Rush as "Ludlow": see David Freeman Hawke, *Benjamin Rush, Revolutionary Gadfly* (1971), pp. 198–200.

"A *natural* right": "Candid and Critical Remarks on a Letter Signed Ludlow," 4 June 1777, vol. 2, p. 274.

78 The four-part "Serious Address to the People of Pennsylvania on the Present Situation of their Affairs" appears in vol. 2, pp. 277–302.

"perfectly cool": p. 279.

"we are a people upon experiments": p. 281.

"If ever we cast our eyes towards England": p. 301.

"the sense of the majority": p. 291.

"Property alone": p. 288.

"Freedom and fortune": p. 285.

"I consider freedom as personal property": p. 286.

79 Hedgehogs and foxes: Sir Isaiah Berlin, *The Hedgehog and the Fox* (1954), p. 1.

"It is a decided point with me": p. 290.

6. "A MOST EXCEEDING ROUGH TIME"

80 TP as "ex officio" member: Lee to Paine, 13 July 1777, Ballagh, *Letters of R. H. Lee*, vol. 1, pp. 310–311.

"styling himself": Sparks, *Life of Gouverneur Morris*, vol. 1, p. 201. Even modern English historians have been fooled by Paine's assumption of authority. Here is Cole-Postgate, *British Common People*, p. 112: "Tom Paine later became the equivalent of Foreign Secretary to the American Congress, and even though he had lost his post through impetuousness and indiscretion, he came back to England with the reputation of being the inspirer and one of the organizers of victory."

"view the matter rather than the parties": "A Serious Address to the People of Pennsylvania on the Present Situation of their Affairs," vol. 2, p. 279.

81 "a very ingenious man": Butterfield, *Adams Correspondence*, vol. 1, p. 303. John Adams to Abigail Adams, 19 October 1775.

"a person of plausible readiness": Butterfield, *Adams Diary and Auto.*, vol. 3, p. 340.

"not genuine": William Williams to John Adams, 30 July 1774, quoted in Oscar Zeichner, *Connecticut's Years of Controversy, 1750–1776* (1949), p. 322.

"in France upon business": Committee of Secret Correspondence to Deane, 3 March 1776, Wharton, vol. 2, p. 78.

82 "If we have but luck": Robert Morris quoted in Smith, *TP*, p. 55.

On Arthur Lee see Hendricks, *Lees of Virginia, passim.*

Deane's recall in Wharton, *Diplomatic Correspondence*, vol. 2, pp. 424, 444.

83 A man "of strong self-esteem": Wallace, *Life of Laurens*, p. 306.

On Shippen, Mifflin, and Greene see Ferguson, *Power of the Purse*, pp. 96–97.

Page

83   "Speculation, peculation": quoted in Flexner, *Washington and the Revolution*,
      p. 335.
      "a civil war in America": Butterfield, *Adams Diary and Auto.*, vol. 2, p. 353.
84   "avaricious and ambitious men": Wood, *Creation of the American Republic*, pp.
      419, 420.
      "The storm increases": Gouverneur Morris to John Jay, 16 August 1778,
      quoted in Burnett, *Continental Congress*, p. 361.
      "Poor little Penny": Wallace, *Life of Laurens*, p. 317.
      "Mr. Laurens, good man that he was": *ibid.*, pp. 322–323.
      "fellow laborers": Laurens to Rawlins Lowndes, 16 August 1778, quoted in
      Burnett, *Continental Congress*, p. 361.
85   "plotted some months before": Lee to Laurens, 1 August 1779, Ballagh, *R.
      H. Lee Letters*, vol. 2, p. 99.
      "corrupt hotbed of vice": Lee to Laurens, 13 August 1779, *ibid.*, vol. 2, p. 118.
      "I cannot": quoted in Burnett, *Continental Congress*, p. 364.
      "that the stores which Silas Deane": TP to the Committee of Claims of the
      House of Representatives, 14 February 1808, vol. 2, p. 1492.
86   "every man thought me wrong": *Crisis No. 10*, vol. 1, p. 197.
      "You will please to observe": TP to Laurens, 15 December 1778, vol. 2, p. 1155.
      "The poor fellow got a beating": Francis Lightfoot Lee to R. H. Lee, 22
      December 1778, quoted in Burnett, *Continental Congress*, p. 367.
      "You may readily suppose": Henry, *Campaign against Quebec*, 143n.–144n.
      "Plain Truth" attacked TP on 17, 19, and 21 December 1778 in the *Pennsyl-
      vania Packet*. TP answered with his "card" on 24 December 1778 in the same
      newspaper.
87   " 'Common Sense' has attacked Mr. Deane": Francis Lightfoot Lee to R. H.
      Lee, 5 January 1779, Burnett, *Letters of Congress*, vol. 4, pp. 9–10.
      "to inquire": Morris in *Pennsylvania Packet*, 9 January 1779. On Morris'
      dispensing of funds to his own firm see Jensen, *American Revolution*, p. 633.
      "Paine was determined": Mifflin to Morris, 26 January 1779, New-York
      Historical Society *Collections*, vol. 1 (1878), p. 441.
      "in handwriting which Mr. Deane": "To the Public on Mr. Deane's Affair,"
      vol. 2, p. 121.
88   "Gérard has fairly bullied": Andrew Elliott to Earl of Carlisle, 14 February
      1779, Historical Manuscripts Commission, *Manuscripts of the Earl of Carlisle*
      (1897), p. 419.
      "My design was": TP to Gérard, 2 January 1779, vol. 2, p. 1155.
      "No member of Congress knows": *ibid.*, p. 1156.
      Gérard thanks TP: 2 January 1779, *ibid.*, p. 1156n.
      "by an early and generous friendship": "To the Public on Mr. Deane's
      Affair," vol. 2, p. 123.
      "indiscreet assertions": Gérard to president of Congress, 5 January 1779,
      Wharton, *Diplomatic Correspondence*, vol. 3, p. 11.
89   "I am under no obligation": TP to Gérard, 2 January 1779, vol. 2, pp. 1155–1156.
      TP before Congress recounted in letter to Committee of Claims, 14 Febru-
      ary 1808, vol. 2, p. 1493. See also Burnett, *Continental Congress*, p. 373.

Page

89 "I cannot in duty": TP to Congress, 7 January 1779, vol. 2, p. 1158.

90 Gouverneur Morris' speech is found in Sparks, *Life of Gouverneur Morris*, vol. 1, pp. 199–202.
"I have betrayed no trust": TP to Congress, 8 January 1779, vol. 2, p. 1160.
Contretemps over Laurens' indiscretion: Ford, *Journals of Congress*, 8 January 1779.

91 "that Congress do fully": *ibid.*
January 16: *ibid.*
$250 was paid 31 March 1779: *ibid.*, p. 393.
"a very lucrative offer": Paine to a committee of Congress (October 1783), vol. 2, p. 1230.

92 "I was sensible of a kind of shame": TP to Laurens, 14 January 1779, vol. 2, p. 1161.
"Mr. Paine, I have always": TP quoting Gérard, *Pennsylvania Packet*, 14 September 1779, vol. 2, p. 184. This essay, pp. 181–186, gives TP's fullest account of the negotiations with Gérard.
"employ his pen": Gérard to Vergennes, 10 January 1779, Meng, *Gérard*, pp. 480–481, translation in Durand, *New Materials*, p. 137.
"Any service I can render": *Pennsylvania Packet*, 14 September 1779, vol. 2, p. 183.
"a private offer": TP to Congress, 23 April 1779, vol. 2, p. 1175.
In *Rights of Man*, vol. 2, p. 406n., TP repeats that he refused the offer to write for Gérard.
"never *labored to prove*": *Pennsylvania Packet*, 16 January 1779, vol. 2, pp. 139, 140.
"He has already entered": Meng, *Despatches of Gérard*, pp. 480–481, translated in Durand, *op. cit.*, p. 137.
Gérard to Congress for "their frank": 14 January 1779, Wharton, *Diplomatic Correspondence*, vol. 3, p. 23.
"I feel myself exceedingly hurt": TP to Laurens, 17 January 1779, vol. 2, p. 1165.

93 "I feel only an *unwillingness*": TP to Laurens, 14 January 1779, vol. 2, p. 1161.
"I have been out no where": TP to Washington, 31 January 1779, vol. 2, p. 1166. A similar note on same day to Greene, *ibid.*
"I have lately met with a turn": TP to Franklin, 4 March 1779, vol. 2, pp. 1167–1168.
Sarah Franklin Bache to Franklin, 14 January 1781, photostat of letter at American Philosophical Society.
"inconsistency and obstinence": quoted in Aldridge, *TP*, p. 70.
"very impertinent": John Fell diary, 3 April 1779, quoted in Burnett, *Letters of Congress*, vol. 4, p. 236.
"Poor Paine": John Armstrong to Horatio Gates, 3 April 1779, *ibid.*, p. 136.

94 "Mr. Robert Morris assured me": TP to Jonathan Williams, 26 November 1781, vol. 2, p. 1200.
"Gouverneur Morris hopped round": *ibid.*
Aftermath of Deane: see Van Doren, *Secret History*, pp. 62–63, 417–418, 431–432.

7. "WE WANT ROUSING"

95 Hired as clerk: TP to Washington, 30 November 1781, vol. 2, p. 1203.
Congress and fisheries: see Burnett, *Continental Congress*, pp. 433–437; Stinchcombe, *American Revolution and French Alliance*, pp. 66–73.
The first letter appears in vol. 2, pp. 188–193. The quotations are on pp. 191 and 193. The second letter is on pp. 193–199.

96 "replied to the piece," p. 208.
The third letter is on pp. 199–208.
A commerce "which interferes with none": p. 200.
"fourth part of the staple": *ibid.*
"*law of nations*": p. 207.
TP "had wormed into notice": *Pennsylvania Evening Post*, 9 July 1779.

97 "Hail mighty Thomas!": *ibid.*, 16 July 1779.
"your inveterate hatred": *ibid.*, 22 July 1779.
"Thomas, you seem": *ibid.*, 24 July 1779.
Towne said "he had not liberty": TP, 16 July 1779, vol. 2, p. 170.
"nothing but a halter": 31 July 1779, vol. 2, p. 176.
"I was delivered": Humphreys in *Pennsylvania Evening Post*, 2 August 1779.

98 Mass meeting's resolutions reported in *Pennsylvania Packet*, 29 July 1779. In the newspaper's 14 August 1779 issue mention is made that "several thousand" were present.
"and as some of them saw me": TP letter in *Pennsylvania Packet*, 29 July 1779.
"less than generally expected": 10 August 1779, vol. 2, p. 176.
"It is sufficient on my part": 31 July 1779, vol. 2, p. 174.
"quibbling pen": "An Epistle," *Pennsylvania Evening Post*, 16 July 1779.

99 "A rich man": TP to Reed, 4 June 1780, vol. 2, p. 1187.
"Though, as a merchant": "The Philadelphia Committee to Robert Morris," 24 July 1779, vol. 2, p. 173.

100 The "Citizen's Plan" appeared in the *Pennsylvania Packet*.
"The consequence was": TP to Danton, 6 May 1793, vol. 2, p. 1337.

101 "I think I have a right": TP to Laurens, 14 September 1779, vol. 2, p. 1178.
Matlack asked: TP to Reed, 18 September 1779, vol. 2, p. 1180.
"I know but one kind of life": *ibid.*
TP's conciliatory note to Gérard, 20 September 1779, mentioned in O'Donnell, *Luzerne*, p. 57n.
"perhaps America would feel": TP to Laurens, 14 September 1779, vol. 2, p. 1178.
"I think I have done better": TP to Reed, 18 September 1779, vol. 2, p. 1181.
Request for loan: TP to Executive Council, 28 September and 11 October 1779, vol. 2, pp. 1181–1183.
Reed to Gérard, 28 September 1779, Reed Papers, vol. 2, pp. 156–157. Gérard to Reed, 11 October 1779, *ibid.*

102 "idleness, uneasiness": quoted in Aldridge, *TP*, p. 80.
Gave "great satisfaction": Charles Willson Peale to Laurens, 6 March 1780, quoted in Sellers, *Peale*, vol. 1, p. 213.
Men "have been without meat": Washington to the president of Congress, 5 January 1780, Fitzpatrick, *Washington Writings*, vol. 17, pp. 357–358.

Page

102 *Crisis No. 8* appears in vol. 1, pp. 158–164.
    "To see women": p. 160.

103 "more than half naked": Greene to Moore Furman, 4 January 1780, quoted in Dangerfield, *Livingston*, p. 120.
    On lopping off second half: *Crisis No. 11*, vol. 1, p. 209.
    "Every idea you can form": Washington to Reed, 28 May 1780, Fitzpatrick, *Washington Writings*, vol. 18, pp. 434–435.
    The loss "is such a blow": TP to Blair M'Clenaghan, May 1780 (?), vol. 2, p. 1184.
    "to defer the matter": TP to Greene, 9 September 1780, vol. 2, p. 1188.

104 TP's draft plan: to Reed, ca. June 1780, vol. 2, pp. 209–210.
    "Something must be done": TP to Reed, 4 June 1780, vol. 2, p. 1187.
    "We must rise vigorously,": *ibid.*
    Laurens' plan: discussed in Wallace, *Life of Laurens*, p. 282.

105 "as it is the rich": TP to Blair M'Clenaghan, May 1780 (?), vol 2, p. 1184.
    TP withdraws pay: Conway, *TP*, vol. 1, p. 157. See also TP to committee of Congress (October 1783), vol. 2, p. 1231.
    "By means of this bank": *Dissertations on Government*, vol. 2, p. 385.
    A full and annotated account of the founding of the bank is found in Hammond, *Banks and Politics in America*, pp. 43–46.

106 *Crisis No. 9* appears in vol. 1, pp. 166–170.
    "Had America": p. 166.
    "Could a person possessed": TP to Greene, 9 September 1780, vol. 2, p. 1188.
    TP also mentions the plan in *Rights of Man*, vol. 1, p. 407n.
    Reed "scarcely knew what to say": TP to committee of Congress (October 1783), vol. 2, p. 1232.
    "collect and furnish myself": TP to the Pennsylvania Assembly, 3 November 1780, vol. 2, p. 1190.
    "dissuading me from it": *ibid.*, p. 1233.
    "composed under our eyes": La Luzerne to Vergennes, 16 December 1780, quoted in Aldridge, *TP*, p. 83.

8. AN INTERLUDE IN FRANCE

107 Franklin "one of those men": Henry Bamford Parkes, *The American Experience* (1959), p. 61.
    "I never had": *Freeman's Journal*, 1 May 1782.
    "on *no account* mix": *ibid.*
    Public Good appears in vol. 2, pp. 303–333.

109 Virginia's claim "has a tendency": vol. 2, p. 326.
    "a frontier state": p. 330.
    "as new emigrants": p. 332.
    "the internal control": pp. 332–333.
    Reactions to pamphlet: Reverend James Madison to his son, 9 March 1781; James Madison to Jefferson, 16 April 1782, in Hutchinson and Rachal, *Madison Papers*, vol. 3, p. 11, and vol. 4, p. 155.

110 "If there is any one circumstance": *Freeman's Journal*, 1 May 1782.

Page

110 "The crisis is extraordinary": Washington to Joseph Reed, 28 May 1780, Fitzpatrick, *Washington Writings*, vol. 18, p. 439.
     Crisis Extraordinary appears in vol. 1, pp. 171–188.

111 "the people generally do not understand": vol. 1, p. 181.
     "I knew I had the ear": TP to committee of Congress (October 1783), vol. 2, p. 1237.
     "for taking up and funding": vol. 1, p. 185.
     Assembly buys ten dozen copies: *Pennsylvania Colonial Records*, vol. 12, p. 503, under date 10 October 1780.
     "all opposition ceased": TP to committee of Congress (October 1783). vol. 2, p. 1237.

112 "drew up a letter": TP to Senate of the United States, 21 January 1808, vol. 2, p. 1490.
     Congress' instructions to Laurens in Wharton, *Diplomatic Correspondence*, vol. 4, pp. 205–206. See also Burnett, *Continental Congress*, pp. 476–477.
     Hamilton "not sufficiently known": John Laurens to Washington, 23 December 1780, quoted in Townsend, *John Laurens*, p. 164.
     On Laurens see Townsend, *John Laurens*, especially chapter 15; Wallace, "Sketch of John Laurens" in *Life of Henry Laurens*, pp. 463–494; and Flexner, *Washington and the Revolution*, pp. 257, 341, 409, 432.

113 Laurens "exceedingly averse": TP to Robert Morris, 20 February 1781, vol. 2, p. 1208. See also TP to Senate of United States, 21 January 1808, vol. 2, p. 1489. Evidence that young Laurens knew Paine in 1778 is found in a letter to his father, 9 February 1778, Wallace, *Life of Henry Laurens*, p. 122.
     Lee accuses Franklin in letter to president of Congress, 7 December 1780, Wharton, *Diplomatic Correspondence*, vol. 4, pp. 185–186.
     Chastellux-Lafayette visit: Chastellux, *Travels in North America*, vol. 1, pp. 175–176, 328–329.

114 Witherspoon would "never forgive": TP to committee of Congress (October 1783), vol. 2, p. 1234.
     TP blackballed: *American Philosophical Society Yearbook, 1943* (1944), pp. 72–73.
     "There never was a man less beloved": Sarah Franklin Bache to Franklin, 14 January 1781, photostat of letter at American Philosophical Society.
     "to avoid contention": TP to committee of Congress (October 1783), vol. 2, p. 1234.
     "I leave America": TP to Greene, 10 January 1781, vol. 2, p. 1191.

115 "The impediment of floating ice": Laurens to president of Congress, 25 January 1781, Wharton, *Diplomatic Correspondence*, vol. 4, p. 249.
     Alliance sails: Allen, *A Naval History of the Revolution*, vol. 2, p. 547.
     Trip across: TP to James Hutchinson, 11 March 1781, vol. 2, pp. 1191–1196. See also Laurens to president of Congress, 11 March 1781, Wharton, *Diplomatic Correspondence*, vol. 4, p. 279.

116 "We agree exceedingly well": Jonathan Williams to Franklin, 18 April 1781, quoted in Aldridge, *TP*, p. 87; King, *TP*, pp. 273–274. A variant reading of the letter is in Smith, *TP*, p. 87.
     Watson's account is in Watson, *Men and Times of the Revolution*, pp. 127–128.

117 "in a state of profound ignorance": TP to committee of Congress (October 1783), vol. 2, p. 1231.

Page

117 On Pownall's *Memorial* see Gilbert, *Beginnings of American Foreign Policy*, pp. 107–111.

118 "There is something ironic": *ibid.*, pp. 110–111.

"with more address": TP to committee of Congress (October 1783), vol. 2, p. 1234.

119 Washington to Franklin: 15 January 1781, Fitzpatrick, *Washington Writings*, vol. 21, pp. 100–101.

Vergennes "exclaimed vehemently": Laurens to president of Congress, 2 September 1781, Wharton, *Diplomatic Correspondence*, vol. 4, p. 686.

TP in Passy and Paris: TP to Franklin, 31 March 1787, vol. 2, p. 1260.

"to write a pamphlet": TP to Robert Morris, 20 February 1782, vol. 2, p. 1208.

120 "the treatment I had received": TP to committee of Congress (October 1783), vol. 2, p. 1234.

"his importunities": *ibid.*, vol. 2, p. 1234.

The voyage back: TP to Greene, 10 September 1781, Gimbel collection; Laurens to president of Congress, 2 September 1781, Wharton, *Diplomatic Correspondence*, vol. 4, p. 692.

Arrival reported in *Pennsylvania Journal*, 12 September 1781.

"We parted the money": TP to committee of Congress (October 1783), vol. 2, pp. 1234–1235.

9. SUBSIDIZED SERVANT

121 "if there is any occasion": TP to Thomas McKean, president of Congress (August or September 1781), vol. 2, p. 1197.

"as I must be obliged": TP to John Laurens, 4 October 1781, vol. 2, p. 1191.

"It is well worth remarking": *Letter to Abbé Raynal*, vol. 2, p. 213n.

Cornwallis "nabbed nicely": TP to Jonathan Williams, 26 November 1781, vol. 2, p. 1201.

122 "situation detached": TP to committee of Congress (October 1783), vol. 2, p. 1236.

TP to Washington, 30 November 1781, vol. 2, pp. 1202–1204.

"affectionately interested": TP to committee of Congress (October 1783), vol. 2, p. 1236.

"small traveling press": Washington to committee of Congress, 19 July 1777, Fitzpatrick, *Washington Writings*, vol. 8, p. 443.

"concerted with a friend or two": TP to Congress, vol. 2, p. 1236.

Morris "had been totally deceived": TP to Jonathan Williams, 26 November 1781, vol. 2, p. 1200.

"his pen to be wielded": Morris diary, 26 January 1782, quoted in Wharton, *Diplomatic Correspondence*, vol. 5, p. 134n.

123 "We want the aid of": Morris diary, February 1782, *ibid.*

"and proposed that he should join me": *ibid.*

Agreement signed 10 February 1782: Conway, *TP*, vol. 1, pp. 182, 195.

"Your old acquaintance Paine": Reed to Greene, 14 March 1783, Reed, *Life of Reed*, vol. 2, p. 393.

124 "not only out of friendship to me": TP to Robert Morris, 20 February 1782, vol. 2, p. 1207.

124   Essay that ridicules King George: later reprinted as the first half of *Crisis
      No. 10*, entitled "On the King of England's Speech," vol. 1, pp. 189–196.
      Aldridge, *TP*, p. 330, has noted that "there is some doubt concerning which
      writing Paine considered to be *Crisis No. 10.*" After *Crisis Extraordinary* in
      October 1780 he published four essays on his return from France. The first
      three, which appeared on 19 and 28 February and 7 March 1782, were arbi-
      trarily combined by an early editor into *Crisis No. 10*. The fourth, published
      in the *Pennsylvania Journal*, 3 April 1782, has never been reprinted.
      "with another piece": TP to Robert Morris (March 1782), vol. 2, p. 1211.
      The second half of *Crisis No. 10* appears in vol. 1, pp. 196–207.
      "*As he rose*": p. 197.

125   "We have given": "To the People," *Pennsylvania Journal*, 3 April 1782.
      "to spend part of an evening": TP to Washington, 17 March 1782, vol. 2, p.
      1209.
      "I have closed it up": TP to Robert Morris, Sunday evening, 7 April 1782,
      New-York Historical Society *Collections*, vol. 1 (1878), p. 480.

126   *A Supernumerary Crisis* appears in vol. 1, pp. 217–220.
      Livingston asks TP to write: TP to committee of Congress (October 1783),
      vol. 2, p. 1236.
      On Asgill case see Flexner, *Washington and the Revolution*, pp. 479–482.
      La Luzerne's gala fete: Benjamin Rush to Elizabeth Graeme Ferguson, 16
      July 1782, Butterfield, *Rush Letters*, vol. 1, pp. 278–282.

127   La Luzerne: "one of the politest": quoted in Stinchcombe, *American Revolu-
      tion and French Alliance*, p. 83.
      "Noble in his expenditures": Brissot de Warville, *Travels in North America*,
      vol. 1, p. 179. Iron bed: *ibid.*, p. 293.
      "an excessive attachment to liberty": quoted in Stinchcombe, *op. cit.*, p. 82.
      "equally inaccessible": Brissot de Warville, *Travels*, p. 179.

128   "Few men": Dangerfield, *Livingston*, p. 114.
      "l'indolence": O'Donnell, *La Luzerne*, p. 58n.
      "the *frenchified* politics of *Master Paine*": *Royal Gazette*, 29 May 1782, quoted
      in Stinchcombe, *op. cit.*, p. 128.
      Raynal's book borrowed: TP to Robert Morris, 26 November 1781, vol. 2, pp.
      1201–1202.

129   "It is yet too soon": *Letter to Abbé Raynal*, vol. 2, p. 215.
      "His mistakes afforded me": TP to committee of Congress (October 1783),
      vol. 2, p. 1236.
      Letter to Abbé Raynal appears in vol. 2, pp. 211–263.
      "It is in vain": p. 220.
      "Here the value": p. 219.
      "Perhaps no two events": pp. 242–243.

130   "We see with other eyes": *ibid.*
      "The true idea of a great nation": p. 256.
      "Her influence on the mind": p. 241.
      "The philosopher of one country": *ibid.*
      American Revolution "distinguished by": p. 256.
      Fifty copies "to send": TP to Robert Morris, 6 September 1782, vol. 2, p. 1211.

Page

See also TP to committee of Congress (October 1783), vol. 2, pp. 1236–1237, and TP to Washington, 7 September 1782, vol. 2, p. 1212.

131 "I have lately traveled much": letter dated 3 February 1783, quoted in Smith, *TP*, p. 100. Authority for number of French editions, Echeverria, *Mirage in the West*, p. 44.

"The scene of active politics": TP to Livingston, 3 October 1782, Livingston papers, New-York Historical Society.

"in terms to induce": Morris diary, 23 October 1782, quoted in King, "TP," p. 309.

132 *Crisis No. 12* appears in vol. 1, pp. 221–229.

"Must England ever be": p. 226.

Laurens and Franklin on *Crisis No. 12*: Benjamin Vaughan to Earl of Shelburne, 26 December 1782.

"I see you are determined": Greene to TP, 18 November 1782, quoted in Conway, *TP*, vol. 2, p. 437.

133 "labors to continue the war": Ferguson, *Power of the Purse*, p. 147.

TP letter to Morris, 20 November 1782, vol. 2, pp. 1213–1215.

All unsigned "because I do not wish": TP to Robert Morris, 20 November 1782, vol. 2, p. 1213.

"What would the sovereignty": second Rhode Island letter, 5 December 1782, vol. 2, p. 345.

"Every man in America": *ibid.*, pp. 345–346.

134 Four prodding letters: TP to Robert Morris, 23 January 1783, vol. 2, pp. 1216–1217. On TP in Rhode Island see Polishook, *Rhode Island and the Union*, pp. 76–78.

"to prevent publication": *ibid.*, p. 1217.

135 No delegate "can say": sixth Rhode Island letter, 1 February 1783, vol. 2, p. 362.

Crisis No. 13 appears in vol. 1, pp. 230–235.

10. FROM RAGS TO RICHES

137 "Trade I do not understand": TP to committee of Congress (October 1783), vol. 2, p. 1228.

138 "Their works are read": Brissot de Warville, *Travels in North America*, vol. 1, p. 179.

"For besides the general principle": TP to Boudinot, president of Congress, 7 June 1783, vol. 2, pp. 1217–1218.

On uprising of Pennsylvania troops see Brunhouse, *Counter-revolution*, pp. 135–140.

139 "a softening measure": TP to Rush, 13 July (misdated 13 June by Foner, as pointed out by King, who read the original in Yale Library) 1783, vol. 2, p. 1219. The petition can be read with signatures in *Pennsylvania Gazette* 6 August 1783 and without them in Foner, vol. 2, pp. 263–265, where it carries the title "The Address of the Citizens of Philadelphia, and of the Liberties Thereof—To His Excellency, the President, and Congress of the United States." TP may have written to others besides Rush about the petition.

Page

Varnum L. Collins, *The Continental Congress at Princeton* (1908), p. 86, quotes a contemporary as saying, "Peale and other persons of his stamp" worked assiduously for signatures.

139 "a just and impartial account": committee report delivered in August, Ford, *Journals of Congress*, vol. 24, p. 413.

140 "will serve to exculpate me": TP to Washington, 2 October 1783, vol. 2, p. 1225.

"confidential opinion": *ibid.*

The essay appears in vol. 2, pp. 1226–1242 under the title "To a Committee of the Continental Congress."

"a very lucrative offer": p. 1230.

Washington "affectionately interested": p. 1236.

"materials and information": pp. 1240–1241.

"For Congress": p. 1240.

"A disposition to serve others": p. 1242.

"whether she will in return": *ibid.*

"The constant coldness": TP to Washington, 2 October 1783, vol. 2, p. 1226.

141 "Your presence": Washington to TP, 10 September 1783, Fitzpatrick, *Writings*, vol. 27, p. 146–147.

Scarlet fever: TP to Washington, 13 October 1783, vol. 2, p. 1243. Same news in letter to Robert Morris, 14 October 1783, only partly printed in vol. 2, p. 1243. Full copy in Gimbel collection, American Philosophical Society.

Stolen coat: John Hall to John Coltman, 16 May 1788, Hall manuscripts, Conway, *TP*, vol. 2, p. 469.

"We had several times been told": "The Cause of Yellow Fever," 27 June 1806, vol. 2, pp. 1062–1063.

142 Washington's arrival in New York: Flexner, *Washington and the Revolution*, pp. 524–526.

"I candidly tell you": TP to Duane, 3 December 1783, vol. 2, pp. 1244–1245.

143 *A Supernumerary Crisis*, 9 December 1783, appears in vol. 1, pp. 236–239. He evinced concern about a commercial treaty with England earlier to Washington, 2 October 1783 (vol. 2, pp. 1225–1226), and Robert Morris, 14 October 1783 (vol. 2, p. 1243). See also TP to George Clinton, 19 December 1783, Gimbel collection, American Philosophical Society.

144 "It is the misfortune of some Whigs": TP to Lewis Morris, 16 February 1784, vol. 2, p. 1247.

"I am shut up here": TP to Lewis Morris, 16 February 1784, vol. 2, p. 1247.

"a fit of gout": TP to Mr. Hyer, 24 March 1804, vol. 2, pp. 1451–1452.

"worth at least": TP to Washington, 28 April 1784, vol. 2, p. 1248.

145 "whatever I may then say": *ibid.*, p. 1249.

"might be construed": Madison to Washington, 2 July 1784, *Madison Letters*, vol. 1, p. 86.

"Can nothing be done": Washington to Madison, 12 June 1784, Fitzpatrick, *Washington Writings*, vol. 27, pp. 420–421. See also Washington to Patrick Henry, 12 June 1784 (pp. 421–422), and to R. H. Lee, 12 June 1784 (pp. 422–423).

146 The ill-advised letter to Congress is in vol. 2, pp. 1251–1252, dated 27 September 1785. TP recalled Gerry's comment in a letter to the Committee of Claims of the House of Representatives, 14 February 1808, vol. 2, p. 1494.

Page

146 "His literary works inspired": quoted in Smith, *TP*, p. 107.

147 "Men of letters": John Dos Passos, *The Best of Times* (1966), p. 241.
"had no idea of purchasing": Hall manuscripts, 3 October 1786, Conway, *TP*, vol. 2, p. 464. Hall mentions bringing the $120 in specie on 24 November 1786 (p. 465).

II. THE BANK WAR

149 Despaired "of seeing an abolition": TP to Anon., 16 March 1790, vol. 2, p. 1286.

150 On the Society of Cincinnati: TP to Washington, 28 April 1784, vol. 2, p. 1249.
"extirpate religion": TP to Congress, 8 February 1780, *Pennsylvania Packet*, reprinted in Aldridge, "Why Did TP Write on the Bank?" p. 313n.
"common sense enough": Hall manuscripts, 4 June 1786, Conway, *TP*, vol. 2, p. 463.

151 "facilitate the management of the finances": Robert Morris, quoted in Hammond, *Banks and Politics*, p. 50. Hammond discusses the bank, pp. 48–64. See also Brunhouse, *Counter-revolution in Pennsylvania*, pp. 173–175, 182–183.

152 "a species of treason": TP to Laurens, 11 April 1778, vol. 2, p. 1142.
"Our plan is commerce": *Common Sense*, vol. 1, p. 20.
"I saw very clearly": Letters on the Bank, 7 April 1786, vol. 2, p. 422.
"that in a government where nothing is certain": TP to Fitzsimmons, 19 April 1785, *Pennsylvania Gazette*, reprinted in Aldridge, "Why Did TP Write on the Bank?" p. 311.

153 "The house is composed of men": *ibid.*, p. 310.
"the most effective participant": Hammond, *Banks and Politics*, p. 60.

154 *Dissertations on Government: the Affairs of the Bank; and Paper Money* appears in vol. 2, pp. 368–414.
"may be altered, amended": p. 376.
"No law made": p. 379.
"by the distresses of the time"; p. 386.
"puts in a nutshell": Hammond, *Banks and Politics*, p. 60.
"The whole community": p. 397.
Praise for paper money in *Letter to Abbé Raynal*, vol. 2, pp. 228–230.
"There may be cases": TP to Fitzsimmons, 19 April 1785, Aldridge, "Why Did TP Write on the Bank?" p. 311.
"Money is money": p. 404.

155 "The republican form": p. 369.
"The term 'forever' ": p. 397. "The next age": p. 397.
"The question, whether one generation": Jefferson to Madison, 6 September 1789, Boyd, *Jefferson Papers*, vol. 15, p. 392.
"that Paine saw a copy": Adrienne Koch, *Jefferson and Madison, the Great Collaboration* (1950), p. 88.

156 "Nothing is more certain": Letters on the Bank, 28 March 1786, vol. 2, p. 416.
"that has been agitated": *ibid.*, 4 April 1786, vol. 2, p. 417.
"an unprincipled author": *ibid.*, p. 418.
"that the people are recovering": *ibid.*, p. 419.

Page

156   "that from the first establishment": "On the Advantages of a Public Bank,"
       20 June 1786, vol. 2, p. 432.
       Smilie, "who loves to talk": Letters on the Bank, 7 April 1786, vol. 2, p. 422n.
       "I have kept cash": Letters on the Bank, 20 June 1786, vol. 2, p. 432.

157   "Atticus" appeared in the *Pennsylvania Packet* on 25 April, 8 and 22 May, and
       28 June 1786. On Wilson and the bank, see Janet Wilson, "The Bank of North
       America and Pennsylvania Politics; 1781–1787," *Pennsylvania Magazine of History
       and Biography*, vol. 66, pp. 10–13.
       "I shall be backward and forward": TP to Hall, 22 September 1786, vol. 2,
       p. 1257.
       "My aim was to quiet": "On the Affairs of the State," *Pennsylvania Gazette*,
       20 September 1786.

158   "Next to gaining a majority": TP to Fitzsimmons, 19 November 1786, vol.
       2, p. 1259.
       Dispute between TP and Coltman: Hall manuscripts, 19 November 1786,
       Conway, *TP*, vol. 2, p. 466.
       "*Janus* is our own": by Peter Markoe, quoted in Sister Mary Chrysostom
       Diebels, S.S.N.D., *Peter Markoe (1752?–1792). A Philadelphia Writer* (1944), p. 99.

       12. EXPERIMENTS OF A DIFFERENT KIND

160   "a people upon experiments": "Address to the People of Pennsylvania," 1
       December 1778, vol. 2, p. 281.
       Mr. Paine "seemed to delight": Hall manuscripts, 27 December 1786, Con-
       way, *TP*, vol. 2, p. 466.
       Experiment with Rittenhouse: "The Cause of Yellow Fever," 27 June 1806,
       vol. 2, pp. 1063–1064.

161   "on exceeding good terms": TP to Franklin, 31 March 1787, vol. 2, p. 1261.
       TP and Henry exchange ideas: letter to Henry mentioned in Hall manu-
       scripts, 22 September 1786, Conway, *TP*, vol. 2, p. 462.
       Welding "appears to me": TP to Jefferson, May 1788, Boyd, *Jefferson Papers*,
       vol. 13, p. 223.
       "lessened the catalogue": TP to Sir Joseph Banks, 25 May 1789, photostat of
       at American Philosophical Society.

162   "adopted political son": Hall manuscripts, 20 April 1787, Conway, *TP*, vol.
       2, p. 468.
       Never "give a deciding opinion": *ibid.*, 22 November 1785, vol. 2, p. 461.
       "Mr. Paine, you may be surprised": anecdote in Epps, *Life of Walker*, pp.
       143–144.
       "In a little time after they are lighted": TP to Franklin, 31 December 1785,
       vol. 2, pp. 1025–1026.
       New Year's Day experiment: Hall manuscripts, 1 January 1786, Conway,
       TP, vol. 2, pp. 461–462.

163   "The European method": TP to Franklin, 6 June 1786, vol. 2, p. 1027.
       On Swan and TP see Brissot de Warville, *New Travels*, p. 258.
       "The only novelty": Aldridge, *TP*, p. 110.

164   Bridge over Harlem River: TP to Franklin, 6 June 1786, vol. 2, p. 1027.

Page

164 TP as employer: Hall manuscripts, 12 December 1785, 28 May 1786, Conway, *TP*, vol. 2, pp. 461, 462.
Wooden model: TP to Franklin, 6 June 1786, vol. 2, p. 1027.
Second, iron, model: TP to Jefferson, 18 September 1789, vol. 2, p. 1296.

165 Quotations regarding Fitch from Flexner, *Inventors in Action*. Women as "greatest torment": p. 135.
"middling glad in liquor": p. 173.
"little Johnny Fitch": p. 128.
"A rickety floor": p. 128.
"to lay at the feet of Congress": p. 75.
Franklin "spoke very flatteringly": p. 77.
Visits to Congress and Henry: Westcott, *Life of Fitch*, p. 138.
"machine to drive boats": Hall manuscripts, 10 March 1786, Conway, *TP*, vol. 2, p. 462.

166 Franklin and "the stone": Biddle, *Autobiography*, pp. 198–199.
"it would benefit the city": TP to Franklin, 6 June 1786, vol. 2, p. 1028.
TP invites the Council: TP to a member of the Pennsylvania Council, June 1786, vol. 2, p. 1255.

167 Agricultural Society and bridge: TP to George Clymer, 19 November 1786, vol. 2, p. 1258.
"I am now flooring": TP to Clymer, 13 December 1786, Gimbel collection, American Philosophical Society.
"This day employed": Hall manuscripts, 14 December 1786, Conway, *TP*, vol. 2, p. 465.
"their sentiments and opinions": Hall manuscripts, 1 January 1787, Conway, *TP*, vol. 2, p. 467. On Rittenhouse's reaction see *ibid.*, 26 December 1786, p. 466.

168 Construction costs for bridge: *ibid.*, 4 January 1787, p. 467.
"not really interested in America": R. K. Webb, *Harriet Martineau: A Radical Victorian* (1960), p. 172.
"whom I am very anxious to see": TP to Franklin, 31 March 1787, vol. 2, p. 1260.

169 On Society for Political Enquiries see Conway, *TP*, vol. 1, pp. 225–226; T. I. Wharton, "Memoirs of William Rawle" in *Memoirs of the Historical Society of Pennsylvania*, vol. 4, part I (1840), p. 25; and Biddle, *Autobiography*, p. 223.
On letters of introduction TP carried to France see Labaree to Gimbel in "Paine and France" file, Gimbel collection, American Philosophical Society.
"We want a bridge": Franklin to Rochefoucauld, 15 April 1787, Bigelow, *Franklin Works*, vol. 11, p. 314.
"more and longer letters": Van Doren, *Franklin*, p. 743.
"Our federal constitution": Franklin to Jefferson, 19 April 1787, Boyd, *Jefferson Papers*, vol. 11, p. 302.

170 "not much" expected: David Franks to Jefferson, *ibid.*, pp. 305–306.
"I am rather a zealot": Edward Carrington to Jefferson, 24 April 1787, *ibid.*, p. 311.

Page

170   "crazy brained politicians": Letters on the Bank, 7 March 1787, vol. 2, p. 435.
      TP's financial situation: TP to Jefferson, 13 July 1789, vol. 2, p. 1294.

13. FRANCE TO ENGLAND AND BACK AGAIN

173   Land "the richest I ever saw": TP to Franklin, 22 June 1787, vol. 2, p. 1262.
      "I have received": *ibid.*
      "The more I see of him": Le Roy to Franklin, 11 June 1787 (?), typescript in
      Gimbel collection, American Philosophical Society.
174   "Determine never to be idle": Jefferson to Martha May, 5 May 1787, quoted
      in Malone, *Rights of Man*, p. 124.
      Jefferson's succinct remarks on the bridge in letter to Benjamin Vaughan,
      2 July 1787, Boyd, *Jefferson Papers*, vol. 11, p. 533. See also his letter to Hopkin-
      son, 1 August 1787, *ibid.*, p. 657.
      "cordial rather than intimate": Malone, *Rights of Man*, p. 143.
      "Je serai très flatté": Moustier to Jefferson, 24 July 1787, *ibid.*, p. 622.
      Bridge retrieved: Morellet says, "I had returned to him his iron bridge," in
      letter dated 3 July 1787, typescript in Gimbel collection, American Philoso-
      phical Society.
      "There is a great curiosity": TP to Franklin, 22 June 1787, vol. 2, p. 1263.
      "skill in rendering judgments:" TP to Royal Academy of Sciences, 21 July
      1787, vol. 2, p. 1264.
175   "I should tell you further": Le Roy to Franklin, 11 June 1787 (?), typescript
      in Gimbel collection, American Philosophical Society.
      Lafayette described: Swiggett, *Gouverneur Morris*, p. 46; Thompson, *Leaders
      of the French Revolution*, pp. 30, 31. On size of his fortune see Lefebvre, *Coming
      of the French Revolution*, p. 11.
176   "the most able and independent": Jefferson to John Jay, 21 June 1787, Boyd,
      Jefferson Papers, vol. 11, p. 489.
      "I think that in the course of three months": Jefferson to John Adams, 30
      August 1787, Cappon, *Adams-Jefferson Letters*, vol. 1, p. 196.
177   "The people of France": *Prospects on the Rubicon*, vol. 2, p. 634.
      "No nation makes war nowadays": Jefferson to John Jay, 3 November 1787,
      Boyd, *Jefferson Papers*, vol. 12, p. 315.
      "seen enough of war": TP to Burke, 7 August 1788, photostat at American
      Philosophical Society. Meeting with Morellet discussed in same letter.
      "superficial publicists": quoted in Appleby, "America as a Model for
      French Reformers," p. 280. For a sketch of Morellet see Claude-Anne Lopez,
      Mon Cher Papa! Franklin and the Ladies of Paris (1966), pp. 284–288. See also Van
      Doren, *Franklin*, pp. 419, 648, 649–650.
      "that I might be assured": *Rights of Man*, vol. 1, p. 246.
178   *Prospects on the Rubicon* appears in vol. 2, pp. 621–651.
      " 'The Rubicon is passed' ": p. 623.
      "Credit is not money": p. 633.
      "There is no real rivalship": p. 630.
      "I defend the cause of the poor": p. 632.
      "the pettish vanity": p. 650.
      "the creation we enjoy": p. 634.

Page

178 "however confused": p. 651.

179 Le Roy on bridge: to Franklin, 11 June 1787 (?), Gimbel collection, American Philosophical Society.

TP was told officially: He may have learned the news unofficially some days earlier. "The committee have among themselves finally agreed on their report which I saw this morning," TP wrote Jefferson, 18 August 1787, Boyd, *Jefferson Papers*, vol. 12, p. 45.

Jefferson's letters to John and Abigail Adams in Cappon, *Adams-Jefferson Letters*, vol. 1, pp. 193, 195. Both are dated 30 August 1787.

"because Trumbull does not paint": quoted in Sizer, *Autobiography of Trumbull*, p. 326.

A reproduction of Trumbull's portrait of Paine, along with comment upon it, can be found in Theodore Sizer, "Tom Paine's Portrait," Yale University Library *Gazette*, 4 April 1956, vol. 30; no pages in reprint at New-York Historical Society.

"perfect likeness": Jefferson to Trumbull, 12 January 1789, Boyd, *Jefferson Papers*, vol. 14, p. 440.

180 "good old woman": TP to Lewis Morris, 4 May 1788, Gimbel collection, American Philosophical Society.

181 "seldom saw the *companions of his youth*": Chalmers, *TP*, p. 56.

"With respect to France": TP to Marquis of Lansdowne, 21 September 1787, vol. 2, p. 1265.

"He has scalded himself": William Stephens Smith to Jefferson, 3 December 1787, Boyd, *Jefferson Papers*, vol. 12, pp. 390–391.

"The viciousness of that nation": TP to Clymer, 29 December 1787, vol. 2, p. 1267.

182 Parker was present: Letter III, "To the Citizens of the United States," 21 November 1802, vol. 2, p. 916. He told a variation of the story earlier to Clymer, 29 December 1787, vol. 2, p. 1266.

"Its color": Sizer, *Autobiography of Trumbull*, p. 147.

TP at Trumbull's described by Royall Tyler, quoted in Conway, vol. 1, pp. 237–238.

"Without wine or other liquor": Carlile, *TP*, p. 27.

183 "most delicious pest," etc.: "Odes to Mister Paine, Author of 'Rights of Man,'" "Song, by Mister Paine," in Wolcot, *Works of Peter Pindar*, vol. 3, pp. 65, 67, 69.

Morris' "affairs appearing to be deranged": TP to Jefferson, 19 February 1788, vol. 2, p. 1268.

"It is very possible that after all": TP to Clymer, 29 December 1787, vol. 2, p. 1267.

"If I can succeed": TP to Lewis Morris, 4 May 1788, Gimbel collection, American Philosophical Society. The Duke de la Rochefoucauld mentions in letter of 6 February 1788, typescript in Gimbel collection, that TP had sent for the model. He also says TP had left London "to help Mr. Beaumarchais."

"my principal object": TP to Jefferson, 19 February 1788, vol. 2, pp. 1267–1268.

184 Lafayette advised "that it would be best": *ibid.*, p. 1267.

Page

184   "for the same price as a wooden bridge": Éthis de Corny, 8 April 1788, quoted in Aldridge, *TP*, p. 113.

"The bridge is to be made in America": TP to Lewis Morris, 4 May 1788, Gimbel collection, American Philosophical Society.

"M. Le Coutenier, the banker": *ibid.*

"You will not be able": Jefferson to TP, 3 July 1788, Boyd, *Jefferson Papers*, vol. 13, p. 307.

TP on the Constitution: letter to George Washington, 30 July 1796, vol. 2, pp. 693, 691, 692, 692n.

185   "Mr. Jefferson, Common Sense, and myself": Lafayette to Knox, 4 February 1788, quoted in Louis Gottschalk, *Lafayette between the American and French Revolution (1783–1789)* (corrected edition, 1965), p. 374.

James Wilson quotation can be found in Boyd, *Jefferson Papers*, vol. 13, p. 7.

"These I conceive to be civil rights": the most authoritative reprinting of Paine's memorandum to Jefferson (January-February 1788) is in *ibid.*, vol. 13, pp. 4–8. It also appears in Foner, vol. 2, pp. 1298–1299. Boyd dates the piece as written between January and February 1788.

186   An eminent biographer: Gilbert Chinard, *Thomas Jefferson: The Apostle of Americanism* (1957 ed.), p. 80.

"He came from Versailles": *Rights of Man*, vol. 1, pp. 304–305.

187   "Jefferson's ideas continued to develop": Palmer, "The Dubious Democrat," p. 398.

"It is difficult to write": TP to Jefferson, 15 June 1788, Boyd, *Jefferson Papers*, vol. 13, p. 254.

14. "IN SOME INTIMACY WITH MR. BURKE"

188   "blossomed somewhat mysteriously": Lucas, *Art of Living*, pp. 135–136.

"I never heard him make a good joke": *ibid.*, p. 139.

"this fierce people": *ibid.*, p. 146.

189   "best talker": *ibid.*, p. 197.

"dirt, cobwebs": *ibid.*, p. 199.

"happens to arrive": TP to Burke, 7 August 1788, photostat at American Philosophical Society.

"but before I do this": *ibid.* TP mentions the planned trip to Wilkinson's works in letter to Benjamin West, 13 July 1788, Gimbel collection, American Philosophical Society.

190   "At a small town": Rickman, *TP*, p. 80. TP tells of visit to Duke of Portland in letter to Jefferson, 9 September 1788, vol. 2, p. 1270, from which "Mr. B——— says," etc., are taken.

"I believe I am not": TP to Jefferson, 26 February 1789, vol. 2, p. 1283.

"I find the opposition as much warped": *ibid.*

191   "He is not without some attention": Burke to Gilbert Elliot, 3 September 1788, quoted in Fennessy, *Burke and Paine*, p. 85.

"a favorite hobbyhorse": TP to Jefferson, 9 September 1788, vol. 2, p. 1268.

"as matters at present appear": TP to Jefferson, 15 June 1787, Boyd, *Jefferson*, vol. 13, p. 254.

Page

191 Patent: Specification of Thomas Paine. A.D. 1788. No. 1667, vol. 2, pp. 1031–
1034.
"the most eminent in England": TP to Jefferson, 9 September 1788, vol. 2,
p. 1269.

192 "we went on rapidly": TP to Jefferson, 16 February 1789, vol. 2, pp. 1039–1040.
Burke's visit to ironworks: TP to Jefferson, 16 February 1789, vol. 2, p. 1281.
Letter is misdated 26 February by Foner; see Boyd, *Jefferson Papers*, vol. 14,
pp. 561–569, for accurate transcription.
"so confident of his judgment": TP to Thomas Walker, 26 February 1789,
vol. 2, p. 1278.
"President of the Board": TP to Jefferson, 16 February 1789, vol. 2, p. 1040.
"making a mockery of the king": quoted in Lucas, *Art of Living*, p. 183.
"to propose a national convention": *Rights of Man*, vol. 1, p. 453. At the time
TP wrote Jefferson, 16 February (vol. 2, p. 1282), "Had Mr. Pitt proposed a
national convention at the time of the king's insanity he had done right, but
instead of this he has absorbed the right of the nation into a right of
Parliament."

193 If Parliament were "permitted": *ibid.*
"there will certainly be a change in ministry": TP to Jefferson, 15 January
1789, Boyd, *Jefferson Papers*, vol. 14, p. 454.
"I had rather see my horse": TP to Kitty Nicholson Few, 6 January 1789,
vol. 2, p. 1276.
"I am in pretty close intimacy": *ibid.*
"I am in some intimacy": TP to Jefferson, 15 January 1789, Boyd, *Jefferson
Papers*, vol. 14, p. 454.
"The greater distance": TP to Jefferson, 26 (i.e., 16) February 1789, vol. 2, p.
1283. See also TP to Jefferson, 17 June 1789, vol. 2, p. 1291, where he repeats
the message.

194 "severest winter": TP to Kitty Nicholson Few, 6 January 1789, vol. 2, p. 1277.
"I have been to see the cotton mills": TP to Jefferson, 17 June 1789, vol. 2,
p. 1292.
On Rumsey: TP to Jefferson, 26 (i.e., 16) February 1789 and 15 September 1788,
vol. 2, pp. 1284, 1272.
"threaten scission . . . awful crisis": Jefferson to TP, 23 December 1788, Boyd,
Jefferson Papers, vol. 14, pp. 375, 376.
"very much rejoiced": TP to Jefferson, 26 (i.e., 16) February 1789, vol. 2, p.
1281.

195 The letter to Staunton, dated spring of 1789, appears in vol. 2, pp. 1040–1047.
That to Banks, 25 May 1789, is a virtual transcript. A microfilm copy from
the Royal Society files is on deposit at the American Philosophical Society.
"if only a fifth of the persons": TP to Jefferson, 17 June 1789, vol. 2, p. 1291.
A complete bridge of five ribs: TP to Congress, June 1803, vol. 2, p. 1053.
"As our works are large": TP to Jefferson, 13 July (1789), vol. 2, p. 1294.
"to find all the materials": *ibid.*

196 "which would be deemed bold": Jefferson to TP, 17 March 1789, Boyd,
Jefferson Papers, vol. 14, p. 672.

Page

196   "as much liberty as they are capable of managing": quoted in Palmer,
      "Dubious Democrat," p. 402.
      "that you may be able to separate": Jefferson to TP, 11 July 1789, Boyd,
      Jefferson Papers, vol. 15, p. 266.
198   "But if it should be *character*": Burke to Charlemont, 9 August 1789, quoted
      in Fennessy, p. 94.
      "death certificate": quoted from Aulard in Lefebvre, *Coming of the French
      Revolution*, p. 150.
      "Mr. Jefferson concludes the letter": TP to Walker, 19 September 1789,
      Armytage, "TP and the Walkers," p. 23.
      "There is yet in this country": TP to Jefferson, 18 September 1789, vol. 2, p.
      1296.
200   In France, "the elements which compose human society": Burke in October
      1789, quoted in Fennessy, *Burke and Paine*, p. 95.
      Whiteside put in prison: Davenport, *Diary of Gouverneur Morris*, vol. 1, p. 177.
      "commodious sponging house": Chalmers, *TP*, p. 60.
201   Belgian baroness mentioned in Aldridge, *TP*, pp. 125–126.
      "do him no good": Davenport, *Diary of Gouverneur Morris*, vol. 1, p. 390.
      TP's essay on central bank: *ibid.*, 5 January 1789, p. 358.
      "how prosperously matters": TP to Burke, 17 January 1790. The letter was
      first published by J. T. Boulton, "An Unpublished Letter from Paine to
      Burke," *Durham University Journal*, vol. 43 (1951), pp. 49–55. Extensive quota-
      tions from it are found in Fennessy, *Burke and Paine*, p. 103.
      "Do you mean to propose": Burke to Paine, no date, quoted in Fennessy,
      ibid., p. 104.
202   The advertisement appeared in the *London Chronicle*, 16 February 1790,
      quoted in *ibid.*, p. 101.
      "I take over with me to London": TP to Anonymous (Benjamin Rush), 16
      March 1789 (i.e., 1790), vol. 2, pp. 1285–1286.

                          15. BUSY WAITING

203   "very pleasant" trip: TP to Anonymous (i.e., Thomas Christie), 16 April
      1790, vol. 2, p. 1300. Copeland, *Burke Essays*, points out, p. 176n., that the
      recipient is Christie.
      Bookseller "informed me": *ibid.*, p. 1301.
      TP's round of visits: *ibid.*, pp. 1300–1301.
204   "deeply infected": Cragg, *Reason and Authority*, p. 262.
      "I am so out of humor with Mr. Burke": TP to Thomas Walker, 14 April
      1790, Armytage, "TP and the Walkers," p. 25.
      "all gay and happiness": TP to Walker, 19 September 1789, Armytage, "TP
      and the Walkers," p. 24.
205   "I am now inclined to think": TP to Anonymous (Christie), 16 April 1790,
      vol. 2, pp. 1301–1302.
      TP and La Luzerne: "Last Sunday evening I was at the Marquise de la
      Luzerne's and I shall dine there on Thursday next." TP to William Short,
      22 June 1790, vol. 2, p. 1310.

Page

205   On Joseph Johnson see Charles Timperley, *Dictionary of Printers and Printing* (1839) and also *Dictionary of National Biography*.

"Paine, in his general habits": Godwin, *Memoirs of Mary Wollstonecraft*, p. 62. Paul, *William Godwin*, vol. 1, p. 69, says Godwin met TP at home of Brand Hollis "sometime before the spring of 1791" but gives no source. An excerpt from Godwin's diary on p. 70 marks the first meeting with Mary Wollstonecraft under the date 13 November 1791: "Dine at Johnson's with Paine, Shovet, and Wolstencraft; talk of monarchy, Tooke, Johnson, Voltaire, pursuits, and religion."

206   On Christie see Cameron, *Shelley and his Circle*, vol. 1, p. 122n.: also TP to Benjamin Rush, 16 March 1790, Kramer, "My Much Loved America," p. 20. Christie's mention of TP in *Letters on the Revolution in France* occurs on p. 65 in a preface dated 1 January 1791. The quotations from his *Miscellanies: Literary, Philosophical and Moral* (1788), are found on pp. 220, 270.

On TP as honorary member of SCI see Cone, *English Jacobins*, p. 106.

"Men may get into": Howell, *State Trials*, vol. 25, p. 330.

"an old-fashioned radical": quoted in Yarborough, *Tooke*, p. 192.

"the most effectual method": TP to Jefferson, 26 (i.e., 16) February 1789, vol. 2, p. 1282.

207   "His good humor": Stephens, *Memoirs of Tooke*, vol. 2, p. 462.

"He was accustomed to sneer": *ibid.*, pp. 423–424.

Quotations from Davenport, *Diary of Gouverneur Morris*, come from vol. 1. April 19 (p. 486), April 21 (p. 487), May 3 (p. 502), May 15 (p. 516), May 17 (p. 517), May 21 (p. 520), June 1 (p. 533).

208   "it appears from the king's speech": *ibid.*, July 12 (p. 559).

Jones's visit to Morris on May 3: *ibid.*, vol. 1, p. 502.

On Nootka Sound controversy see Malone, *Rights of Man*, pp. 309–314; Flexner, *Washington and the New Nation*, pp. 256–258; Ritcheson, *Aftermath of Revolution*, pp. 97–102.

209   "France has nothing to do": TP to Short, 1 June 1790, vol. 2, p. 1307.

"The preparations for war": TP to Short, 4 June 1790, vol. 2, p. 1308.

"I know the character of this country": TP to Short, 22 June 1790, vol. 2, p. 1309.

Pamphlet "recommending an attack": TP to Short, 22 June 1790, vol. 2, p. 1309.

"press gangs at work": TP to Short, 24–25 June 1790, vol. 2, p. 1312.

"The English fleet": TP to Short, 28 June 1790, vol. 2, p. 1313.

"the British ministry have insisted": Davenport, *Diary of Gouverneur Morris*, 12 July 1790, vol. 1, p. 559.

210   TP's visit to Burke: *Letter Addressed to the Addressers*, vol. 2, pp. 497–498.

"so formidable a people": Washington diary, vol. 4, p. 136, quoted in Flexner, *Washington and the New Nation*, p. 136.

"we wish to be neutral": Jefferson to Morris, 12 August 1790, quoted in Malone, *Rights of Man*, p. 312.

"I think I see this": Davenport, *Diary of Gouverneur Morris*, 8 August 1790, vol. 1, p. 570.

211   "I do not permit": TP to Jefferson, 20 April 1805, vol. 2, p. 1465.

211 "War, should it break out": TP to Washington, 31 May 1790, vol. 2, p. 1305.
"a slender opinion of myself": TP to Jefferson, 18 September 1789, vol. 2, p. 1295.
Davenport, *Diary of Gouverneur Morris*, vol. 1: June 12 (p. 540), June 14 (p. 540), June 30 (p. 552), August 1 (p. 568), August 14 (p. 572).
TP on raising of bridge: to Thomas Walker, 8 August 1790, Armytage, "TP and the Walkers," pp. 26–27.

212 "Paine's bridge is not so handsome": Davenport, *Diary of Gouverneur Morris*, 11 September 1790, vol. 1, p. 589.
"I think the floor will be capital": TP to Thomas Walker, 25 September 1790, Armytage, "TP and the Walkers," p. 28.
Bridge "was exhibited": *Gazette of the United States*, 5 January 1791, reprinting an article from London datelined 20 October 1790.
"Paine's bridge sired many others": Armytage, "TP and the Walkers," p. 29.
"several new and original features": Smiles, *Life of Telford*, p. 173.
"one of the most daring": *Encyclopedia of Britannia* (1958), article on bridges.
"a structure which": Robert Stephenson, quoted in Smiles, *op. cit.*, p. 173.

213 "suggested by Mr. Paine's": "The Construction of Iron Bridges," June 1803, vol. 2, p. 1054. See also TP to Jefferson, 1 October 1800, vol. 2, p. 1411.
"magnificent obsession": Armytage, "TP and the Walkers," p. 30.
TP on mint to Jefferson, 28 September 1790, vol. 2, pp. 1314–1315. Jefferson to TP, 29 July 1791, vol. 2, p. 1320n. TP essay on the mint appears in vol. 2, pp. 901–908. It can also be found in Boyd, *Jefferson Papers*, vol. 17, pp. 534–540.
"I can scarcely forbear": TP to Jefferson, 15 September 1789, vol. 2, p. 1295.

16. REFLECTIONS ON RIGHTS AND REVOLUTIONS

215 "tribute of fear": *Rights of Man*, vol. 1, p. 256.
On Burke's slowly mounting antipathy to the French Revolution see Cone, *Burke and the Nature of Politics*, pp. 294–302.
"I looked on that sermon": Burke, *Reflections*, pp. 10–11.

216 "There is no foreign court": TP to Burke, 17 January 1790, quoted in Fennessy, *Burke and Paine*, p. 103.
"the Revolution was not a sequence": Cone, *English Jacobins*, p. 93.
"very bad taste": Rogers, *Recollections*, p. 76.
"Read it": George III quoted in Lucas, *Art of Living*, p. 156.
"*There is no loss of friendship*": quoted in Fennessy, *Burke and Paine*, p. 190.

217 "one of the best-hearted men": *Rights of Man*, vol. 1, p. 249.
Burke in *Reflections* on Price: as "spiritual doctor," p. 13; "porridge," p. 10; "Pisgah," p. 65.
"think that government may vary": *Reflections*, pp. 88–89.
"The total contempt which prevails": *ibid.*, p. 25.

218 "To make a revolution": *ibid.*, p. 168.
"Power, not principles": *Rights of Man*, vol. 1, p. 258.
"Whatever each man can separately do": *ibid.*, p. 59.
"We are afraid to put men to live": *ibid.*, p. 88.

Page

218   "It is one thing to make an idea clear": Burke in *The Sublime and Beautiful*, quoted in Boulton, *Language of Politics*, p. 109.
"I thought ten thousand swords": *Reflections*, p. 76.
Burke's association of revolution with disease and drunkenness pointed out by Boulton, *Language of Politics*, p. 118.

219   rotten borough system "perfectly adequate": *Reflections*, p. 56.
"He pities the plumage": *Rights of Man*, vol. 1, p. 260.
"The imperative tone": Boulton, *Language of Politics*, p. 104.
"It is a partnership in all science": *Reflections*, p. 97.
"Formal government": *Rights of Man*, vol. 1, p. 358.
"We wished to derive": *Reflections*, p. 31.
"I am contending": *Rights of Man*, vol. 1, p. 252.
"a graceful ornament": *Reflections*, p. 141.
"Titles are but nicknames": *Rights of Man*, vol. 1, p. 286.

220   "I wished to know": *ibid.*, pp. 348–349.
"Mr. Burke does not call": *ibid.*, p. 260.
TP on Burke as literary craftsman: *ibid.* "a composition of art": p. 260.
"a theatrical representation": *ibid.*, pp. 258–259.

221   "dramatic performance": *ibid.*, p. 268.
"tragic paintings": *ibid.*, p. 258.
"It suits his purpose": *ibid.*, p. 268.
"Never, never more": *Reflections*, pp. 76–77.
"In the rhapsody of his imagination": *Rights of Man,* vol. 1, p. 259.
"They have sent theirs to be blown about": *Reflections*, p. 195.
"As the wondering audience": *Rights of Man*, vol. 1, p. 319.
TP vernacular phrases: *"swabbed the deck"*: p. 318.
"The duty of man": p. 275.
"a kind of fungus": p. 308.
"A sort of mule-animal": p. 292.

222   "I was then standing": p. 305.
"I will here cease": p. 294.
"pathless wilderness": p. 272.
"A French bastard": *Common Sense*, vol. 1, p. 14.
Representative governments: *Rights of Man*, vol. 1, p. 344.
"he would answer in *four days*": *General Evening Post* (London), 8 March 1791.
"Common Sense is writing for you": Lafayette to Washington, 12 January 1790, quoted in Aldridge, *TP*, pp. 126–127.

223   A detailed analysis of the publication of the first part of *The Rights of Man* can be found in the Gimbel collection, American Philosophical Society.
TP borrows from Scott: Godwin's diary, 14 May 1791, quoted in Aldridge, *TP*, p. 135.
"fitted by them for the press": *ibid.*, pp. 18–19.
"freed from some obnoxious passages": *General Evening Post* (London), 8 March 1791.
"I have got it": quoted in Colby, *Life of Holcroft*, vol. 1, p. xli.
"a consultation of the law officers": *Gazeteer*, 27 April 1791.

224   "Reprehensible as that book was": Howell, *State Trials*, vol. 22, p. 381.

224 "But mum—We don't sell it": Colby, *Life of Holcroft*, vol. 1, p. xli.
"It is written in his own wild style": Samuel Romilly to M. Dumont, 5 April 1791, Romilly, *Life of Romilly*, vol. 1, pp. 317–318.
The age "is too productive": Charles Harrington Elliot, *The Republican Refuted* (1791), p. 2.
"the spirit of puritanic malignity": Anonymous, *A Defence of the Constitution of England* (1791), p. 64.
"What I own has a good deal surprised me": Romilly to Dumont, 5 April 1791, Romilly, *Life of Romilly*, vol. 1, pp. 317–318.
"full of spirit and energy": *ibid.*
"coarse and rustic" language might "seduce": Isaac Hunt, *Rights of Englishmen* (1791), p. 85, quoted in Fennessy, *Burke and Paine*, p. 216.
"Many applications were made to me": *Letter Addressed to the Addressers*, vol. 2, p. 486.

225 "for his most masterly book": *The Oracle* (London), 25 March 1791.
"There was certainly an apparent inconsistency": Batley to Wyrill, 14 April 1792, quoted in Fennessy, *Burke and Paine*, p. 228.
Horne Tooke compares to parts of Bible: Howell, *State Trials*, vol. 25, p. 116.

17. "BIG WITH A LITTER OF REVOLUTIONS"

226 "wretched" apartment; TP a "little mad": Davenport, *Morris Diary*, 11 and 16 April 1791, vol. 2, pp. 159, 163.
"I could easily excuse": Étienne Dumont, *Recollections of Mirabeau*, pp. 261–262.
"good things" in *Rights of Man*; Morris as TP's enemy: Davenport, *Morris Diary*, 8 and 10 April, vol. 2, pp. 156, 159.
Kingship as working title: *The Oracle*, 8 July 1791. Expects to be done by summer: *Morning Chronicle*, 29 May 1791. Twenty thousand copies sold: *Gazeteer*, 6 June 1791.

227 TP at Versailles: *Morning Chronicle*, 29 May 1791.
"The birds are flown": Rickman, *TP*, p. 84.
"I hope there will be no attempt": Rickman, *TP*, p. 84.
"You see the absurdity": *Morning Chronicle*, 29 June 1791. A variant version can be found in Rickman, *TP*, p. 84.

228 "His flight is equivalent": "A Republican Manifesto," 1 July 1791, vol. 2, p. 517.
"This society opposed": "Reasons for Preserving the Life of Louis Capet," 15 January 1793, vol. 2, p. 552.
Essay for the *Républicain* reprinted as open letter to Condorcet, Bonneville, and Lanthenas, June 1791, vol. 2, pp. 1315–1318.

229 "simply Louis Capet"; "The facts show": "A Republican Manifesto," 1 July 1791, vol. 2, p. 518.
"a young thoughtless member": Étienne Dumont, *Recollections of Mirabeau*, p. 261.
Manifesto ripped down: "Reasons for Preserving the Life of Louis Capet," 15 January 1793, vol. 2, pp. 552–553.

Page

229 "against all the hell of monarchy": TP to Abbé Sieyès, July 1791, vol. 2, p. 520.

"to spend a portion of this summer in England": TP to Bonneville, Condorcet, and Lanthenas, June 1791, vol. 2, p. 1315.

"inflated to the eyes": Davenport, *Morris Diary*, 4 July 1791, vol. 2, pp. 212–213.

230 "The work has had a run": TP to Washington, 21 July 1792, vol. 2, p. 1318.

232 "This pamphlet is": Anonymous, *An Impartial Sketch of the Life of TP*, n.p.

"At this time": Rickman, *TP*, p. 101.

233 "Being on wood butments": TP to Hall, 25 November 1791, Hall manuscripts, Conway, *TP*, vol. 2, p. 470. Also in Foner, vol. 2, p. 1321.

Burke "will not attempt": quoted in Copeland, *Burke Essays*, p. 179.

"I see the tide is yet the wrong way": TP to Hall, 25 November 1791, vol. 2, pp. 1321–1322.

234 "I have but one way": TP to Short, 2 November 1791, vol. 2, p. 1321.

"By what I can find": *ibid.*, p. 1322.

"I have received a letter": TP to Hall, 25 November 1791, vol. 2, p. 1322.

"drew a red-hot plowshare": Thomas Wentworth Higginson, quoted in Parrington, *The Colonial Mind*, p. 327.

235 Adams on reception of *Discourses on Davila*: *ibid.*, p. 316.

New York Advertiser printed *The Rights of Man* and the ode. See Conway, *TP*, vol. 2, pp. 331n.–332n.

"I am extremely pleased": quoted in Malone, *Rights of Man*, p. 357, along with the printer's encomium.

Jefferson's apology to Adams, 17 July 1791, in Cappon, *Adams-Jefferson Letters*, vol. 1, pp. 245–246.

236 "He should have pointed out": *Annual Register for 1796*, quoted in Aldridge, *TP*, p. 144.

"Mr. Jefferson and myself": Randolph to Madison, 25 July 1792, quoted in John C. Hamilton, *History of the Republic of the United States of America as Traced in the Writings of Alexander Hamilton and of his Contemporaries* (7 vols., 1857–1864), vol. 4, p. 515.

"The duties of my office": Washington to TP, 6 May 1792, Fitzpatrick, *Washington Writings*, vol. 32, pp. 38–39.

18. HOUNDED BY THE GOVERNMENT

238 Christie gets Chapman for TP: Howell, *State Trials*, vol. 22, pp. 400–401.

"when the town will begin to fill": TP to Short, 2 November 1791, vol. 2, p. 1320. See also *Letter Addressed to the Addressers*, vol. 2, p. 472.

"loitered in the press": Chalmers, *TP*, p. 152.

239 TP's account of publication in *Rights of Man*, vol. 1, pp. 455–458; Chapman's version is in Howell, *State Trials*, vol. 22, pp. 401–403.

240 "author and publisher of that work": TP to Jordan, 16 February 1792, vol. 2, p. 1324.

"Secretary for Foreign Affairs": title page of first edition.

First printing of five thousand copies: Chalmers, *TP*, p. 108n.

"It appears to general observation": *Rights of Man*, vol. 1, p. 368.

Page

240   Dedication of Lafayette: *ibid.*, pp. 347–348.
      Second part of *Rights of Man* appears in vol. 1, pp. 346–458.
241   "It is not worth making changes": p. 353.
      "reforms, or revolutions": p. 451.
      Alterations "in the principles and practices": p. 354.
      Bill of Rights "a bargain": p. 383.
      Monarchy: p. 393.
      The monarch: p. 366.
      Aristocracy: p. 412.
      Constitutions: p. 375.
      Bill of Rights: p. 383.
      Representative government: p. 367.
      Commerce: p. 400.
      "Mr. Burke, who, I fear": pp. 434, 445.
242   "jovial ferocity . . . terrific onslaught": Williams, *Sansculottes*, p. 14.
      "Gentlemen, you will be pleased to take into consideration": Howell, *State
      Trials*, vol. 22, p. 383.
      "monarchy and aristocracy": *Rights of Man*, vol. 1, p. 352.
      "may be considered the *order of the day*": p. 355.
      "hunted round the globe": p. 354.
      "a morning of reason": p. 396.
      "To use a trite expression": p. 449.
      "formal government": p. 358.
      "ten shillings a year": p. 428.
      Twenty shillings ought "to be given": p. 429.
243   "It is painful to see old age": p. 426.
      Excise officers' pay: p. 441.
      "Why not leave them as free": pp. 439–440.
      "it would not only be wrong": p. 446.
      "It is now toward the middle": pp. 453–454.
244   Sent a dozen copies: TP to Jefferson, 13 February 1792, vol. 2, pp. 1322–1323.
      TP to Washington, 13 February 1792, vol. 2, p. 1323.
      Paine would be punished: Davenport, *Morris Diary*, 16 February 1792, vol.
      2, p. 368.
      "the riots and outrages": *ibid.*, 23 February 1792, p. 370.
245   On Friends of the People see Cone, *English Jacobins*, pp. 126–127.
      "was a performance totally different": quoted in Cone, *ibid.*, p. 100, Fen-
      nessy, *Burke and Paine*, p. 242.
      "they were critical": Palmer, *Age of Democratic Revolution*, vol. 2, p. 461.
      In December "five or six mechanics": quoted in Williams, *Sansculottes*, p. 59.
      Hardy and founding of LCS: Thompson, *English Working Class*, p. 17.
246   "The endeavor to inflame": J. Gifford, quoted in Fennessy, *Burke and Paine*,
      p. 246.
      "If Mr. Paine should be able": Christopher Wyvill, quoted in *ibid.*
      "The countryside was ruled by the gentry": Thompson, *English Working
      Class*, pp. 51–52.
247   "They went in a hackney coach": Knowles, *Life of Fuseli*, vol. 1, pp. 374–375.

Page

247 "He went seldom into town": Chalmers, *TP*, p. 158.

Newspaper accounts of TP's arrest: *Columbian Centinel*, 25 June 1792, *Morning Herald*, 18 April 1792. TP admits he had been living in Bromley in *Letter Addressed to the Addressers*, vol. 2, p. 487.

248 Quotations from royal proclamation found in Cone, *English Jacobins*, p. 131.

"Principles had been laid down": Pitt, 25 May 1792, quoted in Fennessy, *Burke and Paine*, p. 243.

"sedulously inculcated throughout the kingdom": quoted in Aldridge, *TP*, p. 163.

Address to Jacobin Club, 27 May 1792, appears in Conway, *TP et la Révolution*, pp. 210–212; translation and emendations in Gimbel collection, American Philosophical Society.

249 "frequent associates" of Talleyrand, *Times*, 28 May 1792.

TP to Mr. Secretary Dundas, 6 June 1792, vol. 2, pp. 446–457.

"It is earnestly recommended to Mad Tom": *Times*, 12 July 1792. Boast that "the matter of charge" had been omitted in cheap edition appeared in August 8 edition.

"As we have now got the stone to roll": Blanchard Jerrold, *The Original* (1874), quoted in Thompson, *English Working Class*, p. 111.

250 TP's offer reported in *General Evening Post*, 7 July 1792.

"No one loves armed missionaries": Palmer, *Age of Democratic Revolution*, vol. 2, p. 13.

"people of Paris without frosting": *ibid.*, p. 47.

251 "Down with the fathead": *ibid.*, p. 41.

"I am an American citizen": Lafayette to Short, 26 August 1792, in Davenport, *Morris Diary*, vol. 2, p. 551.

Honorary citizens are listed in Palmer, *Age of Democratic Revolution*, vol. 2, pp. 54–55.

"who, by their writings": *Le Moniteur*, 28 August 1792, translation in Gimbel collection, American Philosophical Society.

252 Quotations from *Morris Diary*: 2 September, p. 537; 3 September, p. 537; 4 September, p. 538.

"beheaded and emboweled": Morris to Jefferson, 10 September 1792, *ibid.*, p. 540.

TP elected from Calais: Aldridge, *TP*, p. 171.

Oise election of "Peenn": *Procès Verbal l'Assemblée*, Archives Nationales, C 180.

"Does not seem to talk much": Hall manuscripts, 6 September 1792, Conway, *TP*, vol. 2, p. 472.

253 "Scarcely had the fatal news arrived": Brissot, *On the Situation of the National Convention under the Influence of Anarchists*, pp. 89–90, translation in Gimbel collection, American Philosophical Society. Brissot introduces the quotation thus: "Listen to the testimonies which are not suspect: 'I was in England,' writes Thomas Paine in a work which is going to appear, 'during the massacres of September 2 and 3.' " If the work appeared, it has not been identified.

France "wished to gain": TP to Monroe, 10 September 1794, vol. 2, p. 1347.

Page

253   "Would you believe it possible": Jefferson to TP, 19 June 1792, Ford, *Jefferson Writings*, vol. 6, p. 87.
      Letter Addressed to the Addressers appears in vol. 2, pp. 469–511.
      "By this, the will of the nation": p. 499.

254   "it was necessary to take precautions": *Le Moniteur*, 23 September 1792, translation in Gimbel collection, American Philosophical Society. Statement that the party departed at night is found in the *General Evening Post*, September 13.
      Dover affair: TP to Mr. Secretary Dundas, 15 September 1792, vol. 2, pp. 466–469.
      "He was hissed a great deal": J. Mason to J. B. Burges, 13 September 1792, Fortescue, *Manuscripts*, vol. 2, pp. 316–317.

19. CITIZEN PAINE

256   "He is the very picture of a journeyman tailor": J. Mason to J. B. Burges, 13 September 1792, Fortescue, *Manuscripts*, vol. 2, pp. 316–317.
      "All the soldiers on duty were drawn up": Carlile, *TP*, pp. 14–15. See also William Lindsay to Lord Grenville, 27 September 1792, Fortescue, *Manuscripts*, vol. 3, p. 472, where it is remarked that Sir Robert Smythe said TP "received with great honors in Calais."
      Trip to Paris: Frost to Horne Tooke, 20 September 1792, Howell, *State Trials*, vol. 24, p. 535.

257   Stay at White's Hotel: Smith, *TP*, p. 179.
      TP visits Morris: Morris to Pinckney, 23 September 1792, Davenport, *Morris Diary*, vol. 2, p. 555.
      "the Austrians and Prussians": TP to Monroe, 10 September 1794, vol. 2, p. 1350.

258   On Cloots, see Palmer, *Age of Democratic Revolution*, vol. 2, pp. 55, 118; Williams, *Letters of the Politics of France*, vol. 2, pp. 18, 21, 176.
      "Kings are in the moral order": Mathiez, *French Revolution*, p. 228.
      TP "gave his voice": Davenport, *Morris Diary*, vol. 2, p. 555. On the king's fate, *ibid.*, p. 566 under date 23 October 1792.

259   "From this place and this day": Mathiez, *French Revolution*, p. 221.
      "No man could make a greater show of zeal": quoted in Lydia M. Child, *Memoirs of Madame De Stael, and of Madame Roland* (1847), p. 192.
      "Let the people choose": Mathiez, *French Revolution*, p. 229.
      Goupilleau translates for TP: Browning, *Despatches of Earl Gower*, p. 253, under date 22 September 1792.
      "not fortunate": *Morning Chronicle*, 4 October 1792.

260   "at daggers' drawing": Morris to Alexander Hamilton, 24 October 1792, Davenport, *Morris Diary*, vol. 2, p. 573.

261   "is that the Girondins": Thompson, *Robespierre*, p. 52.
      "an owl in a room filled with monkeys": Smith, *TP*, p. 182.
      Lettre de Thomas Paine au Peuple Français appears in Foner, vol. 2, pp. 537–540, under the title *Address to the People of France*.

262   "I was elected the second person": TP to Monroe, 18 August 1794, vol. 2, p. 1342.

Page

262 "Look at the appointments": Smith, *TP*, p. 182–183.
Brissot "an honest but weak man": Williams, "Missions of David Williams,"
p. 655.
"I think him better fitted": Roland, *Mémoires*, pp. 290–291, translation from
typescript in Gimbel collection, American Philosophical Society. See also
Cheetham, *TP*, 61n.

263 "I always understand my own thoughts best": TP in undated letter it has
been assumed to Danton, a colleague on the committee who read and spoke
English fluently. It was found among Danton's papers in the Archives
Nationales, item #5 under AF II 49, Dossier 380.
"was charged with the declaration of rights": Barère, *Memoirs*, vol. 2, p.
229.
"as a mathematical problem": Schapiro, *Condorcet*, p. 97.
"*le peuple* became a reality": *ibid.*, p. 94.
"One could describe Condorcet's intelligence": *ibid.*, p. 96, quoting from
Mme. Roland's *Mémoires* (1884 ed.), vol. 2, p. 297.
Robespierre dismissed him: *ibid.*, p. 97, quoted from *Le Moniteur*, 8 May 1794.

264 "The late constitution": TP in undated letter to Danton, Archives Na-
tionales, item #5, AF II 49, Dossier 380.
"Paine offers a bet": Davenport, *Morris Diary*, 1 October 1792, vol. 2, p. 562.
"The National Convention declares": Mathiez, *French Revolution*, p. 284.

265 Banquet at White's Hotel: Palmer, *Age of Democratic Revolution*, vol. 2, p. 58;
Smith, *TP*, p. 184; Byrne, *Fitzgerald*, p. 113.
Ballads about TP: in Ray B. Browne, "The Paine-Burke Controversy in
Eighteenth-Century Irish Popular Songs," pp. 83, 84–85.
"the more I see of his interior": Byrne, *Fitzgerald*, p. 113.

266 "as I do not speak French": TP to Le Brun, 4 December 1792, vol. 2, p. 1501.

267 "All who are privileged": Mathiez, *French Revolution*, p. 286.
Indictment against TP: See *The Trial of Thomas Paine for Writing a Libel called
the Second Part of the Rights of Man* (1792). Also Howell, *State Trials*, vol. 22,
pp. 358–380. The seditious passages are cited on pp. 407–410.
"Have you read this little work": Thompson, *English Working Class*, p. 103.
"to one printer alone": John Gifford, *A Plain Address to the Common Sense of
the People of England, Containing an Interesting Abstract of Pain's Life and Writings* (1792), p. 13n.
"can be no other than the people of England": "TP to the English Attorney-
General on the Prosecution Against the Second Part of *Rights of Man,*" 11
November 1792, vol. 2, pp. 511–513.

268 "The court was crowded": *Times*, 19 December 1792.
The British Museum has several pamphlets that offer purportedly short-
hand versions—most of them give variant renderings of Macdonald's and
Erskine's speeches—of TP's trial. The two used here are *The Trial of Thomas
Paine* (1792) and *The Trial of Thomas Paine for Writing a Libel called the Second
Part of the Rights of Man* (1792). The *Times* for 19 December 1792 gives a long
account. For a modern secondary account see Cone, *English Jacobins*, pp.
137–139.

270 "unwell or pretending to be so": report dated 17 December 1792, in Browning, *Despatches of Earl Gower*, p. 260.

Page

270 "Paine looks a little down": Davenport, *Morris Diary*, 20 December 1792, vol. 2, p. 587.
"It is the office of royalty": "An Essay for the Use of New Republicans in Their Opposition to Monarchy," 20 October 1792, vol. 2, p. 542.
"If the king is not guilty": Lefebvre, *French Revolution*, vol. 1, p. 270.

271 "On the Propriety of Bringing Louis XVI to Trial" appears in vol. 2, pp. 547–551.
"I think it necessary": p. 548.
"the trial of Louis XVI": p. 550.
"only a weak and narrow-minded man": pp. 550–551.
Louis' trial: scene described in Gershoy, *Barère*, pp. 139–144.
"the king might have need of him": quoted in Sears, *Washington and the French Revolution*, p. 31.

272 "to make sacrifices for peace": Davenport, *Morris Diary*, 23 December 1792, vol. 2, p. 587.
To give "Mr. Pitt": *ibid.*, 24 December.
"He has I think": Morris to Washington, 6 January 1793, *ibid.*, vol. 2, p. 595.
"Bad, very bad": Conway, *TP et la Révolution dans les deux mondes*, p. 442, translation in Gimbel collection, American Philosophical Society.
"If we silence today": quoted in Smith, *TP*, pp. 199–200.

273 "Reasons for Preserving the Life of Louis Capet" appears in vol. 2, pp. 551–555.
Every American "feels the debt of gratitude": p. 554.
"It has already been proposed": p. 555.
The voting: the most vivid account is Smith, *TP*, pp. 188–190. See also Conway, *TP*, vol. 2, pp. 4–5.
TP's plea for mercy appears in vol. 2, pp. 555–558 under the title "Shall Louis XVI Be Respited?" with Marat's and Thuriot's interruptions interpolated.

276 "a king had been put to death": Lefebvre, *French Revolution*, vol. 1, p. 272.

20. THE TERROR BEGINS

277 "If the French kill their king": *Mr. King's Speech at Egham, with Thomas Paine's Letter to Him on it, and Mr. King's Reply, as they all appeared in The Morning Herald* (1793), quoted in Gimbel, "TP Fights for Freedom," p. 426.
"As to Thomas Paine": Barère, *Memoirs*, vol. 2. p. 238.

279 "He was so plagued": Rickman, *TP*, p. 129.
TP at St. Denis: *ibid.*, pp. 134–135.

280 Fellow boarders and visitors: Conway, *TP*, vol. 2, p. 66. See also Cameron, *Shelley and His Circle*, vol. 1, pp. 125–126.
TP describes the house in "Forgetfulness," vol. 2, pp. 1123–1124.
"Friends, we are betrayed": Thompson, *French Revolution*, p. 385.

281 "the violence of party": TP to Monroe, 18 August 1794, vol. 2, pp. 1342–1343.
"Is it really possible": Thibaudeau, *Mémoires*, vol. 1, p. 111, translation in Gimbel collection, American Philosophical Society.

282 "much to the displeasure of the supposed suicide": letter of Sampson Perry in Archives Nationales, W 269, item #16.

Page

282 "Before dying": *Le Patriote*, 16 April 1793, quoted in Conway, *TP*, vol. 2, p. 49.

The trial: *Le Moniteur*, 3 May 1793, gives a full report; translated excerpts are in the Gimbel collection, American Philosophical Society. See also Conway, *TP*, vol. 2, p. 50. The attempt to bring Brissot to the stand is mentioned in Ellery, *Brissot*, p. 334.

283 "It is difficult to contain": Gottschalk, *Marat*, p. 160. TP goes unmentioned in Gottschalk's account of the trial.

Encounter with "stout young man": Rickman, *TP*, p. 151.

284 TP on Miranda in letter to Anonymous, 20 March 1806, vol. 2, p. 1481. On proposed expedition to South America see TP to O'Fallon, 17 February 1793, vol. 2, pp. 1328–1329. On Miranda's trial see Aldridge, *TP*, pp. 198–199, who draws on *Archivo del General Miranda* (15 vols., 1929–1938), vol. 12, pp. 170–172 for TP's testimony.

Christie's testimony: TP to Anonymous, 20 March 1806, vol. 2, p. 1481.

285 "The dispute was then compromised": TP to Anonymous, 20 March 1806, vol. 2, p. 1482.

"Had this revolution been conducted": TP to Jefferson, 20 April 1793, vol. 2, p. 1331.

Jacobins "act without prudence": *ibid.*, p. 1330.

"Most acquaintances that I have": TP to Danton, 6 May 1793, vol. 2, p. 1338.

286 "If every individual": *ibid.*, p. 1337.

TP on price controls: *ibid.*, p. 1337.

287 "in case the Convention refused": Mathiez, *French Revolution*, p. 325.

Danton warns TP: Aldridge, *TP*, p. 201, drawing on Lewis Goldsmith, *Antigallican Monitor*, 13 February 1814.

Lanthenas "too chicken-hearted": Sydenham, *Girondins*, pp. 54–55.

288 "At present I am told": Gouverneur Morris to Robert Morris, 25 June 1793, Davenport, *Morris Diary*, vol. 2, p. 48.

Signers to the petitions of June 6 and 19 are given in Sydenham, *Girondins*, Appendix A, List VIII, p. 219.

"in those childish amusements": vol. 2, pp. 1124–1125.

"Any individual who usurps": Thompson, *French Revolution*, p. 394.

"Respect a pillar of liberty": Smith, *TP*, p. 201

289 TP-Barère encounter: TP to Monroe, 20 October 1794, vol. 2, pp. 1365–1366.

"To succeed with Americans": foreign office memorandum quoted in Aldridge, *TP*, p. 204. TP praises Jefferson and censures Morris in letter to Barère, 5 September 1793, vol. 2, pp. 1332–1333.

He "showed us the way": Barère, *Memoirs*, vol. 2, pp. 114–115.

"return to America": TP to Barère, 5 September 1793, vol. 2, p. 1332.

"Make terror the order of the day!" Palmer, *Twelve Who Ruled*, p. 52.

290 "The National Convention was fighting": Barère, *Memoirs*, vol. 2, p. 103.

"dishonored himself": Conway, *TP*, vol. 2, p. 93; Aldridge, *TP*, p. 206.

"I trusted in the morality of Thomas Paine": quoted in Smith, *TP*, pp. 210, 211. This is a loose translation of one of Manuel's answers in the interrogation which took place on 23 Brumaire at "onze heure du matin." The entire interrogation can be found in Archives Nationales, W 295, item # 246.

290   "Demand that Thomas Paine be decreed": *Age of Reason*, vol. 1, p. 516.

21. PRISON

291   Calendar: Palmer, *Twelve Who Ruled*, pp. 111–113.
Dechristianization program: *ibid.*, pp. 117–120.
"I demand": *ibid.*, p. 122.

292   "Do you seriously believe": John Adams to Benjamin Rush, 12 April 1809, Schutz and Adair, *Spur of Fame*, p. 144.
"and I every day expected": TP to Samuel Adams, 1 January 1802, vol. 2, p. 1436.
Lanthenas' statement found in a letter to Thionville in Archives Nationales, F 7 4774 64. Paine's appears in a letter to Daniel Isaac Eaton, which was published by Eaton as part of an advertisement in the *Morning Chronicle*, 19 December 1795. See also Richard Gimbel, "The First Appearance of Thomas Paine's *The Age of Reason,*" *Yale University Library Gazette*, vol. 31 (1956). The apparently sole surviving copy of the suppressed first French edition is at the American Philosophical Society.
He believed in God: TP to Samuel Adams, 1 January 1802, vol. 2, p. 1435, 1436.

293   The first part of *Age of Reason* appears in vol. 1, pp. 463–512.
"Whenever we read the obscene stories": p. 474.
"tail of the heathen mythology": p. 467.
"a species of atheism": pp. 486–487.

294   "It is only in the CREATION": p. 483.
"whole cartloads of trumpery": John Adams, 18 February 1756, Butterfield, *Adams Diary and Auto.*, vol. 1, p. 8.
"consists in the freshness": Stephen, *English Thought*, vol. 1, p. 390.
"saw Paine's latest offense": Thompson, *English Working Class*, pp. 97–98.

295   "I saw the landlord going": "Forgetfulness," vol. 2, p. 1125.
"It is certain that in one point": *Age of Reason*, vol. 1, p. 512.

296   TP's report on his arrest: *Age of Reason*, vol. 1, pp. 512–514. Government agents' report: Conway, *TP*, vol. 2, pp. 104–107. The original report, which has TP's name spelled as "peine," is in the Archives Nationales, F 7 4774 64. The slip signed by the jailer Benoit acknowledging TP's arrival at the Luxembourg is in *ibid.*

297   On the Luxembourg see Smith, *TP*, p. 230; Aldridge, *TP*, p. 214; and especially Williams, *Sketch of the Politics of France*, vol. 1, *passim*.
"level with the earth": "To the Citizens of the United States," Letter III, 29 November 1802, vol. 2, p. 921.
"If the citizens of the United States": Washington to Acting Secretary of State, 23 September 1795, Fitzpatrick, *Washington Writings*, vol. 34, p. 312.
Americans' petition with signature: Conway, *TP*, vol. 2, pp. 107–109. See also *Le Moniteur*, 29 January 1794.
"Not a few members hissed": Thomas W. Griffith in Latimer, *My Scrap-Book*, p. 51.

298   Vadier's reply to petition: Conway, *TP*, vol. 2, p. 109. Perry on the reply: *Argus*, p. 559.

298 "on terms of the best harmony": TP to Morris, 24 February 1794, vol. 2, p. 1339.
"In the best of times": Morris to Jefferson, 6 March 1794, Sparks, *Gouverneur Morris*, vol. 2, p. 409.

299 "Thomas Paine has just applied": Morris to Deforgues, 14 February 1794, Sparks, *ibid.*, vol. 2, pp. 401–402.
"The application, it must be confessed": Sparks, *ibid.*, vol. 1, p. 416.
Deforgues' reply: Foner, vol. 2, pp. 1338n.–1339n.
"They have nothing against me": TP to Morris, 24 February 1794, vol. 2, p. 1339.
Robespierre "has more than once been heard to say": Perry, *Argus*, p. 559.
November decree: *Le Moniteur*, 18 November 1793, mentioned in Echeverria, *Mirage in the West*, p. 168.

300 "The paid journalists": memorandum in Thompson, *Robespierre*, p. 76.
"all communication from persons imprisoned": letter to Washington, 30 July 1796, vol. 2, p. 698.
"From about the middle of March 1794": *ibid.*
Cloots berates TP "for his credulity": Williams, *Sketch of the Politics of France*, vol. 2, p. 176.

301 "That which you did": Conway, *TP*, vol. 2, p. 129.
"His cheerful philosophy": Williams, *Sketch of the Politics of France*, vol. 4, pp. 55–56.
TP's prison writing: Cobbett-Bonneville manuscript, Conway, *TP*, vol. 2, p. 440.
"and every night when Mr. Bond left him": Rickman, *TP*, p. 194.

302 "Many a man whom I have passed": TP to Monroe, 25 August 1794, vol. 2, p. 1344.
Benoit removed: Conway, *TP*, vol. 2, p. 134.
"nearly terminated my existence": letter to Washington, 30 July 1796, vol. 2, p. 699.
"My illness rendered me": TP deposition in Archives Nationales, W 189.
Robespierre brought to the Luxembourg: Palmer, *Twelve Who Ruled*, p. 378.

303 "That hypocrite" Robespierre: TP to National Convention, 7 August 1794, vol. 2, p. 1340.
"It is not the nation": *ibid.*
Lanthenas' appeal, dated 18 Thermidor, in Archives Nationales, F 7 4774 64.
Audibert's can be found in Conway, *TP*, vol. 2, p. 139.
"As I believe none of the papers": TP to Monroe, 17 August 1794, vol. 2, p. 1341.
Morris, *"my inveterate enemy"*: *ibid.*

304 *"I shall be very glad"*: TP to Monroe, 25 August 1794, vol. 2, p. 1344.
"Citizens Representatives: I offer myself": TP quoting himself in letter to Monroe, 20 October 1794, vol. 2, p. 1365.
"Bourdon de l'Oise is the most inveterate enemy": *ibid.*, p. 1365.
"entirely without money": TP to Monroe, 25 August 1794, vol. 2, p. 1344.
Monroe "has no orders": TP to Monroe, 10 September 1794, vol. 2, p. 1345.
See also TP to Madison, 24 September 1795, vol. 2, p. 1379.

304   Forty-three-page essay: TP to Monroe, 10 September 1794, vol. 2, pp. 1345–
        1354.
305   Nearly "the oldest inhabitant": TP to Monroe, 4 October 1794, vol. 2, pp.
        1356–1357.
        "The weather was becoming damp": letter to Washington, 30 July 1796, vol.
        2, p. 700.
        "By being with us": Monroe to TP, 18 September 1794, reprinted by TP in
        his letter to Washington, vol. 2, p. 701.
        "has relieved my mind": TP to Monroe, 4 October 1794, vol. 2, p. 1355.
        "I have not a candle to burn": TP to Monroe, 13 October 1794, vol. 2, p. 1359.
306   "In short, sir": *ibid.*, p. 1361.
        "I cannot rest any longer": TP to Monroe, 20 October 1794, vol. 2, p. 1374.
        "invite some of the Committee": *ibid.*, p. 1370.
        "Matters and even promises": TP to Monroe, 2 November 1794, vol. 2, p.
        1374.
        "I forwarded it immediately": Monroe to Secretary of State Randolph, 7
        November 1794, quoted in Conway, *TP*, vol. 2, pp. 150–151.

                          22. MR. MONROE'S DIFFICULT GUEST

307   "young, beautiful" wife: Latimer, *Scrap-Book of the French Revolution*, p. 59.
        "till his death or departure": Monroe to Madison 20 January (more likely
        June or July) 1796, Hamilton, *Monroe Writings*, vol. 2, p. 440.
        Paris described: Ammon, *Monroe*, pp. 131–132.
308   A list of all those placed on trial for selling or publishing Paine's books or
        espousing his principles is in the Gimbel collection in packet labeled "Tri-
        als."
        "I have never heard": Thibaudeau, *Mémoires*, pp. 108–109, typescript transla-
        tion in Gimbel collection, American Philosophical Society.
        TP, that "cherished colleague": Chénier speech before Convention, 3 Janu-
        ary 1795, quoted in Aldridge, *TP*, p. 224. The original is in Chénier's *Oeuvres*
        (8 vols., 1823–1827), vol. 5, pp. 180–181.
309   "abyss of misery": Mme. Lafayette to TP, Woodward, *TP*, p. 280. Illustra-
        tive letters revealing TP's willingness to help friends: to Citoyen Pelet, 27
        February 1795, in Gimbel collection; to Citizen Minister re. Robert Smith,
        13 August 1796, vol. 2, pp. 1383–1384.
        Information "is of such great importance": Monroe to Committee of Public
        Safety, 4 January 1795, Conway, *TP*, vol. 2, p. 154. TP also mentions the
        proposal in "Letter to Citizens of the United States," 6 December 1802, vol.
        2, pp. 926–927.
310   "Had a constitution been established": *Dissertation on First Principles of Gov-
        ernment*, vol. 2, pp. 587–588.
        "We should be governed by the best": Lefebvre, *French Revolution*, vol. 2, pp.
        160–161.
311   A constitution "repugnant to reason": speech to National Convention, 7
        July 1795, vol. 2, p. 589.
        "to the people of Holland": *ibid.*

Page

311   *Dissertation on First Principles of Government* appears in vol. 2, pp. 570–588. The quotations come from pp. 579, 580.

312   "In my opinion, if you subvert": speech to National Convention, 7 July 1795, vol. 2, p. 594.

"The Christian religion is, above all": Butterfield, *Adams Diary and Auto.,* 26 July 1796, vol. 3, p. 234.

"For the sake of public and private comfort": Henry, *Campaign Against Quebec,* pp. 145n., 146n.

313   The second part of *The Age of Reason* appears in vol. 1, pp. 514–604.

"I proceed to examine": p. 520.

"Having thus far": p. 523.

"I proceed": p. 531.

"Is it because ye are sunk": p. 537.

"but to return": p. 583.

Ruth "an idle, bungling story": p. 535.

Moses "detestable": p. 528.

Solomon "witty": p. 550.

Jeremiah "a medley": p. 556.

Isaiah "wild and disorderly": p. 552.

"detected and proved": p. 537.

314   "I have gone through the Bible": p. 570.

"Were any girl": p. 574.

"It is assassinating the dignity": p. 598.

"Morality is injured": p. 598.

"Of all the systems": p. 600.

"I here close": p. 604.

Ordered fifteen thousand copies: TP to Fellows, 20 January 1797, vol. 2, p. 1384.

In August "out of cash": TP to Monroe, 15 August 1795, vol. 2, p. 1502. See also Conway, *TP,* vol. 2, p. 270n. On TP's debt to Monroe see Wilmerding, *Monroe, Public Claimant,* pp. 102–104.

315   Monroe praised for "his conduct": Hamilton Rowan, quoted in Aldridge, *TP,* p. 223.

"At first he drank": Cheetham, *TP,* p. 189.

Nurse "who had for him all the anxiety": Cobbett-Bonneville manuscript, *ibid.,* p. 441.

"the prospect now is": Monroe to Joseph Jones, 15 September 1795, Conway, *TP,* vol. 2, p. 166.

"I owe this illness": TP to Madison, 24 September 1795, vol. 2, p. 1378.

"Take from the mine the hardest": Cheetham, *TP,* p. 208n. Also in Eugene Perry Link, *Democratic-Republican Societies, 1790–1800* (1942), p. 196.

316   "did not entertain a favorable opinion": Monroe to Madison, 20 January (more likely June or July) 1796, Hamilton, *Monroe Writings,* vol. 2, p. 441.

"for though my residence in Mr. Monroe's house": TP to Madison, 24 September 1795, vol. 2, p. 1381.

Suffering "incurably": C. F. Cramer, 26 November 1795, quoted in Aldridge, *TP,* p. 238.

Page

316 "I am a notorious liar": *The Last Dying Words of Tom Paine, Executed at the Gullotine* [sic] *in France on the 1st of September 1794* (n.d.), p. 2.

317 Monroe on TP and Pinckney to Madison, 20 January (more likely June or July) 1796, Hamilton, *Monroe Writings*, vol. 2, p. 442.
Adams hears rumor: John Quincy Adams to John Adams, 4 April and 6 June 1796, Ford, *J. Q. Adams Writings*, vol. 1, pp. 482, 492–492.
On Monroe's suspicions of TP see memorandum of an interview with Dr. Enoch Edwards, 19 August 1796, King, *Life of Rufus King*, vol. 2, pp. 79, 81.
Decline and Fall appears in vol. 2, pp. 651–674.

318 "that the English system of finance": p. 674.
"I have not *made*": p. 657.
"and on this slender twig": p. 663.
In a letter to the Directory asking a favor for Smyth, Paine revealed, through his translator Lanthenas, the part Smyth had played in the pamphlet when he said, "l'a essentiellement servé dans la composition de son dernier pamphlet sur *la décadence et la chute du système des finances de l'angleterre.*" Archives Nationales, AF III 369.
A "Minute d'Arrêté" of the Directory calling for promotion of Paine's pamphlet, dated 8 Floréal (1796), is in the Archives Nationales, AF III 365, p. 19. Mention of a German translation is in AF III 374, p. 29. A broadside by Bonneville advertising the French edition is in AF III 365, p. 21.
"This subject warms him so much": Joseph Pitcairn to John Quincy Adams, 20 October 1796, Ford, *Writings of J. Q. Adams*, vol. 2, p. 21n.

319 "This I did, but all in vain": Latimer, *Scrap-Book of the French Revolution*, p. 61.
Letter to George Washington appears in vol. 2, pp. 691–723.
"and John it is known": p. 695.
"and this John": p. 696.
"prating, insignificant pomposity": p. 707.
"the grossest adulation": p. 695.
"a cold deliberate crime": p. 710.
"he can serve or desert a man": p. 698.
No "talent for inspiring": p. 719.
"You slept away your time": p. 695.
"And as to you, sir,": p. 723.
"A better man than any king": TP to Secretary Dundas, 6 June 1792, vol. 2, p. 452.
Friend named Barnes: TP to Fellows, 20 January 1797, vol. 2, p. 1384.
"because it was my intention": *ibid.*

321 "Tom, you are surely mad": "No-Painite," 17 August 1796, quoted in De Conde, *Entangling Alliance*, p. 358.
"How Tom gets a living I know not": quoted in Woodward, *TP*, pp. 295–296.
"Making allowance for the asperity of an Englishman": Washington to David Stuart, 8 January 1797, Fitzpatrick, *Writings*, vol. 35, pp. 358–359.

322 TP calls on Pinckneys: Mrs. Pinckney to Mrs. Gabriel Manigault, 13 December 1796, quoted in Zahniser, *Pinckney*, p. 142.
"The recall of Mr. Monroe": TP to Jefferson, 1 April 1797, vol. 2, p. 1387.

Page

323 "mercantile wiseacres": TP to Madison, 27 April 1797, vol. 2, p. 1393.
"I am mortified": *ibid.*, p. 1395.
"says that he is going with Mr. Monroe": John Quincy Adams to John Adams, 3 April 1797, Ford, *Writings of J. Q. Adams*, vol. 2, p. 156.
TP dissuaded from traveling with Monroe: Ammon, *Monroe*, p. 137.
"I have sustained so much loss": TP to Fellows, 20 January 1797, vol. 2, p. 1385. TP gives a full accounting of his finances in an unpublished letter to Monroe, undated but clearly written shortly before Monroe leaves for America, in Gimbel collection, American Philosophical Society.
"He is vain beyond all belief": MacDermot, *Life of Tone*, vol. 2, p. 172, entry dated 3 March 1797.
"ever since Mr. Jay's *treaty of surrender*": TP to Jefferson, 1 April 1797, vol. 2, p. 1386.
"but I liked neither the captain nor the company": TP to Madison, 27 April 1797, vol. 2, p. 1394.

324 "that searched every part of it": "To the Citizens of the United States," 6 December 1802, vol. 2, p. 927.
"and should a revolution begin in England": TP to Madison, 27 April 1797, vol. 2, p. 1395.

23. GADFLY

325 Permission granted for TP to reside in Paris: Archives Nationales, AF III 369. Order dated 13 May 1797. Two of the directors who signed were Carnot and La Révellière-Lépeaux.
"It is a want of feeling": "A Letter to Camille Jordan," vol. 2, p. 757.
"more on his theology than his politics": MacDermot, *Tone*, vol. 2, p. 172.

326 "A Letter to Mr. Erskine" appears in vol. 2, pp. 728–748.
Theophilanthropy: See Smith, *TP*, pp. 282–283; Conway, *TP*, vol. 2, p. 254, for summaries on. A typescript copy of the "Manual of the Theophilanthropists, or Loves of God and Friends of Men, Containing the Exposition of their Dogmas, Morality, and Religious Practices, with the Information on the Organization and Ceremonies of the Cult" is in the Gimbel collection. A copy of Rickman's *A Discourse Delivered by Thomas Paine at the Society of the Theophilanthropists at Paris* (1798) is in the British Museum, along with Johnson's *Atheism Refuted*.
"It is the only society": *Letter of Thomas Paine to the People of France, and the French Armies, on the Event of the 18th Fructidor, and its Consequences*, vol. 2, p. 603.

327 "and in the style for which Madame Roland": John Quincy Adams to John Adams, 11 September 1797, Ford, *Writings of J. Q. Adams*, vol. 2, p. 201.
Letter . . . on the 18th Fructidor appears in vol. 2, pp. 595–613.
"It was impossible to go on": p. 605.
"the *best organized system*": *Agrarian Justice*, vol. 1, p. 607.
On Babeuf see Lefebvre, *The Directory*, pp. 35–40.

328 "Le départ precipité": appears opposite the title page of the first French edition of *Agrarian Justice*, published in 1797. Colonel Gimbel believed that

it was published shortly after TP left Paris in late March of 1797 for Havre.
328   *Agrarian Justice* appears in vol. 1, pp. 606–623. It is likely that Paine was
indebted to Bonneville for many of the ideas in it. On this point an extended
quotation from Mathiez, *French Revolution*, p. 208, is called for. In 1792
Bonneville, he writes, "brought out a new edition of a curious book entitled
On the Spirit of Religions (De l'esprit des religions), the first edition of which had
appeared just after Varennes, but attracted no attention; this time, however,
it found an atmosphere already prepared for it. In it a whole plan for a
future commonwealth was set forth in passages of an oracular cast, but of
unmistakable significance, in the middle of which was laid down the necessity for an agrarian law." From a chapter in the book entitled "Of a Means
of Execution for Preparing for a Universal Sharing of the Land" Mathiez
takes this excerpt: "The only possible means of arriving at the great social
Communion is to divide inherited lands into fixed or equal shares for the
children of the deceased and to call in all the remaining relatives to share
in the rest. Fix the limits of inheritance, from today onwards at five or six
acres *(arpents)* for every child or grandchild, and let the other relatives make
an equal division of the remainder of the inheritance. You will still be far
removed from justice and from the admissions which you have made regarding the equal and imprescriptible rights of all men."
"The first principle": p. 610.
"spectacles of human misery": *ibid.*
"The rugged face of society": pp. 618–619.
"It is not charity": p. 617.
"It is only by organizing civilization": p. 618.
329   "Though I care as little about riches": p. 617.
"It is necessary as well": p. 620.
"shall be paid to every person": pp. 612–613.
TP as "a worker of miracles": Erdman, *Blake*, p. 277.
"A revolution in the state of civilization": *Agrarian Justice*, vol. 1, p. 621.
"shall be so organized": *ibid.*, p. 622.
330   "It will be best": TP to Talleyrand, 28 September 1797, vol. 2, p. 1401.
"a non-importation convention": TP to Talleyrand, 30 September 1797, vol. 2,
p. 1401.
331   On the XYZ Affair as it developed in Paris see De Conde, *Quasi-War*, pp.
46–59.
332   Bonneville offers to put TP up: Cobbett-Bonneville manuscripts, Conway,
TP, vol. 2, p. 443.
"He rose late": *ibid.*
333   Bonaparte's visit: Woodward, *TP*, p. 297.
Gunboat scheme: TP to Jefferson, 30 January 1806, vol. 2, pp. 1474–1475. See
also Aldridge, "TP's Plan for a Descent on England," pp. 74–84. The memorandum to Bonaparte is in Foner, vol. 2, pp. 1413–1416, misattributed as letter
to Jefferson, 1 October 1800. Plan for voluntary contributions revealed in TP
to Council of Five Hundred, vol. 2, p. 1403.
"the expedition was abandoned": "To the People of England on the Invasion of England," 6 March 1804, vol. 2, p. 680.

Page

334 "I am certain that Bonneville": Archives Nationales, AF III 544.
On Dr. Logan in Paris see Smith, *TP*, pp. 290–291 and particularly Tolles, "Logan's Mission to France," pp. 12, 18, 19n. Logan "carefully avoided Thomas Paine, feeling that the linking of his name with that of the elderly and embittered radical would only discredit him in both French and American eyes," Tolles reports, adding that the doctor "indignantly disclaimed to Talleyrand any association with Paine." The source is Talleyrand to Pichon, 28 August 1798, Archives des affaires étrangères: Correspondance politique, États-Unis, L., 202.

335 TP's plan for invading America appeared in *le Bien informé*, 12 September 1798. John Bristed printed a translation of the essay in *Hints on the National Bankruptcy of Britain and on her Resources to Maintain the Present Contest with France* (1809), pp. 267–271.
TP seldom "went into the society of the French people": Cobbett-Bonneville manuscripts, Conway, *TP*, vol. 2, p. 444.
"Let them alone": Epps, *Life of John Walker*, p. 142.

336 "the duty I owe to justice": TP to Citizen President, 24 Germinal, year 6, vol. 2, p. 1400.
On Ebenezer May and wife see Archives Nationales, F7 7310 Dossier B4.
On Barlow: TP to Sotlin, minister of police, 1 Vendémiaire, year 6, *ibid.*, F7 7300 3245.
TP as "a man of gigantic political genius": Epps, *Life of John Walker*, p. 132.
"sad, vulgar wretches": Tone, *Life of Tone*, vol. 2, p. 347.
"Paine dines almost every day": *The Anti-Jacobin Review and Magazine* (1799), vol. 1, p. 146n.
Tricolor flag, might it "float on the Tower of London": Epps, *Life of John Walker*, p. 133.
TP's "Appeal of Ireland to the Directory" (18 June 1798), in Edward Desbrière, *Projets et tentatives de débarquement aux Îles Britanniques* (1901), vol. 1, pp. 40–41, translation in typescript in Gimbel collection.

337 These bridges "are progressively expanding": Robert Fulton, *A Treatise on the Improvement of Canal Navigation* (1796), p. 56.
"to return to America": TP to Anonymous, 12 Thermidor, year 8, vol. 2, p. 1406.
Visit to Vanhuele: TP to General Brune, 8 Brumaire, year 8, vol. 2, p. 1405.

338 "the wisest and happiest nation": De Conde, *Quasi-War*, p. 224.
Washington's "memory": Echeverria, *Mirage in the West*, p. 253.
"the police are informed": Archives Nationales, AF 194, pp. 41–42.
"The English are all alike in every country": Yorke, *Letters from France*, vol. 2, p. 369.
"Whether in negotiating a treaty": TP to Jefferson, 30 January 1806, vol. 2, p. 1475.

339 "Paine entertains the most despicable opinion": Yorke, *Letters from France*, vol. 2, p. 369.
"If it had not been for us": Lewis Goldsmith, *Antigallican Monitor*, quoted in Aldridge, *TP*, p. 266.
Told his companion "to hold his tongue": *ibid.*, p. 267.

Page

24. MR. JEFFERSON SENDS A PUBLIC VESSEL

340   "If the chance of the day": TP to Jefferson, 1 October 1800, vol. 2, p. 1410.
      "If you should be in the chair": TP to Jefferson, 4 October 1800, vol. 2, p.
      1417.
      Debt to Haley: memorandum headed "N. Haley's account against Thomas
      Paine," Gimbel collection, American Philosophical Society.
341   "as soon as I can pass": TP to Jefferson, 1 October 1800, vol. 2, p. 1412.
      "if any American frigate should come": *ibid.*
342   *Compact Maritime* was published in the city of Washington in 1801. It con-
      sisted of twenty-four pages, as compared to the French edition "of about
      forty pages," and of four essays—"Dissertation on the Law of Nations" (pp.
      3–9), "On the Jacobinism of the English at Sea" (pp. 10–15), "Compact Mari-
      time for the Protection of Neutral Commerce, and Securing the Liberty of
      the Seas" (pp. 16–21), and "Observations on Some Passages in the Discourse
      of the Judge of English Admiralty" (pp. 21–24). Paine later reprinted the
      compact in Letter VII, "To the Citizens of the United States" (21 April 1803,
      vol. 2, pp. 939–945), and though he included all ten articles the wording
      differs in a number of places from the pamphlet Jefferson had printed. For
      example, in Article 3 in the pamphlet (p. 17) it is stipulated that neutrals will
      cease to import from any offending nation all goods "forever." That word
      is dropped by Paine in the later version and several other changes are
      incorporated in the paragraph.
      Jefferson's election: TP to Skipwith, 3 February 1801, Gimbel collection.
      Urges appointment of Vanhuele: TP to Skipwith, 29 September 1801, *ibid.*
      We are determined not to waste "the energies of our people": Jefferson to
      Paine, 18 March 1801, Ford, *Writings of Jefferson*, vol. 8, p. 18.
343   "after the manner of a minister": Yorke, *Letters from France*, vol. 2, pp.
      339–340.
      "gave me the real sensation": TP to Jefferson, 9 June 1801, vol. 2, p. 1419.
      "It would be a curious circumstance": Yorke, *Letters from France*, vol. 2, p.
      345.
344   "*a very affectionate letter*": *Gazette of the United States*, 21 July 1801.
      "What! Invite to the United States": *The Mercury and New-England Palladium*,
      quoted in Woodward, *TP*, p. 309.
      "no more than that Thomas Paine": *Gazette of the United States*, 13 August
      1801, quoting the Jeffersonian *Aurora*.
      "to feel charity for the misfortune of a fellow mortal": *National Intelligencer*,
      3 August 1801.
      "appeared like a half denial of the letter": Aldridge, *TP*, p. 271.
345   "I give up all hope that any good will be done": TP to Skipwith, 29 Septem-
      ber 1801, Gimbel collection.
      "Why, they are worse off": Yorke, *Letters from France*, vol. 2, p. 342.
      "Indeed, he seemed to dislike": *ibid.*, p. 360
      "*The Age of Reason* has lost you": *ibid.*, p. 361.
      "which, if I mistake not": TP to Elihu Palmer, 21 February 1802, vol. 2, p.
      1426.
      Promised "*to be discreet*": *Letters from France*, pp. 362–363.

Page

346 "Many travelers called upon him": Cobbett-Bonneville manuscripts, Conway, *TP*, vol. 2, p. 443.
"He received us with the greatest good humor": Wilmot, *An Irish Peer*, pp. 56–57.

347 "This was the most pleasant amusement for him": Cobbett-Bonneville manuscripts, Conway, *TP*, vol. 2, p. 445.
"because, I suppose": TP to Jefferson, 25 June 1801, vol. 2, p. 1047.

348 "If the power": *ibid.*, p. 1048.
"a method of building houses": Wilmot, *An Irish Peer*, p. 56. See also TP to Jefferson (October, 1801), vol. 2, pp. 1425–1426.
"collection of discourses": TP to Skipwith, 14 December 1801, Gimbel collection.
"Make your will": Cobbett-Bonneville manuscripts, Conway, *TP*, vol. 2, p. 446.

349 "the numerous and respectable list of friends": TP to Livingston, 22 May 1802, New-York Historical Society, Livingston papers.
On Burdett see M. W. Patterson, *Sir Francis Burdett and His Times* (2 vols., 1931). Bosville's disparagement of TP's drinking in Conway, *TP*, vol. 2, p. 60.
Gift of five hundred louis d'or: Lewis Goldsmith, *Antigallican Monitor*, 28 February 1813.
"As it is now peace": TP to Jefferson, 17 March 1802, vol. 2, p. 1427.

350 "objected to any spirits": Rickman, *TP*, p. 11.

25. THE "LOATHSOME REPTILE" RETURNS

353 "our pious President": *Baltimore Republican; or The Anti-Democrat*, 18 October 1802, reprinted in *New-York Evening Post*, 3 November 1802.
"we know it is requisite to make oath": *New-York Evening Post*, 4 November 1802.
"smiling friendly expressions": *American Patriot*, 6 November 1802, quoted in Aldridge, *TP*, p. 272.
"after sipping well of brandy": *New-York Evening Post*, 3 November 1802.
"whose writings *vindicated America*": *Aurora*, 8 November 1802.
"most rancorous *foe*": *Columbian Centinel*, Boston, 22 August 1801, quoted in Malone, *Jefferson the President*, p. 195.

354 "the agitation my arrival has occasioned": TP to Rickman, 8 March 1803, vol. 2, p. 1439.
"*so notorious a drunkard*": *Columbian Centinel*, Boston, quoted in Malone, *Jefferson the President*, p. 195.
"His nose is a blazing star!" *New-York Evening Post*, 10 January 1803.
"as with an hydrophobia": Letter I, "To the Citizens of the United States," 15 November 1802, vol. 2, p. 911.
"these Terrorists of the New World": Letter III, "To the Citizens of the United States," 29 November 1802, vol. 2, p. 920.
"Years have made more impression": *Aurora*, quoted in Smith, *TP*, p. 307.

355 On Washington at the time of TP's visit see Young, *Washington Community*.
"It may be compared": p. 41. "Where monuments had been planned": *ibid.*

355 "refused to remain in the house": King to William V. Murray, 12 November 1802, King, *Life of Rufus King*, vol. 4, p. 182.
"The members who are there": Manasseh Cutler to Joseph Torrey, 3 January 1803, Cutler, *Life of Manasseh Cutler*, vol. 2, p. 119.

356 "Mr. Paine is not": Randall, *Jefferson*, vol. 2, p. 644.
"civilly received by the President": William V. Murray to Rufus King, 12 November 1802, King, *Life of King*, vol. 4, p. 182.
He "is not despised": *Aurora*, 11 December 1802.
"Mr. Paine is not now": *ibid.*
"that *the story of the birth*": *Recorder*, Richmond, 8 December 1802, quoted in Knudson, "Rage Around TP," p. 53.
"In a few moments after our arrival": William Plumer to Judge Smith, 9 December 1802, Plumer, Jr., *Life of William Plumer*, p. 242.

357 Letter I, "To the Citizens of the United States," 15 November 1802, appears in vol. 2, pp. 909–912.
"with what dignity": *Aurora*, 29 November 1802.
"*chosen vessel*": Richmond, *Recorder*, 8 December 1802, quoted in Knudson, "Rage Around TP," p. 54.
Letter II, 22 November 1802, appears in vol. 2, pp. 912–918.
to "be always master": Letter IV, 6 December 1802, vol. 2, p. 926.

358 "I never had one friend contradict": John Adams to Benjamin Rush, 14 November 1812, Schutz and Adair, *Spur of Fame*, p. 252.
Letter III, 29 November 1802, appears in vol. 2, pp. 918–923.
Letter IV, 6 December 1802, appears in vol. 2, pp. 923–928.
"has seen him devoting his time": *Aurora*, 9 December 1802.

359 "I have not heard of his being at the President's": Manasseh Cutler to Dr. Joseph Torrey, 3 January 1803, Cutler, *Life of Cutler*, vol. 2, p. 118.
"in imitation of the President": William Plumer to Jeremiah Mason, Plumer, Jr., *Life of Plumer*, p. 243.
"cordial reception": *National Intelligencer*, quoted in Woodward, *TP*, p. 310.
Evening at the Gallatins': "Dr. Mitchill's Letters from Washington," p. 745.
Evening at the Dearborns': *Aurora*, 17 February 1803.

360 "all this *war-hoop*": TP to Samuel Adams, 1 January 1803, vol. 2, p. 1436.
"Do you think": Samuel Adams to TP, vol. 2, p. 1433n.
TP's answer to Adams, 1 January 1803, vol. 2, pp. 1432–1433.

361 conversation with Dr. Leib: TP to Jefferson, 25 January 1805, vol. 2, pp. 1462–1463.
TP on Louisiana to Jefferson, 25 December 1802, vol. 2, pp. 1431–1432.

362 "I will be obliged": TP to Jefferson, 12 January 1803, vol. 2, p. 1439.
"You have certainly misconceived": Jefferson to TP, 13 January 1803, Ford, *Writings of Jefferson*, vol. 8, p. 189.
Essay on construction of iron bridges appears in vol. 2, pp. 1051–1057.

26. AN ''OBSCENE OLD SINNER'' SETTLES IN

365 "They take off *heads here*": *Port Folio*, quoted in Knudson, "Rage Around TP," p. 57.

366 "from whom you will receive": TP to Mme. Bonneville, 15 November 1802, vol. 2, pp. 1430–1431.

"I'll be damned if he shall go in my stage": Conway, *TP*, vol. 2, p. 327n.

On Madgett: TP to Monroe (July? 1803), vol. 2, p. 1502.

367 "One day laborer would say": Cheetham, *TP*, p. 233.

"A numerous company of republicans": *American Citizen*, 16 March 1803.

"He is full of whims": Hall manuscripts, 10 April 1803, Conway, *TP*, vol. 2, p. 472.

Tradition holds: Woodward, *History of Burlington and Mercer Counties*, vol. 1, p. 471.

368 Letters VI, 12 March 1803, and VII (on the maritime compact), 21 April 1803, "To the Citizens of the United States," appear in vol. 2, pp. 931–938, 939–948.

"the models to be viewed": TP to Peale, 29 July 1803, vol. 2, p. 1440.

369 "Palled with streams of reeking gore": *American Citizen*, 9 August 1803. Also in Conway, *TP*, vol. 2, p. 329n., and Foner, vol. 2, p. 1102.

Letter VI, "to the Citizens of the United States", 12 March 1803, appears in vol. 2, pp. 931–938.

"I love the restriction": TP to Brackenridge, 2 August 1803, vol. 2, pp. 1443–1444.

"hold the priests in a style of good behavior": TP to Jefferson, 2 August 1803, vol. 2, p. 1441.

370 A procedure "with which the Constitution has nothing to do": TP to Jefferson, 23 September 1803, vol. 2, p. 1447.

"sensible comments": Malone, *Jefferson the President*, pp. 320–321.

English government "tottering": *ibid.*, p. 1448.

371 Baptist visitors: TP to Jefferson, 25 January 1805, vol. 2, pp. 1459–1460.

"I shall be employed": TP to Jefferson, 23 September 1803, vol. 2, p. 1449. Also to Mr. Hyer, 24 March 1804, vol. 2, p. 1451.

"a sort of paralytic affection": Cobbett-Bonneville manuscripts, Conway, *TP*, vol. 2, p. 447. TP called it "a fit of gout" in letter to Mr. Hyer, 24 March 1804, vol. 2, p. 1451.

"*Tom* Paine must be a very bad man": Vale, *TP*, p. 146. Staple on TP: *ibid.*, p. 145.

372 Pintard anecdote: Francis, *Old New York*, p. 139.

Wilburn sued: Vale, *TP*, pp. 146–147.

"What is Barlow about?" TP to Skipwith, 1 March 1804, vol. 2, p. 1451.

373 TP's contributions to *The Prospect* appear in vol. 2, pp. 789–830.

"To the People of England on the Invasion of England": 6 March 1804, vol. 2, pp. 675–683.

"France has now for its chief": p. 679.

"instead of paying his rent": Cobbett-Bonneville manuscripts, Conway, *TP*, vol. 2, p. 447.

374 "help me settle my accounts": TP to Fellows, 9 July 1804, vol. 2, p. 1453.

"There has been so much experience": "To the People of Connecticut on the Subject of a Constitution," 2 August 1804, Gimbel, "New Political Writings of TP," p. 101.

Page

374   "our orator conducts Hamilton": "Remarks on Gouverneur Morris's Fu-
neral Oration on General Hamilton," 7 August 1804, vol. 2, p. 959.
"Will the prisoners they take in war": 1 September 1804, "To the Members
of the Society, Styling Itself the Missionary Society," vol. 2, p. 803.
"They come to us on no other authority": "Of the Books of the New
Testament," 1, 8 September 1804, vol. 2, p. 820.

375   "The word Sabbath, means REST": "On the Sabbath-Day in Connecticut,"
15 September 1804, vol. 2, p. 804.
"You are arriving at freedom": "To the French Inhabitants of Louisiana,"
22 September 1804, vol. 2, pp. 964–965.
"the printing of thousands": John Randolph to Albert Gallatin, 14 October
1804, Conway, *TP*, vol. 2, p. 339.
"on a good ground": TP to Jefferson, 25 January 1805, vol. 2, p. 1459.
"I have six chairs and a table": TP to Fellows, 31 July 1805, vol. 2, p. 1471.

376   "At our arrival": Cheetham, *TP*, pp. 246n.–247n.
"The additional part": TP to Jefferson, 20 April 1805, vol. 2, p. 1057.
"I much doubt whether the open room": Jefferson to TP, 5 June 1805, Ford,
Writings of Jefferson, vol. 8, p. 360.

377   "Tom Paine, as I am a sinner": Smith, *TP*, pp. 317–318.
"I ran immediately out": TP to Carver, 16 January 1805, vol. 2, p. 1455. See
also Cobbett-Bonneville manuscripts, Conway, *TP*, vol. 2, pp. 447–448 and
Cheetham, *TP*, pp. 238, 246.
"I am exceedingly well in health": TP to Carver, 16 January 1805, vol. 2, p.
1456.
"and if it continues": TP to Jefferson, 1 January 1805, vol. 2, p. 1455.

378   "She is now the parent of the western world": *ibid.*, p. 1454.
"I have given up the intention": TP to Jefferson, 25 January 1805, vol. 2, p.
1456.
"Have you forgotten my care of you": Carver to TP, 2 December 1806,
Cheetham, *TP*, p. 267.
"The best way that occurs to me": TP to Jefferson, 25 January 1805, vol. 2,
p. 1464.
"Were I twenty years younger": *ibid.*, p. 1459.

379   "a collection of all the pieces": *ibid.*, p. 1459, 1460.
"a small French penknife": TP to Fellows, 22 April 1805, vol. 2, p. 1467.
Mme. Bonneville "an encumbrance": TP to Fellows, 31 July 1805, vol. 2, p.
1471.
"I supposed, as you have a good deal of leisure": TP to Fellows, 4 June 1805,
Gimbel collection.

380   Letter VIII, "To the Citizens of the United States," 7 June 1805, vol. 2, pp.
949–957.
Constitutions, Governments, and Charters, published as a pamphlet, June 1805.
It appears in vol. 2, pp. 989–992.
"madness in her councils": "Remarks on English Affairs," 8 July 1805, vol.
2, p. 684.
"France, at this time": p. 686.
"two skunks who stink in concert": "Another Callender—Thomas Turner of
Virginia," 24 July 1805, vol. 2, p. 981.

Page

381 "I found myself obliged": TP to Fellows, 9 July 1805, vol. 2, p. 1469.
"The independence of America": Letter VIII, "To the Citizens of the United States," 7 June 1805, vol. 2, p. 956.
Pennsylvania constitution censured: "To the Citizens of Pennsylvania on the Proposal for Calling a Convention," August 1805, vol. 2, pp. 992–1007.

382 "his health is, I think, declining": Palmer to Robert Hunter, 6 September 1805, New York Public Library, manuscript division.
"grant me a tract of land": TP to Jefferson, 30 September 1805, vol. 2, p. 1472.
"I think you will find it proper": TP to Jefferson, 30 January 1806, vol. 2, p. 1478.
Jefferson's reply to TP, 25 March 1806, Ford, *Jefferson Writings*, vol. 8, pp. 436–437.
"nearly the color of tanned leather": Carver to TP, 2 December 1806, Cheetham, *TP*, p. 267.

27. POWDERED WITH SNUFF, STUPEFIED WITH BRANDY

384 "among the lower orders": Thorburn, *History of Cardeus and Carver*, p. 32.
"his countenance was bloated": *Life of Thorburn*, p. 102.
"always in a friendly way": *ibid.*, p. 104.
"here you sit": *ibid.*, p. 102.

385 "The Cause of Yellow Fever," vol. 2, pp. 1060–1066.
"barrelled up": TP to Jefferson, 23 September 1803, vol. 2, p. 1450.
"one of the most sensible performances": Melish, *Travels Through the United States*, p. 150.

386 "attracted considerable attention": *ibid.*, p. 62.
"begins to feel the effects of age": Conway, *TP*, vol. 2, p. 388.
"an uncommonly penetrating eye": Melish, *Travels Through the United States*, p. 62.
Lived "quite retired": Conway, *TP*, p. 388.
"felt exceedingly well": TP to Deane, 15 August 1806, vol. 2, p. 1483. Mrs. Elihu Palmer says he fell on July 27 in a letter to (?), 3 September 1806, New York Public Library, manuscript division.
"an experiment on dying": TP to Deane, 15 August 1806, vol. 2, p. 1483.
"hurt in his leg": Melish, *Travels Through the United States*, p. 61.
"The war must inevitably go on": *ibid.*, pp. 61–62.

387 "Sometimes the room became so dirty": TP to Carver, 25 November 1806, Cheetham, *TP*, p. 255.
Vendetta against Carpenter: See *American Citizen* for 11, 28 October, 5, 19 November 1806. Aldridge has reprinted the last three in "TP and the N.Y. *Public Advertiser*," pp. 367–372.
"A Challenge to the Federalists" appears in vol. 2, pp. 1007–1010, and the piece on liberty of the press, *ibid.*, pp. 1010–1011.
"the old philosopher in bed": Conway, *TP*, vol. 2, p. 388.
TP denied right to vote: TP to Madison, 3 May 1807, vol. 2, pp. 1486–1487.
"As it is a new generation": TP to Clinton, 4 May 1807, vol. 2, p. 1488.

388 "In no case was it friendly": TP to Carver, 25 November 1806, Cheetham, *TP*, p. 256.

Page

388 "As to myself, I suffered": *ibid.*, 25 November 1806, p. 255.

"Mr. Paine's parsimony": Thomas Haynes to Robert Hunter, 30 October 1807, New York Public Library, manuscript division.

"some criminal connection": Carver to TP, 2 December 1806, Cheetham, *TP*, p. 268.

"I am glad to hear that Thomas is a good boy": TP to Dean, 15 August 1806, vol. 2, p. 1485.

389 On Jarvis see Harold E. Dickson, *John Wesley Jarvis*; James Thomas Flexner, *The Light of Distant Skies* (1960); Harold E. Dickson, "The Jarvis Portrait of TP," pp. 5–11.

390 TP at Hitt's: Cheetham, *TP*, p. 281.

"My dear Bonneville": TP to Bonneville, 4 April 1807, Conway, *TP*, vol. 2, p. 448.

"You sometimes hear of me": TP to Barlow, 4 May 1807, vol. 2, p. 1489.

"that your labor is not altogether lost": Thomas Hardy to TP, 15 October 1807, copy in New York Public Library, manuscript division.

"Three Letters to Morgan Lewis," 27 April 1807, vol. 2, pp. 968–975. Earlier in the month he had published letters in the *Public Advertiser* for April 3, 4, 8, and 22.

"shanny-faced Rufus": quoted in Aldridge, *TP*, p. 306.

"I, sir, never permit anyone": Aldridge, *TP*, p. 308.

392 "He looks better than last year": Conway, *TP*, vol. 2, pp. 389–390.

Cost of gunboats: "Of the Comparative Powers and Expense of Ships of War, Gun-Boats and Fortifications," 21 July 1807, vol. 2, p. 1074.

"TOM PAINE has exploded": *New-York Evening Post*, 25 September 1807.

Model "has all the ingenuity": Jefferson to TP, 6 September 1807, Ford, *Writings of Jefferson*, vol. 9 pp. 136–137. For follow-up letter, 9 October 1807, see *ibid.*, pp. 137n.–138n.

393 "he expected to live to a very great age": Cobbett-Bonneville manuscripts, Conway, *TP*, vol. 2, p. 450.

"All the civilized world knows": TP to the Senate of the United States, 21 January 1808, vol. 2, p. 1492.

Moves to cheap tavern: Cheetham, *TP*, p. 287.

Sells Bordentown house: indenture with John Oliver, 6 July 1808, in Gimbel collection.

394 "ignorant, conceited" Cheetham: *Public Advertiser*, New York, 25 August 1808, partially reprinted in Aldridge, *TP*, pp. 311–312.

"His conversation was calm": T. Adams, *Democracy Unveiled . . .* (1813), quoted in *ibid.*, p. 315.

"The penetration and intelligence of his eye": Alexander Wilson to Alexander Lawson, 3 November 1808, quoted in *ibid.*, p. 315.

Previous wills: Cobbett-Bonneville manuscripts, Conway, *TP*, vol. 2, p. 451.

Last will: vol. 2, pp. 1498–1501.

395 "When he could no longer quit his bed": Cobbett-Bonneville manuscripts, Conway, *TP*, vol. 2, p. 452.

"indisposed with fever": Dr. Manly, quoted in Cheetham, *TP*, p. 301.

"I am now in my seventy-third year": Cheetham, *TP*, p. 295.

Page

395 "I have no objection to that": Cobbett-Bonneville manuscripts, Conway, *TP*, vol. 2, p. 451.

396 "I am here alone": *ibid.*, p. 453.
"he must see that he or she was there": Manly, quoted in Cheetham, *TP*, p. 304.
"You have neglected me": Rickman, *TP*, p. 174.
"*I am very sorry*": Cobbett-Bonneville manuscripts, Conway, *TP*, vol. 2, p. 453.
"You have now a full view of death": Vale, *TP*, pp. 153–154.

397 "I don't think he can live till night": Cobbett-Bonneville manuscripts, Conway, *TP*, vol. 2, p. 453.
"Do you believe": Cheetham, *TP*, p. 307. See also Vale, *TP*, p. 156.
"*Oh! yes!*": Cobbett-Bonneville manuscripts, Conway, *TP*, vol. 2, p. 454.

EPILOGUE

399 "I shall secure him to a nicety": Dickson, *Jarvis,* p. 104.
"Death had not disfigured him": Cobbett-Bonneville manuscripts, Conway, *TP*, vol. 2, p. 454.
"to the cause of humanity": *Public Advertiser*, 9 June 1809.

400 "I would sooner take my chance with Paine": quoted in Conway, *TP*, vol. 2, p. 417.
"Stand you there": Cobbett-Bonneville manuscripts, Conway, *TP*, vol. 2, pp. 454–455.
"I am unacquainted with his age": *American Citizen*, 10 June 1809.
"I knew him well": Barlow's open letter to *Raleigh Register*, 18 October 1809, quoted in Harvard, *Connecticut Wits*, p.. 334.
"Didst thee never hear him call on Christ": Vale, *TP*, p. 178.

401 "While he lived": Jefferson to Margaret de Bonneville, 3 April 1813, quoted in Nathan Schachner, *Thomas Jefferson* (1957), p. 924.
"old Billy Carver": Thorburn, *History of Cardeus and Carver*, p. 30. *Beacon*, new series, vol. 1, no. 3, 7 December 1839, p. 24, mentions effort to raise a subscription for Carver.

BIBLIOGRAPHY

Basic List of Books and Articles

Only those works that might be of some direct value to a student of Paine are included in the list that follows. Material of incidental importance is given a full bibliographical reference at the point where it is mentioned in the annotation. Occasionally a book or article that did nothing to enlighten me is included to alert scholars who might otherwise not know of its existence.

Abel, Darrel. "The Significance of the Letter to the Abbé Raynal in the Progress of Thomas Paine's Thought," *Pennsylvania Magazine of History and Biography*, vol. 66 (1942), pp. 176–190.

Adams, Charles Francis, ed. *Works of John Adams* (10 vols., 1850–1856).

Adams, Randolph G. *Political Ideas of the American Revolution* (1922).

Aldridge, Alfred Owen. "The Poetry of Thomas Paine," *Pennsylvania Magazine of History and Biography*, vol. 79 (1955), pp. 81–99.

———. "Some Writings of Thomas Paine in Pennsylvania Newspapers," *American Historical Review*, vol. 56 (1951), pp. 832–838.

———. *Man of Reason: The Life of Thomas Paine* (1959).

———. "Thomas Paine and the New-York *Public Advertiser*," *New-York Historical Society Quarterly*, vol. 37 (1953), pp. 361–382.

———. "Thomas Paine's Plan for a Descent on England," *William and Mary Quarterly*, vol. 14 (1957), pp. 74–84.

———. "Why Did Thomas Paine Write on the Bank?" *American Philosophical Society Proceedings*, vol. 93 (1949), pp. 309–315.

Allen, Gardner W. *A Naval History of the American Revolution* (2 vols., 1913).

Ammon, Harry. *James Monroe: The Quest for National Identity* (1971).

Appleby, Joyce. "America as a Model for the Radical French Reformers of 1789," *William and Mary Quarterly*, vol. 28 (1971), pp. 267–286.

Armytage, W. H. G. "Thomas Paine and the Walkers: An Early Episode in Anglo-American Co-Operation," *Pennsylvania History*, vol. 18 (1951), pp. 16–30. Contains a number of Paine's letters regarding his bridge that are not in Foner.

Baker, W. S. *William Sharp* (1875).

Ballagh, James Curtis, ed. *Letters of Richard Henry Lee* (2 vols., 1911–1914).

Barère, Bertrand. *Memoirs* (4 vols., 1897), translated by De V. Payen-Payne.

Beacon, The. A deistic journal edited by Gilbert Vale during the 1830s and 1840s and dedicated to keeping Paine's memory alive.

Bezanson, Anne. *Prices and Inflation during the American Revolution, Pennsylvania, 1770–1790* (1951).

Biddle, Charles. *Autobiography* (1883).

Boorstin, Daniel J. *The Lost World of Thomas Jefferson* (1948).

Boulton, James T. *The Language of Politics* (1963). A superb book, helpful for understanding both Burke and Paine.

Boyd, Julian P., and others, eds. *The Jefferson Papers* (18 vols. to date, 1950–   ). Contains precise transcriptions of all Paine's letters to Jefferson, some of which are not in Foner.

Breck, Samuel. *Recollections* (1877).

Brinton, Crane. *The Jacobins: An Essay in the New History* (1930). This volume should be read in conjunction with Peter Gay, "Rhetoric and Politics in the French Revolution," *American Historical Review*, vol. 66 (1961), pp. 664–676, to which is appended a "Comment on Gay" (pp. 677–681) by Brinton.

————. "Thomas Paine," *Dictionary of American Biography*. In my judgment the best essay written on Paine.

Brissot de Warville, Jacques Pierre. *New Travels in the United States, 1788* (1964), translated by Mara Soceanu Vamos and Durand Echeverria and edited by Echeverria.

————. . . . *On the Situation of the National Convention under the Influence of Anarchists* . . . (1792).

Brown, Philip Anthony. *The French Revolution in English History* (1918).

Browne, Ray B. "The Paine-Burke Controversy in Eighteenth-Century Irish Popular Songs," pp. 80–97, in Ray B. Browne, William John Roscelli, and Richard Loftus, eds., *The Celtic Cross: Studies in Irish Culture and Literature* (1964).

Brunhouse, Robert L. *The Counter-revolution in Pennsylvania, 1776–1790* (1942). Still the best work on the subject.

Burke, Edmund. *Reflections on the French Revolution* (1929), edited by W. Alison and Catherine Beatrice Phillips.

Burnett, Edmund Cody. *The Continental Congress* (1941).

————. *Letters of the Members of the Continental Congress* (8 vols., 1921–1936). Both these works by Burnett are indispensable.

Butterfield, Lyman H., and others, eds. *The Adams Papers. Adams Family Correspondence, 1761–1778* (2 vols., 1963).

_____. *The Adams Papers. The Diary and Autobiography of John Adams* (4 vols., 1961).

_____. *Letters of Benjamin Rush* (2 vols., 1951).

Byrne, Patrick. *Lord Edward Fitzgerald* (1955).

Cameron, K. W., ed. *Shelley and His Circle 1773–1822* (2 vols., 1961). The annotation is especially helpful in identifying a number of Paine's acquaintances in London.

Cappon, Lester J., ed. *The Adams-Jefferson Letters: The Complete Correspondence Between Thomas Jefferson and Abigail and John Adams* (2 vols., 1959).

Carlile, Richard. *The Life of Thomas Paine, Written Purposely to Bind with his Writings* (3rd. ed., 1820).

Cartwright, John. *England's Aegis; or the Military Energies of the Constitution* (2 vols., 1806 ed.).

Chalmers, George. *Life of Thomas Paine . . . by Francis Oldys* (1791 and 1793 eds.). The most important source for Paine's early life and also for his stay in London during 1791 and 1792. The second edition covers the latter period.

Charlemont, James Caulfield, first earl of. *The Manuscripts and Correspondence of . . .* (2 vols., 1891–1894), in series published by the British Historical Manuscripts Commission.

Chastellux, Marquis de. *Travels in North America in the Years 1780, 1781, and 1782* (2 vols., 1963), revised translation by Howard C. Rice, Jr.

Cheetham, James. *Life of Thomas Paine* (1809). Written within weeks after Paine's death, it concentrates on his last years in New York. It is heavily biased against Paine, emphasizing his drinking, but is nonetheless an important source if used with care.

Clark, Harry Hayden. Clark gave a large part of his academic career to Paine. He never produced a biography, but all the scholarly articles he published call for attention, especially the 107-page introduction to his volume of *Representative Selections*.

_____. "An Historical Interpretation of Thomas Paine's Religion," *University of California Chronicle*, vol. 35 (1933), pp. 56–87.

_____. *Six New Letters by Thomas Paine* (1939). These six essays directed at the people of Rhode Island were discovered by Clark. They appear in Foner, vol. 2, pp. 333–366, but Clark's introduction remains useful.

_____. "Thomas Paine's Relation to Voltaire and Rousseau," *Revue Anglo-Américaine*, vol. 9 (1932), pp. 305–318, 393–405.

_____. *Thomas Paine: Representative Selections, with Introduction, Bibliography and Notes* (1944).

_____. "Thomas Paine's Theories of Rhetoric," *Transactions of the Wisconsin Academy of Sciences, Arts and Letters*, vol. 28 (1933), pp. 307–339.

_____. "Toward a Reinterpretation of Thomas Paine," *American Literature*, vol. 5 (1933), pp. 133–145.

Colby, Elbridge. *Life of Thomas Holcroft* (2 vols., 1925).

Cole, G. D. H., and Raymond Postgate. *The British Common People, 1746–1946* (1961).

Collins, Henry, ed. *The Rights of Man* (1969). Useful for introduction.

Collins, Varnum Lansing. *President Witherspoon: A Biography* (2 vols., 1925).

Condit, Uzal W. *History of Easton from the Earliest Times to the Present, 1735–1885* (1889).

Cone, Carl B. *Burke and the Nature of Politics,* "The Age of the French Revolution" (1964).

――――. *English Jacobins: Reformers in Late 18th Century England* (1968).

Conway, Moncure D. *The Life of Thomas Paine* (2 vols., 1892).

――――. *Thomas Paine (1737–1809) et la Révolution dans les deux mondes* (1900). Contains documents not in the English edition. Translations of this new material, with emendations, can be found in the Gimbel collection.

Copeland, Thomas W. "Burke, Paine, and Jefferson," in *Our Eminent Friend Edmund Burke: Six Essays* (1949), pp. 146–189. A superb piece of scholarship, perceptive, balanced, and wonderfully written.

Corner, George W., ed. *The Autobiography of Benjamin Rush: His "Travels Through Life" together with his* Commonplace Book *for 1789–1813* (1948).

Cragg, Gerald R. *Reason and Authority in the Eighteenth Century* (1964). An excellent book but particularly good on Burke.

Cutler, W. P., and J. P. *Life and Correspondence of Rev. Manasseh Cutler* (2 vols., 1888).

Dangerfield, George. *Chancellor Robert R. Livingston of New York, 1746–1813* (1960).

Davenport, Beatrix Cary, ed. *A Diary of the French Revolution by Gouverneur Morris* (2 vols., 1939). More selective but better edited than Anne Cary Morris' edition of the same material.

Deane, Silas. *The Deane Papers . . . 1774–1781* (5 vols., 1887–1890), in the *New-York Historical Society Collections,* vols. 19–23.

De Conde, Alexander. *Entangling Alliance: Politics and Diplomacy Under George Washington* (1958).

――――. *The Quasi-War: The Politics and Diplomacy of the Undeclared War with France, 1797–1801* (1966).

Dickson, Harold E. "The Jarvis Portrait of Thomas Paine," *New-York Historical Society Quarterly,* vol. 34 (1950), pp. 5–11.

――――. *John Wesley Jarvis* (1950).

Dictionary of National Biography (24 vols. thus far, 1917–). Invaluable for sketches of Paine's friends and acquaintances in England in the 1790s.

Disney, John. *Memoirs of Thomas Brand Hollis* (1808).

Dorfman, Joseph. "The Economic Philosophy of Thomas Paine," *Political Science Quarterly,* vol. 53 (1938), pp. 372–386.

――――. *The Economic Mind in American Civilization, 1606–1865* (2 vols., 1947).

Dos Passos, John. "Citizen Barlow . . ." in *The Ground We Stand On* (1941), pp. 256–380. Unannotated but well worth reading.

Duane, William, ed. *Extracts from the Diary of Christopher Marshall, Kept in Philadelphia and Lancaster, during the American Revolution, 1774–1781* (1877).

――――. *Passages from the Remembrancer of Christopher Marshall* (1839).

Dumont, Étienne. *Recollections of Mirabeau, and the Two First Legislative Assemblies of France* (1832).

Durand, John. *New Materials for the History of the American Revolution Translated from Documents in the French Archives and Edited* (1889).

Durden, Robert F. "Joel Barlow in the French Revolution," *William and Mary Quarterly*, vol. 8 (1951), pp. 327–354.

Duval, Georges. *Histoire de la Littérature Révolutionnaire* (1879). See especially pp. 254–304, which contain a long essay on Nicolas de Bonneville.

Echeverria, Durand. *Mirage in the West: A History of the French Image of American Society to 1815* (1957).

Ellery, Eloise. *Brissot de Warville: A Study in the History of the French Revolution* (1915).

Epps, John. *Life of John Walker* (1831).

Erdman, David V. *Blake, Prophet Against Empire: A Poet's Interpretation of the History of His Own Times* (1954).

Ernst, Robert. *Rufus King: American Federalist* (1968).

Falk, Robert P. "Thomas Paine and the Attitude of the Quakers to the American Revolution," *Pennsylvania Magazine of History and Biography*, vol. 63 (1939), pp. 302–310.

———. "Thomas Paine: Deist or Quaker?" *Pennsylvania Magazine of History and Biography*, vol. 62 (1938), pp. 52–63.

Fennessy, R. R. *Burke, Paine and the Rights of Man: A Difference of Political Opinion* (1963). Invaluable work.

Ferguson, E. James. *The Power of the Purse: A History of American Public Finance, 1776–1790* (1961).

Fitzpatrick, John C., ed. *Writings of George Washington* (39 vols., 1931–1944).

Flexner, James Thomas. *George Washington and the American Revolution, 1775–1783* (1968).

———. *George Washington and the New Nation, 1783–1793* (1970). These two from Flexner's superb four-volume biography, the best work we have on Washington, were especially helpful in filling out the military and political background.

———. *Steamboats Come True* (1944), retitled *Inventors in Action* in the paperback edition (1962) used here. Excellent on Fitch, Rumsey, and Fulton.

Foner, Philip S. *The Complete Writings of Thomas Paine* (2 vols., 1945).

Ford, Paul Leicester. *The Writings of Thomas Jefferson* (10 vols., 1892–1899).

Ford, Worthington Chauncey, ed. *Writings of John Quincy Adams* (7 vols., 1913–1917).

———. *Journals of the Continental Congress, 1774–1789* (34 vols., 1904–1937).

———. *Warren-Adams Letters* (2 vols., 1917, 1925).

Fortescue, J. B. *The Manuscripts of J. B. Fortescue Preserved at Dropmore* (10 vols., 1892–1927), in series published by the British Historical Manuscripts Commission.

Francis, John W. *Old New York; or, Reminiscences of the Past Sixty Years* (1858).

Gershoy, Leo. *Bertrand Barère: A Reluctant Terrorist* (1962).

Gibbens, V. E. "Tom Paine and the Idea of Progress," *Pennsylvania Magazine of History and Biography*, vol. 66 (1942), pp. 191–204.

Gilbert, Felix. *The Beginnings of American Foreign Policy. To the Farewell Address* (1961). Excellent.

Gimbel, Richard. "The First Appearance of Thomas Paine's *Age of Reason*," *Yale University Library Gazette*, vol. 31 (1956).
———. "New Political Writings by Thomas Paine," *Yale University Library Gazette*, vol. 30 (1956), pp. 94–107.
———. "Resurgence of Thomas Paine," *American Antiquarian Society Proceedings*, vol. 69 (1959), pp. 97–111.
———. *Thomas Paine. A Bibliographical Check List of* Common Sense, *with an Account of Its Publication* (1956).
———. "Thomas Paine Fights for Freedom in Three Worlds . . . Catalogue of an Exhibition Commemorating the 150th Anniversary of His Death," Yale University, October 1959, *American Antiquarian Society Proceedings*, vol. 70 (1960), pp. 397–492.
Godcharles, Frederic. *Daily Stories of Pennsylvania* (1924).
Godwin, William. *Memoirs of Mary Wollstonecraft* (1927), edited by W. Clark Durant.
Goldsmith, Lewis. *Secret History of the Cabinet of Napoleon* (1810).
Gottschalk, Louis. *Lafayette between the American and the French Revolution (1783–1789)* (1950).
———. *Jean Paul Marat: A Study in Radicalism* (1966).
Gower, Earl of. *The Despatches of Earl Gower, English Ambassador at Paris from June 1790 to August 1792* (1885), edited by Oscar Browning.
Gummere, Richard M. "Thomas Paine: Was he Really Anti-Classical?" in *Seven Wise Men of Colonial America* (1967), pp. 81–108.
Hall, Walter P. *British Radicalism, 1791–1797* (1912).
Hamilton, Stanislaus Murray. *Writings of James Monroe* (7 vols., 1898–1903).
Hammond, Bray. *Banks and Politics in America from the Revolution to the Civil War* (1957).
Hardy, Thomas. *Memoir of Thomas Hardy . . . Written by Himself* (1832).
Hastings, George Everett. *Life and Works of Francis Hopkinson* (1926).
Hawke, David. *In the Midst of a Revolution* (1961).
Hazen, Charles D. *Contemporary American Opinion of the French Revolution* (1897), in Johns Hopkins Studies in History, extra volume, no. 16.
Hendricks, Burton J. *The Lees of Virginia* (1935).
Henry, John Joseph. *Campaign Against Quebec* (1812), reprinted in *Pennsylvania Archives*, 2nd series, vol. 15 (1893), pp. 59–191. Henry recalls Paine when he lived with his family in Lancaster during the American Revolution.
Hindle, Brooke. *David Rittenhouse* (1964).
———. *The Pursuit of Science in Revolutionary America, 1735–1789* (1956).
Howard, Leon. *The Connecticut Wits* (1942).
———. "The Late Eighteenth Century: An Age of Contradictions," in Harry Hayden Clark, ed., *Transitions in American Literary History* (1953), pp. 51–89.
Howell, Thomas Bayly. *A Complete Collection of State Trials and Proceedings for High Treason . . .* (33 vols., 1816–1826).
Hutchinson, William T., and William M. E. Rachal, eds. *The Papers of James Madison* (7 vols. to date, 1962–   ).

Jay, William. *Life of John Jay, with Selections from his Correspondence and Miscellaneous Papers* (2 vols., 1833).

Jensen, Merrill. *The Founding of a Nation: A History of the American Revolution, 1763–1776* (1968).

———. *The New Nation: A History of the United States During the Confederation, 1781–1789* (1950).

Jordan, Winthrop D., "Familial Politics: Thomas Paine and the Killing of the King, 1776," *Journal of American History,* vol. 60 (1973), pp. 294–308.

Kaplan, Lawrence S. *Jefferson and France: An Essay on Politics and Political Ideas* (1967).

Kenyon, Cecilia M. "Where Paine Went Wrong," *American Political Science Review,* vol. 45 (1951), pp. 1086–1099.

King, Arnold Kinsey. "Thomas Paine in America, 1774–1787," doctoral dissertation, University of Chicago, 1951. An excellent piece of research. King missed little concerning Paine for the years he covers.

King, Charles R. *Life and Correspondence of Rufus King* (6 vols., 1894–1900).

Knight, Frida. *The Strange Case of Thomas Walker: Ten Years in the Life of a Manchester Radical* (1957).

Knowles, John. *The Life and Writings of Henry Fuseli* (3 vols., 1831).

Koch, Adrienne. *Jefferson and Madison, the Great Collaboration* (1950).

Koch, G. A. *Republican Religion* (1933).

Kramer, Sidney. "My Much Loved America," *Library of Congress Quarterly Journal of Current Acquisitions,* vol. 1 (1943), no. 1, pp. 17–22. The article contains a letter of Paine's to Benjamin Rush, dated 16 March 1790; part of it appears in Foner, vol. 2, pp. 1285–1286, addressed to Anonymous and dated 16 March 1789.

Kraus, Michael. *The Atlantic Civilization: Eighteenth Century Origins* (1949).

Landin, Harold W. "Some Letters of Thomas Paine and William Short on the Nootka Sound Crisis," *Journal of Modern History,* vol. 13 (1941), pp. 357–374. The letters are in Foner but Landin's commentary is useful.

Latimer, Elizabeth Wormeley. *My Scrap-Book of the French Revolution* (1898).

Laurens, John. *Army Correspondence* (1867).

Lee, Charles. *Lee Papers* (4 vols., 1871–1874), in *New-York Historical Society Collections.*

Lefebvre, Georges. *The Coming of the French Revolution, 1789* (1957), translation by Robert R. Palmer.

———. *The Directory* (1967), translation by Robert Baldick.

———. *The French Revolution from Its Origins to 1793* (1962), translation by Elizabeth Moss Evanson.

———. *The French Revolution from 1793 to 1799* (1964), translation by John Hall Stewart and James Friguglietti.

———. *The Thermidorians* (1964), translation by Robert Baldick.

Le Harival, Philippe. *Nicolas de Bonneville* (1923).

Link, Eugene P. *Democratic-Republican Societies, 1790–1800* (1942).

Littell, Charles W. "Major William Jackson, Secretary of the Federal Convention," *Pennsylvania Magazine of History and Biography,* vol. 2 (1878), pp. 353–369.

Lucas, F. L. *The Art of Living* (1959). Despite the title the book contains a superb essay on Burke, pp. 131–202.

McCulloch, William. "William McCulloch's Additions to Thomas' *History of Printing,*" *American Antiquarian Society Proceedings,* vol. 31 (1921), pp. 89–247.

MacDermot, Frank. *Theobald Wolfe Tone* (1939).

Madison, James. *Letters and Other Writings of James Madison, Fourth President of the United States* (4 vols., 1865). Will continue useful until the Hutchinson-Rachal edition of Madison's writings is completed.

Maier, Pauline. *From Resistance to Revolution: Colonial Radicals and the Development of American Opposition to Britain, 1765–1776* (1972).

Malone, Dumas. *Jefferson and the Rights of Man* (1951).

———. *Jefferson and the Ordeal of Liberty* (1962).

———. *Jefferson the President: First Term, 1801–1805* (1970).

Mathiez, Albert. *After Robespierre: The Thermidorian Reaction* (1965), translation by Catherine Alison Phillips.

———. *The French Revolution* (1964), translation by Catherine Alison Phillips.

Matthews, Albert. "Thomas Paine and the Declaration of Independence," *Proceedings of the Massachusetts Historical Society,* vol. 43 (1910), pp. 241–253.

Melish, John. *Travels Through the United States of America, in the Years 1806 . . . 1811* (1818).

Meng, John J. "The Constitutional Theories of Thomas Paine," *Review of Politics,* vol. 8 (1946), pp. 283–306.

———. *Despatches and Instructions of Conrad Alexandre Gérard, 1778–1780* (1939).

———. "French Diplomacy in Philadelphia: 1778–1779," *Catholic Historical Review,* vol. 24 (1938).

———. "Thomas Paine, French Propagandist in the United States," *Records of the American Catholic Historical Society,* vol. 57 (1946), pp. 1–21.

Mercer, Caroline Gaston. "The Historical Method of Thomas Paine," doctoral dissertation, University of Chicago, 1951.

Merriam, Charles E., Jr. "Thomas Paine's Political Theories," *Political Science Quarterly,* vol. 14 (1899), pp. 389–403.

Miller, John C. *Sam Adams* (1936).

Mitchill, Samuel L. "Dr. Mitchill's Letters from Washington: 1801–1813," *Harper's New Monthly Magazine,* vol. 58 (1879), pp. 740–755.

Montross, Lynn. *The Reluctant Rebels* (1950).

Morais, Herbert M. *Deism in Eighteenth Century America* (1934).

Morris, Anne Cary. *Diary and Letters of Gouverneur Morris* (2 vols., 1888). Supplements Davenport's edition of the same material.

Nicolson, Marjorie. "Thomas Paine, Edward Nares, and Mrs. Piozzi's Marginalia," *Huntington Library Quarterly Bulletin* (1936), pp. 103–135.

O'Donnell, William E. *Chevalier de la Luzerne, French Minister to the United States, 1779–1784* (1938).

Palmer, Robert R. *The Age of the Democratic Revolution: A Political History of Europe and America, 1760–1800.* Vol. 1, *The Challenge* (1959). Vol. 2, *The Struggle* (1964). The second volume is particularly useful.

———. "The Dubious Democrat: Thomas Jefferson in Bourbon France," *Political Science Quarterly*, vol. 72 (1957), pp. 388–404. A provocative interpretation contested by many historians but which I accept as sound and applicable to Paine as well as Jefferson.

———. "Tom Paine: Victim of the Rights of Man," *Pennsylvania Magazine of History and Biography*, vol. 66 (1942), pp. 161–175.

———. *Twelve Who Ruled: The Year of the Terror in the French Revolution* (1941). A marvelous book that blends scholarly analysis into a fascinating narrative.

Parrington, Vernon L. "Thomas Paine: Republican Pamphleteer," in *The Main Currents in American Thought*, vol. 1, *The Colonial Mind* (1927), pp. 332–336. Still one of the best essays in print on Paine.

Patterson, M. W. *Sir Francis Burdett and His Times* (2 vols., 1931).

Paul, C. K. *William Godwin, His Friends and Contemporaries* (2 vols., 1876).

Penniman, Howard. "Thomas Paine—Democrat," *American Political Science Review*, vol. 37 (1943), pp. 244–262.

Pennsylvania Archives. Selected and Arranged from Original Documents in the Office of the Secretary of the Commonwealth (119 vols., 1852–1933). *First Series 1664–1790* (12 vols., 1852–1856). *Second Series* (19 vols., 1874–1890). *Eighth Series—Votes and Proceedings of the House of Representatives of the Province of Pennsylvania* (8 vols., 1931–1935).

Pennsylvania Colonial Records (16 vols., 1851–1853), formally known as *Minutes of the Provincial Council of Pennsylvania, Minutes and Proceedings of the Council of Safety, and Minutes and Proceedings of the Supreme Executive Council of Pennsylvania, 1683–1790.*

Perry, Sampson. *Historical Sketch of the French Revolution* (1796).

———. *The Argus* (1796).

Persinger, C. E. "The Political Philosophy of Thomas Paine," *University of Nebraska Graduate Bulletin*, C, Series 6 (1901), pp. 54–74.

Plumb, J. H. *England in the Eighteenth Century (1714–1815)* (1950).

Plumer, William, Jr. *Life of William Plumer by his son . . .* (1856).

Polishook, Irwin H. *Rhode Island and the Union, 1774–1795* (1969).

Randel, John. "Residence of Thomas Paine," in D. T. Valentine, *Manual* (1864), pp. 841–846.

Reed, William B. *Life and Correspondence of Joseph Reed* (2 vols., 1847).

Richardson, Lyon N. *History of Early American Magazines, 1741–1789* (1931). Fullest and best account of Paine and the *Pennsylvania Magazine*, pp. 174–196.

Rickman, Thomas Clio. *Life of Thomas Paine* (1819). Though by one of Paine's closest friends, I found it more derivative and less useful than have previous biographers. Rickman's eagerness to protect his hero inhibited his pen.

Ritcheson, Charles R. *Aftermath of Revolution: British Policy Toward the United States, 1783–1795* (1969).

Roland de la Platière, Jeanne Marie. *Memoirs* (1878 and 1884 eds.).

Romilly, Samuel. *Memoirs of the Life of Sir Samuel Romilly* (2 vols., 1842).

Rush, Benjamin. *Observations Upon the Present Government of Pennsylvania. In Four Letters to the People of Pennsylvania* (1777).

Schapiro, J. Salwyn. *Condorcet and the Rise of Liberalism* (1954).

Scharf, J. Thomas, and Thompson Westcott. *History of Philadelphia, 1609–1884* (3 vols., 1884).

Schutz, John A., and Douglass Adair. *The Spur of Fame: Dialogues of John Adams and Benjamin Rush, 1805–1813* (1966).

Scoble, Thomas D., Jr. *Thomas Paine's Citizenship Record* (1946).

Sellers, Charles Coleman. *Charles Willson Peale* (2 vols., 1939, 1947).

Sizer, Theodore. "Tom Paine's Portrait," *Yale University Library Gazette*, vol. 30 (1956).

——. *The Autobiography of Colonel John Trumbull* (1953).

Smiles, Samuel. *Life of Thomas Telford* (1867).

Smith, Frank. "New Light on Thomas Paine's First Year in America, 1775," *American Literature*, vol. 1 (1930), pp. 347–371.

——. *Tom Paine, Liberator* (1938). My admiration for this work is shared by few others. Clark, *Representative Selections* (1944 ed.), p. cxxxi, finds it only "interesting in its enthusiasm."

Smith, Page. *James Wilson, Founding Father 1742–1798* (1956).

——. *John Adams* (2 vols., 1963).

Sparks, Jared. *Life of Gouverneur Morris, with Selections from his Correspondence and Miscellaneous Papers* (3 vols., 1832).

Stephen, Leslie. *English Thought in the Eighteenth Century* (2 vols., 1962).

——. "Thomas Paine," *Dictionary of National Biography*.

Stephens, Alexander. *Memoirs of John Horne Tooke* (2 vols., 1813).

Stevens, B. F. *Facsimiles of Manuscripts in European Archives Relating to America, 1773–1783* (1895).

Stinchcombe, William O. *The American Revolution and the French Alliance* (1969). A thorough and very helpful work.

Stourzh, Gerald. *Benjamin Franklin and American Foreign Policy* (1954).

Swiggett, Howard. *The Extraordinary Mr. Morris* (1952). A good biography of Gouverneur Morris is needed. This is not it.

Sydenham, M. J. *The Girondins* (1961).

Sykes, Norman. "Thomas Paine," in F. J. C. Hearnshaw, ed., *Social and Political Ideas of the Revolutionary Era* (1931), pp. 100–140. Everyone has his favorite essay on Paine. I did not find this one impressive. Clark, on the other hand, *Representative Selections* (1944 ed.), p. cxxxviii, calls it "probably the best brief treatment available."

Thayer, Theodore. *Pennsylvania Politics and the Growth of Democracy 1740–1776* (1953).

Thibaudeau, Antoine Claire. *Mémoires sur le convention et le directoire* (1824).

Thomas, Isaiah. *History of Printing in America* (2 vols., 1874).

Thompson, E. P. *The Making of the English Working Class* (1963). Indispensable. Also a delight to read.

Thompson, J. M. *The French Revolution* (1966). For me this turned out to be the best one-volume survey of the Revolution in English.

——. *Leaders of the French Revolution* (1929).

————. *Robespierre and the French Revolution* (1962).

Thorburn, Grant. *History of Cardeus and Carver or the Christian and Infidel Family: A Contrast* (1847).

————. *The Life and Writings of Grant Thorburn* (1852).

Thorning, Joseph F. *Miranda: World Citizen* (1952).

Todd, Charles Burr. *Life and Letters of Joel Barlow, L.L.D., Poet, Statesman, Philosopher* (1886).

Tolles, Frederick B. "Unofficial Ambassador: George Logan's Mission to France, 1798," *William and Mary Quarterly*, vol. 7 (1950), pp. 3–25.

Tone, Theobald Wolfe. *Life of Theobald Wolfe Tone, edited by his Son* (2 vols., 1826).

Townsend, Sara Bertha. *An American Soldier: The Life of John Laurens* (1958).

Trumbull, John. *Autobiography, Reminiscences, and Letters* (1841).

Tyler, Moses Coit. *Literary History of the American Revolution* (2 vols., 1897).

Vale, Gilbert. *The Life of Thomas Paine* (1841). Useful for the friendly contemporary judgments of Paine during his last years; a counterbalance to Cheetham. The book contains a number of documents missing from Foner.

Van Doren, Carl. *Benjamin Franklin* (1938).

————. *Secret History of the American Revolution* (1941).

Wallace, David Duncan. *Life of Henry Laurens* (1967).

Watson, Winslow C. *Men and Times of the Revolution or, Memoirs of Elkanah Watson* (1857).

Westcott, Thompson. *Life of John Fitch* (1878).

Wharton, Francis, *The Revolutionary Diplomatic Correspondence of the United States* (6 vols., 1889). Invaluable.

Wharton, T. I. "Memoirs of William Rawle," in *Memoirs of the Historical Society of Pennsylvania*, vol. 4, Part I (1840).

Wheeler, Daniel E., ed. *Life and Writings of Thomas Paine* (10 vols., 1908). Worth noting only because the first volume contains several items often difficult to get hold of, such as Rickman's life of Paine, Erskine's speech at Paine's trial for sedition, Stephen's "Paine in the American Revolution."

Willard, Margaret Wheeler. *Letters on the American Revolution* (1925).

Willey, Basil. *The Eighteenth-Century Background. Studies on the Idea of Nature in the Thought of the Period* (1940).

Williams, David. *Observations sur la dernière constitution de la France* (1793).

Williams, David. "The Missions of David Williams and James Tilly Matthews to France (1793)," *English Historical Review*, vol. 53 (1938), pp. 651–668.

Williams, Gwyn A. *Artisans and Sans-Culottes. Popular Movements in France and Britain during the French Revolution* (1968). Brief and excellent.

Williams, Helen Maria. *Letters Containing a Sketch of the Politics of France* (4 vols., 1795).

Wilmer, James. *Men and Measures from 1774 to 1809* (1809).

Wilmerding, Lucius, Jr. *James Monroe, Public Claimant* (1960).

Wilmot, Catherine. *An Irish Peer on the Continent, 1801–1803* (1920), edited by Thomas U. Sadleir.

[Wolcot, John]. *Works of Peter Pindar* (5 vols., 1794–1801).

Wood, Gordon. *The Creation of the American Republic, 1776–1787* (1969).

Woodress, James. *A Yankee's Odyssey. The Life of Joel Barlow* (1958).

Woodward, E. M., and John F. Hageman. *History of Burlington and Mercer Counties* (2 vols., 1883).

Woodward, W. E. *Tom Paine: America's Godfather, 1737–1809* (1945). A heavy-handed work for a professional journalist, but contains some material not found elsewhere.

Yarborough, Minnie Clare. *John Horne Tooke* (1926).

Yorke, Henry Redhead. *Letters from France in 1802* (2 vols., 1804).

Young, James Sterling. *The Washington Community, 1800–1828* (1966). More than a history of the town. An original, perceptive account of government as reflected in the physical setting.

Zahniser, Marvin R. *Charles Cotesworth Pinckney: Founding Father* (1967).

INDEX

475